Counseling Issues

Counseling Issues

*A Handbook For Counselors
and Psychotherapists*

George A.F. Seber

To order additional copies of this book, contact:
Xlibris Corporation
0-800-891-366
www.Xlibris.co.nz
Orders@Xlibris.co.nz
700454

CONTENTS

Preface   **xvii**

1   Brain Matters   **1**

   1.1   Introduction   1
       1.1.1   Mind over Matter   2
   1.2   Brain Structure   3
       1.2.1   Nerve Cells   3
       1.2.2   Brain Function   4
       1.2.3   Memory   5
       1.2.4   Ego States   7
       1.2.5   Body/Mind Techniques   8
       1.2.6   Pain Management   10
   1.3   Personality   11
       1.3.1   Personality Differences   11
       1.3.2   Personality Models   12
       1.3.3   Learning Styles   13
   1.4   Emotions, Feelings, and Thoughts   13
       1.4.1   Introduction   13
       1.4.2   Emotions   13
       1.4.3   Cognitive Processes   17

	1.4.4	Thought Stopping	21
1.5		The Aging Process	22
	1.5.1	Midlife Reassessment	22
	1.5.2	Midlife Counseling	23
1.6		The Aging Brain	23
	1.6.1	The Big News	24
	1.6.2	Four Life Phases	26
	1.6.3	Social Intelligence	27
1.7		Biblical Viewpoint	28
	1.7.1	Metaphors	28
	1.7.2	Positive Messages	29

2	**Wholeness**		**31**
2.1		Introduction	31
2.2		Physical	32
	2.2.1	Nutrition	32
	2.2.2	Exercise	34
	2.2.3	Rest and Recreation	36
	2.2.4	Sleep	36
	2.2.5	Relaxation Techniques	40
	2.2.6	Healthy Sexuality	42
	2.2.7	Touch	44
2.3		Intellectual	44
	2.3.1	Balance	44
	2.3.2	Goals	44
	2.3.3	Resilience	45
2.4		Emotional	46
	2.4.1	Beliefs and Emotions	46
	2.4.2	Identifying Feelings	47
2.5		Social	48
	2.5.1	Importance of Networks	48
	2.5.2	Attachment Issues	49
	2.5.3	Self-Esteem	51
	2.5.4	Assertiveness	54
	2.5.5	Forgiveness	59
	2.5.6	Birth Order	68
2.6		Spiritual	69
	2.6.1	Role of Spirituality	69
	2.6.2	Defining Spirituality	70
2.7		Biblical Viewpoint	71
	2.7.1	Who Am I?	71
	2.7.2	Physical Wholeness	71

	2.7.3	Mental Wholeness	72
	2.7.4	Emotional Wholeness	73
	2.7.5	Social Wholeness	73
	2.7.6	Spiritual Wholeness	75

3   Anger   **77**

3.1	The Nature of Anger	77
	3.1.1 Aspects of Anger	77
	3.1.2 Positives and Negatives of Anger	79
3.2	Expressing Anger	80
	3.2.1 Methods of Expression	80
	3.2.2 Anger From Past Hurts	81
3.3	Some Counseling Strategies for Anger Management	82
	3.3.1 A Management Program	82
	3.3.2 The Reluctant Client	88
	3.3.3 Temper	88
3.4	Relationships Causing Anger	89
	3.4.1 Dealing With Our Own Anger	89
	3.4.2 Other People's Anger	91
3.5	Anger Toward God	92
3.6	Passive-Aggressive Anger	94
	3.6.1 Partner of a Passive-Aggressive Person	94
	3.6.2 Passive-Aggressive Clients	95
3.7	Biblical Viewpoint	96
	3.7.1 Anger in the Bible	96
	3.7.2 God's Anger	96
	3.7.3 Effect of Anger	97

4   Guilt and Shame   **99**

4.1	Introduction	99
	4.1.1 Comparing Guilt and Shame	100
4.2	Guilt	100
	4.2.1 Categories of Guilt	100
	4.2.2 Counseling for Guilt	101
4.3	Shame	103
	4.3.1 Nature of Shame	103
	4.3.2 Toxic Shame	104
	4.3.3 Shame and Intimate Relationships	105
4.4	Assessment of Shame	106
4.5	Counseling for Toxic Shame	107
	4.5.1 Shame from a Family System	107

	4.5.2	Adult Shame	109
4.6	Biblical Viewpoint		112
	4.6.1	Guilt	112
	4.6.2	Shame	113

5   Stress   **115**

5.1	Nature of Stress		115
	5.1.1	Physical Effects of Stress	116
	5.1.2	Stress and Personality Type	117
	5.1.3	Substances Causing Stress	117
5.2	Symptoms of Stress		118
5.3	Time Management		120
	5.3.1	Management Skills	120
5.4	Counseling for Stress		122
	5.4.1	Session Outline	122
	5.4.2	Stress Assessment	122
	5.4.3	Stress Reduction Methods	125
	5.4.4	Sleep	127
	5.4.5	Counseling Style	128
5.5	Biblical Viewpoint		128

6   Anxiety and Fear   **131**

6.1	Introduction		131
	6.1.1	Anxiety-Related Disorders	131
	6.1.2	Worry	132
	6.1.3	Personality Styles	133
6.2	Sleep Problems and Disorders		133
	6.2.1	Introduction	133
	6.2.2	Strategies to Improve Sleep	134
	6.2.3	Sleeping Pills	138
6.3	Counseling for Anxiety		139
	6.3.1	Source of Problems	139
	6.3.2	General Strategies	140
	6.3.3	Assessment and Strategies	141
6.4	Nervous Fatigue and Illness		144
	6.4.1	Four Fatigues	144
	6.4.2	Panic Attacks	146
	6.4.3	Counseling for a Panic Attack	147
	6.4.4	Hyperventilation	150
	6.4.5	Sleep and Nervous Illness	151
	6.4.6	Burnout	151

6.5   Biblical Viewpoint   153
        6.5.1   Worry   153
        6.5.2   Anxiety   153
        6.5.3   Fear   153

7   Anxiety Disorders   155

7.1   Some Background   155
7.2   Generalized Anxiety Disorder   158
        7.2.1   Symptoms and Diagnosis   158
        7.2.2   Counseling Strategies for GAD   159
7.3   Post-Traumatic Stress Disorder   161
        7.3.1   Introduction   161
        7.3.2   Diagnosis and Symptoms   162
        7.3.3   Memory Repression   163
        7.3.4   Counseling for Trauma and PTSD   166
7.4   Panic Disorder   172
        7.4.1   Assessment of PD   172
        7.4.2   Counseling for PD   173
7.5   Phobias   174
        7.5.1   Categories of Phobias   174
        7.5.2   Counseling for Phobias   175
7.6   Agoraphobia   176
        7.6.1   Diagnosis   176
        7.6.2   Counseling for Agoraphobia   177
7.7   Social Phobia   179
        7.7.1   Criteria   179
        7.7.2   Assessment of Social Phobia   180
        7.7.3   Counseling Social Phobia   181
7.8   Specific Phobias   184
7.9   Acceptance and Commitment Theory (ACT)   185
7.10   Biblical Viewpoint   188

8   Compulsive Disorders   189

8.1   Introduction   189
8.2   Obsessive-Compulsive Disorder   189
        8.2.1   Description   189
        8.2.2   Diagnosis of OCD   191
        8.2.3   Counseling for OCD   193
        8.2.4   Hoarding   199
8.3   Tic Disorder   203
        8.3.1   Definition and Background   203

	8.3.2	Classification of Tics	203
	8.3.3	Counseling for Tics	204
8.4	Body Dysmorphic Disorder		207
	8.4.1	General Symptoms	207
	8.4.2	Counseling BDD	208
8.5	Self-harm		209
	8.5.1	The Nature of Self-Harm	209
	8.5.2	Why Self-harm?	210
	8.5.3	Counseling for Self-Harm	212
8.6	Eating Disorders		215
	8.6.1	What are They?	215
	8.6.2	Restrictive Anorexia Nervosa	216
	8.6.3	Bulimia Nervosa	224
	8.6.4	Bulimic Anorexics	227
	8.6.5	Eating Disorder Not Otherwise Specified (EDNOS)	227
	8.6.6	Binge-Eating Disorder (BED)	228
8.7	Other Compulsive Actions		230
8.8	Biblical Viewpoint		230

9   Depression   **233**

9.1	Introduction		233
	9.1.1	Basic Symptoms	235
	9.1.2	Sleep Patterns	236
9.2	Causes of Depression		237
	9.2.1	Models of Depression	237
	9.2.2	Physical Causes	238
	9.2.3	Other Causes	239
9.3	Classifying Depression		240
	9.3.1	The Problem of Classification	240
	9.3.2	Reactive Depression	240
	9.3.3	Major Depressive Disorder	241
	9.3.4	Dysthymia	241
	9.3.5	Bipolar Disorder	242
	9.3.6	Postnatal Depression	244
	9.3.7	Seasonal Affective Disorder (SAD)	244
	9.3.8	Premenstrual Dysphoric Disorder (PMDD)	244
9.4	Counseling Strategies for Depression		245
	9.4.1	General Strategies	245
	9.4.2	Cognitive Methods	246
	9.4.3	Fifteen-Step Program	249
	9.4.4	Counseling for Bipolar Disorder	254
9.5	Biblical Viewpoint		254

9.5.1   Spiritual Effect of Depression   254
9.5.2   Biblical People and Depression   255
9.5.3   Some Misconceptions   255
9.5.4   Counseling Guidelines   256
9.5.5   Biblical Responses to Negative Thoughts   257
9.6   Appendix   257

10   Suicide Risk   **259**

10.1   Some Facts   259
10.2   Self-Preservation   260
10.3   Risk Assessment   261
10.4   Counseling for Suicide Risk   264
10.4.1   Uncovering Suicidal Thoughts   264
10.4.2   Coping With an Impossible Life   265
10.4.3   Some Strategies   266
10.5   Some Specific Suicide Factors   271
10.5.1   Alcohol and Drugs   271
10.5.2   Schizophrenia   271
10.5.3   Bipolar (Manic-Depressive) Disorder   271
10.5.4   Borderline Personality Disorder   272
10.5.5   Trauma   273
10.5.6   Suicide in the Elderly   273
10.6   Suicide Prevention Contracts   274
10.6.1   Do We Need Them?   274
10.6.2   Some Pitfalls of Contracts   275
10.6.3   Informed Consent   276
10.7   Biblical Viewpoint   276

11   Grief and Loss   **279**

11.1   Consequence of Loss   279
11.2   Death of a Loved One   280
11.2.1   Overview   280
11.2.2   Grief Models   281
11.2.3   Some Metaphors   285
11.2.4   Significance of Loss   286
11.2.5   Anger   287
11.3   Counseling Framework   288
11.3.1   Initial Sessions   288
11.3.2   Further Sessions   289
11.3.3   Some Aspects of Grieving   290
11.3.4   Children's Grief   293

		11.3.5	Suicide and Sudden Death	296
	11.4		Death of a Child at Any Age	298
		11.4.1	Miscarriage and Prenatal Deaths	298
		11.4.2	Sudden Infant Death Syndrome	299
		11.4.3	Loss of a Child	300
		11.4.4	Abortion and Grief	301
	11.5		Job Loss	303
		11.5.1	Introduction	303
		11.5.2	Grief Process	304
		11.5.3	Finding a New Job	304
	11.6		Unresolved Grief for a Loved One	305
	11.7		Biblical Viewpoint	307
		11.7.1	Story of Job	307
		11.7.2	Death Not the End	307
		11.7.3	Forgiveness	308

12	**Addictions: General**			**309**
	12.1		Introduction	309
	12.2		The Nature of Addiction	310
		12.2.1	Definition	310
		12.2.2	Substance and Behavioral Addictions	310
		12.2.3	Crossover Effects	311
		12.2.4	Goals and Loss of Control	311
	12.3		Diagnosis of Substance Addictions	311
	12.4		The Aim of an Addiction	312
	12.5		Categories of Addiction	313
	12.6		Addiction Models	314
		12.6.1	Addictive Personality	314
		12.6.2	The Addictive Self	314
	12.7		Counseling Methods	316
		12.7.1	Some General Comments	316
		12.7.2	Motivational Interviewing	317
	12.8		Biblical Viewpoint	325

13	**Substance Addictions**			**327**
	13.1		Introduction	327
	13.2		Smoking	327
		13.2.1	Nicotine Addiction	327
		13.2.2	Products of Cigarette Smoke	328
		13.2.3	Health Aspects	329
		13.2.4	Motivation to Stop	330

		13.2.5	Counseling Process	331
	13.3	Alcohol		334
		13.3.1	Physical and Social Effects	334
		13.3.2	Alcohol Assessment	336
		13.3.3	Counseling Strategies	337
		13.3.4	Harm Reduction	340
	13.4	Other Drugs		342
		13.4.1	Stimulants	343
		13.4.2	Opioids	343
		13.4.3	Cannabis	344
		13.4.4	Hallucinogens	345
		13.4.5	Party Drugs	345
	13.5	Biblical Viewpoint		346
14	**Addictions: Behavioral**			**347**
	14.1	General Comments		347
	14.2	Gambling		347
		14.2.1	When is It Addictive?	347
		14.2.2	Assessment	349
		14.2.3	Understanding Chance	350
		14.2.4	Counseling Strategies for Gambling	352
	14.3	Sexual Addictions		355
		14.3.1	What is Sexual Addiction?	355
		14.3.2	Role of Pornography	357
		14.3.3	Counseling for Sexual Addiction	362
		14.3.4	Sexual Anorexia	363
	14.4	Internet and Electronic Device Addiction		363
		14.4.1	Diagnosis and Assessment	363
		14.4.2	Counseling for Internet Addiction	365
	14.5	Relationship Addiction		366
		14.5.1	Recognizing Relationship Addiction	366
		14.5.2	Counseling for Relationship Addiction	371
	14.6	Workaholism		376
		14.6.1	The Nature of Workaholism	376
		14.6.2	Counseling Strategies for Workaholism	376
	14.7	Compulsive Eating		377
		14.7.1	Relationship with Food	377
		14.7.2	Assessment	379
		14.7.3	Counseling for Compulsive Eating	379
		14.7.4	Relapse Prevention	382
	14.8	Biblical Viewpoint		382
		14.8.1	Gambling	382

14.8.2	Sexual Addiction	383
14.8.3	Workaholism	384
14.8.4	Religious Addiction	384

15 Adults Abused as Children — **387**

15.1	Introduction	387
15.2	Sexual Abuse	388
	15.2.1 What is it?	388
	15.2.2 Stages of Abuse	391
	15.2.3 Effects of Sexual Abuse	392
	15.2.4 Counseling Strategies	398
15.3	Physical Abuse	405
15.4	Psychological Abuse	406
	15.4.1 Effects of Divorce, Legal or Emotional	407
	15.4.2 Adult Children of Alcoholics	409
15.5	Biblical Viewpoint	412
	15.5.1 Child abuse	412

16 Abused Adults — **415**

16.1	Introduction	415
	16.1.1 Control	415
	16.1.2 Counseling the Controller	418
16.2	Physical Abuse	418
	16.2.1 Prevalence	418
	16.2.2 Men's Violence Against Women	419
	16.2.3 Women's Violence Against Men	421
	16.2.4 Counseling for Physical Abuse	422
16.3	Adult Sexual Abuse	425
	16.3.1 Rape	426
16.4	Psychological Abuse	427
16.5	Why People Stay With Abusive Partners	428
	16.5.1 Abusive Men	428
	16.5.2 Abusive Women	430
16.6	Abuse of the Elderly	430
16.7	Spiritual Abuse	431
	16.7.1 Defining Spiritual Abuse	431
	16.7.2 Recognizing an Abusive System	432
	16.7.3 Hallmarks of a Spiritually Abused Person	434
	16.7.4 Why Stay?	435
	16.7.5 Counseling for Spiritual Abuse	435
16.8	Biblical Viewpoint	436

16.8.1   Control Issues   436
16.8.2   Partner Abuse   437
16.8.3   Spiritual Abuse and the Bible   438

17   Dysfunctional Relationships   441

17.1   Introduction   441
17.2   General Boundaries   441
17.2.1   Nature of Boundaries   441
17.2.2   Some Boundary Principles   442
17.2.3   Recognizing Unhealthy Boundaries   443
17.2.4   Counseling for Boundary Issues   445
17.3   Particular Boundaries   449
17.3.1   Boundary Checklist   449
17.3.2   Boundaries with Self   450
17.3.3   Boundaries and Partners   450
17.3.4   Boundaries and Family   451
17.3.5   Boundaries and Friends   452
17.3.6   Resistance to Boundaries   455
17.4   Codependency   456
17.4.1   Definition and Nature of Codependency   456
17.4.2   Assessment   458
17.4.3   Counseling for Codependency   460
17.5   Biblical Viewpoint   463
17.5.1   Boundaries   463
17.5.2   Codependency   464

18   Divorce   465

18.1   General Comments   465
18.1.1   Grief from Divorce   466
18.1.2   Attachment Issues   467
18.1.3   Narcissistic Injury   468
18.2   The Fall-out From Divorce   469
18.2.1   Family and Friends   469
18.2.2   Telling the Children   469
18.2.3   Effect on the Children   470
18.3   Parenting and Divorce   472
18.4   Looking Back   476
18.4.1   Reasons For Breakdown   476
18.5   Forgiveness   477
18.6   Biblical Perspective   479

19   Couple Relationship Counseling   **481**

  19.1   Introduction   481
       19.1.1 Who Should Come to Counseling?   481
  19.2   Models for Counseling   483
       19.2.1 Life-Cycle Models   483
       19.2.2 Psychoanalytic Models   485
       19.2.3 Imago Model   489
       19.2.4 Cohabitation   490
  19.3   General Problem Areas   491
       19.3.1 Couple Issues   491
       19.3.2 Intra-personal Problems   493
       19.3.3 Inter-personal Problems   494
       19.3.4 Environmental Problems   496
  19.4   Some Specific Issues   497
       19.4.1 Forgiveness   497
       19.4.2 An Affair   498
       19.4.3 Sexual Problems   500
  19.5   Counseling Structure   505
       19.5.1 Some General Principles   505
       19.5.2 Setting the Scene   505
       19.5.3 First Session   506
       19.5.4 Other Sessions   508
       19.5.5 Some Dos and Don'ts of Evaluation   510
  19.6   Couple Communication Skills   511
       19.6.1 Conversing   512
       19.6.2 Art of Listening   513
       19.6.3 Feelings Contract   516
       19.6.4 Conflict and Disagreement   516
       19.6.5 Love Languages   519
       19.6.6 Role of Birth Order   521
  19.7   Some Miscellaneous Interventions   522
  19.8   Couple Exercises   523
  19.9   Biblical Viewpoint   525
       19.9.1 Marriage Model   525
       19.9.2 What is Love?   526
       19.9.3 Who Is in Charge?   526
       19.9.4 Love and Respect   527
       19.9.5 Adultery   528

20   Blended Families   **529**

  20.1   Introduction   529

20.2		Stepfamilies from Remarriage and Divorce	530
	20.2.1	Some Problem Areas	531
	20.2.2	Counseling and Blended Families	535
20.3		Stepfamilies from Cohabitation	536
20.4		Blended Families with Same Sex Parents	537
20.5		Adopted Children	537
	20.5.1	How Well Do Adopted Children Do?	538
	20.5.2	Open Adoption	543
	20.5.3	Single Parent Adoption	543
20.6		The Adult Triad	544
	20.6.1	Fathers	544
	20.6.2	Adults Adopted as Children	545
	20.6.3	Adoptive Mothers	546
	20.6.4	Birth Mother	548
20.7		Biblical Viewpoint	551
	20.7.1	Blended Families	551
	20.7.2	Adoption	551

21 Personality disorders: General Concepts — **553**

21.1		Introduction	553
21.2		General Psychological Assessment	556
	21.2.1	Gathering Information	556
	21.2.2	BAATOMI Assessment	558
21.3		Indications of a Personality Disorder	559
21.4		Categories of Personality Disorders	560
	21.4.1	Cluster A	560
	21.4.2	Cluster B	561
	21.4.3	Cluster C	562
	21.4.4	Other Disorders	562
	21.4.5	Treatability	563
21.5		Defense Mechanisms	563
21.6		Biblical Viewpoint	566

22 Personality disorders: Counseling — **567**

22.1		General Counseling Strategies	567
22.2		Cluster A	568
	22.2.1	Paranoid PD	568
	22.2.2	Schizoid PD	570
	22.2.3	Schizotypal PD	572
22.3		Cluster B	574
	22.3.1	Antisocial PD	574

	22.3.2	Borderline PD	575
	22.3.3	Histrionic PD	578
	22.3.4	Narcissistic PD	580
22.4	Cluster C		583
	22.4.1	Avoidant PD	583
	22.4.2	Dependent PD	586
	22.4.3	Obsessive-Compulsive PD	589
22.5	Other Disorders		591
	22.5.1	Depressive PD	591
	22.5.2	Negativistic (Passive-Aggressive) PD	593
	22.5.3	Masochistic (Self-defeating) PD	595
	22.5.4	Sadistic PD	597
22.6	Biblical Viewpoint		598

References   600

Index   627

PREFACE

The aim of this book is to provide a handy look-up reference. It focuses on providing information as well as techniques and counseling ideas for dealing with a variety of psychological problems and issues that an inexperienced therapist might encounter in the counseling room. I hope that the book will also be useful for the more experienced therapist, especially for some of the more difficult counseling issues. It is assumed throughout this book that the therapist is in regular professional supervision. In New Zealand, as in most countries, such supervision is a standard requirement for all therapeutic practice.

This book is not an in-depth psychological book nor a self-help book (though some may find it useful in the latter case), but along with the references and extensive bibliography will I believe be a useful resource. I am well aware that a string of techniques is not counseling as therapy needs to be anchored to sound psychological principles, which I have endeavored to endorse throughout. I therefore assume that the reader has at least a basic knowledge of psychotherapy and counseling methods as well as familiarity with the terminology used. In the latter case I try to explain all terms used as I proceed. Throughout the book I endeavor to give some prevalence statistics. Data on any particular topic can vary a great deal and may not be current or very accurate. However, my aim is not for data accuracy but rather to provide a very rough idea of prevalence for the therapist's interest.

Before proceeding further I want to clarify something about terminology. Some people distinguish between a psychotherapist and a counselor, while others use the words interchangeably. It does depend to some extent on the country, for example psychotherapist is used in the U.S. and counselor in the U.K. A distinction is made in New Zealand because of differing qualifications. As I do not wish to enter into this debate, I have titled this book accordingly and I shall use the generic term therapist to represent both groups. A therapist in this book is simply someone who does counseling.

I want to say something about what led me to write such a book. I began my training as a therapist rather late in life having had a long career as a professor of statistics and mathematical author. The journey into counseling in my later years was for me a real challenge, not only in writing assignments in a completely different field, but also in undergoing exercises about self-awareness. I found that I had to be able to change from a person who told people what to do and how to solve their problems into a person who listened and helped people solve their own problems! Preparing a wide variety of assignments opened the door to the extensive literature on the subject and helped me to appreciate the existence of several hundred therapies or methods of counseling that are available. Reading books like Sexton et al. (1997) and McLeod (1998) from my statistical perspective helped me to realize the difficulty of trying to compare the effectiveness of various counseling methods and interventions and to appreciate that more than one method could be used in any specific counseling session. However, there are specific situations when certain methods tend to be favored, for example, cognitive behavioral therapy for depression and motivational interviewing for addictions. The key element of any counseling is the therapist/client relationship, which is more important than the method used—something I always try to remember.

When I began counseling as part of my training, I often wanted to get some background on a particular issue, for example, anger, and find strategies for approaching this issue. I found two sources to help me; one consisted of books on therapies that I looked through for hints on anger management, and the second was reading books just on anger. Neither source I found completely satisfactory as they both required considerable time in searching for suitable strategies. Although I benefitted from the reading as my custom is to take notes, I had limited time available to read whole books. More recently I have found the internet to be a wonderful resource. Now, some years down the track, I want to remedy the situation that I found then by writing a different kind of counseling book, namely one which focuses on issues and techniques, rather than on therapies. One danger in this approach is that of repetition, as one method can be applied to a variety of issues so that some repetition is unavoidable.

Writing such a book opened up some challenges for me. First, I faced the challenge of a multitude of psychological issues: Which ones should I leave out? Clearly some strategies could be applied quite generally, as in the case of addiction, but they often need to be adapted specifically. For example, individual addictions such as alcoholism, smoking, an averseness to needles, and gambling are all very different. Some topics I have deliberately omitted because of space are family counseling, counseling children, counseling parents with problem children, and some specialized topics within each chapter. Given the perverseness of human nature and the variety of human predicaments, I have no doubt omitted one of your favorite issues! Please let me know of any topic which you would have liked to have been covered (e-mail: seber@stat.auckland.ac.nz or g.seber@auckland.ac.nz).

I have also considered some topics that should be dealt with by an experienced therapist such as, for example, eating disorders, self-harm, and personality disorders. However, it is important for an inexperienced therapist to be able to recognize when such an issue arises so that they can at least refer these clients on to more competent therapists. In trying to cover such a wide field, a related problem I am keenly aware of is oversimplification; for example how does one deal with a subject like depression in a single chapter. As I have had to be selective, one answer is through the references to further reading. My choice of references has been largely determined by what is available from local university libraries (including electronic books) and what books I own myself. Sometimes I have had to make do with a less than recent edition. The internet is also a great source of information and I make frequent references to web sites, though one has to be careful to refer to only authoritative sources.

A second challenge that I met I have already alluded to, namely that we can use more than one method to deal with an issue. We all have our favorite approaches even if our style is eclectic, for example, cognitive behavior therapy, transactional analysis, and narrative therapy are all quite different in the way they deal with client problems. Although I have tried to keep in mind the various approaches in writing this book, some techniques or ideas will need to be adapted to your own favorite counseling style.

A third challenge in covering so many counseling issues is that many of the topics overlap. For example, anxiety, anxiety disorders, stress, and phobias overlap, and sleep problems turn up in various places. The therapist often finds that a client has more than one type of problem (comorbidity). I endeavor to get round these difficulties through cross-referencing.

A fourth challenge was how to cater for the reader who is a Christian therapist. As many biblical principles make authentic psychological sense, I have added a brief section entitled "Biblical Viewpoint" at the end of each chapter that endeavors to comment on the material in just that chapter from a biblical perspective. The spiritual is very important in counseling and I am well aware of different world views in dealing with the religious as opposed to the spiritual— a controversial subject. I have endeavored to keep to basic ideas about spirituality, but there will be those who feel I am not biblical enough while others will ignore this add-on section. I believe that my book will be a useful addition to a pastor's bookshelves.

The first two chapters are general introductions that I will refer back to in later chapters, when needed. In Chapter 1 I give some aspects of physiology and brain function to provide a background for thoughts, emotions, behavior, and mind-body interactions. The effect of aging is also mentioned. Chapter 2 is a large chapter about wholeness in the various areas of our lives, namely the physical, mental, emotional, social, and spiritual areas. Topics like the sleep process, relaxation techniques, attachment, assertiveness, self-esteem, and forgiveness are included for later reference. In Chapters 3–6 I refer to issues relating to the common emotions of anger, guilt and shame, stress, and anxiety and fear. The so-called Axis I disorders, like anxiety disorders, phobias, and trauma are in Chapter 7 with compulsive type disorders in Chapter 8. Depression in its various forms is discussed in Chapter 9 while the related topic of suicide risk follows in Chapter 10. Grief and loss are considered in detail in Chapter 11, where the focus is on a variety of losses that one can meet. Addictions are the subject of the next three chapters 12–14 including general addiction counseling, and substance and behavioral addictions. The next two chapters are about abuse; Chapter 15 focussing on adults abused as children and Chapter 16 dealing with adults and various forms of adult abuse. The four chapters 17–20 deal with relationship issues, namely dysfunctional relationships, divorce, couple counseling, and blended families (including adoption). The book concludes with two chapters that deal with personality disorders.

In conclusion, there are several people I wish to thank. My special thanks go to Brian McStay, my supervisor and friend, who has continually encouraged me in the writing of this book and has given me time from his busy schedule to read a first draft of this book and provide valuable comments. I also thank Siobhan Whiting for reading some of the earlier chapters and providing helpful input. I am very grateful to Amy Hendrickson for the use of her Latex electronic package and her technical assistance. Last, but certainly not least, I am most grateful to my wife Jean for her patience and long suffering support while I wrote a book of this size.

GEORGE A. F. SEBER

Auckland, New Zealand
January 2013

CHAPTER 1

BRAIN MATTERS

1.1 INTRODUCTION

I decided to start this book where it all begins—in the brain. With modern developments in brain physiology we are beginning to find that many psychological problems have a physiological basis. We also find that the brain is an organ capable of changing and adapting itself in remarkable ways—described as brain plasticity.[1] The brain has a capacity to reorganize itself and find new ways to perform lost functions. Richard Faull, a neuroscientist at Auckland University, New Zealand, provided first evidence that the diseased human brain can repair itself by the generation of new brain cells. This new knowledge about the brain has been particularly helpful with, for example, stroke victims using constraint induced movement.[2] The brain's plasticity provides a reason why a person gets locked into a particular behavior (e.g., obsessive compulsive disorder, pornography); the structure of the brain becomes altered. Doige says: "The plastic paradox is that the same neuroplastic properties that allow us to change our brains and produce more flexible behaviors can also allow us to produce more rigid ones."[3] The key is to help the brain reorganize itself again; an idea that has considerable repercussions for the future of

---

[1] See the fascinating book by Doige (2007).
[2] For details see the internet.
[3] Doige (2007: 242).

Counseling Issues: A Handbook for Counselors and Psychotherapists. By George A. F. Seber **1**
Copyright © 2013 G. A. F. Seber

counseling and treating people with, for example, compulsive psychological problems.[4]

In this chapter I wish to consider a number of topics about the human brain to provide some background to when they merge later in this book. I will address some relevant aspects of brain structure, function, and memory, ego states, and body/mind techniques as they relate to counseling. This is followed by a discussion on personality, and the connections between emotions, feelings, and thoughts as they too relate to counseling. The chapter finishes with an extensive section on the aging process, including midlife reassessment and aspects of the aging brain that can be helpfully used in counseling older people. I conclude with a biblical viewpoint of this topic.

In future chapters I shall consider a number of disorders that have their origin in brain function. Psychological problems can be categorized by, for example, the Diagnostic and Statistical Manual of Mental Disorders (DSM) as Axis I, II, III, IV, and V disorders. Axis I refers to depression, anxiety disorders, compulsive disorders, phobias, and addictions, Axis II to personality disorders, Axis III to medical conditions, Axis IV to current stressful events, and Axis V to functioning.[5] Although all five categories are generally covered in this book, my chapter divisions will be different. It should be noted that there are some problems with the DSM mentioned in the report of the American Psychiatric Association planning committee for DSM-V. For example:

> The goal of validating these syndromes and discovering common etiologies has remained elusive. Despite many proposed candidates, not one laboratory marker has been found to be specific in identifying any of the DSM-defined syndromes.[6]

What is more concerning is the following comment:

> Epidemiological and clinical studies have shown that extremely high rates of comorbidities among disorders, undermining the hypothesis that the syndromes represent distinct etiologies. Furthermore, epidemiological studies have shown a high degree of short-term diagnostic instability for many disorders. With regard to treatment, lack of specificity is the rule rather than the exception.[7]

Referring to the DSM system, Elfert and Rorsyth (2005: 7–8) note that: "The 'comorbidity' rates among disorders are so high as to challenge the basic definitional integrity of the entire system," and "A syndrome focus has led us to develop treatment approaches that over emphasize symptom reduction and downplay functional and positive markers of psychological health." There is a tendency to view distressing states of mind as signs of disorder and disease but this does seem to work very well. There is a strong focus on disease models.

1.1.1   Mind over Matter

We are all aware of how our minds affect our bodies. Our psychological health can affect our physical health and the physical effects can linger on well after the

---

[4]See Doige (2007: chapter 6).
[5]A helpful overview and assessment is given in a downloadable form called the Psychotherapy Assessment Checklist (PAC) at http://www.affectphobia.org/pacforms.html (accessed November 2010). It is not used for making a final diagnosis.
[6]Kupfer et al. (2002: xviii).
[7]Kupfer et al. (2002: xviii).

psychological problems have gone. For example, reactive depression can set in after we experience a significant loss in our lives. Stress can also affect us physically in many ways. Ailments arising from psychological sources are referred as *psychosomatic* illnesses[8] and are due to complex mind/body/spirit interactions as well as the interaction between heredity and environment. So often people express their pain in bodily symptoms. Terrifying physical symptoms can occur with panic attacks (Section 6.4.2) and post traumatic stress disorder or PTSD (Section 7.3). Addictions are related to substances produced in the brain called *neurotransmitters*. For example, the so-called *reward system* of the brain is involved with the neurotransmitter dopamine.

Given this brief selection of body–mind interactions, I felt it would be appropriate to discuss some physiology of the brain as a prelude to discussing psychological issues. As this is a complex and, at times, a controversial subject, I will be giving only a brief and rather simplified overview of some aspects of brain physiology and related topics.[9] Some aspects are technical, but they can help us understand some of the theory behind counseling.

1.2 BRAIN STRUCTURE

1.2.1 Nerve Cells

Nerve cells or *neurons* are electrically excited cells that process and transmit information and are the core components of the brain, spinal chord, and peripheral nerves. Extending out of each neuron like branches of a tree are a large number of *dendrites*,[10] each covered with small "knobs" called *dendritic spines* that increase the number of possible interconnections. Many neurons have just a single nerve fiber called an *axon* that carries primary messages away from the body of the cell or *soma* to another neuron, muscle cell, or cells in some other organ. Most axons divide many times and the branches connect with other neurons via their dendrites. The axons are in effect the primary transmission lines of the nervous system and, as bundles, help make up nerves. At the ends of the axon branches there are so-called terminal buttons each followed by a "gap" called a *synapse*, which is chemical in nature. When an electrical message hits the synapse it is transported across the gap by a chemical called a *neurotransmitter* on route to the next neuron; such messages generally move in one direction only. Thus each neurotransmitter is like a key that fits into a special "lock" called a receptor and when a neurotransmitter finds its receptor it activates the receptor's nerve cell.

It has been estimated that the brain has approximately 100 billion neurons[11] and each neuron has on average 7,000 synaptic connections to other neurons.[12] Different synapses have different neurotransmitters and it is these substances that have a major effect on how the brain functions and on our emotions. One transmitter, for

---

[8]From *psyche* (soul) and *soma* (body).
[9]For a summary of the various parts see the website
http://www.enspirepress.com/writings_on_consciousness/brain_physiology/brain_physiology.html
by Mark Bancroft (accessed November 2010), and also LeDoux (1998).
[10]Dendron is Greek for tree.
[11]See the table in http://hypertextbook.com/facts/2002/AniciaNdabahaliye2.shtml (accessed November 2010).
[12]http://en.wikipedia.org/wiki/Neurons#Neurons_in_the_brain (accessed November 2010).

example, that is involved in many functions, including muscle movement, breathing, heart rate, learning, and memory is acetylcholine. An important group of common neurotransmitters called monamines include dopamine, adrenaline (epinephrine), noradrenaline (norepinephrine), serotonin, and melatonin.[13] The names in brackets are alternative names used in the U.S. Dopamine plays an important role in addictions,[14] adrenaline and noradrenaline are involved in stress, serotonin is associated with the feeling of well being and its lack can lead to depression, and melatonin plays an important role in sleep. These substances will be discussed specifically elsewhere in relation to therapy. In general, "every addictive drug mimics or blocks some neurotransmitter."[15]

1.2.2   Brain Function

There are several key areas of our brain that relate to how we react to situations. The first has been called our "emotional brain" and has been described as being located in the *limbic system* that includes two important areas, namely the *amygdala*[16] and the *hippocampus*.[17] However, this location has been called into question as the brain is much more complicated and LeDoux believes that the concept of the limbic system should be abolished.[18] The second key area is the *neocortex*, our "thinking brain." It is part of the cerebral cortex, the outermost layer of the brain (commonly called the "grey matter" because of its color), that is the source of our rational thinking and is where most of the memory is stored. The amygdala performs a primary role in the processing and memory of emotional reactions, for example trauma, and it is discussed in more detail in Sections 1.2.3 and 1.4.2 below. Another concept that has been criticized by LeDoux is the evolutionary idea of an old and new part of the cortex.

The view that the brain is divided into thinking and feeling parts, which has received a lot of past support is now being criticized as being too simplistic. Lazarus[19] maintains that we only have one mind, not two, that combines both thought and feeling; Damasio[20] says a similar thing, but in more technical language. As Baker comments, "Emotions and cognition both develop together as mutually interacting systems. The two become fused as part of our total experience."[21] Greenberg[22] uses the metaphor of two selves—one drives cognition and the other, which is more automatic, drives emotions. These two selves don't necessarily get along and one goal of therapy is to integrate the two; the integration of head and heart.

Two Hemispheres

The brain is divided into two hemispheres, and the communication between them takes place through the *corpus callosum*. The left hemisphere controls the right half

---

[13]See http://en.wikipedia.org/wiki/Neurotransmitter (accessed November 2010).

[14]For a fascinating article on the topic see Nash (1997).

[15]Goldstein (2001: 34).

[16]Amygdala is Greek for "almond" describing the shape of this cluster of neurons.

[17]Greek for "sea horse."

[18]See http://www.columbia.edu/~lep1/rry/w3410/LeDoux/NYT.Nov.96.html (accessed November 2010) and LeDoux (1998: 99–101).

[19]Lazarus, R. (1999).

[20]Damasio (1994).

[21]Baker (2007: 35).

[22]Greenberg (2002: ix-x).

of the body and is more about doing so that it involves reasoning and the logical, mathematical, and language based skills. The right hemisphere controls the left half of the body and is more about being so that it involves comprehension, imagination, creativity, insight, and relaxation. The way they work together is interesting. For example, the left side hears the words, whereas the right side appreciates the moral or metaphor of the story and the punch line of jokes. The left side reads the music score, while the right side determines the pitch and quality of the tones. The left brain assesses facts and the right brain appears to be more concerned with moral values.

Gender Brain Differences

There are some differences in male and female brains, the result of different testosterone levels. A clear difference is the size with the male human brain being on average, larger; however in females, who generally do not have as high a testosterone level, the corpus callosum is proportionally larger. This means that the effect of testosterone is a greater overall brain volume, but a decreased connection between the hemispheres.[23]

1.2.3   Memory

The good news is that we never run out of memory, as there are no known limits for memory storage. Our brain's memory is essentially limitless! We tend to think of memory as two types. The first is short term, which is better described as "working memory," where we temporarily keep information required for a task at hand. This is limited and temporary. To retain such memories they need to be transferred to "long-term" memory. This is not a single storage location as long-term memories are distributed right throughout the brain, and different parts are devoted to different types of memory functions.[24]

Long-term Memory

Long-term memory comes in two broad types (alternative names in brackets): declarative (explicit) and procedural (implicit or non-declarative), which acquire and store different kinds of information for long periods of time.[25] Explicit or conscious memory is where we store "how-to" information like driving a car or playing a musical instrument. Some explicit memories, called semantic memories, are facts about the world, while others are more image-based and represent scenes or episodes from our experience (episodic memories). Here the recall is intentional and conscious, and information stored in explicit memory is about a specific event that happened at a specific time and place. In forming and storing explicit memories, associations are made with previous related stimuli or experiences so that they can be remembered and recalled. On the other hand, implicit memory refers to remembering that occurs without effort or conscious awareness and usually relates to habits and skills, like riding a bike. It is best demonstrated when performance is improved on a task. We note that the hippocampus in the brain seems to play a critical role in storing information in our long-term memories. High levels of

[23]Solms and Turnbull (2002).
[24]LeDoux (1998: 180).
[25]Papalia, Olds, and Feldman (2001: 175–176). See also wikipedia.

stress hormones in the bloodstream may shrink the hippocampus and reduce its performance.[26]

Implicit or unconscious memories play a role in alerting us to dangerous or threatening situations and are created through fear conditioning. We may be aware that the fear is there, but we don't have control over its occurrence or have access to its workings. Implicit memories cannot be looked up or remembered in order to use them for actions and reasoning. These memories are linked to the amygdala system. The conscious explicit memory of the fear response, namely the set of unemotional facts relating to the response that generally occurs at the same time, has been called "the memory of the emotion," while the unconscious implicit memory of the emotional response can be termed the "emotional memory."[27] Sometimes these two systems don't communicate as for example with people who have not recovered emotionally from a traumatic event. The resolution of the trauma involves integrating these two memory systems.

Amygdala in Action

In general, when we have an emotional situation, the amygdala system gives rise to an implicit emotional memory and the hippocampal system gives rise to an explicit memory about the emotional situation. The current arousal from the amygdala combined with the explicit memory of past emotions can reinforce fear conditioning,[28] thus making various disorders such as phobias difficult to deal with. Furthermore, when the amygdala system is activated, it turns on all sorts of body systems such as the autonomic nervous system, which in turn activates the adrenal gland that releases adrenaline into the bloodstream. This adrenaline ends up influencing various parts of the brain including the hippocampus, thus strengthening the explicit memories created there so that such memories are stronger than explicit memories of unemotional situations.

If a person faces prolonged stress or trauma, the hippocampus can be damaged, thus explaining why some traumatic events may not be easily recalled. In the case of child abuse, the problem is compounded by the fact that the amygdala matures in a child before the hippocampus.

Memory Association

It should be noted that the brain doesn't store a photographic record of our life that we can access at will. In fact most of our stream of consciousness passes through our brains unpreserved. The key idea is that memory is a phenomenon of association so that the more links we can make in our brain with a particular item the better we will remember it. We can remember a name better if we can also link that person with other items of information about them. Although working memory and and the "episodic" form of declarative memory can decline over time, semantic and procedural memories are quite stable. However, the ability to lay down new memories can be improved with mental exercise. By making lists and using mnemonic tricks, for example, we can augment our more vulnerable working memory. Memoirs, scrapbooks, photos, and so forth, can also be helpful.

---

[26] Papalia et al. (2001: 668).
[27] LeDoux (1998: 182, 202).
[28] For further details see http://serendip.brynmawr.edu/exchange/node/1749 (accessed November 2010).

Linked with the memory are the important concepts of fluid intelligence and crystallized intelligence. Fluid intelligence is on-the-spot reasoning ability that does not depend completely on prior learning. It is the sort of "native" intelligence that IQ tests sometimes strive to measure. Crystallized intelligence is what we accumulate throughout life and arises out of experience. Many studies have shown that fluid intelligence slowly declines with age, but crystallized intelligence often improves and expands. We can learn new skills as we get older.

Information from an event is slowly assimilated into long-term memory over time until it reaches a relatively permanent state.[29] During this consolidation period, the memory can be modulated by the amygdala. For example, emotional arousal following an event can increase the strength of the memory of that event, the greater the arousal the stronger the memory. We see this in the persistence of traumatic memories.

1.2.4 Ego States

Through brain activity, neurons connect up together to form a neural network that relates to a particular state of mind.[30] If an overwhelming trauma occurs or a particular (positive or negative) state of mind is repeated, the state of mind engendered in both cases becomes engrained in a single network called an *ego state* that we can describe as a part of self with a point of view.[31] Berne defined an ego state as "a consistent pattern of feeling and experience directly related to a corresponding consistent pattern of behavior."[32] For example, with certain events one can consistently experience uncomfortable childhood memories and then feel panicky; experience and feelings consistently occur together.

Ego states reflect positive or negative experiences depending on caregiver-child interactions and can change with time, generally becoming more engrained (for better or worse) as new events are interpreted in the light of past experience. Those positive parts tend to live in the present while negative wounded parts due to painful experiences such as childhood neglect or abuse remain stuck in the past. These states vary in complexity. For example, a single event can give rise to several states, or a single state can include a large area of one's life making up many events (e.g., recreation). Our parts of self can disagree, leading to ambivalence (i.e., "Shall I or shall I not ...."), which we all experience. The stuck-child part can conflict with an adult part. Child ego states can form to mimic other people, called *introjects*, and these can have a profound impact on the adult later. For example, life events can trigger a child ego state causing an adult to act inappropriately.

Various ego-state therapies have been developed and some are briefly described below:

---

[29]Referred to as *memory consolidation.*
[30]Siegel (1999).
[31]See http://www.shirleyjeanschmidt.com/aboutdnms.html by Shirley Jean Schmidt and http://www.clinicalsocialwork.com/overview.html by Helen Watkins (both accessed November 2010) for some helpful comments about ego states.
[32]Berne (1966).

1. Transactional analysis or TA (with Parent, Adult, and Child, or PAC states) was developed by Eric Berne (1961).[33] Two key ideas of this method are the PAC model and the life-script.

2. Ego-state therapy, generally regarded as being attributed to John G. Watkins, utilizes family and group-therapy techniques along with hypnosis for the resolution of conflicts between the different ego states that constitutes a "family of self" within a single individual.[34]

3. Inner-child therapies became popular in the late 1980's and are aimed at finding healthy ways to heal the wounded inner child by nurturing child ego states. There are a number of writers associated with this development such as Bradshaw (1990), Napier (1993), Paul (1992), and others.[35]

4. Eye Movement Desentization and Reprocessing (EMDR) was developed by Francine Shapiro in the early 1990's[36] and it is described in the following section.

5. Developmental Needs Meeting Strategy (DNMS) was developed by Shirley Jean Schmidt.[37] It uses the nurturing and protective adult parts of self along with the spiritual core self to deal with introjected caregivers (stuck ego states that mimic significant childhood role models) and child reactive parts.

Ego-state methods need to be carried out with care as they can lead to creating even more parts of self and an increasing ego-state isolation, especially if a person has dissociation problems.

1.2.5 Body/Mind Techniques

There are a number of techniques that seem somewhat strange when first encountered. I mention them because they indicate certain subtle connections between mind and body that open up new possibilities in counseling.

Alternating Bilateral Stimulation (ABS)

ABS refers to a method of stimulating both sides of the brain by applying alternating stimuli of various kinds. This was first introduced as part of a method of psychotherapy called Eye Movement Desensitization and Reprocessing (EMDR), already mentioned above. Clients were asked to move their eyes rapidly back and forth (e.g., tracking the therapist's fingers as they are moved from side to side) while they concentrated on disturbing or upsetting emotional material.

Other forms of stimulation have since been introduced, a popular choice being alternating bilateral tactile stimulation where the therapist taps the client's knees, hands, or feet, or the client uses an electronic device where two hand-held pulsars

---

[33] Helpful introductions are http://en.wikipedia.org/wiki/Transactional_analysis (accessed November 2010), Stewart (2000), and for greater detail, Stewart and Joines (2003).
[34] See Watkins and Watkins (1997).
[35] A helpful article on the topic is http://www.livestrong.com/article/14692-inner-child/ (accessed November 2010).
[36] See Shapiro (2001) and Shapiro, Kaslow, and Maxfield (2007).
A brief description is given at http://www.emdr.com/briefdes.htm (accessed November 2010).
[37] Schmidt (2004).

vibrate in an alternating fashion.[38] Some clients prefer auditory ABS using a headset that provides beeping sounds or music patterns alternately to each ear. Clients can also tap their own knees.

The idea behind ABS is that the alternating movement is thought to affect the way the memory is accessed and treated so that any disturbing affect is neutralized by "desensitization" and "reprocessing." It enables clients to get fully in touch with their memories and accompanying feelings, so care is needed in using ABS or EMDR as feelings are intensified. The method should therefore be used only by personnel trained in its use.

ABS seems to be particularly useful in dealing with trauma, especially single incident events (e.g., seeing horrendous accidents and acts of violence), post traumatic stress disorder, and childhood abuse.[39] However, it has been used in many other areas as well.[40] In dealing with adults who suffered as children, EMDR can be combined with ego state ideas as it activates the child part.[41] An important feature of ABS is that it also helps strengthen positive beliefs about self, which is the basis for its use in both EMDR and DNMS (mentioned in the previous section).

We now consider some body/mind methods based on tapping certain parts of the body.

Tapping Techniques

There is an unconventional technique called thought field therapy (TFT) for dealing with emotional problems that involves tapping with the fingertips at the end points of the body's so-called "energy meridians." The theory behind the method is that the cause of all negative emotions is a disruption in the body's energy system that is fixed by tapping.[42] A similar method based on the same principles has joined forces with TFT called emotional freedom technique (EFT), where EFT is an emotional version of acupuncture.[43] At the time of writing this there seems to be a need for further well-designed scientific studies on the usefulness of these methods.[44] One complicating factor pointed out by some skeptics is the possible existence of a placebo effect. However, there is anecdotal evidence that people have been helped by these methods. They have been used, for example, to deal with traumatic thoughts and uncomfortable emotions. For further details see, for example, Bender, Britt, and Diepold (2004).

[38]For an example of such a device see www.theratapper.com (accessed November 2010).
[39]Parnell (1997). She gives a fascinating collection of case studies demonstrating the applicability of EMDR and the rapid recovery of clients.
[40]See http://www.emdr.com/pop.htm (accessed November 2010) for some applications.
[41]Parnell (1997: chapter 5).
[42]For a description of the method see, for example, http://www.trauma-pages.com/s/tft.php (accessed November 2010).
[43]See http://www.eftuniverse.com/ or http://www.eftwellbeing.co.nz/ (accessed November 2010).
[44]See for example http://en.wikipedia.org/wiki/Thought_Field_Therapy (accessed November 2010) for some critical comments.

1.2.6   Pain Management

I want to say something about pain management as pain can have a serious effect on our well-being.[45] Alternating Bilateral Stimulation, described above, has been used to help a person cope better with chronic pain.[46] An interesting aspect of pain is that there is a so-called *pain gateway* that can be used to ameliorate its effects. An unpleasant stimulus like a cut or sting, is detected by peripheral nerves in that area sending a signal to the spinal chord. The signal is then sent to the brain via a gateway and the brain then relays the message of pain to the effected area. In the spinal chord there are specialized nerves acting like "gatekeepers" that sort the signals according to their severity. For a life threatening signal, the gate is wide open and the signal follows an express route to the brain. For a weak signal (e.g., scratch), the gate may be partially closed or completely closed. However, the brain can work in reverse and close the gate by sending an inhibitory message back down. Pain management is using distraction to close the gate as much as possible, minimizing the signal to the brain.

There are three factors involved in the opening and closing of the gate; physical, emotional, and mental conditions.

Open

    (a) Physical conditions.

        • the extent of the injury
        • any inappropriate physical activity to stir up other nerves

    (b) Emotional conditions.

        • anxiety or worry
        • tension
        • depression

    (c) Mental conditions.

        • focusing on the pain
        • boredom
        • catastrophizing (e.g., "I am not going to get better," or "Life is not not worth living")

Closed

    (a) Physical conditions.

        • medications
        • counter stimulations (e.g., heat, cold, massage)

    (b) Emotional conditions.

        • positive emotions (e.g., self assurance, good information about what has happened)
        • relaxation exercise

---

[45] I write from personal experience as I have a rare genetic arthritic disease called ankylosing spondylitis.
[46] See, for example, Grant (2009).

- rest

(c) Mental conditions.

  - intense concentration as a distraction
  - involvement and interest in life activities

Using up all our attention with distracting thoughts or activities is one key to pain management. The aim is to involve all our senses. Some distracting thoughts and activities are:

- pleasant peaceful image, dramatized image incorporating pain as part of the script (e.g., an escape), or a neutral image (e.g., plans for the weekend)

- focusing on the environment instead of our body (e.g., reorganize the house, study, or garden)

- rhythmic activity (e.g., counting, singing, playing a musical instrument)

- solving problems (e.g., mathematics, chess, crosswords)

Finally I want to briefly mention the so-called phantom limb phenomenon where a person feels a pain in a limb that is no longer there, having been amputated. Various explanations have been put forward[47] and a recent one is the idea already alluded to at the beginning of this chapter that it is because of the brain's plasticity.[48] There are exercises available to help a person with this pain or sensation problem.

1.3 PERSONALITY

1.3.1 Personality Differences

We all think and behave differently because we are different genetically and we are molded by different life experiences. Personality can be defined as a dynamic and organized set of characteristics possessed by a person that uniquely influences his or her thinking, motivation, and behavior.[49] The word "personality" originates from the Greek *persona*, which means mask, and in ancient theatre it originally referred to a mask that typified a character rather than disguising the character. True personality is the person behind the mask he or she wears.

Since personality is such a broad and difficult concept, it is perhaps not surprising that there are a number of different models that endeavor to categorize personality.[50] We meet terms like temperament, traits, and types, which sometimes overlap in their meaning.[51] Temperament has been defined as "a person's characteristic way of approaching and reacting to people and situations"[52] and focuses on not what people do but how they go about doing it. It is largely inherited and tends to

[47]See http://www.painclinic.org/nervepain-phantomlimbpain.htm (accessed November 2010).
[48]Doige (2007: chapter 7).
[49]Ryckman (2004).
[50]For a historical summary see www.businessballs.com/personalitystylesmodels.htm (accessed November 2010).
[51]See wikipedia for some definitions of these words and various models.
[52]Papalia et al. (2001: 202).

be fairly stable throughout life;[53] it has been described as the part of personality that is genetically based. Personality also has a certain stability, but it is molded by circumstances and environment.

1.3.2   Personality Models

One of the earliest personality models, dating from Hippocrates in ancient Greece, consists of the categories choleric, sanguine, phlegmatic, and melancholic. This model has been revived by LaHaye (1988) and Littauer (1992; she uses the terms powerful, popular, peaceful, and perfect).[54] Another model uses the categories of lion, beaver, otter, and golden retriever.[55] A questionnaire along with details for this model is available on the internet.[56]

One other model that has been quite popular is the Type A and Type B personality model, where a Type A person has characteristics like impatience, excessive time consciousness, being unable to relax, and needing to be on the go. Type B people, however, are patient, easy going, and relaxed.[57] A test for type A or B is given on the internet.[58] In using such models, and I am uncertain about the statistical validity of some questionnaires, they can be useful in a "relative" fashion for determining the difference in say the personality profiles of members of a couple, as well as quickly providing some "inside" knowledge on an individual client. Many people have found some of the models mentioned above very helpful.

One popular traits model called the "Big Five" has a five-factor model consisting of factors that seem to underlie five groups of associated traits, and generally persist regardless of language and culture.[59] They are: (1) Openness to experience, (2) Conscientiousness, (3) Extraversion, (4) Agreeableness, and (5) Neuroticism (with acronym OCEAN).[60] A popular personality test based on the Briggs-Meyers test uses four types based on the typology model of Jung involving the pairs **E**xtraversion/**I**ntroversion, **S**ensing/i**N**tuition, **T**hinking/**F**eeling, and **J**udging/**P**erceiving, giving 16 possible categories, for example ENFJ.[61]

There is one personality trait called alexithymia[62] that varies in severity from person to person. It includes difficulty in identifying feelings and distinguishing between feelings and the bodily sensations of emotional arousal as well as difficulty in understanding other people's feelings. Alexithymia places individuals at risk for other medical and psychiatric disorders while reducing the likelihood that these individuals will respond to conventional treatments for the other conditions. It is frequently comorbid with other disorders and overlaps with Asperger's syndrome.

---

[53] Papalia et al. (2001: 204).
[54] For a questionnaire see http://72244.netministry.com/images/PersonalityScoreSheet.pdf (accessed November 2010).
[55] Smalley and Trent (2006).
[56] For example, http://www3.dbu.edu/jeanhumphreys/SocialPsych/smalleytrentpersonality.htm (accessed November 2010).
[57] Friedman (1996) and Friedman and Rosenman (1974).
[58] See http://discoveryhealth.queendom.com/cgi-bin/tests/type_a_personality.cgi (accessed November 2010).
[59] Papalia et al. (2001: 523–524).
[60] For a free personality test based on this model see www.outofservice.com/bigfive/.
[61] For a questionnaire see http://www.humanmetrics.com/cgi-win/JTypes2.asp.
[62] See http://en.wikipedia.org/wiki/Alexithymia (accessed November 2010) for helpful details. It is not classified as a mental disorder in the DSM-IV.

1.3.3   Learning Styles

Another area where we can differ is in our primary way of receiving or giving information. We can be one of three types of people, namely visual, auditory, or kinesthetic/tactile (i.e., seeing, hearing, and handling). Although we can do all three, one tends to dominate, which determines our learning style.[63] The visual person says, "Do you get the picture?"; the auditory person says, "Do you hear what I am saying;" and the kinesthetic person says, "Do you grasp what I am saying?" Sturt and Sturt[64] note that there are other clues about their style such as the profession or recreation they are attracted to. Their movements also differ when asked a question. For example, the visual person will usually look up before answering (just a slight flicker of the eyes), the auditory person will look to the side, and the kinesthetic will look down. Information about learning styles may or may not be useful in counseling a client. However, body language will sometimes give useful cues.[65]

1.4   EMOTIONS, FEELINGS, AND THOUGHTS

1.4.1   Introduction

This whole subject is a difficult one as there isn't agreement in the literature on the relationships between all three of the above concepts and how they interact. There is little agreement as to the nature of an emotion, and emotions are notoriously difficult to verbalize.[66] Part of the problem is that we don't fully understand the nature of consciousness and how it occurs.[67] It seems that emotions can be regarded as unconscious processes that may give rise to conscious content and feelings; the memory is also involved. However, because of lack of clarity in the literature, I shall not enter into the debate but simply use the words "feelings" and (conscious) "emotions" interchangeably.

1.4.2   Emotions

As noted at the beginning of Section 1.2.2, the so-called limbic system making up certain parts of the the brain has been described as the source of emotions in the brain, that is the "emotional brain." However, LeDoux[68] maintains that it is not just this traditional system that is involved in emotions but that different brain networks are also involved with different emotions. There are some cognitive processes that LeDoux[69] refers to as the "cognitive unconscious" whereby the brain does things like analyze the physical properties of a stimulus, help us play a ball game (e.g., table tennis), or help us to talk reasonably grammatically without awareness on our part. Also, the emotional meaning of a stimulus can begin to

---

[63]See http://www.chaminade.org/INSPIRE/learnstl.htm (accessed November 2010) for a short questionnaire. There is a great deal of internet information under the title of "learning styles."
[64]Sturt and Sturt (1988: 15).
[65]http://www.businessballs.com/body-language.htm#body-language-introduction (accessed November 2010) gives a useful summary.
[66]LeDoux (1998: 23, 71).
[67]For some idea of the complexities see LeDoux (1998: chapter 9) and Prinz (2005).
[68]LeDoux (1998: 99–101).
[69]LeDoux (1998: 29–34).

be appraised by the brain before the perceptual systems have fully processed the stimulus so that "the brain can know something is good or bad before it knows exactly what it is."[70]

From the above we see that much of brain processing is unconscious. What is perhaps more important however from a counseling point of view is whether a thought or an emotion comes first. The answer seems to be that either can be first, depending on the circumstances, and we begin by considering the relationship between the two. One aspect of this begins with the amygdala that is linked to our survival mechanism. It is part of the brain that initiates fight, flight, or fright responses in the face of danger and is deeply involved in responding to traumatic events. Sensory signals from the skin, ears, and eyes are received and processed by the thalamus.[71] One part of the information is sent to the amygdala while the major part is sent by a much slower route to the neocortex, our "thinking brain," for an appropriate and meaningful response. If the response from the neocortex is emotional, a signal goes to the amygdala to activate the emotional centers.

If the amygdala senses danger, it sounds the alarm and stirs the body into readiness for action before there has been any thinking and, soon after, the neocortex conveys a response to the amygdala. For example, if I see a projectile heading towards me I instinctively duck, or if I see a stick in my path that looks like a snake I take evasive action, but then I realize it is just a stick and begin to calm down. In addition to the fear aspect, which is closely linked to anxiety, there are times when we are swamped with feelings, apparently without cognition. The reason for this is that the connections from the cortical areas to the amygdala are far weaker than the connections from the amygdala to the cortex so that our conscious thoughts can get invaded by emotional information. The rapid response by the amygdala can, in some cases, be lifesaving while in others integration with the cortex is better. According to LeDoux,[72] we have little direct control over emotional reactions and it is futile to fake an emotion.

Role of Memory

Memory plays a critical role in traumatic situations. During such a situation, LeDoux[73] notes that "conscious memories are laid down by a system involving the hippocampus and related cortical areas, and unconscious memories established by fear conditioning mechanisms operating through an amygdala-based system." If a stimulus happens that was present with the initial trauma, both systems have the potential to retrieve memories of the event. The amygdala's emotional memories tend to be deeply ingrained and underly anxiety disorders. We see then that one memory system stores conscious information about events, while another stores the emotional memories. In counseling it can be a matter of helping clients to use their cortex to control the amygdala and ameliorate those memories. Cognitive processing endeavors to help us make sense of an emotion or regulate it.

One model that is used to describe a response to a stimulus is the SIR (stimulus, image, response) model that follows the pattern *stimulus → image → response*. For example, whenever Joan walks into a crowded room she feels anxious. It tran-

---

[70]LeDoux (1998: 69).
[71]This is a large, dual-lobed mass of grey matter cells located at the top of the brain stem.
[72]LeDoux (1998: 19).
[73]LeDoux (1998: 239).

spires that she always has an image of herself fainting in a crowded environment as many years ago this happened to her. It is not the crowded room that causes the anxiety but the embarrassing image of her sprawled on the floor in front of everybody. A more general model is the SOR model where "O" is for organism and it represents an input from variety of processes from a person such as thoughts, beliefs, motivation, and so forth.

Basic Emotions

Are there such things as basic emotions? As might be expected, there seems to be no clear consensus as to what might be on a basic list.[74] However, given the variations in word meaning, the different lists available have a great deal in common and generally include anger, happiness, sadness, and fear (sometimes referred to as mad, glad, sad, and bad) or close relatives of these emotions. For example, Greenberg[75] found the emotions of anger, sadness, fear, and shame among the most important in therapy. Ekman[76] has given some evidence that certain emotions including anger, disgust, fear, joy, sadness, and surprise have universal facial expressions. For example, an angry face is recognizable in any culture.[77] He pointed out that universal facial expressions can be regulated by what he calls "display rules" that refer to modifications by learning and culture.[78] However, the role of culture and language in formulating emotions is not straightforward and some of these difficulties are discussed by Prinz.[79]

The above basic emotions are also referred to as primary emotions and generally are felt first as a first response to a situation. These tend to followed by so-called secondary emotions which, confusingly, can also be other primary emotions. Such emotions can be reactions to the primary emotions or to thoughts about them, and clients find them troublesome, wanting to get rid of them.[80] They also cause problems for the therapist as they can obscure what is happening deep down with a client (e.g., depression or anxiety can hide anger, anger can hide fear, and so forth). According to Greenberg,[81] primary feelings feel right even if painful, while secondary emotions are more disturbing and puzzling. A key aspect of therapy is for a client to name and experience a disturbing emotion and determine whether or not that emotion is primary—but more below. The only way to get rid of a problem emotion (e.g., fear) is to experience it first before it can be changed.

Emotional Processing

When it comes to isolated small or large disturbing emotional experiences, they are generally satisfactorily dealt with and the accompanying distress dissolved. This process by which emotional disturbances are absorbed or decline so that they no longer interfere with normal living is referred to as *emotional processing*, a term introduced by Jack Rachman (1980). Incomplete emotional processing is evident, however, when there are intrusive memories of the upsetting event (e.g., as in post

---

[74]See, for example, http://changingminds.org/explanations/emotions/basic%20emotions.htm (accessed November 2010).
[75]Greenberg (2002: 43).
[76]Ekman (1993).
[77]For further comments and additional basic emotions see Ekman (1999).
[78]Ekman (1980).
[79]Prinz (2004).
[80]Greenberg (2002: 45–46).
[81]Greenberg (2002: 111–112).

traumatic stress disorder), re-experiencing the original emotions (e.g., as in sexual abuse), ruminative recycling of the event, poor sleep, nightmares, preoccupation with the event, and so forth.

An integral part of counseling is helping clients to recognize and process their emotions with the idea that "in the body, feelings, sensations and impulses are able to indicate what is most significant in life and where a problem lies *before* it has consciously been worked out."[82] The sense that something is not right can be brought into consciousness through emotional focusing of the body. A first step towards awareness might be to ask clients " How is your life going right now?" and then ask them to simply observe their feelings without analyzing them. This can be then followed up by a phrase, image, or metaphor that captures the feelings, for example "an uphill climb." This metaphor may then need to be sharpened up with details until there is an "ah ha" moment of understanding. The next question, which explores the connection, may be something like, "In what way does your life feel like an uphill climb?"

Baker[83] uses the following model to describe emotional experience:

$$input\ event \rightarrow appraisal \rightarrow emotional\ experience \rightarrow emotional\ expression,$$

where *appraisal* means appraisal of the meaning of the event. An attempt to control the emotion can occur at the input, at the experience, and at the expression stages, and inappropriate control can be damaging. For example, control at the input stage can lead to avoidance and phobias, while control at the experience stage can lead to repression and disassociation. In the case of unresolved emotions, the aim is for a client to re-experience the emotional pain, then grapple with it and stay with it long enough for it to lose its terrifying impact and to start the process of considering solutions.[84] Baker sums up the process in three steps: facing the memories and emotions; expressing the emotional feelings; and working through all the details by understanding what has happened.

Greenberg,[85] in his so-called Emotion-Focused therapy (EFT), aims at (1) helping clients to process their experiences more deeply and (2) integrating cognition and emotion by using cognition to make sense of emotion. People need to feel their feelings and make sense of these feelings. They also need to re-author and reorganize their life script so that it is more coherent and more beneficial. Greenberg describes the approach as "emotion coaching" and gives a helpful exercise for recognizing and dealing with difficult emotional states; this is given in Section 2.4.1. He suggests the following steps for helping clients to understand their emotions:[86]

1. Face one's emotions.

2. Trust one's emotions.

3. Reduce the intensity of one's emotions.

4. Sort out and identify one's emotions.

[82]Baker (2007: 42); italics are the author's.
[83]Baker (2007: 69).
[84]Baker (2007: 100).
[85]Greenberg (2002: xii).
[86]Greenberg (2002: 71–72).

5. Overcome avoidance of one's emotions.

6. Re-own one's emotions (once they have fallen into place).

7. Emotions can promote change.

EFT has also been used effectively for couples.[87] For further information and references see Greenberg, Warwar, and Malcolm (2010).

A similar problem can arise when people sometimes procrastinate about a certain task or avoid a particular situation because of the emotions that get stirred up at a subconscious level. It usually the case that such feelings are an echo from the past. A helpful approach is to identify the task or situation that is hated or avoided, determine what memories from childhood are raised by the task (e.g., abused or nagged while doing it as a child, or humiliated over it), and consider what feeling the task now represents. Then ask why such feelings are still threatening, and consider how such feelings can be reinterpreted.

I need to say a bit more about rumination. Ruminating over emotional events that have happened is perfectly normal and "mentally replaying the original incident is a normal element in the emotional processing of a difficult event."[88] However, rumination becomes maladaptive when it continues to rigidly recycle the same patterns of thinking like a cracked record with little change in beliefs, no resolution, and the same emotions being recycled without being disrupted or faced for a reasonable length of time. What is needed is reconstruction, not repetition.

There are many emotions that we could discuss, but I have decided to concentrate in the next few chapters on anger, guilt and shame, stress, and fear and anxiety. These seem to be the most common areas of dysfunction. Fear is a core emotion in psychological problems underlying anxiety, which often presents as a fear of what may happen.

1.4.3   Cognitive Processes

There is another aspect to the above discussion about emotions. We know that certain thoughts and beliefs can lead to emotions and behaviors. This is the basis of several cognitive approaches.[89] Since there is some confusion about terminology I shall now give a summary in this section.

Rational Therapy

The first of the cognitive approaches, called rational therapy, was introduced by Albert Ellis and the therapy was successively called rational emotive therapy in 1959 and then Rational Emotive Behavior Therapy (REBT) in 1992. The ABC part of his model begins with an Activating event (external or internal) or Adversity that triggers the Beliefs that in turn lead to a Consequence of feelings and behavior. This is followed by D, Disputing and changing irrational beliefs, which leads to E, an Effective philosophy and a change in F, Feelings and behavior.[90] Disputing can be be logical ("How does it logically follow...?"), empirical ("What evidence

---

[87]See, for example, Johnson (2008).
[88]Baker (2007: 135).
[89]Corey (2009: chapter 10).
[90]See, for example, Ellis and Dryden (2007) and Dryden and Neenan (2005).

is there ...?"), and pragmatic ("Where is holding on to this belief going to get ...?").[91] Some authors just use the ABC model but subdivide C into C (emotions) and D (behavior). REBT focuses on looking for dogmatic "musts," "shoulds," and "oughts" leading to irrational beliefs of which three major ones, usually in various disguises, are as follows:[92]

1. "I absolutely *must* perform well and/or win the love or approval of significant others or else I am an *inadequate worthless* person."

2. "You and other people *must* under all conditions and at all times be nice to me and treat me fairly or else *you* are a *rotten, horrible* person."

3. "Because it is preferable that I experience pleasure rather than pain, *conditions* under which I live absolutely *must* be comfortable, safe and advantageous or else the world is a rotten place, I *can't stand it*, and life is horrible and hardly worth living."

These three beliefs are about self, others, and the world, respectively, and are sometimes referred to as Beck's triad.

Cognitive Distortions

A slightly different approach, called cognitive therapy, which focuses more on the therapeutic relationship, was developed by Aaron Beck in the 1960's with his work on depression[93] and later extended to other psychological problems.[94] His focus is on *cognitive distortions* (rather than use the term irrational thoughts) such as: arbitrary inferences (e.g., jumping to unfounded conclusions); selective abstraction (e.g., acting on a detail taken out of context); overgeneralization (e.g., holding an extreme belief on the basis of one incident); magnification (e.g., catastrophizing) and minimization; personalization (e.g., inappropriate application of external events to self); labeling and mislabeling (e.g., determining one's identity on the basis of negatives); and dichotomous (black and white, all or nothing) thinking.[95] Behavioral methods were later integrated as well to give a number of techniques collectively called Cognitive-Behavioral Therapy (CBT).[96] I use the terms CBT and cognitive restructuring generically throughout this book to denote the previous methods, ignoring some of the finer distinctions. It should be noted that the interactions of emotion, cognition, motivation, and behavior are complex so that CBT only covers one aspect of understanding the relationship of thoughts and emotions.

In CBT clients can be given a list of some of the common distortions given above to see if they recognize any they regularly use and then be encouraged to dispute them using some of the following methods, adapted from Burns:[97]

[91]Dryden and Palmer (1995: 62).
[92]Ellis, Gordon, Neenan, and Palmer (1997: 8–9); italics are the authors.
[93]For example, Beck (1972); see also Beck et al. (1979).
[94]Two such examples are Beck et al. (2004, 2005); for more general applications see J. Beck (1995).
[95]Beck and Weishaar (1995: 238–239); see also http://en.wikipedia.org/wiki/Cognitive_distortion, and http://powerstates.com/?p=129 for some counter arguments; both accessed November 2010.
[96]For example, Trower, Casey, and Dryden (1988).
[97]Burns (1999: 118–110). I have included this list for later reference.

1. *Identify any obvious distortions.* Monitor negative thoughts and identify any recognizable distortions.

2. *Examine the evidence for the negative thought.*

3. *Check for any double standard.* Would the client want to apply the same self-condemnation for an action to someone else for doing the same thing?

4. *The experimental approach.* Carry out an experiment to see if a negative thought is true. This would be useful in anxiety producing situations.

5. *Using grey instead of black and white thinking.* Is there a middle road for assessing a situation?

6. *The survey method.* The client asks friends to see if they agree with the client's negative thought or beliefs.

7. *Define emotive and extreme terms used to describe self and others.* For example, what is a "loser"?

8. *Change the language.* For example replace words like "must" and "ought" by less extreme words such as "preferable" or "helpful."

9. *List the pros and cons of having a particular negative thought or behavior.*

10. *Reattribution.* Instead of blaming self or others for a problem, look for other contributing factors.

Some helpful questions for challenging mistaken beliefs are as follows.[98]

1. What is the evidence for this belief?

2. Does this belief always hold true for you?

3. Does this belief look at the whole picture including positive and negative ramifications?

4. Does this belief promote your wellbeing and/or peace of mind?

5. Did you choose this belief on your own or has it come from your family of origin?[99]

Multimodal Therapy

Lazarus[100] extended the above ideas of CBT to a more eclectic approach called *multimodal (behavioral) therapy*. It focuses on more than just cognition and behavior and uses other aspects as well, as described in the following checklist with the acronym BASIC ID:

- **Behavior** (What would you like to change or start/stop doing? What is holding you back from doing the things you want to do? What behaviors are preventing you from being happy?)

---

[98] Bourne (2005: 201).
[99] For example, from critical parent messages.
[100] Lazarus (1973, 1981, 2004).

- Affect (What makes you emotional, for example angry, sad, happy, depressed, anxious, and so on?)

- Sensation (What do you like/dislike to hear, taste, and so on? How do you feel emotionally about any of your sensations?)

- Imagery (What do you see yourself doing in the future, short-term and long-term? Can you describe your self-image (or body-image)? Are there any vivid memories that disturb you?)

- Cognition (What beliefs are important to you, especially your musts and shoulds about self, others, and the world out there? How do your thoughts affect all the other six areas listed here?)

- Interpersonal (How do you get on with other people, for example, friends, relatives, work colleagues, lovers, and acquaintances? Have you any concerns about how people treat you or how you treat them?)

- Drugs/biology (Are you on any medication? What about smoking, alcohol, caffeine or drugs? Any worries about your health? What changes would you like to make concerning diet, exercise, and recreation?)

The idea is to assess each of the above to get a client profile on problems in each of the above seven areas[101] and then note suitable interventions for each problem.[102] For example, if under Affect there were anger, anxiety attacks, and guilt, then the proposed interventions might be anger management, relaxation techniques, and disputing irrational beliefs, respectively. It important to examine the interaction between the interventions and the order in which they "fire up" (so-called *tracking*) in any particular problem situation. The idea is to tune into the client's preferred interventions (called *bridging*). Occasionally the interventions do not fully work and a particular problem remains unresolved. One can then obtain a so-called "second-order" BASIC ID that concentrates solely on certain aspects of the resistant problem.

Neuro-Linguistic Programming (NLP)

I wish to briefly mention this controversial topic here as it occasionally appears in the psychological literature and is linked to some of the above ideas about thinking and behavior. NLP was developed in the 1970s by Bandler and Grinder and is based on a supposed theoretical connection between neurological processes ("neuro"), language ("linguistic"), and behavioral patterns that have been learned through experience ("programming"); the idea is that these can be organized to achieve specific goals in life. It is not easy to define NLP as the language used by its practitioners is vague at times and NLP means different things to different people; it is hard to find a consistent description from those who claim to be experts at it.

NLP is essentially a model of interpersonal communication that mainly deals with the relationship between successful patterns of behavior and the underlying

---

[101]For an example of such a profile for a client presenting with high blood pressure see http://www.freewebs.com/multimodalpsychology/multimodalarticle.htm by Stephen Palmer (accessed November 2010).
[102]For a helpful compendium of interventions listed under the above BASIC ID categories see Dryden and Palmer (1995).

subjective experiences (for example patterns of thought). The aim is to educate a person in self-awareness and effective communication in order to change mental and emotional behavior.[103] A basic premise of NLP is that the words we use reflect an inner, subconscious perception of our problems. However, if these words and perceptions are inaccurate, they will create an underlying problem as long as we continue to use and to think them. By analyzing words used, perceptions can be changed and unhealthy patterns of thought and interactions with people changed. In essence, NLP claims to help people change by teaching them to program their brains; it is a series of tools that work at "how" people achieve their results.

Despite its popularity, the method has not gained widespread acceptance in psychotherapy and there is little coverage in the psychological research literature. This is because the underlying scientific theory at the time of writing this is unsupported and there is a lack of empirical evidence.[104] Part of the problem in trying to research the subject is the variability in training standards and methods used by practitioners and the fact that the method is eclectic with ideas drawn from other established therapies. NLP is regarded by its practitioners as a pragmatic discipline with the focus on what "works" rather than existing theory. What "works" means is uncertain and the success of NLP as a therapy is, at the time of writing, mainly anecdotal.

This does not mean NLP is not successful. For example, it has gained considerable support in the business area, sports, coaching, public speaking, and negotiation as a means of providing a set of communication and influencing tools. It is used all over the world by professionals who seek more resourcefulness within their roles, and NLP courses are provided in some universities. Many organizations in the U.K. Europe, and the U.S. require their managers to have an understanding of NLP.

1.4.4 Thought Stopping

Problems with obsessive or unwanted thoughts are discussed in later chapters. It is well-known that the more we try not to think about a certain thing the more likely we are to think about it![105] One technique uses thought-stopping. The client thinks of an obsessional thought and the therapist claps or shouts "stop." If the thought has disappeared, the volume of noise used can be successively reduced to nothing, with the clients eventually learning to say stop in their minds or imagining a big stop sign. Alternatively, they can imagine flicking the "off" switch in their head. Another idea is to count backwards or some other variation of counting. One technique that can be useful in public is tweaking a rubber-band that is around a person's wrist whenever he or she has an unwanted thought. The question of dealing with intrusive thoughts that become obsessive is discussed in Section 8.2.3. Rassin (2005) provides an interesting summary of the research on thought stopping and its relationship to obsession and trauma.

[103] For details see, for example, Bandler (2008) and
http://www.businessballs.com/nlpneuro-linguisticprogramming.htm (accessed November 2010).
[104] See http://en.wikipedia.org/wiki/Neuro-linguistic_programming (accessed November 2010).
[105] See the pioneering paper of Wegner et al. (1987), later supported by further research referenced in Purdon and Clark (2002: 33).

1.5   THE AGING PROCESS

1.5.1   Midlife Reassessment

We have all heard about the so-called "midlife crisis" that everyone is supposed to go through. Cohen[106] believes this is a myth as most adults experience a quest in midlife when there is a reevaluation and a desire to find meaning in life and do new things. It's not so much the middle age producing the crisis, but rather the mind telling us to do something about our life. Hart describes the mid-life crisis as follows:

> In its essence, the mid-life crisis is both a period of life and a process of reassessment in which one explores and tests new choices, generally evoked by a deep pessimism about one's existence.[107]

Pessimism can strike when it is realized that youth is over and maturity starts to take place. The lack of achievement and discontentment about one's life in the past can set in and the future may not look much better. This disillusionment may even lead to depression. We all want to recapture our youthfulness and for men it may mean doing something wildly different and adventurous or becoming romantically and sexually involved with a younger woman. People who go through this phase of life are usually unaware of it being a crisis at all. It needn't be sexual, but it just may lead to disillusion with work and a sense of not having got where they want to be. Hart mentions the following possible areas that can lead to a reassessment:[108]

Values. In early adulthood many troublesome issues, perhaps from adolescence, can be put on hold but if not resolved can resurface later (e.g., "Who am I?", and existential loneliness).

Spouse. The relationship may have changed through, for example, overfamiliarity and the person may need to rediscover his or her spouse. This can be a danger time for affairs.

Children. Children leave home or do not come up to one's expectations.

Work. There may be a realization that life's ambitions are not going to be fulfilled so that goals need to be reevaluated. Perhaps there is a need for a work change or a new direction.

Aging parents. Here we have a role reversal, which may lead to a feeling of restriction as parents become more dependent.

Let go. We go through a transition where we let go the feeling of youthfulness.

Faith and meaning. All past beliefs are open for scrutiny.

Menopause

For women, menopause, which typically occurs in the age range of about 40–55 years (average about 51 in the U.S.), can be a major factor in mid-life. Menopause

[106]Cohen (2005: chapter 3).
[107]Hart (1987: 207).
[108]Hart (1987: 208–212).

symptoms are varied[109] and psychologically they can, for many, symbolize the end of creativity. It signifies, for example, the end of child-rearing years. For those women whose significance and worth is in their reproductive cycle and role as a primary caregiver, this time can be more of a hurdle incurring grief, distress, and loss of identity.

The belief that beauty depends on youthfulness can lead to a fear of losing sexual youthfulness and may lead to being ashamed of one's body. For those who believe sex equals reproduction may think that post-menopause sex is "dirty." Unpleasant experiences of sex in earlier years may mean that when menopause ceases, so does sexual intimacy. For others, however, menopause means a new sexual freedom; freedom from the fear of pregnancy. In male-dominated societies, women may need to reassess their roles and step outside the society's accepted norms about what they can and should do, measuring success in terms of female rather than male norms.

1.5.2   Midlife Counseling

In counseling, therapists need to educate clients about the nature and causes of the mid-life reassessment and to normalize this stage in their life, pointing out that it is only a stage and not permanent. Clients may come with feelings of inadequacy and being unaccepted, or they may believe they have little or no value. Earlier unresolved life conflicts may need to be explored and losses dealt with. This may mean allowing a grieving period and giving permission to feel sad. The different areas of life described above in the previous section can be discussed and strategies for dealing with any changes explored. Ideas related to wholeness[110] can also be bought into the picture. Journaling may be helpful for some clients as they work through issues and establish goals. Value conflicts may need to be resolved and the spiritual person may need to find resources for strengthening his or her faith.

The mid-life period overlaps with Erikson's seventh stage of generativity versus stagnation (35 to 65 years) so that some of the comments about this stage also apply here. For example, in middle adulthood there is a concern to establish and guide the next generation and to leave some sort of a legacy. There is a need to feed something back into society rather than stagnate into self-centeredness. This leads me into the question of coping with growing old, the subject of the next section.

1.6   THE AGING BRAIN

I have not found it easy to locate helpful material for counseling older people but I have included some information about the aging process that I hope might be useful. Before taking a positive line I need to remind readers that some older people find the aging process very difficult and this age group has the highest prevalence of suicide. This is discussed further in Section 10.5.6. There is also a high percentage of older people who have problems with depression. This may be due to grief as people lose partners and close friends as they get older. My father, who lived to 97

---

[109] http://www.project-aware.org/Experience/symptoms.shtml lists 35 symptoms and see http://www.mayoclinic.com/health/menopause/DS00119/DSECTION=symptomspsychologically for a basic list; both accessed November 2010.
[110] See Chapter 2.

years, said that he was outliving all his friends! Anorexia can be a problem with the elderly, especially men.

Care is needed with alcohol and it is recommended by the New Zealand Institute on Alcohol Abuse and Alcoholism that over 65s should drink no more than one or two drinks a day. Older people who have been regular drinkers are likely to need to cut down their consumption by at least a half. For some older people with health problems or those taking medicines, it may be best not to drink alcohol at all. As people age, their body's ability to signal thirst deteriorates, and when combined with a diuretic like alcohol, the risk of dehydration is increased. Also falls are a common problem with the elderly.

1.6.1   The Big News

In counseling or talking to older people (and that includes the author in his seventies) it is encouraging to be able to refer to recent research on the aging brain; it gives us all hope! The following quotation gets to the heart of it:

> The big news is that the brain is far more flexible and adaptable than once thought. Not only does the brain retain its capacity to form new memories, which entails making new connections between brain cells, but it can grow entirely new brain cells—a stunning finding filled with potential. We've also learned that older brains can process information in a dramatically different way than younger brains.[111]

As with all other parts of our bodies, age does affect our brains and affects processes like reaction times, short-term memory storage, and the speed of doing some mental activities. However, much of the degradation is not caused by aging as such but by specific illnesses and small strokes. We can also add stress, excess alcohol use, smoking, inactivity, obesity, malnourishment and social isolation.[112]   What are encouraging are the following positive findings:[113]

- The brain is continually reorganizing itself in response to experience and learning.

- New brain cells (neurons) do form throughout life.

- Our emotional system becomes more balanced with age. The amygdala settles down and reacts less to negative emotions and stimuli. Older people can be calmer in the face of life's challenges.

- The brain's two hemispheres are more equally used by older adults. Some tasks can be performed better by an older person as a younger person may only use one hemisphere.

- Physical exercise boosts brainpower, especially aerobic exercise that is continuous, rhythmic, and uses large muscle groups.

We know that learning actually causes physical changes in a brain, and not just with children. The parts of the brain continually used by older adults have a greater

---

[111] Cohen (2005: xv).
[112] Cohen (2005: 8).
[113] Cohen (2005: 4).

density of brain cells than those of a young person — there are not only more cells but more connections. In 1998, scientists showed that the adult human brain produces new neurons, a process called neurogenesis, and many regions of the brain have primitive cells that, under certain conditions, can mature into neurons and supporting brain cells called glia. As we get older, we therefore need to engage in challenging and creative activities. Cohen[114] mentions dancing, playing board games, playing a musical instrument, doing crossword puzzles, and reading, for example; both variety and challenge are the key ingredients. Doige[115] says that when people age they don't tend to engage in tasks that focus their attention so sharply as they did when younger. Some of their activities are mostly a replay of mastered skills rather than learning. He suggests, for example, that learning a new language is good for improving and maintaining the memory generally. A common problem with aging is having trouble finding words. These kinds of activities can help with this problem and reduce the risk of dementia and cognitive decline. Hands-on activities are also helpful as hands, eyes, and ears are our main means of accessing our world.[116] A number of exercises are available on the internet.[117] Like other parts of our body, the brain is also a use-it-or-lose-it organ!

Two things particularly boost our minds. One is mastery and control in some area of our activities, and the second is forming strong social networks. Both are shown to be beneficial to our health, boosting our immune system and lowering our stress levels. Social activity also helps to combat loneliness. Not only can our brains develop, but also our minds can develop psychologically as well. Here the therapist can encourage an older client to suggest ways to increase these two levels of activity.

The Inner Push

As we get older there are certain drives that develop within us, which Cohen calls the "inner push." Some of the more common ones are:

- to finally get to know oneself and be comfortable with oneself

- to learn how to live well

- to have good judgment

- to feel whole at all levels, despite loss and pain

- to live life to the fullest, right to the end

- to give to others, one's family and community

- to tell one's story

- to continue the process of discovery and change

- to remain hopeful despite adversity

---

[114]Cohen (2005: 26).
[115]Doige (2007: 87).
[116]See http://merzenich.positscience.com/ by Michael Merzenich (accessed November 2010).
[117]See Posit Science on the internet.

Associated with these drives is developmental intelligence. This is defined as "the maturing of cognition, emotional intelligence, judgment, social skills, life experience, and consciousness and their integration and synergy."[118] This higher level of intelligence, which we might call wisdom, is characterized by three related thinking styles.

1. *Relativistic thinking.* We can accept opposing views and recognize that answers can be relative rather than absolute. We can accept some uncertainty.

2. *Dualistic thinking.* We can suspend judgment while we hold opposing views at the same time before making a decision.

3. *Systematic thinking.* We can take a broader perspective and see the forest instead of the trees.

Emotions play an important role in our developmental intelligence. As we age the potential is there to become more self-aware of our emotions and, as mentioned above, to pay less attention to the negative.

1.6.2   Four Life Phases

Picking up where Erikson left off, Cohen formulates four phases for the second half of life, namely (1) midlife reevaluation (discussed above in Section 1.5.1) under the title of "Midlife Reassessment," (2) liberation, (3) summing up, and (4) encore. With retirement there can come the second phase of liberation. It is not a time for disengagement or dimming vigor, but a time for experimentation, exploration, and new beginnings. The inner push to test limits becomes stronger.

The summing up phase, phase three, occurs more towards seventy, though it can occur earlier in different forms. It is a stage in life when people want to find a larger meaning in their lives "through a process of review, summarizing, and giving back."[119] The summing up can take a variety of forms such as writing memoirs and autobiographies, personal story telling, and compiling photographs. Cohen believes that it is the ability to use both hemispheres more effectively that makes such activities more pleasurable. The giving back to the family, the community, or the world at large is reflected in philanthropy and volunteerism. We want our life to count! Psychologists have learned that reviewing one's life is part of normal aging, and the review process can lead to self-awareness and self-acceptance.

The final encore phase four, which generally starts in the late seventies, combines the other three in some sense. By this stage people are getting better at adapting to their conditions regardless of their health status. Aging should be accompanied by more positive and less negative emotions so that well-being rises or remains stable.

Four aspects of aging that are important are cognition, wisdom, memory, and social intelligence. As already mentioned, our cognitive skills can improve with age. A key ingredient of cognition related to wisdom is what contemporary psychology calls *post-formal thought*. This is beyond formal thinking where one uses pure logic in solving a problem. Rather it is the ability to "think outside of the square" and

[118]Cohen (2005: 35).
[119]Cohen (2005: 75).

handle ill-defined, ambiguous problems for which there may be several solutions. This kind of thinking uses the three types of reasoning mentioned above, namely relativistic thinking, dualistic thinking, and systematic thinking. Memory is the foundation of wisdom and Cohen states that,

> neuroscience offers some comforting findings. While the overall processing speed of brain cells and certain specific types of memory do decline gradually with age, other forms of memory robustly resist degradation.[120]

1.6.3 Social Intelligence

Growing old should not be a time to disengage from society, although adverse health and loss of loved ones can help create isolation. We need to remain socially active as it benefits our brains and well-being. All the processes described in the above four phases and our developmental intelligence all add to our social intelligence, which simply is the ability to interact effectively with others. With aging we should be more discriminating and make better social choices. Also there is a change with regard to gender and social roles. For example, men may become more people and relationship oriented, while women can be more active and assertive in societal issues.

A good idea is to have a social portfolio like the following in Table 1.1 below.[121] The idea is to help the client fill in the boxes with their own ideas. The social portfolio should be like a financial portfolio—diversified, balanced, and resistant to changes in circumstances. As we age we need to replace the things we can't do by the things we can do! Also we need to start building "assets" early in life in preparation for later life, which may mean taking up new skills. This was one of the reasons why I took up counseling after an academic university life of mathematics and statistics.

Table 1.1   Social Portfolio.

	Group Efforts	Individual Efforts
	Group/High Mobility	Individual/High mobility
High Mobility	Walking group	Create a garden
High Energy	Dance or walking group	Aerobics
	Group/Low Mobility	Individual/Low Mobility
Low Mobility	Bridge club	Computing
Low Energy	Film night	Photo album

Retirement

Cohen[122] has come up with the following ingredients for successful retirement.

1. Need for planning.

---

[120]Cohen (2005: 106).
[121]Cohen (2005: 127–128).
[122]Cohen (2005: chapter 7).

2. Need to know what is available in the community.

3. Having a good balanced social portfolio.

4. Do more, not less. (Responding to the inner push).

5. Recognize value in long-term regular activities, e.g., once a week.

6. Overcome the problem of forming close relationships. Recognize the need to make new friends.

7. It is important to give back.

8. Recognize the importance of life-long learning.

Summing up[123] we need to develop over time a balanced social portfolio and look for activities that involve repeated interactions. We also need to be creative, keep as fit as possible, and find ways of challenging our mind and body. Being creative may be just continuing with what we already do or by finding new outlets; the latter are particularly needed when loss occurs. Creativity is beneficial to our health.

Aging and Sex

Older people who are interested in sex have tended to be adversely stereotyped in the past. Recent research indicates that aging does not significantly diminish the need and desire for sex.[124] Ability to fulfill that desire, however, does depend on a number of factors including age and health. Men reach their sexual "peak" around 18 years and after that there is a very slow decline in sexual functioning, becoming more noticeable in the 40s and 50s and particularly so in the 60s. However most men, unless they have certain health problems, are able to participate in and enjoy sex for their entire life span. The capacity to do so has been enhanced by various medications that help with erections and overcome any psychological effects of previous erectile difficulty. Some medications to treat organic conditions such as blood pressure can have side effects that are inhibitory. For women, although menopause usually occurs between 45 and 55 years of age, a women's interest and capacity for sex can still continue after this and even with increased enjoyment knowing that the possibility of pregnancy is longer a worry. There are also lubricants available to help them with some effects of aging.

1.7   BIBLICAL VIEWPOINT

1.7.1   Metaphors

The Bible uses a number of different Hebrew and Greek words that are translated as "mind." For example, focussing one's mind (or imagination) on God brings peace.[125] Other Hebrew words used in the Old Testament are heart, soul, and spirit. In the New Testament Jesus repeated the Old Testament command to love

---

[123]Cohen (2005: 164).
[124]See, for example, http://health.discovery.com/centers/sex/sexpedia/ageingandsex.html (accessed November 2010).
[125]Isaiah 26:3.

God with all our heart, soul, strength, and mind, where mind here means intellect or "full mind." Other Greeks words usually translated as "mind" add further shades of meaning such as purpose, thought, will, and inclination. There are several New Testament passages that relate to the mind. For example, Paul tells us not to be squeezed into this world's mold but rather be transformed by the renewing of our minds.[126] He also tells us that our mental focus should be on wholesome attributes[127] and on the things of the Spirit rather than the things of the flesh.[128] He emphasizes that true wisdom comes from the Spirit of God who searches all things including the deep things of God, and through the Spirit we have the mind of Christ.[129] However, Paul found that the purposes of the mind and body are sometimes in collision![130]

Given our knowledge of the brain today, which is still in its infancy and at times metaphoric, we can expect the Bible to be metaphorical when it comes to ideas about thoughts and emotions. For example, the word "heart" is used to describe a whole range of ideas including both thoughts and emotions.[131] Other parts of the body are also linked to the emotions.[132]

1.7.2   Positive Messages

Scripture can be a powerful tool in counseling Christians and, in fact, some clients find memorizing verses very helpful. The word "remember" is mentioned 167 times in the NIV translation. Having verses in long term memory when a person is young can lead to them resurfacing at a fortunate time in adult life. The Bible has many positive messages and Dr Peale's reprinted book[133] is still a good source of positive thinking.[134]

In the Bible there is encouragement not to lose heart even though outwardly we are wasting away.[135] Age is not seen as a hindrance, and in fact God often waited until a person was quite old before fulfilling some particular purpose through that person.[136] Older people can be encouraged to see that God can use them at any age.

---

[126]Romans 12:2.

[127]Philippians 4:8.

[128]Romans 8:5–6.

[129]1 Corinthians 2:6–16.

[130]Romans 7:25.

[131]For example, Proverbs 16:9; Matthew 12:34; Romans 10:10;1 Chronicles 16:10; Jeremiah 17:9; and Luke 6:45.

[132]For example, bowels and kidneys ("reins") referred to in Philippians 1:8; Philemon 7, 20; Psalms 16:7; and Proverbs 23:16 (see the Authorized Version for the original meanings).

[133]Peale (1994).

[134]For example, Romans 8:31; Isaiah 26:3, 40:29–31; and Philippians 4:7,13.

[135]2 Corinthians 4:16–18).

[136]For example, Abraham, Moses, and Caleb.

CHAPTER 2

P   hysical
E   motional
m   mental
S   social
S   spiritual

WHOLENESS

2.1 INTRODUCTION

With the current interest in brief therapy and the fact that there are often fewer counseling sessions available than one would like, therapists may find they need to narrow their focus to just the issue in hand. However, it can be helpful to encourage clients to look beyond their presenting issue and see how they are functioning in all other areas of their life. It seems therefore that a chapter on "wholeness" and how to lead a "balanced" life is appropriate early in this book. A number of things can block a person's journey towards wholeness, for example, lack of vision, poor parental modeling, childhood hurts, low self-esteem, emotional immaturity, unforgiveness and bitterness, grief and loss, and and fear of change.[1]

Many therapists use the following five aspects of the whole person, namely the physical, emotional, mental (intellectual), social, and spiritual (acronym PEMSS). One way of introducing the topic is to draw a circle with ME inside the circle and have five branches coming off the circumference. A client can be asked to assess how well they are doing in each of these areas. A simple way is to draw five same-sized rectangles and ask the client to shade in the proportion of each rectangle to represent how well they think they are doing in each area. Here the interest is on comparing the five proportions shaded to indicate the degree of balance in a person's life as well as on the individual proportions. Another pictorial method suggested

[1]Sturt and Sturt (1998: chapter 3).

by Barrow and Place[2] is to use a circle with inner equally spaced concentric circles with the outer circle area divided up into equal five segments. Proportions of the segments are shaded from the center outwards.[3] They also suggest a pie chart with four segments representing the proportions of time devoted to self, work, play (recreation), and significant others.[4] The question can be asked, "How balanced is this chart?"

From the therapist's point of view, in dealing with the whole person there are many structured skills that can be used such as anger management, anxiety control, assertiveness, cognitive awareness, distress tolerance, emotional regulation, impulse control, interpersonal skills, problem-solving, sensitivity reduction, and thought stopping. Some of these are mentioned throughout this book. Although the main emphasis of this chapter is on providing information, some aspects of counseling will be included in the section on the social aspects of life, namely self-esteem, assertiveness, and forgiveness.

Below I will now consider separately each of the five aspects of wholeness: physical, emotional, intellectual, social, and spiritual and include a number of topics that don't have a ready home in other chapters or else occur briefly in a number of chapters, for example, attachment and forgiveness to name just two.

2.2   PHYSICAL

If we don't look after our bodies, then the other four areas of our life may be seriously affected. Some of the key dimensions to physical wholeness are: nutrition, exercise, rest and recreation, sleep, relaxation, healthy sexuality, and touch.[5] We shall now consider each one of these.

2.2.1   Nutrition

This subject is a complex one as there are many opinions about nutrition and diet and new research continues to suggest new changes. I will therefore try and keep to a few broad principles that seem to be well established. In 1992 the U.S. Department of Agriculture (USDA) officially released the Food Guide Pyramid and in 2005 the USDA followed up with an improved version called MyPyramid, both of which were intended to help the American public eat healthily. Unfortunately both pyramids have been found to fall short in some areas and they have now been replaced by the Healthy Eating Pyramid devised by faculty members in the Harvard School of Public Health.[6] This pyramid will no doubt be modified from time to time as new research becomes available. As eating patterns vary from country to country, other useful local pyramids are also available including a vegetarian pyramid. The new healthy eating pyramid has seven layers instead of the original four and its bottom layer is daily exercise and weight control.

[2]Barrow and Place (1995: 63–64).
[3]The authors use the segments occupational/professional, financial, educational/cultural, social, creative, personal, sport/physical, plus one of the client's own.
[4]Barrow and Place (1995: 66–67).
[5]Sturt and Sturt (1998: chapter 4) add touch.
[6]See Willett (2001) and the internet for details (especially
www.hsph.harvard.edu/nutritionsource/pyramids.html; accessed October 2010).

We now realize that not all carbohydrates are good and not all fats are bad, which has to some extent turned the original pyramid on its head! It comes down to having the right mix of carbohydrates, protein, and fats. In the past there has been an overemphasis on carbohydrates and some people have benefitted from increasing the ratio of protein to carbohydrate at each meal. We note that the body needs a steady supply of amino acids derived from proteins to make neurotransmitters (especially serotonin) for the brain (see Section 1.2.1).

The debate about the role of supplements (e.g., vitamins and minerals) and whether we should take them continues. Some nutritionists also recommend sources of essential fatty acids like omega-3 (e.g., fish oil and flaxseed oil) as they have a number of physical and psychological health benefits. Care is needed not to overdose on some supplements if they are being taken. The need for supplements depends very much on the availability and variety of good food so as to provide a balanced diet.[7]

Role of Insulin

It is important to be aware of the role of the "storage" hormone insulin in our eating. Insulin controls the processing of blood sugar and must be "in balance." Everything we eat and drink is absorbed from the small intestine and passes into the portal vein, which takes the nutrients from the meal straight to the liver. There fats are broken down into the starch glycogen and fatty acids, while protein is broken down into amino acids. Carbohydrates are converted into glucose, which is then rapidly absorbed into the bloodstream. This rise in sugar triggers the release of insulin from the pancreas, and the insulin binds itself to receptor sites on our cells, where it allows the glucose to be absorbed and later burnt as energy. If there is an excess of glucose, the insulin turns some of it into glycogen, which is stored in our muscles and liver. There it can be turned back into glucose quickly and easily whenever we need energy. However, once the stores of glycogen are full and there is still glucose in the blood, insulin converts the excess into triglyceride (fat), which is carried in the blood stream to the fatty tissues where it is deposited as more fat. Also elevated insulin levels stimulate our cells to produce abnormally large amounts of cholesterol.

Complex carbohydrates, like vegetables, are broken down into glucose much more slowly than simple carbohydrates like cakes and sweets, thus avoiding a rapid build-up up of glucose. If insulin is out of balance, good cholesterol (High Density Lipoprotein or HDL) levels can be low and bad cholesterol (Low Density Lipoprotein or LDL) levels high. In contrast, protein foods require only a little insulin to process, whereas fat requires virtually no insulin.

When a lot of fats and carbohydrates are eaten together, the fats effectively reduce the cells' ability to use the glucose released by the carbohydrates. The fats are burnt as fuel but, as noted above, the excess glucose ends up ultimately as fat. Eaten on their own or together with protein, but without an abundance of carbohydrates, the right kind of fats will not lead to the laying down of fat in our bodies. This is contrary to what many believe; it is not the intake of fat that causes overweight but a high carbohydrate intake in the presence of fats.

---

[7]In New Zealand we have seen an explosion in the variety of breads, spreads, fruit, and vegetables that are now available.

Physical Causes

For a client with psychological problems it is important to first rule out any possible physical causes. One cause can be the food we eat.[8] For example, too much caffeine can cause palpitations and anxiety symptoms, while too much salt, sugar, preservatives, and hormones in meat can stress the body. Some people can have anxiety type problems when their blood sugar (glucose) level drops too quickly or too low; this is called hypoglycemia and it can bring on or aggravate a panic attack.[9] The reverse is also true in that stress can cause a rapid depletion of blood sugar.

Food Allergies

Food allergies can create psychological symptoms such as anxiety, depression or mood swings, insomnia, and disorientation, as well as physical symptoms like dizziness, headaches, nausea, and fatigue.[10] For example, in Western culture two common sources of allergic reaction are casein in milk and gluten in wheat products and these together with eggs, peanuts, tree nuts (e.g., cashews, walnuts, and so forth), fish, shellfish, and soy account for about 90% of all food-allergic reactions.[11] What is surprising is that we tend to crave and be addicted to the very foods we are allergic to. Various tests can be used to detect allergies or else one can use a process of elimination. Substances other than foods can also cause allergic reactions. Correct hydration is important as thirst is sometimes mistaken for hunger and at those times we will tend to reach for the foods to which we are allergic as a "quick fix" when a glass of water will alleviate the "hunger."

2.2.2   Exercise

Exercise helps to lower blood pressure, assist weight control, and improve respiration. As noted in Section 1.6.1, exercise also helps the growth of new brain cells as we age. An exercise program should have at least the three following components: flexibility, strength (resistance) training, and an aerobic component.[12] Flexibility comes from stretching-type exercises (e.g., a pilates program) that should be carried out after the muscles have been warmed up, and strength exercises can consist of "natural" exercises such as knee bends, press-ups and sit-ups, or one can use aids such as various elastic bands or weights. Aerobic exercise should be for about half an hour for at least three or four times a week and, for maximum effectiveness, it needs to be rhythmic, continuous, and involve the large muscle groups (primarily located in the lower part of the body). A useful measure of intensity is at a heart rate of $(220 - \text{your age}) \times x$, where x is 0.6, 0.7, or 0.8 depending on the desired fitness level. It does not have to be continuous, but can consist of several shorter sessions of at least ten minutes each. However a single longer session may be more beneficial for weight control. Any exercise program should contain a warm-up phase, an exercise phase, and a cool-down phase. Although not that many calories are burned up during the exercise, recent research has shown that

---

[8]For example, see Bourne (2005: chapter 15).

[9]Bourne (2005: 311).

[10]Bourne (2005: 313).

[11]See http://www.emedicinehealth.com/food_allergy/article_em.htm; accessed October 2010.

[12]See for example www.primusweb.com/fitnesspartner/library/activity/startexercise.htm and http://www.hoptechno.com/book11.htm; accessed October 2010

fat burning continues for 24 hours after the exercise is finished, while the person is at rest.

Exercise is also extremely beneficial psychologically. For example, walking is a great exercise because it alleviates stress, helps dissipate anger, and lifts depression through the production of natural substances (endorphins) in our body. It can also significantly lower blood pressure for 24 hours. If the walking is vigorous and for a reasonable length of time, say 20 minutes to an hour, then it has an aerobic effect. Long Irregular bursts of exercise, for example playing squash once a week, are not helpful and can be stressful. For some, a sporting interest is a good idea not only from a fitness point of view but also because it usually provides social contact as well. Short bursts of activity can be beneficial, and it is a good idea to have "energy breaks," especially if you spend a lot of sitting.

It is my experience that clients with psychological issues often do little exercise. A simple walking plan can do wonders for well being! Common excuses for not exercising are:[13]

1. "I don't have enough time." For some people this is a real problem, but in the end it is a question of priorities!

2. "I feel too tired to exercise." Provided there are no health problems, tiredness may be more a problem of lethargy due to lack of fresh air, poor diet, and poor circulation. The tired feeling can be worked through and any effort to overcome it will be rewarded with a feeling of well-being.

3. "Exercise is boring." For some, exercise is boring and they may find it better to exercise with others or use a variety of activities. However, I believe boredom is a state of mind. I have ankylosing spondylitis (a bit of a mouthful!), a rare genetic-based form of arthritis that I control through exercise. When I am tempted to be bored with my program I remind myself of its benefits as I know that my positive mental attitude to health promotes health.

4. "There is nowhere I can exercise." Although some people prefer to go to a gym, you can exercise in your own home as you don't need a gym to exercise. You can always exercise or do aerobics to a video or DVD of which a number are available, or wear headphones while you run on the spot, do pretend skipping, exercycling, and so forth. All that is needed is a little imagination!

5. "I am too unfit and overweight. Exercise might do me some harm." Exercise, done gently, and slowly increased over time will always benefit a person. The way to go is to start with low impact, low aerobic exercises like light swimming and walking.

6. "I tried exercise once but it didn't work." The question to consider is why it didn't work. Some people try to do too much too soon and end up with aches and pains in places they didn't know existed! Having SMART goals (Section 2.3.2 below) is what is needed.

---

[13]Bourne (2005: 99).

2.2.3   Rest and Recreation

This can be achieved through, for example, daily time out, a regular day off, proper vacations, and creative hobbies. Relaxation techniques are considered below.

Time Out

Short breaks during the day can help prevent the build up of stress, especially if combined with relaxation techniques considered below.[14] Being alone and quiet can be helpful during such a break, but that is not always possible in the workplace environment. If we sit in one place for too long (e.g, studying[15] or working at a computer) we can develop a kind of tunnel vision that lowers our working efficiency; we can also develop postural problems. It is important therefore to change one's position frequently and take short breaks as this can also help release stress. For some a short afternoon nap (say 20 minutes) can be beneficial. Falling into a deep sleep should be avoided as it may interfere with sleep at night and the sleep cycle described below.

Regular Day Off

The idea of a sabbath rest seems to be a sound psychological principle regardless of any religious connotations. Some people have to work on Sunday so it is the principle of a regular day off that matters, not which day.

Vacations

When people skip on having adequate longer-term breaks from their work, fatigue and stress can quietly build up. At least two weeks away from usual routines seems to be a reasonable period of time as it often takes several days to fully unwind.

Creative Hobbies

Unless our job is creative, most of us are able to gain more balance in our lives if we are involved in a creative hobby like music, writing, painting, sewing, handcrafts, and so forth. A hobby helps us to take our minds off work and personal problems, and helps us to relax.

2.2.4   Sleep

Adequate sleep is necessary for good physical and mental health; for example, it brings physical healing, strengthens our heart against strokes and heart disease, replenishes our brain, helps with problem solving, and enhances the memory. Sleep can be a contributing factor in weight control as it can help keep our appetite hormones in balance. Insomnia is a major problem in society, and some strategies for dealing with it are referred to in Section 6.2.2. I will now provide some information about the sleep process.

Sleep Cycles

Research has shown that every 1.5–2 hours we go through a pattern of non-dream sleep (NREM or non-rapid eye movement sleep) followed by a short period

---

[14]Stress is discussed in Chapter 5.
[15]See "study methods" on the internet.

of dream sleep (REM or rapid eye movement sleep). The NREM consist of four stages 1–4 that cycle through 1,2,3,4,3,2.[16] Stages 1 and 2 are essentially light sleep and 3 and 4 deep sleep, depending on the brain waves. When we go to bed we find that after about 15 or so minutes of relaxation we reach a stage of semiconsciousness that is neither waking nor sleeping (stage 1) for a few minutes then we suddenly fall into a light sleep (stage 2). After about thirty to forty-five minutes in stage 2 we go into the deeper stages 3 and 4. We then go back through stages 3 and 2, and enter dream sleep. As the night progresses, the deeper stages of sleep gets shorter and the REM stage gets longer. As we go through these cycles, it is normal to have short periods of waking of 1 or 2 minutes between cycles. We are not usually aware of them unless we are anxious or disturbed. The short periods of being awake feel much longer than they really are so we may feel that we are not sleeping as much as we actually are.

An important question is: "How much sleep do we need?" The answer is: "Usually more than we think," though we are not very good at gauging how much sleep we actually get. Although there is considerable individual variation, the general consensus seems to be that we need at least 7–8 hours on average, and women usually need more sleep than men. Older people need the same amount of sleep, but will often only have one period of deep sleep during the night, usually in the first 3 or 4 hours, after which they wake more easily. They also take longer to fall asleep, with the amount and length of their waking points during the night increasing with age, and the time spent in deep sleep decreases. We also tend to dream less as we get older. One way to find out how much sleep we need is to try adding half an hour at a time (after about a week) until there is no improvement on waking; a good time to experiment is when on holiday.

We may not be getting enough sleep if we experience the following:[17] We always need an alarm clock to wake us up; we habitually sleep late on weekends; and we fall asleep during meetings, watching TV, and reading. We eventually pay for a lack of sleep if we draw too much on our sleep bank. Deep sleep is apparently the most important part of the sleep cycle as it is not only restorative, but we make up for it if there is sleep deprivation. Sleep problems are discussed in Section 6.2. Stress (Section 5.4.4), anxiety (Section 6.2) and depression (Section 9.1.2) can affect the sleeping pattern.

There a two systems in our brain that regulate both sleep and wakefulness; a wakefulness system that dominates during the day and keeps us awake, and a sleep system that dominates at night.[18] However the wakefulness system is always "on guard" even in our deepest sleep so that we are never completely oblivious to the outside world. A person with a weak sleep system or an over-strong wakefulness system may be more vulnerable to sleep problems.

Body Temperature and Light

Body temperature is a key to how we sleep. It goes through a daily cycle (circadian rhythm) closely linked to our activity levels and sleep pattern,[19] reaching

---

[16]See the graph under "Normal sleep" at www.aafp.org/afp/990501ap/2551.html; accessed October 2010.
[17]Jacobs (1999: 76–77).
[18]Jacobs (1999: 20).
[19]Jacobs (1999: 19).

its maximum around 6 p.m. and then dropping a few hours later until we go to sleep. Our temperature then declines more rapidly to its minimum around 4.00 a.m. and then begins to increase just before sunrise. It continues to increase until mid-afternoon and then drops somewhat before increasing until 6 p.m. The higher temperatures are linked to activity and alertness and lower temperatures to sleepiness, irrespective of how we slept the night before. Sleep and body temperature are directly influenced by the daily cycles of sunlight and darkness and their effect on the neurotransmitter melatonin.

When the amount of light entering our eyes goes up, melatonin levels go down and our body temperature goes up, and vice versa. Different body temperature cycles explain why some people function best in the morning ("larks"), while others function better in the evening ("owls"). Since our sleep is related to our body temperature it is important that we get up the same time every morning to start our body-temperature rhythm. If we sleep in, we delay the rise in our body temperature in the morning and delay the fall at night. Sleeping in on Sunday morning may affect our sleep on Sunday night, especially if we try to go to bed earlier to prepare us for the week ahead. It would be better to go to bed later.[20] It should be noted that the average circadian rhythm is 25 hours long so that our internal clock is telling us to wake up an hour later every day and sleep difficulties can push the sleep cycle forward even further.

Jet Lag

A similar process occurs with jet lag.[21] If you are going to spend several days in a different time zone, start to adjust meals and bedtime to the new time zone before leaving home, then adjust meal times and sleep schedule to the new time zone immediately on arrival. If the adjustment is several hours earlier, we can use sunlight and activity or a short nap to stay awake for the longer day. I always found it difficult to adjust to the reverse situation of a shortened day as it meant going to bed very late in the new time zone to get the body temperature down, but getting up at the usual time. The key is to adjust the body temperature cycle as soon as possible. The same applies to shift workers as they frequently have sleep problems. Endeavoring to adjust in advance when there is a change in shift time coming up and making use of bright light or conversely avoiding it by wearing sunglasses are strategies that can be used to shift the temperature cycle.[22]

Infants

As an aside it is interesting to note that stabilizing the body-temperature cycle is also important for infants. This can be helped by exposing infants to bright lights, activity, and stimulation during the day and quiet and darkness at night. Day-time naps can be shortened as they get older and similar strategies used by adults for winding down in the evening also work for infants.[23]

Dreams

A discussion about sleep would not be complete without a mention of dreams, especially as some therapists engage in dream therapy. Although we don't under-

[20] Jacobs (1999: 93).
[21] See Jacobs (1999: 198–200) for suggestions.
[22] See Jacobs (1999: 195–196).
[23] For further information on strategies see, for example, Ferber (1999).

stand the nature of sleep, we know that dreaming is important to our health. One theory is that dreams are simply the result of random activity of our brain to clear itself. There is now however a greater understanding about dreams that is leading to a renewed interest in the subject. The recurrence of certain themes in some of our dreams, and especially nightmares (e.g., in post traumatic stress disorder), would suggest that our subconscious is trying to send us a message.[24]

The problem with most dreams is that they are hard to remember. Women recall more dreams than men and the older one gets the less dream recall is reported. However, with some conditioning, dreams can be remembered long enough to be written down. This must be done immediately on wakening, and even then memories will be fragmented and a lot of detail forgotten. To help the process we can tell ourselves a few times in a row that we will remember our dreams before we fall asleep. To understand the symbols in the dream there are some dictionaries of standard interpretations available. Their use however is questionable as all dreams are individual with their own symbolism, though such dictionaries might provide some triggers as to possible meanings. The person who has the dream is the best person to interpret the dream, perhaps with some guidance from a therapist.

It appears that dreams can do a lot of things, for example, state and solve problems, express emotions, express hidden feelings through images and stories (especially those that are most difficult to think or talk about when awake), and portray current problems, past dilemmas, and future possibilities. When we are concerned about some aspect of our lives or relationships, the unconscious continues to work on the problem while consciousness is busy doing other things. For example, a woman may dream that her husband is having an affair, whereas the dream is expressing a feeling that she is betrayed by him.

Without going into details, some brief comments as to how the dream might be processed will give some idea of dream therapy. It is a good idea to get a dreamer (D) to sketch the dream and clarify any details that are not clear. Usually D is the lead person in the dream (the dream ego or DE), and the feelings of the DE can be observed and compared with anything recently on D's mind. Next, DE's actions can be considered and questioned for their appropriateness as well as whether the dream ending was satisfactory. If not, D considers what advice might one of the other characters in the dream give to the DE and what would D choose to do next to continue the story. It is helpful to examine the very end of the person's dream just before he or she woke up. The dream might be regarded as a rehearsal of potential behavior or as an insight into D's current concerns. One can then explore other aspects of the setting, mood, plot, characters, and so forth.

In conclusion, there is one other related topic that has some promise called lucid dreaming, namely when you are aware you are dreaming. It is a hybrid state between sleeping and being awake. As well as some apparent psychiatric connections, one possible application of this is helping people who have nightmares to dream lucidly so that they can consciously wake up.

---

[24]For further details about dreams see Kramer (2006).

2.2.5 Relaxation Techniques

Many people suffer from "hurry sickness" and find life very stressful.[25] The key is to prevent stress from building up during the day by taking brief time-out moments and using some relaxation techniques. There are three important aspects to relaxation techniques: correct breathing, muscle relaxation, and thought control. There are a variety of breathing and relaxation techniques in the literature and I shall mention some of these as I refer to them in several chapters. With breathing, the basic idea is to breathe from your diaphragm through your nose while you are sitting comfortably (or lying down).[26] You fill the upper part of your abdomen as you breathe in by pushing the upper part of your stomach out and then totally relax as you breathe out; you can also say a word like "one," "peace," or "relax" in your mind as you breath out. Once you have learned to do this you can gradually slow down and deepen your breathing.

Diaphragm breathing has many advantages because of the increased oxygen supply to one's brain and muscles;[27] it is the method of breathing when sleeping. When you are tense you tend to have shallow breathing high up in your chest. Some people find this kind of exercise difficult as their diaphragms have almost fallen into disuse through bad breathing habits. A good way to start is to have one hand on your naval just below your rib cage and the other on your upper chest. As you use your diaphragm, your chest should not move as you breath in. This type of breathing can be done anywhere either standing or sitting, for example while waiting in your car for the traffic lights to change.

There is a lot of information on the internet about diaphragm breathing and some recommend breathing out either through the nose or through pursed lips, whichever is preferred. Breathing out through the mouth may be helpful initially for some, but nose breathing is preferred in yoga practices. I personally find breathing out through my nose more relaxing. Eyes are closed throughout the whole process to encourage the production of melatonin. You can also put on dark glasses or, if you wear glasses, you can stuff a handkerchief behind the lenses.

If you are lying down on your back,[28] some muscle relaxation can be incorporated with the breathing. Some recommend successively tightening then relaxing your muscles in order, starting with various parts of the body.[29] For others, tightening the muscles can be disruptive to concentration, so an alternative is to simply relax the muscles progressively from the feet up to the head and face (or in reverse order) breathing out any tension; it's easy to forget to relax the facial muscles and jaw. You also tell yourself that your arms, legs, body, and head are getting heavier and heavier; a related popular technique is *autogenics*,[30] where you add a further phase where you imagine your solar plexus, arms, and legs getting warmer as well as heavier. This way it is possible to obtain some level of self-hypnosis.[31] Whatever

---

[25]See Chapter 5.

[26]Men find diaphragm breathing easier than women.

[27]See Bourne (2005: chapter 4) for example.

[28]Some may find it more comfortable to have a cushion under their knees or bend their knees.

[29]Introduced by Jacobsen (1938); see http://en.wikipedia.org/wiki/Progressive_muscle_relaxation. Accessed October 2010.

[30]Linden (1990, 2005) and http://www.guidetopsychology.com/stress.htm; accessed October 2010.

[31]For the use of hypnosis by a therapist see Palmer (1993) and Palmer and Dryden (1995: 118–126).

method is used, your hands can be on their backs or on your chest and diaphragm. After the exercise, stretch and get up slowly.

One can go through a similar process if sitting in a chair, but with particular focus on relaxing neck, shoulder, and facial muscles, often the source of tension especially after sitting at a computer. If we choose a chair with arm rests, we can let our hands hang loose over the ends of the arm rests; otherwise we can place one hand on our navel and the other on top. By relaxing head, hands, and feet, and imagining our body is getting heavier and heavier, we can achieve a good overall relaxation. If possible, it is a good idea to "dedicate" a particular chair to relaxation so that when we sit in it we associate relaxation with it. Finally, if we are standing, then as we breath out we can flop our head and shoulders forward and relax.

Relaxing the mind can be a lot more difficult, though a relaxed body helps the mind to relax. If there is not a lot of time available, then focusing on something moving like a waterfall can help as a short term measure. Otherwise, we can imagine a peaceful scene like a beach for example and concentrate on using all our senses such as seeing, feeling (e.g., the sand beneath our feet, the breeze in our hair), hearing (e.g., the sound of the waves, the sounds of birds or of children playing) and smelling (e.g., the salt air). We could also apply the sensing principles to a forest, a brook, or mountains. For those with a good imagination, perhaps a ride in a hot air balloon or flight on a magic carpet might be good alternatives.[32] A number of visualization techniques are described by Bourne.[33]

If a client is having problems with obsessive thoughts, one simple technique is to hold up his or her hands to ear-level and wiggle the index (first) finger of each hand. This helps to keep each hemisphere of their brain occupied. Alternatively, one can devise a number of simple distraction techniques such as counting backwards in threes (e.g. 100, 97, 94, and so on), going though the alphabet making up a positive word for each letter (e.g., able, brainy, creative, and so on), or going through the alphabet backwards. The key is to let go of thoughts about the immediate past and the future, and enter into the here and now. These methods can be combined with some of the above relaxation techniques.

Dr Herbert Benson, a pioneer in the area of body/mind relationships and the author of several books and numerous research papers, especially in the area of re-laxation, introduced what he calls the *Relaxation Response*.[34] His steps are similar to the above, namely:

1. Sit comfortably in a quiet place with your eyes shut.

2. Relax all your muscles from your feet up to your face, and keep them relaxed.

3. Breath through your nose and say a word like "one" or "peace" (or a religious phrase) as you breath out; this eventually becomes a trigger for relaxation. While breathing, focus on this word or phrase for ten to twenty minutes. You may open your eyes to check the time, but do not use an alarm. Alternatively, you can count up to a certain number.

[32]Johnston (1998: 41–42).
[33]Bourne (2005: 228–233).
[34]Benson (2000).

4. Assume a passive attitude to intrusive thoughts. When distracting thoughts occur, try to let them float away by not dwelling on them and return to repeating your chosen word.

5. When you finish, sit quietly for several minutes, at first with your eyes closed and later with your eyes opened. Do not stand up for several minutes.

6. Practice the technique once or twice daily, but not within two hours after a meal as the digestive process seems to interfere with the relaxation process. (Possible times are before lunch, after work, and last thing at night.)

The key is not to worry about how successful you are in achieving a deep level of relaxation and not to force relaxation. It gets easier with practice. Initially about 20 minutes can be spent on a session and it should be practiced once or twice daily until the skill has been mastered. If necessary, the time can eventually be reduced down to 15 or even 10 minutes. Through practice one can build up a "relaxation memory bank" of the mental and physical sensations of being completely relaxed and therefore be able to quickly slip into the relaxation mode using the triggering word mentioned above.[35]

There are many variations on the above programs such as (a) keeping your eyes open, looking at your diaphragm, and then imagining the air being drawn downwards, (b) holding your breath for several seconds after breathing in, and (c) practicing the exercise for short spells (mini relaxation response) and for at least ten or fifteen times a day to master the skill. Palmer (1993) gives a similar program involving progressive relaxation beginning with the eyes and working down to the feet, followed by relaxed breathing and peaceful thoughts. Further ideas are given by Girdano et al.[36] I find that in many counseling situations, my client may have very little opportunity to practice a relaxation technique for any length of time during the day or even find a place where they can do it. In this case they can also use the mini relaxation response for a few seconds or minutes, sitting or standing, using the diaphragm breathing, relaxing head and shoulders, and focusing on a word. This can be done several times a day to prevent tension build up. With some people deep relaxation can bring up suppressed feelings with an accompanying anxiety. By using short spells of relaxation and stopping when feelings of anxiety arise, this problem will generally diminish with time and practice.

2.2.6   Healthy Sexuality

This is a topic for which there will be many diverse opinions especially as to what is meant by healthy sexuality.[37] In this section I will briefly discuss some physiology and endeavor to address the issue of masturbation. Further background information, especially relating to sexual dysfunction, is given in Section 19.4.3 in relation to couple counseling.

Testosterone is a steroid hormone primarily secreted in the testes of males and the ovaries of females, and it is the main sex hormone for men. It plays a key role

[35]Barrow and Place (1995: 44).
[36]Girdano, Everly, and Dusek (1997).
[37]For a frank and informative overview of male sexuality see Zilbergeld (1999) and http://www.sebringsil.com/sex.htm (accessed October 2010).

in health and well-being, for example, enhanced libido, increased energy, increased production of red blood cells and protection against osteoporosis, as well as in sexual functioning. On average, an adult male produces about forty to sixty times more testosterone than an adult female,[38] but the overall ranges are so wide that they overlap.

Masturbation

Masturbation has had a lot of bad press in past centuries along with a great deal of misinformation.[39] According to some of the literature, masturbation is normal behavior and is not only physically harmless but it can actually be beneficial with the reduction of stress and the release of endorphins, provided it is not too frequent or becomes addictive. However, there is the problem of deciding what is too frequent. Most men masturbate for most of their lives, depending to some degree on their marital status, while a majority of women (say two-thirds) masturbate at some stage in their lives; this is true right across all societies studied. For men, it is a release of sexual "pressure" caused by the steady build up of substances in their sex organs and also may be used as a release from daily stresses as a kind of pacifier. However, masturbation needs to be kept in perspective as it can cause problems. For instance, some men see this as an easy way out of avoiding trying to sort out sexual difficulties in a relationship. It can interfere with a partner's relationship and become a substitute for sex with a partner; it can then become selfishness.

Another problem with masturbation already alluded to above is that it can become an addictive habit or even a full-blown addiction that takes over a person's life and dominates his or her thinking. This can happen very easily when it is used as a stress reliever as one may masturbate to cope with successively smaller and smaller stresses. Pornography is particularly dangerous as it can take a man out of the real world into fantasy.[40] Also, people can confuse a normal sexual response with an adrenaline "high" so that as the adrenaline becomes addictive so the sex has to become more exciting, and perhaps more bizarre. Sexual appetite like any other appetite needs some discipline; eating can be good for us but we can overdo it. In a relationship there is a danger that sex becomes reduced to what can I get out of it rather than what can I contribute to the other person; other-centeredness will increase the enjoyment of the experience without taking away personal enjoyment. Sex is best enjoyed in a caring and loving relationship.

There is some other information relating to masturbation that is probably not so well known. During sexual activity, the neurotransmitter dopamine brings about excitement and after orgasm the body knows to release the hormone prolactin to suppress the dopamine and bring a feeling of relaxation and satisfaction. However, with both men and women, about four times more prolactin is released after orgasm with a committed sexual partner than when orgasm is done alone.[41] Masturbation can therefore leave people feeling discontented and unfulfilled as they may feel that their body is not being used in the way it was intended. It may also be followed by

---

[38]Though females are more sensitive to the hormone.
[39]Not only from the church but also from some psychiatrists, cf. Zilbergeld (1999: 71–72).
[40]See Section 14.3.2.
[41]Brody and Kruger (2006); for further references see
http://www.reuniting.info/science/research/sexual_hangover#prolactin; accessed October 2010.

guilty feelings. What happens is that the feeling of unfulfilled satisfaction and the return of arousal can lead to repeating the masturbation. Because the emotional connection is missing, there is the danger that masturbation can therefore become addictive and depressive.

2.2.7   Touch

We all need healthy, non-demanding touches in our lives, for example a touch on the arm. It could be said that the largest sex gland on our bodies is our skin! Well-known psychologist Virginia Satir suggested that we need at least 12 hugs a day. I am not sure about this figure but it emphasizes the importance of human contact, which we need from an early age. The need for touch in an adult also depends on the person's love language, discussed in Section 19.6.5. So much for the physical, what about the mental?

2.3   INTELLECTUAL

2.3.1   Balance

In Section 1.2.2 I referred to the two hemispheres of our brain. It seems that most people tend to be dominated by one side or the other.[42] The significance for wholeness lies in the importance of keeping a balance between the hemispheres, which means developing our less preferred side. For example, a person with a left brain emphasis could consider taking up activities like music, painting, or pottery, while a person with a right brain emphasis could take up activities like learning a foreign language, computing, or doing cross-word puzzles. Creativity and relaxation are right brain functions.

2.3.2   Goals

Two important keys to intellectual wholeness are having a positive mental attitude and having suitable attainable goals. Having achievable goals makes life more doable and helps to create a sense of achievement and purpose. Achieving goals provides encouragement and helps to build self-esteem and self-respect. A helpful metaphor for counseling on goal setting and balance is to describe life like a railway track with the positive and good things on one rail and the negative and bad on the other. As we are human we always have some negative stuff, but we can choose which we rail we get on! In the case of goals, they can be general life goals relating to one's mission statement,[43] or particular goals. These latter goals need to be SMART, namely:

1. **S**pecific (not vague).

2. **M**easurable (you know when you have achieved them).

3. **A**chievable (some authors use the word attainable).

---

[42]There are a number of accessible tests on the internet to determine which side is dominant (e.g., enter "Left and right brain").
[43]Covey (1989: Habit 2) talks about having a mission statement for every part of our lives, for example, what sort of a parent, spouse, work colleague, etc. do I want to be?

4. Realistic.

5. Timely, that is, have a time frame for accomplishing the goal.

A goal like, "I want to get fitter" needs to be replaced by something more specific such as I will walk for 20 minutes every day. It helps to have some steps to take on the way to the goal The next step can be to determine how our improvement in fitness can be measured, for example, by slowly increasing the distance walked in the same time. Clear criteria should be put in place for measuring progress. The goal must be achievable so that there needs to be a 20 minute slot of time available each day (or most days) irrespective of the weather (wet-weather gear may be needed). The goal won't be realistic if it does not help me to get fitter. A five minute walk is certainly achievable but not realistic for getting fitter. A date needs to be set when a certain target is reached, for example walking 50% further in 20 minutes. Sturt and Sturt[44] suggest that the way to produce an effective goal is to ask the questions what, why, where, how, and when. Goals need to be prioritized and planned on a daily and/or weekly basis and they need to set us up for success, not failure. Time management skills like those discussed in Section 5.3 play an important role in setting and achieving goals.[45]

The role of goals in addictions is discussed generally in Section 12.2.4 and more specifically in the case of gambling in Section 14.2.4.

2.3.3 Resilience

Resilience is the ability to cope with stress and adversity, and be able to "bounce back" and function normally again. Padesky and Mooney (2012) give the following four-step program as part of a Strengths-Based CBT to help people to build positive qualities.

Step1: Search for Strengths. The following areas are correlated with resilience and can therefore be regarded as possible strengths for resilience.

1. Good health and an easy temperament.
2. Secure attachment and basic trust in other people.
3. Interpersonal competence including the ability to recruit help.
4. Cognitive competence that encompasses the ability to read, capacity to plan, self-efficacy and intelligence.
5. Emotional competence including diverse emotional skills such as the ability to regulate one's emotions, delay gratification, maintain realistically high self-esteem and employ creativity and humour to one's benefit.
6. The ability and opportunity to contribute to others.
7. Holding faith that one's life matters and life has meaning, including a moral sense of connection to others.
   Unfortunately clients are often unaware of their strengths so that therapists need to search for the client's hidden strengths within everyday activities and bring them to the client's awareness. A helpful question

[44]Sturt and Sturt (1998; 124–127).
[45]See, for example, Covey (1989: Habit 3 of putting first things first).

might be: "What is one thing you do every day because you really want to do it?" The therapist then needs to investigate this activity in detail and look for the positive aspects of the activity. A regular activity will encounter obstacles and these can be explored as a window into discussing resilience.

Step 2: Construct a Personal Model of Resilience (PMR) The client and therapist can work together to create a PMR in the client's own words using the strengths found in Step 1. The activity identified in Step 1 can be used to make a client aware of his or her resilience in dealing with associated obstacles and then see how the resilience demonstrated here can be applied to other difficulties in the client's life.

Step 3: Apply the PMR The client is now asked how the PMR can be used to help maintain resilience in areas of difficulty. Common challenges in problem areas can be considered and written down. The emphasis is in staying resilient rather than success in solving or overcoming the problems.

Step 4: Practice Resilience The aim now is to help the client to devise behavioral experiments to practice resilience.[46]

2.4 EMOTIONAL

2.4.1 Beliefs and Emotions

In Section 1.4.2 we considered the interaction of beliefs and emotions, pointing out that one part of our brain stores the facts about an experience and another part stores the memories of the accompanying emotions. What happens is that the intensity of an emotion has virtually gone after 15 seconds but the memory of it can last for years, particularly if the emotion is deliberately perpetuated and reinforced. Difficult emotions and feelings never go away unless they are dealt with. A helpful exercise described by Greenberg[47] for recognizing and dealing with difficult emotional states is as follows:

1. Identify and focus on a problem state in which you spend a lot of time, perhaps without recognizing that you do (e.g. angry, hurt).

2. Take notice of the emotion and allow yourself to feel it in your body.

3. What do you feel about the emotion, accepting or rejecting?

4. Welcome and accept the emotion.

5. Explore how this state feels.

6. Identify the voice and the thoughts that accompany this state.

7. What specifically triggers this state?

8. Is this state related to any past experience?

---

[46]See Padesky and Mooney (2012) for further details.
[47]Greenberg (2002: 191).

9. Identify what this state is saying now.

10. Interact with this state by talking to it and notice any changes in the state. Cooperate with the state instead of trying to control it.

A more cognitive approach for clients who feel trapped by their feelings is for them to have a look at their belief system. Negative feelings such as inappropriate anger, bitterness, resentment, melancholy, despair, fear, and grief can destroy a person's wholeness if they are continually recycled and not processed adequately; the aim is to recycle positive feelings. Memories can become distorted so that our emotions can also become inappropriate over time, but are nevertheless "real" to us.

Clients need to realize that people can't make us feel a certain way as we are responsible for our own feelings. We need to say, "I feel angry when..." rather than "You make me angry." Our attitude can be "You can only hurt me and I choose to be angry in response. You therefore can never make me angry. You can only hurt me or frustrate me." It helps to get into the habit of using "I" statements rather than "You" statements. If we let people affect us, then they are controlling us. By the same token, we can't be responsible for other people's feelings.

2.4.2 Identifying Feelings

As noted in Section 1.4.2, the four basic emotions can be summarized as glad, sad, mad and bad (afraid) and it is helpful if the therapist can identify variations on these four like those in the Table 2.1 below. We process feelings by identifying them, owning them, and hopefully sharing them with someone whose sensitivity we can trust. This does not mean dumping them on others. Clients also need to learn to listen to other people's feelings. As an aside I would like to stress the importance of judicious humor. It's beneficial, and in a counseling situation can sometimes help to settle difficult feelings without minimizing the seriousness of the situation.

Some clients can be so emotionally immature that they can't identify and express their feelings clearly; they tend to be black-and-white in expressing themselves. In helping clients to identify their feelings, a "word matrix" like that in Table 2.1 can be helpful.

Further categories can be added if need be; I added "strong" and "weak" to the four basic emotions. Clients can be encouraged to also embrace feelings by developing their listening skills and reflecting feeling words as is done in counseling.[48]

If feelings are not identified and processed, they can even lead to physical ailments (so-called somatization).[49] Symptoms might be stomach discomfort ("I can't stomach him"), sore throat ("I find that hard to swallow"), and itchy skin ("She gets under my skin"). For example, hate directed at an abuser can surface as a psychosomatic illness. Children often carry anger and anxiety in their stomachs, due to an excess of adrenaline.

---

[48]See also Section 19.6.2 on listening skills.
[49]There is a psychological disorder called somatization disorder or Briquet's syndrome.

Table **2.1**   Mood Matrix.

Mood						
Intensity	GLAD	SAD	BAD	MAD	STRONG	WEAK
HIGH	elated	depressed	terrified	furious	powerful	helpless
	delighted	distressed	scared	incensed	forceful	powerless
	excited	wretched	afraid	mad	strong	defenseless
MEDIUM	happy	miserable	anxious	angry	confident	drained
	cheerful	sad	disturbed	cross	capable	weak
	glad	unhappy	uneasy	resentful	positive	fragile
LOW	pleased	low	apprehensive	irritated	firm	limp

2.5   SOCIAL

2.5.1   Importance of Networks

We were not designed to live in isolation and we all can benefit from a network of good friends. We also need people who will listen without offering advice. Research shows that interaction with social support groups improves health and increases longevity.[50] It also appears that the benefits of being socially involved are enhanced if the person is also religious. A religious organization can be regarded as a social support group,[51] and there is increasing research evidence that religious involvement is associated with better physical health, better mental health, and longer survival. We all need to feel accepted, valued, and have a sense of belonging; we cannot achieve these on our own. People can become stunted in their social development because of a lack of trust engendered when they were children, and they may not have grown out of their childhood self-centeredness.

As noted by Sturt and Sturt,[52] social wholeness develops in stages beginning with dependence, then moving to independence through to interdependence.[53] However, there are cultural and sexual differences; for example, Western cultures tend to emphasize individualism, while other cultures emphasize interdependence and collectivism. Women tend to network better than men, so that we find that many men are very isolated. In Section 1.6.3 I mentioned the usefulness of a social portfolio as we age; we can apply this idea at any age.

I believe that true social wholeness is achieved by moving from being self-centered to being other-centered. Sturt and Sturt[54] comment that, "This is not done by negating ourselves, but through developing a sense of self-worth. Only then we can

[50]Death rates for single, widowed, and divorced people of all races and ages are significantly higher than for married individuals, cf. Ortmeyer (1974: 159–184) and Lynch (1985: 69–70).
[51]Wallis (1996).
[52]Sturt and Sturt (1998: 166).
[53]Covey's (1989: 261) seven habits are based on this model.
[54]Sturt and Sturt (1998: 165).

forget ourselves and focus on the needs of others." A key to good relationships is learning to listen rather than giving advice, and being prepared to being vulnerable enough to share something of ourselves.

There a number of key issues that impinge on our interpersonal relationships, including (a) the type of attachment we had to our caregivers, which may affect the current attachment we have to our significant others, (b) the degree of assertiveness we can exercise within our relationships, (c) the level of our self-worth and self-esteem, and (d) the extent to which we are able to forgive others and ourselves. One other topic, birth order, is briefly mentioned for information only because of its popular interest; its relevance to counseling is uncertain. These four topics are now discussed below.

2.5.2 Attachment Issues

Attachment theory argues that we have an innate predisposition to form attachment relationships, and an infant cannot survive healthily without care and protection. Our psychosocial development and psychological health therefore depend on the type of attachment we had with our caregivers as children. Attachment is based on how sensitive and responsive parents are to a child's needs. It is therefore helpful to consider the various attachment styles of children proposed by Bowlby, Ainsworth, Main and others when counseling; some healing may be needed. These attachment styles consist of one secure style and three insecure styles as follows:[55]

1. *Secure attachment.* This is the most common form of attachment (about 55–65% of the population). Infants with secure attachment get minimally distressed when mother leaves them and greet her happily on returning. She is their secure base that they can wander from but occasionally return to for reassurance. As adults they show greater physical and resilience and are less likely to experience health and psychiatric problems than those with insecure styles.

2. *Insecure avoidant attachment.* Avoidant infants don't usually cry when mother leaves and avoid her when she returns. They dislike being held but dislike being put down even more; they tend to be angry. Such children often have abusive or neglectful parents and therefore avoid seeking help. This occurs in about 20–25% of the population.

3. *Insecure anxious resistant (ambivalent) attachment.* Infants with this form of attachment get very upset when mother leaves but are ambivalent when she returns both wanting contact but also resisting it. This form of attachment is usually the result of poor maternal availability with the child not being able to depend on the mother being there when needed. This occurs in about 10–15% of the population.

4. *Insecure disorganized/disoriented attachment.* Infants with this form of attachment show a mixture and oscillations of both resistant and avoidant behavior. They greet mother brightly on returning but then turn away or approach without looking at her. They seem dazed, confused, and afraid, and

---

[55]There is a very extensive literature on attachment (see, for example, the internet for some general ideas). Percentages are from Goldberg, Muir, and Kerr (1995: 11).

their attachment appears to be the least secure. Such behavior can occur if the child feels both comforted and frightened by the mother, who may be insensitive, intrusive, or abusive. This occurs in about 15–20% of the population.

There are a few attachment patterns that don't quite fit any of the above.

Bowlby believed that attachment is not only a theory of child development but that the attachment phenomena are lifelong. He wrote, "attachment behavior is held to characterize human beings from the cradle to the grave."[56] Consequently we find that there are also different adult attachment styles in adult romantic relationships that have some overlap with child-parent attachment styles.[57] One working definition of adult attachment is as follows:

> Adult attachment is the stable tendency of an individual to make substantial efforts to seek and maintain proximity to and contact with one or a few specific individuals who provide the subjective potential for physical and/or psychological safety and security.[58]

The four styles usually mentioned are described below[59] and can also be categorized by the two dimensions of anxiety about their relationship and how avoidant they are in their relationships;[60] the two dimensions are included below.

1. *Secure.* These people are comfortable with both intimacy and autonomy and cope with both extremes of closeness and distance. They trust themselves and others, and are comfortable in depending on others and others depending on them. They don't worry about being alone or having others not accepting them. They have positive views of self and others. The two dimensions are low anxiety/low avoidance.

2. *Preoccupied/anxious.* These people are preoccupied with relationships. They feel that they can't get close enough to others and are very sensitive to any suggestion of rejection or abandonment. They can therefore be very clingy and possessive and need constant reassurance of their acceptance, value, and belonging, often worrying that their partner doesn't really love them or won't want to stay with them. They are less positive about their partners as they don't trust people's good intentions. They are more likely to be emotionally expressive. The two dimensions are high anxiety/low avoidance.

3. *Dismissive/avoidant.* These people are dismissive of intimacy and don't like others to get too close. Their partners may want to be closer and more intimate, but this scares them and they want to move away. They are strongly independent and don't like being dependent on others nor for others to depend on them. They often deny needing close relationships and may even view close relationships as relatively unimportant. Also they are the least emotionally expressive. The two dimensions are low anxiety/high avoidance.

[56]Bowlby (1977: 203).
[57]Hazan and Shaver (1987). See also http://www.psych.uiuc.edu/~rcfraley/attachment.htm by Fraley; accessed October 2010.
[58]Berman and Sperling (1994: 8).
[59]Bartholomew and Horowitz (1991) based on thoughts about self and thoughts about partners; there are some differences in terminology in the literature.
[60]Collins and Freeney (2004).

4. *Fearful/avoidant.* People with this attachment style are fearful of intimacy and may feel they are being smothered if others get too close, while they may feel abandoned if others get too distant. Although wanting emotionally close relationships, they find it difficult to trust others completely, or to depend on them. They also seek less intimacy from partners, frequently suppress and hide their feelings, and are socially avoidant. The two dimensions are high anxiety/high avoidance.

People may have aspects of more than one attachment style.

The different styles can be acted out in the counseling situation, for example, some clients appear anxious and needy, others withdrawn and distant (even hostile), and others oscillate between both styles. For a free on-line questionnaire to determine a person's adult attachment style see the internet.[61] We can expect attachment styles to affect such things as partner choice, how much partners are "in tune," and ultimately marital success (see also Sections 19.2.2 and 19.2.3).

2.5.3   Self-Esteem

Although self-concept and self-esteem are often used interchangeably, Girdano et al.[62] prefer to distinguish between the two and describe self-concept as having six major components: self-awareness, self-worth, self-love, self-esteem, self-confidence, and self-respect. We can also add self-image. Self-concept can be regarded as the overall view we have of ourselves and it includes our appearance, ability, temperament, attitudes, and beliefs, and how we see ourselves in terms of other people's perceptions of us. However, when it comes to all these self-words there seems to be a general confusion in the literature over the meaning of some of them. I am choosing here to focus on self-esteem which has been defined as a favorable or unfavorable attitude toward one-self.[63] This involves the evaluation of the self-concept, is often unrelated to one's true abilities, and can vary in different areas of one's life.[64] It begins with our self-image or what we *think* about ourselves, which is formed from an early age; this affects how we *feel* about ourselves, which helps to establish our self-esteem.

Self-worth is often used interchangeably with self-esteem, but some writers maintain that there is a difference, for example, one may have a very high level of self-esteem and yet have a very low sense of self-worth. Self-worth can be defined as the evaluation of one's own worth. From a counseling viewpoint I don't distinguish between self-esteem and self-worth.

If I suspect that my client has low self-esteem, I find it helpful to use a self-administered questionnaire. Care is need in interpreting the results as some clients are not always fully self-aware or are overoptimistic, thus tending to skew the results toward high self-esteem. There are a number questionnaires on the internet, but

[61]For example http://www.web-research-design.net/cgi-bin/crq/crq.pl (accessed October 2010), which uses scores on the two dimensions.
[62]Girdano et al. (1997: 127–129).
[63]Rosenberg (1965: 15).
[64]Plummer (2004: 14).

some of these are more reliable than others. For the popular Rosenberg's scale and other questionnaires see the internet under "self-esteem questionnaire."[65]

The roots of low self-esteem are often found in childhood often because of inadequate parenting.[66] Parents may have been over-critical (the child is never good enough), neglecting (the child feels worthless, lonely, and insecure), rejecting (the child feels unwanted and is self-rejecting), or abusive. Parental divorce or drug abuse, including alcoholism, can have a profound affect on a child's self-esteem. At the opposite end of the spectrum, an overprotective or overindulgent parenting can produce an an adult who feels insecure, unsure about the world or is unwilling to take personal responsibility for his or her life. This can also lead to low self-esteem. For adults, the basis of self-esteem is taking care of one's self and recognizing the importance of our "inner child" (Section 1.2.4). Bourne states that "It's possible to overcome deficits from your past only by becoming a good parent to yourself."[67]

Counseling for Low Self-Esteem

The first thing to consider is what is the client's self-image like—is it positive and realistic? Where does a client's self-esteem come from: personal performance and achievements, the love of someone else, or the approval of others? The personality traits mentioned in Section 1.3.2 are also relevant to one's self-esteem, especially perfectionism and an excessive need for approval. Negative self-esteem often goes round in a reinforcing circle: I think I am inferior, therefore I feel inferior and act inferior, then others believe it and treat me as inferior, which confirms I am inferior, and so on.[68]

Some common distorted thought patterns are:[69]

- black and white thinking (e.g., "I lost my temper, therefore I am a bad person")
- self-labeling (e.g., "I am a born loser")
- viewing the world through dark glasses (e.g., "I'm overweight... no one would be interested in me")
- jumping to conclusions (e.g., "He didn't ring me ... he doesn't care about me")
- maximizing weaknesses and minimizing strengths (e.g., "I achieved that ... but it is nothing" or "I didn't thank her ... I'm an ungrateful person")
- having a slave-driver mentality using words like "should," "ought," and "must" (e.g., "I must please everyone").

Counseling can be a vital process in helping a client to identify, challenge, and change distorted messages of self and deal with those things that prevent change. These can be fear of change, learned helplessness, rationalizing and denial, blaming

---

[65] For example, http://www.insight-psychology.co.uk/Self-Esteem.pdf and
http://www.theselfesteeminstitute.com/Files/Self-EsteemQuestionnaire.pdf (both accessed October 2010).
[66] Bourne (2005: 276–277).
[67] Bourne (2005: 276).
[68] Sturt and Sturt (1994: 27).
[69] Sturt and Sturt (1994: 27).

others or one's background, projecting one's faults on to others, self-deception, and self-sabotaging behavior.[70] A low self-esteem will aggravate depression, cause stress, and may lead to false guilt, anger, and jealousy of others (e.g., of one's partner if they have good self-esteem and relate well to others).[71] Other signs of low self-esteem are boasting or exaggerating (to bolster one's image), wanting to be the center of attention (to compensate in some way), being dogmatic (can't stand being proved wrong), having workaholic tendencies (to gain acceptance), and directing anger inwardly (because of feelings of inadequacy).

Plummer[72] notes that people with low self-esteem generally have problems in forming close attachments, often because they don't feel worthy of them. Misunderstandings readily occur and there is a tendency to have a distorted view of self and others. Such persons undervalue their abilities, often deny their successes, and find it difficult to set goals and problem-solve. They will usually be unwilling to try anything new for fear of failure or rejection.

Plummer suggests exploring the following areas of life with a client to establish and maintain a healthy self-esteem:[73]

1. *Self-knowledge.* This relates to who I am, where I fit in, where I am the same as or differ from others.

2. *Self and others.* This involves understanding how relationships function and being aware of my own and others' emotions and how they are expressed.

3. *Self-acceptance.* I accept my strengths and weaknesses and feel happy about my physical body.

4. *Self-reliance.* I know how to care for myself, establish my independence, and be self-motivated.

5. *Self-expression.* I know how we communicate verbally and nonverbally and being creative in our expression.

6. *Self-confidence.* This means having a right to be me and to express myself, and my opinions count.

7. *Self-awareness.* I am aware of my feelings, know my capabilities, and can learn to set realistic goals.

It is important for a client to have a healthy network of friends, especially close friends who are accepting and supportive because in these relationships we learn to maintain appropriate boundaries and this promotes good self-esteem.

A helpful exercise for a client who has some negative thoughts about self is to use the Big I/Little i diagram of Lazarus.[74] The therapist draws a large capital I in block form and then begins to fill it in with lots of little i's that stand for various things about the client. These are obtained by asking the client to give some positive things that people might say about them (e.g., the way he or she

[70]Sturt and Sturt (1994: chapter 6).
[71]Sturt and Sturt (1994: 74–77).
[72]Plummer (2004: 19).
[73]Adapted from Plummer (2004: 20–23).
[74]Ellis, Gordon, Neenan, and Palmer (1997: 112).

smiles), some negative things, and some neutral things. The therapist can then point to the little i's that initiated this exercise and note that they do not represent the big I.

Another exercise is to help clients to list things they like about themselves (internally and externally) and then ask them to read the list three times a day with meals for at least a month, as with a medical prescription! Care is needed with just using general positive statements as clients may regard them as unrealistic and they may actually have a detrimental effect on those with low self-esteem.[75] Some examples of positive statements are given on the internet.[76] Satir[77] has a helpful self-esteem poem that can be used for clients.[78] Also, images can be used constructively both to explore current inappropriate behaviors and to develop new behaviors.[79] The following famous five freedoms proposed by Satir are relevant to self-esteem and self-care:[80]

- to SEE AND HEAR what is here, rather than what was, will be or should be

- to SAY what one feels and thinks instead of what one should

- to FEEL what one feels, instead of what one ought

4. to ASK for what one wants, instead of always waiting for permission

5. to TAKE RISKS on one's own behalf, instead of choosing to be only "secure" and not rocking the boat

2.5.4   Assertiveness

Appropriate assertiveness can play a significant role in interpersonal relationships and consequent personal wellbeing. There are many books and internet sites about assertiveness and the topic is often introduced under a life-skill heading. For example, a person might need help in giving criticism, giving compliments, asking for a rise, promotion or career move, being interviewed, making a presentation, and chairing meetings.[81]

It is important to remember that assertiveness is culturally defined so that what works in one culture will not necessarily work in another. Assertiveness issues can arise in counseling when a client is finding life difficult because of inappropriate aggressiveness in family, work, and other relationships.[82] Assertiveness is also linked to self-esteem. In this section I shall bring together some ideas from the literature for improving one's assertiveness.

Assertiveness is a behavior style that strikes a balance between aggression at one end of the scale and being totally passive or submissive at the other end. Under

---

[75]Wood, Perunovic, and Lee (2009); further research with larger samples is needed on this topic.
[76]See, for example, http://www.innerworkspublishing.com/inventory.htm, which is a self-esteem inventory focused around positive statements; accessed October 2010.
[77]Satir (1975).
[78]See http://www.kalimunro.com/declaration-of-self-esteem.html for a copy; accessed October 2010.
[79]For more details see Plummer (2004: chapter 3).
[80]From Satir (1976).
[81]For example, see Bishop (2000: chapter 13).
[82]For further ideas with regard to difficult dyadic relationships see Chapter 17.

the heading of aggressive we can also include passive-aggressive, where anger and aggressive feelings are expressed covertly through passive resistance, for example, procrastinating and being awkward, being unreliable, and being "forgetful" (see Section 3.6 about passive-aggressive anger). Another non-assertive style is the manipulative style whereby manipulative people get what they want by using various indirect strategies such as making others feel sorry for them or guilty toward them, being intimidating using anger, or even feigning indifference. Assertive behavior, however, involves standing up for your right to be treated fairly without having to apologize or feel guilty, without violating the rights of others, and not being aggressive. It is also expressing your opinions, needs, and feelings, without ignoring or hurting the opinions, needs, and feelings of others.

A helpful tool for the therapist is a "personal bill of rights" with twenty-five "rights" given by Bourne, which can be downloaded from the internet.[83] For example, "I have the right to ask for what I want" and "I have the right to say no to requests or demands I can't meet." Therapists can use these rights to devise suitable questions such as "Do you find yourself saying 'yes' to requests when you should really say 'no,' as you don't want to disappoint people?" or "Do you find it hard to voice a difference of opinion with others?"

Ladder of Exercises

For general assertiveness, Girdano et al.[84] described an assertiveness ladder of exercises where we begin at the bottom with the least difficult exercise and, once having practiced at a particular rung, move up to the next rung. If we experience anxiety, we drop back a rung for a while. The list is summarized in Table 2.2 and the exercises in the list are described briefly as follows:

Table 2.2 Assertiveness Ladder.

Eye Contacts
Disagreement
Feelings
"Why"
"I"
Compliments
Greeting Others

Exercise 1. *Greeting others.* We initiate conversation (at least two per day) with a person who is not one of our close friends.

Exercise 2. *Complimentary statements.* We give others compliments, and endeavor to do it more often.

[83]Search under "personal bill of rights," for example,
http://www.adoptioncrossroads.org/PersonalBillofRights.html (accessed October 2010). There are several different lists on the internet, each adapted for a specific purpose.
[84]Girdano et al. (1997: 147–150).

Exercise 3. *The use of "I" statements.* This shows ownership; we don't be afraid to take a position in regard to our preferences and disagreements. Disagreement with an "I" statement by someone else may be seen by an unassertive person as a rejection of him or her personally, which is not usually the case.

Exercise 4. *Why?* This involves asking "why?" It does not represent a challenge but simply asks for additional information. We should ask "why" at least two times per day from people we consider to be "above" us in some way. If we feel the word "why" is too threatening to that person, substitute "What makes you think that?" or "How is that so?" or possibly "Could you help me to understand that better?"

Exercise 5. *Spontaneous expression of feelings.* We try to express our emotional reaction at least twice a day and we don't repress our feelings.

Exercise 6. *Disagreement.* This involves disagreeing with someone when we feel the person is wrong. But we need to be sure that we believe in what we are saying.

Exercise 7. *Eye contact.* This is one of the most difficult things for the unassertive person to do. We begin with eye contact for 2-3 seconds and eventually extend it up to 10 seconds. It is important not to stare as it may be interpreted as a challenge. When we break eye contact we don't look down but maintain our basic eye level.

A key aspect in using these exercises is to maintain positive thinking and a positive self-image.

Assertiveness Techniques

Bourne[85] has some very helpful comments about being assertive, particularly in a problem situation. Some of the following suggestions overlap with those in the above ladder:

1. We develop nonverbal assertive behaviors. This can be achieved by looking directly at another person when addressing them without staring, and maintaining an open rather than a closed posture. For example, if sitting, we avoid crossing our arms or legs, while if standing, we stand up straight and face the person directly (not off to one side). It is important for us to stay calm, breathe normally, and not back off or move away when talking. This can be practiced in the counseling room.

2. We speak clearly and firmly at a normal conversational volume (i.e., don't yell or whisper) and avoid long sentences. We should allow pauses for feedback. It is important not to interrupt the other person when they are talking, and we try hard to listen and understand their point of view. We ask the other person to show us the same respect and attention. We avoid whining or using an apologetic tone of voice.

3. We recognize and exercise our basic rights (these are discussed above).

[85]Bourne (2005: chapter 13).

4. In order to know what to ask for, we need to be aware of our own feelings, needs, and wants. We can't expect people to be mind readers, which often happens with couples.

5. We practice assertive responses. To do this we first define the problem situation in specific and not vague general terms, and then formulate an assertive response as follows:

   (a) We evaluate our rights within the situation at hand.

   (b) We set up a convenient time for discussion with the person concerned (unless, of course, we have to be assertive on the spot).

   (c) We state the consequences to us of the problem situation using "I" statements, avoiding judging or blaming, and making our feelings clear.

   (d) We make our request (not a demand or command) for change very specifically using assertive nonverbal behavior (see (1) above). For example, instead of "I would like you to help me more around the house" say "I would like you to help me in the house by doing the vacuuming inside and sweeping outside". The request should be simple and not ask for too many things at once, preferably one thing at a time. In the case of a relationship, it is helpful to validate self and the other person, for example, validate specifically and honestly what is good in the relationship and try to sandwich the request for change between two positive statements.

   (e) In our request, we focus on the behavior and not the person, and we don't apologize for our request.

   (f) We state the consequences of gaining (or not gaining) the other person's cooperation (if appropriate).
   In the case of having to be assertive on the spot, we evaluate our rights and then make our request, bearing in mind the other steps above.

6. We learn to say no by (a) acknowledging the request by repeating it, (b) explaining the reason for declining, and (c) saying no. For example, "I would like to go to the show with you, but I have had too many late nights lately so I will have to say no." It is important not to feel guilty, which may show up through, for example, excessive apologizing.

Another popular assertiveness ladder, based on the acronym LADDER[86] can be used in a specific situation to help decrease stress, namely:

L Look at your rights and what you want, and understand your feelings about the situation. Define what you want and keep it in mind when negotiating for change.

A Arrange a time and place with the other person to discuss the situation. This step will be skipped in unplanned situations in which you choose to be assertive (e.g., you receive the wrong food at a restaurant).

D Define the problem simply and specifically, without assuming any prior knowledge of the other party about the problem.

---

[86]From Davis, Eshelman, and McKay (2000: 197–220).

D Describe your feelings so that the person understands how you feel about the situation using "I" messages. An "I" message expresses your feelings without blaming others. Say "I am feeling frustrated," rather than "You frustrate me."

E Express your request specifically and be brief and firm. For example, instead of asking your husband to be "more considerate," ask him to call if he'll be more than 15 minutes late.

R Reinforce the idea of getting what you want by showing the other person that your request might be of mutual benefit.

To apply this process, it is a good idea to write out a script, with one or a few statements for each step in the process. You then practice the script by yourself out loud until it feels comfortable. Then try it out it in a real situation just keeping the principles in mind and not worrying too much about the details. A key issue is tension control through relaxation techniques. When we are assertive we may experience a reaction from others, and I now want to consider some resulting types of reaction.

Diversionary Tactics

The person on the receiving end of assertiveness may adopt one or more of the following diversionary tactics:[87]

- denial

- change the subject

- put off until another time

- react strongly (e.g., angrily to gain control or tearfully to gain sympathy)

- denigrate the request, or even laugh it off

- question or criticize the legitimacy of your request

- ask you why you want what you ask for

- reverse the guilt to try and make you feel guilty

- respond with a threat

In response we can do the following:

1. Keep repeating the request (so called "broken-record" technique). This is a somewhat aggressive technique that should be used only when all attempts to be assertive have failed and one's rights are being infringed.

2. When criticized, use a statement like "You could be right—it might be easier to walk. " By partially agreeing you defuse the criticism and avoid argument; you then repeat your original request. This is known rather aptly as "fogging." It is particularly effective if the other person's opinion can be restated in a

---

[87] Adapted from Bourne (2005: 291, 296).

way that could be true of anyone or everyone. For example, a response to "You're stupid" might be "That could be true as we all have a stupid side."

3. Use negative assertion, which involves accepting the truthful part of any criticism, but stating it in more positive terms, perhaps with humor. For example, a response to "You're aggressive" might be "I certainly don't let people walk all over me, " or respond to "You always make mistakes" with "I have to admit I am not perfect."

4. Use negative enquiry, which involves asking for some constructive comments about any negative criticism. For example, in response to "You're lazy" one could ask, "What is it you think I should be doing?" It requires some confidence to do this.

5. Respond by saying that it is beside the point or it is a side issue to be discussed later.

6. Sometimes it might be best to say, "I can see you are upset; we can discuss it later," though the issue of control mentioned above needs to be considered. Using anger is a very common control ploy for a person wanting to get their own way.

2.5.5   Forgiveness

Introduction

There has been an increasing interest in forgiveness "as a way to feel better by letting go of past hurts"[88] and the literature on the subject is extensive. However, I have found this section a difficult one to write for a number of reasons. First, the subject is still in its infancy with inputs not only from psychology and religion but also from philosophy, and its literature is growing rapidly.[89]

Second, from the mid-1980s, forgiveness began to be studied scientifically using statistical models and empirical techniques,[90] and with a focus on the idea that forgiveness can possibly benefit a person's mental health and well-being (or at least indirectly). Some studies support this idea statistically as forgiveness and unforgiveness are linked to some physiological variables,[91] but some questions remain about actual causality and the effect of changes in other variables like resentment and anger that can be detrimental to health.[92] There is some evidence that rumination may play a causal role in impeding forgiveness over time.[93] Even if forgiveness is not possible, a reduction in "unforgiveness" can have a positive effect.

Third, although there seems to be a general consensus about what forgiveness is not, there are many different definitions as to the nature of forgiveness.[94] This is perhaps not surprising as there are a variety of situations where the question

---

[88]Benner and Hill (1999: 1152).

[89]The extensive nature of the subject is reflected in the edited volume of Worthington (2005a); see in particular the extensive bibliography of Scherer, Cooke, and Worthington (2005).

[90]See, for example McCullough and Root (2005).

[91]See, for example, Witvliet (2001), Harris and Thoresen (2005), and Toussaint and Webb (2005).

[92]Statistical studies of this kind have some difficulties, c.f. Flanigan (1998) for some comments.

[93]Toussaint and Webb (2005: 357–358).

[94]For example see Worthington (2005b: 3–5).

of forgiveness arises, for example in marriage, families, sexual and physical abuse, trauma, genocide, desecration, and so forth. Enright and Fitzgibbons (2000) show that forgiveness can play a role in a wide range of psychological disorders including depression, anxiety, addictions, and mental and personality disorders; in fact whenever there is an anger problem it can be reduced with the exercise of forgiveness. It is therefore difficult to give a definition to cover all the various cases, though I will make some suggestions below. As there are many different definitions, there are also many different models for the forgiveness process.[95]

Fourth, forgiveness has generally been linked to religion and has it roots there, but it has to be noted that different religions, although having common threads, bring different perspectives to the nature of forgiveness.[96] For example, Christianity tends to concentrate on unilateral forgiveness, that is, forgiving without any requirement from the offender (though there is some debate, depending on the nature of the offense), Judaism focuses on the need for repentance by the offender, while Islam is somewhat in between the two.[97]

Fifth, the role of forgiveness in society depends very much on culture and whether the world view is individualistic or collectivistic. For example:

> Forgiveness and reconciliation are likely to be closely related or synonymous in collectivistic cultures. Self-forgiveness is likely to be implausible from a collectivistic world view because the self is socially defined and socially sustained.[98]

Sixth, there is some disagreement among therapists about the role of forgiveness in counseling. For example, McMinn[99] selected three distinct perspectives on psychologists' attitudes to forgiveness: (1) There are those who oppose any kind of forgiveness in therapy, (2) some see forgiveness as beneficial as it promotes the mental health of the forgiver and they treat forgiveness as just a clinical technique to give relief, and (3) some Christian therapists see forgiveness as a Christian duty; the last two groups may overlap. A valid concern of those in the first group (including philosophers) is that forgiveness may be offered for the wrong reasons such as (a) wanting to please the therapist so that forgiveness is merely intellectual and does not bring emotional release but can leave behind confusion about what has been accomplished, and (b) the topic of forgiveness may lead the client to confusing forgiveness with reconciliation, which could evoke a fear of possible further harm. Those in the second group remind us that counseling is practical so that there is a need to teach specific skills of forgiveness in the process of helping clients repair damaged relationships. The third group reminds us that forgiveness plays a key role for those who desire to live the Christian life (see Section 2.7.5). With regard to the third group, there is a balance in counseling between just raising the issue of forgiveness on the one hand and being too directive or simplistic on the other. Forgiveness is a dynamic process that needs to engage the emotions as well as the intellect, and it may ebb and flow with the passage of time. Some differences in viewpoints by researchers are discussed further below.

---

[95]Worthington (2006 : 15–28).
[96]Sandage and Williamson (2005).
[97]See http://en.wikipedia.org/wiki/Forgiveness and McCullough and Worthington (1999: 1145).
[98]Sandage and Williamson (2005: 45).
[99]McMinn (1996: 208–212).

Finally, we note that there is a similar interest in the notion of "restorative justice" that also involves concepts like forgiveness,[100] thus broadening the subject of forgiveness even further. Clearly I cannot cover all aspects of forgiveness as each client may have a different understanding of the issue. In this section I will focus on just some general concepts, noting that some specific applications will occur in other chapters (e.g., divorce, couple counseling, abuse). For convenience, I shall use the terms "victim " and "offender" (or "perpetrator"), though these terms may not always be quite appropriate.

Why Forgive?

The first question to consider is why we should (or should not) forgive. The answer will of course depend on the therapist's world view, the client's world view, the nature of the wrongdoing to be forgiven, and the possible effect of unforgiveness or forgiveness for the client. It can be argued that a victim is chained by unforgiveness to the offender by the memory and experience of the offense. The victim experiences a lot of negative feelings, and the pain of the offense coupled with the memory of the offender can dominate and control the victim's life. For example, it can lead to the victim avoiding the offender, which may cause difficulties. If avoidance is not always possible, the victim may get angry or upset whenever he or she sees the offender or even just thinks about the offender. What is happening is that the offender is indirectly exercising control over the victim like a puppet on a string and the client may decide to forgive in order to deal with the anger.[101] At a deeper level, we may find that without forgiveness in our lives we can become stuck, not able to move on. Time does not heal all wounds.

Changing the metaphor, we can end up building walls as a form of self-protection in our lives rather than bridges. Months and even years later it may appear on the outside that there has been recovery but, deep within, anger, guilt, and resentment may be bottled up and may present in destructive forms. Lack of forgiveness can lead to bitterness, which like an acid eats out its container.

Forgiveness, then, can be seen as a means of cutting the puppet strings and breaking a victim's connection with the offender. Forgiveness, however, is an individual decision and should not be premature or forced on anyone. The therapist needs to proceed cautiously and be aware of possibly other therapeutic paths before raising the issue of forgiveness. Deciding not to forgive remains a client option and the question may be whether it is a safer bet or not to forgive.[102]

We may discover that a client has one or more of three "resentment bank accounts," namely, one each for others, self, and God.[103] In the "others account" we store all the hurtful things people have done to us. In the large "self account" we have our failures, stupid mistakes, and our hurtful actions against self and others. We may even have a "God resentment account" where we feel that God has let us down and has not protected us or those close to us. This simple metaphor may provide some ideas for counseling. Without the healing power of forgiveness these accounts may remove any peace and calm in one's life and hinder or destroy loving relationships.

[100] For example, see Marshall (2001). I have found his ideas helpful in this chapter.
[101] Many of the case histories in Enright and Fitzgibbons (2000) illustrate this motivation.
[102] For further comments see Smedes (1984: 175).
[103] I am grateful to Pearman (2007) for some ideas from his local church booklet.

Any resentment can generate anger, which may be difficult to deal with or resolve. Murphy and others[104] sound a cautionary philosophical note about hasty and uncritical forgiveness. Referring to comments by Bishop Butler of the 18th century, Murphy points out that, as an initial response, resentment, anger, and the desire to see the wrongdoer punished are not unnatural or unreasonable emotions; resentment has some positive aspects relating to one's self-respect, self-defense, and respect for moral order and justice. Once self-respect has been recovered, forgiveness can then be regarded as "a sign of self-respect and an allegiance to moral order."[105] Further helpful comments on these issues are given by Enright and Fitzgibbons.[106]

We note that forgiveness can be problematical in the case of those who are involved with caring for partners with addictions, especially where codependency is an issue. The "caretaker" can continue to hear promises and may keep on trying to forgive, but grow weary of trying. An addict needs treatment more than forgiveness,[107] though that does not suggest an unforgiving attitude is appropriate. Clearly each situation needs to be dealt with individually.

It is helpful to normalize a client's desire to retaliate as a sign of how damaged the victim feels. Malcolm et al. state that: "Owning one's intense feelings of anger and desire to make the other suffer as one has suffered generates a sense of self as a person of worth who has been treated unfairly and deserves to be treated differently."[108] By accepting one's emotions, a client is more able to tolerate their emotions and work with them rather than against them. Holmgren maintains that "genuine forgiveness and self-forgiveness are *always* morally appropriate and desirable goals of psychotherapy for those clients who are willing and able to achieve them."[109] However, she emphasizes that such a goal can only be achieved after any necessary work has been done to address the wrong.

Dr. Robert Enright,[110] a pioneer in the scientific study of forgiveness, and others proposed a "forgiveness triad," namely forgiving others, receiving forgiveness, and forgiving self. I will consider these topics separately with aspects of forgiveness by God and "forgiving God,"[111] after having described the nature of forgiveness itself.

What is Forgiveness?

We observe that the reaction by a victim to wrongdoing elicits

> emotional responses (e.g., anger or fear), motivational responses (e.g., desires to avoid the transgressor or harm the transgressor in kind), cognitive responses (e.g., hostility toward or loss of respect or esteem for the transgressor), or behavioral responses (e.g., avoidance or aggression) that would promote the deterioration of goodwill toward the offender and social harmony.[112]

Forgiveness can therefore be described as a process involving both the will and the emotions whereby there is a positive change in attitude, motivation, and behavioral intentions toward the offender (decisional or cognitive forgiveness), and a

---

[104]Murphy (2003, 2005) and Lamb and Murphy (2002).
[105]Freedman, Enright, and Knutson (2005: 400).
[106]Enright and Fitzgibbons (2000: chapter 16)
[107]Beattie (1987: 197).
[108]Malcolm, Warwar, and Greenberg (2005: 382).
[109]Holmgren (2002: 116); author's italics.
[110]Enright (1996).
[111]This is discussed further in Section 3.5 on anger toward God.
[112]McCullough and Worthington (1999: 1142–1143).

replacement of negative emotions by positive, other-oriented emotions like empathy, compassion, and sympathy (emotional forgiveness). Forgiveness can be regarded as a gift to the offender and will generally include cancelation of the offender's debt. If, however, the victim repays in kind, then the victim becomes the offender. Unilateral forgiveness requires nothing in return from the offender and does not depend on the offender nor on any proximity to or involvement with the offender.

Forgiveness will generally take place over time in stages with lots of feed-back loops, and may be somewhat up and down, rather than in a straight line.

What Forgiveness is Not

There seems to be a general agreement about what forgiveness is not. The following are some misconceptions about the nature of forgiveness.

1. Forgiveness does not involve forgetting. We can't magically forget wrong doing after offering forgiveness; what happens is that the nature of the memory can change so that the memory is transformed rather than erased.[113] Hopefully the memory of the act of forgiveness helps to lessen and begin to erase the impact of the offense.

2. Forgiveness is not denial or passive acceptance or minimizing the hurt (e.g., "It really was only a small matter after all"). Refusing to confront when there is an offense or keeping peace at any cost is not forgiveness. Nor is it a matter of denying the offense by redefining it; we may have to acknowledge that the impact of an offense can be very different from the nature of the offense.

3. Forgiveness is not condoning inappropriate behavior nor is it an approval of injustice (e.g., "They can't be blamed for their weaknesses"). It does not absolve wrong doing.

4. Forgiveness is not excusing wrong doing (e.g., "They didn't know what they were doing"). Excusing can be somewhat automatic and casual, while forgiveness requires long-term effort.

5. Forgiveness is not self-blame as we don't have to accept responsibility for the wrong doing (e.g., "I caused them to react that way").

6. Forgiveness is not the same as reconciliation. A relationship is not always restored by forgiveness, but it can create a healthier interaction. In some situations it may be right to forgive, but unwise to enter back into a relationship with someone who is unrepentant and is liable to offend again. We can also have reconciliation without forgiveness, for example, call a truce. An alternative to reconciliation could be acceptance.

7. Forgiveness does not rule out taking action to change a situation.

8. Forgiveness does not require verbal communication directly with the person forgiven.

9. Forgiveness is not weakness. It requires strength and courage and is not for cowards.

---

[113] However, it is possible to forget without forgiving by repression.

Walrond-Skinner[114] considers a number of types forgiveness that are *not* what she calls "authentic" forgiveness, namely: (a) instantaneous forgiveness (given before any account of the offense), (b) arrested forgiveness (denied by one or both parties in conflict), (c) conditional forgiveness (forgiveness with a proviso), (d) pseudo forgiveness (premature forgiveness), (e) collusive forgiveness (unconditional capitulation by the victim to avoid opposition or conflict without a behavior change by the offender), (e) repetitious forgiveness (successive incomplete attempts to deal with the problem).

The Process of Forgiveness

Various models have been proposed for how a therapist might guide a client through the forgiveness process. Usually a number of steps are listed and various programs list different numbers of steps, which is confusing. One well-known model of twenty steps, described by Enright and Fitzgibbons,[115] consists of four phases each with several steps, namely: (1) uncovering phase (acknowledging the damaging effect of the offense and its mental rehearsal); (2) decision phase (understanding the nature of forgiveness and choosing to forgive); (3) work phase (reframing how the offender is viewed including empathy and compassion); and (4) deepening phase (recognizing we all have needed forgiveness in the past; knowing we are not alone; finding meaning in suffering; finding healing, new self-meaning, and purpose in the forgiveness process).

To assist the therapist with some ideas, the following list endeavors to incorporate some of the common steps in the literature that a client might carry out if forgiveness is likely to be an option.

1. Identify and acknowledge that a wrong has been done to you. It may help to make a list of what was actually done and not just what you felt; in fact journalling through the whole process can be helpful.[116] (The therapist might need to help the client recover his or her self-respect by recognizing that she is a valuable person deserving to be treated well, and that the offensive behavior was not his or her fault.[117] It could be helpful to explore what assumptions the client has about the world that have been violated as these may relate to the degree of damage done.[118] There is also the problematic situation where the victim may be permanently damaged while the offender is off scot free. On the other hand, the therapist might need to explore any over-reacting to the hurt.)

2. Access and face your own pain, and focus on what hurts now, not on the past. The therapist can help the client to work through those painful feelings, especially anger and resentment, and discuss the pros and cons of hanging on to the resentment. When the client is upset, anger management (Section 3.4.1) or a relaxation technique (Section 2.2.5) may be helpful. A useful question might be, "What specifically was there about the perceived hurt that caused the most pain?"[119] Forgiveness should not be the only goal as

[114]Walrond-Skinner (1998: 10).
[115]Enright and Fitzgibbons (2000: 68).
[116]Enright and Fitzgibbons (2000: 17).
[117]Holmgren (2002: 118–119).
[118]Flanigan (1998: 102).
[119]Hebl and Enright (1993: 661).

other aspects like grief or shame, for example, may need to be considered. Continual ruminating about the hurt can be unproductive.

3. Recognize that if there is to be any change, you must make it first. If you wait until the offender apologizes, you may remain stuck in unforgiveness. It is better to make a decision to claim back your personal power by deciding to forgive the offender and let go of your anger and resentment. The therapist can first raise the idea of forgiveness as an option and explain what forgiveness is and what it is not. Once cognitive forgiveness is offered it may need to be repeated on a regular basis until some of the following steps begin to lead to emotional forgiveness.

4. Acknowledge any part you may have played, for example, were you honest about your hurt or did you excuse, minimize, or deny the hurt and seek peace at any cost? Did you stay when you should have left? In any conflict it is rare that one is totally blameless, though care is needed, in cases of sexual abuse, for example, where the victim may have difficulty in relinquishing blame. In such situations, self-forgiveness is important.

5. Be empathetic toward the offender. He or she may have acted out of ignorance, fear or pain, or may have a problem from the past. This involves cognitive restructuring and reframing whereby the client endeavors to see the other person in a different light, perhaps seeing him or her as being an imperfect person like everyone else, yet of value. Being empathetic towards the offender represents a change of heart by the victim and it is one way of separating the wrong doing from the wrongdoer.

6. What did you gain from the relationship? Were there any positives? Through reframing, the therapist again encourages a change in the client's perspective. However, nothing might have been gained from the relationship.

7. Recognize that we all need forgiveness, including the victim, for what we have done to others. The therapist can ask the client whether he or she ever wronged someone else, and if so was forgiveness extended, and how did it feel.

8. Inform your offender of both your hurts and your painful feelings and offer forgiveness. One method of doing this is by writing a letter to the offender (which you don't need to mail and can be destroyed later) and express forgiveness for the hurts. Writing a blank cheque listing the offenses and then writing "Canceled" over the top may be helpful. Another method is to use the empty chair technique whereby you address the offender as though he or she was sitting in a chair opposite. By imagining what the offender might feel if he or she was capable of understanding the effect of the hurt on you, a helpful step is to then sit in that chair and express what you think the offender would say in reply. Then go back to your own chair and offer forgiveness for the hurt.

Clearly not all the above steps will be appropriate as it will depend on the situation. The client may need to go through aspects of the above process several times as anger and resentment can reoccur. Also the client may need to set boundaries to avoid being hurt again. Whether to confront the offender will depend on the relationship with the offender. An acronym which captures much of the above is FORGIVE which refers to: Face the wrong, Out with feelings, Recognize own contribution, Give benefit of the doubt, Identify any positives, Vow to forgive, and Extend forgiveness. Another simple acronym due to Worthington is REACH, namely Recall the hurt, Empathize with the one who hurt you, offer Altruistic gift of forgiveness, make a Commitment to forgive, and Hold on to the forgiveness.[120]

Self-forgiveness

When we are an offender, we can experience feelings of guilt and shame. Such feelings "serve as a moral barometer, alerting us when we have violated important personal, societal, and moral standards. These feelings and the *anticipation* of these feelings often inhibit us from yielding to temptation."[121] However, unresolved feelings of guilt, shame, and remorse can psychologically cripple a person. One way forward is to encourage self-forgiveness and reparation where possible. However, before doing so, we need to acknowledge the wrong done and our responsibility for it and fully experience the feelings of guilt and regret. Hall and Fincham comment on this:

> Attempts to forgive oneself without cognitively and emotionally processing the transgression and its consequences are likely to lead to denial, suppression, or pseudo-forgiveness .... True self-forgiveness is often a long and arduous process that requires much self-examination and may be very uncomfortable.[122]

Because of the difference between guilt and shame (see Chapter 4) with guilt relating to a specific behavior and shame affecting the whole person, shame can have a greater impact on the process of self-forgiveness as "bad behavior is easier to change than a bad self."[123] A shamed person may respond defensively, deny responsibility, and externalize blame, holding others responsible for failure. Tangney et al. note that "research has shown that such painful and debilitating feelings of shame do not motivate constructive changes in behavior."[124]

Enright defined self-forgiveness as "a willingness to abandon self-resentment in the face of one's own acknowledged objective wrong, while fostering compassion, generosity, and love toward oneself."[125] In comparing forgiveness of self and forgiveness of others, both are processes that take time and both are freely given. True forgiveness of others is generally regarded as unconditional and is not the same as reconciliation with the offender. However, self-forgiveness requires reconciliation with self and can be conditional on, for example, reparation or changing one's behavior in the future.[126] If I forgive self, then I may be able to identify better with my offender and be more able to forgive him or her. Some argue that self-forgiveness is a necessary introduction to forgiving others. What about a self-imposed injury? Here the focus of self-forgiveness is not on the hurt but rather on the actions leading to the hurt, for example, "I can't believe I did X".[127]

---

[120] For further details http://www.mindpub.com/art471.htm by Vijai Sharma (accessed October 2010).
[121] Tangney, Boone, and Dearing (2005: 143)—authors' italics.
[122] Hall and Fincham (2005: 627).
[123] Tangney et al. (2005: 147).
[124] Tangney et al. (2005: 147).
[125] Enright (1996: 115).
[126] Hall and Fincham (2005: 623–624).
[127] Hall and Fincham (2005: 625).

Seeking and Receiving Forgiveness

Most of the theoretical and empirical work on forgiveness has focused on granting rather than seeking forgiveness.[128] As noted above, a victim and an offender are both chained together so that an offender needs to be released also; the offender may be bound by guilt and shame[129] and go out of his or her way to avoid the victim, thus being "controlled" by the victim. However, an offender may have difficulty apologizing and asking for forgiveness as deep down he or she may believe that the victim deserved what happened or may excuse or minimize the offense. There is a need for an offender to recognize that the impact of an offense on a victim may be much greater than the nature of the offense, and there are times in our lives when we may also be victims!

Another situation can arise when a client remains stuck, even after asking for forgiveness. So often there is nothing we can do to minimize the pain we may cause others (e.g., the extreme case of a drunken driver killing a child). Even after apologizing, seeking forgiveness, and endeavoring to make some sort of restitution, we may still feel guilty and become a slave to the victim by always trying to make things right and trying to gain approval. However, how a victim responds to this is not the offender's responsibility. The victim has his or her own resentment to deal with. Clearly self-forgiveness is needed here and I now discuss this.

Some steps in the process of seeking self-forgiveness are as follows:[130]

1. *Recognize.* Recognize your wrongdoing and that the victim has a right to retaliate and punish.

2. *Remorse.* Experience "other-centered" remorse or regret for your wrong doing. This is not just feeling sorry for yourself and perhaps regret for being caught out, but is feeling sorry for the victim. (Another word that some might use here is "repentance" as it has the connotation of a decision rather than just an emotion.)[131]

3. *Reform.* You determine to not just avoid doing the same wrong again but also to be a better person. Some measure of self-improvement needs to be recognized.

4. *Reframe.* You may have to deal with feelings of guilt and shame and may feel unworthy of forgiveness. Recognizing that we all make mistakes from time to time (including the victim) and that you are trying to change your life can help you regain your self-respect. The process of self-forgiveness begins here.

5. *Request.* Ask the victim for forgiveness. This will bring some measure of self-forgiveness.

6. *Restitution.* This may need to accompany the request, if appropriate.

7. *Receive.* Accept forgiveness from the victim.

---

[128] Bassett et al. (2006).
[129] This topic is discussed in Chapter 4.
[130] I have drawn ideas from North (1998: 30).
[131] The New Testament Greek word *metanoein* for "to repent" means "to change one's mind," as in the next step.

8. *Reconciliation.* Reconciliation might now be achieved or at least be possible in the future.

Not all the above steps can be achieved or be appropriate, depending on the situation.

2.5.6   Birth Order

There has recently been a surge of interest in birth order[132] as there appeared to be some evidence of a connection between behavior and intelligence of children and their order of birth in a family. Ernst and Angst, who summarized over a 1000 publications from 1946 to 1980 pointed out statistical flaws in previous work and concluded that "Birth order influences on personality and IQ have been widely overrated."[133] In fact their conclusion was effectively that such influences were nonexistent. Their statistical analysis has since been redone using the more appropriate technique of meta-analysis by Sulloway[134] who found that there are some sibling order differences in personality using the 5-factor model as a rough guide.[135] However, these conclusions of trait differences have themselves been challenged by new data suggesting either no association or an inconclusive one.[136] With regard to intelligence, Rodgers et al. [137] using a longitudinal study instead of a cross-sectional one concluded that birth order and intelligence are not related to one another in the U.S. They also concluded: "It appears that although low-IQ parents have been making large families, large families do not make low-IQ children in modern U.S. society."

Clearly there are a number of factors that will confuse the issue, for example, the number, sex, and spacing of the siblings, to begin with, and these are confounded with inherited factors. Parental background and how the parents interact with their children will certainly be major factors. As divorce is very prevalent, parental splits will have different effects on different siblings. Birth order can impinge on behavior and can affect the nurture part of personality, but whether it has an enduring effect on personality is another matter. Harris[138] comments that when people are with their parents and siblings, firstborns behave differently than later-borns, even during adulthood. However, what happens outside the family home can be quite different.

What about children with no siblings; are they generally more intelligent than other children? Again the evidence seems to be inconclusive because of the considerable variability in the data.[139] It is possible that firstborn children may be more intelligent than their siblings but if there is a difference it is likely to be small. Any difference may simply be because of the single loving focus by both parents on the first-born. Other factors may account for the apparent successes of some notable first born children. Also, specific personality factors may be more important than IQ (Intelligence Quotient) if birth order has any effect at all. It has also been sug-

---

[132]See, for example, Kluger (2007).
[133]Ernst and Angst (1983: 242).
[134]Sulloway (1995, 1996).
[135]See Section 1.3.2.
[136]Jefferson, Herbst, and McCrae et al. (1998) and Harris (2006).
[137]Rodgers, Cleveland, van den Oord, and Rowe (2000).
[138]See Harris (1998).
[139]In the past they used the term "only child syndrome," which now seems to be a misnomer.

gested that later born children are more creative. Clearly more careful research is needed as the problem is a statistical one, namely trying to eliminate some of the variability due to other confounding factors. It should be emphasized that even if such connections exist, they are simply trends and probably only apply to "typical" as opposed to "dysfunctional families." The value of birth order knowledge to counseling is therefore uncertain.

There are some general observations that have been made about birth order behavior rather than personality traits initially. For example, being the only child for a while, first born children may be used to being the center of attention and therefore may feel put out, unloved, or jealous when a second child arrives on the scene. Second-born children have never had the parents' undivided attention and always have another older sibling ahead of them that they want to catch up with or overtake. They may be jealous of the attention given to the first child. If a third child is born, they may feel "squeezed," especially if there are only three children altogether. In this case they may feel that they have neither the rights of the oldest nor the privileges of the youngest. On the other hand they may be more adaptable, having learnt to deal with the oldest and the youngest.

The middle children of a family with more than three children may tend to be different from the middle child of three. They may be less competitive as the parents have less time for each child so these children learn to cooperate to get what they want. Youngest children may behave like only children expecting others to do everything for them, being the "baby" of the family. They may be very good at getting their own way.

The only child has to learn to be a child on its own so that it learns to be more independent and entertain itself. Although they don't have to cope with sibling rivalry, only children don't have the immediate availability of others near their own age with whom to interact socially, so they have to work to win friends through other means. Parental attention does not have to be shared with other siblings so they have more adult conversation and interaction. Clearly there are pluses and minuses to being an only child. In counseling such people it may be helpful to ask an open ended question such as what it was like for them growing up.

2.6   SPIRITUAL

2.6.1   Role of Spirituality

Spirituality can be a contentious issue for therapists. Some would argue that spiritual issues should be avoided as they raise the question of which spiritual framework should be used. Others, however, might refer to such things as the 12-step programs for addictions where there is an emphasis on a "higher power." There is also a growing body of scientific evidence that spirituality can have a positive impact on one's health, and Claudia Wallis[140] in her thought-provoking TIME article summarizes some of this evidence. She notes the growing interest in the connection between health and spirituality both in medical training and among the general public.

[140]Wallis (1996).

Dr Herbert Benson, in advocating his relaxation response technique for coping with stress,[141] believes that the effects of his technique are enhanced when combined with the practitioner's philosophical or religious belief system.[142] As some clients have a religious background that is important to them, the therapist may need to address this aspect of their lives at some stage especially if it has a component which impinges on their psychological welfare (e.g., spiritual abuse). It has been suggested that in most situations, spiritual issues are best left to later in the counseling process until empathy has been built up between the client and the counselor so that the client can be comfortable in expressing their spiritual beliefs.[143] Therapists need sensitivity and understanding in these situations.

2.6.2   Defining Spirituality

There are a number of definitions of spirituality. They don't always refer to God in the standard sense as clients often have their own view on it. For example, at a workshop I attended in 2008, Dr David Benner gave the following working definition, "Spirituality is a way of living in relation to something other (or larger) than ourselves that responds to our deepest longings for meaning, purpose and connection."[144] Spirituality is usually distinguished from religion as the former goes much deeper, so that spirituality can be religious or non-religious depending on whether "other" is replaced by some "higher power." It is a lifestyle rather than a set of beliefs; it is being rather than doing. However, it could be argued that spirituality may not proceed very far without religion as there needs to be a communal and historical context for the spirituality.

Ciarrocchi[145] endeavored to provide a model, in the context of gambling addictions, that therapists can comfortably use to help them to locate a client's religious concerns and be able to take a neutral stance. He lists six approaches to religion: through sacred rites, right action, devotion, mysticism, contact with the other world, and reasoned enquiry. For him, spirituality

> represents an individual's attempt to relate his or her ultimate reality in the
> six ways outlined above. A person's spirituality is religious if the ultimate
> reality constitutes an 'other world'.

The question for the therapist is whether the client's spirituality and/or religion is a help or hindrance in his or her development. For example, is one's spirituality an affair of the heart rather than the head and does it have a focus on personal integrity? Sometimes clients are spiritually asleep and need to be awakened, or on the other hand through childhood experiences religion may have been toxic to them.

---

[141] See Section 2.2.5.

[142] See www.vhl.org/newsletter/vhl1997/97dafait.htm by Benson (accessed October 2010).

[143] Some biblical counselors may regard this as the wrong way round and maintain that the spiritual should be foremost in counseling. I shall not enter into this debate.

[144] Reproduced with kind permission of Dr Benner.

[145] Ciarrocchi (2002: chapter 15).

2.7 BIBLICAL VIEWPOINT

2.7.1 Who Am I?

The Bible has a lot to say about wholeness so that my comments will be somewhat brief and selective. What we are ultimately as human beings is a mystery. However, the Bible presents three views of our identity: material and immaterial (e.g., soul or spirit);[146] body, soul, and spirit;[147] and a more holistic Hebraic way of thinking of a person as an integrated unity, where both soul and spirit refer to the person. They all reflect on different aspects of our existence with the integrative model being reinforced by modern science. For example, Wallis (1996) summarizes a number of body-mind links such as the limbic system being linked both to spiritual experiences and to relaxation. She lists studies showing the health benefits of spirituality and quotes from Benson (1996) who believes from his research that "humans are also wired for God", and that "our genetic blueprint has made believing in an infinite Absolute part of our nature."[148] Benson believes that prayer uses the same biochemical pathways as the relaxation response so that prayer is beneficial to us in reducing stress, blood pressure, pulse rate, and respiration, for example.[149]

Another biblical facet of who we are is that humans are described as being made in the image of God (Imago Dei).[150] Although various possible meanings of this concept have been discussed down through history, it does suggest that humans somehow have the stamp of the divine upon them, thus establishing their worth and their spiritual connection. Having talked generally, I now want to focus for a Biblical viewpoint on the five topics discussed in this chapter, namely the physical, intellectual, emotional, social, and spiritual aspects of our lives.

2.7.2 Physical Wholeness

Concerning physical wholeness, the Bible reminds followers of Christ that their bodies are indwelt by the Holy Spirit, and they should glorify God in their bodies.[151] They should also offer their bodies as living sacrifices.[152] Our bodies are therefore regarded as important and need to be looked after. Jesus was concerned about healing the body and healed all kinds of people. He also recognized the close link between body and spirit.[153] Under "Rest and recreation" I mentioned earlier the importance of having a day off. If Christians have to work on Sunday and many people do, then the principle of a day's rest from their usual labors, even if a different day, is a good one. We see one principle at work when the early church

---

[146]For example Genesis 2:7 and Ecclesiastes 12:7. These two references use the Hebrew words *nephesh* and *ruasch*, respectively.

[147]For example, Hebrews 4:12 and 1 Thessalonians 5:23. These texts use the Greek words *pseuche* (soul) and *pneuma* (spirit), respectively.

[148]See   http://www.time.com/time/magazine/article/0,9171,984737-4,00.html#ixzz0ruFkXS1h for the article (accessed October 2010).

[149]It seems that the same pathways are responsible for the "placebo effect" where faith in an ingested inert substance can improve health.

[150]Genesis 1:26–27.

[151]1 Corinthians 6:19–20.

[152]2 Corinthians 12:1.

[153]For example, Luke 5:17–26 where he healed psychologically before healing physically.

shifted their Sabbath from the seventh to the first day of the week. The actual day was not so important as having a day so Christians need to have a balanced view of the sabbath and not be legalistic about it. Jesus debated this question with the Pharisees and closed with the words that the Sabbath was made for us, not we were made for the Sabbath.[154] However I acknowledge that some may disagree with my comments on this issue.[155]

I want to make a few comments about sexuality, as Christianity has been blamed in recent times for putting a dampener on sex. God created sex and saw that it was good.[156] It was meant to be enjoyed.[157] Understanding a spouse's sexual needs is important so as to help maintain self-control.[158] Where does masturbation fit into the picture? Some would argue that if a lustful fantasy with another woman is involved in the act, then the act could be seen as adultery, which is condemned in the Bible.[159] Masturbation of itself is mentioned nowhere in the Bible.[160]

2.7.3   Mental Wholeness

The key to mental wholeness for the Christian is being renewed in one's mind[161] and being positively balanced in one's thinking.[162] The Bible says that nothing is too hard for God or impossible with God.[163] For the Christian there is power through the presence of God who supplies his or her needs.[164] An excellent book on positive thinking that has sound biblical and psychological principles is Peale (1994).

One aspect of positive thinking is humor. Good humor and mental health seem to go well together as laughing releases endorphins that promote a feeling of well-being.[165] As Sturt and Sturt[166] say, "He who laughs, lasts." We should not forget that Jesus used humor, irony, and word plays, such as trying to take a speck out of someone's eye when you have a log in your own eye, straining out a gnat but swallowing a camel, and letting the dead bury the dead.[167] There are many other places in the Bible where there is humor.[168] As people's minds can be a battlefield, they need to identify harmful negative thoughts, capture them, and change them to conform to the will of Christ.[169] Christians also need to learn that Godliness with contentment is great gain.[170]

---

[154] Mark 2:37
[155] For example, seventh day adventists.
[156] Genesis 1:27,31.
[157] Proverbs 5:18–19 and Song of Songs (sometimes referred to as the Song of Solomon).
[158] 1 Corinthians 7:3–6.
[159] Matthew 5:27–30.
[160] Sturt and Sturt (1986: 98).
[161] 2 Corinthians 12: 2).
[162] Philippians 4:11–12.
[163] Jeremiah 32:17, 27; Matthew 19:26; and Luke 1:37.
[164] Romans 8: 31, 37–39; 2 Timothy 1:7; 1 John 4:4; and Philippians 4:13, 19.
[165] Proverbs 17:22.
[166] Sturt and Sturt (1998: 120).
[167] Matthew 7:3, 23,24, and 8:22.
[168] See, for example, http://theologytoday.ptsem.edu/jan1992/v48-4-article1.htm by Doris Donnelly and http://www.paulthigpen.com/humor/causetolaugh.html by Paul Thigpen (both accessed October 2010).
[169] 2 Corinthians 10:45.
[170] 1 Timothy 6:6. and Philippians 4:11–12.

2.7.4   Emotional Wholeness

When it comes to emotions, we note that in the Bible God is described as having feelings and is a God of love and compassion to whom we can pour out our feelings.[171]   Jesus, in his humanity, is described as coming to show people what God is like and experiencing all human emotions, including anger, joy, compassion, tiredness, loneliness, discouragement, and depression.[172]   Through the Holy Spirit Christians can exhibit a wide range of positive emotions as "fruits of the Spirit."[173] When it comes to expressing feelings, Christians need to learn to express the truth in love.[174]

2.7.5   Social Wholeness

Socially, Christians are to be salt and light in their social dealings with others,[175] showing love,[176] and having some responsibility for the less fortunate.[177]   They are also exhorted to be in fellowship with other Christians, welcoming one another,[178] looking out for other's interests,[179] and helping others to bear their burdens.[180]   In counseling a client, Christian or non-Christian, it can be helpful to shift the focus of a client away from self and encourage him or her to reach out to help others.   For example, a frustrated client with cerebral palsy can be encouraged to help others with a disability.   For some detailed studies on aspects of Christian community see Warren (2004).

The ideas of self-esteem and self-love have caused some theological controversy as there has been some unrealistic negative emphasis on teaching that "we are sinners so that we are totally depraved and therefore worthless."   More appropriate teaching is that the Christian is not worthy of God's love, but is not worthless as shown by Christ's substitutionary death, by God's love for us, and by God's grace freely given.[181]   As for self-love, Christians are told to love their neighbors as themselves,[182] and having established their own self-worth in Christ, they are exhorted to deny themselves and follow His example.[183]   The story of Gideon demonstrates that a person's view of self is not necessarily matched by God's view of that person.[184]

Forgiveness

Forgiveness is a key biblical issue and could be the subject of a whole book. However, I will confine myself to what I regard as some key issues.   First, people need to be aware of their offenses,[185] confess their sins to God, and ask for God's

[171]Exodus 34:6; Psalms 40; and 1 John 4:7–12.
[172]John 1:18; Colossians 1:15; Mark 3:5; John 4:6, 12:27; and Matthew 26:38.
[173]Galatians 5:22.
[174]Ephesians 4:15.
[175]Matthew 5:13–16.
[176]1 John 4:20–21 and Matthew 5:43–44.
[177]Matthew 25:45–40.
[178]Romans 15:7.
[179]Philippians 2:1–4.
[180]Galatians 6:2.
[181]Romans 5:6–12 and Ephesians 2:8–9. For a helpful discussion of this issue see Sturt and Sturt (1994: chapter 5).
[182]Matthew 22:39; Romans 13:9; Galatians 5:14; and James 2:8.
[183]Matthew 16:24–25.
[184]Judges 6:12,15.
[185]Psalms 139:23–24.

forgiveness.[186] Second, they need to forgive others.[187] It is both a condition for receiving God's forgiveness[188] and a consequence.[189] It is the only action asked for in the Lord's prayer.[190] The Old Testament argues that one should not seek revenge or bear a grudge, as judgment belongs to God;[191] this is reiterated in Paul's teaching.[192] Because people are continually faced with their own fallibility and God's undeserving grace and mercy towards them, they can learn to offer the same grace and mercy to others. It allows the Holy Spirit to work in others' lives.

Forgiveness is rooted in humility, kindness, and tenderheartedness,[193] and it is a process rather than just an event. It is also one way in which people can love not just their neighbors but also their enemies,[194] thus fulfilling Jesus' commands.[195] The supreme example is Jesus who asked God to forgive those who put him on the cross.[196] This does not mean that people simply ignore injustice and are happy with what has been done to them; sometimes consequences have to be put in place and boundaries established.[197] Also, forgiveness by God does not remove the consequences of one's sin.[198] Old Testament statements like "An eye for an eye" and New Testament verses such as "Turn the other cheek" should not be taken at face value but need careful exegesis.[199]

We have seen then that although divine forgiveness is linked to human repentance, interpersonal forgiveness is not, and Worthington et al. suggested two reasons for the latter.[200] First, only God knows an offender's true motives so we don't need to try and discern those motives before forgiving. Second, if we had to wait for an offender to repent before we forgave the offender, then our forgiveness would be held in hostage by the offender. Logically this could mean that if the offender failed to repent, the victim would not receive the benefits of forgiving in return. It can be argued then that forgiveness is not commended to the Christian just for the benefits to the forgiver but is also aimed at being a blessing to the "enemy." As Worthington et al. note:

> In psychological research, interventions that have promoted selfishly motivated forgiveness seem to be more effective in the short-term, but interventions promoting altruistic forgiveness are more effective in the long-term.[201]

Pingleton proposed a forgiveness model consisting of three parts:

> (a) Forgiveness can only be received from God if given to others, (b) forgiveness can only be given to others if received from self, and (c) forgiveness can

[186]See, for example, Psalms 32:1–5; Psalms 51; Proverbs 28:13; Joel 2:12–17; and I John 1: 5–10.
[187]And not just once (Matthew 18:21–22 and Luke 17:3-4).
[188]Matthew 6:14–15; Mark 11:25; Luke 6:37; and the parable of Matthew 18: 23–35.
[189]Ephesians 4:31–32 and Colossians 3:13.
[190]Matthew 6:9–13 and Luke 11:2–4.
[191]Leviticus 19:18; Proverbs 20:22, 24:29, 25:21–22; and Deuteronomy 32:35.
[192]Romans 12:14–21.
[193]Ephesians 4:32.
[194]Worthington, Sharp, Lerner, and Sharp (2006).
[195]Matthew 5:44 and 22:39; see also Romans 12:14.
[196]Luke 23: 34. See also the words of Stephen, Acts 7:60.
[197]See, for example, Luke 17:3 and John 2:13–16, where Jesus cleansed the temple.
[198]David was forgiven his adultery with Bathsheba and the death of her husband, but his household and descendants suffered the consequences (2 Samuel 12:9–10, 13).
[199]See for example Affinito (2002: 98–100) for a helpful discussion.
[200]Worthington et al. (2006: 33).
[201]Worthington et al. (2006: 33).

only be given to self if received from God. Forgiveness is a cyclical process involving self, others and God.[202]

Thus forgiveness of self and others is linked to our ability to receive forgiveness from God. We note that:

> Although much is offered Biblically in terms of an ethic concerning forgiveness, little is offered in the Bible in terms of how to actually complete the forgiveness process. Thus, the way in which people actually complete the process of forgiveness has been a matter of speculation from theorists from both the fields of psychology and theology.[203]

A helpful 13-step program for forgiveness is given by Dr Stanley.[204]

2.7.6 Spiritual Wholeness

Spiritual wholeness stems from having a right relationship with God, which can be summarized in the two greatest commandments of loving God with all our being and loving our neighbors as ourselves.[205] Some keys to spiritual wholeness are prayer, meditation, contemplation of biblical passages, praise, keeping a journal, and fellowship with other Christians.

---

[202] Pingleton (1989).

[203] Walker and Gorsuch (2004). They compared sixteen models for how the process of forgiveness might be carried out.

[204] See http://www.cbn.com/spirituallife/Prayerandcounseling/Stanley_Forgiveness.aspx, accessed October 2010.

[205] Deuteronomy 6:5; Leviticus 18:18; and Matthew 22:26–40.

CHAPTER 3

ANGER

3.1 THE NATURE OF ANGER

3.1.1 Aspects of Anger

The word "anger" is usually used to cover a very broad spectrum of emotions ranging from mild irritation and annoyance through to intense fury and rage. In this chapter we will be mainly concerned with the milder aspects of anger, though some of the ideas discussed may apply to more extreme forms of anger. There is some debate about the difference between anger and aggression, but for the purposes of therapy we shall not differentiate between them but treat them as similar, closely-linked emotions.[1] Anger does not usually lead to aggression. One can be aggressive without being angry and one can be angry without being aggressive. It appears that humans are hardwired for anger because of its survival functions. In this chapter we shall also consider both personal anger and dealing with anger from others.

Some aspects of anger occur elsewhere in this book, for example as a feature of some personality disorders and also with respect to violence (see Section 16.2). Although not mentioned specifically as a DSM disorder, anger (and irritability) symptoms appear in a wide range of disorders in the DSM-IV-TR. [2] DiGiuseppe and Tafrate.(2007: 184) note that anger is not addressed consistently or systematically

---

[1]See Kassinove and Sukhodolsky (1995: 12–14).
[2]These different aspects of anger are referenced in the index.

in DSM and does not appear in its index. They proposed a new anger disorder called Anger Regulation-Expression Disorder (ARED), which can be predominately of a subjective type or an expressive type or a combination of both.[3] They note that there is a lack of clinical research on anger. Anger can also occur with depression, anxiety, grief, and Post Traumatic Stress Disorder (PTSD), which are mentioned in the chapters involving those topics.

There are many views and theories about anger. For example, some argue that aggression and anger are part of being human (the nature aspect), while others blame society for making us angry (the nurture aspect). Anger is a signal that all is not right within us in much the same way that physical pain is a signal of some physical problem; we need to heed the anger and use it to make positive changes. Some theories of anger are described in DiGiuseppe and Tafrate (2007: chapter 4).

All sorts of things can trigger anger. The most common is an external event (e.g., being cut off in traffic, or some hurtful, unjustified comment), then there are internal anger-laden memories triggered by an external cue (e.g., a rejecting comment by a spouse may trigger memories of rejection by parents), and finally anger may be the result of ruminating about a past or future events (e.g., thoughts of a partner's infidelity or an unfair performance review at work). There are a number of precursors to anger such as frustration, helplessness, indignation, and injustice. A frequent source of anger is the sense of obligation (e.g., "The world should be good to me on my terms"). Such persons can feel unloved and unworthy, and their unrealistic expectations can lead to diminished self-esteem and frustration. They may lash out at those who do not give them what they feel is rightly owed. In the next chapter, the role of anger in guilt and shame is discussed more fully. Guilt is associated with lower levels of anger and tends to impose a restraint on aggression, whereas shame-prone people may have higher levels of anger arousal.[4] Those with physical handicaps (e.g., cerebral palsy) can have anger problems for various reasons. They are sometimes treated as though they are mentally handicapped, or they may become very frustrated with their bodies. They can be smart mentally, but end up having to do menial or repetitive jobs because of their disability.

In many cultures, anger is regarded as being socially and personally unacceptable. Some people feel guilty when they get angry, perhaps because they have been taught by family, teachers, or a religious community that it is wrong to get angry; or that it should be a brief phase passed through as quickly as possible on route to forgiveness, as anger is a waste of time and energy. Anger is also often viewed differently for women than men. Lerner[5] notes that women "have long been discouraged from awareness and forthright expression of anger." She comments that women who openly express anger at men are especially suspect and, when a woman shows her anger, she is likely to be dismissed as irrational or worse. However, Tavris[6] gives evidence that men and women have equal difficulty in expressing anger, although women are more likely to express it privately than publicly.[7]

[3]DiGiuseppe and Tafrate.(2007: Table 14.3, p. 271).
[4]Baumeister and Bushman (2007: 67–69).
[5]Lerner (2004: 1).
[6]Tavris (1989: chapter 7).
[7]See also Fischer and Evers (2010).

A client needs to be aware that holding on to strong anger can be damaging. This damage can include "failure to overcome emotional pain, misdirection of anger toward people who do not deserve it, the excessive expression of anger in relationships, the development of physical illnesses, or continued control by the offender."[8] We need to avoid the popular response to feelings of hurt and insult, namely revenge and violence. So often on TV the response to anger is to break things, which is a way of showing power over an object.

There are several methods for assessing anger and some of these can be found on the internet under "anger questionnaire."[9] However, there seems to be a lack of diagnostic tools for assessing the *level* of anger as there is with Axis I disorders, for example, whether the anger is chronic, moderate, or pervasive.[10] As mentioned above, anger is common with clients who have a personality disorder, especially passive-aggressive (negativistic) personality disorder (see Section 22.5.2), and it is a symptom of several other personality disorders (e.g., in cluster B, see Chapter 21).[11]

In addition to individual counseling for anger, group anger-management workshops can be helpful. They encourage self-disclosure and openness, and provide opportunity for group interactions and role plays. Some clients benefit from having individual counseling as well as belonging to such a group.

3.1.2   Positives and Negatives of Anger

Feeling angry is a normal emotion and, as such, is neutral—neither good or nor bad. Anger is a universal emotion and an angry face is generally recognizable worldwide, although culture and context may make a difference.[12] Frustration is often a stepping stone to anger before we boil over, and we all get frustrated at some time. It is what we do with these angry feelings and how we act on them that determine whether our anger is going to be constructive or destructive. Someone has said that anger should be occasional, brief, controlled, and channeled into problem solving behavior.

According to Puff (2002), anger is there for a reason and we should learn to make it our friend. In many years of dealing with both children and adults, Puff believes that there are only two emotions we can use to respond to difficult and painful situations that will bring about healing for us—anger and sadness. He maintains that if we fail to express our anger or sadness about what has happened to us, then these emotions will persist and grow and may eventually lead to depression, stress-related illness, compulsive behavior, or some form of addiction.

On the negative side, anger can block logical problem-solving thinking, jeopardize careers, and change relationships. On the positive side, anger can rouse us out of lethargy and motivate us to get going or stand up against wrong-doing and injustice. It can lead us to change a pattern of interaction with a significant other like a spouse, relative, or fellow worker. Anger can signal that a boundary has been crossed and

[8]Enright and Fitzgibbons (2000: 119).
[9]For example, http://www.renewalcs.org/Handouts/Anger%20Questionnaire.pdf; accessed October 2010, and http://www.psychology.iastate.edu/faculty/caa/Scales/BussPerry.pdf, which has a measure for anger (accessed November 2012).
[10]Eckhardt and Deffenbacher (1995: 35).
[11]Enright and Fitzgibbons (2000: 241) and DiGiuseppe and Tafrate.(2007: chapter 11).
[12]Russell (1994). See Section 1.4.2.

an appropriate expression of anger can lead to a greater honesty in a relationship. On the negative side, anger can lead outwardly to violence, as is mostly evidenced by men, or it can turn inwardly to depression, numbness, withdrawal, or isolation, resulting in the destruction of relationships. Women sometimes use different styles of anger management that also don't work in the long run, such as silent submission, ineffective fighting and blaming, and emotional distancing.[13]

You have no doubt heard the phrase, "You make me angry." Nobody makes us angry; anger is our response to the pain or frustration, or other real or perceived hurt. We need to take responsibility for our anger as it is our chosen problem. When we respond angrily to someone, then we are allowing them to control us and take away our power. In the context of Post Traumatic Stress Disorder, Enright and Fitzgibbons state that, "The failure to resolve the anger with the offender regularly places the perpetrator in a position of power over the victim."[14]

3.2   EXPRESSING ANGER

3.2.1   Methods of Expression

Anger can be expressed in the following ways:[15]

1. *Vent it.* This explosive expression of anger is usually destructive of relationships and does not solve problems. This method of releasing anger is known as *catharsis.* Unfortunately venting anger does not necessarily dispel it, but tends to feed it. Baumeister and Bushman state that "the facts and findings do not support the catharsis theory."[16] Other ways of letting anger out will be discussed below.

2. *Repress it.* Pushing anger down into the subconscious generally leads to its reappearance later on in various forms such as violence, depression, withdrawal, cynicism, or bitterness.

3. *Suppress it.* We contain anger until it can be processed at an appropriate time. This can unfortunately lead to a delayed volcano eruption process.

4. *Process it.* This means using anger constructively without dumping it on others or ourselves. Strategies for doing this are discussed later. One aim of the therapist is to elicit any buried anger or locate where it is being dumped.

Strategies for handling anger can be divided into self or intra-personal strategies that focus on how a person deals with themselves when their anger threatens to break out, and interpersonal strategies that focus more on the relationships generating the angry feelings. There is plenty of advice in the literature on how to deal with anger and I shall endeavor to describe a number of methods below. Before looking at controlling one's anger in current situations, I will consider dealing with anger from past hurts.

[13]Lerner (2004: 10).
[14]Enright and Fitzgibbons (2000: 152).
[15]Sturt and Sturt (1998: 153–156).
[16]Baumeister and Bushman (2007: 63); see also Tavris (1989: chapter 5).

3.2.2   Anger From Past Hurts

Catharsis

Puff (2002)) introduced the concept of Anger Work as a method of letting go of emotionally painful events through focusing on them and expressing anger about the pain. He found that when people focus on the trauma over and over, the pain will gradually go away, never to affect the person again. We all know that exercise helps us to release tension and dissipate adrenaline when we are angry; also endorphins produced by vigorous exercise have a calming affect. However, as noted by Puff, exercise alone is not enough to heal emotional wounds, but it can be combined with a healthy expression of anger. For example, he suggests that walking or running can be combined with the thought that you are stepping on the person who has hurt you, or stepping on the pain that the person or incident has caused you. It's important to feel the anger, which can provide the energy! We can dream up all sorts of strategies for releasing anger as long as they do not hurt us, others, or property.

Puff emphasized that we must not take out or "act-out" our anger on ourselves or act out our anger on others (this includes animals). He says that learning not to be self-abusive is one of the most challenging parts of the journey to wholeness. We can, at times, get angry with ourselves, but we don't need to be mean to ourselves or direct the full brunt of our anger at ourselves. Guilt about our actions can be a wake-up call, but self-abuse can turn guilt into shame.

Any form of exercise can be used as an effective way to express anger or release angry feelings. Puff suggests a variety of activities such as hitting and throwing things (in a safe way), and screaming or yelling (e.g., into a pillow or in the car with the windows up). If we are with others, he suggests some kind of isometric action such as clenching our hands or tightening some part of our body. It's a matter of focusing on our feelings about some issue or event in our life that still causes us to feel angry, hurt, or sad. We can focus on the event rather than the person causing the anger; sometimes just thinking about some injustice is enough to release the anger.

Another approach to catharsis is a psychological technique through which a client can talk to a therapist about anything and everything that comes to their mind without any inhibition, especially those thoughts that are forbidden by society. As the free flow of thoughts starts, a client might experience emotional outbursts. In the case of anger, the role of the counselor is to provide a safe place where angry emotions can be released. As already noted, however, the form of catharsis whereby a person vents their anger directly at the one causing the injury does not work.

Forgiveness

Clearly the above approach using catharsis does not help everybody. The benefits may only be temporary and the client may be left feeling sad, lonely, and empty. Enright and Fitzgibbons[17] show that anger underlies many psychological problems and recommend forgiveness as a way of dealing with anger. They suggest that the therapist can mention the many benefits of forgiveness such as freedom from the emotional pain of the past, greater mood stability, decreased anxiety, im-

[17]Enright and Fitzgibbons (2000).

proved loving relationships, and so forth.[18] The topic of forgiveness is discussed in Section 2.5.5 and we recall briefly some of the key ideas from there along with some additional thoughts from Richmond (2008).[19]

First, we need to "uncover" the anger and recognize the nature of the frustration or hurt that has lead to the anger. The anger can be a smoke screen that stops us from seeing and feeling the real or hidden hurt. Sometimes the anger that we feel now is compounded by memories of past hurts and past anger so we may need to check back to when we felt the same way. Second, we decide to forgive and continue to forgive on a regular basis or when there are strong feelings of anger. Forgiveness will not always be easy nor quick.

The motivation for forgiveness comes from reframing the way we view others, and forgiveness often starts with an act of conscious intent rather than a feeling. We need to realize that everybody does and says hurtful things as there seems to be a universal tendency for human nature to be selfish and inconsiderate; none of us is perfect.[20] We can be sorry for the misguided person caught up in this "popular" way of behaving. This does not mean rationalizing what happened and thereby justifying the other person's actions so that we don't have to forgive. There are times when we need to speak up and be assertive (see Section 2.5.4). This should happen as soon as we feel the first inkling of injury before it turns into anger. However, people who have other issues may find speaking up very difficult, and this inability may be feeding the anger they feel toward a situation or person. In the end it is important to remember that we cannot control the behavior of others.

3.3   SOME COUNSELING STRATEGIES FOR ANGER MANAGEMENT

3.3.1   A Management Program

Steffgen and Pfetsch suggest four broad ways of dealing with anger: the modification of physiological arousal (e.g., systematic desensitization and relaxation techniques); cognitive processes (e.g., modify inappropriate beliefs, problem solving); behavior and social interaction (e.g., social skills training); and several psychological processes (e.g., combining cognitive and relaxation techniques, mentioned further below).[21] One program for anger management that uses mainly a cognitive approach but incorporates the other aspects as well is listed below:[22]

1. *Identify the angry response pattern.* To help clients do this they can check out the following when they are angry:

   - Emotions.
   - Physical symptoms.
   - Effects on others.

[18] Enright and Fitzgibbons (2000: 119).

[19] See http://www.guidetopsychology.com/anger.htm for his helpful comments (accessed October 2010).

[20] In theological language, we are all *sinful*; in psychological language we all have a *shadow self*. Some would deny the reality of sin but still advocate forgiveness.

[21] Steffgen and Pfetsch (2007: 100–101).

[22] Partly adapted from Geldard and Geldard (1999: 166–173), who use the program for teenagers, and from Tafrate (1995).

Anger involves involves body, mind, and behavior, and there is a need to examine what is achieved or not achieved by the outburst.

2. *Externalize the anger.* This means separating the anger from the person and treating them as separate identities. The ideas of triggers (external events) that act on the client to produce anger, and catalysts (self-destructive beliefs that give power to the triggers) are introduced here to show the process *triggers → catalysts → anger* for the client. This is essentially the ABC method of Cognitive Therapy (see Section 1.4.3).

3. *Identify and list the triggers.* It is important to recognize that triggers will come unbidden and it is a person's response to them that needs to be controlled.

4. *Identify the catalysts.* These beliefs need to be identified, challenged, and replaced by alternative beliefs.

5. *Focus on personal power.* A person can either take control or can give away control to the triggers, catalysts, and anger. Sometimes anger is used as a method of power or control as it has a payoff. Other ways of achieving the same result need to be explored.

6. *Choose control options.* For example:

   (a) Avoid triggers. In the first instance there may be a need to avoid situations or places where triggers might occur, though eventually the triggers need to be faced. In the latter case, it has been suggested that systematic desensitization methods might be used perhaps using a hierarchy of situations, as discussed in Section 6.3.3. Once in a state of relaxation, a client can imagine the least anger-provoking scene and then shift back to relaxation. This is repeated until the scene no longer leads to anger. The second least anger-provoking scene is dealt with in the same way, and so forth. The method is then applied to real-life situations. Part of what happens in desensitization is that the situation is revisited from a safe place and one is able to view it as not as dangerous or arousing. It often adds a perspective to the anger/situation that allows for healing responses. However, the effectiveness of this approach with anger needs further clinical evaluation.

   (b) Recognize physical symptoms of arousal, for example, increased pulse, tension, sweating, stomach churning, and so forth. These can be used as warnings.

   (c) Use thought stopping (e.g., press the stop button or shout stop in one's mind).[23]

   (d) Use distraction by shifting one's focus to something else.

   (e) Use a relaxation technique[24] straight after thought stopping. Novaco (1975) found value in combining relaxation training plus self-instruction for dealing with anger. This idea of combining cognitive restructuring

---

[23]See Section 1.4.4.
[24]See Section 2.2.5.

and relaxation has been the mainstay of many anger management packages.[25]

(f) Challenge distorted and self-destructive beliefs using cognitive therapy. For example: "Someone tries to get me to do something that I don't want to do" (trigger or activating event); "They are trying to take advantage of me" (catalyst or self-destructive belief); and "I am me and I can make my own decisions about what to do" (alternative belief to neutralize the consequences). Another example is: "Someone else doesn't do what I want them to do" (trigger); "Other people *should* live up to my expectations" (catalyst); and "Other people *do not* need to live up to my expectations" (alternative belief). A helpful list of faulty thinking that can lead to anger is given below:[26]

   (1.) Catastrophizing in which a person has an exaggerated view of a perceived threat. Reducing this can lead to a reduced anger arousal. However an exaggerated perception of a threat can lead to other primary emotions such as anxiety and depression, and a person may vacillate among the three emotional states. There is a need to distinguish between them.

   (2.) Thinking that leads to people believing that they are getting less than their fair share of resources or status (e.g., arbitrary inference, selective abstraction, all-or-nothing thinking, and over generalization; see Cognitive Distortions in Section1.4.3).

   (3.) Condemnation, in which another person has done something bad to us and the person is perceived as being worthless or all bad. Changing a person's attitude towards the offender and seeing the offender in a different light can reduce the anger. In this sense the condemnation can be regarded as an overgeneralization.

   (4.) Suspiciousness is another thought that may differentiate anger from anxiety and depression. Here negative intentions are attributed to others which may or may not be true, e.g., "I suspect that people are talking about me behind my back." Thoughts related to suspiciousness can be difficult to replace in angry people as they often interpret challenges to these thoughts by a therapist as siding with the enemy.

   (5) Another major theme in anger is *demandingness* where clients believe that the target of their anger should have acted differently. Words like "must," "ought," and "should" reflect the client's expectations of others. Emotional disturbance results from the discrepancy between a clients expectation and reality.

(g) Deal with internalized anger so it can be released. This can be done through some form of catharsis (discussed above) such as physical activity (e.g., a brisk walk), talking to a friend, and counseling (e.g., using empty-chair work to address the person who created the anger, such as a parent). Childhood wounds may need to be uncovered and an inner child's anger identified.

---

[25] Fernandez (2010).
[26] DiGiuseppe and Tafrate.(2007: 138–139).

(h) Use an appropriate expression of anger. There are times when it is appropriate for a client to express their anger directly to the person causing the upset. This needs to be done with care, that is not raising one's voice or pointing a finger. Also it is appropriate to use "I" statements, not "You make me mad" but "I get mad when you ...."

(i) Find constructive ways of responding and getting needs met, for example using assertiveness training.[27] This avoids the two extremes of aggressive and passive anger. I would also add the alternative of lowering expectations so that a person does not get so frustrated when they don't get what they want. Social skills training can also be used. For example, the therapist identifies through various procedures (e.g., self-monitoring, interview, behavioral role plays) inappropriate social responses and then suggests alternative responses that can be rehearsed in the counseling room. Problem solving, where the focus in on the client collecting information about anger generating situations and then coming up with solutions, is another approach.

(j) Some antidepressants (SSRIs) can help with anger problems,.[28]

(k) Music is useful in regulating anger both for musicians and non-musicians. Kinesthetic movement and percussion are useful add-ons. Other forms of art can also be used.[29]

(l) The empty chair technique is useful in processing anger with another person.[30] The client imagines the person sitting in the chair and is able to safely release the anger. The client can then sit in the chair and see the other person's point of view as well as also seeing herself/himself from the other person's point of view.

There are several other methods that can be used.

(1) Systematic desensitization can be useful in anger management where the therapist uses a hierarchy of potentially anger-provoking scenarios constructed with the help of the client.[31] This topic is discussed in 7.6.2.

(2) One technique called a cognitive-behavioral affective therapy or CBAT for anger has been developed by Fernandez,[32] which incorporates affective (emotional) aspects into CBT. The method consists of three phases, the prevention, intervention, and "postvention" phases.

(a) The prevention phase involves education about anger and its effects followed by the presentation and signing of a behavioral contract. In the contract is set out the goal of minimizing maladaptive anger and a system of points to be awarded depending upon goal attainment. It also involves keeping a diary of angry incidents noting the frequency, intensity, and duration of the incidents. The client also needs to keep away from anger inducing situations.

[27]See Section 2.5.4.
[28]Bond and Wingrove (2010).
[29]Fernandez (2010).
[30]Fernandez (2010).
[31]Fernandez (2010).
[32]See (Fernandez (2010) for references.

(b) The intervention stage involves using some of the techniques described above such as thought stopping, distraction, and relaxation. Also reappraisal can be used to assess the damage of anger episodes and self-culpability.

(c) The postvention phase applies to situations when the previous phases have not been successful. One can use methods such as the empty chair technique to allow the aggrieved person to safely re-experience and express feelings that have been withheld. Drawing therapy can also be useful here.

(3) Novaco (1977) applied a method call stress inoculation to anger management, which was originally applied to anxiety, This method consists of three steps: cognitive preparation, skill acquisition, and application training. It is essentially

> a performance-based intervention during which the client engages in reframing of appraisals, relaxation training, imagery, modeling, and role playing to strengthen his/her ability to cope with anger-provoking situations.[33]

It is helpful for clients to have an anger diary to keep track of situations and the frequency, intensity, duration, and mode of expression of anger. This is particularly helpful for chronically angry individuals as it can help them to see a pattern to their anger.[34] In the diary they need to record the situations when they get angry and also record the early warning signs, the triggers, and the catalysts. Each day they answer two questions:

- How many times was I angry?

- How strong was the anger?

They can also record situations when they have controlled their anger. What did they do? What strategies did they use? Self-awareness is clearly the key. Extending the above idea of using a hierarchy mentioned under Control Options item 6(a) in the previous long list, one exercise[35] is for clients to choose the incident that provoked the least anger and review it in their minds. Using a relaxation technique, they go over this incident and insert an appropriate positive coping-statement at the following four points: before (e.g., "I don't need to get angry in this situation"), physiological arousal (e.g., "I must stay relaxed"), during (e.g., "What is my outcome here?"), and after (e.g., "I did okay"). When they can relive this incident without anger they move onto the next least stressful situation from their diary until they run out of incidents; then they switch to future possible incidents and do the same in their imagination. In this process they can also consider how else they might respond, and ask themselves why they didn't respond in that way.

Anger is generally a learned behavior that then becomes a habit, and it can be unlearned. For this reason it is helpful to explore past experiences and family background, as ways of expressing anger can get passed onto children. Weeks and

---

[33] Fernandez (2010).
[34] Novaco (1975, 1985).
[35] Girdano et al. (1997: 154).

Treat[36] suggest using an anger genogram to trace intergenerational patterns and ask questions like:

- How did your parents deal with anger/conflict?

- Did you see your parents work through anger/conflict?

- What did you learn about anger from each of your parents?

- When you got angry, who listened or failed to listen to you?

- How did members of your family respond when you got angry?

Anger can be used to regulate distance in a relationship and it may result from a fear of being too close or may be used to gain attention when the distance is too great. Also, anger triggers adrenaline, which some people enjoy, but it does not last. In the end anger is a choice.

DiGiuseppe and Tafrate.(2007: 328–329) give the following list of attitudes that are likely to interfere with the counseling process:

(1.) *Appropriateness of Strong Anger.* Clients may see strong anger as being acceptable because of modeling by the family, culture, or peer group, and not see it as deviant.

(2.) *Misinterpretations and Distortions.* Clients may misinterpret ambiguous or benign interactions as hostile. Also statements by the therapist may be misinterpreted.

(3.) *Lack of Emotional Responsibility and Other-Blame.* Clients sees the others as being responsible for their anger and that others need to change. They cant separate the person from his or her actions.

(4.) *Other-Condemnation.* Here clients see the target of their anger as worthy of their condemnation and deserving to be punished.

(5.) *Self-Righteous.* Clients see themselves as aggrieved parties while the transgressors are portrayed as morally wrong: "God and justice are on my side."

(6.) *Cathartic Expression.* Clients believe they must release their anger.

7. *Rigidly held, Demand-Based Assumptions.* This refers to demandingness mentioned above. The therapist needs to be careful in challenging a client's assumptions.

(8.) *Short-Term Reinforcement.* People often comply to a client's anger thus temporarily reinforcing the client's behavior. Clients needs to be aware of the long term negative effect of their outbursts.

(9.) *Reactance and Perceived Lack of Empathy by Others.* Clients may see a therapists attempts to change their anger as siding with the transgressor or disagreeing with the clients moral standard.

---

[36]Weeks and Treat (1992: 140–141).

For reasons like those given above, it can be hard for a therapist to have empathy for an angry client. One of the attributes of angry clients is that they believe that they are always right, and any revenge is justified. Anger can result from the perception of an injustice, lack of fairness, or grievance. When someone goes against the client's moral code, anger is an effective way to reinforce the rules. As noted above, this means that straight-forward challenging by the therapist can backfire, as the client may think that the therapist is taking the wrong side of a moral argument.

3.3.2   The Reluctant Client

A therapist may be faced with clients who do not want to change their behavior. For example, they may use the following excuses, especially if referred by some person or agency rather than coming to counseling on their own volition voluntarily:[37]

1. I don't get angry, just forthright (denial).

2. Anger toward a child is necessary for a parent to achieve discipline (justification).

3. If I give up my anger toward my wife/relative/child, I am condoning inappropriate behavior (self-righteousness).

4. Anger is the only way I can get get my staff to work properly (reinforcement).

5. I need to have an outlet for my anger after work by expressing it to my family (catharsis).

6. You need to help me change the person who I am angry with; she needs changing, not me (other condemnation).

Faced with this kind of client it may be difficult for a therapist to form a therapeutic relationship with the client. Obviously it is important to acknowledge and validate a client's frustration. Then a shift is needed, reminiscent of trying to shift a person from a pre-contemplative stage to an action stage[38] as in addiction counseling. Clearly motivational interviewing has a role here to start the counseling process. Clients need to understand that their anger is dysfunctional in the long run (as with an addiction), even though there is temporary satisfaction, and they need to be able to visualize an alternative behavior that is socially and personally acceptable to them. Inappropriate beliefs like those mentioned above need to be disputed.

3.3.3   Temper

According to Puff (2002), people who describe themselves as having a "temper problem" are generally people who have had some very negative hurtful experiences in the past. Because they have not yet successfully worked through all their feelings about these events, they walk around with "leftovers," that is, leftover hurt and anger from past situations. This is brought into every new situation so that they are

---

[37] Adapted from DiGuiseppe (1995).
[38] DiGuiseppe (1995: 136).

already somewhat angry before anything happens. Therefore when someone does something that might normally be a minor source of irritation, the person with leftovers always over-reacts. They feel the hurt and anger of the current situation plus the leftovers they had in store.

Each time we express our anger in an abusive way we make it that much easier for us to be abusive again in the future, as we build up a tolerance for violence and discord. It begins to feels natural and normal to us, especially if we are in an environment of abusive people. Puff maintains that the biggest stumbling block to healing is not what was done to us by others, but what we did to others. Also he says that how abused we are doesn't generally matter as much as how abusive we have become.

3.4   RELATIONSHIPS CAUSING ANGER

3.4.1   Dealing With Our Own Anger

All relationship combinations, for example, husband–wife, person–parent, parent–child, brother–sister, and person–employer can be a source of irritation and anger. Lerner (2004), although more focused on women, has a very helpful series of such case studies along with strategies for resolving anger issues in each case. It is a learning-by-example approach rather than a set-by-step method of controlling anger, for example: A husband may be too controlling and the wife keeps giving in to him (de-selfing); a wife is continually on her husband's back; an aging parent becomes too demanding (I focus on this one below); a child is rebellious; an employer expects too much; and so forth. When such a relationship leads to us getting angry then the problem is actually *ours*; we need to change as the other party is happy with the status quo.

We find that angry retaliation does not get us anywhere except perhaps into the blame game. Lerner[39] calls it "a circular dance in which the behavior of one partner maintains and provokes the behavior of the other." It doesn't matter who started it as the question is how to break the cycle.[40] The key is to deal with our own anger rather than try and change the other person. Trying to change the other person when they don't want to change is a fruitless task if done in a confronting manner; it simply maintains the pattern. It's a question of learning to change our part in the dance by observing and interrupting the pattern, and then dealing with the flak, namely the countermoves or "change back" reactions.

One common pattern is under-functioning—over-functioning, where the under-functioning of one person allows for the over-functioning of the other person. For example a situation may arise, say over one of the children, where the wife is very concerned and accuses her husband of showing no concern or emotion, while he accuses her of being over-emotional and over-reacting; the more she overreacts and becomes angry, the calmer he becomes, which makes her more angry, and so forth. The wife ends up doing the feeling work for both of them without allowing her husband to feel the emotion for himself with regard to the child.[41]

---

[39]Lerner (2004: 56).

[40]This circular reinforcing behavior (circular interaction) is discussed in more detail in Section 19.5.3.

[41]This type of emotional imbalance is quite common with couples.

Another way of looking at the dynamics of this situation is as an emotional pursuer—emotional distancer scenario. Lerner[42] describes emotional pursuers as "persons who reduce their anxiety by sharing feelings and seeking close emotional contact," and emotional distancers as "persons who reduce their anxiety by intellectualizing and withdrawing." Getting the distance right is a key factor in relationships.

A reverse situation can also take place when it is the woman who underfunctions in some way. For example, the husband vetoes something that she really wants to do and, perhaps after a fight, she gives in to him because she is afraid for her marriage. Lerner describes this as typically a women's subconscious dictum that, "The weaker sex must protect the stronger sex from recognizing the strength of the weaker sex lest the stronger sex feel weakened by the strength of the weaker sex."[43] In other words, women help men to feel stronger by relinquishing their own strength.

How can the cycle be broken? Lerner[44] gives an example where a woman Katy was angered by the demands that her elderly father made on her, making it difficult for her to live her own life. When she tried to gently raise the issue she got all sorts of negative feedback. To break the cycle she needed to have a "difficult conversation" with her father.[45] This topic is discussed in more detail in Section 17.2.4. Lerner described the conversation as going something like this:

> You know Dad, I have a problem. I haven't figured out how to balance the responsibility I feel toward you and the responsibility I feel toward myself. Last week when I took you shopping two times and also drove you to your doctor's appointment, I found myself feeling tense and uncomfortable, because I really wanted some of that time just for me . . . .

Her father followed up with a negative reaction, as expected: "Well, if I'm that much of a burden, I can just stay away." Instead of getting drawn into the usual dance, Katy stuck to her guns and continued to calmly address her own issue.

As every situation is different, it is difficult to give hard and fast rules on how to proceed in general. However, there are a number of key points. First, Katy needed to own the fact that *she* had the problem and *she* needed help. Second, she had to resist the temptation to blame her father or give him advice. Third, she used "I" language rather than "you" language. Fourth, she expected her father to strongly resist any change, and she avoided buying into his counter-arguments or digressions. Finally, she was firm but stayed calm and focused on her own issues.

Lerner[46] referred to Bowen[47] by describing the steps that the opposition will follow with regard to the client, namely: Lots of reasons are given why the client is wrong; the client needs to change back so that he or she will be accepted again, and; if the client does not change back, consequences will be listed. She comments that, "Countermoves are the other person's unconscious attempt to restore a relationship to its prior balance or equilibrium, when anxiety about separateness and change gets too high."[48] This separation anxiety is particularly strong if the relationship

---

[42]Lerner (2004: 57).
[43]Lerner (2004: 22).
[44]Lerner (2004: chapter 6).
[45]See, for example, Cloud and Townsend (2003).
[46]Lerner (2004: 34).
[47]Bowen (1978: 495). He was the originator of Bowen Family Systems Theory.
[48]Lerner (2004: 35).

is close, and the reaction may seem unreasonable and "over the top." Asserting independence can be frightening for the other person. Summing up, "Anger is a tool for change when it challenges us to become more of an expert on the self and less of an expert on others."[49]

In concluding this section I want to comment briefly about anger that arises in a codependent relationship (See Section 17.4). In this context Beattie[50] has a number of useful suggestions that apply quite generally.

- give permission to self and others to feel angry when needed

- feel the emotion and acknowledge the accompanying thoughts (preferably out loud)

- what is anger telling us

- don't let anger control us

- openly and honestly discuss our anger when it is appropriate

- take responsibility for our anger ("I feel angry when you do this because ....")

- burn off anger energy

- deal with guilt

3.4.2 Other People's Anger

The above guidelines for dealing with one's own anger are a first step to understanding what works and doesn't work in controlling anger. We also need to remember that anger fuels anger. In the face of an angry outburst Lindenfield makes the following suggestions for a client:[51]

1. To avoid an angry retaliation use positive self-talk. For practice make a list of positive affirmations such as:

   (a) I am not responsible for the other person's feelings, only for my own.

   (b) Anger is a temporary state so it will pass.

   (c) I don't have to negotiate with an angry person.

   (d) People say things they don't mean when they are angry.

   (e) I can control my physiological response to anger and put a temporary lid on my anger.

2. Check that my body is in a state of "alert relaxation."

3. Check the position of my body. For example, I need to be as much on a level with the other person as possible and maintain a reasonable distance from the other person as being too close can be threatening for both of us. Also, check that I am in the best position for leaving the room, if necessary.

---

[49]Lerner (2004: 102).
[50]Beattie (1987: 145–146).
[51]Lindenfield (1993: chapter 12).

4. I need to acknowledge the other person's feelings calmly and assertively. For example, "I see that you are very upset" or "I can understand that you are angry."

5. I can share my own feelings and fears using "I" rather than "You" sentences. For example, "I find your anger very upsetting" or "I feel very frightened when you shout in that tone."

6. I need to indicate that I am listening. This can be done by repeating back a summary of what the person has said. For example, "I hear you saying that you don't like me being late," or some such statement that does not come across as patronizing.

7. I need to make a conciliatory gesture such as a genuine apology, a statement of regret, a compromise, recognize the other person has a right to their view, and accept responsibility for my share of the problem.

8. I need to express my needs and wants calmly and persistently (e.g. using the broken record or fogging techniques; see Section 2.5.4 under "Diversionary Tactics."). This will help me to protect myself against criticism.

9. I give myself a reward.

After the outburst, an assertive follow-up may be necessary. Lindenfield[52] suggests first getting rid of any residual tension and talking to other trusted people about the experience. Then prepare what you want to say, rehearse the scene using a positive image of yourself, give yourself some positive self-talk, and relax your body. The final step is to initiate a discussion, being aware that there may be a defensive reaction, and ask for a clarification of other's grievances along with some constructive suggestions for resolving the situation.

When it comes to dealing with chronic anger from bosses, partners and so on, clients need to remind themselves of their rights to protect themselves and be very aware of of the first signals of this kind of anger. An appropriate time and place needs to be chosen for a confrontation and one should try and obtain constructive criticisms, for example, asking for specific examples of the offending behavior. A negotiation can be initiated with such questions as, "What do you think we can do about this." For further comments about having such difficult conversations see Section 17.2.4.

3.5   ANGER TOWARD GOD

Although this topic relates to the final section on biblical viewpoint, I mention it here as it has been the subject of some recent research interest in the psychological literature.[53] This topic is connected with the idea of "forgiving God."

Since God is generally not seen as being capable of wrongdoing, a perhaps more appropriate description is "resolving anger toward God." Anger with God often arises, for example, when there is undeserved suffering and injustice, particularly

---

[52]Lindenfield (1993: 153–155).
[53]Exline and Martin (2005)

when there is a big gap between how things are and how they would be if things were fair. Exline and Martin[54] suggest from the literature that three factors have a bearing on this topic: (a) anger toward God may be especially characteristic of those with an inflated, narcissistic sense of entitlement (i.e., believe they merit special treatment), (b) the closer a person is to God the less their anger toward God, and (c) parental abuse and poor attachment can adversely affect one's image of God. They also suggest that "anger toward God can impair health and might also decrease belief in God's existence."

How do we counsel someone who is angry with God because of hurt or suffering but does not want to turn away from God? This can be a difficult issue for a therapist as it depends on the therapist's world view and religious orientation, if any. Some therapists may wish to refer such a client on for spiritual directional help. The following are some thoughts and behavioral suggestions:

1. Suffering may be a consequence of wrongdoing. This wrong-doing may be self-inflicted or caused by others.

2. Acknowledge that suffering is a mystery.[55]

3. God is so much beyond us that we cannot comprehend God's character or his purposes. We can only trust in his infinite wisdom and recognize that we cannot know why certain things happen.[56]

4. Suffering can be reframed using various arguments. For example:

    (a) God has given us free will, which requires an impartial world, thus allowing the entry of suffering and evil, evil being the absence of good. God may not choose or be able to prevent suffering for this reason.

    (b) Suffering arises because the world is a spiritual battleground where satanic evil forces are at work.[57]

    (c) Justice will be restored in the after-life; the answer lies in our eternal destiny.[58]

    (d) Suffering can be a refining process to make us fit people for God's kingdom. It can help to develop character and compassion.[59]

    (e) Suffering can wake us up to ponder the essentials of life.

    (f) Suffering can bring us to the end of ourselves so that we have to rely on God.

    (g) God suffers along with people or on their behalf (e.g., in Christianity we have the atoning death of Christ on the cross; a supreme example of unjustified suffering).

[54]Exline and Martin (2005: 76–77).
[55]God never answered Job's questions about his unfair suffering but simply pointed out that God is creator (Job: chapters 38–41).
[56]Isaiah 55:8–9.
[57]Ephesians 6:11.
[58]Revelation 21:3.
[59]James 1:2–4; 1 Peter 4:12–13; and Romans 5:3.

5. Even natural disasters or so-called "acts of God" can have a human component (e.g., destruction of forests, global warming, pollution). Science teaches us that a tiny change in one part of the world can affect the whole world.

6. Focus on blessings we may have rather than on the suffering and loss.

Some behavioral methods are:[60]

1. Use techniques such as prayer, worship, journaling, writing letters to God, or empty-chair methods in which people imagine themselves talking with God.

2. Meditate on sacred texts written by fellow-sufferers (e.g., the Psalms in Judeo-Christian traditions).

3. Meditate on sacred texts that emphasize God's love and power and use appropriate imagery. We can thank God for the good that is in the world.

4. Ask God for forgiveness as none of us is blameless.

5. Encourage a client to forgive one's parents, if that is appropriate.

3.6   PASSIVE-AGGRESSIVE ANGER

The following two sections can be read together as they have common features.

3.6.1   Partner of a Passive-Aggressive Person

Anger can express itself passively rather than outwardly, and it is then referred to as passive-aggressive anger or simply passive anger. It is usually caused by a need to have control with the least amount of accountability, and it is one of the more destructive interpersonal styles with the anger being expressed in a covert way rather than openly. This form of anger is different from suppressed anger because the person is deliberately doing something knowing it will agitate the other person involved. Common expressions of passive anger are apathy, withdrawal, sabotage, pretending not to see or hear, procrastination, not doing what they agreed to do (e.g., "forgetfulness"), lateness, giving someone the cold shoulder, playing the victim role, being forgetful, or just being plain awkward, stubborn, uncooperative, and unreasonable.[61] They don't mean what they say or say what they mean. Also, they may be chronically late, ambiguous, make excuses for non-performance at work, and generally cause chaos. There is a tendency to blame others for their own failures and not take responsibility for their actions. When confronted they react and complain about the other person.

In couple situations, common expressions of passive-aggressive anger are "forgetting, procrastinating, misunderstanding, and overreading the person's behavior."[62] Forgetting wedding anniversaries or birthdays is an example. One of the main difficulties for people who have a passive-aggressive style is that they are frequently out of touch with their feelings so that they don't know that what they're doing is

---

[60]Some of the following ideas are from Exline and Martin (2005: 82).
[61]For a detailed checklist see Enright and Fitzgibbons (2000: 208).
[62]Weeks and Treat (1992: 144).

being angry. Frequently they are puzzled and resentful of their partner's constant anger and disapproval because of broken agreements and betrayal of trust.

In a marriage, a spouse may pretend that he or she is not angry yet act passively to vent anger in a covert way toward the partner; it can be regarded as a covert form of abuse. He or she may pretend to be loving and understanding while expressing anger in a veiled manner. The most painful way of doing this is by actually withholding love. Those on the receiving end may be unaware that they are subject to covert resentment and may be irritable and frustrated, reporting a variety of uncomfortable feelings such as anxiety, sadness, exhaustion, and anger, as well as various psychosomatic symptoms. The danger is that the victim could end up being seen as the person with the anger problem while the passive-aggressive partner paints himself or herself as calm and relaxed and blames the partner for overreacting—the offender takes on the role of the victim and feels treated unfairly.

Passive-aggressives have dependency needs and a fear of being alone. This can lead them to fight for dependency usually by trying to exercise control and by endeavoring to prove that the other partner is not needed. They also have a fear of intimacy because they are often unable to trust so that they guard against becoming intimately attached to someone. They may have sex with their partner but not make love.

Clients with a passive-aggressive partner need to first of all recognize that their partner is actually passive- aggressive. Second, they can examine how they might be contributing to the problem and consider what changes they need to make. Third, they can try and understand what motivates the partner's behavior and what his or her upbringing was like. Fourth, they can endeavor to find out what does the anger mean to the partner and in what way is the partner afraid of being alone, of expressing anger openly, and of becoming intimate. Fifth, they need to set clear boundaries (see Section 17.2) that are constantly enforced, but done sympathetically without being authoritarian. Although any changes may be strongly resisted, it is important to set firm limits and respect oneself. Finally, they can help the partner to understand that expressing anger is acceptable, provided it is done in constructive manner (see Section 19.6.4 on handling disagreements).

3.6.2 Passive-Aggressive Clients

Enright and Fitzgibbons[63] note that such clients are not easy to counsel as they may not admit to being passive-aggressive or even choose to realize what they are doing. A key step therefore is promoting self-awareness and identifying anger that they might deny. Such clients can be manipulative and highly defensive and use their anger to control and distance their partner. The origin of such anger may be a neglectful or controlling parent that they are still angry with resulting in misdirecting their anger into the marriage. Alternatively, they may have been taught never to show their anger and when they wanted to express anger it was never validated. There can be a conflict of dependency when as children they never separated properly from a parent who did not support their need to grow and experience life independently. They may have learnt to suppress overt expressions

---

[63]Enright and Fitzgibbons (2000: 207).

of anger for fear of damaging the dependent relationship. However, they could assert some measure of control and independence through passive anger. They want and fear both dependence and independence, which causes internal tension. Forgiveness of the client's parents can reduce the anger once the passive-aggressive behavior is clearly identified.

Passive-aggressive behavior stems from an inability to express anger in a healthy way. Such clients need to get in touch with their emotions as they may not even realize that they are angry or feeling resentment, and they may seem sincerely dismayed when confronted by their behavior. They also need to realize that no one is trying to make them do the things they don't agree to; the other party wants their participation to be voluntary. Because of fear of rejection, clients may agree to something they don't want to carry out so they need to learn to say "no" when they don't agree (see Section 17.2.2).

3.7   BIBLICAL VIEWPOINT

3.7.1   Anger in the Bible

A number of people in the people in the Bible had anger problems, for example, Moses killed an Egyptian and was kept out of the promised land because of his anger later,[64] Jonah was angry with God because God saved Nineveh,[65] and Peter got angry when accused of being a follower of Jesus.[66] However, the Bible describes anger as a neutral emotion in the injunction to be angry but without sinning, and this is followed by two further injunctions not to go to sleep at night without dealing with one's anger and not giving the devil any opportunity to get a foot in through one's anger.[67] Christians are also told to be slow to anger, indicating the need for awareness of one's response and self-control[68] to refrain from anger,[69] to stay away from hostile people,[70] and try to live at peace with everyone if at all possible.[71] Proverbs, in particular, has many verses about anger.[72] We are also admonished not to take revenge.[73]

3.7.2   God's Anger

As noted above, there is a place for righteous anger and we see that with regard to God's anger expressed in the Bible,[74] but this is tempered with the fact that God is long-suffering.[75] Jesus expressed anger openly when he rebuked the Pharisees for their hypocrisy and unmerciful interpretations of God's laws[76] and drove out the

[64]Exodus 1:12 and Deuteronomy 32:48–48–52.
[65]Jonah 4:1.
[66]Matthew 27:74.
[67]Psalms 4:4 and Ephesians 4:26–27.
[68]Proverbs 16:32; James 1:19; and Ecclesiastes 7:9.
[69]Psalms 37:8.
[70]Proverbs 22:24–25.
[71]Hebrews 12:14.
[72]For example, Proverbs 14:17, 29; 15:18, 16:29; 19:19; 29:8, 11, 22; and 30:33.
[73]Romans 12:19–21).
[74]Exodus 32:9 and Psalms 7:11.
[75]Exodus 34:6; Psalms 78:38ff, 103:8ff, 145: 8–9; Isaiah 48:9; and Jonah 4:2.
[76]Matthew 23:13–33 and Mark 3:2–5.

money-changers from the temple.[77] Moses was justifiably angry when the Israelites worshipped a golden calf.[78] He stated his reason and position clearly at the time so everyone knew exactly where they stood. It was not a question of loss of emotional control but rather a response to an unreasonable external stimulus. Joseph had every reason to get angry, but instead he channelled it elsewhere, as described in the last few chapters of Genesis.

3.7.3   Effect of Anger

When a Christian is angry with someone it can threaten to break his or her fellowship with God and hinder God's work.[79] It also spoils relationships with others, takes away peace, affects enthusiasm, and affects health. Anger needs to be confessed to God, its nature and source identified and analyzed, and dealt with as quickly as possible. If necessary, anger can be ventilated before God in a private place, telling God exactly how one feels, and God can begin to bring about healing.

Psalms 109 is a good model for handling anger.[80] David defines the problem (verses 1–5), expresses his anger to God (verses 6–20), has a change of attitude after letting go his anger (verses 21–29), and is finally able to praise God (verses 30–31).

---

[77]Matthew 21:13–14.
[78]Exodus 32:19.
[79]Matthew 5:23–24.
[80]Sturt and Sturt (1998: 160).

CHAPTER 4

GUILT AND SHAME

4.1 INTRODUCTION

Systematic empirical research on this subject has been slow in developing. A problem in researching this chapter was that the words guilt and shame are often used interchangeably in the literature, a contributing factor being a lack of adequate language. In counseling, clients will generally present with some other issue so that shame and guilt may initially lie hidden. For example, shame is often associated with depression, eating disorders (e.g., anorexia, bulimia, and bulimarexia),[1] and some personality disorders (e.g., narcissistic and paranoid personality disorders). In fact shame could be associated with any so-called Axis I or Axis II disorders. For example, Bradshaw[2] says that addiction is about an attempt at an intimate relationship with something, for example, the workaholic with work and the alcoholic with alcohol, the aim being to alter the mood and avoid the feeling of loneliness and shame. The acting out creates even more shame, so that the cycle continues. Another reason why shame is often a hidden emotion and directed inwardly is that clients may be ashamed of feeling shame; in contrast, shame is sometimes expressed outwardly as anger.

[1] Kaufman (1989: 133).
[2] Bradshaw (2005: 36).

4.1.1 Comparing Guilt and Shame

Guilt and shame are both moral emotions in that they foster moral behavior and "self-conscious" emotions; they are emotions of self-blame. They influence who we are in our own eyes. The difference between guilt and shame is described in several ways and, as previously mentioned, the distinction is sometimes blurred. The word "shame" tends to be avoided and guilt is often used as a substitute for both guilt and shame. A simple distinction is that guilt is a painful feeling of regret about an action (act of commission) or inaction (act of omission), while shame is a painful feeling about oneself as person. The words "I made a mistake" are internalized as "I am mistake," and "I did a bad thing" as "I am a bad person." A common phrase indicating shame is, "I am a loser." Shame pervades the whole person and can arise as a violation of personal, cultural or social values. An example of the latter is the traditional Japanese society, which may be described as a "shame-based" rather than a "guilt-based" society as the social consequences of getting caught over a misdeed are regarded as more important than the individual guilt feelings or experiences of the agent. The focus may then become more on etiquette rather than ethics, as understood in Western civilization. In many societies shame is related to "losing face." We note that there is a need to distinguish between secondary shame that arises from everyday events and primary shame that is a belief that self is fundamentally flawed.

People may be guilt prone or shame prone. Guilt-prone people are less likely to exhibit anger and are more likely to accept responsibility for interpersonal events. They also tend to make better use of their anger. On the other hand, shame-prone people seem to be more likely to blame others as well as themselves for negative events. They are also prone to anger and express their anger in inappropriate ways. Instead of blaming others they may withdraw from others and internalize shame thereby becoming vulnerable to a host of psychological symptoms. Guilt and shame will now be discussed individually.

4.2 GUILT

4.2.1 Categories of Guilt

Guilt is usually divided into objective guilt and and subjective guilt. Objective guilt is the result of an act violating a set of established laws or rules and it is guilt by fact irrespective of whether there is any remorse. It can be legal guilt (e.g., breaking a law), social guilt (e.g., not conforming to some social ritual or cultural norm, such as being rude), personal guilt (breaking a personal established rule like being home late for dinner), or theological guilt (e.g., breaking God's law by committing adultery). The person then has consequences to face. Subjective guilt has been defined as "an unpleasant emotional reaction by an individual to an actual or presumed negative judgment of himself by others resulting in self-depreciation visa-vis the group."[3] Briefly, objective guilt means a person *is* in fact guilty and subjective guilt is when a person *feels* guilty; a person can have one of these without the other.

[3] Narramore and Coe (1999: 534).

In the literature, subjective guilt is subdivided into various categories[4] using a variety of labels; I shall mention just two broad categories, real (true) or false (neurotic) guilt. Real guilt can be personal, like not going to the doctor when you should, or external, where another is affected such as not looking after a child properly before the child had an accident. False guilt is when a person accepts blame for something they did not do or omit doing. It is an illogical response based on perception rather than reality, and it generally arises from shame stimulated by deep inner conflicts or hidden binds, perhaps buried from childhood. Some writers ascribe false guilt as mainly due to an overactive conscience.

If a client is in a crisis situation, the therapist may need to enquire whether there is any *anticipatory* guilt, where a person predicts that they will feel guilty in the future if certain circumstances occur. Another type of guilt is *existential* guilt. This can be defined as the guilt experienced when one is aware of a discrepancy between one's well-being and the well-being of others. We identify another's plight, compare it with the advantages we have, and then feel helpless to do anything or little about it. A good example of when this can occur is while watching scenes of people starving on TV and enjoying a good meal.[5]

Another form of guilt is *survivor* guilt experienced when a person survives a major event while others don't, for example, war veterans or earthquake survivors. They feel guilty about being alive and feeling relieved that someone else died instead of them; they feel the need to justify their own survival. The feeling is even greater if a person is rescued at someone else's expense. As mentioned in Chapter 11 on grief, death of a loved one can lead to a feeling of guilt with the thought "If only I'd ....." Parents whose child has died may feel a special kind of guilt associated with the idea that as parents they have failed to carry out their fundamental obligation of caring for their children.[6]

Finally, guilt is a typical reaction in victims of abuse irrespective of whether they are children, spouses, the elderly, or in fact anyone. They may wonder how they failed to avoid the abuse and ask themselves if they could have done something else. There can be long term effects such as bitterness, anger, hatred, distrust, or a repeated abusiveness toward others. Abuse is discussed in Chapters 15 and 16.

4.2.2 Counseling for Guilt

Guilt emerges as an emotion in the course of a child's cognitive and social learning, and there are a number of theories about the process. Children take in the standards and expectations of parents and significant others and begin to make them their own to form the core standards of conscience or their ego ideal (ideal self). These ideals will become a standard by which children judge their morality and they will feel guilty any time they violate those standards. Children also take on parents' corrective attitudes and punishments, which may be detrimental. For example, if the parental attitudes are punitive or rejecting, "children adopt these attitudes toward themselves and begin to inflict some other punishment on themselves when

---

[4]See, for example, a detailed decision tree giving types of guilt by Johnson (1987: 46–47).
[5]For some thought-provoking ideas on this topic see
http://www.tc.umn.edu/ parkx032/CY-GUILT.html by James Park (accessed October 2010).
[6]For further comments relating guilt to grief see Johnson (1987: 40–43).

they fall short of their ideals. These punitive and self-rejection emotions formed the core of neurotic guilt feelings."[7]

Guilt is a very pervasive emotion in our lives as many incidents stir up feelings of guilt and it is not always easy to distinguish between true or false guilt.[8] From a counseling perspective, a first step is to listen for any guilt statement(s) from the client and see whether the cause is based on a present, past, or future act, or whether the person just feels guilty for no apparent reason. If a client does not come to realize that false guilt has no reality, they will not be able to make restitution or resolve the guilt and have forgiveness. Resolution or release may be attempted in a variety of ways, for example, by blaming or projection.[9]

People deal with guilt in different ways. One way is to redirect it elsewhere, for example, by rationalizing one's behavior (e.g., "He deserved it anyway") or blaming someone else (e.g., "They started it"). A second way is to endeavor to bury the guilt through denial, hoping that it will go away, but it doesn't. A third way is to try and pay for it in some way by working harder at doing good things. Unfortunately some things can't be paid for (e.g, not being reconciled with a parent before he or she died). A fourth way is to confess it and ask for forgiveness.

A key question is: When does a person need therapeutic help for guilt? Clearly a client has a problem if he or she feels guilty all the time or the guilt interferes with the way he or she functions. Some symptoms of toxic guilt are: a person becomes over responsive (e.g., gives too much of self to keep every body happy); over conscientious (e.g., becomes fearful that every action may hurt others); over sensitive (e.g., becomes over sensitive about the rightness and wrongness of actions and to any cues from others implying personal wrong doing); becomes immobilized (e.g., too afraid to do anything in case it is wrong); and can't make decisions in case they are the wrong ones.[10] Then, of course, people sometimes stir up feelings of guilt in others to achieve their own purposes.

Overcoming Toxic Guilt

Some steps for helping clients to overcome toxic guilt are as follows:[11]

1. Help clients to recognize the role of guilt in their lives by choosing a current problem and answering the following questions (say in a journal).

    (a) Who is responsible for the problem, and whose problem is it really?
    (b) How did I make this problem worse for myself?
    (c) How much guilt do I feel about this problem, and how much does my guilt make it worse?
    (d) If my guilt was removed, what would my problem now look like?
        If (d) is the response go to step 2.

2. Help clients to redefine the problem without the guilt. They then decide whether the problem is interpersonal or intrapersonal and see if they can set

---

[7] Narramore and Coe (1999: 535).
[8] For a detailed exposition on the extent of guilt see Tournier (1974).
[9] See Section 21.5 for "projection."
[10] Adapted from http://www.livestrong.com/article/14689-handling-guilt/ (accessed October 2010).
[11] http://www.livestrong.com/article/14689-handling-guilt/ (accessed October 2010).

aside guilt to resolve the problem. Again ask whose problem is it, really? If a client is taking on another person's responsibility in order to protect the person in some way, he or she should go to the next step.

3. If the problem is someone else's, give the problem back to them to solve. Help the clients to confront the guilt preventing them from handing on the problem. If the problem is the client's go to the next step.

4. Help the client to see what fears are getting in the way, then dispute irrational beliefs. Positive self-affirmations can then be introduced to build self-esteem.

5. If the guilt is not resolved by now, go back to step 1.

4.3 SHAME

4.3.1 Nature of Shame

Shame can be either a healthy feeling or it can be toxic. Healthy shame can't hurt us as it lets us know our limitations and also helps in the development of our conscience. Natural or healthy shame is an an emotion that lets us know when our sense of modesty/morality is being violated and our core boundary is crossed. For example, we blush when we feel embarrassed and unprotected in a social or public situation. Bradshaw notes that, "Sex and shame go hand in hand because we need our sense of shame as a boundary for our sexual desires."[12] In a permissive society where sex is openly exploited it is much more difficult to deal with such shame.

Natural shame also tells us that we are imperfect and we experience it as a mild to moderate feeling of embarrassment when we notice ourselves making a mistake or being imperfect. It is a good leveler as it keeps us humble and more accepting of others. We can sometimes feel guilt and shame at the same time, for example we can feel guilty if we break our own moral code and feel shame if someone else finds out about it. Shame is a very painful emotion usually accompanied by a sense of shrinking or "being small" and by a sense of worthlessness and powerlessness. It is a fear of being exposed, humiliated, or rejected. Here the concern is with others' evaluation of self as opposed to concern with one's effect on others in the case of guilt. It also reflects the degree to which we fall short of attaining our ideals, and relates to the gap between our ideal self and our actual self.

Mellody et al.[13] refer to a "shame attack" in which we want to run away or crawl under a chair. It seems that everyone is looking at us and we may even feel nauseated or dizzy, or start talking in a childlike voice. There may be a tendency to continually ruminate about what happened and thus increase the feeling of shame. The motivation then is to hide or strike back in contrast to guilt where the motivation is to confess, apologize, or repair. Puff [14] aptly describes shame as a voice that wants to punish us and not let us out of its grip. If we continually tell ourselves that we are bad, then we are going to end up doing bad things. Kaufman describes shame as a "wound made from the inside, dividing us from both ourselves

---

[12]Bradshaw (2005: 16).
[13]Mellody, Miller, and Miller (1989: 98–99).
[14]Puff (2002).

and others."[15] Difficulties with shame are also important for teens to young adults entering into the world more independently as they have to juggle with a variety of different moralities. They may feel acute shame in a situation in which others would feel none; the need to fit in and mask one's true feelings can lead to difficult complications of behavior.

4.3.2   Toxic Shame

Where does toxic shame come from? It usually comes from how we are treated as children such as being taught that we are worthless or inadequate in some way. For example, adults may say, "You'll never amount to anything!" or "I wish you were never born!" They may severely discipline us with the message that *we* don't matter—only what we *do* matters. We may be humiliated for our behavior with comments such as, "What would the neighbors think of you if they knew …?", or "You look ridiculous," or "What is wrong with you anyway!"

As a result of childhood messages, shame becomes stored in memory in the form of scenes along with the affect relating to the scenes. These scenes govern the further development of a person as·well as future behavior and become impediments to self-esteem and to intimacy.[16] Such people live with the deep-down conviction that they are worthless. Also shame can become internalized through faulty attachment and abandonment, and when it has been completely internalized a person may believe nothing about him or her is okay. It can be triggered internally without any attending stimulus. The more one experiences shame, the more one is ashamed. To be shame-bound means that whenever a person feels any need or drive, he or she immediately feels ashamed.

Bradshaw says that a shame-based person will not only guard against exposing oneself to others but also guard against exposing oneself to oneself. He said, "In toxic shame the *self becomes an object of its own contempt*, an object that can't be trusted."[17] He further says that such people can't love themselves and escape from self is necessary, which can be achieved by creating a false self. The false self is always more or less than human, for example a perfectionist or a slob, a family hero or a family scapegoat, and a super-achiever or underachiever.[18] With a false self, intimacy with others is impossible. The authentic self goes into hiding and feels lost.

Shame has a very negative affect on interpersonal behavior as shame-prone individuals are more likely to blame others, as well as themselves, for negative events; are more prone to bitter, resentful kind of anger; and are less able to empathize with others in general.[19] They will tend to deal with the pain of their shame one of two ways.[20] The first way is that they may become angry with the world, attempting to shift the blame on to others as a form of ego-protection. By externalizing shame they can preserve their self-esteem and reduce painful self-awareness. Their anger can help them gain control and authority and help counteract shame induced feel-

[15] Kaufman (1989: 17).
[16] Kaufman (1989: 215).
[17] Bradshaw (2005: 30); italics are the author's.
[18] Bradshaw (2005: 34).
[19] Tangney and Dearing (2002: 3).
[20] Tangney and Dearing (2002: 5, 92).

ings of worthlessness and ineffectiveness.[21] A shamed person is very conscious of what others may think of them so it is a short step to blaming others for the painful shame feelings. The second way is to withdraw from others, but this is only partly effective as the individual is still stuck with loathsome self. Withdrawal leads to internalizing the shame, and this can make one prone to a number of psychological symptoms, especially depression.

Feelings of shame pose a serious threat to self-esteem so that shame-prone people tend to have low self-esteem, but this is not always the case as the relationship between shame and self-esteem is complex.[22] In contrast to guilt, which encourages people to behave morally, shame tends not to inhibit immoral action but seems to promote self-destructive behaviors such as hard drug use and suicide in an attempt to escape the punitive self.

We noted above that guilt and shame can go together. For example, a man can feel guilty for cheating on his girl friend. However, he may view his transgression as likely to affect many aspects of his life and be typical of the untrustworthy and immoral character of his nature that may continue into the future.[23]

4.3.3   Shame and Intimate Relationships

Men and women in relationships can communicate very differently about their problems and worries. Because of the difference in perspective, partners have particular difficulty in communicating their shame experiences, particularly as most personal troubles such as sexual incompatibility, concerns about health or physical attractiveness, job worries, and money issues are shaming situations.[24] Learning to respond appropriately can avoid feelings of shame experienced by the other party. For example, if one member of the couple wants more intimacy and/or more communication than the other, both may feel shame for different reasons. The one wanting more intimacy may feel rejected and shamed for wanting too much, while the other may feel shame for either not being comfortable with more closeness, or for wanting more distance than the other. The shame can then turn into blame (e.g., "You don't love me!", or "You're too needy!") and this can turn into an escalating cycle (see Section 19.5.3 which describes circular interaction).

If just one partner has shame problems, we can have a similar escalation, this time as part of a shame-anger cycle: the victim feels shame, which leads to the externalization of blame, anger, and destructive retaliation against the partner; and the partner then gets angry in turn and retaliates against the victim, thus reinforcing the shame. Shame can therefore cause serious problems in a relationship because of these recurring cycles.

Tangney and Dearing[25] discuss what they refer to as a shame-bound relationship that results when two shame-prone people come together. Here both partners bring into the relationship their own baggage such as, for example, insecure attachment, fear of negative evaluation, and impaired capacity for empathy, so that anger, conflict, and shame characterize their interaction. Little is done to to affirm self-

[21]This is in contrast to guilt, which is not so conducive to anger.
[22]Tangney and Dearing (2002: 59–69).
[23]Tangney and Dearing (2002: 53–54).
[24]Tangney and Dearing (2002: 158).
[25]Tangney and Dearing (2002: 163).

worth or the integrity of the relationship. Interaction becomes a blame game where blame is carefully assigned, and this leads to shame; "If there is a negative outcome, someone is to blame and it must be you!" This attempt at self-protection ends up with each partner getting hurt, but where it hurts most. Such relationships can sometimes become violent where a male offender can be a jealous, insecure person who tries to cover his shame and fear with overt hostility and demands for control. As a shame-prone person, she is likely to believe that she deserves to be treated in this way and feels responsible in some way for the abuse. She internalizes the blame and, by accepting a submissive role, allows her abusive partner to feel less shame.

One place where shame can have a major impact is in the area of of sexual intimacy. Bradshaw observed, "Perhaps no aspect of human activity has been dysfunctionally shamed as much as our sexuality."[26] Some of the sexual hang-ups that a therapist might encounter are discussed in Section 19.4.3. With regard to sexuality, men and women have different vulnerabilities with regard to shame.[27] Men need to perform well sexually and when they don't, especially if impotence rears its ugly head, they can experience shame and humiliation. Just one failure can be devastating and raise all sorts of doubts in a man's mind. Women face two conflicting sexual ideals, the chaste virgin or the sex kitten. They can feel shame if they come across as being too prudish on the one hand or appearing to be a "loose" woman on other hand. Women can also face unrealistic physical images in the media of how they should look. This topic of self-image is mentioned further in Section 8.6.1 in the context of eating disorders. For further details about shame in relationships see Epstein and Falconier (2011).

Couple Counseling

In couple counseling, the therapist can begin by teaching some communication skills as described, for example, in Section 19.6. Tannen makes the following helpful comment:

> Many women could learn from men to accept some conflict and difference without seeing it as a threat to intimacy [or as a devaluation of the self], and many men could learn from women to accept interdependence without seeing it as a threat to their freedom.[28]

It is helpful to focus on what each member of the couple wants or does not want and then reframe these wants to minimize any shame and blame. This discussion can replace the cycle mentioned above that was preventing proper communication and help them to understand what the shame/blame cycle is doing.

4.4 ASSESSMENT OF SHAME

Methods of assessing guilt and shame tend to assess emotional states, the feelings at the moment, or dispositions, namely shame-proneness and guilt-proneness. Many measures have been developed, but often in cases guilt and shame are not separated.

---

[26] Bradshaw (1988: 54).
[27] Tangney and Dearing (2002: 166).
[28] Tannen (1990: 294).

Promising measures are the guilt and shame scales of the Test of Self-Conscious Affect (TOSCA) and its various modifications and updates such as TOSCA 3.[29]

Shame can appear as body shame, relationship shame, competence shame, or character shame,[30] and it is driven by scenes from the past. Kaufman suggests four helpful indicators in identifying shame in the counseling room, namely:[31]

1. *Facial signs.* Except in the case of a culturally driven behavior, some clients avoid eye contact with their eyes or head down, staring at the floor and/or blushing. Some clients become ill-at-ease when looked at directly and look away. Avoidance of mutual facial gazing and direct eye-to-eye contact is usually a definite sign of shame, though in some cultures it can be a sign of respect. Others may adopt a staring attitude and stare directly into the therapist's eyes. During an interview clients may cover their face with their hands.

2. *Affective signs.* Affective signs of shame are shyness, embarrassment, discouragement, self-consciousness, and guilt. The therapist's task is to find a way in to the client's shame; metaphors are helpful. A good question might be, "Have you ever felt that there is something wrong with you inside?"

3. *Cognitive signs.* Statements from a client about being a fraud or an impostor are a good indication of shame. Other signs are low self-esteem, diminished self-concept, deficient body image, feelings of worthlessness or feeling unloveable. Some clients believe that no real self is present inside them while others have a sense of of something vitally wrong within.

4. *Interpersonal signs.* There are many signs that can be looked out for. Denial, perfection, transfer of blame, and internal withdrawal scripts (scripts being a Transactional Analysis term) along with rage, contempt, and power scripts, the latter being frequently directed at the therapist. The client may even endeavor to exercise power by controlling the interview.

4.5   COUNSELING FOR TOXIC SHAME

4.5.1   Shame from a Family System

Following Bradshaw,[32] a therapist can help a client to find toxic sources of shame. For instance, a major source is the family system, as shame can be generated in significant relationships because those are the relationships that we care about. Bradshaw says, "If our primary caregivers are shame-based, they will act shameless and pass their toxic shame onto us. There is no way to teach self-value if one does not value oneself."[33] Shame can get passed on from parents. He points out that shame-based families transfer toxic shame by means of shaming rules such as the following:[34]

[29]Tangney and Dearing (2002: chapter 3).
[30]Kaufman (1989: 94–95).
[31]Kaufman (1989: 178–181).
[32]Bradshaw (2005: chapter 3).
[33]Bradshaw (2005: 45).
[34]Adapted from Bradshaw (2005: 6263).

1. *Control or chaos.* Either there is tight control of all feelings and personal behavior at all times, or the children experience chaos because of family problems (e.g., drugs and alcohol).

2. *Perfectionism or lack of moral and social standards.* One must always live according to some externalized image that no one measures up to, or else the children have no rules to guide them.

3. *Blame.* When things don't go right, blame yourself or others; blame is a cover-up for shame.

4. *Denial of the five freedoms.* Briefly these freedoms are the power to perceive, to think and interpret, to feel, to want and choose, and the power to imagine.[35] You mustn't perceive, think, feel, desire or imagine the way you do, but rather follow the perfectionist ideal.

5. *The "no talk" rule.* You are not allowed to express your true feelings, needs, or wants.

6. *The "no listen" rule.* Everyone is stuck in their roles and don't hear the true self of another person.

7. *Don't make mistakes.* Cover up your mistakes to avoid scrutiny and, if someone else makes a mistake, shame him or her.

8. *Unreliability.* Don't trust anybody and don't expect reliability in relationships.

9. *Don't trust.* Since no one is validated or listened to, no one develops basic trust in themselves or others.

Added to the above, there may have been issues of abandonment, physical absence, narcissist deprivation, abuse of various kinds from parents and/or possibly siblings, and enmeshment in the needs of the family system. Parents who physically humiliate and abuse their children were typically abused themselves when they were young. They have never resolved the internalized shame in their own lives and tend to identify with the shaming oppressor rather than themselves in order to possess that person's power and strength. Sometimes parents shame their child's sexuality by giving the impression that sexuality is disgusting or shameful. They may act with disapproval when a child displays his or her sexuality in any way. Often the parents can't handle it as they had their own sexuality shamed.

A person sets up a number of primary defense mechanisms to cope with shame caused by sexual abuse such as denial, dissociation, displacement, and projection.[36] When the primary ones fail they are followed up by secondary defenses such as inhibition (unable to perform normally), reactive formation, undoing, isolation of affect, and turning against self. Other sources of shame can be school and peer groups (e.g., bullying and belittling, or put-downs by teachers) as children like to tease, especially older siblings, and they can be very cruel.

[35] See end of Section 2.5.3 for further details.
[36] See Section 21.5.

4.5.2 Adult Shame

Divorce or the loss of a relationship can lead to shame as can public failure and the aging process, where there is a bodily and perhaps mental decline. Perfectionism, mentioned above, denies healthy shame as it assumes that we can be perfect. Perfectionists have no sense of healthy shame and have no internal sense of limits, never knowing how much is good enough. Control is important as it avoids vulnerability and exposure, which can allow others to see one's defectiveness and opens the door to shame.

Tangney and Dearing [37] suggest the following interventions for helping a client cope with shame reactions:

1. Help the client to verbalize the episode that led to the feeling of shame. This helps the client to see more clearly and perhaps realize that the event was not cause for shame and perhaps other emotions such as disappointment or frustration might be more appropriate. Shaming scenes need to be relived as completely as possible as well as the client re-experiencing all the associated affects. These scenes need to be reshaped or repaired by creating new positive scenes.[38] A method for doing this due to Bradshaw is described briefly below.

2. Cognitive revaluation (CBT) can be used by the therapist to focus on the bigger picture of the client's life experiences, strengths, and abilities, and address some shame-inducing beliefs. In fact most flaws, setbacks, and oversights don't warrant global feelings of shame.

3. Help the client to understand the difference between guilt and shame and shift the focus away from condemning self (shame) to condemning the behavior (guilt).

4. Empathy from the therapist can provide an accepting, positive environment for the client even though the therapist may not be too happy with the client's actions. The therapist's reaction and acceptance can model an alternative way for the client to respond and accept himself or herself.

5. Light-hearted humor, without minimizing a client's feelings, can be a helpful foil against the deadly serious self-condemnation inherent in shame.

Morrison (2011) notes that the first task in counseling is to recognize and name shame for what it is and for the therapist to overcome any embarrassment in speaking of it. In the counseling room shame may be disguised as some other emotion such as anger, reflecting a narcissistic injury to self and self-esteem. For example, a son may not live up to a fathers expectations, and his first reaction might be shame for letting his father and himself down. Depression can be another manifestation of shame, perhaps arising out of a feeling of helplessness and not being able to live up to expectations. Morrison states that: "Frequently the patient suffering from a shame-based depression feels isolated and alone, and this loneliness and sense of being rebuffed provide a handle to get at his or her conviction of worthlessness.[39] Shame-based depression can lead to suicide and this is discussed in Chapter 10.

[37] Tangney and Dearing (2002: 175–177).
[38] Kaufman (1989: 215).
[39] Morrison (2011: 9).

Envy can also hide feelings of shame resulting in a person feeling inferior to someone else. Another defense method of hiding shame is through grandiosity where a client exhibits the defense of reaction formation, the tendency to act in a manner opposite to the feared emotion. For example, "I am not a failure, but I am really an outstanding person." The therapist needs to look beyond the noisy arrogant grandeur of such a client and focus on cracks in the client's defensive assuredness before attempting entry into areas of self-doubt. For example, "I noticed some hesitation when you spoke of being the best teacher in the school. I wonder if you were feeling some doubt about it."

Shame can be hidden by what Morrison refers to as "withdrawal" in which there is an attempt to hide shame experienced by a client with a comment such as, "I wish the ground opened up and swallowed me." This arises from a client's feeling of public humiliation, and through denial hides the shame the client feels from failure to attain his or her own ideals. Morrison talks about what he calls the language of shame where the therapist needs to recognize the possible presence of shame lurking behind a clients self-descriptions such as "I am a loser," "I am a failure," and "I am a hopeless case," and then identify the shame experience that the client is trying to express. By the therapist exploring, identifying, and accepting the shame he or she finds, the client can begin to tolerate shame so that it becomes more bearable and acceptable. By bringing the shame from the unconscious to the conscious, it can now be explored as a psychological problem. As we have seen in other areas of counseling, naming an issue, that is externalizing it, enables it to be investigated objectively. A client may experience depression at the same time as conscious shame so that both feelings can be considered during the counseling.

Greenberg and Shigeru (2011; chapter 3) discussed how emotion-focused therapy (EFT)[40] can be applied to shame. They note that shame is created in interpersonal relationships so that it needs a special interpersonal relationship to heal and transform it. This is where the therapist comes in to provide an accepting environment where clients can reveal their shortcomings and be exposed to shameful experiences. Clients can then learn to automatically regulate the intensity of their shame arousal, to tolerate distress using for example relaxation techniques, and to take a mindfulness approach to uncomfortable emotions. As always, focusing on the positives and emphasizing ones resilience can help clients to reconstruct their views of the past, present, and future.

Exercises for Shame

Along the line of (1.) in the above list, another approach is to redo toxic childhood scenes. A helpful exercise,[41] which I will just briefly summarize to give the flavor of the method is for the client to begin with relaxation breathing (see Section 2.2.5) and then imagine going back in time through a time portal at the end of a corridor back to the house where he or she lived as a seven year old, taking note of all the details of the house. There is a small child coming out of the front door (note the clothes), so walk over to the child and tell the child you are from his or her future. Tell the child you know what he or she has been through and you will be there for the child, being the only person he or she will never lose. Ask the child if he or she is willing to go home with you and if not tell the child you will

[40]See Section 1.4.2.
[41]Bradshaw (2005: 176–177).

visit again tomorrow. If the child will go with you, take the child's hand and start walking away. As you walk away see your mum and dad come out on the porch. Wave goodbye to them. Look over your shoulder as you continue walking away and see them getting smaller and smaller until they are completely gone. Bradshaw should be consulted for fuller details. Clearly ego state therapies can be used here to resolve past childhood issues (see Section 1.2.4).

Bradshaw gives several other helpful exercises such as dealing with negative self-talk and the critical inner voice that is powerful and generates toxic shame. This voice can be likened to automatic thoughts so that cognitive therapy can be used to challenge the negative thoughts as mentioned in (2.) of the above list. Empty-chair work, as in Gestalt therapy, can also be used to deal with the inner critic; you imagine yourself sitting in the opposite chair and let the inner critic criticize you. Changing places you then answer the critic and repeat the process several times thus keeping the dialogue going. After analyzing the dialogue, translate the critical messages into specific behaviors (e.g., instead of "You are selfish," say "I didn't want to do the dishes") as the critical statements are generalizations, and then challenge these generalizations. Those obsessive shaming thoughts that keep coming up can also be dealt with using thought stopping methods (see Section 1.4.4) and using thought substitutions. Finally, choosing to love and forgive yourself for your mistakes and accepting yourself unconditionally is toxic shame's greatest enemy!

Kaufman[42] mentions another technique that he calls *refocusing attention*, which is an affect tool for releasing affect such as the affect of shame. When shame rears its ugly head and begins to put a client into a kind of internal shame spiral, the client makes the effort to refocus attention back outside of self through, for example, visual and physical sensory experiences. The key is to recognize when the spiral begins, then intervene and stop the spiral.

Counseling Process and Shame

Some important issues concerning our role as therapists are raised by Tangney and Dearing.[43] It is often difficult for shamed clients to come to counseling as they are admitting that they have a problem, which may be a shameful experience for them, especially if they are already shame-prone. This is perhaps why so many people don't make it to counseling; it has made me realize how important it is to affirm those who do make it. Once in the counseling room, a client faces the possibility of bearing all to a therapist who is supposed to have all the answers, and this can be a shaming experience. Transference can be an issue whereby a client transfers perceptions and dynamics of previous relationships on to their relationship with the therapist. These perceptions are typically negative and may be shame laden so that shame-based relationship issues can end up being transferred onto the client-therapist relationship.

How might these shame experiences affect counseling? We have seen above that shame can lead to either withdrawal or anger, which can generate a similar response in the counseling room. Withdrawal and wanting to escape or hide can lead to various sabotaging activities that might be interpreted as "resistance." Such resistance may be a sign of shame, and may be reflected in the client arriving late for

[42]Kaufmann (1989: 183).
[43]Tangney and Dearing (2002: chapter 11).

a session, abruptly changing the subject, or claiming to have nothing to say. Thus when clients become irritated or hostile, question the therapist's skills, or suddenly want to end the counseling program, the question of shame in the client-therapist relationship may be worth considering. It is a good idea to keep a lookout for cues indicating that a client might be discussing a shame episode. Such cues may include downcast eyes, agitation, anger, nervous laughter, face touching, or slumped posture. Other signs are mentioned above in Section 4.4 above on assessment.

Finally, a therapist can be vulnerable to feelings of shame that may arise through counter-transference when he or she develops negative attitudes to the client, or through apparent failure in the counseling room. For example, some clients may terminate prematurely, others may go on for a long time with little sign of improvement, and there is the the ultimate experience of "failure" when a client commits suicide. However, clients may also want to take a break, but knowing they can contact the therapist if the need arises. Morrison comments that the pain of shame "threatens us as therapists, often reminding us of faults or weaknesses that we have experienced at various points in our lives. This shared pain regarding shame can often lead to a collusion between therapist and patient to avoid acknowledging or identifying shame. This shared pain regarding shame can often lead to a collusion between therapist and patient to avoid acknowledging or identifying shame."[44]

4.6   BIBLICAL VIEWPOINT

4.6.1   Guilt

With regard to true and false guilt, true guilt has traditionally been regarded as the judgement of God through conviction by the Holy Spirit concerning a betrayal of a standard (God's or our own) or the violation of relationships. On the other hand, false guilt can be regarded as arising from the judgement of other people, social suggestion, fear of losing another's love, or breaking a "taboo." For example, false subjective guilt could be the product of past learning from parents who expected too much, thus giving rise to unrealistic adult behavior with consequent low self-esteem and guilt. Also rigid and too exacting parental discipline can also lead to unachievable over-high expectations. Social pressure and criticisms from others can lead to feelings of not being able to measure up to society's standards and the resulting guilt. Here the client needs to examine the standards of right and wrong and realize that he or she does not need to feel guilty about those things the Bible doesn't say are sin. It is a matter of asking what God really expects of us.

From a theological perspective, the Bible sees all humankind as being objectively guilty as all have fallen short of God's standard[45] and are therefore worthy of God's judgement.[46] However God has extended grace to the Christian through faith in Christ[47] and what Christ has done on the cross. Christians believe that if they truly repent and confess their shortcomings they shall receive forgiveness and be

---

[44]Morrison (2011: 6).
[45]Romans 3: 23.
[46]Romans 6: 23.
[47]Ephesians 2:8–9 and Romans 5: 1, 8:1.

reconciled to God.[48] They can then move forward in their lives[49] even though they continue to fall short.[50] This is the teaching, but many Christians have difficulty with it because of "the idea deeply engraved in the heart of all men, that everything must be paid for."[51] They find it difficult to accept the fact that God removes their guilt without them having to work for it.[52] A therapist may need to explore this concept with a client. When guilt comes to Christians they can check their fellowship with God and if there is any sin in their lives confess it. They can then walk in fellowship with God and the guilt feelings will go. However, if after confession deep guilt remains, one may need to explore the possibility that such guilt may be false guilt, socially created and not of theological significance.

4.6.2 Shame

According to Allender and Longman[53] the signposts of shame are a painful absorption of self (and its apparent ugliness),[54] flight from exposure, and physical or emotional violence against self or the person who witnessed self's fall. They see shame as a form of idolatry[55] that comes when we invest in others and in ourselves as idols rather than worshipping God.[56] They say that shame is also a gift that can turn a person to God who, through the incarnation in Christ, was humiliated and suffered the shame of the cross.[57] Through forgiveness and redemption the Christian is no longer condemned.[58] If God does not condemn a person, then there is no need to accept self-condemnation or unjustified condemnation from others. Sometimes the church can be a source of shame as church people can put others on a guilt/shame trip by using such terms as "Christian duty," "insincere repentance," and "self-denial."[59]

Christians who struggle with shame should read the story of Mephibosheth[60] in 2 Samuel 9:1–13 who was lifted out of his shame by King David—a picture of God who can lift us out of our shame. The Bible says that if we believe in God and God's son Jesus, we will not be put to shame.[61]

---

[48] 1 John 1:9 and Isaiah 44:22, 55:7.
[49] Philippians 3:12–14.
[50] Romans 7:18–25.
[51] Tournier (1974: 174).
[52] Ephesians 2:8–9.
[53] Allender and Longman (1994: 194).
[54] The Bible describes the shame as affecting our countenance (e.g., Isaiah 29:22, Psalms 44:15 and 83:16–17).
[55] Psalms 97:7 and Isaiah 42:17.
[56] Psalms 4:2.
[57] Hebrews 12:2 and Isaiah 50:6–8.
[58] Romans 8:1.
[59] The more severe form of spiritual abuse is mentioned in Section 16.7.
[60] The name means "puff of shame," or "dispeller of shame or idols."
[61] Psalms 25:1–3; Romans 9:33, 10:11; and 2 Timothy 1:12, 2:15.

CHAPTER 5

STRESS

5.1 NATURE OF STRESS

This chapter is linked with the next as stress and anxiety tend to go together—stress can lead to worry and anxiety, and anxiety can promote stress. Dealing with anxiety and causes of stress and anxiety is therefore an important task for the therapist. Even good things can cause stress and Dr Hans Selye, one of the pioneers of the modern study of stress[1] who introduced the terms eustress (good stress)[2] and distress (bad stress), showed that too much of either type, or *over-stress*, can cause problems. What we do can feel good, but it still may be stressful, and too much can be harmful. In fact any change that disturbs our internal equilibrium (homeostasis) and requires adaption can be stressful, though negative or distressful events are the most harmful. Stress is also caused by how we appraise events.

Holmes and Rahe (1967) provided a self-assessment questionnaire, called the Social Readjustment Rating Scale (SRRS), which gives stress scores to various life events, and the total is used determine susceptibility to illness and mental health problems.[3] A number of other questionnaires relating to stress are given by Girdano et al. (1997: chapter 5).

---

[1]Selye (1978); see also Cooper and Dewe (2004) for historical details.
[2]The prefix *eu* from the Greek means "good."
[3]The SRRS can be obtained from, for example,
http://chipts.ucla.edu/assessment/Assessment_Instruments/Assessment_files_new/assess_srrs.htm
or http:www.emotionalcompetency.com/srrs.htm (both accessed October 2010.

Counseling Issues: A Handbook for Counselors and Psychotherapists. By George A. F. Seber **115**
Copyright © 2013 G. A. F. Seber

5.1.1   Physical Effects of Stress

The heart is the central target for stress, caused by excessive adrenaline (also called epinephrine), and stress can also increase cholesterol levels and atherosclerosis (build up of plaque in the arteries), as well as increase the blood's tendency to clot.[4] More attention needs to be given to these latter aspects of stress. Even when the stress is gone, muscle tension may still remain. The build up of stress can be very subtle because we can continue to adapt to it until finally it becomes too much and we break down. When the stress is severe, some form of temporary medication may be necessary. Frequently a client comes for counseling on the advice of a health professional after they have been started on medication. Sometimes non-specific ailments caused by stress are misdiagnosed or the impact of stress is not appreciated.

Stress can arise internally or externally. Even the healing process can cause stress, for example after surgery. Hart[5] describes what happens when a person is stressed. The brain first sends messages along two pathways: first to the pituitary gland from the amygdala via the hypothalamus, which releases ACTH[6] that travels rapidly in the blood to stimulate the adrenal glands on top of the kidneys, and second through the brain stem and spinal chord to various places including the adrenals. The combined effect of these chemical and neural signals is to stimulate two major parts of the adrenal glands — the core and the cortex (exterior layer). The cortex releases cortisol and cortisone to help fight pain and inflammation. The core releases adrenaline (epinephrine) and noradrenaline (norepinephrine), which stimulate the heart to "fight, fright, or flight." In preparation for action, blood is shunted to the muscles and stomach, leaving cold hands. Short bursts of elevated adrenaline are okay, but high sustained levels can be very harmful. The amygdala, stimulated by adrenaline, can stir up emotional memories and elicit conditioned responses, thus producing a flood of feelings.

Stress can build up through having too much pressure put on us. We should be able to take a reasonable amount pressure without being distressed. Reasonable pressure can produce good stress that motivates us to get going. However, unreasonable pressure can lead to over-stress. Some people seem to cope better with pressure than others although it is unclear why. Clearly genetics and physiology will have something to do with it. However what is going on in our heads is just as important; how we view the pressure will have a lot of bearing on how much we get stressed. If we tell ourselves we can't cope with the pressure, we will get stressed; our self-talk can have a huge effect on how we cope with pressure. Pressure can arise in different areas of our lives such as health, age, responsibilities, time management, environment, and so forth.

When adrenaline is elevated, the body seems to be able to fight off disease and discomfort, and mild stress may enhance explicit memories. But when the adrenaline drops, the body returns all systems to a normal level of arousal. It is at this point we feel let down and symptoms such as headaches, diarrhea, fatigue, illness, rapid heartbeats, skipped beats, depression, and generalized anxiety may be felt, as the adrenaline no longer shields us. This feeling of "blues" is the normal

---

[4] Hart (1991: 15–17, 21, chapter 7).
[5] Hart (1991: 20).
[6] Adrenocorticotrophic hormone.

part of recovery from stress. Some people feel unwell on a weekend when away from work, or virtually "collapse in a heap" for the first few days of a vacation. Migraine sufferers report onsets at such times.

When the adrenaline level remains high for an extended period of time, the outer layer of the adrenal gland becomes enlarged, important lymph nodes shrink, and the stomach and intestines become irritated. The hippocampus begins to falter so that explicit memory is affected. The adrenal system eventually collapses forcing prolonged and severe fatigue—what is sometimes referred to as a "nervous break-down" or "nervous illness." This topic is discussed in detail in Section 6.4 of the next chapter. Prolonged adrenal exhaustion can cause "chronic fatigue syndrome, fibromyalgia, chronic bronchitis or sinusitis, and autoimmune disorders, ranging from lupus to rheumatoid arthritis."[7] Another effect of extreme stress is the sudden arrival of panic attacks, also discussed in the next chapter.

5.1.2 Stress and Personality Type

About 50% to 70% of people have a Type A personality (Section 1.3.2), which tends to produce higher levels of stress hormones, and others may have aspects of this as well. There is some evidence that the Type A behavior pattern is a learned behavior so that it can be unlearned, or at least modified.[8] Hart[9] comments that such people tend to have "hurry sickness," and one can argue that this is very much a characteristic of our present age, irrespective of our personality type. People moved a lot more slowly in the past (e.g., walking or riding, no electricity, wintertime restrictions, and so forth). As already indicated, we need some stress to function and to enjoy life. However, all stress can be dealt with or become good only if we bring ourselves back to a state of tranquillity as soon as possible; challenge and stress must be followed by relaxation and rest.

5.1.3 Substances Causing Stress

Substances like caffeine, alcohol, and nicotine, which can create dependency, and even too much sugar (causing a depletion of B-complex vitamins) or salt (causing an increase in blood pressure through fluid retention), are best avoided when a person is stressed.[10] Alcohol and nicotine addictions are discussed in Chapter 14. With regard to caffeine it is important to know the amount of caffeine consumed by a client since this is sometimes overlooked in dealing with stress symptoms as caffeine triggers adrenaline. A regular high level of caffeine such as 700–1000 mg can cause "caffeinism" (an agitated state induced by excessive ingestion of caffeine) and symptoms of stress.[11] Caffeine has a half-life of about five or six hours depending on a number of human variables so that drinking coffee late in the day can affect sleep. For those who want to kick the caffeine habit, it can take up to five days to recover from the addiction during which time they may experience a need to sleep, headaches, difficulty concentrating, mood changes, and an upset stomach.

[7] Bourne (2005: 333).
[8] Girdano et al. (1997: 1334).
[9] Hart (1991: 28–29).
[10] Girdano et al. (1997: 104–106).
[11] Caffeine in mg per cup is about 70 for instant coffee, 100 for real coffee, and 40 for tea, depending on individual taste.

Symptoms climax at the second day of withdrawal. Caffeine, which stimulates the central nervous system, can have physical benefits for some people with certain conditions.

5.2 SYMPTOMS OF STRESS

These can be many and varied and can include some of the following:

- chronic muscle tension that can act as partial blocks to the flow of blood (e.g., sore neck, shoulders, and back; tension headaches or migraines are common; and muscle cramps)

- disturbance of the digestive system is the most common symptom (e.g., loss of appetite, nervous stomach, stomach pain or ulcer, nausea, constipation, diarrhea)

- lungs affected (e.g., shortness of breath, respiratory problems, hyperventilation)

- insomnia (e.g., difficulty getting off to sleep, waking up too early, broken sleep)

- heart and circulation effects (e.g., rapid pulse, high blood pressure, cold hands and/or feet)

- persistent fatigue

- loss of enthusiasm for life (e.g., lack of excitement or interest in normal activities)

- other psychological difficulties (e.g., depression, anxiety, forgetfulness, loss of libido and other sexual problems such as erectile dysfunction in men and vaginal problems in women, mood swings, hyperactivity, overeating, difficulty concentrating, worrying, feeling "overloaded")

- interpersonal difficulties (e.g., irritability, anger, passive-aggressive behavior, lack of friends, competitiveness)

Stress can also deplete our immune system, deplete naturally produced pain-killing hormones called endorphins, and deplete the body's natural tranquilizers.

All of the above symptoms can be used to monitor our level of stress. However, two simple ones that can be self-administered at any time are my pulse rate (I need to have a base line for what is "normal" for me, say, its level first thing in the morning when I'm properly relaxed) and the skin temperature of my hand, determined by holding my hand to my cheek.[12] The rule is: The warmer the hand the lower the adrenaline arousal, and a cold hand indicates adrenaline arousal. The drop in hand temperature will vary from person to person so we need to experiment a bit to find out our own personal response. We also need to take into account the

[12]Hart (1991: chapter 9).

temperature of our environment as low temperatures will lead to cold hands without there being any stress.[13]

Hart[14] reminds us that stress generally begins in the mind but ends in the body. Our body is designed to protect us from stress with an alarm system (e.g., tension pain), an activation system to respond to the alarm (e.g., release of adrenaline), and a recovery system to help us back to normal. If we ignore these systems then we can get into trouble! Unfortunately, some people can become addicted to adrenaline and some symptoms of this include:[15]

- preferring to be active than sleeping

- feeling restless when activity is stopped

- only feeling good when engaged in activity, and otherwise feeling low

- finding activity helps a person to forget his or her problems

- thinking a lot about one's activity when away from it

A related topic is the addiction of workaholism, discussed in Section 14.6, which can be linked to adrenaline. Sexual addiction may also be driven by adrenaline (Section 14.3).

When withdrawing from adrenaline addiction, typical symptoms are:[16]

- strong compulsion to do something

- obsession with thoughts about what remains to be done

- a vague feeling of guilt when resting

- fidgeting, restlessness, and inability to concentrate for very long on any relaxing activity

- a vague feeling of depression when one stops an activity

A common time when people may feel these symptoms is at the beginning of a vacation. This can lead to a person being very restless for several days.

How much adrenaline do we need to perform tasks? Not as much as we think; in fact, our creativity is increased and our memory improved when we relax. Some people think they work better mentally under pressure, especially when they have a tight deadline to work to. My experience over a long and demanding academic career is that the way I retain my mental stamina and creativity is to continually focus on relaxing and not allow time to dominate my thinking; short breaks are important. We don't allow ourselves to get worked up as time passes and try too hard! However, when it comes to action rather than creative thinking, our efficiency tends to go up with the rise in adrenaline until it reaches a maximum and then begins to fall off as the adrenaline continues to rise further.[17]

---

[13]Two other symptoms are tense muscles, especially around the neck and shoulders, and blood pressure, though not every one has their own monitor to measure it.
[14]Hart (1991: 49).
[15]Hart (1991: 69).
[16]Hart (1991: 71).
[17]This ∩-shaped trend between arousal and activity, called the Yerkes-Dodson law, is fully described on the internet.

5.3   TIME MANAGEMENT

Stress can sometimes be due to poor time management skills (or more appropriately, poor self-management skills). If a client answers yes to any of the following, then he or she may benefit from considering some time management skills.[18]

- underestimating the time to finish a task and not having enough time for the next task

- trying to do too many things in the time available

- unable to stop what he or she is doing in order to do the next task

- having difficulty prioritizing activities

- having difficulty delegating nonessential tasks to others

5.3.1   Management Skills

Bourne suggests developing the following skills for time management:[19]

1. *Prioritization.* List tasks as *essential, important,* and *less important,* and do them in that order. Having had a busy life, I find the greatest temptation is to use the order of easy, moderately difficult, and difficult and go with the easy stuff first. We all have different periods of the day when we are most alert so that, where possible, it might be appropriate to do the essential but difficult tasks then or at a time when there are least interruptions. Some relaxation and downtime need to be part of the *essential* category. The key is planning well in advance; short and long-term goal setting is essential. Breaking large tasks into smaller ones is always helpful.

   In discussing assignment preparation, students sometimes say that they work better under pressure (often as an excuse for leaving things to the last minute). It is true that people work harder if the pressure is increased, but do they work better? As I noted above, stress adversely affects both memory and creativity, and I personally have found that my best ideas have always come when I am relaxed and my mind is at rest. Covey[20] in habit number three, "Put first things first," which deals with time management, uses the table below:

Table 5.1   Time Management Matrix.

	Urgent	Not urgent
Important	I Crises etc.	II Planning etc.
Not important	III Some mail or meetings etc.	IV Time wasters etc.

[18]Bourne (2005: 86).
[19]Adapted from Bourne (2005: 86–89).
[20]Covey (1989).

Covey describes the above table as four quadrants and emphasizes that effective people stay out of quadrants III and IV as they are unimportant, even if urgent. They also spend more time in quadrant II by reducing the time spent in quadrant I. A helpful diagram is to divide up the four regions to reflect the time spent in each, for example:

Table 5.2   Division of Time.

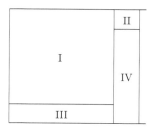

This table indicates a person dominated by crises with little time given to planning; burn out is then likely. Covey emphasizes that his habit 3 depends very much on habits 1 and 2, and his book should be consulted for further details.

2. *Delegation.* This may mean paying someone to do more mundane things that you used to do to free up your time, for example car washing, if you are able to afford it. It also may mean investing some time in training someone else. This may be difficult for someone who likes complete control.

3. *Allow extra time.* A common problem is underestimating the time required to complete a task so that stress builds up. Extra time needs to be allowed for each task so that fewer tasks should be scheduled.

4. *Relinquish perfectionism.* This is also tied up with our personal beliefs concerning expectations of self and others.

5. *Overcoming procrastination.* Often there are essential tasks we don't like doing and we put them off. If we can't delegate, then it may help to do those tasks first. It's best not to think too much about them but simply jump in and get started. My experience is that tasks that we don't want to do, perhaps because we perceive them as difficult, often turn out to be quite straightforward once we begin them. We can ask ourselves why we don't want to do the particular tasks and imagine doing them.

5. *Saying no.* Some people find this difficult to do and it is often associated with the problem of inadequate boundaries.[21] The inability to say no can be tied up with perfectionism or codependency,[22] and it may be linked with our self-image.

---

[21]See Section 17.2 for further details on boundaries.
[22]Section 17.4.

5.4 COUNSELING FOR STRESS

5.4.1 Session Outline

A suggested rough guide for sessions is as follows:[23]

1. After the first introductory session, review the client's present state in follow-up sessions. This involves asking the client how he or she has been since the last session. Progress can be assessed using "scaling" whereby the client uses a number from 0 to 10 to assess his or her performance thus far. Focussing on the positives and giving encouragement is always helpful. How long all this will take depends on the therapist's counseling method. Rather than dealing immediately with any problems that arise, the therapist can move to the next step.

2. Set the agenda. Any issues raised in (1) can be negotiated with the client to put on the agenda in order of priority. Questions can be asked such as, "What would you like to focus on today?", "What changes would you like to make?", and "Is there one part of the problem that, if solved, would help the other parts?" An agreement to review any homework assignments is needed early on as they may affect subsequent counseling. Thoughts and feelings about the last session can also be added, for example, a client may comment on how helpful or unhelpful a particular technique taught in the last session has been. If it seems unlikely that all the issues raised can't be covered in one session, then there can be a mutual agreement to transfer some of the issues to the next session.

3. Review homework assignment(s). It is important for the therapist to keep a clear record of any assignments set in the previous session so that they are not overlooked. Otherwise the client may get the message that homework is not important.

4. Target the problem. Agenda items can now be followed up.

5. Negotiate homework assignment(s). In doing this the client can be asked in what way he or she thinks how a particular exercise might be helpful. For those clients who find the word "homework" unsettling, "assignments tasks" can be used instead.

6. Have a session feedback. Stressed clients can sometimes get things wrong or misunderstand some comments so it is helpful to check for any problems and enquire what was helpful or unhelpful about the session.

5.4.2 Stress Assessment

The aim of stress management is to try and reduce the frequency, intensity, and especially the duration of stress responses. As stress can affect all aspects of life, a first step for the therapist is to carry out a broad assessment to locate the main sources and triggers of a client's stress, bearing in mind that it is often the cumulative effect of minor hassles that causes at least as much stress as the big events.

---

[23] Adapted from Palmer and Dryden (1995: 40).

One method of assessment, used by Palmer and Dryden,[24] is the BASIC ID assessment associated with multimodal behavioral therapy described in Section 1.4.3.[25] Another similar method looks at the following areas of life:

1. *Home.* Difficulties in couple relationships in the immediate and extended family can cause stress. Questions like, "How often do you get angry or irritated by someone at home?" and "How happy are you when you are at home?" can help client focus. Being overloaded with household chores or family care can be a problem.

2. *Work.* Typical questions might be: "Any problems with the boss or other staff?", " Is there too much or too little work to do?", "Are there too many different colleagues telling you conflicting things to do?" and "Are the working conditions satisfactory?" These days, even just commuting to and from work can be very stressful. Such things as lack of financial rewards, promotion opportunities, and career guidance, along with such difficulties as over-specialization, job complexity, lack of a clear job description, lack of training, the setting of unrealistic targets, work overload, discrimination or sexual harassment, internal bureaucracy, boredom, poor internal communication, and poor working conditions (e.g., excess noise, poor lighting, uncomfortable temperature, inadequate working space) all add to stress in the workplace.[26] Some occupations are by nature stressful such as those with low control and high demand, frequent deadlines, serious responsibilities, or crisis situations that need solving. The internet is becoming a source of stress for some as it can involve constant multi-tasking that can lead to shallower thinking, weakened concentration, reduced creativity, and heightened stress.

3. *Health.* Often when clients come with stress problems they may have been referred by a health-care worker such as a physician and may have been put on medication. They can be asked how they feel about that and how the medication is or is not helping. An inappropriate diet can also add to stress.

4. *Recreation.* Exercise and sport are very good alleviators of stress, and being fit can raise one's stress threshold and inoculate a person against future stresses. Such activity enhances the body's ability to adjust and to respond quickly to challenges. As stress prepares our bodies for action, the best way to disperse the stress products formed in our organs is to use the arousal for its intended purpose, namely physical movement. Physical activity also promotes a feeling of well-being through the release of endorphins. However, such activities should not be too intense as the end result might be an increase in stress (e.g., elevated pulse, over-tiredness). Playing a club sport can be rewarding in terms of friendship, but it can also be stressful if you play, for example, in an inter-club competition where there is pressure to win for your team. To get the full stress benefits from exercise, you therefore need to avoid any physical activity that involves competition with others or yourself. A good long walk does wonders for peace of mind and posture!

---

[24] Palmer and Dryden (1995).
[25] See also http://www.managingstress.com/articles/webpage3.htm (accessed October 2010).
[26] Adapted from Girdano et al. (1997: chapter 12).

5. *Intrapersonal.* Here a person's basic beliefs, self-perception, and questions of time urgency, control, and anger can lead to excessive stress. Other personal stressors might include sleep difficulties, pain,[27] addictive practices, poor nutrition, boredom, loneliness, and financial difficulties. Some people have a genetic predisposition for a heightened reactivity to stress, and childhood exposure to traumatic events can have a similar effect.[28]

6. *Interpersonal.* This could include things like neighbor problems, overcrowding, noise, flatting problems, dysfunctional friends and relationships, and bureaucracy (e.g., trying to sort out a problem with a large commercial or governmental organization, or being part of such an organization). Church or some other religious gathering might be included here as religious organizations can sometimes bring stress into people's lives, perhaps because of unreasonable demands.

Two aspects of life that are linked to all of the above areas are time and worry. With regard to time, suitable questions might be, "Do you always feel you must do something before some deadline?" and "Do you have a feeling that time is 'running out' for you?" Worry or "anticipatory stress" is a feeling of anxiety about impending events and is mentioned briefly in Section 6.1.2 in the next chapter.

One approach to the above is to use a type of mind map[29] showing all stressors, called "stress mapping," that can be used along with scaling to summarize the information obtained by exploring the above six areas with the client.[30] Lazarus[31] says that work and family create the two most important sources of daily stress in modern adult life, especially where both husbands and wives work and share in homemaking and raising the children. He notes that work cannot be isolated from other aspects of a person's life. Lazarus says that men often won't tell their wives about their work stress to avoid upsetting their wives, which would stress the men even more. Also, they also don't want to be seen as not being up to work challenges. Unfortunately the work stress is visible to their wives and children, and not talking about it can be upsetting for the wives. Giving advice to her husband can be risky and unhelpful!

Linden[32] describes one way of *categorizing stimuli* that may lead to determining stressors is to use a $2 \times 2 \times 2$ model with three dichotomies, namely external/internal stimulus origin, high/low predictability (or chronic/acute), and high/low control, as set out in the following Table 5.3. For each type of stimulus origin there are four possibilities, giving eight categories in all.

Acute stress is provoked by time-limited, major or minor events that are upsetting at a particular moment or for a relatively brief period. Chronic stress arises from harmful or threatening but stable conditions of life or from a stressful role in life.[33] Linden gives several examples using the $2 \times 2 \times 2$ model and I include two. First, suppose an individual experiences a sudden migraine coming on and knows that he has enough painkillers to get him through the attack. This stimulus

[27]This topic is discussed briefly in Section 1.2.6.
[28]Linden (2005: 18–19).
[29]See "Mind map" on the internet and Buzan (1991).
[30]Palmer (1990).
[31]R. Lazarus (1999: 132).
[32]Linden (2005: 45–49).
[33]R. Lazarus (1999: 144–146).

Table **5.3** $2 \times 2 \times 2$ Model.

Stimulus		Predictability		Control	
Ext.	Int.	High	Low	High	Low

can be described as internal stimulus/acute stress (low predictability)/high control. Second, consider a person involved in a daily traffic jam getting onto a particular bridge then we have a stimulus that can be described as external stimulus/chronic stress (low predictability)/low control. Although somewhat crude, the method does at least give the therapist some ideas for categorizing stressors.

For solution-focused (brief) therapy, one way of focusing clients is to ask them to put their problem into one word and then into a sentence. The problem statement is then converted into achievable goals and activities and the therapist then explores whether any of these activities have happened recently.[34] The "miracle question" can be helpful here, for example, "What would life be like if you woke up tomorrow morning and you were free from stress?" or "If you woke up one morning and all the problems you brought to counseling today were solved but nobody told you, what would you find?" Another opening approach is to ask clients to list the five most stressful things they have to do and then discuss strategies for coping with these.

We should be aware that clients may find it difficult to explain how they feel. Saying they are stressed is not helpful and other additional descriptive words may need to be found, for example, angry stressed or depressed stressed. There will be times of emergency when we want all the adrenaline we can get to go into action (e.g., a life threatening situation), but afterwards we need to get back to normal adrenaline levels by appropriately relaxing. However, not every situation is an emergency situation so that monitoring and preventing a build-up are important. It is helpful for the client to eventually come up with a stress management plan for each of the above areas of life using some of the strategies given below. Some care is needed in dealing with each stressful item. Lazarus[35] gives the example about a man very worried about sitting an exam. Telling him that there is nothing to worry about is challenging the legitimacy of his feelings. Then saying that he passed all previous exams with flying colors adds to the pressure of not just passing but doing well. Instead, looking at the worst possible scenario and how he will manage that may be more help.

5.4.3   Stress Reduction Methods

Once the client is aware of his or her stress triggers and identifies the presence of stress and its effect (e.g., physical or psychological or both), the next step is to consider how adrenaline levels be can lowered and stress reduced to manageable levels. This will vary from person to person and some suggestions follow that the therapist might find useful:

[34]O'Connell (2001: 44).
[35]R. Lazarus (1999: 135).

1. Use relaxation techniques throughout the day to avoid a build up of stress.[36] Also using such a technique can be helpful both before and after a particularly stressful event (e.g., chairing a meeting or public speaking). When we are relaxed we can become more self-aware (e g , of the tense parts of our body), achieve better pain control, and be more in touch with our emotions.[37] For many people it begins with learning to be still; a form of meditation.

2. Learn to cope with what Hart calls the "adrenaline emotions" of anger, frustration, irritation, resentment, and hostility, as they tend to stimulate adrenaline production.[38]

3. Learn to recognize distorted thinking and erroneous beliefs.

4. Have a clear picture of one's goals so as to focus on essentials, rather than get caught up with details that can sidetrack and cause stress. We need SMART goals.[39]

5. Learn to deliberately slow down. We can do this by, for example, walking more slowly and allowing more time in traveling (e.g., driving) from A to B so that we are more relaxed on arrival. We can talk and eat more slowly and learn to be a better listener.

6. Try not to stress others —it is catching!

7. Good self-talk is helpful, like telling myself "I can't solve everybody's problems" or asking myself "If I succeed in this activity, will it be worth it in terms of the stress involved?" The therapist may need to help the client challenge some ingrained destructive beliefs and do some reframing. For example, clients who are harder on themselves than their friends may be asked whether they would say to a friend who faced a similar problem the same negative things they say to themselves and, if not, what would they say instead. They then reframe those negative thoughts and give themselves the same encouraging messages that they would give to their friend.

8. Plan ahead when a time of stress is coming up and try not to do too much just prior to that time (e.g., restrict demands made on me and what I put on myself and aim to have adequate or even extra sleep, if possible). Plan to follow up the stressful period with planned recovery time.

9. Develop some time-management skills if necessary.

10. Learn structured problem solving. This is described in Section 9.4.2 and the steps there may be summarized as follows.

    1. Identify the problem and obtain relevant information about it.

    2. Generate alternative solutions.

    3. List the pros and cons of each solution.

[36] See Section 2.2.5 for details.
[37] Barrow and Place (1995: 32–35).
[38] Hart (1991: 122).
[39] See Section 2.3.2.

4. Make a rational choice.

5. Evaluate the desired outcome. Return to steps 2 or 3 if the outcome is undesirable.

This can be applied to stressors uncovered in the six areas of assessment discussed in the previous section.

11. Clients need to change their attitude towards time urgency, especially if they are of Type-A disposition, by for example having a shorter daily priority list. They need to put their thinking on hold and quieten their minds from time to time. They also need to accept the fact that they will always have unfinished business and need to be relaxed about having some things unfinished each day. Certain beliefs may need to be challenged, for example, thinking involving words like "must," "should," and "ought" can lead to internal stress and the client perceiving something being more stressful than it really is.

12. Use thought stopping when anxious or obsessional thoughts intrude.[40] Other techniques like counting backwards can also help. Regular practice is needed beginning with the least disturbing thoughts.

13. Establish daily routines for home and work, meals, exercise, sleep, rest, and recreation.

14. Be careful about life changes (e.g., giving up something such as smoking) as they can add to the stress. If change must happen, plan well ahead for the desired specific changes.

15. Own a pet. A well-trained animal can lower stress levels. For example, dogs need to be walked daily, thus providing sustained exercise for the owner. Animals can also provide social support.

In negotiating change with a client, the therapist might find it helpful to use the Wheel-of-Change model used in addiction (see Section 12.7.2), as adrenaline can be addictive. Further techniques for managing various kinds of stressors are given by Girdano et al. (1997). In Chapter 2 a number of recommendations are listed under "physical" (Section 2.2), which can be particularly helpful in reducing stress. To minimize any relapse after counseling, some possible future stressors can be discussed and strategies developed.[41]

5.4.4   Sleep

Sleep is an area that will invariably come up when discussing stress as many things can disturb our normal sleep pattern[42] and affect the quality and quantity of a person's sleep. Strategies for improving sleep are discussed in Section 6.2.2. Cognitive restructuring combined with a relaxation technique can be used on nights when daytime stressors are keeping us awake. To wake up tired, if we have slept long, is good news if we are fighting the effects of stress. It means that our body has really switched off and, after several such nights, we will generally wake up refreshed.

[40]See Section 1.4.4.
[41]See also the relapse strategies of Section 12.7.2.
[42]See Section 2.2.4.

5.4.5 Counseling Style

The above discussion focuses on specific interventions rather than a particular approach to counseling. Therapists will bring their own styles to the counseling room and these can be very different in dealing with stress. For example, we have solution-focused therapy[43] and cognitive restructuring,[44] both discussed above, and the eclectic multimodal behavioral therapy.[45] The solution-focused approach combines certain aspects of person-centered with narrative therapy where, for example, the focus is on the following: solutions to problems rather than the cause of problems, present and future not past, change more than just insight, what is wanted rather than what has happened, what is right rather than what is wrong (e.g., looking for exceptions when the stress was less and utilizing client strengths and coping skills), staying with surface rather than deep material, solutions fitting the client rather than the problem, and the counselor learning from the client rather than the other way round. A similar method is structured problem solving discussed in Section 9.4.2.

5.5 BIBLICAL VIEWPOINT

Some scriptural strategies for overcoming stress are as follows.

1. Seek first God's kingdom and God will take care of the necessities of life.[46]
2. Know that God cares for us and provides peace and rest.[47]
3. Set realistic goals and time frames that are based on a realistic assessment of our strengths and weaknesses and available time.[48]
4. Organize our time wisely.[49]
5. Know how to delegate.[50]
6. Look after our bodies.[51]
7. Be content with what we have so that our lives are not dominated by a love of money.[52]

Christian clients need to be aware that God is interested in who they are rather than just what they do, so it is a matter of balancing priorities. From their perspective, it may not be surprising that when they try to live a godly life in a godless world and facing opposition from evil spiritual powers that they become stressed.[53]

---

[43] O'Connell (2001).
[44] Ellis, Gordon, Neenan, and Palmer (1997).
[45] Dryden and Palmer (1995).
[46] Matthew 6: 25–34 and Philippians 4:19.
[47] Isaiah 26:3; Philippians 4:6–7; 1 Peter 5:7; and Matthew 11:28.
[48] Romans 12:3.
[49] Ephesians 5:15–16.
[50] See the story of Moses in Genesis 18:34ff.
[51] 1 Corinthians 3:16, 6:19.
[52] Hebrews 13:5.
[53] For example see Luke 10:38–42.

Unfortunately some Christian workers (and religious workers in general) have inadequate job specifications so that there are no limits on what they think they should do in their work, which can lead to stress and depression. Their self-imposed expectations and even expectations imposed by those they seek to serve may never be met. This problem is especially true for those who are self-employed or for pastors in a sole pastoral role. Jesus was very aware of the need for a recovery time in people's busy lives when he told his disciples to draw aside and rest awhile.[54]

God took rest seriously by instituting the Sabbath rest. Stress can dampen one's spirituality, upset one's prayer life,[55] and bring out the worst in people. It can also lead to confusing adrenaline arousal with true spirituality when Christians become "hyped up."[56] Christians need to ask God to help them to slow down, which they can do by waiting on God.[57]

Many of the problems raised in this chapter can be alleviated by the client having a spiritual approach to life. By turning over their problems and anxiety to a Higher Power they can be more relaxed about their future. This is the basis of step 3 in all 12-step programs (cf. Section 12.7.2); a Christian version is given in Section 12.8. David, the psalmist, certainly knew about this in his eventful life.[58] People also need to be aware that sin in their lives can be a source of stress and stress a source of sin so that seeking God's forgiveness, which God has promised, can help bring peace. Finally, as stress is linked to anxiety, further related Biblical texts are given at the ends of the next two chapters.

---

[54]Mark 6:31.
[55]Psalms 46:10, which speaks about the need to "be still."
[56]Hart (1991: 390).
[57]Psalms 25:5, 27:14, and 62:5.
[58]Psalms 55:22.

CHAPTER 6

ANXIETY AND FEAR

6.1 INTRODUCTION

6.1.1 Anxiety-Related Disorders

We all get anxious from time to time as we live in a rapidly changing world. Many people struggle with anxiety, which seems to be on the increase. Anxiety and fear are closely related, though anxiety comes from within us while fear tends to come from the outside world; anxiety has been described as unresolved fear.[1] Anxiety is universal, and my initial comments about anxiety refer to the general sense of rumination or worry about possible negative future outcomes. Bourne[2] categorizes anxiety as "free-floating" (it occurs for no apparent reason), situational (it arises in response to a specific situation), or anticipatory (worry about what might happen). When the anxiety is more extreme, it can present as a generalized anxiety disorder or it can develop into a full-blown panic attack marked by heart palpitations, disorientation, and terror. Panic attacks are discussed in Section 6.4.2, anxiety associated with specific disorders such as the free-floating generalized anxiety disorder (GAD) is discussed in the next chapter, and obsessive compulsive disorder (OCD) in Chapter 8. Some phobias arise out of fear of panic attacks, and phobias are considered in the next chapter along with post-traumatic stress

---

[1] Öhman (1993).
[2] Bourme (2005: 5–6).

disorder, which involves severe anxiety arising, for example, from some extreme past event. The aim of this chapter is to look at general methods for counseling clients with specific anxiety problems. But first some comments about worry.

6.1.2 Worry

Worry is one of the root causes of anxiety. If something is worrying us, we may believe that if we keep thinking about it we will somehow cope better with it or change it, instead of letting it go. This is particularly the case if we can't do anything about the problem worrying us; we have a choice to be positive or negative about it. Ruminating is not problem solving. We have the example of the person who works hard at the office and when he or she comes home there is an inability to leave worries at the front door. Consequently the person may be irritable and yell at the cat (or his or her partner!) and sleep badly. Sleep deprivation makes the next day worse and a downward spiral begins as stress builds up, with depression not far behind.

Worry can be about "things" or relationships. People who are compassionate may tend to worry more than most about relationships out of their real concern for the well-being of others. However, worry can be experienced as compulsive and very intrusive and may lead to being diagnosed as Generalized Anxiety Disorder (GAD), discussed in the next chapter. The worry might be about future harmful events and often these events are very unlikely to happen. A typical expression is then "What if ...." It is useful for a client to keep a diary so as to identify the things that trigger the worrying and to note which activities and situations help a client to forget their worries, for example exercise and hobbies that fully engage a person's attention. When indecision is a source of worry, problem solving techniques can be used, for example listing pros and cons with scores of importance out of ten. Working with clients on this will often bring to light irrational beliefs and assumptions that can be disputed. The aim is not make a decision for them but to encourage them to come up with their own solutions.

A cognitive approach to a worry is to first identify the worry, then identify the negative beliefs (e.g., over-predicting the likelihood of bad outcomes or thinking one cannot cope if difficulties occur) and look at the emotional consequences of the beliefs, and finally challenge the negative beliefs with alternative ideas and beliefs. A helpful idea is to schedule a fixed time of say 30 minutes called "worry time" when clients repeatedly goes over their list of worries. Clients soon learn that you can't worry on demand or *make* yourself worry so that they realize the fleeting nature of these intrusive thoughts. The idea then is to own the worry and postpone it before beginning to change the habit.

If a client has a worrying decision to make (e.g., whether to leave one's partner or not, or change jobs), but does not want to decide just yet, then he or she can choose a future date when he or she will make the decision. The client is then able to put the decision and the consequent worry aside for the time being.

SLEEP PROBLEMS AND DISORDERS

6.1.3 Personality Styles

Certain personality styles may contribute to worry and anxiety, and Bourne lists the following:[3]

1. *Perfectionism.* It is helpful to ask clients how they determine their worth (by their achievements and accomplishments?). Their thinking style may include should/must thinking (parent messages?), all-or-nothing thinking ("I can't do it" instead of "If I break it down into small steps I can do it") and overgeneralization ("I always get it wrong"). They can be encouraged to focus on the positive things they have done and not on small errors. Goals need to be realistic and clients need to have a bit more fun and recreation in their lives.

2. *Excessive need for approval.* People react to criticism in different ways. Criticism of what we do is not the same as criticism of who we are. If, after careful evaluation, we find that the criticism is valid, then a helpful self-message is "This criticism is a good opportunity to learn something." Another helpful message is: "If someone doesn't like me it doesn't mean I am unlikeable." For example, anger is usually directed at someone and not always at the source of the anger. There will always be people who don't like us, often for irrational reasons. Sometimes people project their own faults on to others! The need for approval can also lead to codependency and Bourne gives a helpful check list for recognizing codependency, for example, "I should keep people I love happy" or "It is usually my fault if someone I care about is upset with me."[4]

3. *Tendency to ignore signs of stress.* When a person is out of touch with their body, they can ignore the stress signals and end up with a breakdown or a range of anxiety problems. Stress is discussed in more detail in the previous chapter.

4. *Excessive need for control.* Life is unpredictable and there are times when we all wish we had a bit more control of our circumstances. One couple I counseled had arguments that escalated until they came to realize that they were both fighting for control because for much of their individual lives they felt powerless over circumstances. Patience and acceptance need to be cultivated, especially if there are unrealistic expectations. I am great believer in using humor in counseling, where appropriate, as people who like control need to take themselves less seriously.

6.2 SLEEP PROBLEMS AND DISORDERS

6.2.1 Introduction

People who have problems with worry and anxiety often have sleep problems. The reader should refer to some general comments about sleeping and the sleep cycle given in Section 2.2.4. A number of things such as anxiety, stress, depression, and medical problems can disturb the normal sleep pattern and affect the quality and

---

[3]Bourne (2005: chapter 10).
[4]Codependency is discussed in Section 17.4 and a related topic is relationship addiction (see 14.5).

quantity of our sleep. If you think your client might have a sleep disorder, and there are a number of them (e.g., sleep apnea, periodic limb movements, restless legs syndrome, delayed phase disorder, bruxism/teeth grinding, and narcolepsy), there are several useful websites for symptoms and diagnosis.[5]

Insomnia is the most common sleep problem and most people have a spell of it at some stage in their life. According to British and American sleep researchers, between 15 and 30% of the population are affected by insomnia.[6] It is more common among women and the elderly, and research suggests that it may linked to alterations in the body temperature and circadian rhythm. Insomnia may manifest itself as difficulty in getting off to sleep, waking up during the night or waking up too early, or having poor quality sleep. The occasional night without sleep won't harm us, except leaving us tired the next day. If insomnia lasts more than a month, then some help may be needed. Insomnia is generally a learned problem that can be unlearned.[7]

6.2.2   Strategies to Improve Sleep

Being anxious or worrying about going to sleep will hinder sleep. The therapist can explore what the client thinks about sleeping. Cognitive behavioral therapy (CBT) can be used to help change faulty thinking and negative thoughts about sleep. For example, we can counter "I need at least eight hours of sleep to cope the next day" with "I don't necessarily need eight hours as everybody is different" or with "I will naturally catch up on my sleep over the next few nights." Another thought might be: "I didn't sleep a wink last night." However, insomniacs are generally not accurate in estimating how much sleep they actually get as they tend to over-estimate how long they are awake during the night.[8] A common thought is: "How will I function today after such a horrible night of sleep?" This can be countered with the fact that provided they get "core" sleep (deep sleep), which is about five and a half hours, they will be able to function adequately the next day.

There are two useful facts that Jacobs mentions that can be passed on to clients:[9] (1) There is no consistent scientific evidence that insomnia causes significant health problems; other factors such as nutrition, stress, exercise, and environmental factors can affect how we are and how we perform during the day, and (2) we have a remarkable tolerance for sleep loss, at least on a temporary basis.

Jacobs[10] suggests a number of sleep scheduling techniques and they are based on the concepts of *prior wakefulness* and *sleep efficiency*. Prior wakefulness is the time between getting up in the morning and "lights out" at night, while sleep efficiency refers to the percentage of time spent in bed that a person is asleep. Good sleepers may have an efficiency of 90% (i.e. asleep for 90% of the time in bed) while a poor sleeper might only manage 65%. For the former group, bed becomes associated with sleep while for the latter bed becomes associated with wakefulness. Because

---

[5] See, for example www.helpguide.org/topic_index.htm (enter "sleep disorders") and www.rcpsych.ac.uk/mentalhealthinformation/mentalhealthproblems/sleepproblems/sleepingwell.aspx (both accessed October 2010).
[6] Johnston (1998: 11).
[7] Jacobs (1999: 12).
[8] Jacobs (1999: 77).
[9] Jacobs (1999: 78–79).
[10] Jacobs (1999: chapter 6).

our sleep pattern is related to body temperature, Jacobs' first rule is that we should get up around the same time every day including weekends irrespective of how we feel or how we slept as this will help stabilize the body temperature cycle. As noted in Section 2.2.4, our sleep cycle is 25 hours long on average so there may be an innate tendency to oversleep. If we sleep in one morning, our temperature cycle will be upset. Strategies for dealing with this are: Don't sleep in for more than an hour, get early exposure to sunlight to raise the body temperature, and go to bed later that night. Similar ideas apply to coping with jet lag.

Jacobs' second rule is to increase our sleep efficiency by reducing our time in bed so that it matches roughly how much time we actually sleep on average (not how much time we spend in bed) plus about an additional hour, which may mean going to bed later. Staying awake long enough may be a problem so that some light activity might be needed earlier on in the evening. This regime is maintained until sleep efficiency is at least 85% for two weeks and then we increase the time in bed by 15 minutes each week while maintaining the 85%. It should be emphasized with a client that reducing time in bed will not reduce sleep time provided at least five and a half hours are allowed for core (deep) sleep.

A sleep diary will be needed to keep track of clients' sleep patterns over a couple of weeks. Information recorded could include bed hours, amount of sleep, time to get off to sleep, breaks in sleep, quality of sleep, feelings, negative sleep thoughts, what they did when awake during the night, what they did and what food and drink they consumed before going to bed, and medications used.[11] This sounds a lot of information. However, the aim is not to get hung up with recording during the night as clock watching can be counter productive, but simply to get a rough idea of sleep patterns. The key information is to find out how many hours of sleep clients get so as to determine what time to go to bed once the getting-up time has been determined.They also need to identify habits that may interfere with sleep.

In addition to going to bed earlier or sleeping later, insomniacs may try a number of things to get off to sleep such as trying harder to sleep, trying to relax in bed by watching TV or reading, drinking alcohol, and reducing physical activity during the day because of fatigue. None of these strategies is appropriate and a number of general suggestions, gleaned from various sources, to help a client with insomnia are listed below (not in any particular order):

1. Have a good supporting mattress and pillow. People with physical problems may need extra body pillows or a special pillow for neck comfort.

2. Don't do anything late at night that stimulates adrenaline (e.g., watch an exciting movie on TV).

3. Take some time to relax properly before going to bed (e.g., switch off the phone). Having a fixed routine can prepare the mind for sleep.

4. Reduce the level of illumination early in the evening. Darkness begins the production of melatonin that tells the body to get ready for sleep. Make sure your bedroom is dark enough (or use a mask). Conversely, soon after waking up in the morning, expose yourself to bright light/sunlight to help regulate your biological clock.

[11] For helpful details and assessment forms see Jacobs (1999).

5. Avoid being too close to electromagnetic radiation as it can interfere with the production of melatonin. For example, have an illuminated electric clock no closer than a meter (three feet) and do not sleep with the electric blanket on.

6. Avoid alcohol as it interferes with sleep patterns. It may help you fall asleep (light sleep) but you will generally wake up during the night and have your deep sleep disturbed. Also avoid caffeine, nicotine, chocolates, large amounts of food or spicy foods that may cause stomach discomfort before going to bed. Caffeine hangs around for many hours after your last drink of tea or coffee so it may be best to stop drinking it by mid-afternoon. However, cheese cubes contain L-tryptophan,[12] a natural amino acid that has been found to promote sleep.[13] Eating turkey on an empty stomach is also helpful for the same reason. Some find milk drinks, cereal, and bananas beneficial for various reasons; hunger should be avoided.[14] Johnston[15] suggests snacking on foods containing tryptophan during the day and evening such as dairy products, bananas, dates, and tuna. Some herbal drinks may also be beneficial, though for some people it may be best to avoid fluids before bedtime (e.g., prostate problems with men). Iron deficient women tend to have more problems sleeping, so a blood test for iron levels can be helpful.

7. Some medications can interfere with sleep (e.g., some antidepressants such as prozac, steroids, some drugs for treating high blood pressure, alpha blockers for enlarged prostate, nasal decongestants that contain stimulants, and thyroid hormones).

8. For women, sleep can be affected by pregnancy (e.g., during the last trimester), menopause, and premenstrual syndrome.

9. Don't try to force sleep. As mentioned above, trying to force sleep can create problems. It is better to lower adrenaline arousal first and go over suggestions from cognitive counseling. Worry about not getting to sleep and fighting sleeplessness will make sleeping more difficult. The key is acceptance knowing that the odd night with little sleep will not hurt you.

10. Achieve quietness, with ear plugs if necessary, though one can get used to certain types of noise (e.g., traffic noise). The hum of a fan can be soothing as it helps to drown out distracting noises. Music may be helpful but it should switch off after about 45 minutes as it can disturb deep sleep. If the slightest noise wakes you up it might be helpful to make a sleep affirmation like "I will sleep deeply and easily throughout the night."

11. Make sure the bedroom temperature is not too hot as it will raise body temperature and affect the sleep cycle.

12. Have a warm bath (perhaps with a few drops of lavender oil in it) several hours before going to bed to ease stress.

[12] A major building block for making serotonin which can be converted to melatonin.
[13] See www.helpguide.org/life/insomnia_treatment.htm then "Food and herbs."
[14] Although dairy products contain a minimal amount of tryptophan, it is generally not enough to affect sleep.
[15] Johnston (1998: 48).

13. Exercising earlier in the day usually promotes sleep. Avoid exercise before going to bed, though stretching can be helpful.

14. Exposure to bright sunlight during the day can also help with sleep.

15. Reduce stress in your life and deal with negative self talk.

16. Reduce anger and enjoy humor.

17. Learn a relaxation technique (see Section 2.2.5) for tense muscles and a racing mind; it can produce a brain-wave pattern similar to stage one sleep. There are a number of tapes and CDs on the market that might be useful.

18. Free up your mind. If something is worrying you and there is nothing you can do about it straight away, try writing it down before going to bed and then tell yourself to deal with it tomorrow.

19. Do not use your bedroom as an office (e.g., have the computer elsewhere). Use the bedroom only for sleep and intimacy. This will strengthen the association of the bed with sleep.

20. Short naps during the day are okay as there is a dip in body temperature after lunch. If you must sleep during the day it is best to restrict it to less than 30 minutes early in the day to avoid going into a deep sleep cycle. However with severe fatigue a longer sleep might be needed.

21. It might help to move the clock so you can't see it as it might make you anxious.

22. You may have to address your partner's sleep problems if they are disturbing you (e.g., there are number of methods for dealing with snoring other than a cork!)

A helpful acronym that summarizes some of the above is ASLEEP, which stands for: Avoid (drugs, nicotine, alcohol, electromagnetic radiation); Sleep (and intimacy, only in the bedroom); Leave (laptop and work out of the bedroom); Empty mind (e.g., write down things to do next day); Early rising; and Plan bedtime routine.

If a client wakens during the night and can't get back to sleep even after using some of the above techniques, recommendations vary, for example:

1. Don't get up unless you must. Relax and enjoy your light sleep. This may be the only viable option if the house is cold or if getting up will disturb others.

2. Get up and repeat your night-time routine before going to bed.

3. Get up, perhaps have a light snack and read or listen to quiet music; avoid television. After a while (20 minutes or so) you should feel tired enough to go to bed again. Repeat this process if necessary. This seems to be the preferred option. You might need to avoid the clock by turning it to the wall. It is important to avoid making the bed a battlefield that stirs up an emotional reaction to sleeplessness.

Clients need to find out what suits them best. Relaxation techniques can be helpful (Section 2.2.5). If the insomnia persists, your client should see a doctor just in case the sleeplessness is caused by a physical problem or a medicine, either prescribed or over-the-counter (e.g., cold/allergy medications, analgesics, and diet pills). Sleeping too much can also be a problem and may indicate a sleep disorder.

Teenagers find it difficult to get up in the morning and there is a good reason for this. During adolescence, the body's circadian rhythm is reset, telling a teen to fall asleep later at night and wake up later in the morning. This change in the circadian rhythm seems to be due to the fact that melatonin is produced later at night in teens than it is for younger children and adults, making it harder for teens to fall asleep earlier.[16]

6.2.3   Sleeping Pills

Sleeping pills (e.g., benzodiazepines) can be a helpful short term crutch for people with occasional sleep problems such as jet lag or a stressful event such as the death of a loved one, divorce, or a medical problem. Jacobs notes that "In these circumstances, sleeping pills may help prevent short-term insomnia from evolving into chronic insomnia."[17] They may also help break the cycle in chronic insomnia. Some experts suggest keeping a few pills in the medicine cabinet to provide a sense of security and minimize the fear of insomnia. However, sleeping pills should only be used for short periods of time (less than 2 weeks) as they have a "hangover" effect and some side effects, are only moderately affective, act for a limited length of time in the night, can be addictive with a build up of tolerance, and can produce withdrawal symptoms on stopping. So-called "rebound insomnia" can also happen when taking a tablet one night leads to wakefulness the next.[18]

Jacobs says that sleeping pills are

> no longer considered a safe or appropriate treatment for chronic insomnia because they can have serious side effects that far outweigh their benefits; ... (they) strengthen the belief that the cure for insomnia comes from external factors; and can lead to physical or psychological dependency, which can cause feelings of helplessness, loss of control, and lowered self-esteem.[19]

Information on the downside of using sleeping tablets is available on the internet.[20] Note that the side effects can be greater for older people. Melatonin is another medication sometimes used for sleep problems, but its usefulness is uncertain and its long term effects and interactions with other drugs is unknown.

If your client is taking sleeping tablets while in therapy with you, Jacobs suggests the following strategies for the person.[21]

1. Use the smallest possible dose.

2. Use intermittently, only after two consecutive bad nights of sleep and never on consecutive nights (i.e., no more than twice a week).

---

[16] Papalia et al. (2001: 418).
[17] Jacobs (1999: 40).
[18] Interactions with other drugs can be a problem. For further information see http://helpguide.org/life/sleep_aids_medication_insomnia_treatment.htm; accessed October 2010.
[19] Jacobs (1999: 7).
[20] See http://www.darksideofsleepingpills.com/ by Daniel Kripke (accessed October 2010.
[21] Jacobs (1999: 40).

3. Don't escalate the dose and try to use sleep medications with a short half-life (hours rather than days).

If a client is wanting to cut out a regular use of sleeping tablets, Jacobs suggests the following strategies:[22]

1. Start the reduction program when life is not too busy or stressful.

2. Begin by cutting the dose in half on one of the medication nights. Choose a low stress night such as a weekend night.

3. Once sleeping reasonably well on this dosage, try a reduction on another low stress night suitably spaced from the first. Continue until all nights are on half dosage.

4. Repeat the process by steadily cutting out all doses.

5. Don't rush the process as it may take a while, especially with long term use.

Some antidepressants, in a lower dose or when there is underlying depression, can be helpful for insomnia and there are some herbal alternatives such as valerian root[23] that have been used. Aromatherapy is also a possibility for some clients.

6.3   COUNSELING FOR ANXIETY

The aim of this section is to provide a general counseling framework that can be used for a variety of anxiety problems and disorders. Further details and more specialized aspects are given under the appropriate headings in this and the next two chapters.

6.3.1   Source of Problems

Anxiety problems are varied, but they have certain underlying themes and ideas that can provide a basis for counseling, as set out by Hallam (1992), for example. As with other psychological problems like depression, it is important to have the patient checked medically for any physical disorders that may produce symptoms felt as anxiety such as hormonal disorders (hyperthyroidism, hypoparathyroidism, Cushing's syndrome, and pheochromocytoma), hypoglycemia (low blood sugar), temporal lobe epilepsy, cardiovascular disorders (pulse irregularities), and balance disorders (e.g., dizziness and nausea).[24] A common physical problem in anxious clients that can trigger a panic attack is over-breathing, and this can lead to a group of effects called *hyperventilation syndrome*. This is discussed later.

A number of processes can produce or maintain anxiety problems such as the following:[25]

1. *Having a chronic source of behavioral disorganization.* This can be an external source (e.g., threat of job loss or relationship breakdown) or an internal source

[22]Jacobs (1999: 41–43).
[23]For more details about this herb see Bourne (2005: 323) and the internet. Its long term effect is uncertain at the time of writing.
[24]Hallam (1992: 9).
[25]Hallam (1992: chapter 2).

(e.g., lack of problem-solving or interpersonal skills; toxic assumptions about self, others or the world; and unresolved trauma).

2. *Fear of fear cycles.* Here various disturbing sensations lead to a tendency to self-observe, and this creates more disturbing sensations, thus causing an escalating cycle of fear. This is fed by perceived threats whether physical (e.g., heart attack), psychological (e.g., losing control), social (e.g., rejection) or material (e.g., loss of earnings). This fear cycle is discussed further in the next section.

3. *Lack of awareness.* There is a need to become more aware of what is driving the anxiety problem and learn strategies to reduce bodily arousal and change behaviors.

4. *Failure to confront.* By not confronting the source of an anxiety problem leads to a perpetuation of the problem.

5. *Tunnel vision.* Symptoms become completely self-absorbing so that a person's mental life becomes consumed with worry, intrusive thoughts, and the effects of bodily sensations.

Hallam explains that any difficulties with an anxious client will tend to reflect the nature of anxiety, for example,

> clients have a need both to *contain* and *express* their worries, a *desire* to be reassured and a *resistance* to reassurance, an *impatience* for quick results and a *reluctance* to confront unpleasant situations.[26]

An approach to counseling is to use one or more of three strategies, namely cognitive therapy (e.g., along the lines of CBT using socratic disputing), behavioral therapy, which looks at the ABC behavior chain of antecedent–behavior–consequence, and medication such as the anti-anxiety drugs benzodiazepines, antidepressants (e.g., tricyclics or monoamine oxidase inhibitors), and beta blockers. A comparison of the three strategies and various combinations is still a subject of ongoing research and the most useful approach will no doubt depend on the nature of the anxiety disorder. An important contributor to anxiety is negative self-talk.

6.3.2   General Strategies

I now want to briefly discuss two of the above three strategies; details will be given later.

Cognitive Therapy

The idea here is that anxiety and associated negative emotions are the products of faulty thinking and the aim is to change the thinking through cognitive restructuring. The first step is to elicit the habitual automatic thoughts, which, if not spontaneously available, can be recalled by two methods. The first is *association*, where there is a focus on other aspects of the behavior such as physical symptoms and behavior and the client is asked for associated thoughts, or there is focus on the image of being anxious and any words that come to mind are relayed. A second

[26]Hallam (1992: 28); the italics are his.

method is backward reasoning where the therapist asks the question, "What kind of thought might have made you feel that way?"

The next step is to identify the underlying irrational beliefs, such as probability overestimation and catastrophizing (i.e., blowing things way out of proportion), which can be done in two ways, the so-called downward-arrow technique and examining thought records for common themes. The downward-arrow technique consists of challenging statements people make about what they think is causing their negative mood states by *repeatedly* asking the question, "If that were true, why would it be so upsetting?" Other questions might be "How certain are you that ... will occur?" and "What is the worst thing that can happen, and how bad is that?" Thought records are records of automatic thoughts compiled by the client between counseling sessions that arise in problem situations. The next steps are to challenge the irrational beliefs and replace them by suitable alternatives. In the case of dealing with troublesome thoughts, the thought stopping techniques of Section 1.4.4 can be used.

Bourne[27] refers to four personality sub-types that commonly promote negative self-talk: the worrier (promotes anxiety, as discussed above), the critic (promotes low self-esteem), the victim (promotes depression), and the perfectionist (promotes stress). Self-talk is very subtle; the client is often not aware of what they are telling themselves. The therapist can help a client to stand back and identify the negative statements and then, as mentioned above, use cognitive therapy to produce counter arguments to these statements.

Behavioral Therapy

Simply providing information about maladaptive thinking (e.g., nonpoisonous spiders are harmless) is generally ineffective in producing change, but it can be very effective when combined with behavioral experience. For example, discovering through handling that spiders are harmless and friendly creatures will generally eliminate fear of them. The key behavioral approach is therefore to use exposure, perhaps with systematic desensitization through rehearsal and role-playing, as described in detail in the next section. This approach is generally referred to as exposure response prevention (ERP) and it appears to be the most powerful method in helping a client overcome a variety of fears by getting the client to face them for a reasonable period of time. This method also applies to trauma and exposure to traumatic memories. It is discussed further below under "Exposure Methods."

6.3.3   Assessment and Strategies

The aim of this section is to set the scene for some broad strategies that can be used in this and the next two chapters. To begin, the first stage in counseling is to obtain a list of common fears and anxieties, along with the usual background information, and determine the main problems and what sort of events elicit and maintain them. The problem might be the occurrence of panic attacks (see Section 6.4.2 below) or some sort of compulsive behavior driven by anxiety. The absence

---

[27]Bourne (2005: 175–176).

of a desired behavior can also be a problem. In the case of using behavioral and cognitive strategies, the aim would be to identify the following:[28]

1. The behaviors/thoughts/feelings that are unwanted and problematic.

2. The behaviors/thoughts/feelings whose absence is problematic.

3. The stimulus antecedents (events preceding the stimulus) and the short and longer-term consequences of the above.

4. The surface thinking and core beliefs associated with (1) and (2).

5. General styles of coping with problems that are creating difficulty for the client.

A chronology of events relating to the main problems, together with surrounding circumstances, is helpful in looking for causes, patterns, and connections. It is helpful to solicit "the history, current impact, future implications, frequency, duration and situational specificity"[29] of the problems. Situational antecedents can be determined by asking when, where, and with whom. Other assessment information can be obtained from behavioral observation (in simulated or real situations), self-observation (e.g., diary recording of distressing events), and guided fantasy whereby the client, with eyes closed and reasonably relaxed, is asked to imagine vividly the problem situation and describe sensations, thoughts, and behavior. A client's thoughts that arise when describing anxiety-provoking imagery can be very revealing both to the counselor and the client, and can show the chain of thoughts that lead to the behavior. There are also a number of anxiety related self-administered questionnaires that the reader might find useful.[30]

Exposure Methods

Once the problems have been formulated, the next stage is to set goals (especially those suggested by the client) and determine whether a behavioral and/or cognitive strategy is best, depending on the client. Following Hallam,[31] the problems can be divided into themes or categories, for example, meeting new people, discomfort in an enclosed space or in a crowded place, and fear of insects. The major behavioral intervention is confrontation for an appropriate period of time, as repeated exposure to the same kind of stimulus can lead to a weakening of the response. In the case of phobias, one simply exposes the client to the phobic stimulus for 30–45 minutes in real life; too short a time won't help. It is a matter of repeatedly facing the fear. It is important to explain to a client what the aim of this approach is all about.

One method used is the hierarchical exposure approach, the idea being to begin with the mildest form of confrontation and steadily increase the intensity of the stimulus in steps. This can be done by taking one theme at a time, listing real (or imaginary) situations relating to the theme and asking the client to rate each situation from 0 to 10 where 0 is no distress and 10 is extreme distress; the list is then reordered with increasing score giving an *anxiety hierarchy*.[32] For example,

[28] Hallam (1992: 43).
[29] Hallam (1992: 53).
[30] For an extensive collection of questionnaires see Antony, Orsillo, and Roemer (2001).
[31] Hallam (1992: chapter 6).
[32] This type of measurement is sometimes referred to as a SUDS (Subjective Units of Disturbance Scale). Some may prefer a scale of 0–100.

given the general theme of fear of insects, a hierarchy with the score in brackets might be finding: a small dead insect (2), a large dead insect (4), a live small insect (5), a large non-flying live insect (7), a large flying insect (9), and so forth.

Each theme and its hierarchy will generally need to be treated separately, and within each hierarchy, confrontation (either real or imagined) can begin with a low score situation and then move to the next situation with a larger or the same score. The therapist needs to inform the client that he or she is expecting the client to become distressed, so as to "normalize" and then reframe the response, for example: "I am sure your anxiety is very stressful but it will not physically harm you." Each client will respond differently and may need to be able to opt out of the confrontation (e.g., using an escape route in real life) if the client finds it too distressing. However, the client should be encouraged to make an effort and be exposed for a sufficient length of time as reactions do subside relatively quickly.

Confrontations can take the form of actual encounters or imagined encounters, and are either self-managed by the client or organized by the therapist. They should be planned so that the client is prepared for them as much as possible and they are manageable for the client. Progress can be monitored by any reduction in the hierarchical scores when reassessed. The top scores in a hierarchy should be reduced almost to zero for imagined scenarios and to low scores (e.g., 3 or 4) for real situations, the latter being more effective.[33] Because some anxiety may return between sessions, Hallam suggests starting the next session at a hierarchical level below the final level reached in the previous session. Helping a client to prevent a defensive response is a key part to the therapy. Here training in using the relaxation response (see Section 2.2.5) may be helpful so that the client can pause and use a rapid relaxation response (taking 15–20 seconds) when tensed up. However, the literature suggests that the relaxation response may not be of additional help.

Having described a general procedure for confrontation, I now mention some variations of this procedure.[34]

Systematic desensitization. Using the above hierarchy approach, the client is asked to relax with their eyes shut (e.g., imagine a peaceful scene) and the therapist describes a situation listed on the hierarchy. The client is asked to imagine the situation and to signal (e.g., by raising an index finger) when the image is clear and vivid. After imagining the scene for a short period of time (30 seconds to one minute) the client stops the fantasy, relaxes again, and signals whether the image invoked anxiety. If it failed to do so on three consecutive occasions, then the therapist moves up one item on the list. (This procedure can be practiced by a client on their own once they have done it a few times.)[35]

Covert Rehearsal. Here the approach is similar to that above except that the focus is now more on what the client imagines himself or herself *doing* in the fantasy and there is some interaction between the client and the therapist, who gives instructions for the client to imagine actively coping in the situation. The client reports back to the therapist on the way the image develops and the therapist then suggests modifications to the fantasy in subsequent scenes.

[33] Hallam (1992: 78, 82).
[34] Hallam (1992: 82–86).
[35] See Bourne (2005: 159–160).

Prolonged fantasy. Here the therapist confronts the client with a whole range of anxiety-provoking images for at least forty minutes; this is usually referred to as *flooding* and is ineffective if its duration is too short . Here the client is extended in a creative manner by the therapist to visit difficult situations, and the imagery is repeated until it ceases to be upsetting.

Guided fantasy. This involves a prolonged fantasy in which the client is instructed to describe aloud, in the first-person present tense, a relevant episode of distress.[36] As the scene unfolds, the client is asked to elaborate on various details such as circumstances, events happening, bodily reactions, and thoughts. The therapist can invite the client to to respond to new elements added to the scenario.

Self-managed confrontation. For some anxiety problems that inevitably arise between sessions, for example fear associated with public places and social occasions, the preferred approach is a program of self-managed confrontation. Here clients face real-life situations as part of their homework along with keeping records of thoughts, bodily sensations, and so on, and practicing relaxation techniques, if necessary.

Exposure methods are referred to again in the next chapter on anxiety disorders.

6.4   NERVOUS FATIGUE AND ILLNESS

When discussing anxiety and fear it is important to mention what happens to the nervous system when it is stressed. Dr Claire Weekes has written a number of very useful books on the subject and I will refer to her work often in this section.

6.4.1   Four Fatigues

When our nervous system is stressed to its limit, we suffer what is sometimes described as a nervous "breakdown" when nervous fatigue becomes crippling and several frightening symptoms occur. Weekes[37] described four kinds of nervous fatigue: muscular, emotional, mental, and a kind of fatigue of the spirit. These fatigues do not operate in isolation; it is likely that a person will be experiencing several of them at different levels all at once.

With regard to muscular fatigue, we are all aware of it and the aches and pains that may follow after strenuous exercise. However, it is not generally realized that stress can produce similar sensations, as prolonged tension allows chemicals of fatigue to build up in muscles causing tiredness and aching. Small muscles in the eyes can be affected leading to blurred vision, while tension in the neck and shoulder muscles can lead to headaches.

Emotional fatigue arises as the result of our nervous system[38] becoming over-sensitized and trigger-happy through prolonged stress. As a result, very strong emotions, especially fear, are released very easily along with frightening bodily

---

[36]For an excellent demonstration of the method with dialogue see Hallam (1992: 56–60).
[37]Weekes (1997).
[38]Generally the so-called "sympathetic" part of our involuntary (autonomous) nervous system.

sensations such as those described under panic disorder below. When our nervous system has been pushed to the limit, it can react back at us, particularly at an unguarded moment when we are taking time out, or when we are going off to sleep. We can describe it as an "attack" (e.g., anxiety or panic attack) as it usually happens with little or no warning. Because the symptoms are so scary, people are not only bewildered by them but they become more afraid of them than of the cause of the original stress. This makes things worse. The extra stress of fear gets added to the original stress with the result that even more adrenaline is released with the fear-adrenaline-fear feedback cycle pushing the person towards nervous fatigue and possibly towards a nervous illness.

When the nervous system is severely sensitized, all emotions become exaggerated such as sadness, impatience, guilt, love, and joy, and even noise is amplified because of sensitized auditory nerves. Also we become more aware of our beating heart. Such intensification of emotions leaves a person emotionally drained and fatigued. Weekes[39] notes that the emotional reaction is hard to understand as it is so incapacitating with little relationship to physical effort and little relieved by resting. It is also hard to describe to family, friends, and even the doctor.

Mental fatigue begins to set in when a person's anxious thoughts about what is happening to them begin to take over and turn inward and the fatigue can descend like a fog in the mind or be like a dark low ceiling. Upsetting thoughts go round and round obsessively and won't go away leaving a person mentally exhausted, confused, and struggling to concentrate. It is in this kind of thinking accompanied by fear that can pave the way for many obsessions and phobias to develop.

Weekes[40] mentions three types of obsession. The first is a habit of repeating a ritual, for example, hand washing for fear of contamination by germs, in which the fear of the ritual is not as fearful in itself as the fear of the state in which the obsessed person finds himself or herself. The second holds much more fear, as in the case when a nervously ill mother is obsessed with the idea that she might harm her child. The third is when a person becomes obsessed with himself or herself and his or her nervous illness. In the first case the person adds further fear, namely being afraid of his or her compulsive state of mind, and it is this second fear that causes the brain fatigue and keeps the brain stuck. In the second case, when a harming thought comes to mind and fear of the idea rises up, the mother should accept the fear and "float" through it while endeavoring to glimpse the truth that she would never harm her child. With practice, the obsessive thoughts can be replaced by true thoughts. In the third case, it is a matter of accepting that the obsession is no more than a symptom of the mental fatigue. These three fears are related to obsessive compulsive disorders discussed in Chapter 8.

Fatigue of the spirit starts to set in when the sufferer begins to give up the struggle and lose hope of ever feeling normal again. Every task is just too hard to carry out.

A person can still get by and manage their life even when hampered by nervous problems or nervous fatigue. The question Weekes asks is when do the nervous symptoms get so bad that they lead to an illness or a breakdown. Her response is when "a person's 'nervous' symptoms are so intense that they cope inadequately

[39] Weekes (1997: 16).
[40] Weekes (1997: 120).

with their daily work or do not cope at all."[41] The original stress may have been due to some physical trauma like surgery or an accident, or to some overwhelming problem (e.g., guilt or grief), but either way the fear-adrenaline-fear cycle eventually traps the person in a state of continuous fear and tension. In the end, a nervous breakdown "is no more than emotional and mental exhaustion usually begun and maintained by fear."[42]

6.4.2 Panic Attacks

We all experience palpitations at sometime in our lives, for example having a fright or even drinking a cup of strong coffee. However, when the palpitations begin to occur frequently there is often the fear of heart trouble. As the fear-adrenaline-fear cycle gets stronger a person may experience a full-blown panic attack that can leave them wondering if they are having a heart attack or a nervous breakdown. When it happens for the first time it is a terrifying experience that can leave a person reeling! If the attacks happen more than once, the sufferer can become afraid of them, and this can generate even more attacks. The attacks usually come on suddenly, and may have no obvious triggers; a bit like having a fight or flight response out of context.

An attack often strikes when things seem to be going well and can happen in seemingly harmless situations such as while we are asleep. They can be as short as 1–5 minutes, but symptoms may last up to half an hour, though their intensity usually reduces after a few minutes. Their pattern of occurrence varies from person to person and the frequency varies considerably from just occasionally to regularly, with several a week. A person might have a panic spasm every few minutes and this may continue for hours.

Panic attacks often strike in mid to late thirties, with women being more vulnerable than men, though the attacks frequently begin during late adolescence and early adulthood. The strongest people are often the most vulnerable as they fight the attack!

Some symptoms of a panic attack are:

Physical. These are varied and can include headaches, dizziness, blurred vision, sweating, fatigue, weak knees or legs, trembling, dry mouth, vague aches and pains, palpitation, skipped heart beats, chest pain or chest tightness, shortness of breath, sensation of choking or smothering, nausea, and churning stomach.

Behavioral. These can include lack of concentration, loss of memory, compulsive behavior, restlessness, lack of motivation, and irritability.

Emotional. These can include fear of dying, worry, tearfulness, nervousness, panic feelings, fear of impending doom, and fear of going crazy.

Cognitive. There is as strong connection between body symptoms and catastrophic thoughts. The terrifying body symptoms can lead to thoughts like, "I will have a heart attack," "I will faint," or "I am going crazy."[43]

---

[41]Weekes (1997: 27).
[42]Weekes (1997: 158).
[43]For a list of catastrophic thoughts see Bourne (2005: 113).

Panic attacks are not uncommon and if a person experiences just one or two then there is probably no cause to worry; being afraid of their reoccurrence is more serious.

Panic disorder

People who have repeated, persistent attacks or feel severe anxiety about having another attack are said to have panic disorder, discussed in the next chapter. However, before diagnosing panic disorder, other possible problems need to be ruled out as there a a number of possible triggers and causes of panic attacks such as heredity, some physical and psychological conditions, phobias, stressful life events such as loss or separation, hyperventilation syndrome, substance abuse, and some medications.[44] Bourne mentions that medical causes such as hypoglycemia, hyperthyroidism, reaction to excess caffeine or nicotine, or withdrawal from alcohol, tranquilizers and sedatives, need to be ruled out.[45] According to DSM-IV criteria[46] other mental disorders also need to be ruled out such as social or specific phobias, obsessive-compulsive disorder, post-traumatic stress disorder, or separation anxiety disorder. Unfortunately, in a majority of cases, panic disorder is complicated by the development of agoraphobia (discussed in the next chapter). In the next section, strategies for coping with panic attacks are discussed.

6.4.3 Counseling for a Panic Attack

In counseling a client with a nervous illness and especially with the extreme symptom of panic attacks, the first thing to do is to check that they have seen a doctor and confirm that there is nothing physically wrong, especially with regard to heart, blood pressure, thyroid, and so on. Usually they will have already done this. If the medical check-up reveals there is nothing wrong organically, then the good news is that the attacks can't hurt them, and the problem is eminently treatable. For example, the scary palpitations are not dangerous, any lightheadedness won't mean you will faint, you won't lose your balance or fall over even if you feel "weak in the knees," and you won't lose control of yourself or your mind![47]

The therapist needs to deal with any catastrophic thinking by explaining the role of the nervous system in body symptoms. In the case of panic attacks it is helpful to make an inventory of bodily sensations and thoughts experienced just before, during, and after a panic attack. For the therapist to really appreciate the severity of an attack, he or she should realize that a panic attack is physiologically indistinguishable from the adrenaline-driven arousal that occurs when drowning! When clients understand the nature of their problem and realize that their symptoms are simply the result of an over-sensitive nervous system and especially a fear of fear, some of the tension usually disappears. We need to remind our client that without fear they are invulnerable!

The next step is to give the client a coping strategy (which may be likened to first aid) for when an attack occurs and, if necessary, develop a long term program

---

[44]For further details see en.wikipedia.org/wiki/Panic_attack.
[45]Bourne (2005: 8).
[46]American Psychiatric Association (2000a,b).
[47]Bourne (2005: 109–111).

of lifestyle changes to deal with the problem(s) that gave rise to the initial stress. Weekes[48] describes such a coping strategy in four steps.

- facing
- accepting
- floating
- letting time pass

Rather than be afraid of a panic attack, the first step is to face it, as shying away from it makes the symptoms worse, and fear can precipitate another attack. If we face our symptoms and even consciously try to make them worse, we will find that they won't get worse, and in fact may improve when looking at them with interest rather than fear. Instead of fighting an attack we simply accept it, examine and analyze it, relax the muscles (especially in the chest and stomach), take a deep breath and exhale slowly[49] while imagining that we are floating forward without resistance. We do this until the attack finishes, which it will. We need to say such things as "I accept and float", "I am floating through and beyond this panic," and "I am accepting and relaxed, and it will pass."

Acceptance is more than just putting up with the attack but rather taking the role of a detached observer similar to the mindfulness approach in handling cravings arising with addictions.[50] By continually going through the four steps we can come to a point when we can tell ourselves that it doesn't matter that the attack is happening. After all, it is just our own body complaining because of over-sensitization, so we need not be afraid of our own body. Although we may not get as much relief initially as we would like, if we let sufficient time pass we will get better. We can expect our bodies to take a while to become less sensitive so we need to be patient with ourselves, knowing that our nervous system will eventually settle down. Impatience means tension, which is the enemy of healing. However, some medication may be necessary in the short term to give some respite, especially at night; antidepressants can be helpful. It is also helpful if a client can learn to recognize antecedents of a panic attack by noting what happened before an attack (e.g., stress level the preceding day, prior mood and emotions, diet, cognitions, and so forth).

The sympathetic nervous system is the one of our two nervous systems that is the main culprit, but there may be a rare occasion when the parasympathetic nervous system takes over with pulse and blood pressure falling. Although a very slow pulse can be just as scary as a rapid one, it can be handled in the same way, as it is still the result of over-sensitization and there is no need to be afraid of it.

It is important to not be afraid if we get a sudden recurrence when we think we are well again, as it can take a while for our negative memories and triggers to become blunted. As an old physical injury can give us the odd twinge of pain, so our nervous system can give us the odd nervous "twinge." If we are not afraid, the attack will pass; we need not fear a recurrence. If a person is afraid of a future

[48]Weekes (1997).
[49]See relaxation breathing in Section 2.2.5.
[50]See Section 12.7.2 under "Relapse Strategies."

breakdown, then they are still controlled by fear; fear alone makes them vulnerable.

Barrow[51] gave another version of the above steps using the acronym ARFT (Accept, Relax, Float through, and let Time pass). She mentions the importance of applying a relaxation technique that, through practice at other times, can be applied quickly and relatively easily. However, the key is not to *strive* for relaxation.

The above methods apply to any nervous symptoms and associated strange feelings and not just the extreme one of a panic spasm or attack. For example, we can accept the fact that, although our heart is "misbehaving" because of palpitation and thumping, there is nothing organically wrong with our heart and we need to realize that we are oversensitive to its every beat.[52] With regard to those intrusive and obsessive thoughts, the more we fight them the harder it is to get rid of them. Weekes suggests a slogan of "float" not "fight."

Some people who are paralyzed by fear can learn to free muscles by floating past obstructive thoughts; they float their legs out of bed, float on their clothes, float down the hall, and even float food to their mouth! Thoughts of fear can be floated away off the top of their head![53] Weekes also mentions the helpfulness of occupation, especially in the company of other people,[54] for someone coping with a nervous breakdown. Even when a person feels exhausted, they need some light occupation and avoid just going to bed. It is a matter of accepting all the tricks their nerves play on them while attempting to get absorbed in an occupation.

It is important for clients to also look carefully at their lifestyle and consider the physical, emotional, mental, social, and spiritual aspects of their life as discussed in Chapter 2. For example, physical exercise (especially aerobic) can help relieve stress[55] while activity or moving around can forestall a panic attack. Appropriate eating and nutrition can reduce the stress on the digestive system and circulation, and eliminating caffeine and nicotine (and reducing sugar intake) can reduce palpitations. Relaxation techniques (e.g., the relaxation response) can help desensitize the nervous system; recognizing and dealing with the role of frustration and anger can help calm emotions. Positive self-talk and adopting more positive beliefs can help relax and refocus the mind, especially at the onset of a panic attack. Finally, using meditational and spiritual exercises can alleviate anxiety.

With regard to positive self-messages it is generally best for a client to come up with their own positive statements, and then read them aloud several times three times a day for at least thirty days. These new positive statements begin to come back to the conscious mind instead of the tired old negative statements that have been sitting in the subconscious mind for some time.

[51] Barrow (1985).

[52] A healthy heart can beat rapidly for hours without putting a person at any risk (Bourne (2005: 111).

[53] Weekes (1997: 64).

[54] Weekes (1997: 158).

[55] However, too much exercise can leave the body stressed later.

6.4.4   Hyperventilation

In the context of this chapter, hyperventilation or over-breathing is quite common in clients with a stress or anxiety problem, occurring in about 50% of those with a panic disorder and in 60% of those with agoraphobia.[56] The incidence is a lot higher among women than among men. What happens is that a person's breathing becomes faster and/or deeper than necessary, bringing about lightheadedness and other undesirable symptoms often associated with panic attacks. Breathing switches from diaphragm to thoracic (upper chest) breathing that leads to an excess of oxygen and a drop of carbon dioxide in the lungs. The brain then gets the message to shut down the rate of breathing, which may be experienced as an inability to breathe or as difficulty in breathing and a shortness of breath. This can cause the client to breath even faster, which makes things worse and can lead to a vicious cycle of panic, rapid breathing, and more panic. If a person regularly hyperventilates then the condition is generally described as *hyperventilation syndrome* (HVS).

Some clients may not be aware of their hyperventilating, but they will be aware of some of the varied associated symptoms such as dizziness or lightheadedness, sighing and yawning, dry mouth, lump in the throat, weakness, confusion, sleep disturbances, numbness and tingling in their arms or around their mouth, muscle spasms in hands and feet, chest pain, and palpitations. If a person has HVS it is important they have a medical check-up to rule out any physical problems (e.g., heart or lung problems). HVS is a common cause of dizziness and about 25% of medical patients who complain about dizziness are diagnosed with HVS.

If a person starts to hyperventilate, and he or she has been cleared of any organic problems, the goal is to raise the carbon dioxide level in one's blood, which will put an end to most of the symptoms. The traditional and quickest intervention is to ask the client to breathe into a paper bag over nose and mouth so that re-breathing takes place and carbon dioxide levels are restored. However, some physicians are not happy with this method (or at least limit its use to one or two minutes) as it may lead to inhaling too much carbon dioxide. The method may not be successful as the client may have difficulty complying with the technique. Also carbon dioxide may itself be a chemical trigger for anxiety. An alternative approach is to breath through pursed lips (like blowing out a candle) or cover one's mouth and one nostril and breath through the other nostril, thus reducing the oxygen intake. A longer term approach is to slow down the breathing using diaphragm breathing along the lines of the relaxation response described in Section 2.2.5. One suggestion is to eventually inhale to the count of 7 seconds (or counts) and exhale very slowly to the count of 11 (or as long as possible). A person with HVS can benefit by doing this twice a day for five minutes at a time. The gaol is to reduce breathing to no more than five breaths per minute.[57]

It is important to explain the role of hyperventilation in panic. One practical way of demonstrating this is to have the patient breath rapidly at a rate of about 30 breaths a minute (instead the normal 8–12 breaths) for two minutes through nose and mouth, fully expelling the air with each breath, although the client is allowed

---

[56]http://www.emedicine.com/EMERG/topic270.htm by Brian Kern and Adam Rosh (accessed October 2010).
[57]http://en.wikipedia.org/wiki/Hyperventilation_syndrome.

to stop sooner if the rate cannot be maintained The aim of the exercise is to show clients that over-breathing is responsible for the symptoms and thus relieve their anxiety about their symptoms. If the therapist is conducting the test for the first time, it is a good idea for him or her to have a practice run of the breathing either alone or with a colleague to get an idea of what happens. The method may not be appropriate with some clients and care is needed in using it.

6.4.5   Sleep and Nervous Illness

I now want to make a few more comments about sleep in the context of a nervous illness or fatigue.[58] Night-time can mean different things to different people suffering from a nervous illness. Some sufferers feel so much better in the evening that they may feel almost cured. Others, however, may dread the night because panic feelings return leaving the person in a bed of panic and sweat. What can happen is that just as they are about to drop off to sleep their heart suddenly starts to race leaving them wide awake. They then quieten down, go to drop off, but go through the whole process again and again, leaving them exhausted. Applying the principles described above throughout the day and night using acceptance, floating through, and a relaxation technique in bed will in time help the person to sleep. However, if the symptoms are too disturbing and exhausting, some medication may be needed initially. A common problem is having to go to bed very early because of exhaustion and then waking very early in the morning and not being able to get back to sleep; a short nap during the day can be helpful. Making some changes in the bedroom can sometimes be helpful to break old behavior patterns.[59] Lack of sleep can eventually lead to depression (see Chapter 9).

Finally, I want to say something about the morning.[60] With a sensitized nervous system, the smallest shock can set the heart bumping, for example, even just the shock of waking up in the morning![61] In the morning it is best to get up immediately on awaking to prevent the dreaded morning feeling, remembering that a difficult morning does not necessarily mean a difficult day. Instead of lying in bed being miserable it is best to get mobile and perhaps put on some music or the TV. Keeping occupied can be really helpful in the recovery from a nervous illness.

6.4.6   Burnout

I wish to mention this topic separately as the term "burnout" is heard quite often in relation to the workplace. It is a form of emotional depletion and is similar to a nervous illness. It can stem from a variety of causes such as grief, stress, and overwork. We need to recognize the early signs of burnout. Self-care is important for those in the helping ministries such as social work, counseling, and pastoral work. Some early signs gleaned from various sources are:[62]

- chronic fatigue not fixed by sleep (a kind of weariness of the soul)

---

[58] See Weekes (1997: chapter 24).
[59] See Section 6.2.2.
[60] Weekes (1997: 127).
[61] This can be a shock to the sufferer, particularly if they felt pretty good when they went to bed the night before.
[62] For example, http://www.trans4mind.com/life-coach/life-challenge14/neils1.shtml by Henry Neils (accessed October 2010).

- inability to concentrate and prioritize

- loss of enthusiasm for life

- demands, even small ones, cause anger and anxiety

- self-criticism for putting up with demands

- a feeling of being trapped or being besieged

- cynicism, negativity, and irritability

- exploding easily at seemingly inconsequential things

- problems with one's family who are upset about one's lack of attention

- frequent headaches and gastrointestinal disturbances

- weight loss or gain

- mild depression

- shortness of breath

- suspiciousness

- feelings of helplessness

- increased degree of risk taking

There are many reasons for burnout by people including intra-personal problems such as childhood wounds or perfectionism, where self-worth depends on achievements, or there may be interpersonal problems such has wanting to please everybody as they are afraid of conflict or rejection. In counseling, ideas from the previous chapter on stress can be used here. Further suggestions for a client are as follows:[63]

Stop running. Face up to your fears and permit yourself to experience that hideous feeling. What thought comes to mind when you think of taking time out?

Do a reality check. Are your expectations realistic? Are you overoptimistic? You need to cultivate some "healthy pessimism."

Learn to say no. This idea is discussed more fully in Section 17.2.3.

When the mind is tired exercise the body. When the body is tired only exercise the mind. When both are tired rest or go to bed.

Don't work harder—work smarter. Time management skills can be helpful here (Section 5.3).

You should protect yourself from people you are afraid of and stop anticipating their criticism, anger or rejection. Take your worth out of the hands of the person who makes your life crazy.

[63]Based on Riddell (2007).

6.5   BIBLICAL VIEWPOINT

6.5.1   Worry

In Matthew 6:25–34 Jesus emphasizes that worry and anxiety can be dealt with by having faith and trust in God's provision and by focusing on God's kingdom. Jesus talks about trusting God with the details of life, especially food and clothing—of supreme importance to the listeners of his day (verse 25). The notion of gathering into barns indicates that worrying about the future effects how one feels today (verse 26); in fact worry gets us nowhere (verse 27). It is a matter of realizing that God does not ignore those who have faith in God's provision of *things* (verses 28–30, 33b). Worry can show a lack of faith in and understanding of God (verses 31–32) and the key is to seek God's kingdom and righteousness (verse 33). Living one day at a time is still the recipe for keeping one from being consumed with worry (verse 34). It should be remembered that we are not all the same and some people through childhood or rough life experiences find it much harder than others to just let go and trust.

6.5.2   Anxiety

Paul sounds a similar note about God supplying every need[64] and earlier exhorts readers not to be anxious for any *thing* but to bring all their requests to God in prayer, who gives them peace that guards their minds and their emotions.[65] Because God cares for them, they can cast all their anxieties on God [66] knowing that Jesus is their burden bearer.[67]   However, when a person is suffering from extreme anxiety, stress, or a nervous illness, he or she may find it difficult to pray or even have a devotional time. A verse that emphasizes not being anxious about anything can actually make anxiety sufferers feel worse as they can't stop feeling anxious and now believe they are disobeying God. Care is therefore needed in deciding what verses need to be introduced and how they are introduced. In the end it becomes a matter of living by faith and taking hold of God's promises.[68]

6.5.3   Fear

The Bible talks about overcoming fear by recognizing that God provides security,[69] help and support,[70] as well as God's presence,[71] peace of mind,[72] and contentment. It is important to realize that the saying, "Jesus first, others second, and yourself last" is not scriptural; it can lead to burnout from obligation, which often happens in Christian ministry.

---

[64] Philippians 4:19.
[65] Philippians 4:6–7: see also John 14:27.
[66] 1 Peter 5:7
[67] Matthew 11:28–30.
[68] For example Isaiah 40:28–31, 41:10, 43:1–3; Romans 8:26–28, 38–39; Philippians 4:19; and Hebrews 13:6.
[69] Proverbs 3:21–26 and Hebrews 4:16.
[70] Psalms 23:4, 27:4; Romans 8:31; and Hebrews 13:6.
[71] Psalms 23:4 and Matthew 28:20.
[72] John 14:27; Romans 15:33; and Philippians 4:6–7.

CHAPTER 7

ANXIETY DISORDERS

7.1 SOME BACKGROUND

Anxiety disorders are among the most prevalent emotional mental disorders in the general population, which some estimate to be about 18% in a lifetime, and in some sense they represent an irrational distortion of a normal anxiety response. Because of overlapping symptoms and comorbidity with other problems, anxiety disorders can be difficult to accurately diagnose. For example, they can be comorbid with depression, though anxiety usually precedes depression.[1] It is suggested that all clients with anxiety should be assessed for depression. Statistics about anxiety disorders also vary somewhat as criteria are not always definitive. Disorders discussed in this chapter are usually referred to as Axis I disorders according to the DSM-IV criteria. However, there have been some problems and controversy over the use of the DSM for anxiety disorders, and a history of the developments is given by Wolfe (2005). There is a striking difference between the criteria of DSM-IV (U. S.) and those of ICD-10 (Europe). A useful introduction to the subject of anxiety disorders is given by Nydegger (2012), and for further background reading see Stein and Hollander (2002). There are a number of different counsellng methods for anxiety disorders, and Wolfe (2005) considers five theoretical perspectives that have contributed significantly to an understanding of anxiety and anxiety disorders: psy-

---

[1]Stein and Hollander (2003).

choanalytic, behavioral, cognitive and cognitive-behavioral, experiential-existential, and biomedical.

This chapter builds on the previous chapter about anxiety and discusses a number of key disorders that have their roots in anxiety. We include Generalized Anxiety Disorder (GAD), Post Traumatic Stress Disorder (PTSD), Panic Disorder, and then consider a range of phobias. Obsessive-Compulsive Disorder, which is usually included in such a list, is dealt with in the next chapter. Many of the counseling procedures mentioned in the previous chapter about fear and anxiety can be applied to these disorders, along with some additional techniques specific to each disorder. A useful method of assessing a person is the BAATOMI list given in Section 21.2.2.

Many of the disorders are similar in their presenting symptoms and some people have more than one anxiety disorder so that some care is needed in making an appropriate diagnosis. Depression is often co-morbid with an anxiety disorder. The causes of anxiety disorders are varied and include heredity (e.g., personality type, the nature of the serotonin transfer gene), some childhood circumstances (e.g., inappropriate parenting, emotional insecurity and dependence), cumulative stress over time (e.g., difficult life events), biological causes (e.g., medical conditions, allergic reactions, and dietary factors), and combinations of these.[2] Initially, substance use and abuse needs to be ruled out. The role of substance use in anxiety disorders is discussed by Stewart and Conrod (2008), and the role of illness by Zvolensky and Smits (2008).

A comprehensive approach to recovery includes the wholeness approach set out in Chapter 2, namely the physical, emotional, mental, social (interpersonal), behavioral, and spiritual balance. Bourne[3] provides a helpful check list of the following: relaxation, nutrition, exercise, coping techniques (e.g., for panic), exposure (fantasy or real), self-talk, mistaken beliefs, expressing feelings, assertiveness, self-esteem, meaning/spirituality, and medication. All or some of these may be relevant to a particular disorder. A useful resource which is being used more and more in counseling is motivational interviewing.[4]

As exposure methods are frequently mentioned in this chapter, a word of caution is appropriate. Wolfe found that although exposure therapy was helpful in over 300 of his patients with anxiety disorder, "exposure therapy led to the rapid reduction of symptomatology in approximately 30% of cases.[5] He found that with exposure therapy, clients typically experienced outcomes such as finding the treatment too frightening to complete even if done very gradually, finding their symptomatic relief did not last, and continuing to experience substantial anxiety whenever they confronted their feared object or situation, even though they were able to reduce their avoidance behavior. This suggested to Wolfe that there were underlying issues connected to the phobia that need to be addressed, and that the so-called simple phobias mentioned below were not so simple. Concentrating on just the symptoms fails to focus on the personal meaning of the symptoms of anxiety. A more eclectic and integrative approach is required that all of us need from time to time when facing difficult clients. As clients want symptom relief, the place to start is with a

[2]Bourne (2005: chapter 2).
[3]Bourne (2005: 69).
[4]Westra (2012).
[5]Wolfe (2010: 5).

symptom-focused treatment that helps the patient gain a sense of control over his or her anxiety. Wolfe chooses the treatment by assessing the client's most comfortable area of functioning, what he calls an access point, for example a behavioral intervention for an action client, a cognitive intervention for the cognitively oriented client, or an emotion-focused intervention for the few emotionally inclined. In the end all three approaches can be used.

Medication

With regard to medication, benzodiazepines seem to be the most popular treatment of anxiety disorders at present, though there is some debate over their use as they can be quite addictive. They are not effective however in treating depression, which may be comorbid with the medication.[6] Benzodiazepines are not first choice with panic disorder because of the high doses required.[7] Antidepressants such as the selective serotonin reuptake inhibitors (SSRIs) are also popular in treating anxiety disorders and are often recommended as first-line medications. In the past tricyclic antidepressants were found useful, but their unfavorable side-effect profile has made them less favorable these days.[8]

General Questionnaires

A downloadable questionnaire for assessing anxiety is the Hamilton Anxiety Rating Scale (HAMA-A).[9] Another self-report questionnaire is the Beck Anxiety Inventory (BAI), also downloadable.[10] Several other questionnaires are used but they are not in the public domain.

Assessment

Some useful general questions that can be used for an overall assessment of an anxiety disorder are:[11]

- Under what circumstances does the anxiety show itself?
- Are there any things that trigger or maintain the anxiety disorder?
- What does a client do when becoming anxious?
- What bodily sensations go with the experience of fear?
- What are the client's thoughts before and after a period of anxiety?
- What are the short-term consequences of any avoidance behavior?
- What are the long-term consequences of any avoidance behavior?

When there is more than one problem area, a flow diagram is helpful in linking up these areas. Finally, the role of parental upbringing should not be overlooked in counseling as parents may have been overly critical with unreasonably high standards, overprotective and dampening childhood exploration, always telling them to be careful, and so forth.

[6] Favaravelli, Rosi, and Truglia (2003: 315, 326).
[7] Favaravelli et al. (2003: 328).
[8] For a list of available medications see Nydegger (2012, Table 7.1, 113–114).
[9] http://www.atlantapsychiatry.com/forms/HAM-A.pdf (accessed October 2010).
[10] It is listed in several places on the internet, e.g., http://www.anxietyclear.com/beck-anxiety-inventory-scoring.html (accessed October 2010).
[11] Emmelkamp, Bouman, and Scholing (1989: 56–57).

7.2   GENERALIZED ANXIETY DISORDER

7.2.1   Symptoms and Diagnosis

Generalized anxiety disorder (GAD) has been a topic of considerable debate in the mental field and this is reflected in the Diagnostic and Statistical Manual of Mental Disorders (DSM) symptoms list being continually revised.[12] It is seldom diagnosed correctly because of associated chronic physical conditions,[13] and it is is often an array of physical symptoms that prompts a visit to a clinician, perhaps leading to an uncovering of GAD. The underlying cause of GAD is not fully understood and it may go unrecognized for years.

One assessment method that is downloadable is the self-report set of scales called the Depression Anxiety Stress Scales (DASS); this instrument also gives a measure of depression and stress as well as anxiety.[14] Cut-off points for the severity of each scale are not given, but the scores may be helpful. The Hamilton Anxiety Rating Scale mentioned above is helpful for monitoring GAD, though it has a limited coverage of worry.[15]

GAD develops slowly (and insidiously) at any age, though often during the time between childhood and middle age. It is one of the most common anxiety disorders with a lifetime prevalence of about 4–5% in the U.S., and women are about twice as likely as men to have the disorder. It is characterized by a persistent, excessive, unrealistic, uncontrollable, and exaggerated worry and anxiety about everyday life events, but is unaccompanied by panic attacks, phobias, or obsessions. Clients with this problem expect everything to go wrong, have an unrealistic view of problems, and can't stop worrying about almost everything, for example, health, finances, family, work (or school), and especially relationships. Although they usually realize that their anxiety is more intense than the situation warrants, they can't seem to get rid of their concerns. Eventually the anxiety may so dominate their thinking that it interferes with daily functioning.

When their anxiety is mild, people with GAD can function socially and hold down a job. As worry and anxiety are common symptoms in other psychiatric problems it is not always easy to separate normal worry and anxiety from pathological worry. GAD tends to be a lifelong condition if left untreated. Antidepressants and benzodiazepines are currently useful forms of medication.[16]

Clients with GAD sometimes suffer from other psychological problems that can make the diagnosis difficult, for example Major Depressive Disorder (Section 9.3.3) is comorbid with GAD almost two thirds of the time. In addition to frequent worry, along with its significant interference with normal functioning and the anxiety symptoms mentioned above, a person is diagnosed with GAD if they experience at least three of the following six symptoms for more days than not over the past six months:[17]

[12]Monnier and Brawman-Mintzer (2003: 51).
[13]Portman (2009: 8).
[14]See www2.psy.unsw.edu.au/groups/dass/down.htm (accessed October 2010).
[15]Vanin and Helsey (2008: Table 2.17, p.31).
[16]Favaravelli et al. (2003: 329).
[17]http://en.wikipedia.org/wiki/Generalized_anxiety_disorder, from DSM-IV-TR (American Psychiatric Association, 2000a,b).

- restlessness

- easily fatigued

- difficulty concentrating or mind going blank

- irritability

- muscle tension and aches

- sleep problems

The above list, which focuses on physical symptoms, can be combined with the following summary, namely: (1) excessive worry and anxiety occurring more days than not for a period of 6 months, (2) impairment in social and occupational functioning, (3) difficulty in controlling the worry, and (4) frequency, intensity, and duration of the worry are out of proportion to the probability of the feared event.[18] Other possible anxiety disorders need to be ruled out, for example, symptoms present only during a panic attack can be excluded. Hazlett-Stevens notes that "the individual eventually develops fundamental beliefs that the world is dangerous and that he or she is unable to handle adversity. Worry becomes the primary strategy to cope with perceived threats ...."[19]

GAD sufferers have poor coping strategies including avoidance, procrastination, and poor problem-solving skills. In general, GAD is one of the most difficult disorders to assess and diagnose consistently. Helpful introductory questions might be, "Have there been days at a time when you felt extremely tense, anxious, or nervous for no apparent reason?" If the answer is yes then the next question might be, "Have you felt this way even when you were at home with nothing in particular that you have to do?" Again if the answer is yes, then, "Have these anxious or nervous feelings bothered you for at least 6 months?"

Other problems that might cause chronic anxiety need to ruled out such as medical problems like hyperventilation, thyroid problems, some cardiovascular, metabolic, and neurological conditions or drug induced anxiety (e.g., wrong medication dosage, withdrawal too quickly from a medication, illegal drug use), and other anxiety disorders and phobias. Possible causes of GAD are genetic factors (knowledge of family history is therefore important), neurotransmitter imbalance in the brain, and environmental factors like trauma and stressful events such as a loss or a major life change. It most often begins in childhood or adolescence, but can begin in adulthood.

7.2.2   Counseling Strategies for GAD

Counseling and treatment strategies include the following:[20]

1. Exercise, relaxation techniques, and lifestyle changes (see Section 2.2), particularly for the physiological symptoms. Relaxation techniques can be used

---

[18]Schulz, Gotto, and Rapaport (2005).
[19]Hazlett-Stevens (2008: 9).
[20]Adapted from Bourne (2005: 16–17).

to interrupt anxiety spirals by releasing anxious thoughts and sensations, and to release muscle tension.[21]

2. Cognitive-behavioral therapy (CBT). This involves countering distorted and negative beliefs about worry (cf. Section 1.4.3), for example, "If I worry about it, it won't happen," and in dealing with catastrophic thoughts. GAD sufferers also view the world as a dangerous place and have a need to to constantly look out for threats. In Beck's tradition they need to identify those automatic thoughts and core beliefs about self, the world, and others—the "cognitive triad." Using a diary, thought tracking can be used between sessions to capture automatic anxious thoughts as they occur in daily life. Clients can learn to challenge these thoughts later. It is helpful to determine whether a particular worry is about the past or future and what they are telling themselves about it. They can also consider alternative ways of interpreting the past and predicting the future, and consider the chances (probabilities) of certain events happening. The downward-arrow technique (Section 6.3.2) can be used to lead to the bottom core belief of a worry chain that brings about catastrophic thinking. The client can be then asked to estimate the probability of each step and think of two alternatives for each step in the chain.[22]

3. Worry exposure. This uses some of the exposure methods involving imagination, fantasy, and real life (*in vivo*) exposure described in Section 6.3.3 to face fearful images and worst-case scenarios.

4. Reduce worry behaviors. An example of worry behavior is frequently checking up on the safety of a person using, for example, cell phone calls or texting. It is a matter of determining these and helping clients to resist urges to carry them out. The general comments about worry in Section 6.1.2 are relevant here.

5. Structured problem solving. This means finding solutions to problems that can be solved (e.g., using the methods of Section 9.4.2) and accepting the problems that can't be solved.

6. Distraction. This involves using a variety of activities, especially those that have been neglected, to shift the focus away from worries.

7. Mindfulness meditation. This method, discussed in Section 12.7.2 under "Relapse Strategies," involves not fighting or judging the worrying thoughts but simply observing them with dispassionate interest. This can help break the cycle of incessant worry.

8. Medication. The most common drugs used are anxiolytics, with benzodiazapines being the most common ones prescribed as they act as tranquilizers bringing a feeling of calm and helping to relax tense muscles. Because they can be addictive and can have long term effects, they are more suited to short term use; they can also cause sleepiness and sexual problems. Antidepressants are also used for treating GAD such as the SSRIs.

---

[21] A helpful resource relating to GAD is Hazlett-Stevens (2008: chapter 5).
[22] For further details see Hazlett-Stevens (2008: chapter 6).

Another approach is to target interpersonal problems and use emotional processing as well as some or all of the above, especially CBT.[23] This can involve exploring past and current relationships, teaching clients alternative ways to handle interpersonal relationships, and making use of the client-therapist relationship. Role playing, using homework to practice new behaviors outside of therapy, and using the therapist to disclose how the clients's interpersonal style is affecting the therapist are all useful tools for helping the client to become more self-aware. Emotional processing is discussed in Section 1.4.2 and here consists of encouraging a client to experience and express his or her emotions as GAD suffers tend to ignore or be afraid of their emotions, including positive ones. It is also a matter of dealing with unfinished business by going back to situations that evoked reactions. A 16-session program using CBT is described by Hazlett-Stevens.[24] She also emphasizes the importance of establishing a written relapse prevention plan (cf. Section 12.7.2).

Summing up, GAD is difficult to treat because of its chronic nature, and unfortunately it is probable that a significant number of people with GAD cannot be cured. Most, however, can be helped a great deal to manage their problem. A reasonable goal is to aim for remission from GAD. Clients need to realize that everyone experiences anxiety and worry to some degree on occasion so that counseling won't help to remove it all. It is a matter of preventing it from becoming excessive, chronic, and difficult to control.

7.3   POST-TRAUMATIC STRESS DISORDER

7.3.1   Introduction

Post-Traumatic Stress Disorder (PTSD) is an anxiety disorder with disabling psychological symptoms that can develop after exposure to a terrifying event or ordeal in which grave physical harm occurred or was threatened. PTSD is often triggered by some event that recalls the original trauma. Such traumatic events include violent personal assaults (e.g., rape), abuse, life-threatening illness, natural or human-caused disasters, accidents to self or others, terrorism, war, or military combat (e.g., shell shock).[25] It is noted that PTSD symptoms seem to be worse if the event that triggered them was deliberately initiated by another person, as in a mugging or a kidnapping. PSTD can occur at any age, including childhood, affecting about 1-9% of the population; women are much more likely to suffer from it than men. There is some evidence that susceptibility to the disorder may run in families. Although the majority of people experience trauma over a lifetime, only about 8% develop full PTSD.[26] There are a number of other disorders that are associated with trauma.[27]

---

[23]Portman (2009: 52).
[24]Hazlett-Stevens (2008: 56–58).
[25]For a detailed list see Briere (2004: chapter 1).
[26]A particularly informative article on PTSD is given by
Wikipedia at http://en.wikipedia.org/wiki/Posttraumatic_stress_disorder.
[27]Briere (2004: chapter 2).

7.3.2   Diagnosis and Symptoms

The diagnostic criteria for PTSD from DSM-IV-TR[28] may be summarized as follows:[29]

1. Exposure to a traumatic event that is life threatening to self or others.

2. Person's response involved intense fear, helplessness, or horror.

3. Persistent re-experience such as recurrent distressing recollections of the event, flashbacks and/or nightmares of the event. The flashbacks may consist of images, sounds, smells, or feelings, and are often triggered by ordinary occurrences, such as a door slamming or a car backfiring on the street. A person having a flashback may lose touch with reality and believe that the traumatic incident is happening all over again.

4. Persistent avoidance of stimuli associated with the trauma so that there is an inability to talk about things even related to the experience and especially those that trigger flashbacks and the re-experiencing of symptoms. There is also a fear of losing control.

5. Persistent symptoms of increased arousal such as sleep problems, irritability, outbursts of anger, being easily startled, finding it difficult to concentrate, and hyper-vigilance.

6. Symptoms last more than 1 month.

7. Significant impairment in social, occupational, or other important areas of functioning such as problems with work and relationships.

8. Efforts to avoid any thoughts, feelings, activities, or places that remind one of the trauma.

9. Feeling of detachment or estrangement from others, especially in relation to people with whom they used to be close.

If the symptoms subside in less than one month, then we use the term *acute distress disorder*.[30] If others died as the result of the trauma there may also be survivor guilt. Other anxiety disorders or depression may be comorbid with PTSD.

The above criteria can be divided into symptoms of intrusion (3, 4, 7), which may happen at least weekly, often daily, or several times a day, avoidance (8, 9), which can include a diminished interest in significant activities or a reduction in emotional responses, and arousal (5). Some helpful lead-in questions are, "Have you ever had any experience that was so frightening, horrible, or upsetting that, in the past month, you had nightmares about it or thought about it when you didn't want to?" and "Have you tried hard not to think about the experience or went out of your way to avoid situations that reminded you of it?" Also, since the experience

---

[28] American Psychiatric Association (2000a,b).
[29] The criteria have changed with each edition of DSM, reflecting some lack of agreement.
[30] Full details of the actual criteria are available at
http://www.behavenet.com/capsules/disorders/ptsd.htm (accessed October 2010).

"Have you been constantly on guard, watchful, or easily startled?" or "Have you felt numb or detached from others, activities, or your surroundings?" Yes to three of the above four questions indicates PTSD.

Not every person who is traumatized develops full-blown or even minor PTSD. Although symptoms usually appear within three months of the incident, they occasionally emerge years later. Some people recover within six months, while others have symptoms that last much longer and the condition may become chronic.

According to Girdano,[31] there are two main underlying factors of PSTD, namely a neurological hypersensitivity leading to a lowered threshold for excessive arousal and a psychological hypersensitivity. The slightest annoyance can lead to abnormal brain activity resulting in rage, panic, and impulsive actions. The amygdala becomes overactive. Trauma often violates, challenges, and sometimes shatters important assumptions or presuppositions about how one sees life and the world around us, thus creating a psychological void. For example, a belief that good always triumphs may be destroyed. This topic is discussed further below under counseling.

One important question is: "When should counseling for trauma take place?" Baker[32] suggests that counseling should not take place immediately after trauma, as in trauma debriefing, as it is not the right time to explore and discuss one's emotional pain. Rather, the memory of the trauma needs to be registered and consolidated first, and ruminating about the event again and again has a natural part to play.

Debriefing

Finally a word about debriefing, which can best be done in groups. This is a controversial subject as there is some evidence to suggest that debriefing does not prevent PTSD and that single session debriefing is not a useful treatment. There is also evidence that it can be harmful for some people.[33] One recommendation is that the compulsory debriefing of victims of trauma should cease and, if it is used, individuals should be screened first to see if it is appropriate for them.

7.3.3 Memory Repression

This topic is highly controversial so my coverage will be limited and is an extension of the discussion on the memory in Sections 15.2.3 and 15.2.4 in relation to child abuse. Excluding sexual abuse for the moment, trauma (especially events that strongly activate the amygdala in the brain) are generally very well remembered, though not infallibly so; generally the greater the trauma the better the memory of it. Some believe there is a lack of evidence to support the idea that some memories of trauma are unconsciously repressed and may argue that memories can be consciously repressed as, for example, in sexual abuse. There is confusion here over the terminology as voluntary forgetfulness is usually referred to as suppression while involuntary forgetfulness is usually called repression. In the debate, a more recent term used than repression is amnesia.[34] Jim Hopper[35] has a very extensive list of

---

[31] Girdano, Everly, and Dusek (1997: 1657).
[32] Baker (2007: 136).
[33] Lilienfeld (2007); see also http://en.wikipedia.org/wiki/Debriefing.
[34] Dissociative amnesia is listed with DSM-IV.
[35] http://www.jimhopper.com/memory/ (accessed November).

references on the subject, for example, Scheflin and Brown (1996) list 25 studies in which there was total or partial amnesia with some child-abuse victims.[36] From a counseling point of view, the question of voluntary versus involuntary forgetfulness is not critical so I will not enter the debate.

Most people who were sexually abused as children remember all or part of what happened to them, although they may not have fully understood or disclosed it. As suggested above, it is not rare for them to experience amnesia and delayed recall for the abuse and, since recall is a process of reconstruction, it therefore involves some degree of distortion. A cautionary note therefore needs to be sounded as there is strong evidence that people can sincerely believe they have recovered a memory or memories of abuse by a particular person, but actually be mistaken. Such mistaken memories and accusations have caused extraordinary pain and damage to individuals and families.

Why the memory gap and delayed recall with abuse? The natural tendency of an abused child is to remain silent because of toxic shame and the fact that a small child has limited vocabulary. Some have argued that the child wants to be rescued from the abuse but it is not possible so the need to forget or dissociate in some way is strongly reinforced, especially if the abuse continues over a period of time. It is also suggested that those with a memory gap may have a delayed onset of PSTD that is triggered by some event that lets loose dormant feelings and memories. They may have severe depression or start having anxiety attacks without any previous history of either of these. Certain situations or objects that cause fear or distress for no apparent reason may indicate forgotten memories. Such feelings can be triggered both in people who remember their abuse as well as those who do not remember. Those who do remember are more able to process what is happening while those who don't can be bewildered by what is happening. As mentioned elsewhere, we can remember feelings but forget the event giving rise to them. What happens is that "Emotional memories are not simply erased. Oppressive negative memories need to be actively replaced by positive memories."[37] Some of the above ideas are still under debate. For example, in other areas of trauma there is evidence that repetition sharpens the memory.[38]

Sometimes there is memory recall through therapy using a form of *repressed memory therapy* (e.g., hypnosis), and there is evidence that such memories may be false (called confabulations) unless there is additional corroboration.[39] The Royal College of Psychiatrists in Britain has officially banned its members from using therapies designed to recover repressed memories of childhood abuse. However, the British Psychological Society does not have such a ban, but in a 1995 report warned about drawing conclusions from memories recovered during therapy. In the end it is not currently possible to distinguish a true memory from a false one without corroborative evidence.[40] There can also be a recall of nightmares, TV or movie scenes, or drug induced hallucinations. Similar care is needed with group therapy

---

[36] For a recent discussion in which the repression theory is negated see http://skepsis.no/?p=638 by Mona Hide Klausen (accessed October 2010).

[37] Quoted by Professor Mansuy, University of Zurich, in ETH Zurich (2008).

[38] See for example Schacter (1996).

[39] For some comments from professional groups see http://www.religioustolerance.org/rmt_prof.htm (accessed October 2010).

[40] For 12 myths about false memories see http://www.bfms.org.uk/site_pages/myths_page.htm (accessed October 2010).

as it can become a communal reinforcement of delusions. The group might not originate the repressed memory, but it might facilitate the birth and nourish the growth of horrendous fantasies.

A working group from the American Psychological Association stated that,

> Clients who seek hypnosis as a means of retrieving or confirming their recollections should be advised that it is not an appropriate procedure for this goal because of the serious risk that pseudomemories may be created in trance states and of the related risk due to increased confidence in those memories.[41]

They went on to say that,

> recollection of trauma is only helpful insofar as it is integrated into a therapy emphasizing improvement of functioning. Therapists should avoid endorsing such retrievals as either clearly truthful or clearly confabulated. Instead, the focus should be on aiding the client in developing his or her own sense of what is real and truthful.

Narrative therapy can be a useful approach in helping to deal with memories and one's story. This is a major part of the counseling methods of Cloitre et al. (2006) discussed in more detail in Chapter 15.

A client who wants to recover (more) memories needs to ask questions like, "Why do I want to recover (more) memories and what will it do for me?" and "How important is it for me to know for sure that I was abused and what in my life will be changed by knowing?" Memories are of course useful and need to be made sense of, especially those disrupting life. However, they are only part of the therapy and clients can move on from there. Memories are little pieces of a jigsaw puzzle. It all depends on how essential it is to have the complete picture.

For those who want to recall memories, Hopper[42] offers the following cautions.

- If abuse memories don't come spontaneously, the body may be providing protection as a defense mechanism from them.

- Trying to forcefully dig up abuse memories is not helpful and can cause harm (e.g., false memories).

- Recovering abuse memories through hypnosis and other mind-altering techniques is almost never a good idea; there is a risk of distorted or false memories.

- Care is needed in focusing on abuse memories that one already has, as a person can be re-traumatized.

- If new memories emerge, they also need to be made sense of, but recovering memories should not be the goal of therapy.

When trying to determine whether or not a client has been abused as a child, some false memory traps based on unproved statements need to be avoided, for example:[43]

---

[41] American Psychological Association (1998).
[42] Adapted from http://www.jimhopper.com/memory/ (accessed October 2010).
[43] See http://www.skepdic.com/repress.html.

1. If you doubt whether you were abused as a child or think that it might be your imagination, it doesn't necessarily prove that it is a sign of "post-incest syndrome."

2. If you can't remember specific instances of abuse, but still have a feeling that something abusive happened, it does not mean that it did.

3. When a person can't remember his or her childhood or has fuzzy memories, it doesn't mean that incest should be considered as a possibility.

4. If you have any vague suspicion or memory relating to abuse it doesn't mean that it happened or that you are merely blocking the memories and denying them.

Summing up, it is very important not to help a client call forth traumatic memories unless the therapist and the client are confident that everything that may arise including anxiety, emotions, and body sensations can be contained at will and that the client has the necessary skills (e.g., the Skills Training in Affective and Interpersonal Regulation (STAIR) method of Cloitre et al (2006) to build resources). This will make trauma therapy safer and easier to control. It is up to the client as to what he or she wants to do about memories.

7.3.4   Counseling for Trauma and PTSD

Assessment

This discussion on counseling will include trauma in general, as not all experiences of trauma lead to PTSD. Careful assessment is important here. In addition to the DSM criteria, some clients may wish to use a helpful questionnaire instead of a structured interview. The Impact of Event Scale-Revised (IES-R) has been found to be a particularly reliable tool even though it does not cover all the criteria.[44] Although various cut-off points have been given in the literature, the scale's main use is to provide information on the intensity of intrusions, avoidance, and hyperarousal.[45]

A so-called structured interview can involve carefully worded logical questions and following a prescribed order of topics. It seeks specific information about symptoms (e.g., prevalence, incidence, duration, and so on) and such things as the client's level of arousal and his or her fragility. One advantage of this approach is that clients can tell their story without interruption. Being familiar with PTSD symptoms, the therapist can slip in the appropriate questions as part of an informal conversation to help the client describe his or her experience more freely.

Spiers emphasizes that it is important to make the counseling experience as "ordinary and as normal as possible to reduce the extraordinariness of the client's experience."[46] Normalizing a client's reaction to a trauma brings reassurance, particularly when they learn that stress symptoms are not a weird, and even a healthy, reaction and will generally fade within 4 to 6 weeks. Some experience

[44]This is readily available on the internet, for example
http://members.iinet.net.au/ gmt/IES-R-Scales.pdf (accessed October 2010).
[45]Other assessment methods are described by Briere (2004: chapter 4).
[46]Spiers (2001a: 49).

genuine relief to know that the disturbing symptoms are due to a traumatic state. The therapist can ask simple questions like, "What has it been like for you since the incident?" and "How are you at home and at work?" Telling the story may be very difficult for some clients so the therapist needs to establish a relationship of safety and be sensitive to any signs of extreme arousal.

Both the immediate symptoms and the activating traumatic wound need to be addressed, though some clients may have difficulty in separating the two. It is important for a therapist to also recognize any developmental wounds having occurred as the child grew up or have occurred in a client's relationship with family and the world; these can become entwined with traumatic woundings. Dissociation, that is splitting away parts of self, may have occurred from the developmental wounds and these can leave significant residual effects that may resurface later.

Defense Mechanisms

There are various defense mechanisms that clients might use to deal with trauma. One defense alluded to briefly above is dissociation from the experience, where the experience is numbed out and sidelined out of awareness, ready to be awakened by future traumas or triggers. Another is denial, a refusal to accept the unwelcome reality and importance or significance of the original experience. This can lead to blocking or repressing specific feelings like sadness, anger or guilt. The therapist needs to be aware of which feelings are absent when working with a client and gently acknowledge the missing feelings. Other defense methods may include splitting, projection, fixation, and regression (see Section 21.5).

Four-Stage Model

Dunn (2001) has developed a four-stage (four-session) counseling model used for trauma aftercare that has many helpful ideas. She gives a detailed description of the model, so I hope I can do justice to some of the ideas in my brief summary. She combines features of various counseling methods beginning with the client-centered approach of Carl Rogers to develop a safe therapeutic relationship. With this modality, clients are encouraged to express what they need to do. The narrative of the client is followed rather than pushing a reluctant client to tell his or her story. Clients can be asked what they would like to talk about in the session or asked how comfortable they are in telling their story.

The client-centered approach can be combined with the psychodynamic method of working with the impact of the past, including previous traumas and developmental problems. Exposure methods can then be used where appropriate and cognitive restructuring can be used to deal with unhelpful beliefs. Care is needed in using exposure methods as some clients are in such distress that they are unable to revisit the trauma even imaginatively; they fear being overwhelmed and losing control of their feelings. If they are overwhelmed, they effectively become retraumatized and may drop out of therapy. On the other hand, some clients can't wait to talk all about the trauma so that their experience can be heard, acknowledged, and processed. The therapist needs to carefully observe if a client is becoming too aroused. Stress reduction techniques are particularly valuable and can be incorporated as part of a holistic approach using ideas from Chapter 2. Clients need to be encouraged to maintain a good daily routine including regular meals and exercise and have a good supportive network of friends, all of which can help towards stress reduction.

In the first session there will be all the usual introductory information that therapists discuss concerning appointments, privacy, and so on. Clients can also be asked how they feel about coming to counseling and what they hope to get from it. As already mentioned, achieving a degree of ordinariness is important and this can be done by initially talking about everyday things. Therapy is to proceed slowly and not be rushed as there can be a strong temptation for the counselor to do something because of the counter-transference often triggered by the client's desperate need of help. This is particularly the case with hyper-aroused clients; clients need to be in control of the pace and when to take a break or stop. If the client becomes too aroused, he or she can be asked to walk around the counseling room touching objects in it, or the therapist can switch to talking about things the client likes such as family or hobbies. Another idea is to ask the client to describe the therapist's physical appearance (e.g, eye or hair color) or some other feature of the counseling room. The client can then be asked what is happening to his or her body. It is a matter of keeping the client grounded and in touch with the real world so that the client can learn to "apply the brakes" in therapy.[47] Assessment is the ultimate aim of the session.

Exposure can begin as early as the first session if the client is willing and able to talk about what happened. To ease the situation it may help if the client looks at how the day had been going before the incident and possibly immediately afterwards. What is important here is not just familiarity with the traumatic experience; exposure "allows for the measured emergence of the traumatic experience in its entirety allowing new information to be available to the client thus enabling new learning to take place."[48] This helps to break down any dissociation and allows a client to process emotionally and cognitively what he or she couldn't do at the time of the incident. When asking about symptoms, the client can be encouraged to go into details (e.g., content of nightmares). Also a client can be encouraged to be aware of his or her bodily reactions as, for example, in body-centered therapy promoted by some therapists.

In the second session the therapist continues to focus on assessment, noting what progress has been made by the client. The story can be retold in more depth giving more details such as sensory information (e.g., sounds), bodily sensations, thoughts, and feelings.

In session three the intrusion symptoms can be dealt with by retelling the story (in chapters, if necessary) and, using exposure. Avoidance can be worked through by setting homework on exposure. Arousal can be reduced through relaxation, breathing, and grounding. As with exposure methods, it is important for the client to stay in the process until the anxiety subsides, possibly revisiting the physical location of the event. This can be done in stages if necessary, and perhaps even visiting more than once. Session four is described as either winding up the counseling or preparing the client for PTSD work.

With regard to PTSD counseling, the counseling and treatment strategies described under generalized anxiety disorder above can also be used here. As already noted, care is needed in using exposure methods as there is a danger of re-traumatizing a client. Using fantasy, the aim is to repeatedly go over the memories

[47]See, for example, Rothschild (2000, 2003).
[48]Spiers (2001b: 19).

of everything associated with the trauma (e.g. antecedent events, circumstances, objects, people, and aftermath). This will need to be done in small steps so that at each step the process stops when the image becomes too uncomfortable.

Two techniques can be helpful, namely, Eye Movement Desensitization and Reprocessing (EMDR) and Traumatic Incident Reduction (TIR). EMDR, mentioned in Section 1.2.5, seems to be a useful method for clients who can tolerate some exposure as it leads to desensitization, while TIR, developed by Gerbode,[49] involves a client repeatedly going over an incident and reporting what is happening. With each viewing, different things are mentioned or noticed, feelings and sensations begin to change, and the incident becomes less disturbing. TIR is also useful for clients who have past traumas not adequately dealt with. In this case clients can confront their past traumas by repeatedly engaging the present incident and linking it back to previous but re-stimulated incidents, which can then be worked through in a similar fashion to the present incident. The therapist, referred to as the facilitator, follows a number of rules[50] such as not interpreting or evaluating for the viewer (client). Dunn has found that TIR works well with clients who can tolerate exposure, are reasonably robust, and have good outside support.[51] Both techniques require specific training. Nydegger (2012: 122) comments that:"A major meta-analytic by the Institute of Medicine did not find that EMDR was an effective treatment for PTSD and the the the effects, if any, were not strong." This suggests that further research is needed.

Throughout the sessions it is important to be aware of the resources that clients have. Turner and Diebschlag[52] suggest a number of resources that are available to help a client, some of which we shall now consider.

Client Resources

The therapist can discover what things or activities in a client's life helps him or her to feel good and then ask the client to imagine carrying out such an activity. The client is then asked to comment on what the body feels, the idea being to get the client to stay with those good sensations and get familiar with recalling them. Another idea is that the therapist, by noting an item of jewelry or clothing, may open up a warm response from a client (e.g., "My favorite pendant"). Also teaching a client to stop and think about their breathing as in the relaxation response (see Section 2.2.5) and using deep muscle relaxation can slow down the client and reduce the stress.

Another available skill clients can learn from a therapist who has practiced the art is to apply to themselves what is called "tracking." This involves being aware of the physical aspects of a person, for example, body language, breathing, habitual gestures, voice tone, changes in skin coloring and moisture, changes in eye pupils, and especially signs of arousal. One other resource for clients is learning to understand their bodily sensations. When they are stuck in the moment of the intrusive traumatic event they have, to some degree, lost connection with "now" and their mind and emotions are caught up in the past. When clients describe a feeling they can be asked what the sensation is in their body, for example, "What

---

[49] See http://www.healing-arts.org/tir/issues.htm by Frank Gerbode (accessed October 2010).
[50] See http://www.healing-arts.org/tir/rules.htm by Nancy Day (accessed October 2010).
[51] Dunn (2001: 123).
[52] Turner and Diebschlag (2001: chapter 3).

sensation in your body is telling you that you are so afraid?" It is like the method of mindfulness (Section 12.7.2 under "Relapse Strategies") in which a person takes a detached nonjudgmental view of what is happening.

World View

A trauma can distort a client's view of others and the world as it cannot be incorporated into a client's schemas or assumptions. This can lead to negative and distorted thinking, for example, the belief that world is safe place may be replaced by the belief that the world is always a dangerous place, and I am a good person replaced by I am a bad person. This can lead to an existential crisis. Cognitive methods can be used and the following are some strategies for dealing with the disturbance caused by violated assumptions.[53]

1. Reinterpret the traumatic event. This involves trying to find something positive about the event such as revealing a previously unknown inner strength.

2. Reinterpret my role in the trauma, for example, favorably comparing myself with others on how well I have survived, or that I have recovered much better than expected. If I am fully or partly responsible for the trauma, then I can learn from it, and give some meaning to the trauma, thus helping to restore my world assumptions.

3. Through appropriate activities I increase my control of the trauma by reducing the likelihood of a repeat of the trauma or similar events (e.g., seek justice or protection, install an alarm system).

4. Use any activity that helps me to increase my personal sense of control (e.g., increasing my self-esteem or assertiveness training) in a world that now seems uncertain.

5. Obtain social support. This will help to restore feelings of safety and security.

6. If the trauma is so great, my assumptions and world view may have to be altered or even radically changed.

Trauma and the Therapist[54]

Coping with the suffering of the traumatized client can be difficult for therapists as they are open to absorbing the profound loss and suffering from their clients through countertransference, which can manifest itself in physical symptoms or even a reaction in anticipation of sessions. Maintaining a balance between being there for the client but not being lost in the client's experience is not easy. There are times when therapists may feel helpless as clients struggle with the existential crisis triggered by the trauma. On such occasions therapists need to accept the role of "being" rather than "doing" along with the inherent insecurity of such a position. Here the person-centered approach means listening and "being" rather than "doing something" with the client, and understanding what is happening.

The relationship is not a question of the therapist knowing it all but rather it is more like two people going on a difficult journey together where both the therapist

---

[53] Adapted from Girdano et al. (1997: 169–171).
[54] The material below is adapted from Berger (2001).

as well as the client may struggle with vulnerability and uncertainty. Past personal experiences such as developmental wounds may be triggered for the therapist. The desire to somehow rescue the client can be very strong and may inadvertently lead to trying to "fix" the client or to disempowering the client, for example, wanting to become an advocate in a disagreement with authorities. The therapist may experience other responses such as avoidance by taking an analytical approach to avoid managing feelings or may pick up some of the client's dissociation. Another response may be some form of denial or minimization through not believing the client or because the client is difficult to reach.

Earthquakes

There are many natural disasters, such as floods, fires, and earthquakes that leave countries devastated and their peoples traumatized. The degree of traumatization will be depend on the nature of the disaster, but perhaps the most difficult disaster to cope with is an earthquake where the threat of aftershocks is very real and unknown. This was brought home to me by an earthquake in Christchurch, New Zealand, where aftershocks have continued for a long time. I wish therefore to digress and make a few additional comments about helping victims of disasters with a focus on earthquakes. This topic is also related to crisis intervention.

Traumatic events are events that are overwhelming, shattering our basic feelings of safety, security, and control. They lead to flash-backs, emotional avoidance, emotional numbing, and hyper-vigilance, with an inability to relax and let go— the fright aspect of fear rather than flight or fight. There is invariably a second earthquake, and the aftershocks can be more traumatic than the original shocks as they hit people who are already sensitized, jumpy, not sleeping, and fearful of the future; one's body says here we go again. If the quakes continue unpredictably, people of all ages have to endure them and manage anxiety and fear, and cope with frustration and anger. The continuing tensions that people hold in their minds and bodies may lead to all sorts of unsettling bodily symptoms that can be hard to deal with. They may develop PTSD. Some general suggestions, not in any particular order, to add to the above for counseling such clients follow:

1. *Grieve.* As noted in Chapter 11, whenever there is a loss, grief will follow. Grieving allows you to process what has happened and to move on more quickly with your life.

2. *Help others.* Let your heart prompt you as to the good you can do. Helping others shifts the focus away from self and ones personal problems.

3. *Maintain a network of friends.* We all need someone's shoulder to cry on, as well as listening to others also suffering their losses. There is a need to team together and share experiences when ready to do so.

4. *Take care of self.* It is important to do the basics with regard to eating, sleeping, and exercising. The latter will help in coping with stress and depression. Keep a daily routine is helpful and getting out into nature and perhaps going for a walk in the park can be therapeutic. There is the temptation to try and fix everything at once as there is usually so much to do, so take your time. It is helpful to have daily goals, and it is important to get enough rest. Do some things that you enjoy doing, e.g., listening to music.

5. *Use relaxation techniques to cope with stress.*

6. *Limit media exposure about the earthquake.* This is with regard to radio, TV, and the newspaper. Instead, tune into specific programs that give you just the information you need.

7. *Become more aware of your surroundings and the here and now.* This helps you to become more grounded. It means using all your senses of smell, hearing, taste, and touch to savor life. Wear something that you like (e.g. jewelry or clothing) that is comforting.

8. *Begin restoring order.* No matter how big the task of recovery, celebrate each small step, and pace yourself as you do it. Have realistic goals (see Section 2.3.2). Making small decisions (e.g., what I shall eat for the next meal, what music I shall listen to) can help restore some feeling of control again.

9. *Begin to be hopeful.* Hopefulness helps us to deal with depression and negative thinking.

10. *It may be helpful to write down your thoughts, memories, and experiences.* This helps to eternalize what is going on inside.

It seems that people have a natural ability to recover from a crisis provided that they have the support, guidance, and resources that they need. Awareness of the impact of a crisis on oneself is an important part of being able to move on. It can lead to the unlocking of one's potential. Although the above focuses on earthquakes, it applies to other disasters as well.

7.4   PANIC DISORDER

Panic Disorder (PD) was briefly alluded to in the previous chapter (Section 6.4.2) where panic attacks were discussed in detail. The lifetime prevalence rate of PD is about 3–5%, and females are about twice as likely to be affected by it as males. Comorbidity rates are high especially for other anxiety disorders (e.g., GAD, social phobia) and depression. PD can be confused with hypochondriasis (the persistent emotional conviction of having a disease) and GAD, especially because of the fear or tension between attacks. A key difference of PD from other anxiety disorders is that the panic attacks are unexpected or uncued, whereas with other disorders the attacks tend to be cued by some thought (e.g., worries with GAD) or exposure to some situation or trigger (e.g., certain social situations or facing a feared object).

7.4.1   Assessment of PD

The DSM-IV-TR criteria for panic disorder require recurrent unexpected panic attacks plus at least one month of persistent concern about experiencing additional attacks, worry about the implications or consequences of attacks (e.g. losing control, having a heart attack, "going crazy"), or a significant change in behavior related to attacks. Panic disorder may occur with or without agoraphobia, though most people with PD have at least some degree of agoraphobic avoidance. Substance abuse, medical conditions, and other disorders need to be ruled out.[55]

A helpful downloadable self-report version of the the Panic Disorder Severity Scale (PDSS-SR) for assessment is available.[56] A total score above 8 out of a possible 28 suggests panic disorder.[57] However, the interpretation of the PDSS total score differs according to the presence or absence of agoraphobia. When the clients are not agoraphobic, score ranges 0–1 correspond with "Normal," 2–5 with "Borderline," 6–9 with "Slightly ill," 10–13 with "Moderately ill," and 14 and above with "Markedly ill." When the clients are agoraphobic, score ranges 3–7 mean "Borderline ill," 8–10 "Slightly ill," 11–15 "Moderately ill," and 16 and above "Markedly ill."[58] As far as counseling is concerned, I believe that the fine divisions of the scores are not as important as the general qualitative information gleaned from the questionnaire answers. The questionnaire can also be used to track progress when repeated later.

Clients with PD have many physical complaints (e.g. chest pain, shortness of breath) tending to be convinced that they are physically ill (e.g., have heart trouble) and resisting the thought that their disorder may be psychiatric. PD is associated with high levels of subjective distress, frequent use of emergency services, impaired social functioning, substance abuse, and a high rate of suicide attempts. There is no single cause for panic disorder, but it has been found to run in families suggesting a genetic effect, though the connection is not clear.[59]

7.4.2 Counseling for PD

It is important to get a very detailed history from the client with regard to such things as the duration of the PD, the degree of functional impairment, any previous treatment, and any family history. Information is also needed on the severity of the PD as indicated by the frequency, intensity, and duration of panic attacks as well as the degree of anticipatory anxiety and phobic avoidance of situations and places. The primary goals of treatment for PD are: diminution of the frequency and intensity of panic attacks, decrease of anticipatory anxiety, reduction of phobic avoidance, and acquiring the skill to focus on something else to break the cycle of distress. The methods mentioned in the previous chapter for panic attacks are relevant here. Using cognitive therapy and education about panic attacks is well supported in the literature.

A major concern with people suffering panic attacks is the threat of loss of control that can occur in four areas of their lives, namely:[60]

1. *Somatic Loss of Control.* They fear such things as a heart attack, stroke or fainting, and that their body will let them down. This results in them

---

[55]For details of the DSM-IV-TR criteria see, for example,
http://en.wikipedia.org/wiki/Panic_disorder.
[56]See http://goodmedicine.org.uk/files/panic,%20assessment%20pdss.pdf:accessed October 2010.
[57]Estimated by Shear et al. (2001).
[58]Furukawa et al. (2009). See the abstract at
http://onlinelibrary.wiley.com/doi/10.1002/da.20532/abstract (accessed October 2010).
[59]For a collection of abstracts from research studies see
http://www.neurotransmitter.net/panicgenetic.html (accessed October 2010).
[60]Emmelkamp et al. (1989: 6).

making demands on medical services even when they are reassured that there is nothing organically wrong.

2. *Psychic Loss of Control.* They may believe they are going mad and losing their grip on situations.

3. *Behavioral Loss of Control.* This is a very a frightening idea as they may be afraid of throwing away their inhibitions and doing crazy things under a panic attack like yelling or screaming, throwing things, or hurting themselves.

4. *Loss of Control in Social Respect.* Here they often feel ashamed about alleged signs of increased arousal or of their sensations that actually occur such as nervousness, trembling, and wanting to leave. They have thoughts like, "People will think I'm mad" and visualize all sorts of embarrassing behavior like lying on the ground.

Looking at these four areas may help therapists to decide where to focus their efforts. The direction of counseling will depend on whether the client has agoraphobia or not. What happens is that panic attacks predispose a person to engage in avoidance behavior that often leads to agoraphobia.

If a client has agoraphobia as well as PD, then Section 7.6 on agoraphobia is appropriate and both cognitive therapy and the exposure methods discussed in the previous chapter can be used. Emmelkamp et al.[61] emphasize the following facts about exposure methods: (a) exposure in vivo (real life) is more effective than exposure in imagination, (b) prolonged exposure is more effective than brief exposure, (b) fast exposure is more effective than slow-paced exposure, and (d) practice in more frequent counseling sessions is more effective than practice in more spaced sessions. If hyperventilation is a problem and it often is, then education about its role in panic attacks (see Section 6.4.4) and the learning of breathing exercises is helpful.

7.5 PHOBIAS

Phobias[62] are probably the most common anxiety disorder and affect a substantial proportion of the population. A phobia is an irrational, intense, and persistent fear of certain situations, activities, things, or persons along with an unreasonable and excessive desire to avoid the feared subject. When the fear is out of control and is interfering with daily life, then a diagnosis under one of the anxiety disorders can be made.

7.5.1 Categories of Phobias

Phobias are usually classified as follows:[63]

1. Agoraphobia (with or without panic disorder).

---

[61]Emmelkamp et al. (1992: 88–89).

[62]From the Geek word *phobos* meaning "fear".

[63]I have given some of the more common ones their technical names. For an extensive list see http://en.wikipedia.org/wiki/-phobia#Psychological_conditions.

2. Social phobia.

3. Specific phobias. The DSM-IV defines the following four main subtypes of specific phobia:

   (a) Animal type, for example, spiders (arachnophobia), insects, dogs, cats, rodents, snakes, birds, and fish.

   (b) Natural environment type, for example heights (acrophobia), water (aquaphobia), lighting and thunderstorms.

   (c) Blood-injection-injury type (e.g., seeing blood, getting an injection or blood test, and watching surgery).

   (d) Situational type, for example enclosed places (claustrophobia), the dark, driving, flying, elevators, and bridges.

   (e) Other type (e.g., phobic avoidance of situations that may lead to choking, vomiting, or contracting an illness; in children, avoidance of loud sounds or costumed characters).

7.5.2 Counseling for Phobias

The methods of the previous chapter using cognitive restructuring and exposure (real or imagined) can be used for all the phobias. We recall from that chapter that a client can accept the disturbing bodily symptoms using Weekes' four steps of Section 6.4.3 knowing that the fear always subsides. With regard to exposure, a client needs to feel fear and anxiety before they can become desensitized to these feelings. The client can reframe any anxious thoughts with "This anxiety is good as it means I am beginning to desensitize" or "I need this anxiety as I can't desensitize without feeling it."[64] Repeated exposure usually works provided it is regularly practiced. In Chapter 9 on depression I emphasize the importance of positive self-talk; the same can be true with anxiety problems. Negative self-talk can reinforce the avoidance behavior and can be a catalyst for a panic attack. Bourne[65] has some useful suggestions for a client to make the most of real-life exposures, such as the following:

1. Be willing to take risks, talk yourself out of any resistance, and be prepared for some discomfort. However, be prepared to retreat from too much exposure if necessary.

2. Don't start too high on the anxiety scale, and take your time. Repeat exposures several times before moving up a hierarchy.

3. Plan your exposures in advance and plan for any contingencies or worst-case scenarios.

4. Know how to cope with early stages of panic, and keep repeating positive coping statements before and during exposures.

5. Don't let any setbacks discourage you, but treat them as a learning experience.

---

[64]Bourne (2005: 149).
[65]Bourne (2005: 144–148).

6. Accept any strong feelings and allow them to surface.

7. Don't stop the process until you are over all your problems and free of any props (e.g., support people, medications).

The above general principles, which apply to all phobias, will be incorporated into the following discussion of the more better-known individual phobias.

7.6 AGORAPHOBIA

7.6.1 Diagnosis

Agoraphobia[66] initially meant a fear of open spaces, though its definition has widened to refer to a fear of public or unfamiliar places. When there are associated panic attacks, which is usually the case (85% to 95% of agoraphobics), the anxiety felt is really a fear of having a panic attack in these places (and this can include being embarrassed as well), rather than a fear of the places themselves. Typically, these attacks are experienced when client is experiencing feelings of being trapped, insecure, out of their comfort zone, or out of control, with no escape routes. Agoraphobia can start suddenly with an unexpected panic attack, which generally leads to the place of attack being avoided. This sets up the avoidance pattern that can end up with such clients being confined to their home, being afraid to go out from their "safe place." Alternatively, they may not be able move too far away from home, only on well-travelled routes, and sometimes only with certain people. Agoraphobia occurs about twice as commonly among women as it does in men and tends to begin in early adulthood.

General criteria for a diagnosis of agoraphobia can therefore be described as follows:[67]

1. There is an anxiety about being in places or situations from which escape might be difficult (or embarrassing) or where they might get caught out with an unexpected panic attack or panic-like symptoms. Typical situations include crowded public places (e.g., shops, stores, restaurants, and railway stations), enclosed or confined places (e.g., cars, tunnels, bridges, and elevators), and public transport (e.g., trains, subways, buses, and planes), or even simply being alone and away from home.

2. The situations are either avoided so that life is restricted or else they endure the situations with marked distress, or need a companion with them.

3. For a specific diagnosis, other anxiety disorders need to be ruled out such as social phobia (e.g., avoidance limited to social situations because of fear of embarrassment), specific phobia (e.g., avoidance limited to a single situation like elevators), obsessive-compulsive disorder, post-traumatic stress disorder or separation anxiety disorder (e.g., avoiding leaving home or relatives).

[66] From the Greek word *agora* meaning "market place."
[67] For the specific DMS-IV-TR criteria for a diagnosis of agoraphobia see
http://en.wikipedia.org/wiki/Agoraphobia, from American Psychiatric Association (2000 a,b).

As with other such disorders, we have to rule out any direct physiological effects of the abuse of a substance (e.g., alcohol, drugs, medications) or a general medical condition.

Two features from the above criteria deserve comment.[68] First, the strength of the phobia can vary greatly from person to person, and the list of possible anxiety-producing situations is extensive. However, travel is usually involved and the distance from "home" or even from one's car can be an important factor. Second, phobic anxiety can occur when a person is separated from significant attachment figures. With severe agoraphobia, this need for help and understanding from significant others can put a great strain on friends and family. It should be noted that a major affect of agoraphobia is depression.

7.6.2   Counseling for Agoraphobia

The general methods of counseling in Section 6.3 can be adapted for agoraphobia. Education concerning misconceptions about the problem will be invaluable. For example, a person may believe that his or her problem is solely due to an undiagnosed physical problem (e.g., diabetes) and therefore has a physical solution. Clarke and Wardman[69] describe a number of misconceptions such as: agoraphobia is a panic disorder and not a real phobia, it is a fear of open spaces, it is an attention-seeking device (certainly a lot of support is sought by the sufferer), it is a form of depression, it is a mental illness, and it can be cured by "will power." The difference between an agoraphobic and a claustrophobic—and these can be confused—is that the former wants to be near a door so that there is an escape route while the latter wants to be near a window. If panic disorder is also present, then Section 7.4 is relevant here. We now consider several therapeutic methods for agoraphobia.

Anxiety Hierarchy

There are two parts to the counseling process: first, providing coping skills to manage the fear and the panic and anxiety episodes, and second, dealing with the extent and degree of avoidance. We can use the direct exposure approach or the anxiety hierarchy of Section 6.3.3 in which situations causing anxiety are listed with increasing scores and then we add another category for each item, namely the degree of avoidance using categories like "none", "slight" avoidance, "usually" avoid, and "always" avoid. For example (with scores and categories in brackets), going to a local shop with a friend (2, none), going to a local shop on one's own (3, none),..., having coffee with a friend at the local mall (7, usually),..., having coffee on one's own at a local mall (10, always). By tracking such scores, any long term progress made can be measured, as often clients forget how far they have progressed. For the same reason, a *brief* diary of events and reactions in association with homework activities is also a useful tool for assessing short term progress with both planned and unplanned activities.

An additional approach is to take a particular situation and break it down into small stages, giving a separate hierarchy for that situation. For example, if going to a shop has a score of 9, then simpler stages might be: go to the shop then come

---

[68]Clarke and Wardman (1985: 10–11). This book gives a powerful story of a doctor and his struggle with agoraphobia.
[69]Clarke and Wardman (1985: 46–53).

away immediately; go to the shop and spend some time at the doorway or gazing in the window; go into the shop halfway, look briefly at an item, then leave; go into the shop and look around for five minutes; and so on. By working through the stages, progressive desensitization can be achieved and both scores for that situation thus reduced; the key is repetition, especially for routine activities. The idea is to stay in a stage long enough for any anxious feelings to subside so that the score for that stage eventually drops low enough for the person to move to the next stage. Goal setting is important.

The therapist should be aware that exposure therapy is not easy for clients so that any progression may need to be made gradually with small steps. Some anti-anxiety medications can bring relief when necessary, but they are a temporary crutch only and a "reasonable" rather than a drugged exposure is essential. Low doses of tranquilizers may be used to help a client negotiate the early stages of exposure. It is important to have a clear contract for each step and to stick to the contract, especially when the temptation arises for the client to cancel out because anticipatory anxiety increases as the time for the exposure exercise approaches. Nicotine, caffeine, and immoderate drinking should be avoided. In times of sickness and other difficult life events it is best for the client to ease back a bit, but not stop the program altogether. Group therapy can also be helpful.[70]

Fantasy and visualization in the safety of the counseling room can be extremely helpful along with therapeutic techniques for handling panic attacks, but in the end the client has to function in the real world so that eventually a self-managed program is the key. Everyday activities will provide their own challenges, and there are usually opportunities to incorporate various strategies such as choosing a favorable venue with an "escape route" in mind (e.g., a table near an exit or a toilet), and varying the duration of the exposure and the time of the day. There may be times when it is helpful for the therapist to be physically present at a real-life desensitizing situation (e.g., go to the shop initially with the client).

Cognitive restructuring in the counseling process can be an important part of the therapy program for all phobias in terms of neutralizing threats, but the behavioral component plays a key role in eliminating avoidance so that imagination is engaged (with the main input from the client) in devising suitably graded or alternative behavioral experiments. Some of the client's irrational beliefs can be tested by an appropriate experiment (e.g., "Are people are always watching me at a restaurant?" and "If they do look at me, does it matter?")

Meditation

Another helpful program for the client is meditation. This is essentially the relaxation response of Section 2.2.5 carried out for an extended period of time (say 20 minutes twice a day) with eyes closed. The aim of meditation is to step back from intrusive and self-destructive thoughts rather than trying to fight them. The thoughts are not probed, analyzed, or disputed as in cognitive restructuring, but we simply draw away from them by concentrating on breathing and using a particular word such as "relax" when breathing out. Our minds will continually wander off in inappropriate directions but we keep coming back to our routine and, with practice, our attention control and focus will improve. The key is not to try too hard or strive to do it perfectly—you just let it happen with as little effort

---

[70]There are a number of agoraphobia support groups available.

as possible. The client should be warned that although it is essentially an easy task, especially in the safety of the therapist's office with the reassuring voice of the therapist, it can be difficult at first even in a client's own home. The aim is not tranquility but a refocusing. There will be "good" and "not so good" meditation days, but persistence is important, as with practicing anything in life.

Clarke and Wardman[71] recommend keeping a daily record of a client's meditations that includes the duration and degree of difficulty for each meditation. They also suggest having "mini-meditations," which are also called rapid relaxation responses, throughout the day when the environment is not conducive to a full meditation. For example, one can count ten focused breaths.

7.7 SOCIAL PHOBIA

7.7.1 Criteria

Social phobia or social anxiety disorder is one of the more common anxiety disorders with the rates being similar for men and women.[72] Its onset typically occurs between 11 and 19 years of age, with the onset after 25 years much less likely.[73] There is evidence that social phobia runs in families through heredity and environment, although the genetic connection is probably more in terms of a predisposition rather than a direct transmission.[74] Some people have very specific social anxieties, while others have more pervasive anxieties (generalized social phobia) affecting a wide range of social activities. The problem is diagnosed as social phobia if the following conditions, summarized from the DSM-TR-IV[75] are met:

1. A marked and persistent fear of one or more social and performance situations in which the person is exposed to unfamiliar people or to possible scrutiny by others, and embarrassment may occur. The most common social phobia is a fear of public speaking, which affects a lot of people and is equally prevalent among men and women.

2. Exposure to the feared social situation almost invariably provokes anxiety, which may result in a panic attack.

3. The person recognizes that his or her fear is excessive or unreasonable.

4. The person avoids the feared social or performance situations or else endures them with intense anxiety or distress.

5. The diagnosis is appropriate only if the avoidance, anxious anticipation, or distress in the feared social or performance situation interferes significantly with the person's normal functioning (e.g., with work, social activities, or important relationships), and/or there is marked distress about having the phobia.

---

[71] Clarke and Wardman (1985: 85–87).
[72] Up to 14% of adults in the U.S. experience social phobia at some time in their lives (Bourne (2005: 12).
[73] http://en.wikipedia.org/wiki/Social_phobia.
[74] Heimberg and Becket (2002: 25).
[75] American Psychiatric Association (2000a,b).

6. In individuals under the age of 18 years, the symptoms must have persisted for at least 6 months.

7. The fear or avoidance is not due to any of the following: (a) the physiological effects of any substance (e.g., medication or drug abuse), (b) a general medical condition, and (c) some other mental disorder such as panic disorder with or without agoraphobia.

8. If a general medical condition or another mental disorder is present, the fear in criterion (1) at the beginning of this list is unrelated to it, for example, the fear is not of stuttering, trembling in Parkinson's disease, or exhibiting abnormal eating behavior in Anorexia Nervosa or Bulimia Nervosa.

As well as public speaking, some common social phobias include fears such as: blushing in public, choking on or spilling food while eating in public, being watched at work, using public toilets, writing or signing documents in the presence of others, fear of crowds, and the fear of taking examinations.[76]

Social phobia is very similar to avoidant personality disorder (APD) and there is no agreement in the literature as to how different the two disorders really are.[77] A person with APD is characterized by an avoidance of social interaction for fear of being ridiculed, humiliated, rejected or disliked, and they often consider themselves to be socially inept or personally unappealing.[78] A person with social phobia on the other hand may experience panic attacks, though in contrast to panic disorder the attacks occur only during or in anticipation of feared situations rather than spontaneously (i.e., unexpectedly and apparently out of the blue).

Social phobia is often comorbid with other psychiatric disorders such as panic disorder, generalized anxiety disorder, post-traumatic stress disorder, and clinical depression. A lack of personal relationships combined with long periods of isolation because of avoiding social situations, can lead to low self-esteem and depression. A sufferer may then turn to alcohol or other drugs for relief.[79] While social phobia can have its origins in a variety of situations such as family background, trauma, illness, and being teased or rejected by peers, it is however basically a learned behavior resulting from life's experiences. The good news for a client is that it is possible for the behavior to be unlearned and replaced by new behaviors. The social phobia/social anxiety association provides a helpful website.[80]

7.7.2   Assessment of Social Phobia

In determining the social fears experienced by a client, we need to explore a couple of fears, namely, the fear of interacting in dyads and groups (social interaction anxiety) and the fear of being observed and scrutinized by others (performance anxiety). As in agoraphobia, there are also two aspects of the phobia, the fear (or anxiety) and avoidance, thus giving four categories for assessment. Heimberg and Becker[81] give a number of assessment scales including the Liebowitz Social Anxiety

---

[76]Bourne (2005: 11).
[77]Heimberg and Becker (2002: 34).
[78]Avoidant Personality Disorder is discussed in Chapters 21 and 22.
[79]For further general information see http://en.wikipedia.org/wiki/Social_phobia.
[80]http://www.socialphobia.org/whatis.html (accessed October 2010).
[81]Heimberg and Becker (2005: chapter 6).

Scale (LSAS), which is readily accessible,[82] can be self-administered, covers the four categories, is reliable, and gives an overall score for diagnosis. For those items where the client has not experienced a particular situation, Heimberg and Becker recommend simply imagining being in that situation and scoring accordingly.

7.7.3 Counseling Social Phobia

The methods in the previous chapter and in the previous section on agoraphobia can be used for dealing with social phobia, for example, using a combination of cognitive restructuring and various exposure methods (EPR). Social skills training, including assertiveness training, can also be of value. The exposure can be progressively less controlled beginning with covert rehearsal in the counseling room using fantasy and simulated incidents, then perhaps incorporating role play with the therapist, and finally encountering the actual social situation or a hierarchy of situations. Medication using anti-depressants and low doses of tranquilizers can be helpful and group therapy is particularly relevant for social phobia as it allows direct exposure to social situations.[83]

Poor social skills can be uncovered from examples of difficult situations given by the client, perhaps from a diary of incidents. These incidents can be used for role-playing to help the client to acquire new behaviors and new social skills. The client might find such activities artificial and a bit awkward at first so that beginning with the less difficult skills will encourage self-confidence. The client may of course even disagree with the therapist about an appropriate response in a given situation, and that is okay.

The anxiety response has three interacting components, a physiological component (i.e., feeling), a behavioral component (i.e., doing), and a cognitive component (i.e., thinking). It is therefore important for the client to keep a diary record of incidents causing anxiety along with accompanying feelings, behavior, and those automatic thoughts that play a role in cognitive therapy. A hierarchy of anxieties, referred to in the previous section, may be difficult to put together for some day-to-day activities, but the concept can be used imaginatively such as taking an everyday or regular activity and adding some social interaction to increase the anxiety score. The idea is for the client to try and do something every day such as interacting with another person or doing something when others may be watching.

In dealing with the client's feared situations, the therapist may find it helpful to be aware of the following.[84]

1. *The perceived audience.* Here the client will feel threatened by the "audience" that can consist of a single individual, a group of peers, or some strangers simply observing the person in public. The client thinks that he or she is being evaluated.

2. *Perceived audience reaction.* Clients construct a mental picture of how they will be viewed by the audience, even of one person, and this forms the basis of how they think they will be evaluated. Typically the picture is negatively dis-

---

[82]See http://www.socialanxietysupport.com/disorder/liebowitz/ (accessed November 2010).
[83]See, for example, Heimberg and Becker (2002: part II).
[84]Heimberg and Becker (2002: 98–103).

torted by the client, for example, "Because she is so beautiful and so engaging, she will expect too much from me."

3. *Too much attention is given to the audience and their possible reaction.* Clients focus so much on every little thing about themselves, including the perceived audience reaction, that they can't relax and give full attention to the actual social interaction. They will therefore look for anything that will confirm their negative image, for example, "She's looking all around so she thinks I am a loser," so that they end up interacting badly, thus confirming their worst fears!

4. *Comparing one's image with the appraisal of the audience's expected standard.* The extent to which a client believes his or her behavior matches audience expectations depends on a variety of factors such as behavior and social demands. This comparison generally leads to a negative evaluation and consequent mental pain; social situations that trigger such responses are then avoided.

We have seen that negative thoughts and negative self-assessments need to be challenged, as well as using exposure methods. Typically the client's automatic thoughts will be negative, illogical thoughts about himself or herself, others, the world, or the future. Clients usually lack self-esteem, have poor social skills, and may having upsetting bodily reactions that they think everybody is noticing. In fact the effect of their reactions on others is usually negligible. They will probably blame themselves unnecessarily for unsuccessful social encounters.

Cognitive restructuring can help clients change unhelpful beliefs and counteract some of the negative feedback that they give themselves. It also enables them to think less about audience reaction and more about their performance of the social task as well as being more positive in looking back on the event. Heimberg and Becker[85] suggest two helpful approaches to eliciting more rational responses from a client, the "non-equation" for undermining over-generalization, and focusing on the worst possible outcome and seeing it in a more positive light. They give the following non-equations: "Looking nervous does not equal ($\neq$) looking foolish," "Not getting this job $\neq$ Never getting a job," and "Feeling anxious $\neq$ Looking anxious."

Methods of Exposure

Exposure to feared situations has several advantages.[86] First, it bypasses the avoidance problem and allows clients to experience the natural reduction in anxiety that comes with them being in the situation long enough on repeated occasions. Second, exposure allows clients to practice their behavioral skills in situations that may have been long avoided (e.g., eating in a restaurant). Third, exposure gives clients the opportunity to test the reality of their dysfunctional beliefs (e.g., "People always stare at me when I eat in public" or "I won't think of anything to say when I take this person out to lunch.")

The question is which type of exposure works best, in-session exposure or real-life exposure; both have advantages and disadvantages depending on the nature of the

[85] Heimberg and Becker (2002: 194–195).
[86] Heimberg and Becker (2002: 129–130.

anxiety. For example, Hallam[87] advocates focusing more on homework assignments relating to actual incidents in the client's life, drawn from the diary recordings, as many clients find it impossible to completely avoid all social situations. However, what clients might do is have a minimal participation in the feared situations and simply endure the situations at some cost, resulting in withdrawal rather than experiencing the full exposure. Although behavioral exposure is taking place, it is not helping as clients need to be able to analyze their problem and perhaps reassess the standards by which they judge their own performance and that of others. The therapist needs to keep closely in touch with the client's experiences and slow down the process if necessary.

Sometimes social exchanges are so brief that clients are not able to see a reduction in their anxiety through exposure but may simply be left "hanging." Even if they are exposed long enough, there is still the problem of a fear of a negative evaluation by the audience. In some situations they may not be able to discern how they are being evaluated so that the exposure may not provide the information needed to help set aside the fear of a negative evaluation. On the other hand, in-session simulated exposures are always available, able to be scheduled, controllable, and moldable to the needs of the individual client. Whilst less easily avoided than homework assignments, in-session work is easily integrated with cognitive restructuring activities, and are under the observation of the therapist.[88] The therapist can employ role-play to rehearse difficult situations recorded in the client's diary and then easily observe the client's behavior first-hand. However, some situations are obviously very difficult to simulate in the counseling room and group sessions might be more helpful here. Clearly both types of exposure are important with in-session exposure perhaps being more appropriate at the beginning of the counseling process.

Automatic Thoughts

We now turn our attention to automatic thoughts mentioned above. When challenging these, care is needed to start with more peripheral ones as these can be more easily challenged or changed. By nibbling away at the edges, a structure of deep-seated faulty thinking can be brought down! Arguing with the client about believing an alternative rational response must be avoided. The aim remains to encourage the client to keep an open mind about the possibility that the alternative rational response is true. The therapist might find it helpful to have a list of the usual erroneous thinking such as that given in Section 1.4.3 under the title of "Cognitive Distortions." An erroneous thinking list can be supplied by the therapist or provided by the client from his or her own experiences. I now want to say something about homework.[89]

Homework

As already stated, homework is important for encouraging the client to face anxiety-causing situations in real-life and I have already mentioned the importance of trying to confront something every day. Before doing so, the client's homework can be to prepare by visualizing the situation, record automatic thoughts (ATs) and rate the degree of belief for each thought (e.g., 0–10), then check out each AT

---

[87]Hallam (1992: 145–147).
[88]Heimberg and Becker (2002: 201).
[89]See Heimberg and Becker (2002: chapter 13).

for thinking errors using a list of disputing questions compiled by the therapist. Examples of questions are: "How can I tell?", "Do I know for certain that ...?" , "What evidence do I have that ...?", "What is the worst that can happen? How bad is that ?", and "Is there an alternative explanation?" There is ample evidence from therapists that client homework speeds recovery.

7.8   SPECIFIC PHOBIAS

Specific (simple) phobia is a generic term for any kind of anxiety disorder that involves an unreasonably strong fear and avoidance of one particular type of object or situation. Consequently the affected person tends to actively avoid direct contact with the object or situation, and, in severe cases, avoid any mention or depiction of the object or situation. The fear or anxiety may be triggered both by the presence and the anticipation of the specific object or situation, and direct exposure to the feared object or situation may elicit a panic attack. However, there are no spontaneous panic attacks or fear of them (as in agoraphobia) and no fear of embarrassment in social situations (as in social phobia). There is a recognition that the fear is excessive and unreasonable and there is an inability to overcome it. There is a fear of harm, concerns about losing control, having a panic attack, or having bodily symptoms like a racing heart, or fear of fainting. The fear and avoidance are strong enough to interfere with normal routines and cause significant distress. Specific phobias affect about 10% of the population, but only a minority of people seek treatment.[90] Specific phobias can coexist with other disorders, the latter usually being the focus of clinical attention. Medications generally do not appear to be useful as a first-line treatment for specific phobias.

Referring to the list of specific phobias given in Section 7.5.1 above, animal phobias often begin in childhood when they are considered normal fears. However, if they persist into adulthood and cause considerable disruption and distress, then they are classified as specific phobias. The same can be be said for natural environmental phobias. Blood-injection-injury phobias can arise out of painful past experiences or some physical trauma, or even from vivid unpleasant TV or movie scenes that have stuck in one's mind, and can extend to a doctor's or dentist's surgery. Situational phobias can cover a wide range of situations, though the more common ones involve a fear of heights and especially a fear of flying.

As with other phobias, the counseling approach is to use cognitive restructuring and progressive exposure as used above and discussed in the previous chapter; relaxation techniques are also helpful. Fearful thoughts can be challenged and coping statements help, for example, "I have handled this kind of thing before and I can do it again" and "This is just an intrusive thought and I don't need to act on it." Bourne[91] gives a number of interesting examples of hierarchies. For example if elevators are a problem, then a sequence might be: watch elevators go up and down; stand in a stationary elevator with a support person, and then alone; go up or down one floor with and then without the support person. Clients can be asked for suggestions.

[90] Bourne (2005: 14).
[91] Bourne (2004: 139–141).

Needles

The fear of needles is worthy of specific mention. It is a bit different from other phobias and affects a substantial proportion of the population ranging from 3%–10%.[92] The difference lies in the fact that avoiding needles can lead to a person not accessing proper medical or dental care, which can even be life threatening and has certainly lead to deaths.[93] A fear of pain is not generally the phobic's main focus, though there are some who have inherited a pain sensitivity (hyperalgesia) and may need some form of anesthesia. Fainting is quite common with people who have a blood or injection phobia (about 50% of them) as their blood pressure and heart rate may drop sharply, and sufferers are often more afraid of this reaction than the needle itself.[94] This needle fear may be an inherited condition that can grow through repeated needle exposure so there is a learning component as well. One method of dealing with this problem is for clients to tense all the muscles of their body, thereby increasing their blood pressure and preventing fainting. Another approach is to lie down with feet elevated. Beta blockers can also be used. Progressive exposure techniques need to be used here with great care in a non-medical setting as conjuring up images of needle procedures can evoke a full needle-phobic reaction.[95] Avoiding visual exposure, providing topical anesthesia, or using anti-anxiety drugs (e.g., a quick acting one like diazepam) are alternative treatments.

Other causes of the phobia can be childhood trauma associated with needle procedures or a repressive upbringing leading to a fear of being controlled. Cognitive and exposure methods are also helpful here. Inappropriate health care by professionals can also have a negative impact on children. Two helpful questions to ask are: "What would need to be different about the experience of needle sticks in order for you to accept them without disabling pain, fear, or anxiety?" and "When did you first realize that you had this problem and what do you think caused it?" Clients need to helped to begin to understand why they are afraid of needles.

7.9   ACCEPTANCE AND COMMITMENT THEORY (ACT)

The above methods and those in the next chapter describe traditional ways of counseling anxiety and compulsive disorders. Although this book is not about counseling modalities, some mention should be made of a more recent modality called Acceptance and Commitment Theory (ACT), developed during the 1980s and expanded in its scope in the last decade. ACT therapy can be combined with the traditional methods of exposure therapy, but with the goal of feeling rather than feeling better. It embraces both traditional behavior therapy and traditional CBT, and endeavors to look past anxiety symptoms and symptom alleviation to the client's life situation. The aim is to ask questions like, "What are the so-called symptoms of anxiety a sign of?" and "What processes turns normal anxiety into the devastating problems that we refer to as anxiety disorders?" It turns out that the disorders are more similar than what is apparent so that there is a need for one

[92]Hamilton (1995) gives at least 10%.
[93]Children of such people can also be at risk; pregnant women with the phobia are of special concern.
[94]Referred to as vaso-vagal syncope.
[95]Use in a medical situation with a hierarchy of steps is described by Fernandes (2003); also available at http://psy.psychiatryonline.org/cgi/content/full/44/3/253 (accessed November 2010).

overall approach. We also need to look more closely at the role of anxiety and fear
in our lives. According to Elfert and Forsyth (2005), on which this section is partly
based, the basic goal of ACT "is to help the client become better at living a full,
rich, and meaningful life, rather than becoming better at feeling good (i.e., being
symptom free) in an attempt to have such a life."[96] This involves helping clients
to do three things:

(1.) **A**ccept Thoughts and Feelings. This means, through various mindfulness exercises, clients accepting and embracing thoughts and feelings, especially the
unwanted ones. They no longer struggle with them nor attempt to eliminate
or change them, and by not acting on them ultimately let them go. Mindfulness therefore plays an important role in ACT therapy and involves the
client remaining psychologically present in the here and now, something humans don't find easy to do. It also involves making direct contact with our
experiences, with acceptance and without judgment. It should be noted that
mindfulness is not used here as a method of controlling anxiety as such. We
have already mentioned its role elsewhere in this book (see the index).

(2.) **C**hoose Directions. This step aims to help clients to focus on the goal of
attaining what they value in life and then help them to choose directions to
achieve that goal. This means accepting whatever happens on the way.

(3.) **T**ake Action. This is about making a commitment to take action and change
what can be changed. Clients are encouraged to behave in ways that move
them in the direction of their chosen values. This means committing to the
things you want to do and accept the feelings that go with it, no matter
how difficult. Living good is more important than feeling good. Standard
therapies focus on the opposite idea of feeling good in order to live good by
avoiding the pain.

A number of assessment forms are available, e.g., LIFE (Living in Full Experience)[97], AAQ (Acceptance and Action Questionnaire as a measure of acceptance
and willingness[98]), daily activity ratings, WBSI (White Bear Suppression Inventory,
to measure a person's tendency to not accept unwanted thoughts and feelings[99])

Clients with an anxiety disorders evolve strategies to avoid difficult thoughts,
feelings, and memories. Unfortunately avoidance is built into our culture and we
are taught it at an early age as part of our social learning. At all costs we must
avoid certain feelings and thoughts and regard unpleasant ones as the enemy. Anxiety disorders are essentially experiential avoidance disorders and, from an ACT
perspective, become disordered when people[100] (1) don't accept the reality that
they will experience certain emotions, thoughts and memories they don't like, (2)
be unwilling to experience such emotions, thoughts and memories, (3) take delib-
erate steps to avoid the circumstances leading to such experiences, (4) and do so
rigidly even at significant personal and interpersonal cost. Thus, as summarized by
Elfert and Forsyth:

[96] Elfert and Forsyth (2005: 6–7).
[97] See http://www.integrativehealthpartners.org/downloads/LIFE%20FORM_correct%20Version.pdf.
[98] http://contextualpsychology.org/acceptance_action_questionnaire_aaq_and_variations.
[99] http://www.scribd.com/doc/53076993/4/White-Bear-Suppression-Inventory-WBSI.
[100] Elfert and Forsyth (2005): 64.

Anxiety becomes problematic when we do not accept its presence, when we are unwilling to have it, when actions are geared to not having it, and when such actions disrupt or impede movement toward valued goals.

The problem then is accepting what we have even though it is aversive at first. Another problem is that emotions cannot be controlled, but it is what we do with them that matters. This is true with anger for example. The first step is to notice the anger and accept its presence. The second step is determining how we will respond to it. We can only control an emotional experience to a point, and attempts at control usually lead to a stronger emotional experience and with an increase in the chances of it reoccurring. Therefore a first step in regulating emotions is to let go of our attempts at control and simply acknowledge the presence of the emotion. As mentioned in Section 6.4.2, the first step in coping with panic attacks is to accept them. Being afraid of fear and anxiety makes us even more afraid of them and turns normal fear and anxiety into disordered fear and anxiety.

ACT means accepting the good and the bad, in fact the whole deal, irrespective of whether it includes anxiety, anger, joy and memories, while staying committed to doing what needs to be done to live a fulfilled life. This is irrespective of what thoughts or feelings occur, so that anxiety need not stand in the way. Although clients who move in this direction may feel more anxiety at first, they will in the end generally feel more enjoyment and less anxiety. Traditional methods involve struggle for control, but often control efforts can be very life restricting, for example not going to the shops because of the fear of panic attacks. Unfortunately control may not work. We cannot turn emotions on and off at will, and it is a useful exercise to try and do this with clients, for example ask a client to try to be extremely happy just for the sake of it, that is without the use of imagery. Although it would seem a sensible strategy to be able to control unpleasant thoughts and feelings, research indicates that attempts to control unwanted thoughts and feelings tends to increase the unwanted thoughts and feelings.[101] Not thinking about something is still a thought about that something.

Counseling the anxiety disorders described above focuses on helping clients to face rather than avoid anxiety-producing situations in an endeavor to achieve control and reduce the pain. Recently, as with ACT, the focus has been on a more general type of avoidance called *experiential avoidance* in which the aim is to avoid or deal with the accompanying negatively evaluated private events such as bodily sensations, emotions, thoughts, worries, and memories. This means avoiding the effects of such events rather than the events themselves. A person with agoraphobia, for example, avoids certain places not because of the places themselves but because of the associated thoughts and feelings. In the case of specific phobias like elevators, the aim is not to avoid elevators as such, but rather the accompanying feelings of panic. According to ACT, controlling anxiety is the problem, not a solution. Control is obtained by giving up control! Giving up does not mean giving in.

---

[101] In Section 8.2.3 under "Intrusive Thoughts" we considered an exercise about pink elephants.

7.10 BIBLICAL VIEWPOINT

Biblical comments about anxiety from the previous chapter apply here as well. One suggestion has been found to be helpful, especially with extremely agitated Christian clients, is to take a verse like, "The Lord is my shepherd" or "I can do all things through Christ who strengthens me" and briefly meditate on each word. I have found that such an exercise can be calming. Reading the Psalms can also be helpful as most people can identify with the psalmist in real life situations.[102] Psalm 23 is a particularly powerful one. When the Lord is your Shepherd who looks after you his sheep, you won't be in want (verse 1). He leads you into a place of rest (verse 2) bringing restoration and opening the door to righteous living (verse 3). He also walks with you through dark and shadowy valleys so that you need not be afraid; the rod and staff are symbols of a shepherd's protection (verse 4). There will always be conflicts in life but God will be there for you both to heal your wounds (the anointing with oil) and to satisfy your needs (verse 5). Finally you have the reassurance that the Lord will be with you for the rest of your days and safely into eternity (verse 6).

Life may seem impossible for a client with an anxiety disorder, but nothing is impossible with God.[103] Christians believe that God is always there for them and God is their refuge.[104] Reading through Philippians 4:4–13, where the focus is on rejoicing (remember Paul is in prison), thanksgiving, peace, and meditation on things positive, can provide a life focus.

Natural disasters raise the question of why God allows suffering. I do not propose to try and answer this deep question here as suffering is a mystery,[105] but simply make a few comments. The exercise of free will and personal sin can lead to interpersonal suffering, while natural disasters can arise from a world that is not what it is supposed to be having become "fallen" in some way. Suffering can also lead to character building, drawing us closer to God in a trust relationship, turning our thoughts to eternity, and enabling us to help others. An earthquake is not an act of God but simply the earth doing what the earth does; we live in a groaning world.[106] We need to remember that God is about recovery. Nehemiah wept for days when he heard about the destruction of Jerusalem[107] but then God called him to rebuild.

---

[102]For example, Psalms 4:8, 34:4, 37:8, 42:5, 46:1–3, 55:22, 94:19, and 121:1–8.
[103]Luke 1:37.
[104]Psalm 9:9–10.
[105]I am writing elsewhere on this topic.
[106]See Romans chapter 8.
[107]Nehemiah 1; 4.

CHAPTER 8

COMPULSIVE DISORDERS

8.1 INTRODUCTION

In this chapter I have gathered together a number of disorders that are sometimes included with other conditions such as anxiety disorders or addictions. The common theme here is that of compulsion and we include Obsessive-Compulsive Disorder (OCD) and hoarding, tics, body dysmorphic disorder, self-harm, and eating disorders. Wilson[1] gives reasons as to why the addictive model may not appropriate for eating disorders, especially binge eating.

8.2 OBSESSIVE-COMPULSIVE DISORDER

8.2.1 Description

Obsessive-Compulsive Disorder, or OCD, is among the most common anxiety disorders.[2] It is characterized by recurrent, distressing, unwanted thoughts (obsessions) and/or repetitive behaviors or rituals (compulsions). Repetitive behaviors such as hand-washing, counting, and in particular checking or cleaning, are often performed with the hope of preventing obsessive and intrusive thoughts or making them go

---

[1]Wilson (1995: 165-166).
[2]For extensive research references on OCD see Frost and Steketee (2002) and Menzies and de Silva (2003).

Counseling Issues: A Handbook for Counselors and Psychotherapists. By George A. F. Seber **189**
Copyright © 2013 G. A. F. Seber

away.[3] However, performing these so-called rituals (a process referred to as "neutralization") provides only temporary relief, and not performing them markedly increases anxiety. A number of theoretical models endeavoring to explain the origin of OCD have been proposed,[4] but there are still many unanswered questions on this topic.

A distinction needs to be made between cleaning and checking compulsions. In the case of cleaning, the compulsion can be stimulated by a sense of smell and the cleaning ritual is carried out to neutralize anxiety about such things as a fear of illness, or a sense of dirtiness or mental pollution (defined as a sense of internal uncleanness), or the overall need for perfection.[5] Checking, on the other hand, involves discomfort and is generally linked to an inflated sense of responsibility to avoid harm and is neutralized by more covert (hidden) activities.[6] Repeated requests for reassurance are generally regarded as a disguised form of compulsion and are often a disguised form of compulsive checking.

OCD has a a lifetime prevalence of about 2–3% in the U.S. and often begins in childhood, adolescence, or early adulthood, usually with a gradual onset. If untreated, it tends to become chronic with symptoms waxing and waning in severity, often in response to any stressful life events. It is commonly co-morbid with other disorders such as other anxiety disorders, mood disorders, eating disorders, tics, trichotillomania, Tourette's disorder, substance use disorders, and obsessive-compulsive personality disorder (OCPD). The symptoms therefore need to be carefully distinguished from similar symptoms found in other disorders such as "depressive ruminations, the worries of generalized anxiety disorder, the intrusive thoughts and images of post-traumatic stress disorder, and schizophrenic and manic delusions."[7]

OCD differs from OCPD in that a major factor of OCD is anxiety about the feared consequences of forgoing compulsive behaviors (e.g., burglars may get in if the house is not locked properly, and this needs to be checked many times). In OCPD (Obsessive-Compulsive Personality Disorder), however, the focus is on control and doing things "my way," which is the "correct way."[8] In OCD, perfectionism and preoccupation with rules are usually focused and limited to feared events, whereas in OCPD these traits tend to be global and effect all of one's life. Also, in OCPD the concerns and behaviors are regarded as normal and are considered as useful attributes rather than needing to be resisted or changed. Such people are not aware of anything abnormal about themselves and are happy with their obsession or compulsions. OCPD is discussed in detail in Section 22.4.3.

Is OCD inherited? Although no specific genes for OCD have been clearly identified at the time of writing, research suggests that genes may well be involved as childhood-onset OCD runs in families, sometimes in association with tic disor-

---

[3] For helpful articles see http://en.wikipedia.org/wiki/Obsessivecompulsive_disorder and http://www.emedicine.com/med/topic1654.htm.
[4] See Taylor (2002).
[5] Jones and Krochmalik (2003).
[6] Rachman (2003).
[7] American Psychiatric Association. (2007: 9); comorbidity is discussed in great detail in this book.
[8] OCD is ego dystonic, meaning that it is incompatible with the person's self-concept or ego, while OCPD is ego syntonic meaning that it is compatible with ego.

ders.[9] There is an increased but modest risk of OCD in the children of parents with OCD.[10] The cause of OCD is unknown to date, though brain chemistry seems to be involved, for example, insufficient serotonin as serotonin-enhancing antidepressants help and there is evidence of excessive activity in certain parts of the brain.[11]

There is a wide spectrum of obsessive-compulsive type disorders.[12] For example, there are those concerned with a preoccupation with bodily appearance or sensations such as body dysmorphic disorder (BDD), anorexia nervosa, and hypochondriasis. A second group involves impulse control disorders like pathological gambling, kleptomania, sexual compulsions, trichotillomania, and self-harm. A third group involves neurological conditions such as Asperger's syndrome, simple tics, and Tourette's disorder (or syndrome). We will address tic disorders, BDD, self-harm, eating disorders, trichotillomania, and miscellaneous compulsive actions below, while some of the others will be dealt under behavioral addictions in Chapter 14.

8.2.2   Diagnosis of OCD

OCD tends to be under-diagnosed and under-treated for various reasons such as its similarity to other disorders (see below) and clients are often secretive about their condition and its symptoms. According to the DSM-IV-TR diagnostic criteria,[13] to be diagnosed with OCD a person must have either obsessions or compulsions alone, or both obsessions and compulsions, that satisfy certain criteria[14] that can be summed up as follows:

> Obsessions are intrusive, persistent, unwanted thoughts, impulses, or images that give rise to marked anxiety or distress. Compulsions are mental or physical acts that the patient feels driven to perform in order to magically prevent some feared event, to undo some thought, or to reduce anxiety or distress.[15]

Also the client must realize that his or her obsessions or compulsions are unreasonable or excessive, and are products of his or her own mind. Moreover, the obsessions or compulsions must be time-consuming (e.g., taking up more than one hour per day), cause distress, or cause impairment in social, occupational, or school functioning. Obsessions and compulsions that are not severe enough to meet the above criteria are generally common in society and tend to be less frequent, shorter in duration, and less stressful or restrictive.[16]

Typical Obsessions and Compulsions

These include:

Fear of contamination or dirt: This can also take the form of of disgust with bodily waste or fluid and can lead to hand-washing, showering or brushing teeth over and over again, and endless cleaning, with possible eventual skin damage.

---

[9]http://www.ocfoundation.org/causes.aspx (accessed October 2010); see also American Psychiatric Association (2007: 39).
[10]American Psychiatric Association. (2007: 9).
[11]Bourne (2005: 18).
[12]Veale (2003: 221–222).
[13]American Psychiatric Association (2000b).
[14]See American Psychiatric Association (2007: 15, Table 1).
[15]American Psychiatric Association, (2007: 13).
[16]Taylor (2002: 2).

Repeated doubts: These can lead to endless repeated checking of drawers, door locks, and appliances to be certain that they are shut, locked, or turned off.

Repetitive behavior: Examples of this are repeating going in and out of a door, sitting down and getting up from a chair, or touching certain objects several times. Also there may be counting over and over to a certain number, or counting in certain patterns.

Having things orderly and symmetrical: This can lead to ordering and arranging items in certain ritualistic ways (e.g., pillows, rugs, and tassels on a rug).

Compulsive hoarding: This may consist, for example, of saving newspapers, mail, or containers when they are no longer needed. The discovery or self realization of hoarding can indicate that counseling is going to be difficult, especially if hoarding is having a major effect on the client's life. Hoarders frequently do not view their behavior as unusual and exhibit less insight into their behavior than those with other OCD symptoms. Partners of hoarders however usually consider the issue as very serious! Research suggests that hoarding should perhaps be treated as a separate factor.[17] It is discussed in more detail later in Section 8.2.4.

Need for constant reassurance: This leads to continually seeking assurance and approval.

Fear of harming someone: Such a fear can lead, for example, to continually driving back to a certain place to check that no one has been run over. The client may have reoccurring vivid dreams of such an occurrence.

Uncomfortable mental images: Examples are images of hurting one's child, repeated sexual images, or mentally replaying pornographic images, again with unpleasant dreams of such events.

Disturbing impulses: One example of this is wanting to shout obscenities in inappropriate situations.

Rachman[18] proposed that

> obsessions are caused by catastrophic misinterpretations of the significance of one's thoughts, images, and impulses. The obsessions persist as long as these misinterpretations continue and diminish when the misinterpretations are weakened.

He described three categories of of misinterpretations, namely ones that are mad (insane, illogical), bad (immoral, evil, or a bad thought implies a bad person), and dangerous.

Compulsions can persist for several reasons.[19] First, when carried out there is an immediate stress reduction and a temporary removal of the unwanted thought, however both reinforcing the compulsion. Second, a person is prevented from learning that his or her appraisal is unrealistic because the intrusive thought does not

[17] Kyrios, Steketee, Frost, and Oh (2002: 270).
[18] Rachman (1997: 793).
[19] Taylor (2002: 5).

lead to actual harm. Third, the absence of the feared consequence after performing the compulsion reinforces the belief that the performance of the compulsive activity is responsible for removing the threat. The compulsion or ritual can therefore maintain the intrusion and provide a feedback cycle that escalates. It can be driven by beliefs such as "Having a bad thought about an action is the same as performing the action," and "Failing to prevent harm is the same as having caused the harm in the first place."[20] All societies have a whole range of superstitious rituals seemingly dating from earliest recorded histories.

When is a compulsion terminated? Salkovskis and Forrester suggest two main solutions:

> (a) repeat the action until it feels right; or (b) conducting the activity in such a way as to ensure some feeling or token of completeness. The latter involves introducing some distinctive sequence to ensure that the neutralizing is recalled clearly enough 'to be sure'.[21]

Unfortunately a sequence can become subject to the same doubts, as the greater the repetition the less distinctive any particular instance becomes. This means that the more you check the less sure you become that you have checked. Repeated checking "can fuel a self-perpetuating cycle by inflating the person's sense of responsibility, increasing the perceived chances of harm and decreasing confidence in one's memory."[22] Summing up, Rachman describes four aspects that drive compulsive checking:[23]

1. Clients are unable to achieve certainty, so that checking has no natural end.

2. Clients have no confidence in their memory of the checking that declines as the checking continues. Such a person's memory span can be very short—only a matter of seconds.

3. Clients have a cognitive bias where they believe that the probability of harm occurring increases when they are responsible or on duty.

4. Clients have another cognitive bias in which they experience an increase in responsibility after completing a check for safety. This sets off a self-perpetuating mechanism in which the more they check, the more responsible they feel, the greater the perceived threat, and the worse their memory gets.

8.2.3   Counseling for OCD

Clients with OCD need to be assessed for their potential for self-harm or suicide as they have a higher suicide attempt rate than individuals in the general population.[24] In order to determine a client's progress, it is helpful to have some sort of baseline measurement.

Baseline Measurements

One such measurement is the client's estimate of the number of hours spent obsessing and performing compulsive behaviors, along with the effort involved in

---

[20]Salkovskis (1985).
[21]Salkovskis and Forrester (2002: 54).
[22]Rachman (2003: 152).
[23]Rachman (2003: 154–155).
[24]American Psychiatric Association (2007: 10).

trying to escape obsessions and resisting behaviors. Also, noting items or situations actively avoided can be helpful. Another assessment method is the ten-item Yale-Brown Obsessive-Compulsive Scale (Y-BOCS).[25] Alternatively, the client can be asked to give a score from 0 to 100% to describe how incapacitating are the OCD symptoms. This helps the client to become more self-aware. Asking questions about items on the list of compulsions and obsessions in the previous section can help with the screening, for example: "Do you have unpleasant thoughts you can't get rid of?", "Do you have to count things, or wash your hands, or check things over and over?" and "How do these worries and behaviors interfere with your life."[26]

The next stage in counseling is to deal with the problem of intrusive thoughts.

Intrusive Thoughts

Most people have intrusive and irrational thoughts at times. In fact "about 90% of the general population report intrusive thoughts in the absence of OCD and that the form and content of normal intrusive thoughts and obsessional thoughts is indistinguishable."[27] What counts, however, is the significance attached to the thoughts; usually they are dismissed as meaningless.[28]

A first step would be to inform clients that intrusive thoughts are a normal phenomenon and perhaps provide a list of intrusive thoughts that commonly occur in the general population. It is helpful to ask clients what they think people are more likely to be troubled by and then refer to typical subject areas such as inappropriate aggressive thoughts (e.g., violence against the elderly, someone close, children, or animals; rude or abusive behavior), sexual thoughts (e.g., about sexual violence, sexual activity with all sorts of of people including children, or painful sexual practices), and blasphemous religious thoughts (e.g, about obscene images, blasphemous words or acts, or performing a ritual incorrectly).[29] This may help them to feel less guilty about their own intrusions. Clients can be asked whether intrusive, automatic thoughts might have any advantages. The effect on mental life if every thought had to be deliberately conjured can be discussed. They may also be helped by the realization that someone who is religious is more likely to be disturbed by blasphemous thoughts than someone who is irreligious; or that someone who respects children would be more distressed at having sexual thoughts about them than a child sex offender would be.[30]

A helpful exercise in the problem of thought redirection or suppression is to ask the client to think about something in the session for a given period of time (e.g., pink elephants) and then to resist thinking about it. The therapist can then explore with the client how difficult it was to keep thoughts about pink elephants out of his or her mind and whether trying to forget them had a paradoxical effect. This will help the client see that it is not necessary to try and control one's intrusive thoughts but rather trying to control them can contribute to the maintenance of such symptoms.

[25]See http://home.cogeco.ca/ ocdniagara/files/ybocs.pdf (accessed October 2010).
[26]For a helpful questionnaire that also provides some ideas for questions to ask the client see http://psychcentral.com/ocdquiz.htm (accessed October 2010).
[27]Marks (2003: 276).
[28]For helpful information on intrusive thoughts in general see Baer (2001) and http://en.wikipedia.org/wiki/Intrusive_thoughts.
[29]For several lists of such thoughts that a client might find helpful in normalizing intrusive thoughts see Rachman and de Silva (1978).
[30]Marks (2003).

A second step would be to help clients to distinguish between intrusive thoughts and the negative appraisal of them. The goal here is to eventually change the appraisal rather than get rid of the thought. For example, an intrusive thought like harming self or another with a knife might be triggered by the sight of a sharp knife. Normally one would regard the thought as irrelevant and dismiss it, with no harm-related implications. However, such an intrusion could develop into an obsession if it is appraised as having serious consequences for which the client is personally responsible. For example, such a thought might be: "Having thoughts about stabbing my child must mean I really want to hurt her so I am a dangerous person who needs to take special precautions and remove all sharp objects from the house." The therapist can explain that such thoughts do not reveal an aspect of the personality but rather a relationship with the individual's value system. A negative interpretation occurs most frequently when the intrusive thought contradicts the person's values.[31] The client can be encouraged to question the catastrophic significance of the intrusive thought and to come up with an alternative less catastrophic interpretation. Identifying the pros and cons of the client's interpretation of the thought can also be helpful.

With a checking compulsion, a client can compare seeing the problem as one of actual harm and one's responsibility for it with seeing the problem as one of worry about that harm and an excessive concern about one's responsibility for preventing it. The differences and similarities can be highlighted. With checking, a simple procedure can be for the client to keep a notebook and write down the day and time he or she, for example, locked the door and refer to it before checking.

Having set the scene, the next stage is to consider how to modify appraisals and to provide methods for dealing with compulsions.

Therapeutic Methods

Cognitive-behavioral therapy (CBT), especially with an emphasis on the behavioral technique of exposure and response (ritual) prevention (ERP) and/or a selective serotonin re-uptake inhibitor (SSRI) provide a basic starting approach for the treatment of OCD. The advantage of medication is that it may diminish the symptoms sufficiently for the client to engage in CBT, though the medication may take 4–6 weeks to take effect. The psychodynamic approach does not appear to be as effective, except perhaps in managing some aspects of the disorder rather than the core symptoms.

The idea of ERP is to help the client to learn to tolerate the anxiety associated with not performing the ritual behavior (called habituation), that is, not to "neutralize" the anxiety. For example, a client with a locking up ritual can leave the house and check the lock only once (exposure) without going back and checking again (ritual prevention). The next step might be not to check the lock at all. Apparently the more you check something the more uncertain you can become about whether you did what you were supposed to do or not! Another example might be touching something that may be considered mildly "contaminated" (e.g., a trash can) without hand-washing afterwards and then moving on to touching items that are considered to be more "contaminated." The client can use a hierarchy of events as described in Section 6.3.3 whereby one begins with an exposure that provokes

[31]Rachman (1997).

mild anxiety followed by exposures of increasing difficulty. These exposures can either be imagined or take place in real life and need to be targeted at an appropriate anxiety level. After such an exposure, it is helpful to discuss the client's experiences during the task and check on the use of any new neutralization strategies.

In addition to using a hierarchy, some examples of response prevention strategies are as follows:[32]

Response delay. In hand-washing or cleaning rituals, this involves extending the period between "contamination" and cleaning or washing. With checking switches of various kinds, this involves delaying the time between the action and the checking.

Ritual restrictions. In hand-washing or cleaning rituals, this involves reducing the cleaning or washing time and the number or intensity of washing or cleaning activities. With checking one reduces the period or number of checks.

Extension strategies. In hand-washing or cleaning rituals the idea is to touch part of oneself or one's clothes instead of hand-washing to undermine avoidance. For checking, one can whistle a happy tune!

Distraction methods. For visual checking, these can consist of turning and walking away, closing one's eyes, looking straight ahead, or using alternative visual imagery that is not related to the content of the checking concern. In the case of mental checking, singing a song, counting backwards by three from 101, going "blank," or meditational techniques can be used.

Refocusing techniques. In the case of mental checking and compulsive counting, one can use alternative visual imagery that is not related to the content of the intrusive thought.

In addition to the exposure tasks mentioned above, other behavioral experiments can be designed to test whether a feared event will really take place, for example, testing whether leaving a tap dripping can lead to a flood. Such experiments are particularly useful to test out the prediction that thoughts are equivalent to action. For example, a client who has thoughts of harming young children, and who might therefore avoid them, would be asked to test whether having these thoughts leads to any such acts. A client who fears screaming out his or her blasphemous thoughts during church would be asked to go to church and allow such thoughts to occur.[33]

Clients may find anxiety-reduction techniques helpful such as relaxation and breathing control before coping with anticipatory anxiety leading up to an exposure session and with post-exposure (refractory) anxiety, which is likely to increase the urge to neutralize. The techniques may also be helpful in maintaining the exposure during active ERP, but as a rule the client needs to feel the major force of the stressful event.[34] It should be noted that about 25% of clients reject ERP after therapy and another 25% may drop out of it.[35]

In the case of of obsessive ruminators, where people receive a particular thought or question which they tease over and over in their mind, the ERP approach can also

[32] Kyrios (2003: 264).
[33] Marks (2003: 286).
[34] Kyrios (2003: 271).
[35] See http://emedicine.medscape.com/article/287681-treatment (accessed November 2010).

be applied on a cognitive level. Here the client focuses on the thought (exposure) and then internally tries to refrain from carrying out the ruminative activity (response prevention).[36] This idea relates to covert compulsions, which are discussed further below.

Cognitive therapy can also be used to dispute dysfunctional beliefs or appraisals such as the following:

Overestimation of the probability of feared events. For example, "If I don't check and recheck the handbrake on my car and turn the wheels into the curb when leaving the car on the flat, it may roll away." Also, "If I am responsible, things are bound to go wrong."

An over-importance of thoughts. If a thought comes into one's mind it is therefore important and deserves attention. Typical thoughts might be, "If I have bad thoughts it means I am bad person," "If I think something bad it's the same as if I had actually done it," and "If I think something it feels as if it will occur," so that the presence of a "bad" thought can produce a "bad" outcome.

Need to control thoughts. For example, "It is important for me to have complete control over my intrusive thoughts." There might be a false belief that others do not have intrusive thoughts.

An overinflated sense of personal responsibility. For example, "If I don't continually ... then someone might be harmed."

Perfectionism. For example, "All the cushions must be perfectly placed, otherwise I am an untidy person and out of control" and "I mustn't make a mistake."

Hoarding. For example, "If I don't keep that newspaper, I might need it one day."

An intolerance for uncertainty. For example, "It is possible to be absolutely certain about the things I do if I try hard enough."

Magical thinking. For example, "If I am close to that hand rail I might be contaminated by it" or "If I touch something that touches a contaminated object, I need to shower, change my clothes, and clean my watch and my glasses."

The client may also have inappropriate core beliefs about self-worth and identity, and lack confidence to cope with or tolerate discomfort. The therapist can help the client to devise behavioral experiments like those described above to test and evaluate strongly held false beliefs.

Some strategies for modifying some of the above appraisals are as follows:[37].

Modify the inflated risk appraisal. The aim here is to modify inflated probabilities of harm taking place so that they are seen to be negligible. The process begins with the the client estimating the probability of a feared event occurring. Next, the therapist and the client work out the sequence of events or steps that lead to the feared outcome. Then a probability is calculated to represent the chance of going from each step to the next.[38] To calculate the probability

---

[36]De Silva (2003).
[37]Van Oppen and Arntz (1994) and Marks (2003: 283–285).
[38]Technically this is called a "conditional" probability.

of getting to the final step of the sequence the probabilities are multiplied together. An example of the calculations is demonstrated in Table 8.1 below for a client who is afraid of his or her car rolling forward and causing harm after having turned the front wheel into the curb, put on the handbrake, and left the car in "park" (or in gear if a manual car). The client continually checks all three steps.

Table 8.1   Probability of a Feared Event.

Event	Probability	Cumulative Product
Brake on	$\frac{1}{10}$	$\frac{1}{10}$
Wheels turned in	$\frac{1}{100}$	$\frac{1}{10} \times \frac{1}{100} = \frac{1}{1000}$
Park (in gear)	$\frac{1}{1000}$	$\frac{1}{10} \times \frac{1}{100} \times \frac{1}{1000} = \frac{1}{1,000,000}$

One obvious difficulty is getting acceptable estimates of the probability of each step, which a client may over-inflate.

Modify responsibility appraisals. Even with a low probability of the feared event, as in Table 8.1, clients may still feel compelled to continue their rituals. This could be because they feel over-responsible for negative events and overestimate the consequences of being responsible. For example: "If I do not wash after going out I will bring germs into the house, which will contaminate my whole family, and if they become ill it will be my fault for being careless." One suggestion is to list all the factors that might contribute to the feared outcome, for example, a child becoming ill. A percentage is then assigned to each factor and the percentages are displayed on a diagram like a pie chart[39] where each segment of the pie reflects the percentage. The client is then asked to decide from the chart what would be the likely cause if his or her child became ill. Another helpful follow-up question might be, "How strongly would you rate your responsibility for your child having become ill?" Usually clients reassess their own roles as being less than originally thought.

Cognitive continuum. Here clients are asked to rate how bad the consequences of a feared event are compared to consequences for other events. This approach will help with modifying responsibility appraisals and the overestimating of the severity of consequences. For example, clients are asked to score on a 0–100 scale how bad it would be if they left the tap dripping, if the bath overflowed, and they were blamed for being careless. They might then be asked about other things that could be worse than this, and where these would rank on a continuum of severity; for example, leaving the front door open overnight, not locking the entrance to a communal property, or not telling neighbors one has seen an intruder looking into their home. With regard to clients with worries about bringing germs into the house, they can be asked how bad not washing would be compared to not feeding their children, not putting them to bed on time, not ensuring they have vaccinations, not sending

---

[39] One can also use a histogram, which can be easier to draw.

them to school, and various other measures performed by a responsible parent. In the case of having intrusive sexual or violent thoughts, clients can be asked to rank how bad this is to acting on these thoughts, viewing adult or child pornography, stealing, or carrying out violent acts.

Comparison with others. Clients can be asked to judge someone else who had intrusive thoughts but did not act on them yet had the same record of lawful behavior. This may help expose the fact that the client judges himself or herself more harshly than he or she judges others.

ERP can be used to deal with intrusive thoughts; acceptance rather than suppression is the key. Trying to prevent such thoughts is not appropriate as they come uninvited anyway. The key is to experience them without distress. Those that trigger unwanted sexual obsessions, for example, can be very distressful for a OCD person.

Some methods used by clients to control thoughts are: distraction (e.g., think pleasant thoughts, call positive images to mind, physical action, talk to someone else), self-assurance (i.e., convince self that the thought is not important), social control (e.g., reassurance from others, assess the normality of the thought), refocusing (e.g., focus on different negative thoughts or on other worries), punishment (e.g., slap or pinch self, or get angry at self), re-appraisal (e.g., try to understand and reinterpret the thought, or analyze the thought rationally), thought replacement, and thought stopping.[40]

A distinction needs to be made between overt (external) and covert (internal) compulsion. As already noted, in the case of an overt compulsion, trying to stop the intrusive thought can be self-defeating and it is generally better to experience the thought (exposure) and then refrain from trying to neutralize or carrying out the compulsion (response prevention). Dealing with covert compulsions where it is all going on in the client's head is much more difficult as it is the compulsive thought that is set in motion rather than a compulsive action. To prevent carrying out the neutralizing process by giving into compulsive thinking, a stop needs to be put on the compulsive thought (this is not the same as the original intrusive thought). Here thought stopping and other distractive methods such as some kind of mental arithmetic or word search puzzles can be used.[41]

Saturation is another technique that can be used. With saturation, the client is directed to to do nothing but focus on one obsessional thought that he or she has complained about, say, for 10–15 minutes at a time over 3-5 days and the thought may then lose some of its strength.

8.2.4   Hoarding

It appears that about 1 to 2% of people in the U. S. have a problem of compulsive hoarding, and it tends to run in families. Such people often don't present for treatment until late middle age, when they have had sufficient opportunity to accumulate overwhelming clutter. Because of difficulties in dealing with hoarding,

---

[40]See Section1.4.4.
[41]De Silva (2003: 206–207).

often a symptom of OCD,[42] some attention needs to be given to this topic.[43] Those OCD people who exhibit excessive responsibility for the safety of others might be more concerned about their responsibility for storing possessions or for ensuring availability of possessions when others may need them, thus having an exaggerated sense of responsibility. They may feel guilty if they don't have an item possibly needed by someone else. Hoarding can be seen as a means of avoiding painful consequences and also as an opportunity that should not be missed. Compulsive hoarders often place excessive importance on remembering unrealistic amounts of seemingly superfluous information so they collect material to avoid memory failure. Because each item is regarded as unique, hoarders have problems in organizing and categorizing their material so that similar objects are not grouped together, leading to clutter and chaos. They may want to keep items in sight so that everything gets covered. Indecisiveness has been found strongly related to compulsive hoarding behaviors and may be linked to a perfectionistic fear of making a mistake and avoiding having to decide what to discard. Hoarders may not recognize that the clutter is unreasonable or be unaware of insanitary conditions.

Attachment may also play a role in compulsive hoarding where there is a greater level of the need for emotional attachment than shown by non-hoarders. Disposing of possessions might feel like losing a loved one. The objects may provide a comforting and pacifying quality as well as satisfying a sense of responsibility, a sense of safety and security (like having old friends), the wish to remember, and the need to control the environment. The possessions may be regarded as an extension of the self and therefore need to be protected and not to be moved or touched by unauthorized persons to prevent loss of control or violation of privacy.

Other types of hoarding include the obsessive collecting of books that are of no use to the collector (bibliomania), collecting digital computer files, and collecting animals. We must not forget that the world is full of healthy hobby collectors who collect from bells to teaspoons!

Although there are currently no accepted diagnostic criteria for compulsive hoarding, the following defining features are helpful:[44]

1. The client accumulates disorganized clutter in the active living areas of the home like the living room, kitchen, bedroom etc.

2. The client has difficulty now or in the past to resist the urge to collect, buy, or acquire free things that add to the clutter.

3. The client is reluctant to part with the clutter, even if it is not useful or has any monetary value.

4. The accumulation of items interferes significantly with the clients basic activities such as cooking, cleaning, walking through the house, and even sleeping, so that it may even become a dangerous problem (e.g., fire risk, and health problems), especially for elderly people. Other areas affected may be the workplace, family and social activities, and interpersonal relationships such as family, neighbors, authorities, work supervisors, and landlords.

---

[42]Whether hoarding is a symptom of OCD or is a symptom in its own right is open to debate.
[43]The immediate comments are based on Kyrios et al. (2002).
[44]Steketee and Frost (2007a).

5. Parting with any items causes distress.

6. The problem has persisted for at least 6 months and is not the result of a temporary situation like recently moving house, having house repairs, or accumulating items from a deceased estate.[45]

7. The problem is not the result of some other mental disorder like OCD, dementia, major depressive disorder, drug abuse, medical condition, and so forth.

The book and accompanying manual of Steketee and Frost (2007a,b) provide an extensive and detailed program along with assessment forms for helping clients with hoarding problems. They believe that some in-home sessions are important to encourage clients in their efforts and to enable the therapists to take photos to check on progress. They emphasize that it is important not to blame clients for their hoarding or make them fearful in the beginning about the prospect of having to get rid of hoarded items. They suggest that it is a good idea not to use terms like discarding or removing because of underlying connotations. Alternative terms are: letting go, getting rid of, recycling, selling or giving away. The help of family friends or family members who are empathetic and that the client is happy with can be enlisted. They also propose developing along with the client a model of the client's hoarding behavior that deals with the separate problems of organizing, acquiring, and discarding, and emotional reactions to the same, as well as, for example, family histories, comorbidity, special vulnerabilities, traumatic events, information processing deficits, and the meaning of possessions and the client's attachment to them.

In counseling, Frost and Hartl[46] suggest focusing overall on six general themes: education about hoarding, training of organizational skills, training in decision-making, cognitive restructuring of hoarding-related beliefs, and ERP for both non-acquisition and discarding. One of the problems in working with hoarding clients is their inability to work by themselves. Frost and Hartl (2003) and Steketee and Frost (2006a: 63–64) suggested the following goals:

1. Increase the client's understanding of compulsive hoarding and what happens when changes are introduced.

2. Evaluate beliefs about possession.

2. Encourage the client to develop a plan to create more living space and better organize possessions in order to improve efficiency. This should generally be acceptable, as clients usually are totally against discarding anything. They may have problems in reorganization and may need to keep things in sight. Problems in categorization and focusing on too many attributes of the possession are also reoccurring factors.

3. Encourage the client to increase appropriate use of cleared living space so that it is used for its intended purpose.

4. Teach the client to organize possessions so that they are more accessible. This means learning to put items into categories, including wanted and unwanted

---

[45]I am tempted to add "and storing children's possessions when they leave home!"
[46]Frost and Hartl (2003).

items (for throwing out, recycling, giving away) and developing filing systems. How long to save paper items may be important (e.g., receipts, bank and credit card statements, tax material, wills).

5. Help the client to improve decision-making skills, by seeing how things can be sorted and moved immediately to their planned location.

6. Encourage the client to reduce compulsive buying or acquiring so as to avoid and replace these behaviours with other more pleasurable activities. This is to avoid filling up the newly created space. An ERP approach to compulsive shopping might be to ask clients to pick a department store and item and imagine approaching (even handling) the item to increase their urge to acquire it. They then imagine walking out of the store without buying the item and keep track of their urge and discomfort for the next few days. The therapist can use a hierarchy of approach behaviors to deal with the urge to acquire, going from the easiest to the hardest shop or item in it.

7. Help the client to reduce clutter. This will tend to happen naturally when the previous goals are put in place. (It is important not to double-handle items so that they are simply shifted from one pile to another.)

8. Work with the client to develop discarding strategies. One technique is to ask the client to bring a box or bag of possessions to the counseling room, then get the client to select an item. The consequences of subsequently discarding the item can then be discussed and beliefs about the loss of the item identified. Using cognitive therapy, dysfunctional beliefs can then be challenged. An example is the following "downward arrow" technique[47] to identify core beliefs about the importance and meaning of possessions:[48]

Therapist: "Why did you save this old newspaper?"

Client: "I just might need it someday."

Therapist: "What would happen if you threw it out and later discovered you needed it?"

Client: "That would be terrible!"

Therapist: "What would be so terrible about it?"

Client: "It would mean I made a mistake."

Therapist: "Why would that be so bad?"

Client: "Because it would mean I'm a bad person."

9. Teach the client problem-solving skills. These will arise with the pursuit of the previous goals. Any failure to complete homework can be labelled as "a problem to be solved" to avoid self-blame and guilt.[49]

10. Develop strategies to prevent future hoarding. The relapse methods and other techniques associated with addictions[50] can be used here.

---

[47] See Section 6.3.3.
[48] Frost and Hartl (2003: 176–177).
[49] See Section 9.4.2 for structured problem solving.
[50] See Section 12.7.2 and "Relapse Strategies".

Summing up we see that two main approaches can be used for hoarding. First, CBT is used to examine hoarding beliefs, and these are assumed to come from such things as personality traits, past experiences and core beliefs about possessions, and accompanying emotions associated with acquiring and discarding. Second, ERP is used to overcome fears of losing items or losing sight of items. For example sorting and filing should begin with items (e.g., a certain type of possession) or place (the target area) that are low on the discomfort hierarchy. Then raise the discomfort. As described in previous chapters, visualization and imagery about discarding items can be used in preparation for beginning the real thing.

8.3 TIC DISORDER

8.3.1 Definition and Background

DSM-IV-TR defines a tic as "a sudden, rapid, recurrent, non-rhythmic, [and] stereotyped motor movement or vocalization involving discrete muscle groups." The onset occurs in childhood before the age of 18 and is not caused by the effects of medication or medical condition.[51] Motor tics are movement-based tics that can occur in any body part such as face, shoulders, hands, or legs, while phonic (vocal) tics are involuntary sounds produced by moving air through the nose, mouth, or throat.

About 1% of people may experience some form of tic disorder in their lifetime, usually before the onset of puberty; most cases are not severe and the severity will likely decline through adolescence. Often children and adults do not recognize that they have tics so that the tics may be undiagnosed. Adults with tic disorders are mainly those who had the disorder at some stage during childhood, though there are some for whom the disorder is secondary to an environmental incident (e.g., trauma, accident). Some people's tics are most obvious when the person is in a relaxed situation such as quietly watching television. Tics tend to wax and wane spontaneously irrespective of treatments or interventions. There appears to be a genetic linkage to tic disorders as well as environmental factors.

Tics can have comorbid conditions such as OCD (discussed above) and attention-deficit hyperactivity disorder (ADHD), which can be a major source of impairment. For example, OCD has been diagnosed in a substantial proportion of individuals with Tourettes disorder (discussed below). In patients with co-occurring OCD and Tourettes disorder, use of a rating scale such as the Yale Global Tic Severity Scale (YGTSS) may be helpful.[52] This scale provides anchor points for rating the number, frequency, intensity, complexity, interference, and impairment associated with motor and phonic tics.

8.3.2 Classification of Tics

Tics are classified by type as simple or complex.[53] Simple tics involve only one group of muscles such as eye blinking, head jerking, and shoulder shrugging; there is an extensive variety of movements. Simple phonic tics consist of elementary, mean-

[51]For a helpful information on the subject see Woods and Miltenberger (2001) and http://www.minddisorders.com/Py-Z/Tic-disorders.html (accessed October 2010).
[52]See www.pandasnetwork.org/TIC-YGTSS-Clinician.doc (accessed October 2010).
[53]For two extensive lists see http://www.tourettesnz.com/Types.html (accessed October 2010).

ingless noises and sounds, for example, such as throat clearing, tongue clicking, and sniffing. Complex motor tics involve coordinated patterns of movement such as jumping, smelling, and arranging, ordering, touching, or making objects symmetrical. Complex phonic tics include meaningful words or phrases (out of context), saying socially unacceptable words (coprolalia) or repeating a sound, word or phrase just heard (echolalia). Tics need be distinguished from small twitches. The latter merely involve almost invisible twitches of a few muscle fiber bundles rather than of a whole muscle.

Tics are also classified by duration as follows:

1. *Transient tic disorder.* This consists of multiple motor and/or phonic tics lasting at least four weeks but less than a year. Most tics are of this type.

2. *Chronic tic disorder.* This consists of either single or multiple motor or phonic tics, but not both, which are present for more than a year, with no more than three consecutive tic-free months.

3. *Tourette's Disorder.* This is the more severe expression of a spectrum of tic disorders and is diagnosed when several motor tics and at least one phonic tic are present for more than a year. Tics that begin after the age of 18 are generally not considered symptoms of Tourette's disorder.[54]

4. *Tic disorder NOS (Not Otherwise Specified).* This is diagnosed when tics are present, but do not meet the criteria for any specific tic disorder.

People with Tourette's disorder have a normal life expectancy and intelligence (though there may be learning disabilities), and in most cases the disorder is mild. Although the symptoms may be lifelong and chronic for some, the condition is not degenerative or life-threatening. The disorder is three to four times more common with males than females. Medication is generally not needed except in the rare cases where symptoms are sufficiently severe to interfere with functioning.

8.3.3   Counseling for Tics

Differentiating compulsions from complex motor and/or phonic tics can sometimes be difficult. For example, repeating an action until "it feels right" (e.g., repeatedly closing a door until the right sound or sensation of closure is achieved) may be a complex tic or a compulsion, or reflect elements of both. However tics, unlike compulsions, are neither preceded by thoughts nor aimed at relieving anxiety or preventing or undoing an external, undesired event. Tics are often preceded by premonitory sensations such as muscular tension or urges that may involve repeating an action until an unpleasant, localized, physical tension or a sense of incompleteness is relieved. An example of such an urge is the feeling of having something in one's throat leading to the need to clear one's throat; a bit like wanting to scratch an intolerable itch.

Although there is no "cure" for tics or Tourette's disorder, there are some strategies that can alleviate the problem and manage the more troubling symptoms. For example, focusing on a tic can make it worse whereas distraction, ignoring the

[54]For further information see http://en.wikipedia.org/wiki/Tourette_syndrome.

tic, and not allowing one to get embarrassed or angry by it can help minimize its effect. It is important to avoid stress and get plenty of sleep as being tired can make tics worse; tics tend to reduce during sleep. Strong negative or even positive emotions such as excitement or anticipation can increase the occurrence of tics. It helps not to try and hold back a tic otherwise the tension builds up to intolerable levels; the advice is to just let it happen. Tics have been described as suppressible but irresistible! Education about the problem, reassurance, and good family and community support are important.

Apart from medication[55] the main treatment for tics is behavioral therapy, and especially habit reversal training (HRT)[56] either in its "complete" form or in one of several "simplified" forms. This training requires only a few sessions (e.g., three). In its complete form, the steps are:[57]

1. *Awareness training.* This has four components.

    (a) Response description. The client gives a very detailed description of what each tic looks like or sounds like.

    (b) Response detection. The client needs to learn to identify the occurrence of each tic. The daily frequency of each tic is estimated and the tics are ranked from least to most distressing to give a treatment hierarchy; therapy begins with the least distressing. Self-monitoring can be done using a diary of events or a suitable recording sheet provided by the therapist.

    (c) Early warning. This involves the client recognizing and describing preceding sensations and behaviors just before the tic occurs. Also finding out what situations, both external and internal, that trigger the tic is important, especially if environmental and cognitive changes can be introduced.

    (d) Situation awareness training. Here the client learns to acknowledge the tic by the therapist mimicking the tic; it is easier to spot things in other people than in oneself. Then the client acknowledges his or her own tics by being asked to point out occurrences of his or her own tic and warning signs.

2. *Competing response training.* This key aspect of habit reversal involves the client doing something physically incompatible to the tic that can be maintained for at least a minute on the occurrence of the tic or one of the warning signs. The action should also do the following: produce awareness by tensing opposing muscles, be hidden from the public eye, and strengthen muscles antagonistic to the tic. The method involves three steps: the therapist and client determine an appropriate competing response; this is demonstrated by the therapist and practiced by the client.

    Examples, in brackets, of competing responses for motor tics are: arm movements (push hand down on one's thigh and elbow in towards one's hip),

---

[55] For example, the use of neuroleptics, which can have serious side effects.
[56] Originally developed by Azrin and Nunn (1973).
[57] Adapted from Woods (2001) and Miltenberger, Fuqua, and Woods (1998); see also http://www.nil.wustl.edu/labs/kevin/move/HRT.htm by Kevin Black (accessed October 2010).

eye blinking (voluntary blinking at a rate of one blink per 3–5 seconds), hand/wrist movements (push hands on an solid object or leg), head movements (press chin into sternum), leg movements (feet flat on the floor and push downward or lock knees if standing), facial movements (clench jaw and press lips together), and nose movements (upper lips pulled down slightly and lips pressed together).[58] For phonic tics, and these are more difficult, possibilities are controlled diaphragm breathing (see Section 2.2.5), pressing lips firmly together, or lowering one's chin slightly and tensing neck muscles.[59]

There is no "correct" competing response so a little imagination can be used to find something the client is happy with.

3. *Motivation procedures.* This is also called contingency management and involves at least three motivation techniques.

   (a) Inconvenience review. Here the client reviews with the therapist all of the ways in which the tic is inconvenient or embarrassing.

   (b) Social support. This involves choosing and teaching a support person (e.g., a spouse, relative, or close friend) about the competing response exercises whose job it is to make sure the client is aware when the tic occurs and remembers and correctly implements the exercises, and praising the client when the exercises are done well.

   (c) Public display. Here the client is encouraged to go into situations where the habit is likely to occur and to practice the competing response, thereby controlling the habit behavior and generating approval from significant others.

4. *Imagined rehearsal.* This involves imagining the tic beginning to appear in likely situations, stopping the tic, and then using the practiced competing response; the entire sequence is imagined.

The simplified version of the above involves some of the described components, for example, awareness training and competing response training (and possibly social support) may be sufficient to achieve similar results as the complete form.

Two other behavioral therapies that I will mention are differential reinforcement and relaxation training. Differential reinforcement involves reinforcing alternative behaviors, for example, after finding that attention exacerbated a particular tic the client uses an alternative behavior of continually withholding attention from the tic every time the tic occurred. Other alternatives might include reading, conversation, and eye contact. Although relaxation training is essentially superseded by competing response training, it can be a useful adjunct to other procedures. The idea is to teach clients to become aware of tension in the muscles involved in the tics and then teaching them to relax those muscles. Another method, called massed negative practice, is currently not supported by sufficient evidence.[60] Relapse strategies may also be used (Section 12.7.2) as part of the maintenance program.

[58] Woods (2001: 111-112, Table 6.3).
[59] Woods (2001: 112, Table 6.4).
[60] Watson, Howel, and Smith (2001: 76).

8.4 BODY DYSMORPHIC DISORDER

8.4.1 General Symptoms

Body dysmorphic disorder (BDD),[61] also known as body dysmorphia, is classified as a somatoform disorder by DSM-IV (rather than as an anxiety disorder, though there are similarities with it). It is defined as a preoccupation with an imagined or slight defect in appearance in a person and the person is severely distressed by his or her supposed flaws.[62] This disorder should not be confused with other disorders such as an eating disorder where weight concern is a problem.

It is estimated that 12% of the world's population suffer from BDD. Typically the imagined or minor flaws are of the head and face, particularly the hair, the skin, and the nose, and there may be complaints about acne, scarring, wrinkles, paleness, excessive facial hair, hair thinning, or the shape or size of body parts such as hips, thighs, legs, nose, lips, or teeth. However, any body part can be the focus of concern including body asymmetry and seeing oneself as small and weak when in fact one is quite muscular and large.[63] In a sense, BDD clients compare three different images of themselves: what they first see in the mirror, their ideal body image, and their desired body image. Repeated comparisons result in further uncertainty in their body image and the more they look the worse they feel. The projected images on glossy magazines and TV create unhealthy stereotypes for both sexes.

Individuals with BDD describe their preoccupations as painful, tormenting, difficult to control, and very time consuming; some spend several hours a day thinking about their supposed defect. Apparently about 90 percent of such individuals perform repetitive behaviors, intended to check, improve, or hide the supposed defect so that in this respect there are some similarities with OCD. They appear to have a love-hate relationship with mirrors or other reflecting surfaces, such as store windows or car bumpers. On the one hand they may want to check their perceived flaw in mirrors and on the other hand may want to avoid looking and remove mirrors from their home. Many camouflage the perceived flaw with make-up, hair, body position, or clothing (e.g., wearing a hat to hide protruding ears or balding). Others may engage in excessive grooming behaviors, such as combing, cutting, or styling their hair, or they may pick at their skin for several hours per day, trying to remove blemishes.[64] Such individuals may seek reassurance about their imagined defect and may also frequently compare their appearance in a ritualistic way with that of other people. A high proportion of sufferers believe that others take special notice of their perceived defect such as staring at it or mocking it.[65]

BDD can lead to extensive occupational and social disability, including unemployment, absenteeism, lost productivity, and marital dysfunction. It can be so incapacitating that a person withdraws socially sometimes becoming housebound (similar to social phobia) and can initiate the onset of severe depression and anxiety

---

[61] This section draws heavily on Wilhelm and Neziroglu (2002).
[62] For the actual DMS-IV criteria see http://en.wikipedia.org/wiki/Body_dysmorphic_disorder, which also gives extensive lists of symptoms and compulsive behaviors.
[63] Usually referred to as muscle dysmorphia.
[64] They may damage their skin so much that hospitalization is required.
[65] This can be serious when done to children with such defects as a cleft palate.

as well as other anxiety disorders. Many individuals with BBD have a delusional aspect, and possible suicide risk needs to be kept in mind as the rate of suicide ideation is high here.

The onset of symptoms generally occurs in adolescence or early adulthood, where most personal criticism of one's own appearance usually begins. BBD tends to be chronic, lasting for decades, and affecting males and females about equally.

What leads a person to have BDD? It seems that there may be a genetic and/or an environmental disposition that is triggered by life events such as excessive teasing or criticism about one's appearance, inappropriate parenting, childhood abuse, trauma, or conforming peer or media pressure to look fantastic! Certain personality traits such as avoidant and schizoid traits or perfectionism may also act as triggers. A chemical imbalance in the brain may also contribute to BDD.

There are some major differences between OCD and BDD. The thoughts of individuals with BDD are often not experienced as intrusive or senseless as is the case with obsessions in people with OCD. The former are less likely to resist the thoughts. The thoughts of clients with BBD are limited to imagined physical flaws, and insight is often limited or absent. Compulsive behaviors in BDD also tend to increase anxiety rather than relieve it, though there are exceptions such as reassurance seeking, which can be anxiety decreasing. Unlike OCD, BDD also shares many features with social phobia.

8.4.2 Counseling BDD

Methods used for OCD can also be useful such as exposure response therapy, cognitive therapy, and medication. Individuals with BDD generally think that other people share their view of the perceived defect and are disgusted by it. They have confusing evaluations about their self-worth and their personal appearance. Typical unhelpful beliefs to be challenged might be:[66]

- "If my appearance is defective, I am inadequate."
- "If my appearance is defective, I am worthless."
- "If I am unattractive, I will be alone and isolated all my life."
- "If I looked better, my whole life would be better."
- "Happiness comes from looking good."
- "If there is one flaw in my overall appearance, then I feel unattractive."
- "If my (body part of concern) is not beautiful, then it must be ugly."
- "The first thing that people will notice about me is what is wrong with my appearance."

Objective outside opinions can be sought as these will typically give a different perspective than that held by the client. These other persons might even deny that such defect is noticeable or in some cases simply not there. There is usually an element of perfectionism with BDD as indicated in a statement like, "I have to have perfection in my appearance."

[66]Wilhelm and Neziroglu (2002).

8.5 SELF-HARM

8.5.1 The Nature of Self-Harm

Self-harm (also called self-injury) refers to self-inflicted attacks on the body. Some people harm themselves once or twice, or spasmodically at a particularly difficult time as a way of coping with a specific problem and they stop once the problem is resolved. For some it is an ongoing way of coping with current problems and may occur at irregular intervals or regularly, on a monthly, weekly, or even daily basis, depending on circumstances. The definition of self-harm can obviously be extended to include some harmful compulsions and addictions such as eating disorders, alcoholism, and smoking, but these are considered elsewhere; we can all engage in harmful behaviors from time to time (e.g., overworking) to cope with emotions.[67]

Self-harm is sometimes linked to other underlying psychological problems such as severe depression, eating disorders, or personality disorders, which may require referral to an experienced health professional. For example, a very high proportion of people with borderline personality disorder (80%)[68] engage in self-harm. However, label pinning should be avoided as there is a lack of consistent adherence in the various labels used. The behavior also is not generally explained or even helped to be understood by using a label.[69]

Self-harm takes a number of forms: cutting, burning, hitting, biting, scratching or picking at one's skin (dermatillomania), pulling out hair or eyelashes (trichotillomania), overdosing, inhaling, sniffing harmful substances, or risk taking. In the case of cutting, young women usually used a razor or a knife and generally cut their arms and legs (especially their thighs), though they occasionally may cut other places like their face, abdomen, breasts, and even genitals. Usually the cutting is done very carefully and deliberately so as not to be life threatening. Some people may even be resorting to tattooing as some form of symbolic gesture.

It can be very unsettling for a therapist dealing with client self-harm, especially when they realize that their client will probably continue to self-harm while undergoing therapy. However, there is some comfort in the fact that although a few people who self-harm go on to commit suicide, generally this is not what they intend to do, though it can happen accidentally. In fact, self-harm can be seen as the "opposite" of suicide as it is often a way of coping with life rather than ending it. As Gardner puts it, "the damage inflicted signifies a desire to continue to live and get on with life."[70] In fact self-harm is one way of averting suicide and can therefore be seen as extreme self-constraint. However, client self-harm can be a helpful clue to deep inner distress which untreated can lead to suicidal tendencies.[71]

There are some things self-harm is not. It is very seldom mere attention-seeking,[72] nor is it manipulative behavior. It is not something that you just "grow out of." It does not mean that a person who self harms has a personality disorder (e.g., borderline personality). The severity of self-harm doesn't depend on the

---

[67]For a helpful web site see www.selfharm.org.uk (accessed October 2101).
[68]Miller, Rathus, and Lionhan (2007: 8).
[69]Gardner (2001: 9).
[70]Gardner (2001: 14).
[71]Miller et al. (2007: 48).
[72]Most self-harmers want to hide their injuries.

severity of a person's underlying problems. The person who is self-harming becomes more tolerant to their self-inflicted pain and consequently harm themselves
more severely to get the same level of relief. Both tolerance and withdrawal may
be features of self-harm, as in the case of addictions.

There is a great deal of information about self-harm on the internet. However,
care is needed before referring clients to a website as this may trigger a self-harm
episode, especially if they log onto graphic pictures or a video. The profile of a
person who engages in self-harm is now discussed.

Who Does it?

It is hard to give accurate statistics as those who self-harm usually want to keep
it secret and scars are hidden under clothing. Most people who harm themselves do
so in adolescence. The majority seem to be young women, although the percentage
of young men seems to be on the increase. Young men may well engage in other
forms of self-harm that are not so obvious. The main age range is from 15 to 25
years and clients who have mental health problems or are faced with a number of
major life problems (e.g., homeless or a single parent) are at risk. Recent research
focusing on young people suggests that about 10 per cent of 15 to 16 year olds
have self-harmed, usually by cutting themselves; they tend to have low self-esteem,
be depressed and anxious. Also they tend to drink and smoke too much and use
more recreational drugs. They confide in few people including parents and other
adults, and don't tend to ask for help. Sometimes groups of young people self-harm
together. A person who self-harms has a reasonable chance (say 40%) of repeating
some form of self-harm if not helped.

Diagnosis

It is not easy to discover if a person is self-harming. Neither the DSM-IV-TR
nor the ICD-10 provide diagnostic criteria for self-harm; it is often seen as merely
a symptom of an underlying disorder. People who self-harm may feel ashamed,
afraid, or worried about other people's reactions so they usually conceal what they
are doing and wear clothing that will hide the scars, or they may give alternative
explanations for their injuries. Being covered up at all times, even in hot weather,
can be a sign of self-harm. The key issue is whether there is a repetitive nature
about their self-harming. They can be asked, for example, "If you say your self-
harm is not compulsive, do you often think about it even when you're relatively
calm and not doing it at the moment?" A "yes" answer would suggest you have a
repetitive self-harmer as your client.

8.5.2   Why Self-harm?

Self-harm becomes one way of coping with unbearable emotional feelings such as
rage, sadness, emptiness, grief, self-hatred, fear, loneliness, and guilt. A person who
self-harms is likely to have gone through very painful experiences as a child or young
adult.[73] They probably had no one to confide in or had no emotional outlet. The
experience may have involved various forms of abuse (physical, emotional, psychological or sexual), bullying, or separation from someone they loved. Contributing
factors include: being made homeless; being sent into care, into hospital or other

---

[73]Gardner (2001: 20).

institutions; being under pressures and expectations from family or peer groups to perform a certain way; having low self-esteem, or having a poor body image.

One theory is that abused people can use self-harm to express the horror of their abuse. For those with low self-esteem, self-harm might be an expression of self-hatred. Through self-harm the overwhelming emotions can be released through the body, where they can be seen and dealt with; it's a way of getting the pain out and also a way of keeping memories at bay. In the act of self-mutilation the focus is on that act and this releases the focus from the distressing memory or event. By turning emotional pain into physical pain it is more easily dealt with. The pain therefore provides some form of distraction so that a person feels better afterwards and more able to cope with life again, for a while. Unfortunately the act of self-harm adds another event to be ashamed of in doing the harming act.

Self-harm can also be a means of self-punishment to relieve feelings of guilt or shame, or it can be an attempt to gain some control over life when other parts of life are out of control. Cutting can make the blood take away bad feelings, and pain can make someone feel more alive when feeling numb or dead inside. A badly traumatized person may end up feeling quite detached from their feelings and their body so they self-harm to feel something and know they are alive in a real world. When it is too difficult to talk to anyone, self-harm can be a form of communication about unhappiness—a cry for help. Sometimes a person does not know why they self-harm. It can be a means of communicating what can't be put into words or even into thoughts, and has been described as an inner scream. There is often an absence of pain during self-harm;[74] the body produces natural opiates, like beta endorphins, that numb the pain and mask the emotions.

Gardner,[75] whose main focus is on young women, provides one explanation for self-harm in terms of mother-daughter relationships where there is a desire by the daughter for fusion with her mother, but there is a fear of being smothered and "stuck with the malevolent figure of the avaricious, overwhelming mother;" the mother is both loved and hated. Counselors report that this can also be a factor in father-daughter relationships. Subconsciously the fear of rejection clashes with the fear of being taken over, and this can apply to other relationships (including transference to the therapist when the client wants to bond with the therapist but not be taken over or let down by the therapist). The trigger could be a row within the family or with a friend that contained the threat of abandonment. This psychic conflict leads to intolerable emotions, with self-harm symbolizing an act of aggression. Cutting, for example, could be a symbol of cutting loose and breaking free. In the case of sexual abuse, the client may use self-harm to make themselves physically unattractive or punish themselves for the abuse they felt partly responsible for, or had enjoyed. Gardner says that "Self-punishment can reflect a sexualization of aggression, and there is a clear sexual aspect to penetration and opening up of the skin, whether by razor, knife, cigarette or through piercing."[76]

Self-harm can be addictive since it can bring a measure of relief. Also the first experience produces a certain excitement, which may never be regained but is longed for—hence the repetition. Gardner notes that, "When the behaviour becomes addictive and is regularly repeated, ceremonial symbolism and ritual around

[74]This is like the absence of sensation that often occurs during abuse or trauma.
[75]Gardner (2001: 8–10).
[76]Gardner (2001: 55).

the actual harming may in turn become crucial, or even addictive in their own right."[77] There can be a special attachment to the implements used and the way the ritual is carried out.

According to Gardner,[78] self-harm can also be associated with adolescent development. She lists five states of mind that are not only familiar in adolescence but are also characteristic of self-harming behavior. These are described briefly as follows:

1. *Intensification of aggressive impulses.* Self-harm is aggression turned inwards.

2. *Narcissism.* Gardner says that, "Such narcissism can be linked to difficulties in giving up the gratifying parent, and also to the dilemma of breaking free from a tyrannical inner object relationship," where the parent is the "object."

3. *Hypersensitivity and heightened feelings.* This can mean being more sensitive to triggers for self-harm, thus heightening any unbearable emotions.

4. *Action oriented, rather than ruminating.* Self-harm is an action that takes precedence over thinking and reflecting.

5. *Preoccupation with death.* Although self-harm is not about killing the body, it is destructive.

When a young person becomes stuck and self-defeating instead of maturing normally through the above phases, their actions can be directed outwardly in the form of delinquency or inwardly in the form of self-harm. There are also uncontrollable powerful body changes during puberty that can lead to self-harm as a way of obtaining control. Self-harm can also be a way of punishing the body for sexual urges.[79]

Summing up, it is clear that the reasons for self-harm can be varied, and it is hoped that the above brief comments will give at least some idea as to the complexity and deep-seated nature of the psychology of self-harm.

8.5.3 Counseling for Self-Harm

Short term therapy may be satisfactory if the acting out is not too serious and the client seems to be able grasp in a few sessions what is behind his or her problems. However, therapy will generally be long term and details of life history will need to be carefully explored. We should not expect change to happen quickly; clients can't stop self-harming just because we want them to. People who self-harm are trying to resist feeling the full weight of their emotions and our aim is to strengthen their self-esteem and help them explore their feelings so that they come to realize that their feelings will not destroy them. It is important to pay due attention to their injuries so as to affirm that they and their body are important, but the focus should not remain there. When working with a young client there may be communication difficulties in getting below the surface and the therapist may need to be ready to cope with periods of silence.

[77] Gardner (2001: 28).
[78] Gardner (2001: chapter 4).
[79] One can think of the flagellants in the monasteries of the middle ages.

Initially three safety nets can be put in place. First, although suicide is generally not the intent of a client, the therapist needs to check for suicidal ideation (Chapter 10). Thoughts of death may not be inappropriate for the healing process and may need to be explored. Also, as with all destructive behavior, the therapist needs to have arranged for medical and psychiatric back-up and good contacts for possible referral. The issue of confidentiality and privacy of treatment may need to be dealt with, especially if the client is young, say under 16 years. Second, the therapist needs to check that a client knows basic first aid[80] so that they can immediately take proper care of any self-damage caused (e.g., avoid infection in the case of cutting) and know how to handle emergencies. Third, the client should be encouraged to stay safe while hurting themselves, for example, keeping the cuts shallow and doing only the minimum damage required to ease their distress. They should be encouraged to set limits beforehand and keep within them.

A key issue here is not to dismantle a person's defense mechanism before replacing it by something else. A client may not want the therapist to try and stop them self-harming as the client may believe that they have a solution for their problem.[81] Clients need to understand that they do not need to be overwhelmed by shame for what they are doing. Self-harm is the only tool they have at present to deal with these overwhelming feelings and helps them maintain psychological integrity, even though the tool is crude and ultimately self-destructive. We can, however, suggest some other ways of handling emotion or inflicting pain that do not do so much damage and I now refer to a number of alternatives, depending on the mood.[82] The first step is to determine the mood or feeling when the urge to self-harm comes, and then match the activity to the feeling, as in the following examples.

1. *Angry, frustrated, or restless.* Do something violent with an inanimate object, for example, slash a plastic bottle or old item of clothing, cut and tear a soft cloth doll, bang a pillow against the wall, rip up an old newspaper, use a red marker to mark on a sketch of yourself in red what you want to do and cut or tear the picture, hit a punching bag, or engage in a vigorous activity such as dance or sport. It may help to rant at the thing you are cutting/tearing/hitting, starting out slowly and explaining why you are feeling like you do, then venting fully.

2. *Craving sensation, or feeling unreal or dissociated.* Do something that hurts, for example, squeeze an ice cube hard (putting ice on a spot you want to burn gives you a strong painful sensation and afterwards leaves a red mark, like a burn), put a finger into a frozen food like ice cream for a minute, bite something hot or unpleasant (e.g., a hot pepper), rub liniment under your nose, snap your wrist with a rubber band, stomp your feet, or take a cold shower or bath.

3. *Wanting to see blood.* Do "red things" to yourself, for example, use a red marker or mimic cutting with a bottle squeezed to let red food coloring trickle out.

[80]See for example www.selfharm.net/fself.html and click on First Aid (accessed October 2010).
[81]One client said to Gardner (2001: 17), "Don't try and stop me cutting, I'll die if I can't cut."
[82]See www.selfharm.net/fself.html under "So what do I do instead?" (accessed October 2010).

4. *Wanting to see scars or pick scabs.* Get a henna tattoo kit, put the henna on as a paste and leave it overnight. The next day you can pick it off, and it leaves a mark behind.

5. *Wanting focus.* Focus the mind on something else.[83] Any kind of distraction that requires a lot of concentration but little effort (like counting the colors in the immediate environment or going through the alphabet backwards) can be helpful. Concentrating on relaxation breathing is another possibility.

The above strategies can work, as the intense emotions that provoke self-harm are transient (as in cravings with addictions). The key is to break the cycle by changing the coping mechanisms and thus provide a moment of mastery.

A client may find a daily diary helpful to record events and coping methods used for dealing with emotions. The idea is to write down thoughts and feelings before, during, and after a self-harm episode. It also provides a means of determining situations to be avoided. Care is needed in exploring painful emotions that lead to self-harm. The client can also fill out a table like Table 12.2 under "Relapse strategies" in Section 12.7.2 about the benefits of stopping or not stopping, and so forth. If anger is involved, then empty chair work can be used to address the people who caused the anger (see also Chapter 3). The therapist can help the client to focus on other physical aspects of his or her life, as outlined in Section 2.2. One helpful approach is to see the therapeutic process as "own the problem, postpone the problem, before beginning to change the problem."

Once clients stop hurting themselves, they may find they still think obsessively about injuring themselves. One approach is to use controlled desensitization in which the clients obsess regularly for a fixed period of time (say 10 or 15 minutes) during the day about hurting themselves and then stop. They would think about what it would feel like to self-harm, how they would feel afterwards, and how much they want to do it; namely, those thoughts they've been trying to suppress. If the thoughts occur at some other time, they don't fight the thoughts but simply acknowledge them, remind themselves to think about the thoughts later, and then let the thoughts go. Some safeguards may need to be put in place during these times (e.g., having a friend a phone call away); the client can be asked for suggestions. There will be a number of other issues such as confiding in others, answering intrusive questions, and hiding and healing scars. Questions can be deflected with light humor (e.g., "I got run over by a lawnmower" or "It's a long story" with a laugh).[84]

In conclusion, we note that Gardner[85] gives a word of warning about the effect a client can have on us as it can lead countertransference and projection. She says that "the disturbing patient will unerringly find our most deeply repressed and carefully defended danger spots ...."

---

[83]Some suggestions are given at www.selfharm.net/fself.html/ (accessed October 2010).

[84]Some strategies for handling such issues are discussed at www.selfharm.net/fself.html (accessed November 2010).

[85]Gardner (2001: 115–116).

8.6 EATING DISORDERS

8.6.1 What are They?

In this section we will consider five eating disorders: restrictive anorexia nervosa (abbreviated to anorexia),[86] bulimia nervosa (abbreviated to bulimia), bulimic anorexia where they occur together (sometimes referred to in the past as bulimirexic), eating disorder not otherwise specified (EDNOS)[87] that is a category introduced by DSM-IV that does not quite fit the criteria for the previous three disorders, and binge eating. A related disorder is overeating, which is dealt with in Section 14.7 on behavioral addictions. The boundary between it and the eating disorders is somewhat blurred and the material there also has relevance to this section.

The activity of dieting, which is essentially cultural, plays an important role in the development of eating disorders for susceptible individuals; for example, it can lead to an insensitivity to various internal cues such as hunger. The anorexic or bulimic, however, uses dieting to give life direction, obliterate emotional pain, and help solve a problem of identity.[88] Exercise, being extolled and glamorized in contemporary Western culture, also adds to the pressure. Here, the ideal is the lean, physically fit body; thinness equals attractiveness and beauty is linked with femininity. Body image plays an important role in recovery from an eating disorder, being the most consistent predictor of either improvement or relapse for anorexia and bulimia. For this reason these eating disorders have much in common with body dysmorphic disorder (BDD) discussed in Section 8.4 above.

The disorders are not mutually exclusive as a person can have a combination of them. They are all serious and include physical dangers and complications; they can affect both males and females of all ages. Therefore counseling should only be done by experienced therapists, usually associated with a clinic. However, all therapists need to be at least aware of the treatment available for eating disorders and know what to look for so that they can refer a client on to an appropriate program or therapist, if necessary. These disorders share a number of common causes and emotional aspects, even though their signs and symptoms may differ. For example, the most common element is the inherent presence of a low self esteem. The literature on treating eating disorders strongly supports the use of cognitive-behavioral therapy, especially in the case of bulimia.[89]

A useful self-report questionnaire for detecting an eating disorder is the Eating Attitudes Test (EAT-26). This is readily available on the internet.[90] Other questionnaires like EDE-Q, EDI-2, and BULIT-R are used, but full details are not available in the public domain at the time of writing this chapter.

There is a tendency for those with eating disorders to delay getting help,[91] for example, having difficulty telling their doctor. They may not view the disorder as a

---

[86]I refer here to the so-called restricting type with no regular engagement in binge-eating or purging behavior.
[87]Also referred to as an atypical eating disorder.
[88]Gordon (2000: 156).
[89]Collins (2005: 256).
[90]For example, http://www.montanamentalhealth.org/documents/eatingattitudestest.pdf (accessed October 2010).
[91]Adapted from Fairburn (1995: 291).

problem or being severe enough to merit treatment, or may not believe they deserve help. Also they may be afraid that others will find out or fear that the treatment will take away their defense mechanism (e.g., anorexics and weight gain). A general goal of counseling is to (a) aim for a healthy diet rather than a particular weight, (b) encourage reasonable activity and exercise, and (c) allow the occasional indulgence of eating "forbidden" (usually high energy) foods.

8.6.2 Restrictive Anorexia Nervosa

Anorexia is an eating disorder that is characterized by a drive for thinness, extremely low body weight, distorted thinking about body image, and an obsessive fear of gaining weight.[92] This is a difficult disorder as it can be seriously life threatening and, being often hidden by the sufferer, may only be presented when the disorder is in an acute stage, perhaps requiring hospitalization or care in or from a clinic.

Anorexics generally do not seek professional help because they may deny they have a problem so that often a diagnosis is not made until medical complications have developed. Family members may alert a professional only after a marked weight loss has occurred; by then the sufferer may be so malnourished as to lack insight into the problem and be unreliable in providing accurate information about themselves. Information may be required about weight loss and the extent of the disorder from family members. Early diagnosis can improve the overall prognosis as the longer the disease goes on, the more difficult it can be to treat. One of the problems with starvation is that it can lead to a range of abnormalities that perpetuate the disorder.[93] For a heart-wrenching and informative story of a woman's struggle to help two anorexic daughters see the first chapter of Claude-Pierre (1997).

Some Facts and Figures

Most anorexics are female and, according to the U.S. Institute of Mental Health, about 0.5%–3.7% of women will suffer from this disorder at some point in their lives. However, males are not exempt with 5–10% of diagnosed cases being male. Anorexia is primarily a disorder of female adolescents, though it is also seen in young children and adults. Before puberty, appetite is characterized by a stronger preference for carbohydrates in females and for protein in males. After puberty there is a sharp increase in appetite for fat by both sexes, though it is more dramatic for females.[94] The big difference is that the boys experience an accelerated growth of their fat-free mass, while girls experience an accelerated growth in their fat mass. For females, there is a preferential distribution of fat to the hips, thighs, and buttocks for successful reproduction, which most females don't want.[95] In the U.S. and other countries with high economic status about 1% of adolescent girls have anorexia, and the incidence is rising world-wide.

Anorexia is a psychiatric condition with one of the highest mortality rates, having about 5%-20% dying from complications of the disorder (e.g., cardiac arrest,

---

[92] Anorexia comes from the Greek and means lack of desire to eat.
[93] Z. Cooper (1995: 25).
[94] Liebowitz (1995: 6).
[95] Wilmore (1995: 43–44).

electrolyte imbalances, and so forth) and suicide.[96] With appropriate treatment, about half of the sufferers will recover fully, some will experience fluctuations of weight gain followed by a relapse, others will experience slow deterioration over many years, while some will never fully recover. It is estimated that about 20% of anorexics remain chronically ill from the condition.

With regard to females, Gordon's hypothesis[97] is that the contradiction between the cultural ideal (standards of thinness becoming more stringent) and biological reality (women are becoming heavier) plays a key role in the rising incidence of eating disorders. Thinness is a symbol of status in affluent societies. Striegel-Moore makes the following comment:

> Given the greater importance of a woman's physical appearance in achieving interpersonal success, and given that women seem to care more about other's opinions and approval, it is not surprising that women make appearance and weight high priorities in their lives.[98]

Men, on the other hand, are less concerned about dieting and tend to describe themselves as overweight only when more than 15% overweight.[99] Body shape is also of less concern with men.

Body insecurity for women is driven by various media, advertising, and Western culture where "women's bodies have been regarded as objects of beauty as well as symbols of what constitutes beauty."[100] A woman's identity is deeply entwined with how she sees herself as an attractive person.

Research suggests that genetics plays a susceptibility role with the environment being the trigger, and imbalances in neurotransmitter levels along with possible brain dysfunction may also contribute. Risk factors for anorexia include feeding problems as an infant, childhood abuse, a general history of under-eating, maternal depression, a high level of negative feelings, a poor self-image, and perfectionism. Anorexics often grow up in families where there is considerable emphasis on all forms of achievement, external appearance, and weight control, and they may be predisposed to value these attributes because of their temperament or experience. There may have been enmeshment with the parents, especially the mother, so that adolescent autonomy may have been a goal. Family disorder, high family demands, or non-expression of feelings (no talk rule) can sometimes be factors. The typical feeling of worthlessness is not related to how successful the anorexic may be, but rather is "the consequence of an identity that is based on pleasing and supporting others, rather than behaving according to one's own needs and self-chosen goals."[101]

Confirmed Negativity Condition

Claude-Pierre presents a strong case for the idea that an eating disorder (including bulimia discussed further below as well as anorexia) is a symptom of a deeper affliction that she calls a Confirmed Negativity Condition (CNC), the predisposition for this beginning early in life.[102] A child's predisposition toward CNC is

[96] The statistics vary considerably in the literature; for one source see http://www.state.sc.us/dmh/anorexia/statistics.htm (accessed October 2010).
[97] Gordon (2000: 120–121).
[98] Striegel-Moore (1993: 148).
[99] Anderson (1995: 177).
[100] Orbach (1986: 70).
[101] Gordon (2000: 101).
[102] Claude-Pierre (1997: 36).

reflected in an exaggerated sense of responsibility for others and the woes of the world; perfectionism can drive the child's need to please others before himself or herself and lead to a strong sense of worthlessness. For sufferers of eating disorders there is a civil war going on in their minds between their being and their "heads." Claude-Pierre describes the process as having two minds, the Negative Mind that attacks the positive Actual Mind with negative, destructive, often vile, self-hateful thoughts and, as a tool of CNC, begins a take-over of the sufferer's identity. It can be the cause of abusive and bizarre behavior. When the Negative Mind gets control, the Actual Mind is prohibited from seeking help as any help is undeserving. She argues that although societal attitudes about being thin can be a trigger, they don't explain the extreme thinness of anorexics; the Negative Mind is the real culprit. Everything is twisted to confirm negative thoughts about self; she emphasizes that sufferers see their need to be the best at being the least deserving! She mentions that sufferers in an acute stage can go into a trance when under the attack of the Negative Mind. Also the Negative Mind is good at encouraging deceit and deception like cheating at weigh-ins. In the end, anorexics don't believe that they deserve to live; anorexia is an unconscious form of slow suicide.

Role of Dieting

Anorexia often begins with dieting to lose weight because of social pressure to be thin and attractive, but over time the weight loss can become a sign of control for both internal and external reasons.[103] Internally, it provides a sense of mastery and euphoria for a person who previously felt weak, depressed, and empty. Externally, it provides the triumphal achievement of a thin body shape in a culture that values thinness. However, once set in motion, anorexia has a life of its own irrespective of how it began. Becoming thinner is not as important as concerns about control and/or fears relating to one's body, which leads to an endless cycle of restrictive eating. This can then be accompanied by other behaviors such as the overuse of diet pills, diuretics, laxatives, and/or enemas, and excessive exercising in order to reduce body weight, often to a point close to starvation. Once anorexics have lost a significant amount of weight, they will strenuously defend their achieved low weights using deception, secrecy, and ingenious methods of disposing of food to avoid eating it.

Associated Disorders

In many ways anorexia resembles an addiction disorder as it involves dependency on and obsessive preoccupation with oral behavior (food refusal). The initial triggers may be psychological and developmental but once anorexia is established it involves difficult and often intractable physical complications. Anorexics may have had prior anxiety disorders, particularly social phobia, which is reflected in the fact that they are anxious about eating in the presence of others. Also the disorder has many parallels with obsessive-compulsive disorder (OCD) and may be comorbid with obsessive-compulsive or avoidant personality disorders. Depression may also be present.

Sexuality

A key aspect of anorexia is a negation of one's body. With females this is often related to female sexuality where fatness is connected to the emergence of

[103] Gordon (2000: 23).

sexuality in adolescence. Also repressive sexual attitudes by parents or others may lead to a denial of the female form by anorexics trying to become more male looking with less shape, less sex appeal, reduced bust size, and so forth through weight loss. For adults, it can also be driven by the need to compete with men in the work place and have equal power by setting aside femaleness. Their role model is the idealized "superwoman" who is competent, achieving, and ambitious, but also feminine, sexual, and nurturing. Either female intellect and ambition are discounted, or are regarded as too aggressive and unfeminine, thus creating a dilemma for the anorexic of intellectual aspirations versus femaleness.

With males, anorexia is frequently related to doubts or confusion about sexual identity and orientation. The gay community regard thinness as an important criterion for attractiveness.[104] A significant number of males with eating disorders are obese or overweight during childhood and adolescence.

Assessment of Anorexia

The DSM-IV-TR criteria for determining anorexia may be described as follows:[105]

1. *Very low body weight.* Anorexics refuse to maintain at least a minimal normal weight for age and height and maintain their body weight at less than 85% of their expected weight.[106]

2. *Obsessive fear of gaining weight or becoming fat.* This is true even if the person is grossly underweight.

3. *Distorted body image.* They may see themselves as fat and ugly and minimize or refuse to acknowledge their weight loss and its seriousness.

4. *Endocrine disorder.* A woman who has already begun her menstrual cycle has three consecutive missed periods (amenorrhea), or menstrual periods occur only after a hormone is administered. ICD-10 criteria adds that if the onset is before puberty, then puberty is delayed, and for men there is a loss of sexual interest and potency.

Unfortunately the above criteria are no way representative of what a sufferer feels or experiences in living with this illness. Food is not the real issue. The underlying factor is a distorted self image that leads to an obsessive fear of gaining weight and is driven by faulty thinking about one's body, food, and eating. Such people may be very thin but are somehow convinced they are overweight.

In making an assessment, there is a helpful selection of questions (other than asking women about their periods) listed below that can assist the therapist form his or her own interventions. These also apply to bulimia.[107]

1. Have you been dieting, not because you are overweight (according to standards based on your age, sex and height), but because you desire to be more slim in your appearance?

[104]Gordon (2000: 114).
[105]See, for example, http://www.eatingdisorders.org.nz/index.php?id=763 or http://casat.unr.edu/docs/eatingdisorders_criteria.pdf (both accessed October 2010).
[106]Represents a Body Mass Index of less than 17.5.
[107]Adapted from McGee and Mountcastle (1990).

2. Do you claim to feel fat when others tell you that you obviously are not overweight?

3. When others tell you that you are not overweight, do you ever feel annoyed or irritated? If so why?

4. Do you often think about food, calories, and body weight, to the extent that you are distracted from other important, though unrelated responsibilities and tasks?

5. Does physical exercise occupy a disproportionate amount of your time each day?

6. Do you weigh yourself frequently, even going out of your way to do it?

7. Do you fast, induce vomiting, or use laxatives or diuretics in order to lose weight?

8. Do you go to the bathroom immediately after meals? Do you get angry or irritated if it is occupied or if you must delay for some other reason?

9. Do you often hide or hoard food that you prefer others not know about?

10. Do you occasionally binge on food and then feel ashamed of yourself and atone for your overeating by subsequently starving yourself totally for a period of time?

Symptoms and Signs of Anorexia

Being seriously underweight will eventually lead to all sorts of serious health problems involving most organs and systems in the body. Depression, anxiety disorders, personality disorders, and social withdrawal are also likely to occur.[108] Anorexics can become irritable and easily upset and have difficulty interacting with others.

Sufferers generally sleep badly so that they can become fatigued during the day and have problems with attention and concentration. Most of them continually think compulsively about food and eating rituals and attempt to maintain strict control over food intake. Sometimes they will seem to eat normal meals with only periods of restriction and may even eat junk food, particularly candy, drink a lot of coffee or tea, and/or smoke.

Anorexics may deny hunger, make excuses to avoid eating, and will often hide food they claim to have eaten. They may cut their food into tiny pieces, eat painfully slowly, add excessive condiments, collect recipes, prepare elaborate meals for others yet not eat anything themselves, refuse to eat in front of other people, or hoard food. In addition, they may exhibit other obsessions and compulsions about food, body weight, or body shape that satisfy the criteria for an obsessive-compulsive disorder. Depression and anxiety are common symptoms of anorexia.

---

[108] For some physical symptoms see http://www.medicinenet.com/anorexia_nervosa/article.htm (accessed October 2010).

Anorexics will often disguise the fact that they are not eating by the clothes they wear, for example, wearing big or baggy clothes or dressing in layers. Physical symptoms, other than the obvious loss of weight, can be seen such as dry, flaky skin that takes on a yellow tinge, and fine, downy hair growing on the face, back, arms, and legs. Despite this new hair growth, loss of hair on the head is not uncommon.

About 75% of anorexics have what might be called activity anorexia where exercise is valued more than food, and time is stolen from work, school, and relationships to exercise. There may be obsessive calorie counting, avoiding food-related social situations, and using athletics as an excuse not to eat. Such people define self-worth in terms of physical performance and are rarely or never satisfied with athletic achievements. There are many sports (e.g., gymnastics, ballet, figure skating, diving, and endurance sports) where thinness and low body weight are emphasized so that their participants are prone to eating disorders. Sports that have weight classifications (e.g., wrestling, horse racing) and those where the clothing is revealing (e.g., swimming, cheerleading, body building) have a high percentage of athletes with eating disorders.

Many anorexics overexercise deliberately to burn calories and induce weight loss. They may exercise surreptitiously such as getting off public transport early and walking the rest, or else engage obsessively in a strenuous physical activity such as aerobics, jogging, or swimming, This is usually done on their own and performed in a regular and rigid sequence. They feel guilty if they don't do the exercise and may feel entitled to eat a certain amount of food if they burn it off with exercise, or vice versa. A second kind of overactivity is a persistent restlessness typical of most anorexics when they have become emaciated. This can lead to sleep disturbance.

Therapy for Anorexia

An initial aim should be create a very safe environment in the sessions to get to know the person really well as he or she is liable to be withdrawn and suspicious. In some cases, it can be helpful to suggest that the client not lose any additional weight so that therapist and client can continue to discuss the situation unchanged as it is at the time. The basic principals of treatment remain similar for females and males.

Depending on the seriousness of the disorder, anorexia may require hospitalization, especially with starvation and impaired organ function where intravenous or tube feeding may be urgently needed to correct the effects of serious malnutrition. Weight gain can sometimes be achieved by appropriate eating schedules, decreased physical activity, and increased social activity, either on an inpatient or outpatient basis. In addition to obtaining professional help, Orbach[109] maintains that self-help has a role to play in recovery from anorexia and proposes a self-help model along with themes for consideration in group therapy. She sums up the general aims of therapy as follows:[110]

1. The creation of an understanding of the food refusal.

2. Focusing on the body.

[109] Orbach (1986: chapter 6).
[110] For details see Orbach (1986: chapters 8,9,10).

3. Restarting the development of a self.

Claude-Pierre believes that the key approach in counseling is to address the Negative Mind mentioned previously and create an alliance with the sufferer against it so that the Actual Mind can regain supremacy again. She suggests, for example, that the client write what the Negative Mind (the "condition") is saying in one column and what the Actual Mind ("Me") or logical part responds with and questions in the second column. This helps the Actual Mind to get stronger and in time it will have more to say.

Tracking the weight of an anorexic is eventually important but, initially, target weights are best not mentioned and information about his or her weight can kept from an anorexic to avoid any pressure and remove any ammunition for the Negative Mind. The focus must be on more than just gaining weight as this will not be permanent if the underlying psychological problems are not addressed. Sufferers can talk a lot as their heads are full of it and any negative thoughts need to be answered with positive expressions; it requires patience and unconditional love from the therapist. Claude-Pierre describes five stages of recovery and the reader is referred to her book for further details.

Depression is very common here because of semi-starvation and is generally regarded more as a symptom of anorexia rather than as separate disorder, which will improve with nutrition improvements. An important aspect of counseling is the difficult task of helping the client to acknowledge that they have a problem. Encouraging self-acceptance is vital. Anorexics often have a tremendous need to control their surroundings and emotions as they feel life is out of control. Controlling one's body by obsessive dieting and starvation is one way of regaining some empowerment. They may therefore be afraid of losing their control over the amount of food they eat, accompanied by the desire to control not only their weight but also their feelings and actions regarding the emotions attached. Some also feel that they do not deserve pleasure out of life, and will deprive themselves of situations offering pleasure (including eating). Orbach[111] says that the female anorexic cannot tolerate feelings as she experiences her emotional life as an attack on herself. As mentioned above, by getting control of her body she may believe she can similarly control her emotional neediness; rigorous discipline is part of her attempt to deny an emotional life and negate who she is so that she finds herself more acceptable.

In addition to the need for control, anorexics may have various irrational beliefs that fuel their obsession with food and weight loss. For example:

- "The best way to stay thin is what I am doing it now."

- "The worst thing that could happen to me would be to gain weight or get fat."

- "I have to continue this pattern otherwise my friends won't care about me if I'm well and don't have this problem anymore."

- "My favorite escape from my problems is food. If I give up this area of my life, I'll have to deal with those other sore spots that I don't want to deal with."

[111] Orbach (1986: 14).

- "My eating disorder doesn't affect other people."

Therapies used for anorexia can be individual, group, or family therapies (with the family being part of the solution), and cognitive behavior therapy addressing irrational beliefs has been found to be helpful. Clients "are not asked to concede the irrationality of cherished values but simply to take a closer look at the *means* they have chosen to secure them and the full range of *consequences* that result."[112] Medication (e.g, SSRIs) to stabilize the mood can also be helpful. Orbach notes:

> The anorexic position is a highly tenacious one because it holds in check the frail false self created to keep in the hated needs and to defend the as-yet-underdeveloped self. Thus anticipating rapid change in self-image or in eating behavior is extremely unlikely.[113]

Olmsted and Kaplan[114] emphasize the importance of psychoeducation, especially in a group context, for example, knowing the effects of laxative and diuretic abuse together with starvation on one's body along with non-dieting and nutritional information. They also mention the need for knowledge about the consequences of dieting and the so-called *set-point theory*.[115] This theory maintains that the body naturally gravitates toward a given weight largely determined by genes. The set point tends to keep weight fairly constant at a particular weight in opposition to attempts at dieting when that weight is reached. In addition, understanding the role of advertising and the media on body image issues can serve to arouse righteous indignation about the ways women's bodies are objectified. They also mentioned that clients should realize that what led to their eating disorder may be quite different from what is maintaining the problem. Given recovery takes time with ups and downs, an understanding of relapse prevention[116] and differentiating "slips" from relapse can also be helpful in therapy.

In group therapy Orbach[117] suggests that topics for discussion might include: the role of food in the family and eating patterns of family members, feelings about food and eating, routines and rituals, control and lack of control, secrecy, relationships, dependency, body size and body image, sexuality, and inclusion/exclusion. Such topics also provide ideas for individual therapy.

As mentioned above, athletes are at risk from eating disorders because of various pressures such as: performance pressure (e.g., over contracts and scholarships), coach-athlete relationships (e.g., pressure experienced by coaches is transmitted to athletes), value incongruence (e.g., pressure to intimidate or even injure opponents), visibility of participation (e.g., all actions are scrutinized by many others), time demands and social isolation (e.g., tough training schedules), fatigue-related stress (e.g., stress fractures with running), injury, academic pressures (e.g, conditions of a scholarship), and discrimination by race and gender.[118] Such pressures can be investigated and exposed to the client by the therapist.

---

[112]Vitousek (1995: 326); the italics are the author's.
[113]Orbach (1986: 145).
[114]Olmstead and Kaplan (1995: 299–302).
[115]See the internet, for example, http://medweb.mit.edu/pdf/set_point_theory.pdf (accessed October 2010).
[116]See Section 12.7.2.
[117]Orbach (1986: 124).
[118]Lopiano and Zotos (1992).

8.6.3   Bulimia Nervosa

Bulimia is characterized by episodes of binge eating followed by inappropriate methods of weight control (purging) such as vomiting, fasting, enemas, diet pills, excessive use of laxatives and diuretics, or compulsive exercising.[119] Binge eating is when a person eats a great deal more than what would be regarded as normal in response to problems like depression, anger, stress or anxiety, and self-esteem issues, and not because of intense hunger. They may feel overwhelmed in coping with their emotions, or want to punish themselves for something they feel they should (unrealistically) blame themselves for.

What happens in an episode is that tension builds up prior to a binge eating episode; between episodes little is eaten or there is a struggle to resist eating. There is then an obsession with thoughts about the next binge and these become more insistent as time goes on. Rumination about details of the next binge such as when, where, and so forth may occur. The binge begins under extreme compulsion, and once it begins there is a release of tension. During the episode bulimics lose control and feel as though they have been taken over or possessed; such feelings may ultimately lead to them getting help. However, feelings of guilt, shame, self-loathing, and anxiety about possible weight gain begin to take hold. Food now becomes the enemy thus leading to purging, which provides some calm. However, this is short lived as the feelings of distress return and the cycle is repeated.

About 90% of bulimics are women, typically young females, and they tend to be high achievers. About 1% to 3% of young women are estimated to have bulimia, largely developing their symptoms between the ages of about 16 and 20. Bulimia has been described as mainly a developmental disorder perhaps related to the psychological separation from the family and entry into the adult world with all its challenges to the sense of personal identity. New research indicates that for a percentage of sufferers, a genetic predisposition may play a role in a sensitivity to develop bulimia, with environmental factors being the trigger. Bulimics are generally seen as outpatients. With appropriate treatment, about 50% of clients in the U.S. become symptom free and 25% are much improved, though still resorting to the occasional binge; relapse rates are about 30%. The majority of patients remain afflicted for the rest of their life.[120]

Many bulimics have experienced some form of significant emotional deprivation in their early life, for example, parental unavailability, illness, or psychological problems, separation and divorce. Their childhood emotional needs that are ignored result in food becoming a comforter. Bulimia has addictive characteristics in that it is compulsive, secretive, and the person becomes ultimately dependent on it for solving life's difficulties. It can easily become a chronic relapsing condition, and the longer it is maintained, the more difficult it is to overcome. Bulimics tend to be ambivalent about getting help and may wait a long time before this happens. Shame and the fear of losing the freedom to binge and purge may prevent them from taking such action. The role of the Negative Mind discussed above in relation to anorexia also applies to bulimia.

Unlike anorexia, most women with bulimia can look perfectly normal having normal or excess weight for their height and age, and tend to hide their bingeing

---

[119]Bulimia comes from the Greek and means "ox-hunger".
[120]Silverstone (2005: 56).

and purging. Bulimia is therefore more difficult to detect. Bulimics are usually aware that they have an eating disorder and, fascinated by food, they sometimes buy magazines and cook-books to read recipes, and enjoy discussing dieting issues. Unlike anorexics, who tend to be phobic about sex and avoid sexual encounters, bulimics tend to be sexually active and oriented to pleasing males, though their sexual and interpersonal relationships tend to be troubled especially with regard to issues of intimacy and loss. On the surface they give an appearance of being positive and managing, but underneath is a different story, being for example ashamed of feeling needy, childlike, and dependent. Bulimics often fluctuate wildly from overweight to underweight reflecting their ambivalence about issues of gender and identity.

Assessment of Bulimia

The DSM IV-TR criteria for bulimia can be described as follows:[121]

1. *Binge eating.* This accompanied by a feeling of not being able to stop eating or control what or how much is eaten.

2. *Preventing weight-gain.* This can take the form of purging (e.g., self-induced vomiting or misuse of laxatives, diuretics, and enemas) or non-purging (e.g., fasting, excessive exercise).

3. *Recurrent behavior.* The binge eating and inappropriate compensatory behavior both occur, on average, at least twice a week for 3 months.

4. *Undue preoccupation with shape and body weight.* There is a tendency to evaluate self according to shape and weight.

5. *Anorexia ruled out.* The bulimic behavior does not occur exclusively during anorexia episodes. The difference between anorexia and bulimia is not the purging, but the cycle of bingeing and purging.

The essential feature of bulimia is the desire to be slender, which leads to restrictive eating and resulting constant thoughts about food. The eating alternates between fasting or extreme dieting on the one hand and binge-eating episodes on the other. Self-induced vomiting and laxative abuse generally occur after the bingeing behavior has been established.

As with anorexia, a selection of questions that might be asked in the assessing process are as follows:[122]

1. How afraid are you of being fat?

2. Do you try to diet repeatedly but end up being sabotaged by bingeing activities? How do you feel when this happens? (e.g, ashamed)

3. How often do you binge/purge a week?

4. Do you hide and hoard private stashes of food for later bingeing?

5. What sort of food do you binge on?

---

[121] See, for example, http://www.eatingdisorders.org.nz/index.php?id=763 or http://casat.unr.edu/docs/eatingdisorders_criteria.pdf (both accessed October 2010).
[122] Adapted from McGee and Mountcastle (1990).

6. Do you keep your binges secret?

7. How much time do you spend thinking about your next binge?

8. Do thoughts about food occupy much of your time?

9. Do you induce vomiting or take laxatives and/or diuretics to get rid of "binge" food?

10. Do you exercise to work off a binge?

Symptoms and Signs of Bulimia

Physical symptoms arising from bulimia relate to the effects of both overeating and purging, for example, heartburn, bloating, indigestion, constipation, and throat, dental, stomach, and esophagus problems. There is a preoccupation with body weight, and depression or mood swings. Also frequent trips are made to the bathroom immediately following meals and this is sometimes accompanied with water running in the bathroom for a long period of time to hide the sound of vomiting. Some bulimics take diet pills in an attempt to keep from bingeing. They may hide or "store" food for later binges, will often eat secretly, and can have large fluctuations in their weight.

Depression is very common with bulimics though it generally does not precede the eating disturbance but rather tends to be a consequence of the eating problem.[123] Also Beumont[124] states: "A significant proportion of bulimics have pre-existing personality difficulties, a history of disturbed interpersonal relations, and difficulties in impulse control and substance abuse."

Therapy for Bulimia

It is important to educate clients about the long term health impact of dieting, bingeing, and purging on one's health. Comments above about the value of psychoeducation in dealing with anorexia also apply to bulimia. Nutritional counseling is particularly important early in the course of treatment as bulimics have a chaotic eating pattern and often have lost the ability to eat in a balanced fashion. Beumont and Touyz[125] point out that clients should know that good health requires not just nutritionally sound foods but also the addition of some high-energy, less "nutritious" foods. A little of the latter occasionally may prevent bingeing on them later. Another helpful piece of information is that fluctuations in body weight are quite normal and can be demonstrated by weighing in the morning and in the evening and before and after a rich meal.

An effective method for treating bulimia is cognitive-behavioral therapy that challenges the clients' distorted views of body weight and shape and their relationship to self-worth, encourages self-monitoring of eating behavior and the elimination of dieting, and provides techniques for controlling bingeing and purging episodes (e.g., substituting new behaviors and replacing reminders or cues for stimulus control). A manual for therapy is given by Fairburn, Marcus, and Wilson (1993).[126] SSRI's such as fluoxetine (prozac) has been found helpful in treating bulimics.[127]

[123] P. Cooper (1995: 161).
[124] Beumont (1995: 157).
[125] Beumont and Touyz (1995: 311).
[126] A helpful article with practical suggestions is Mines and Merrill (1987).
[127] Silverstone (2005: 64).

Clients need to realize that they will improve considerably with therapy, but in times of stress they may slip back temporarily and will always be a bit sensitive about eating, shape, and weight. Also helpful is interpersonal therapy to deal with interpersonal problems, thus addressing the bulimia symptoms indirectly. Both of these methods encourage a problem-solving approach. However, such therapies might not work so well when a client also has a personality disorder, which is common with bulimics.[128] Some of the ideas used for counseling addiction can be used here. For example, the transtheoretical model[129] with its stages of change can be helpful.[130]

In contrast to anorexics who tend to be enmeshed with their mothers, bulimics may attempt to distance themselves from their mothers, perceiving them as weak compared to powerful fathers. Thinness becomes associated with masculine power, fatness with feminine weakness so that the bulimic has an identity problem—being powerful and in control, yet being nurturing, submissive, and pleasing to men.

8.6.4   Bulimic Anorexics

It is not uncommon for people suffering with anorexia to have periods of bulimia as well. Up to 50% of patients with anorexia nervosa develop bulimic symptoms, and a smaller percentage of patients who are initially bulimic develop anorexic symptoms. The occurrence of bulimic episodes combined with the anorexic pattern of denial and fierce resistance to external intervention makes anorexia a great deal more resistant to treatment. Also, those with this problem tend to be more seriously psychologically distressed than restrictive anorexics.[131]

There are many similarities in both illnesses, the most common being the cause. Sexual and/or physical and emotional abuse may be a factor for some people with eating disorders. There also seems to be a direct connection in some people to clinical depression. The eating disorder sometimes causes the depression or the depression can lead to the eating disorder.

8.6.5   Eating Disorder Not Otherwise Specified (EDNOS)

There are many people with serious eating addictions that satisfy some but not all the criteria in any of the above eating disorders. Such people are diagnosed as having EDNOS; [132] an alternative name suggested by Gordon[133] is "subclinical eating disorders," suggesting a lesser degree of severity. For example, a woman may satisfy the criteria for anorexia but still has a normal menstrual cycle and/or restricts food but is not yet underweight by the weight criterion. A second person may experience episodes of bingeing and purging, but may not do so frequently enough to warrant a diagnosis of bulimia nervosa. A third person may be involved with bingeing episodes without other compensatory behaviors such as purging, and this is usually referred to as binge-eating disorder (BED). All three people would be

[128]Tobin (2000: 18).
[129]See Section 12.7.2 under the title of "Wheel of Change."
[130]Tobin (2000: 22–23).
[131]Gordon (2000: 36).
[132]For the criteria see, for example, http://casat.unr.edu/docs/eatingdisorders_criteria.pdf. (accessed October 2010).
[133]Gordon (2000: 76).

technically classified by DSM-IV-TR as being in the category of EDNOS, a category that obviously needs further research as it can contain people who are basically anorexic or bulimic. People diagnosed with EDNOS may frequently switch between different eating patterns, or may eventually satisfy all the diagnostic criteria for anorexia and/or bulimia. All the above eating disorders need to be treated with equal seriousness irrespective of labels, as they can be all life threatening and there can be a change from one disorder into another over time.

Some people believe that binge eating should be categorized as a disorder in its own right, which we do now, or else treated as a subset of bulimia or of EDNOS.

8.6.6   Binge-Eating Disorder (BED)

BED is surprisingly common, perhaps 2–3% of women in U.S. and Western Europe. It often begins with dieting, being a little more common in women than in men; three women for every two men have it. People of any age can have BED, but it is seen more often in adults age 46 to 55. About 20% to 30% of people who seek treatment for obesity report serious problems with binge eating.[134]

Assessment for BED

Some of the signs of BED are as follows:[135]

- Periodically doesn't exercise control over food consumption including what is eaten and how much.

- Eats a very large amount of food at one time, even when not really hungry.

- Eats more quickly than normal during binge episodes.

- Eats until feeling uncomfortable due to the amount eaten.

- Eats when depressed or bored.

- Usually eats alone when bingeing, as embarrassed at the amount of food eaten.

- There is marked distress regarding binge eating.

- May eat alone during normal eating because of being embarrassed about food.[136]

- Feels disgusted, depressed, or feeling very guilty after binge eating.

- Has a rapid weight gain and/or sudden onset of obesity.

- Engaged in binge eating, on average, at least 2 days a week for 6 months.

The first two signs involve the consumption of a large amount of food and the loss of control. However, it is not easy to determine both of these as they rely on client self-assessment and the context of the eating. Although similar to compulsive overeating, those with BED do not have a compulsion to generally overeat or spend

[134]Marcus (1995: 441).
[135]See, for example, http://en.wikipedia.org/wiki/Binge_eating_disorder.
[136]This could also be an aspect of social phobia.

a lot of time fantasizing about food. Unlike in bulimia, those with BED don't purge, fast, or engage in strenuous exercise after binge eating and are more likely to be overweight or obese, though a minority have normal weight. Bingeing episodes frequently include foods that are high in fat, sugar, and/or salt, but low in vitamins and minerals so that people with the problem can become ill through poor nutrition (e.g., have Type 2 diabetes, hypertension, high cholesterol, arthritis, and so on). Some people miss work, school, or social activities to binge eat. They feel ashamed of their eating pattern, may avoid social gatherings, and try to hide their problems. They may also have an alcohol problem, act impulsively, not feel in charge of themselves or feel part of their communities, and may not notice and talk about their feelings.

Sufferers may use binges as a way to regulate difficult emotions such as depression, anger, sadness, and feelings of inadequacy, to reward themselves, to fill a void they feel inside, and to cope with daily stresses and problems in their lives. They eat to feed their feelings, rather than their bodies. Bingeing can also be used as a way to keep people away, to subconsciously maintain an overweight appearance to cater to society's sad stigma "If I'm fat, no one will like me," as each person suffering may feel undeserving of love. As with bulimia, bingeing can also be used as self-punishment for doing "bad" things, or for feeling badly about oneself.

Therapy for BED

As far as clients are concerned, the therapies used for depression can also be used here to deal with the cause of the binge eating and their obsession with weight and shape, as well as engaging in a healthy eating program to improve their health and self-esteem. Such therapies are cognitive-behavioral therapy (CBT) to keep track of their eating and determine what triggers their bingeing, interpersonal psychotherapy (IPT) to examine problem relationships with friends and family, and possibly some drug therapy using antidepressants. Here IPT has a role as a woman's basic sense of self-worth is said to be closely tied to her ability to form relationships that are mutually empathetic and empowering. This means that women can be highly vulnerable to others' opinions of them and behaviors toward them.[137]

CBT can be used to design three or more meals a day, gradually introduce feared foods into the diet (exposure therapy), and deal with distorted thinking about food intake, weight, and body shape. Some of the ideas for dealing with addiction and particularly overeating addiction can be used here (see Section 14.7). Relapse prevention methods can be introduced later. It should be noted that Wilson[138] maintains that binge eating does not satisfy some of the usual criteria for an addiction, especially the disease model of addiction with its absolute avoidance of certain foods.

[137]Striegel-Moore (1993:147).
[138]Wilson (1993: 103–104).

8.7   OTHER COMPULSIVE ACTIONS

There are a number of other repetitive compulsive-behavior disorders such trichotillomania,[139] oral-digital habits (e.g., nail biting, thumb or finger sucking, skin
picking), stuttering, bruxism (teeth grinding), and kleptomania. Trichotillomania,
which generally leads to a noticeable hair loss (alopecia), is caused by chronic, repeated hair pulling usually from the head possibly followed by the eyelashes and
eye brows. It may begin by simply stroking one's hair. The hair of any part of
the body may be pulled and multiple sites may be involved; the hair may even be
ingested by some sufferers. Additional criteria include an increase in tension that
occurs prior to the act of hair pulling or that corresponds with attempts to inhibit
the act, a sense of gratification following the act, absence of a causal medical or
psychological condition, and significant distress or impairment.

Techniques similar to those given above for tics such as habit reversal training mentioned in Section 8.3.3 can be used to help clients with repetitive disorders
involving the body.[140] The major components of habit reversal are awareness training, competing response training, and social support. In the case of hair pulling,
a competing response might be making a fist, folding hands in one's lap, grasping
an object, or putting hands in one's pockets. The idea is to begin the competing
response when one's hair is touched and then learn to do it earlier and earlier until
just the thought of hair pulling begins the response.[141]

As part of the awareness training, clients can be given self-monitoring sheets
to record frequency, duration, number of hairs pulled, their emotional state at the
time, and so forth. In addition, clients can be instructed in how to graph the
number of pulling episodes they have had on a daily basis. This information will
provide some insight as to their pattern of hair pulling. When the urge to pull
occurs, progressive muscle relaxation and diaphragm breathing (see Section 2.2.5)
can also be used prior to using the competing response. Changing routines to avoid
triggers (stimulus control) can be used along with appropriate self-statements like
"Every hair counts" or "I don't have to give myself permission to pull."[142]

For stuttering, an appropriate competing response is to use deep relaxed breathing with a slight exhale just prior to speaking. This is practiced while speaking
briefly, say one or two words only, to achieve control. When the stuttering is controlled, speech duration can be steadily increased. When a stutter occurs, the client
stops speaking, takes a deep breath, exhales slightly, and resumes speaking.

The internet is a useful source of information on these and similar topics.

8.8   BIBLICAL VIEWPOINT

Some people suffer from *scrupulosity*, which alludes to the torment of an oversensitive conscience. It often involves mistakenly thinking that innocent or unavoidable
things are sin and the sufferer ends up feeling needlessly guilty; it is like a moral or

---

[139]See, for example, http://www.answers.com/topic/trichotillomania or
http://www.healthofchildren.com/T/Trichotillomania.html (both accessed October 2010).
[140]See, for example, Woods and Miltenberger (2001) for details.
[141]For further details see Miltenberger (2001).
[142]For further details see Penzel (2003).

religious form of OCD. It takes away love, damages self-esteem, and makes the life of faith difficult. Exposure and response prevention therapy (ERP) described above may be helpful, while cognitive therapy can be used to look at a client's spiritual beliefs, especially beliefs about God, God's expectations, and God's grace.

The Bible says nothing about OCD specifically, but it does talk about freedom[143] and peace[144] through God's healing; this can be either directly or indirectly through a health professional/therapist. Christians put their trust in God knowing that God cares,[145] provides strength,[146] and helps them overcome fear,[147] an ingredient of OCD. Positive statements like "Christ will help me to drive safely" and "Christ will not let me do anything wrong" can be helpful. Some commentators believe that OCD is merely a spiritual problem and unfortunately ignore the physical factors such as brain chemistry.

There is an interesting story in the Old Testament that some refer to as the first documented case of anorexia and its associated infertility. It describes a woman called Hannah who was under such pressure to conceive that she wept and would not eat. She overcame her problem through prayer and spiritual support.[148]

Those struggling with eating disorders frequently have difficulty viewing God as a friend and someone that cares about them. They may tend to see God as one who blames them for their problems rather than as one who loves them, even when they are starving themselves. It can be helpful for clients to focus more on the personal nature of God in Jesus of the gospels rather than the Jehovah aspect of God in the Old Testament. The Bible says our bodies *are* important. It teaches that we are to honor our bodies as temples of the Holy Spirit and to present them as living sacrifices; not to be starved in order to ease emotional pain, nor to be mutilated in any way as in self-harm.[149]

We read that God heals the brokenhearted, binds up wounds,[150] and is close to those whose spirits are crushed.[151] God is described as a refuge[152] and Jesus promises rest to those who come to him.[153]

---

[143] John 8:36.
[144] Philippians 4:6–8.
[145] Matthew 7:11 and Psalm 6
[146] Philippians 4:13.
[147] 1 John 4:18 and 2 Timothy 1:7.
[148] 1 Samuel 1:3–19.
[149] 1 Corinthians 3:16, 6:19–20.
[150] Psalms 147:3.
[151] Psalms 34:18.
[152] Psalms 62:5–8. The whole Psalm is about the Lord's deliverance.
[153] Matthew 11:28–30.

CHAPTER 9

DEPRESSION

9.1 INTRODUCTION

Clinical depression is one of the most common mental health disorders in society today. It is estimated that about one in five people will develop a depressive illness at some time in their life. Women seem to be about twice as prone to depression as men, and the elderly are more prone as the life-span has been significantly lengthened. Separated and divorced people show a higher incidence of depression than others. Single people have a higher incidence than married people. The incidence is higher among lower socioeconomic groups and the incidence among children and teenagers is on the increase.

Depression is often comorbid with other issues like anxiety disorders, compulsive disorders, addictions, social anxiety, and schizophrenia. Stein and Hollander (2003) suggest that a client with depression should also be assessed for anxiety. Depression has a high incidence rate among people with a chronic illness (e.g., cancer, diabetes, chronic pain) and cardiac problems. The challenge is to determine whether or not the depression is just a normal reaction to the stress of having the illness. Although depression is not always considered life-threatening, it often does lead to thoughts of and even attempts at suicide. As many as 70 % of suicides in the U.S. are related in some way to depression, and up to 15% of severely depressed people will commit suicide. The positive risk of suicide therefore needs to be taken into account in counseling depressed clients. A combination of a desire to harm self and a sense of hopelessness and helplessness are possible warning signs. Some antidepressants can sometimes cause an increase in suicidal thoughts in those with severe depression during the first few treatment weeks or when changing the dose. The topic of suicide risk is discussed in Chapter 10.

The good news is that depression is treatable and a very high percentage of depressed people are treated effectively through antidepressants, psychotherapy, or a combination of both. The not so good news is that depression tends to reoccur (about 50% of people) so that a maintenance program needs to be established with the client. The counseling therapies which seem to be most popular are CBT (Cognitive-Behavioral Therapy), IPT (Interpersonal Psychotherapy),[1] or a combination of both.[2] Here IPT looks at interpersonal issues connected with the depression, focusing on one interpersonal issue at a time. Depression can arise through a loss of interpersonal connectedness with significant others. People with depression tend to engage in few social activities and have difficulty in experiencing such activities as pleasurable; self-esteem can be affected. IPT can include four areas of interpersonal focus: grief, role disputes, role transitions, and social skills.

Kiser (2003) maintains that psychodynamic approaches that encourage people to introspect about what they were unhappy about in the past will deepen depression. Trower et al. make the comment:

> In CBT it can be helpful to explore early experiences to enable the client to place his problems in a historical context, but this is not seen as a major part of the counseling. The CBT view is that people are not disturbed so much by past events as by the way that these events are viewed in the present.[3]

Downing-Orr states: "Therapies such as humanistic and client-centered approaches should be avoided, because they increase suffering."[4] However, early negative beliefs can be activated by life events, and attachment theory may have a role in the understanding of a client's depression.[5] As we are all different, it is clear that one hat size does not fit all heads, and we have to adapt to each individual's needs.[6]

The main types of antidepressants are SSRIs (serotonin selective re-uptake inhibitors) such as fluoxetine (prosac) and paroxetine, the TCAs (tricyclics) such as amitriptyline, and the MaOIs (monoamine oxidase inhibitors), the latter requiring some dietary restrictions. They all lead to an increase in certain neurotransmitters that elevate the mood: the SSRIs reduce the absorption (re-uptake) of serotonin, while the other two promote an increase in noradrenaline (norepinephrine) and serotonin.[7] These drugs can sometimes have side effects (e.g., wakefulness when taken at night), and the long term effects of many drugs are unknown.[8] Clients of all ages taking antidepressants need to be monitored closely, especially during the first few weeks of treatment to watch out for worsening depression, any unusual changes in behavior, or suicidal thinking. If a client does not find their particular drug helpful, they should be encouraged to go back to their doctor to change the dose or their drug regime. The medical profession is unclear about the exact nature of depression and the way antidepressants actually work!

[1] Also referred by some as interpersonal therapy.
[2] Other therapies may be effective and Reinecke and Davidson (2002) discuss 12 approaches.
[3] Trower, Casey, and Dryden (1988: 7–8) .
[4] Downing-Orr (1998: 153).
[5] Gilbert (1992: 19–21).
[6] A powerful and personal description of depression is given by Solomon (2001).
[7] These drugs are described in greater detail on websites using the search word "antidepressants".
[8] For detailed comments about this topic see Downing-Orr (1998: 123–127).

Psychotherapy has proved to be as effective as drug treatment in mild cases and it is commonly used in conjunction with drug therapy. If just a drug regime is used, there is the danger that when there is an initial improvement, the major problems underlying the depression may get pushed aside by the client. This may exacerbate the possibility of a later relapse. In the case of mild depression, some people have found the herbal remedy St. John's wort (hypericum) helpful as it tends to have less side-effects than some antidepressants. However, it should be used with care as it can interact with other drugs and the quality of the product can vary.[9]

An interesting alternative view about serotonin has been proposed by Griffin.[10] He maintains that a low serotonin level is an index that a person's life is not going well—feeling stuck with needs not met—rather than wrong brain chemistry; brain chemistry is then in his view an effect, but not the cause!

9.1.1 Basic Symptoms

Depression is usually described as a mood ("affective") disorder with wide ranging symptoms that vary from individual to individual. The basic symptoms may be listed as follows:[11]

(1) Emotional symptoms (e.g., feelings of misery, lack of self-esteem, a sense of hopelessness, unhappiness, shame, worthlessness, uselessness, guilt, extreme sadness, excessive crying, feeling emotionally flat, loss of pleasure, inability to enjoy anything, and irritability).

(2) Motivational symptoms (e.g., apathy, lack of motivation, inertia, boredom, uncertainty, indecision, discouragement, and lack of control).

(3) Thought symptoms (e.g., negative self-appraisal, bleak outlook for the future, sense of failure, thoughts of inferiority and inadequacy, thought distortions, suicidal thoughts, self-blame, concentration difficulties, memory problems).

(4) Physical symptoms (e.g., appetite disturbances, weight change such as a gain or loss of 5% or more in a month, sleep disturbances, loss of sexual drive, fatigue, anxiety and panic, and bodily aches and pains). There may also be psychomotor agitation or retardation where a person is observed to be either agitated and restless or physically slowed down in their movements.

Two key symptoms are sleep difficulties and not being able to shake off certain thoughts. One can also add any history of depression in family members; endogenous depression (see below) tends to run in families.

As might be expected, cultural variations will exist.[12] A major difference is that Western cultural traditions promote individualism, which leads more readily to isolation, loneliness, narcissism, and perceived helplessness. However, in non-Western cultures there is a collective identity or collectivism that can mitigate

---

[9]For example, some believe it should be standardized for the ingredient hyperforin. There is plenty of information about St. John's wort on the internet.
[10]Kiser (2003).
[11]Adapted from Downing-Orr (1998: 92).
[12]Marsella and Kaplan (2002) provide a checklist to see if conventional Western psychology can be used with a particular client.

against existential problems (e.g., meaninglessness) and against an over-emphasis on the individual's moral fiber — "It's up to you to pull yourself out of it." CBT may not work so well with cultures that do not place a high value on rationality but instead favor such things as intuition. For example, Asian cultures may adopt a more holistic stance and rely less on formal logic.

There are several "inventories" or questionnaires for testing the severity of depression. Two common ones are the Beck Depression Inventory Second Edition or BDI-II[13] (0–13 minimal range, 14–19 mild, 20–28 moderate, and 29–62 severe depression) and the Hopkins Symptom Checklist-90 (HSCL-90), both from the perspective of the client (i.e., self-reporting). There is also the Hamilton Rating Scale of Depression (NHRD) which should be administered by a professional.[14] Another inventory called the Goldberg questionnaire[15] may be useful for a client to use to monitor their own personal progress in overcoming depression. Several other useful inventories are available on the internet (e.g., CES-D).

Male Depression

It is worth making some comments about male depression as it is sometimes difficult to detect, especially as it has been regarded in the past as a woman's problem. Men have tendered to be diagnosed using the same women's pattern of symptoms. However, women tend to feel their depression and try to connect with others, while men act out their depression through frustration, anger, and hostility, and have a tendency to withdraw from others. There are a number of ways that men mask depression:[16]

(1.) *Anger, rage, and pent-up resentment.* Stress or major loss can be the trigger, and it can surface in road rage, work rage, and even school rage.

(2.) *Workaholism.* Work can be both a cause and a mask for depression. Overwork is the most significant cause of stress in society today, which can upset the serotonin neurotransmitter system in the brain, causing depression.

(3.) *Avoidance of Intimacy.* Depression can lead to a shut down of intimacy with partner, family, and friends. However, as sex, for the typical male, is not necessarily an expression of intimacy, sex isn't necessarily excluded with a partner. This withdrawal from intimacy may also lead to the man trying to fault others for the way he is feeling.

(3.) *Sexual Compulsions.* Sex can alleviate stress and depression, so that a man may become obsessed with sex.

9.1.2   Sleep Patterns

A change in one's normal sleep pattern, with either sleeping too much (approximately 15% of sleep problems) or too little, and having broken sleep throughout the

---

[13] Available at http://www.ibogaine.desk.nl/graphics/3639b1c_23.pdf (accessed October 2010).
[14] See http://healthnet.umassmed.edu/mhealth/HAMD.pdf (accessed October 2010).
[15] See http://counsellingresource.com/quizzes/goldberg-depression/index.html (accessed October 2010).
[16] http://www.ministrymagazine.org/archive/2002/November/unmasking-male-depression.html by Archibald Hart, accessed June 2012, and Hart (2001).

night, can be a very useful diagnostic aid for depression. Many depressed clients complain that their minds go round and round when they try to go off to sleep. A person suffering from depression has the pattern reversed with regard to REM and non REM sleep: REM sleep happens much more quickly after first falling asleep and decreases towards the morning.[17] Depressed people have excessive REM sleep, and antidepressants suppress REM sleep, delay its onset, and decrease its duration thus helping to normalize the sleep pattern. Why the excessive dreaming? Dreaming seems to be a kind of "clearing-house" for our brains, and Griffin[18] maintains that depressed people do so much worrying and negative thinking during the day that there is an overload of dreaming that uses a lot of energy in the brain. There is then less of the recuperative deeper sleep so that they wake up exhausted and unable to get going. According to this view, people generate their own depression and the key to overcoming this problem is to change daytime thinking and ruminating.

9.2   CAUSES OF DEPRESSION

With the variety of possible symptoms, it is clear that the causes of depression are complex and each diagnosis needs to be done carefully. Given the right diagnosis, we noted above that most people can be helped, but unfortunately a significant proportion of people are misdiagnosed. We now look briefly at some models about causes.

9.2.1   Models of Depression

There are a number of models or theories employed to explain the origins of depression and the following is a somewhat simplistic overview to give the flavor.[19]

1. Psychoanalytic model. Here there is an object loss[20] or loss of self-esteem, which may be due to a difference in one's actual ego state (who we are) and one's ideal ego state (who we would like to be). The psychoanalytic approach was first introduced by Freud and developed by others.

2. Cognitive model. Beck[21] ascribes depression to irrational and negative thought patterns, the patterns being referred as schemas.[22] Here one has negative perceptions of self (e.g., "I must be perfect and never make a mistake"), the world (e.g., "People must act the way I want"), and the future (e.g., "Life must always go the way I want it to").[23]

3. Behavioral model. Behaviors are positively or negatively rewarded so that an inadequate reinforcement such as deprivation, or learned helplessness (in which, for example, stress cannot be removed) can lead to depression. Further comments about this model are given by Downing-Orr.[24]

---

[17] Downing-Orr (1998: 41–42); see Section 2.2.4 on the sleep cycle.
[18] Kiser (2003).
[19] Hart (1987: 50).
[20] Object also referring to a person.
[21] Beck (1972, 1980).
[22] Also called schemata.
[23] For a mistaken-beliefs questionnaire see Bourne (2005: 210–213).
[24] Downing-Orr (1998: 53–55).

4. Sociological models. Social factors such as loss of role status and an inability to balance one's needs against those of others can lead to depression. This seldom appears in third world poverty.

5. Existential model. Here the individual may feel not only alone in society but also alone in an apparently purposeless universe; life has lost its meaning.

6. Biological model. Here the underlying cause of depression is physical: this is called endogenous depression.

Although each model can produce useful insights, no single model gives a totally adequate description. For example, Reinecke (2002) mentions four types of factors involved in depression: biological and genetic factors, interpersonal and environmental factors, development history, and social-cognitive variables. Gilbert (1992) refers to the biopsychosocial model of depression. In the past there has been a tendency to regard depression as either a psychological illness (e.g., emotional disorder) or a biological illness (e.g., neuro-chemical imbalance in the brain). However Downing-Orr[25] suggests that a better description of depression is that it is really a combination of both, that is a *psychobiological* illness.

9.2.2 Physical Causes

Listed below are some physical causes of depression.

1. Problems with the action of certain neurotransmitters such as serotonin, noradrenaline (also called norepinephrine) and dopamine.[26] There may be an insufficient production of the neurotransmitter, insufficient release of it from the sending side across the synapse, insufficient receiving of it at the receptor side, degradation of it during transmission, insufficient return (re-uptake) of it from the receiving to the transmitting side, and/or excessive removal of it from the synapse by monamine oxidase, a chemical that is believed to regulate the balance of the neurotransmitter.

2. Imbalance of hormones produced by the endocrine glands, for example, hypothyroidism (underactive thyroid).[27] Some neurotransmitters are also hormones so we can add pre-menstrual syndrome.

3. Adrenaline exhaustion after the body has experienced a high adrenaline demand. The adrenaline switches off when the demand is over and can lead to depression, forcing the body to rest. This effect can occur with post-traumatic stress disorder (see Section 7.3).

4. Diseases of the central nervous system (e.g., dementia, Alzheimer's disease, and multiple sclerosis).[28]

5. There are many drugs which can cause or contribute to depression, for example, beta blockers for high blood pressure, steroids, oral contraceptives, anti-inflammatory drugs for arthritic conditions, antibacterials, anti-hypertensives,

[25] Downing-Orr (1998: 27).
[26] See Section 1.2.1.
[27] Downing-Orr (1998: 40-41,68).
[28] Downing-Orr (1998: 67–72).

and various over-the-counter drugs (e.g., diet pills, cold and cough suppressants, and laxatives).[29]

6. Illegal drugs (e.g., marijuana depletes serotonin causing depression). The literature establishes that long term use from teen years can produce psychosis.

7. Excessive alcohol, especially with alcoholics who may try using alcohol to medicate their emotional distress. It however makes things worse.

8. Nutritional problems, such as an inadequate intake of vitamins and minerals, and reduced levels of omega-3 fatty acids. A deficiency of the B vitamins can produce depressive symptoms, and this deficiency is not uncommon. A lack of vitamin C can also lead to symptoms of depression. Students on poor diets would do well to take note here.

9. Cancer.

10. Some infectious diseases such as glandular fever and hepatitis.

11. Chronic fatigue syndrome or chronic pain such as chronic back pain.

12. Environmental poisons (e.g., carbon monoxide, organophosphate insecticides, and solvents).

Many healthcare professionals use the DSM-IV as a guide in interviewing patients about their symptoms, but they may fail to rule out some of the above causes.

9.2.3 Other Causes

It appears that genetics may have some role in one's risk of suffering from depression. There seems to be a link between families and depression, and of course environment will play a role. One has to be careful not to stereotype, for example, the gender or age difference already alluded to at the beginning of the chapter.

Causes of depression are many and varied. A crisis or traumatic event can sometimes set depression in motion or trigger a latent malaise with the full force of depression occurring some time after the presenting event, as it can take time to accommodate and process what has happened. There may even be a succession of difficult events that a person survives, and when it is all over depression may hit him or her, seemingly out of the blue. Stress is a frequent trigger for depression and, again, depression usually occurs after the stress; it can catch people unawares as they did not realize what has been happening to them. With stress it is very easy to ignore the warning signals our body gives us, and part of a coping strategy is becoming more self-aware of where our body is at. We need to recognize the symptoms of stress and know how to cope with it.

As already noted, depression is often a major factor in various other conditions. Further, it can have an acute onset (within days or weeks) or come on gradually; it can be chronic (e.g., lasting over two years) or short-lived (recovery in weeks or months) or even show cyclical patterns.

---

[29] Downing-Orr (1998: 69–74).

9.3 CLASSIFYING DEPRESSION

9.3.1 The Problem of Classification

The first problem is to determine whether the depression is due to a mood dis-order ("primary" depression) or a physical disorder ("secondary" depression) like those listed in Section 9.2.2 above. Although the clinical assessment of depres-sion will generally be done by an appropriate healthcare professional, it is helpful for counsellors to be acquainted with some of the labels given to various types of depression. Gilbert comments: "Generally, a counsellor rarely makes a detailed diagnosis of type, and some counsellors even wonder about the wisdom of distin-guishing depression from other psychological difficulties."[30] Some professionals find the categories helpful while others ignore them altogether. A very detailed sum-mary of the symptoms of the various categories of depression discussed below is given by Hart.[31]

Wearing my hat as a past professional statistician, I would point out that try-ing to establish various categories of depression is fraught with statistical difficul-ties.[32] If you can imagine a set of symptoms that a person may have is somehow summarized as a single point (dot) representing the person on a two-dimensional graphical plot, and we have lots of such points, with one for each person, then the aim of categorization is to look for clusters or groups of points and then give the clusters descriptive labels; some clusters may even overlap. A little imagination will make it clear that there will be some points, that is people, that don't fit anywhere! Downing-Orr states that "this question of categorizing depression still remains controversial, conflicting, and unresolved."[33] There is also some variation in categorization and terminology with different countries. For example, the DMS-IV-TR is the main source of diagnosis used in the United States and the ICD-10 (International Classification of Disease) is more influential in Europe and elsewhere. Finally, the boundary between normal and clinical depression is not clear-cut and depends on the number, severity, and persistence of the symptoms over time. The following are the usual categories of depression.

9.3.2 Reactive Depression

This is the most common form of depression and it results from a reaction to life events such as job loss, bereavement, divorce, and so forth. It can helpfully be viewed as a grieving process that follows loss or deprivation. Hart[34] gives the following useful steps for dealing with this type of depression:

1. Identify losses, which may have many different facets.

2. Understand each facet. We need to remember that we all see losses differently.

3. Separate the concrete from the abstract losses and use the following categories:

    • concrete losses (real, imagined, and threatened)

[30] Gilbert (1992: 3).
[31] Hart (1987: 68–72).
[32] In statistics this topic is referred to as cluster analysis.
[33] Downing-Orr (1998: 100).
[34] Hart (1987: chapter 9).

- abstract losses (real, imagined, and threatened)

4. Separate real, imagined and threatened losses; one can only grieve for real losses. For example, a threatened loss might be, "I might die under anesthetic." By examining their beliefs, clients can determine what aspects of the loss are real (sensible and rational) and what are imagined.

5. Convert imagined and threatened losses into real losses or else help the client to discard them. The reality of each such loss needs to be tested. Imagined abstract losses are more common, for example, "I imagine that I might lose my job," even though the job is going well.

6. Help the client through the grieving process; Chapter 11 can be helpful here.

7. Encourage the client to develop a perspective on the loss, separating out the essentials from the nonessentials and distinguishing between the unchangeables and the changeables in life.

8. As with all depression, encourage the client to avoid negative thinking.

9.3.3 Major Depressive Disorder

A major depressive disorder (MDD), also referred to as clinical depression or major depressive episode, is characterized by a severely depressed mood or a loss of interest or pleasure in daily activities consistently for at least a two week period together with most of the basic symptoms given above. It is described as either "a single episode" or "recurrent," and as mild, major, or severe. If the client has already had an episode of mania (markedly elevated mood), a diagnosis of bipolar disorder (see below) can be made instead of MDD. Depression without periods of elation or mania is sometimes referred to as unipolar depression because the mood remains at one emotional state or "pole."[35]

9.3.4 Dysthymia

Dysthymia is a chronic, mild depression in which a person suffers from a depressed mood almost daily over a span of at least 2 years without episodes of major depression. This type of depression used to be called *neurotic depression* and is also referred to as a persistent affective disorder. The symptoms are not as severe as those for major depression.

A subset of dysthymia is Atypical Depression (AD), the most common subtype of depression. In addition to the basic symptoms of depression, AD is characterized by DSM-IV-TR as the ability to feel better temporarily in response to a positive life event, plus any two of the following criteria: excessive sleep, overeating, a feeling of heaviness in the limbs, and a sensitivity to rejection. Some clients with AD have intense cravings for carbohydrates. A mineral supplement, chromium picolinate, can reduce these cravings.

---

[35]The term unipolar now seems to be generally avoided.

9.3.5   Bipolar Disorder

Description

Bipolar Disorder (BP), also known as manic depressive illness, is a brain disorder that causes unusual shifts in mood, energy, activity levels, and the ability to carry out day-to-day tasks.[36] BP is often difficult to diagnose as the symptoms, which are severe, might appear to indicate separate problems. People with BP experience unusually intense emotional states that occur in distinct periods called "mood episodes." An overly joyful or overexcited state is called a manic episode, or, if milder, hypomania, and an extremely sad or hopeless state is called a depressive episode. The latter may be absent, or in the case of "mixed episodes," mania and depression may occur at the same time. The depression may be severe, moderate, or mild (dysthymia, if chronic or long term). Those with BP may experience a long-lasting period of unstable moods rather than discrete episodes of depression or mania. Others who present with at least four alternating depressive-hypomanic cycles per year are said to have *rapid cycling* BP; this is usually a transient phase.

Bipolar Disorder generally lasts a life-time with the episodes typically coming back over time; it tends to get worse if not treated. The onset of full symptoms usually occurs in late adolescence or young adulthood. People with BP may be symptom-free between episodes or have lingering symptoms. With proper diagnosis and treatment they can lead healthy and productive lives.

The risk factors for BP are not clearly understood. The literature suggests BP tends to run in families suggesting a possible genetic connection; brain development and environmental factors can also play a part. Substance abuse is common among people with BP who may try to treat their symptoms with alcohol or drugs; the latter possibly triggering or prolonging the symptoms. Anxiety disorders such as post-traumatic stress disorder and social phobia, or attention deficit hyperactivity disorder (ADHD), may be comorbid with BP. There may be physical illnesses such as thyroid disease, heart disease, and diabetes, for example, that can cause symptoms of mania or depression.

Symptoms of Mania

The symptoms for depression have been discussed above, while those for mania involve mood and behavior. The mood may be a long period of feeling "high," (e.g., overly happy or outgoing), or extremely irritable, agitated, and "jumpy." The behavior may include restlessness, fast talking, jumping from one idea to another, impulsiveness, being easily distracted, having an unrealistic belief in one's abilities, taking on new projects, and impulsively taking part in a lot of pleasurable, high-risk behaviors (e.g., spending sprees, impulsive sex, and impulsive business investments). People having the milder hypomanic episode may feel very good, be highly productive, and function well, not believing that anything is wrong, even when friends and family suspect BD. They may have episodes that last less than a week and do not require emergency care. However, without proper treatment they may well develop severe mania or depression.

[36]For details, see for example,
http://www.nimh.nih.gov/health/publications/bipolar-disorder/complete-index.shtml (accessed October 2010).

Those with mixed episodes can feel extremely energized yet feel very sad or hopeless at the same time. They can be agitated, suicidal, having trouble sleeping, and having major changes in appetite. Those with severe episodes of mania or depression can also have psychotic symptoms such as hallucinations or delusions (e.g., believing they are rich and famous with special powers), so that BD in this case can be confused with schizophrenia.

Assessment

A person may be having an episode of bipolar disorder if he or she has a number of manic or depressive symptoms for most of the day, nearly every day, for at least one or two weeks. DSM-IV describes a spectrum of disorders under the BP umbrella along with criteria, namely:[37]

1. *Bipolar I.* The occurrence of one or more manic or mixed episodes that last at least seven days, or manic symptoms that are so severe requiring hospitalization. Usually there are depressive episodes as well.

2. *Bipolar II.* The occurrence of one or more major depressive episodes accompanied by at least one hypomanic episode, but no full-blown manic or mixed episodes.

3. *Bipolar Disorder Not Otherwise Specified (BP-NOS).* The symptoms may not last long enough or be too few to diagnose as Bipolar I or II, but they are certainly outside a person's behavioral norms.

3. *Cyclothymia.* This is a mild form of BP where episodes of hypomania cycle back and forth with mild depression for at least two years.

Bipolar III has also been mentioned in the literature, referring to when hypomania has been brought on by medication for depression.

A diagnosis needs to be made by a doctor or mental health professional such as a psychiatrist. People with BP are more likely to seek help when they are depressed than when experiencing mania or hypomania. In the U.S. there is roughly a lifetime prevalence of about 5% or 6% for the BP spectrum; there are considerable variations in the data and how it is collected. BP can also lead to suicidal ideation, especially when depression is a major factor.

Treatment

BP is a lifelong and recurrent illness, and at present there is no cure for it. However, treatments are available to help people gain better control of their mood swings and related symptoms. Medication using a mood stabilizer is a first choice, for example lithium or anticonvulsants, though the former can affect the thyroid and the latter have associated risks such as suicide. An antidepressant may also be added to a mood stabilizer, though any additional effectiveness is uncertain; atypical antipsychotics may also be used. It important to get the dosages right, and discontinuing or lowering the dose can cause problems. Adherence to a medication program can be a problem for those with BP. Caffeine and an inconsistent sleep schedule can cause instability while excessive stress can lead to a relapse. In addition

---

[37]For extensive details, criteria, and definitions see
http://www.fortunecity.com/campus/psychology/781/dsm.htm (accessed October 2010).

to the general strategies for counseling depression (Section 9.4), further comments for counseling for BP are added below in Section 9.4.4.

9.3.6 Postnatal Depression

Postnatal depression (PND) is an intense, sustained, and sometimes disabling depression experienced by women after giving birth. It has an incidence rate of about 10-15%, though it may be much higher (some say 25%) as it is sometimes undiagnosed. PND typically sets in within three months of labor and it can last for as long as three months.[38] Typical symptoms are irritability and anger.[39] For many mothers, PND is a physiological imbalance of neuro-transmitters (primarily serotonin) often intensified by REM (rapid-eye-movement) sleep-deprivation. A downloadable assessment tool is the Edinburgh Postnatal Depression Scale (EPDS).[40] A score of 9–12 is borderline depression, while 13 or more suggests clinical depression.

9.3.7 Seasonal Affective Disorder (SAD)

This form of depression has a seasonal onset (autumn and/or winter) with relief in spring and summer, and in the U.S. affects about 4% to 6% of people, usually over the age of 20 years. It is caused by a biochemical imbalance in the hypothalamus due to the shortening of daylight hours and the lack of sunlight in winter. This lack of sun can lead to an imbalance in the body's natural circadian rhythm that governs the timing of sleep, hormone production, body temperature, and other biological functions. In addition to depression, associated symptoms include anxiety, increased appetite (especially for carbohydrates), weight gain, difficulty concentrating, loss of energy, social withdrawal, and oversleeping.

An important feature of SAD is that too much melatonin is produced so that exposure to sunlight or bright white light can be an effective form of treatment in combination with antidepressants. There is a photo receptor in the human eye responsible for reacting to light and controlling the production of melatonin. Light, particularly in the range of 447-484 nanometers (for about 30 minutes), can suppress this melatonin production, releasing serotonin, and shifting circadian rhythms. Typically light therapy is done in the morning as it can cause insomnia if too late in the day.[41] Commercial light boxes for treating SAD are available especially in Scandinavia where the winters are so long and depressing.

Some people however experience summer SAD (spring and summer depression) with associated symptoms including anxiety, insomnia, agitation, poor appetite, weight loss, and increased sex drive.

9.3.8 Premenstrual Dysphoric Disorder (PMDD)

About 3% to 5% of menstruating women suffer from premenstrual dysphoric disorder (premenstrual depression). Symptoms, including depression, can be irritability,

---

[38] It is also called *postpartum depression*.
[39] Enright and Fitzgibbons (2000: 131).
[40] See the internet, e.g., http://www.fresno.ucsf.edu/pediatrics/downloads/edinburghscale.pdf (accessed October 2010.
[41] For some specific details of the light therapy see
http://www.mayoclinic.com/health/sad/MY00371 by David Mrazek (accessed October 2010).

being on edge, anger, tension, verbal outbursts, and increased sensitivity to rejection or criticism. There can also be an increased need for emotional closeness, an increase or decrease in sex drive, fatigue, some difficulty concentrating, and sleep problems. Further symptoms include food cravings and binge eating, and crying spells for no reason. Some physical symptoms include breast tenderness, headaches, and joint or muscle pain. The distinguishing factor (from say major depression) is that the symptoms appear a week or two before menses and then disappear a few days after the onset of menses. The diminished level of function for the woman is in strong contrast to how she is at other times of the month.

To diagnose the disorder a client needs to keep a journal or diary for several months to assess the severity, timing, onset, and duration of the symptoms. Those who already suffer from depression may need a slight increase in their dosage of antidepressant premenstrually. Treatments can include antidepressants, oral contraceptives, some nutritional supplements, exercise, and cutting back on caffeine. A milder form of PMDD is premenstrual syndrome (PMS) experienced by 20% to 50% of women between the ages of 30 to 40 with regular menstrual cycles.

9.4 COUNSELING STRATEGIES FOR DEPRESSION

9.4.1 General Strategies

The counsellor–client relationship is particularly important for depression as clients often feel separate or cut off from people and think that people don't really understand them or can be bothered with them. Family members may have reacted very negatively towards them as the family members may be tired of being with someone who is a a "kill joy" and can't pull themselves together!

At an early stage it is helpful to find out the history of the client's depression, family, and medical background. I like to construct a genogram as we proceed, and the client can be asked whether there are other members of their extended family with related problems. It is also important to see whether they have had a thorough medical check-up to rule out some of the physical causes mentioned previously. Therapists might have in mind their own instant diagnosis of the type of depression their client might have, but l believe labels should generally be avoided. Although drugs play an important role in treating clinical depression, therapists need to deal with the whole person. This involves looking at the mental, emotional, physical, social, and spiritual well-being of the client as I have done in Chapter 2. As depression tends to reoccur, a maintenance program is needed for clients to follow for the rest of their lives. They will still have their daily ups and downs, which is normal, but through a balanced program their "downs" can become short-lived and happen less frequently.

Related emotions are, for example, anxiety, anger, and guilt or shame; any of these can lead to depression, which is often linked to a painful sense of disappointment and/or a sense of hopelessness. Depression tends to steal hope so that hope plays an important role in recovering from depression. I like the following quote:

> Never doubt for a moment that you will get well and be your old self again.
> In fact, you will be better than your old self. All that separates you from
> where you are now and a state of well-being is a little time and effort. Allow
> yourself to hope, for you have every reason to do so. It is very important that

you believe you can be fit, well and inwardly content. Believing that we can and will recover is the first important step towards healing. It is the catalyst that initiates the healing process.[42]

Important areas for exploration are self-esteem[43] and social relationships, which can play an important role both in the cause of depression and in the recovery from it. Barrow[44] mentions a number of attitudes that feed depression and anxiety. These are: harboring resentments and hurts; self-pity; passive behavior (allowing people to walk all over us); lack of forgiveness of ourselves, of God (it's God's fault I am like this), and of others; and habitual loneliness through withdrawal.

9.4.2   Cognitive Methods

In discussing Beck's Cognitive Therapy mentioned in Section 1.4.3, Reinecke states that:

> The schemas of depressed individuals are rigid and are characterized by perceptions of personal inadequacy and loss, the belief that others are unreliable or uncaring, that the future is bleak, and that they lack control over important outcomes in their life.[45]

In using cognitive methods such as the ABC of REBT (Section 1.4.3), it is helpful to assess the intensity of the emotions felt by the client; this can be done by, for example, asking the client to score the intensity of an emotion on a scale of 1 to 10 or as a percentage; discussing bodily sensations at the time is also helpful. It is important to distinguish clearly between beliefs and emotions, which are often confused by the client. A small shift in a belief can lead to a big shift in consequences.

J. Beck[46] divides beliefs into three levels: automatic thoughts, intermediate beliefs (rules, attitudes, and assumptions), and, at the deepest level, core beliefs. I have found it difficult sometimes to distinguish between the bottom two levels, which is not critical as it is a matter of definition. However, it is helpful to determine those rules passed down from a family of origin. The strength of a belief can be measured by a percentage and then tested again to see if there is a drop after alternative and challenging beliefs have been raised.

Trower et al.[47] suggest alternative categories of inferences and evaluation (of self and others) while Gilbert[48] considers the cognitive approach of interpersonal psychoherapy (IPT) and replaces the category of core beliefs by self–other beliefs. This approach focuses on the fact that social relationships play an important role in depression, not only in its cause and maintenance, but also in its recovery.[49]

Gilbert[50] summarizes the interpersonal dimensions of depression and refers to the work of Klerman et al. (1984) who emphasize the role of social life events and the significant current and early relationships of a client. They link depression to

---

[42] Barrow (1985: 12–13).
[43] See Section 2.5.3.
[44] Barrow (1985: Chapter 4).
[45] Reinecke (2002: 252).
[46] J. Beck (1995: 14).
[47] Trower et al. (1988: 3).
[48] Gilbert (1992: 35).
[49] For details see Weissman, Markowitz, and Klerman (2007).
[50] Gilbert (1992: chapter 2).

specific causes such as grief and loss, interpersonal role transitions, role conflicts, and social skills deficits. Cognitive counselors will emphasize how attitudes and beliefs can affect important relationships. As noted in the introduction to this chapter, early negative beliefs arising from early experiences with parents/caregivers and significant others can activate depression later. Problems with early attachment can lead to a negative view of self and others.[51] Some basic interpersonal schemas include approval, achievement, self-worth, efficacy/entrapment, affect, and power. These schemas or belief systems are discussed by Gilbert [52] and a brief commentary on them follows.

The need for approval arises for clients who have an anxious attachment style. They don't function without a close relationship(s) and love. Achievers endeavor to gain approval and respect by achievement. For them success and the subsequent recognition is everything, and without it they believe they are a failure.

The development of self-worth begins in childhood and if children do not receive sufficient praise, attention, love, and so forth, they develop as adults who believe that they have nothing to contribute to relationships and society as a whole. For example, a mother who is always late in picking up her daughter produces in the child a perception that she is not important enough for her mother to be on time. Later on, the grown-up girl may believe that she is worthless and is unaware of the source of that belief.

Another source of depression is a perception of helplessness, lack of control, and hopelessness. The client may feel trapped in a situation such as a relationship or job and sees no way out. A client can be depressed about his or her feelings and the confusion they cause. The therapist can help the client to verbally express these feelings openly and therefore examine them with the client.

There is also the issue of power. The client may feel inferior to others or make excessive accommodation to others in order to obtain approval. Believing one is inferior to others may lead to inhibited and cautious social behavior.

The above ideas of interaction with others need to be carried over to interaction with self. We can be accepting of others yet remain non-accepting of self and vice versa. Often, in depression, the relationship with self is hostile or down-putting, and the client needs to recognize negative self-talk (see below). Any negative self-judgments need to be recognized and disputed and hopefully replaced. Some negative beliefs can be self-fulfilling! A person has a certain negative self-belief that leads to a certain behavior, which in turn produces a certain reaction from others thus confirming the initial negative belief. Gilbert[53] gives the following example: "I am boring, so people won't be interested in what I have to say, therefore I won't say anything and people lose interest in me as they find me boring." In essence, a client can elicit the very action from others that they complain of; this is an example of a *recursive feedback loop* which can be drawn as a circle for the client.

Gilbert gives a number of other techniques such as role play; empty-chair work; replacing words like "I should" and "I must" by "I prefer;" and the advantages–disadvantages of changing a certain belief. Depressed clients may also engage in

---

[51]See Section 2.5.2 for various attachment styles.
[52]Gilbert (1992: 23–33).
[53]Gilbert (1992: 45).

"yes-but" style of thinking. For example, " If I do ... I could achieve ..., but I might not be liked by ...."

Structured Problem Solving

Depressed clients have difficulty in dealing with everyday problems. One method of dealing with problems is Structured Problem Solving (SPS). There are four basic steps to this method.[54]

1. *Identify Problems.*

   (a) Write down all the problems and give a short statement for each (e.g., relationships, grief, stress, unemployment, harassment, addictions, illness, financial or legal problems).

   (b) Choose a problem.

   (c) Define the problem by asking why, what, when, where, and why (e.g., Why is it a problem and what effect is it having on your life?).

   (d) Write a single "I" sentence that includes an action word like try, learn, or work that summarizes the problem.

2. *Generate Solutions.*

   (a) List any potential solutions no matter how impractical or silly.

   (b) Evaluate the list.

   (c) Choose the best looking idea.

   (d) Evaluate the idea under the headings: advantages, disadvantages, and neutral (e.g., ask questions like "How will the solution affect my well-being or of those close to me?" and "Are there any financial costs or benefits?").

   (e) If the idea shows promise, write a summary of it; otherwise choose another solution and compare the two.

3. Make an action plan to carry out the solution.

   (a) Write a description of the plan.

   (b) Check that is a SMART plan (see Section 2.3.2).

   (c) Write a list of the steps needed to carry out the plan.

4. Review progress with the plan (e.g., what worked or didn't work) and give yourself a pat on the back if every step above was followed, irrespective of the result. Move on to the next problem on the list.

Homework

Homework is important part of the cognitive approach as the client is able to practice and develop the necessary skills. Gilbert[55] suggests the following four "mottoes" about homework that will prevent it from being sabotaged.

---

[54]http://www.depression.org.nz/ContentFiles/Media/PDF/structured_problem_solving_workbook.pdf (accessed October 2010).
[55]Gilbert (1992: 73).

- challenging but not overwhelming

- getting better rather than feeling better (the client may feel worse at first)

- dealing with the fear of getting better

- avoiding trivializing achievements

Topics for homework can be gleaned from the following fifteen-step program outlined in the next section. It can also be very helpful for clients to suggest their own homework.

9.4.3 Fifteen-Step Program

The following fifteen-step program using a holistic approach was developed by Iris Barrow (1985) for depression; the order and progress rate through the steps will depend on the individual.

1. *Relaxation.*
   When stress builds up we run on adrenaline (epinephrine), which tends to protect us from how our body is really coping. However, if the stress becomes too great or continues for too long, the adrenaline stops, our bodies shut down, and we become fatigued and depressed. Our body is then telling us how we really are. Using relaxation techniques to cope with stress are discussed in Section 2.2.5. If a person has a tendency towards depression, then a stressful event can trigger a bout of depression, often some time after the event.

   Stress can lead to over-sensitivity and over-reaction. It can also lead to fear of losing control or even going mad. Clients may even think they are the only people who feel like this. Feeling a bit depressed after a period of intense adrenaline-driven activity is perfectly normal and even healthy as it is telling them that they are letting go and coming back to normal.

   Stress can surface when our guard is down, for example when we are going to sleep, and our body reacts in some way. This is what can happen with anxiety and panic attacks. Unfortunately we cannot force the healing process, as nature has to take its course. All we can do is create the right environment in which healing can take place. The key is to regularly destress ourselves during the day through relaxation exercises and so prevent the build up of stress in the first place. If we carry out a relaxation exercise, our blood pressure drops, sometimes quite substantially. A relaxation exercise is not just doing something relaxing like reading but deliberately going through a process involving correct breathing, relaxing muscles, and redirecting thoughts. This needs to be practiced several times a day so that one can slip into it easily.

2. *Daily exercise.*
   Exercise is a great stress reliever and depression lifter. As stress affects the heart, other organs, and our immune system, prolonged stress is physically harmful. However, exercise leads to the release of biochemicals such as endorphins, which can produce a feeling of well-being being after the exercise. Not surprisingly, regular exercise along with relaxation exercises are very good for one's blood pressure. If the exercise gets people outside as well, they receive

the benefits of sunlight, for example the production of vitamin D, which helps the absorption of Calcium. It is important to slowly build up one's program and eventually aim for a minimum of half an hour exercise each day. For further comments see Section 2.2.2.

3. *Replacing negative thoughts with positive ones.*
   We all engage in self-talk and what we tell ourselves will determine how we feel and how we will act. Although depression makes it difficult to be positive, we do have a choice to be positive or negative. When we catch ourselves with a negative thought we can pretend we have a switch in our head to turn off the thought and replace it by positive one. The key is to be self-aware of how we respond to situations that arise.

4. *Coping with panic and feelings of fear.*
   We saw in Section 6.4.3 that when a person's nervous system has been pushed to the limit, it can react back at the person in the form of a panic attack, particularly at an unguarded moment when he or she is taking time out, or when going off to sleep. We described it as an "attack" because it often happens with little or no warning. Counseling for such attacks is discussed in Section 6.4.3.

5. *Accepting and expressing one's feelings.*
   If people repress or deny their feelings they can become depressed. In particular, if powerful negative emotions such as anger, jealousy, and resentment are not dealt with in healthy ways, they can turn inwards and be damaging, just like acid can damage its container. Once people own their feelings and release them in a safe place, they will feel much better. A therapist can listen to a person talk out suppressed feelings with the view of working through them and letting them go.

6. *Using imagination to work for one.*
   Our imagination is a powerful force for changing how we feel and act. Emotions and behavior stem from our beliefs. You have heard it said, "We become what we eat." I would like to add, "We become what we believe." Many books have been written about positive thinking because it really does work. If we continually imagine ourselves as not really coping, we won't! If we continually put ourselves down, we will stay down. We need to start imagining ourselves as coping, being successful, and achieving our goals. We need to imagine ourselves as being happy, positive and outgoing, not on the way to becoming, but having actually become, this person. If we regularly feed these positive messages into our subconscious for three or four weeks, our subconscious begins to feed those messages back to us and we begin to feel and act positively.

How do we feed in our positive messages? Barrow suggests two ways. The first is visualization where we picture how we want to be. The second is to repeat the words describing how we want to be eight times, and each time concentrating on their meaning. In my counseling I often encourage a client to write out positive statements (particularly about his or her best personal attributes) then read them three times a day with meals, like other medicines! Whichever method is used (or both), it is important to carry out the task when fully relaxed, for example, during a relaxation exercise or going to sleep at night, as this is when autosuggestion works best. If clients do this every day they won't be the same. They may have to shake off negative thoughts from time to time, but if they persevere they will find it's worth it in fighting depression and many other problems.

7. *The importance of eating sensibly.*
Because of the intricate relationship between our body and mind, what and how we eat can have a big effect on our psychological well-being. Depression can have a major effect on our eating habits; in fact having a 5% change in weight in a month is regarded as a symptom of depression. For example, depression can lead to a loss of interest in food, which in turn leads to eating less and often to eating the wrong kind of food. Our bodies are then running on inadequate fuel, which leads to more lethargy and even less interest in food. This downward spiral needs to be halted.

In contrast, however, people may overeat because of depression and anxiety, as eating becomes a comfort to help cope with negative feelings. A craving for carbohydrates can arise, for example, with seasonal affective disorder. I guess this can happen to all of us at times when we come under pressure. Nutrition is discussed in Section 2.2.1 and the key mentioned there is our insulin balance, which controls our blood sugar levels. This means watching our carbohydrate intake (especially junk food with high levels of fat and sugar) with a major emphasis on different colored fruit and vegetables, and making sure that we have the right intake of protein and essential fatty acids. Breakfast is extremely important, and should include some protein to put fuel in the engine for the day. Several smaller meals seem to be better that a few large meals, for example, three basic meals plus morning and afternoon tea, and supper if needed. With depression, the under-eater may find it hard to eat much and Barrow suggests having a "six mini-meal" menu. Although a person may not be hungry, eating does help to create an appetite.

For the overeaters it is important that they never allow themselves to get too hungry. If they have a sweet tooth, then they need to find healthy substitutes, for example, a few dried apricots. Some nuts or seeds can help with cravings and will not affect glucose levels if taken on their own without carbohydrates. Supplements can be helpful as stress can rob the body of B and C vitamins.

8. *Letting go of anxiety.*
Worrying or being anxious about what we are doing or going to do does not help us at all, and in fact hinders our performance. A job becomes more difficult when we add anxiety to it! We need to separate the anxiety from the action; the problem doesn't change, but our attitude to it can. When we have a lot of things to do we simply put them in order and focus on them one at time without worrying about coping with the rest. It is important to be decisive as depression can make a person indecisive and fearful and afraid of doing the wrong thing, so one begins with small decisions. Time management is discussed in Section 5.3.

9. *Facing and overcoming problems.*
If there are things in people's lives that stress and depress them, they need

to write down a "problem-list" including symptoms of depression and "life-problems." A therapist can help clients to come up with some strategies for reducing or eliminating the problems. Suppressed problems tend to get worse and bring a feeling of powerlessness, while if they are faced logically they are often not so big after all. A method for doing this is Structured Problem Solving described above.

Very often a large task can be broken down into a number of smaller more manageable tasks. For example, the house needs a big tidy and clean up. This can be done two ways; either one room at a time or focus on one aspect at a time for the whole house (e.g., tidy up all paper and clothing, dust the whole house, and so on). By having a list a person can enjoy ticking off each item that is completed. A second example relates to attending an evening function. The list could begin with ringing up and confirming attendance, followed by a step by step timetable for organizing all aspects of tea, dressing, checking where to go, and leaving at the right time. Each item can be ticked when completed and, after a successful evening, a double tick can be used to celebrate success.

10. *Taking constructive action despite negative feelings.*
    If people allow themselves to be totally governed by their negative feelings, they won't be able to lift themselves out of depression. Feelings are often transient and once people have acknowledged them they need to put them aside and get on with life. They may not feel like doing something but they do it because they know it is good for them and will help them to make progress. It is important to make small decisions and small gains before making big decisions. It is important for the therapist to identify all achievements no matter how small.

11. *Building one's self-esteem and affirming oneself.*
    Poor self-esteem and depression are often linked together. How people cope with life, handle stress, and interact with others hinges on their self-concept, which depends very much on their childhood conditioning and their self-esteem. For example, if they were rejected as children they may reject themselves now and have poor self-respect. However, they don't need to be stuck there, but as adults they can move on by engaging their willpower, giving themselves positive messages (as already discussed above) and examining the options and choices that they have. Every day is a new day with its potential and possibilities. Also they need to not only love others unconditionally but they also need to extend this unconditional love to themselves. At the same time they should never allow ourselves to be put down without responding assertively,[56] and they need to teach people how to treat them and respect their boundaries.[57]

12. *Setting one's goals and motivating oneself.*
    Depression can stifle motivation so people need to establish some goals to get motivated. They need to learn to take action in spite of how they feel. If they wait to be in the mood for action, nothing may happen at all!

[56]See Section 2.5.4.
[57]See Section 17.2.

The first goal is to look for the "high" spots of the day, the little things that are sometimes missed or not appreciated like the warm sun in one's face, a good television program, a new flower in our garden, a nice cup of tea or coffee, and so on. The next step is to set specific small goals along with a detailed series of steps as to how they can be achieved. As mentioned in (9) above, each step on one's list can then be ticked off with two final ticks for finally achieving the goal. Initially the aim is to achieve one small goal daily and one larger goal each week; the list of seven small goals are called "movers" by Barrow. My list of different activities in the Appendix at the end of the chapter may be helpful for counseling ideas. It can also be a good idea to keep a diary and write in it only one's successes.

Having achieved one' small goals for a month, a client can set weekly goals; these need to provide some challenge and stretch the client a bit more. They should be SMART goals, as described in Section 2.3.2. After, say, three months the client may be ready to think about long-term goals, provided he or she is not still over-anxious or depressed. The key is not to rush the process but to proceed at the client's own pace. It is better to begin small and achieve the goal rather than begin big and fail!

13. *Meeting one's own needs.*
Too often we rely on other people to meet our needs rather than take personal responsibility for our needs. This is particularly the case in relationships when we need to be careful we do not have unrealistic expectations of others. It is important to distinguish between needs and wants. A good place to start is in the following areas of one's life: emotional, mental, physical, social and spiritual. Dealing with each area at a time, therapists can help clients to make a list of their needs and do the following:

(a) State how clients are trying to meet these needs at present.

(b) List the ways that these needs are not being met.

(c) List the ways in which clients can begin to meet them.

Alternatively a therapist can use the "WDEP" system of reality therapy where W=wants and needs; D=direction and doing; E=evaluation; and P=planning and commitment.[58] In addition to such exercises clients need to consider one of the very basic needs of simply being needed. They do this by considering ways in which they can help others.

Finally people need to do something nice for themselves every day. Give themselves a treat! My list in the Appendix below may be helpful. Engaging in pleasant events can lead to a significant mood improvement.[59]

14. *Thinking and acting well, not sick.*
Essentially this is a reiteration of things discussed previously; we need to condition ourselves mentally to be well. If someone says to us, "How are you?", how do we respond? Clients also need to look after their appearance as when they don't feel so good they can get lazy with their dress habits and

[58] Corey (2001: 240–244).
[59] Lewinsohn and Gotlib (1995).

they may begin to look like how they feel. As Barrow comments, when life is going well we can sometimes neglect our appearance and get away with it, but when we are depressed we cannot afford to neglect ourselves as our self-esteem won't handle it too well.

15. *Having a realistic expectation of oneself.*
    If I have an unrealistic expectation of myself I continually put myself under pressure and set myself up for failure. Impossible standards and perfectionism can lead to depression and compulsive behavior. It can also lead to inertia, as I don't start something because I am afraid of failure. In the end it is down to having a balanced life, where there is balance between work and play, mental and physical activities, social interaction and time alone, creative outlets and structured activities.

9.4.4   Counseling for Bipolar Disorder

Once a client's mood swings are under control with medication, therapy can provide additional support, psychoeducation, and guidance for the client and his or her family using the above methods for depression. Thus we can use cognitive-behavioral therapy to change harmful or negative thought patterns or behavior and manage daily routines, interpersonal psychotherapy to help improve relationships with others, or a combination of both. We can also add family-focused therapy to enhance family coping strategies. Psychoeducation can be used to teach people about the illness and is usually done in a group. Having regular daily routines and sleep schedules may protect clients against manic episodes. Clients can be helped to identify any return of the symptoms, and have actions that will prevent the symptoms from getting worse.

9.5   BIBLICAL VIEWPOINT

9.5.1   Spiritual Effect of Depression

The effect of of depression on a person's spiritual life can be quite devastating. Prayer, meditative reading, worship, and focus on one's Higher Power can be difficult because of obtrusive thoughts and negative feelings. However, in spite of this, Barrow in the final chapter of her book reminds the readers that they should not neglect the spiritual part of themselves. Coming from a Christian worldview, she recommends daily communication with God and highlights the need for a person to praise and thank God—yes, even when the person is depressed as there are always things one can be thankful for. Prayer, meditation, and a verse of scripture can provide a focus for Christians even when they don't feel like it, and especially when they don't feel like it! Christians believe that they are not alone in this universe and God is there for them.[60] Section 2.7.3 on mental wholeness from a biblical perspective has some helpful scriptures about positive thinking.

[60]Romans 8:38–39.

9.5.2   Biblical People and Depression

The Christian client can be encouraged by the fact that the Bible mentions a number of people who suffered from depression. For example Elijah[61] went through a major crisis at Mount Carmel where he saw the power of God demonstrated, but then succumbed to "post adrenaline depression;" he was in a black mood and needed sleep.[62] God did not criticize him but looked after his physical needs at Beersheba and then counseled him at Mount Horeb giving him an object lesson about God's presence and provided encouraging words about other prophets. Hughes[63] pointed out four things that God did in counseling Elijah: (a) God waited until Elijah had enough food and sleep, (b) God waited until Elijah had enough rest before asking him what he was doing there, (c) God encouraged him to talk about his problem and ventilate his feelings, and (d) God gave him a task to do.

David the psalmist had difficulties with depression and many of the psalms reflect this.[64] He talks about God who took him out of a bog in a pit, set him securely on solid ground, and gave him a new song;[65] the God who heals the brokenhearted and binds wounds.[66] Psalm 103 is a good antidote for depression beginning and ending with praise. It spells out the benefits of knowing God (verses 2–5), emphasizes God's compassion (verses 8, 13), and God's willingness to forgive (verses 9–12).

Jonah became angry with God because the people of Nineveh were going to be saved, and this anger turned inwards on himself leading to depression.[67] God challenged his belief system and gave him an object lesson about a plant that protected Jonah but died.

Job suffered from what seems to be reactive depression when everything was taken away from him including his health and he felt unjustly treated by God.[68] God challenged Job who came to realize that it was not up to him to question God but rather to submit to a sovereign God; God then restored him.

9.5.3   Some Misconceptions

There are misconceptions that some Christian clients might have about depression. An important one is the belief that Christians shouldn't get depressed and if they do it must be because of sin in their lives, or because they are not walking close enough to God, or they lack faith; other Christians may add to their misery by telling them to pray and read the Bible more. If such misconceptions surface in counseling, the following are some arguments that a therapist might find useful;

1. It is true that sin can lead to depression.[69] However, should a Christian ever get sick? If the answer is yes, then a chemical imbalance in our brain is no different from some imbalance elsewhere in our body such as a virus or organ deterioration, which can also cause depression. How different is being

[61] 1 Kings 18:16–46, 19:1–18.
[62] 1 Kings 19:4–7.
[63] Hughes (1991: 23).
[64] For example, Psalms 5:1, 6:6, 13:1, 22:1, 34:18, 42:5, and 69:1–3
[65] Psalms 40:1–3.
[66] Psalms 147:3.
[67] Jonah 4:3.
[68] For example, Job 19:8–9.
[69] Galatians 6:7 tells us that we reap what we sow and king David certainly did this.

depressed from having a sore leg, as pain and depression both originate in the brain? We may take a painkiller for a sore leg and an antidepressant for a sore psyche.

2. In the same way that we need to separate a pain from the cause (e.g., disease), we need to separate depression (pain) from its cause.

3. Should a Christian ever suffer grief and loss, as grief can lead to depression? The answer of course is yes. God allows difficult things to happen to us as part of being human and because of free will. Not all sickness will be healed as we have to die some day. God can also use suffering as a refining process.[70]

4. There are number of famous preachers and teachers, for example Calvin, Luther, Wesley, Kierkegaard and Spurgeon, who suffered bouts of depression, and we saw above that several biblical people struggled with various aspects of depression. People who are continually giving out can experience the post-adrenaline let-down, as did Elijah.

For those Christian clients who are concerned about the length of time needed to treat depression is taking we can refer them to the story in Luke chapter 24. Here Jesus used what we today would call cognitive-behavioral therapy to help two depressed clients process their condition while walking with them. The walk probably took a couple of hours with the same Jesus who *instantly* healed other sicknesses and even death. In this case he took his time.

9.5.4   Counseling Guidelines

Finally, some guidelines for the spiritual counseling of depression are:[71]

1. Explain to clients that depression can exacerbate any spiritual problems they might have so that they should withhold judgment on themselves until the problem is explored in depth.

2. Assure clients that our Higher Power is still in control and understands their pain. They can pray to God for their healing.

3. Encourage clients to stop trying to figure out why God allows depression and accept the fact that suffering is a mystery.

4. Encourage clients to exercise faith even when doubts seem overwhelming.

5. As mentioned in Section 9.4.1, we need to create hope and convince clients that they will come out of their depression sooner or later. God is with us to uphold us[72] when we pass through deep waters or through the fire.[73]

---

[70]See, for example, 2 Corinthians 12:7–10.
[71]Adapted from Hart (1987: 34–35).
[72]Isaiah 41:10.
[73]Isaiah 43:2.

9.5.5 Biblical Responses to Negative Thoughts

As negative thoughts can dominate a Christian with depression the following are biblical responses to some typical thoughts.

- It's impossible (Luke 18:17).

- I'm exhausted (Isaiah 40:31).

- I can't go on (2 Corinthians 12:9).

- I don't know what to do (Proverbs 3:5–6).

- I can't do it (Philippians 4:13).

- It's not worth it (Galatians 6:9).

- I'm afraid (Proverbs 3:24).

- I can't make ends meet (Philippians 4:19).

- I can't handle this (Psalms 55:22).

- I'm all alone (Hebrews 13:5).

- I'm not smart enough (James 1:5).

Christian therapists can be encouraged to develop their own lists.

9.6 APPENDIX

I find it helpful to have an extensive list of things a depressed client might like to do as a treat. The following is a selection from my own list, but put into approximate categories to save space and to give the general idea. You will no doubt think of items to add to your own list and the list can be compiled with the help of the client.[74]

Physical: Swimming or paddling; walking on a scenic path in a park or on a beach; practicing yoga, karate, or judo; playing tennis, going bowling, or playing bowls; tramping; gardening; fishing; and bike riding.

Relaxation: Lying or sitting in the sun; stopping and smelling/admiring some flowers; reading a book containing jokes; doing a crossword or jigsaw puzzle; surfing the internet; watching sport live or on television; soaking in a hot bath; going for a drive; going to the hairdresser; playing with animals; and eating something sweet.

Shops: Buying a new tool; window shopping; buying or cutting flowers for oneself; going to a pet shop and playing with the animals; buying gifts, books, or clothes; buying a CD; and finding a bargain.

---

[74]For further ideas see
http://www.letsthrive.co.nz/SELF/Self-development/101+Ways+To+Feel+Happy.html
by Annabel Candy (accessed October 2010).

Social: Smiling at people; spending an evening with good friends; meeting new people; doing something for someone else; going to plays, concerts, or movies; going to the zoo, museum, or garden show; playing cards or board games; traveling or going on a bus or train trip; going out for coffee; dancing; discussing books; and talking on the phone.

Hobbies: Sorting and labeling photos; creating a scrap book; working on the car or bicycle; playing a musical instrument or listening to music; photography; drawing, painting, needlework, pottery, or sewing; and reading the newspaper, magazines, or novels.

Spiritual: Going to church; meditating; praying for someone; and listening to religious music.

House: Taking care of plants; making a list of tasks; repairing things around the house; tidying a room; cooking; decorating; planning a garden or getting plant boxes.

Mental: Planning activities; planning a career change; thinking about past trips; remembering deeds of loving people; thinking about pleasant events; remembering beautiful scenery; thinking I have a lot going for me; writing letters; and planning something new to do.

CHAPTER 10

SUICIDE RISK

10.1 SOME FACTS

Suicide, the most taboo of topics, is becoming increasingly prevalent in Western society (just over 1% of all deaths in the U.S.), especially among men and youth.[1] Men
are at least four times more likely than women to die by suicide, while women are
approximately three times as likely as men to attempt suicide, a pattern common
to most countries.[2] Men have a tendency toward violent behavior while women are
less violent. Methods of suicide vary greatly among different countries, depending
on cultural traditions and social and political conditions.

In the U.S., using a firearm is the most common form of death with men while
women use an overdose or poisoning. Certain psychological problems mentioned
below predispose a person to suicide; in fact approximately 95% of people who die
by suicide experienced a mental disorder at the time of death.[3] Suicide seems to
run in families so there appears to be a genetic component to suicidal behavior
(e.g., through the serotonin system and through family traits). In most countries
and cultures, suicide rates increase with age. Immigration can be a factor as it can
lead to a person feeling disconnected, being no longer part of one's mother country.
Unfortunately there are sick websites that promote suicide as well as euthanasia.

---

[1]For details see Joiner (2005: 29–30, 155–162).
[2]Suicide rates are more even between males and females in Asian countries.
[3]Cavanagh, Carson, Sharpe, and Lawrie (2003).

Counseling Issues: A Handbook for Counselors and Psychotherapists. By George A. F. Seber **259**
Copyright © 2013 G. A. F. Seber

Chiles and Strosahl[4] list various views that one might have of suicide. For example: (a) suicide is wrong because it violates the dignity of life, adversely affects its survivors, and is no different than homicide; (b) suicide is sometimes permissible if the alternatives are unbearable or there is extreme and incurable pain; (c) suicide is not a moral or ethical issue but just a phenomenon of life; (d) suicide is a person's right if based on rationality and logical thinking; and (e) suicide has positive value in reuniting a person with loved ones or ancestors. Attitudes to suicides have changed drastically over the past centuries.[5]

A therapist needs to be aware of any sign that a client is contemplating suicide (referred to as suicidal ideation) and take appropriate action, if necessary (e.g., hospitalization). Unfortunately most therapists have inadequate training and experience in assessing and treating suicidal behaviors. However, regardless of one's experience, it is important to be able to recognize when a client is at risk. In this chapter I look at factors that relate to increased suicide risk, then consider some signposts that indicate suicidal ideation, and finally give some suggestions for counseling clients at risk. As the subject is an extensive one I shall give a number of different strategies from the literature.

10.2 SELF-PRESERVATION

In determining suicide risk one needs to be neither dismissive nor alarmist. Referring to the latter case, many people who have mood disorders will have suicidal ideas, but the vast majority will not attempt suicide or die by suicide. Joiner (2005) develops a very convincing model for describing key risk factors for suicide, which I now describe.

People are not born with a developed capacity to injure themselves, but rather the opposite is true, namely there is self-preservation to avoid pain, injury, and death. However, there are those who over time develop the ability to overcome the urge toward self-preservation through exposure to self-injury and similar experiences (e.g., through previous suicidal behavior and self harm, or through violence, pain, and injury) and are consequently more able to carry out lethal self injury. They lose their fear of death and become habituated to risk and injury. Some people who attempt suicide and survive say they regretted the act of attempted suicide when in the middle of it, so strong is self-preservation. Other risk factors are feeling disconnected from others, for example such as experiencing a thwarted belongingness, and seeing oneself as ineffective and a burden to others.

Joiner links the above ideas to other models. For example, the above may be seen as specific features of what Shneidman[6] calls psychache or psychological pain that reaches an intolerable intensity. Hopelessness is another related factor used by Beck, Brown, Berchick, and Stewart (1990). Being unable to regulate emotions can lead to self-harm and suicide, and Linehan (1993a,b) developed Dialectical Behavior Therapy (DBT) to provide techniques to change self-destructive ways of regulating emotions into more constructive ways.

[4]Adapted from Chiles and Strosahl (1995: appendix).
[5]For an extensive discussion of the pros and cons of suicide see
http://plato.stanford.edu/entries/suicide/ (accessed November 2010).
[6]Shneidman (1996: 4).

10.3   RISK ASSESSMENT

Before doing a risk assessment it is important to recognize that assessing suicidal ideation is a complex issue with no one correct method of assessment. Jacobs et al. maintain that the "reliable prediction of individual suicide at a specific time is impossible."[7] This was clearly demonstrated in a classic paper by Pokorny (1983). Given the uncertainty of prediction, the aim of an assessment is to give the therapist some guidance as to what to do next in an endeavor to minimize risk. A look at key websites will unearth a large number of risk factors, some being more critical than others. It is important that therapists are very familiar with the risk factors not only if they are involved with suicidal clients but also with other clients as well. Clients who are not suicidal during initial sessions and are wanting counseling for a relatively minor problem may, during the course of therapy, become suicidal. External events can increase suicidal risk.

It is important to remember that risk factors are related to probabilities that apply to a large sample of people, but don't necessarily apply to individuals. There is no such person as a "typical" suicidal client. Risk factors or not, people kill themselves because they decide to do it, usually after a difficult weighing of the pros and cons.[8] Questions like how, when, the degree of pain expected in committing suicide, and whether or not to write letters or a suicide note are considered. Two key questions are, will it work (e.g., "Will suicide result in damnation in an after life so that my pain and problems will not be resolved?") and is it the right thing to do (e.g., "Does committing suicide hurt other people or break my underlying code of ethics?" or "I am too much of a burden to my family.")[9] Gaining access to a client's planning for suicide is critical for the therapist to be of effective help.

Because writers give different priorities to risk factors I will give several ways of listing risks. The first list combines risk factors from those referred to above as well as some demographic and clinical risk factors.[10] We need to remind ourselves that everybody is unique so that more knowledge of the client is required than simply adding up risk factors.[11]

1. Multiple previous suicide attempts.

2. Exposure to experiences that may habituate a person to lethal self-injury (e.g., multiple surgeries, repeated tattoos and piercings, exposure to violence, and self-injecting drug use).

3. Having resolved plans for suicide including the following symptoms: being courageous and competent enough to make an attempt, having the means and opportunity to carry it out, having specific plans and preparations for an attempt, and duration and intensity of suicidal ideation.

4. Voicing suicidal desire, wishing to die, frequent ideation, and wanting to attempt suicide.

5. Feeling of not belonging.

[7] Jacobs, Brewer, and Klein-Benheim (1999: 3).
[8] This ignores the exceptions of impulsive acts.
[9] Adapted from Shea (1999: 36–37).
[10] From Jacobs et al. (1999).
[11] For a similar list see http://kspope.com/suicide/#copy (accessed November 2010).

6. Belief of being a burden to others.

7. Hopelessness.

8. Psychological (mental) pain and anguish (e.g., life stressors; thwarted love, acceptance, and belonging; lack of achievement and autonomy; shame and humiliation; loss of people one depends on to hold one together; and excessive anger through frustrated needs).[12] Emotions become intolerable.

9. Impulsivity. This personality trait is a tendency to act without thinking and can lead to a person experiencing various provocations.

10. Having a psychiatric problem (e.g., affective disorders such as depression and bipolar disorder, post traumatic stress disorder, panic disorder (indirectly), schizophrenia, self-harm, antisocial personality disorder, borderline personality disorder,[13] and comorbidity). Suicide is generally not intended with self-harm (see Section 8.5), but it can happen accidentally. Some authors regard a mental or addictive disorder, especially depression (having a lifetime suicide risk of about 15%), as the strongest risk factor.

11. Physical illness (e.g., restricted function and loss of independence), especially with older people.

12. Alcoholism and substance abuse, especially when linked with depression.

13. Family history of suicide, mental illness, or substance abuse.

14. Childhood maltreatment.

15. Lack of social support.

16. Drop in social or economic status (e.g., suffering humiliating events like financial ruin associated with scandal).

17. Some antidepressant medications.

18. Demographic-type variables.

    (a) Being male for suicide and female for attempted suicide.
    (b) Being aged 60 years or older.
    (c) Being widowed, divorced, or single.
    (d) Presence of firearms. Their use is the most common form of suicide in the U.S.
    (e) Living alone.
    (f) Being unemployed.

According to Joiner, (1) or (3) taken with most any other additional risk factor (e.g., substance abuse) or (4) taken with two other risk factors implies at least a moderate suicide risk. With regard to (3), the degree of planning should be followed up carefully by the therapist.

---

[12] Adapted from Shneidman (1999: 89–90).
[13] This is the only personality disorder with suicidal ideation as a criterion for diagnosis.

About 70% of suicide victims communicate their thoughts about suicide shortly before their death.[14] However, there are those who consistently deny active suicidal thoughts and who seem to be living and working normally yet suddenly commit suicide as they are emotionally exhausted. Witnessing a suicide can lead a person to suicide (the copycat phenomenon). In the case of young people, some rock cultures romanticize suicide; the suicide of a friend may provide a model.

In assessing suicidal ideation, a common feature is ambivalence about wishing to die and wishing to live. This is reflected in the first two questions of a downloadable questionnaire for assessment called the modified scale for suicidal ideation (MSSI).[15] Another questionnaire, called the Suicide Behaviors Questionnaire-Revised (SBQ-R) is also available.[16]

The factors (10) and (11) are linked to a major proportion of the suicides so that such problems need to be addressed, especially when there is comorbidity.[17] It is important to remove any potential means of suicide from the home of a suicidal patient, especially firearms and prescription medications.

Another way of grouping key risks of suicide is the following:[18]

Knowledge of the Person. Has the person experienced any of the following: recent loss or recent break-up of a relationship, a major disappointment or failure, a major change in circumstances, and a physical or mental illness? Also, has there been any previous suicide attempt, any history of suicide in the family, and any tidying up of affairs (e.g., making a will)?

Visual Clues. Is the person withdrawn, low-spirited, finding it difficult to relate to others, taking less care of themselves, unusually cheerful, or showing symptoms of depression?

Things to Listen for. Does the person talk about feeling suicidal, seeing no hope in the future, feeling worthless and a failure, feeling alone and isolated, sleeping badly (especially waking early), and losing his or her appetite or over-eating?

A third way of listing risks for clients is the following, which uses the easy to remember acronym of PLAIDPALS.[19]

- **P**lan. Do they have one?

- **L**ethality. Is the plan lethal, leading to death?

- **A**vailabiity. Do they have the means to go through with it?

- **I**llness. Do they have a mental or physical illness?

- **D**epression. Are there chronic or specific incident(s) of it?

- **P**revious attempts. How many and how recent?

[14] Jacobs et al. (1999: 20).
[15] See http://www.gpsouth.com.au/downloads/MSSI.pdf (accessed November 2010).
[16] See http://www.cqaimh.org/pdf/tool_sbq-r.pdf. (accessed November 2010)
[17] Jacobs et al. (1999: 7).
[18] Charles-Edwards (2005: 111–112).
[19] From http://www.sfsuicide.org/prevention-strategies/warning-signs/p-l-a-i-d-p-a-l-s/ (accessed November 2010).

- **A**lone. Are they alone or do they have a partner or support system?

- **L**oss. Have they suffered a loss, e.g., death of a significant person, loss of a job, relationship or self esteem?

- **S**ubstance abuse (or use). Are they involved with drugs, alcohol, or prescription medicine, and is the problem current or chronic?

10.4   COUNSELING FOR SUICIDE RISK

10.4.1   Uncovering Suicidal Thoughts

The key aspect of counseling is the therapeutic relationship, as in times of crisis it may be the only thing that keeps a client alive. This may mean taking phone calls at awkward times, having extended sessions, or even making home visits. Havens[20] suggested that it is important to protect a client's self-esteem by being willing to admire the client through finding something one can enjoy and appreciate in the client. He also adds that understanding is needed and this means validating a client's experiences and seeing them from the client's point of view. Even if the therapist believes that the client's behavior and suicidal ideation are unreasonable, it is important for the therapist to express understanding of the client's pain. Because of the taboo on suicide, a therapist's calm and matter of fact discussion on the topic can enable the client's long endured silence and taboo about suicide to be broken. Sometimes clients may not want to share their suicidal thoughts and Shea[21] lists the following beliefs they might possibly have.

- Suicide is seen as a sign of weakness and is shameful.

- Suicide is immoral or a sin.

- The client may be perceived by the therapist as crazy.

- If suicidal ideation is admitted, the client may fear being locked up.

- The client really wants to die without anybody knowing.

- The client thinks he or she is beyond help.

Therapists need to ask themselves how they feel about the above list and how much of it applies to them. There is a need to be aware of possible countertransference issues as their beliefs may unconsciously make a client uneasy when discussing suicide. They could ask themselves questions like, "Do I feel that suicide is a sign of weakness and/or is immoral or sinful?" and "Is this topic taboo and do I overreact when a client reveals suicidal thoughts?" Having clients express suicidal intent can raise thoughts about the cost of dealing with such a person in terms of time, effort, and stress. Such thoughts can lead to feelings of aversion and anger toward the client.

[20]Havens (1999: 211).
[21]Shea (1999: 111–112).

Clear language should always be used (e.g., "kill yourself," "commit suicide," or "take your life") when discussing suicide. Shea[22] gives the following hints for uncovering suicidal intent when asking the client about suicidal ideation.

1. A slightest hesitation of the client in responding may suggest suicidal thoughts.

2. Answers like, "No, not really" or "Really none" usually indicate some past suicidal ideation.

3. Body-language clues (e.g., anxiety, increased fidgeting, aversion of the eyes) can indicate discomfort with the question.

4. The therapist should avoid note taking during the discussion so as to give the client full attention.

5. The therapist should avoid conveying discomfort with the topic of suicide.

6. The interview should be unhurried as the clients may disengage if they feel they are not being listened to. This is particularly true with clients who have borderline personality disorder. Telling clients to take their time and acknowledging the difficulty of talking about suicidal thoughts can be helpful.

7. Therapists should check up on their own feelings during the discussion to avoid any inappropriate countertransference mentioned above.

8. Do not accept the first "No." The therapist can add a question about fleeting thoughts of suicide.

Shea[23] makes an important point about clients with high level defenses who are able to hide their pain from others and the therapist as well. If such a client expresses suicidal ideation, it is important to keep that window open until it is no longer needed. No matter how well therapy is going or how well the client looks, suicidal ideation needs to be enquired about during every session so that it becomes a natural part of the therapy.

10.4.2 Coping With an Impossible Life

Therapists need to recognize that some clients have good reasons for wanting to be dead as their lives are perceived by them to currently not be "livable." Such clients have too many life crises, environmental stressors, difficult interpersonal relationships, physical or mental problems, or dysfunctional habitual behaviors that cause stress. Clients may even try to convince their therapists that suicide is a good idea. What is needed is a life improvement program that provides a future; part of this is finding those things that a client feels good about and also working with the client's strengths.

An important step is a recognition by the client of the negative effects of suicidal behavior on others, and clients can be asked who wants them to live? Finding out the true attitudes of relatives and possibly friends can be helpful in case these are negative. It is important to work with the client to create an actively supportive

[22]Shea (1999: 120–122).
[23]Shea (1999: 52–53).

environment and to know what resources are available to the client. While trying to help clients develop new strategies for dealing with their problems, therapists sometimes need to encourage clients to tolerate some of the negative affects.

In looking at external losses I find it important to realize that we all view losses differently so that we should never underestimate the effect of a loss on a client. The loss or death of someone close can have a major impact. Apart from specific questions about the impact, scale of pain (from 1 to 10), and asking will the resulting pain lessen or end, more general questions can be asked. For example, does the client believe in an afterlife and the possibility of seeing the loved one again in heaven? Also what is his or her belief about God's attitude to suicide and whether it is forgivable provide valuable information on suicidal ideation.

The most dangerous word one can hear from a potentially suicidal client is the quietly said word *only*, for example, "It's the only thing I can do." Other factors that should raise alarm bells are a client giving away important belongings, or a client suddenly recovers, becoming very relaxed and cheerful, which can happen when the client has finally decided to end it all and is now at peace with the decision. It is important to always take seriously what a client has to say and be able to hear the client's message.

10.4.3   Some Strategies

Most therapists insist on a contract with the client such as "Do you agree to phone me if the stress gets too great?" or else negotiate other actions the client can contract to do between sessions. Contracts and their usefulness are discussed in detail in Section 10.6 below.

Cognitive Methods

Any fantasies that the client has about suicide need to be explored and unrealistic beliefs about what suicide will and will not accomplish reevaluated. Cognitive therapy aimed at restructuring negative thoughts is recommended by Joiner[24] using the acronym ICARE as follows.

- **I**dentify the thought.

- **C**onnect the thought to general categories of cognitive distortion (Section 1.4.3).

- **A**ssess the thought for evidence for and against.

- **R**estructure the thought, that is, replace it by a more positive thought.

- **E**xpress, that is act in ways that flow from the restructured thought.[25]

The above approach is like the ABCDE part of Rational Emotive Behavior Therapy.[26] Joiner again emphasizes focusing this method on thoughts concerning burdensomeness and failed belongingness. We now look at some writing methods for dealing with certain feelings.

[24] Joiner (2005: 214–215).
[25] Joiner uses the word Execute which doesn't seem appropriate!
[26] See Section 1.4.3.

Writing Methods

Joiner[27] gives several methods to help take the edge off distress as anyone under stress may be at risk. The first, called symptom-matching hierarchy, involves simply listing symptoms and feelings beginning with those that are the most upsetting. Some strategies for alleviating the top few symptoms or feelings are then given, for example, sleep techniques for insomnia and relaxation techniques for stress.

A second method is to target feelings of burdensomeness and low belongingness with appropriate questions such as, "I see that you perceive yourself as a burden on your family, but do they see it in the same way?" The therapist can then summarize the outcome of the discussion onto an index card that the client takes home and later adds to. The idea is to destabilize and slightly reduce these feelings.

A third method is to use a "crisis card," which involves writing down a crisis plan for dealing with suicidal thoughts and feeling upset, especially with feelings of burdensomeness and low belongingness. For example, "I can use what I have learnt at therapy to identify what is upsetting me and I can come up with some reasonable non-suicidal responses to what is bothering me. I can also try to do things that in the past have made me feel better (e.g., music). If the suicidal thoughts become too much then I contact an emergency person."

A fourth method is to draw a mood graph when negative moods are intense in which the client uses the x-axis to represent time and the y-axis to represent the intensity of a negative mood. The client plots the rating for their mood once every minute or two for around 15 –20 minutes. This will show that negative moods lose some of their intensity by simply sitting down with the graph; an important learning experience for the client.

Validation Techniques

Shea[28] gives the following methods that are also useful for other problems besides suicidal ideation.

Behavioral Incidents. This is any question asking about concrete behavioral facts or trains of thoughts. For example, "How many pills did you take?" instead of "So you took an overdose of pills", and "When you placed the gun in your mouth, did you take the safety catch off" instead of "When you took the gun out, were you close to killing yourself?" The idea is to ask for facts rather than opinions. Such questions can be followed up by by asking the client to describe what happened next or what the client was thinking.

Shame Attenuation. This involves attempting to ask a question so that the client does not feel overly self-incriminating. For example, "Do you find other men tend to pick fights with you when you are trying to enjoy yourself?" instead of "Do you have a bad temper and tend to pick fights?"

Gentle Assumption. Here the therapist makes the assumption that a behavior is occurring and frames a question based on the assumption. For example, "What other ways have you thought of killing yourself?" or "How often have you found yourself in a fist fight, if at all?" Questions beginning with the words "Have you ever ..." are not gentle assumptions as nothing is assumed!

---

[27] Joiner (2005: 211–217).
[28] Shea (1999: chapter 5).

Symptom Amplification. This technique is based on the idea that clients downplay the frequency or amount of their disturbing behaviors (e.g., amount drunk or gambled). Here the therapist suggests a specific number that is set well on the high side, for example, "How many times have you struck your wife in any fashion—20 or 30 times?" and "On the days when your thoughts of suicide were most intense, how much of the day did you spend thinking yourself, 50% of the day, 80%, 90%?" By exaggerating the number the client is more likely to give an accurate answer.

Denial of the Specific. Here the therapist asks a specific question rather than a generic question as the former is harder to deny, for example, "Have you thought of overdosing?" instead of "Have you thought of committing suicide?"

Normalizing. This method involves letting a client know that others feel the same way. Thoughts about suicide can be normalized by comments like, "When people are extremely upset, they sometimes have thoughts of killing themselves. Have you had any thoughts of wanting to kill yourself?"[29]

CASE Method

Shea[30] describes a method for eliciting suicidal ideation and the degree of lethality potential, which I shall endeavor to describe briefly. The first step is to set the scene for suicide enquiry. The key is to avoid simply "popping" the question of suicide but rather raising the topic as naturally and unobtrusively as possible. This can be done more easily through moments of strong emotion such as depression and hopelessness or when there is a sense of crisis, anger, anxiety or confusion. When the pain is close to the surface the question can be asked, "Have you ever thought of bringing it to an end by killing yourself?" as the pain can overcome any taboos the client may have about suicide.

The second step is to use Shea's Chronological Assessment of Suicide Events (CASE) method to examine suicidal ideation and past suicide experiences and thoughts in detail. Using the validation techniques described above, the CASE method endeavors to break down the mass of information about a client into smaller more manageable amounts. This is done by dividing up the client's life into four time frames, namely: the presenting suicidal ideation and behavior unearthed in step one above; any suicidal ideation and behaviors over the previous eight weeks; past suicidal ideation and behaviors; and immediate suicidal ideation as well as future plans for its implementation (e.g., "Right now, are you having any thoughts about wanting to kill yourself?") These four areas need to be explored in considerable detail and include not just suicide events but thoughts as well, even if fleeting ones.

In the case of earlier suicide attempts, specific questions can be asked like what was the method used (e.g., where and how deep was the cut), whether the client was alone or with others, how successful was the attempt, how well planned was the attempt, was anybody told beforehand, any alcohol of drugs involvement, why did the attempt fail, and "What are some of your thoughts about the fact that you are still alive now?"

[29]Shea (1999: 112).
[30]Shea (1999: chapter 6).

In carrying out the above assessment over time, a particularly useful technique is to use a sequence of behavioral incidents. For example, if the client admits to having thoughts about using a gun, a sequence might look like this:[31]

- "Do you have a gun in the house?"

- "Have you ever got out the gun with the intention of thinking of using it to kill yourself?"

- "Have you ever loaded the gun?"

- "Have you put the gun up to your body or head?"

- "How long did you hold the gun there?"

- "Did you take the safety catch off?"

- "What stopped you from pulling the trigger?"

The above approach helps the therapist to assess the client's degree of suicide risk and it can often encourage clients to spontaneously discuss the pros and cons of killing themselves.[32] Using the gentle assumption technique, the therapist can then ask about another mode of suicide such as "Have you ever thought about taking an overdose?" and if the answer is yes, another sequence of behavioral incidents can be used like the one above.

After establishing the list of suicide methods the client considered and the action taken on each one, the therapist can then ask about the frequency, duration, and intensity of suicidal ideation over the previous two months. Care should be taken in assessing this time period as a suicidal person usually spends considerable time planning the suicide.

In conclusion there is an interesting suggestion used by Puff (2002). When clients who are suicidal page him, he listens to them on the phone and then asks them to go for a walk for half an hour or more. He then makes them promise that if they are still suicidal when they finish their walk, they will give him a call back. He found that the call back was not needed. When he saw the clients again he was told that they felt much better after the walk and did not need to talk to him again until their next meeting.

Dialectical Behavior Therapy

Dialectical Behavior Therapy (DBT) was originally introduced by Marsha Linehan to deal specifically with a chronically suicidal client, that is a client

> who is unremittingly high in suicidal ideation, frequently threatens suicide or talks about taking his or her own life, has difficulty articulating any reasons for living or staying alive, and may attempt suicide or self-injure on multiple occasions.[33]

Her treatment manuals[34] describe the method as a treatment for borderline personality disorder (BPD) because of the overlap between BDP and suicidal behavior.

---

[31]Shea (1999: 166–168).
[32]Shea (1999: 174).
[33]Linehan (1999: 147).
[34]Linehan (1993a, b).

Linehan believes that such severely suicidal clients need to be looked after by more than one experienced therapist and not treated alone.

Treatment strategies involve combining those methods that are acceptable to a client through validating a client's current capacities with those related to change. The client learns to become comfortable with ambiguity and change, which are viewed as inevitable aspects of life. The goal is to bring out opposites, both in therapy and in the client's life, and provide conditions for a synthesis. At any point an opposite position can be held and the client is helped to move from an "either-or" position to "both-and." Problem solving such as finding alternative responses to precipitating events leading to suicidal behaviors is also a key aspect.

As the aim of this book is to discuss issues and not counseling modalities I refer the reader to Linehan's manuals and Linehan (1999: chapter 9) for further details of DBT.

Hospitalization

When should a client be hospitalized? Before making such a decision it is important to explore all the drawbacks as fully as the benefits and weigh up the likely long-term and the immediate effects of this intervention. Clearly, if there is a strong therapeutic alliance, it is possible to have a collaborative discussion between client and therapist. In any case, both therapist and client should have a clear idea right from the beginning what circumstances might lead to hospitalization. Other alternatives might be to increase the number of sessions, use the day hospital or respite services, or mobilize family members to maintain a 24 hour watch on the client.

Hospitalization, which means taking away a client's freedom without warning, separation from family, and possible disruption of work, does have its risks, especially immediately after admission and after discharge; family support should be initiated immediately after the discharge.[35] It can sometimes be helpful for therapists to keep clients in their stressful environments and go in themselves to help the client to cope with life as it is—an example of on-the-spot learning.[36]

What if a chronically suicidal client wants to be hospitalized but the therapist is not in favor? Linehan suggests the following strategies:[37]

1. *Maintain one's own position.* The therapist does not have to always agree with the client.

2. *Validate the client's rights to maintain his or her position.* Therapists must humbly recognize that they could be wrong. The client should evaluate both positions and be encouraged to maintain a position independent of the therapist.

3. *Insist that the client takes care of himself or herself.* The therapist tells clients to do what they think is best. Clients should pursue hospitalization if they believe it is important. The message is that clients are ultimately responsible for their own lives.

[35]Qin and Nordentoft (2005).
[36]Linehan (1999: 169).
[37]Linehan (1999: 179).

4. *Assist clients to getting themselves admitted.* In these situations, therapists should teach clients how to get themselves admitted to an inpatient acute-care facility without the therapist.

4. *Don't punish the client who gets admitted against therapeutic advice.* It is a matter of considering whether the client is acting in accord with his or her best judgment.

10.5 SOME SPECIFIC SUICIDE FACTORS

10.5.1 Alcohol and Drugs

Alcohol use is strongly related to impulsive suicide attempts, especially with acute intoxication. The latter increases aggressiveness, impairs judgment, and leads to the erosion of constraints on self-destruction.[38] Suicidal ideation is more common with clients for whom depression is comorbid with alcohol dependence. It appears that antisocial personality disorder (Sections 21.4.2 and 22.3.1) is common among substance abusers and this adds to the risk of suicide.

If a person is persuaded or coerced to stop drinking as a suicide prevention measure (e.g., a wife threatening to leave), the risk of suicide can paradoxically increase.[39] Note that the use of drugs or alcohol can exert a short-term suicide prevention influence as a sort of defense mechanism so care may be needed when such use is stopped.

10.5.2 Schizophrenia

Those with schizophrenia have about a 10% lifetime risk of suicide and a 60–80% occurrence of suicidal ideation. The risk decreases with advancing age and the typical schizophrenic suicide is young, unmarried, and has never lived independently.[40] People with this disorder (or any psychotic disorder) are most at risk when they are in a period of remission as they can see clearly that the disorder is not going to go away and they will have to cope with it indefinitely. This is particularly true with young people whose illness developed after several years of normal function. Those who have a history of previous suicide attempts or struggle with hopelessness, depression, or a fear of deterioration and progressive mental decline are at greater risk. Schizophrenics apparently fail to communicate their suicidal intentions to the same degree as other psychiatric clients so that their suicide may be unexpected and inexplicable.[41] People who need careful attention are those who hear voices commanding them to kill themselves.

10.5.3 Bipolar (Manic-Depressive) Disorder

Suicide accounts for up to 20% of deaths among those with severe bipolar illness.[42] It depends to some extent on the severity of the depressive part of the illness. From

---

[38]Weiss and Hufford (1999: 302).
[39]Motto (1999: 227).
[40]Tsuang, Fleming, and Simpson (1999: 291).
[41]Tsuang, et al. (1999: 291).
[42]Jamison (1999: 251).

Jamison,[43] the risk periods for suicide are first of all the early part of the illness during and after the first episode when denial and noncompliance with medication are most substantial. The other risk periods are when the client is in a mixed state (combination of depression symptoms along with mental alertness and tense, apprehensive, and restless behavior), a depressive phase, a recovery period, and during the period following psychiatric hospitalization. Lithium significantly reduces the suicide rate,[44] but a high proportion of bipolar people stop taking lithium at least once during their lives against medical advice. Anticonvulsant drugs are also being used instead of lithium. Further information on bipolar disorder is given in Section 9.3.5.

10.5.4   Borderline Personality Disorder

The discussion on this topic is based on Davis, Gunderson, and Myers (1999). As noted above, borderline personality disorder (BPD)[45] is closely connected with suicide along with such factors as self-harm, sexual promiscuity, reckless behavior, and substance abuse, all adding to the risk. Although suicide is not usually the aim of self-harm, impulsivity and hopelessness can add to the risk. Attachment to significant others (including the therapist) is an important aspect of BPD as there is an intolerance for aloneness. Clients with BPD are manipulative and like to test a therapist's willingness to look out and care for them, and this can lead to more dangerous behavior such as an escalation of self-harm, substance abuse, and suicidal activity. Such clients want to be important to their therapist and exercise control over them. People with BPD also tend to act covertly without asking explicitly for some intervention. The therapist needs to find out what this is and make the request explicit.

A major problem for the therapist is achieving a balance between being too supportive and yet remaining sufficiently objective so as not to take away the client's opportunity for psychological growth. There is a similar problem for family members of the client as they can end up being held hostage to the fear of the borderline's harmful acts. They need to know they cannot be held responsible for such acts. Once families begin preventative actions, they are assuming a responsibility that belongs to the client or the therapist. However, families should not ignore evidence of any kind relating to self-harm or inappropriate activity, but should convey their fears to the client and inform professionals.

It is important to treat the client as a potentially competent adult as this will help determine which of the dichotomous positions such as good versus bad, strong versus weak, and responsible versus irresponsible the client takes up. This dichotomy that can shift from one pole to the other depending on the interpersonal context is indicative of the borderline's self-concept. Where possible, a borderline client should be actively involved in any decision making.

One approach to suicide prevention proposed by Stone (1993b) focuses attention on the four A's: aloneness, anger, alcoholism, and antisociality. Aloneness can be dealt with by encouraging clients to strengthen their social skills and engage in appropriate hobbies and group-based recreational activities (e.g, playing bridge,

---

[43] Jamison (1999: 256).
[44] See Baldessarini and Tondo (1999) for details.
[45] See Sections 21.4.2 and 22.3.2.

a reading group, or a walking group). Anger therapy can be used with a focus on developing more supportive and harmonious relationships along with realistic expectations, while Alcoholics Anonymous can provide an effective treatment for alcoholism as well as providing a supportive network that will help reduce feelings of anger and aloneness. Antisociality is much more of a challenge and is generally treated indirectly such as by encouraging a client to join a group that emphasizes a strict adherence to a certain code of behavior (e.g., a religious organization).

Although medications are not particularly helpful in treating BPD, they can be usefully used to treat comorbid conditions such as major depression or panic disorders. The possibility of an overdose needs to be kept in mind when a medication and its dosage is chosen. As already mentioned, clients need to make their own decision about medication rather than just give consent, as they can have either positive or negative feelings about medication.

10.5.5 Trauma

People who have been chronically maltreated in childhood often have two funda-mental traits, namely profound mistrust and self-hate, and these can place them at substantial risk of suicide. Severe post-traumatic symptoms can cause considerable distress that can lead to suicidal impulses. It is a good idea for clients to have a crisis plan for the times when they feel particularly overwhelmed. Such a plan needs to be developed prior to a crisis and can consist of a list of possible interventions such as calling friends, taking a walk or exercising, reading or watching television, calling a hot line or a therapist, or using emergency services.[46] Clients also need to learn strategies to help them stay grounded, that is maintain contact with reality. Chu[47] states that eye contact in interpersonal situations is enormously grounding as is visual or bodily contact with familiar objects (such as clothing, jewelry, furni-ture, stuffed animals, or pets). Therapists, by asking clients to simply look at them and to make eye contact, can help clients to resolve crisis situations. Therapists can also remind clients that they are safe and in the present in the counseling room. For further details about trauma see Section 7.3.

10.5.6 Suicide in the Elderly

Steffens and Blazer[48] mention that acute suicide, which involves taking a decisive action leading to death, such as hanging oneself, overdosing, or crashing one's automobile in a single car accident may be interpreted with the older person as a natural or accidental cause of death due to some acute medical event rather than suicide. A more difficult scenario for a therapist working with older adults is attempted chronic suicide. Examples are failure to eat, leading to starvation and death, sustained drug and alcohol abuse, refusal to take life-sustaining medications, and self-neglect. Recognizing such forms of slow suicide need to be recognized by all those caring for the older person, even though the idea may be unpalatable to some.

[46] Chu (1999: 344).
[47] Chu (1999: 344–345).
[48] Steffens and Blazer (1999: 445).

Some elderly use indirect methods of suicide by putting themselves in dangerous or even reckless situations such as tramping in the bush on their own without adequate clothing, or refusing adequate medical care for a potentially fatal condition. Some older clients express so-called passive death wishes such as "I'd be better off dead," "I am tired of this life," or " I have asked God to take me." Such comments are usually more of an expression that life is difficult rather than an indication of suicidal intent.

Psychiatric disorders are the most important risk factors for suicide in the elderly, especially depression and alcohol abuse or dependence. Physical illness, loss of ability for self-care, and disability are also strongly contributing factors as a client may fear having to face suffering or being kept alive for no purpose. As older clients are more likely to complete a suicide attempt than with younger people, any previous suicide attempts should be taken very seriously.

In assessing suicide with older clients, Steffens and Blazer[49] suggest asking the following four questions instead of using the more direct questionnaires:

- "Have you ever felt life is not worth living?" If "yes," go to the next question.

- "Have you ever thought of hurting or harming yourself? If yes, go to the next question.

- Have you ever considered specific methods of harming yourself?" If yes, go to the next question.

- "Have you ever made a suicide attempt?"

Safety contracts (discussed below) can be helpful with older clients as the latter are generally faithful to their word (in the U.S.). Such clients need to be cognitively intact and the therapist needs to be able to be readily contacted. Usually the crisis of suicide is brief as immediate suicide intentions rarely last more than a few days, so it is a matter of protecting the client through the crisis.[50] Telephone contact can be used effectively including home visits by volunteers and people familiar to the client. Families play an important role in screening the environment of a client for possibly harmful objects and medications during a crisis period. However families should realize that they do not have the responsibility of preventing an older person from harming himself or herself.

10.6   SUICIDE PREVENTION CONTRACTS

10.6.1   Do We Need Them?

No-suicide or safety contracts, as they are commonly called, can take various forms ranging from a formal written and signed document to verbal informal agreements. The extent and duration of the contract needs to be clear. An informal approach can be used, for example, by asking "Can you manage okay until our next appointment?" or provide a safety net with "If things get too much to cope with, will you please phone me?" Such contracts are most effective when they are made face to

[49] Steffens and Blazer (1999: 454–455).
[50] Steffens and Blazer (1999: 454–455).

face with direct eye contacts, along with a genuine affect, a firm handshake, a natural and unhesitant tone of voice, and with the therapist sensing a sincerity about the agreement, even if the client is somewhat reluctant. The reaction of a client to a contract proposal can also be used as an assessment tool on suicidal intent.

If the client wants the therapist to commit to the relationship so that they can work together, then it is reasonable to expect the client to make some commitment to stay alive so as to maintain the relationship for now without taking away the client's ultimate control of the decision to live. Therefore an effective intervention might be the therapist interpreting suicide with the client as an abandonment of the relationship.[51]

How helpful are such contracts? The answer seems to be "not always" and there is evidence that they can cause harm with some clients. Shea[52] suggests that unless bonding takes place quickly, a contract with a client met for the first time may have little, if any, effect. Miller[53] comments that such contracts, although widely used, are infrequently studied, overvalued as a risk management device, limited by the unpredictability of suicide and the multiple factors leading to completed suicides, and can be motivated by a therapist's fear of litigation. There is also limited or no formal training in the use of contracts. Motto notes that: "Protection from legal liability arising from the treatment of suicidal patients requires documentation that the risk was recognized, assessed, and managed in a nonnegligent manner."[54] Simply just mentioning that there is a safety contract will not give much legal protection. As there are often unrealistic expectations on the part of the therapist, client, and family members relating to the fallacy of suicide prediction, there may be a fear of a lawsuit from family members if the client commits suicide. Where appropriate, it is therefore important for the therapist to work closely with family members and alert them to the suicide risks.

With appropriate clients and a good therapeutic alliance, however, such contracts can be very effective for relieving therapist anxiety and client ambivalence about lethal behavior. Such contracts are invariably time limited as few clients agree to a long-term indefinite contract as it can compromise their sense of control. A contract needs to be renewed at agreed-on intervals without fail. A depressed client, for example, may feel he or she can hang on for a short period of time rather than try and face an eternity of depression. It is important to remember that an agreement to a contract does not abolish risk and in fact may not make much difference with regard to risk.

10.6.2   Some Pitfalls of Contracts

Miller[55] mentions several pitfalls of a safety contract. It may lead to clients not talking frankly about suicidal thoughts as they may feel that such a discussion is a violation of the contract. This can lead to the client using more indirect methods of communication such as behavior rather than conversation, for example, suicidal behavior, regression, or some form of manipulative behavior. Another pitfall is

[51] Chu (1999: 343).
[52] Shea (1999: 182).
[53] Miller (1999: 464).
[54] Motto (1999: 235–236).
[55] Miller (1999: 471–2).

that the client may even think that the therapist is more interested in formal and administrative matters than in the client's distress or treatment. There is also the possibility that the client may feel coerced, which can affect the therapeutic alliance. Miller suggests not using the word "contract" as it is not a legal contract and the therapist does not offer anything in exchange other than what would normally be expected from a therapist. What then does the client gain from such a contract other than perhaps knowing that the therapist may feel better about it or thinking that it lets the therapist off the hook?

10.6.3   Informed Consent

Miller suggests an alternative approach that he calls "informed consent." The idea is for the therapist to review various treatment options with the client, clarifying the risks and benefits of each option, and encouraging full participation by the client. A frank acknowledgment of the risk of death from suicide can also be included in the discussion as well as other risks such as overly restrictive plans. An important factor in this approach is the client's competence to give informed consent. We note that Joiner prefers to use the crisis card idea described above as no-suicide contracts only tell clients what not to do instead of what to do.[56]

10.7   BIBLICAL VIEWPOINT

The Bible does not condemn nor condone suicide; nor does it contain the word suicide so it is perhaps not surprising that there are a variety of opinions about suicide. The occasions of such deaths in the Bible are described simply, briefly, accurately, and without condemnation. For example:[57] Abimelech, seriously hurt and not wanting the disgrace of being killed by a woman, killed himself; Samson brought the temple of the Philistines down upon himself in order to kill his captors, dying for a cause he believed in and for revenge; Saul, badly wounded, facing capture, disgrace, and torture in a defeat by the Philistines, fell on his own sword; Ahithophel chose to hang himself after he supported Absalom's unsuccessful revolt against King David and found that his advice was not followed; Zimri chose to burn himself because of the evil he had done; and Judas Iscariot went and hanged himself when he realized he had betrayed an innocent man.

Arguments for and Against Suicide

The Christian church generally condemns suicide on various grounds, and in the past considered suicide to be a great moral sin, a view still held by some parts of the church. Others view suicide as devil inspired.[58] The sixth commandment says, "You shall not kill"[59] and this is often taken to include killing oneself, though the exceptions of self-defense or war are generally allowed. However, it has also been argued that in keeping with the two great commandments of loving God and your neighbor,[60] the first four commandments are about one's relationship with God

---

[56] Joiner (2005: 213).
[57] Judges 9:54, 16:28–31; 1 Samuel 31:1–6; 2 Samuel 17:23; 1 Kings 16:15-20; and Matthew 27:3–5.
[58] See James 4:7.
[59] Exodus 20:1–17 and Deuteronomy 5:6–21.
[60] Matthew 22:36–40.

and the remaining six about one's relationship with others. With this view, the sixth commandment is about murdering another person, not killing oneself.

Other arguments against suicide are indirect being based on the Bible's view of the sanctity of life. For example, Paul says that our body is the temple of the Holy Spirit and we are not our own but bought with a price, so we need to honor God with our bodies.[61] We are made in God's image,[62] which implies we are of value. It can also be argued that the "survival instinct," which is very strong, is a gift from God.

Biblical Heroes

Many of the greatest heroes of the Bible faced overwhelming depression and sometimes wished they had never been born. King David, the prophet Jeremiah, and Job all reached low points where they despaired of their very lives.[63] However, all these men persevered through suffering and injustice keeping their faith in God, and God blessed them. There were others who wanted God to take their life such as Moses, Jonah, and Elijah,[64] but they also had hope in God and God dealt kindly with them.

The solution to despair and hopelessness is not suicide, but faith in God who is "our help and shield."[65] People need the power of God to set them free from hopeless ways of thinking and such things as anger, resentment, bitterness, unforgiveness, fearfulness, despair, worthlessness, and self-pity. The Bible teaches that one day we will give account of ourselves before God.

There are many positive messages in the Bible about life. God has plans for God's people that provide hope and a future, and plans for individuals.[66] The purpose for one's life is yet to be fulfilled. Also Jesus wants his people to have life to the full[67] and promises relief to those who are burdened.[68]

Suicide and Salvation

If a true believer does commit suicide, it can be argued that there is nothing in the Bible which says that his or her salvation is necessarily lost, as salvation is by faith,[69] and nothing can separate a true Christian from God's love.[70] Murder (if a person truly repents[71]) and suicide are not described as unpardonable sins. However, contemplating suicide may lead to a severed relationship with Christ, which can put one's salvation at risk.

---

[61] 1 Corinthians 6:19–20; see also 1 Corinthians 3:16–17.
[62] Genesis 1:27, 9:6.
[63] Psalms 13:2–4; Jeremiah 20:14–18; and Job 7:15–16.
[64] Numbers 11:12-15; Jonah 4:4, 8; and 1 Kings 19:4.
[65] Psalms 33:20–22.
[66] Jeremiah 29:11; Psalms 139:13–16; Isaiah 49:1,5; Jeremiah 1:5; and Galatians 1:15.
[67] John 10:10.
[68] Matthew 11:28–30.
[69] John 5:24 and 1 John 5:13.
[70] Romans 8:38–39.
[71] See the story of David and Uriah and 2 Samuel 12:13.

CHAPTER 11

GRIEF AND LOSS

11.1 CONSEQUENCE OF LOSS

Whenever there is a loss or change, grief stalks close behind with the depth of grief depending on the significance of the loss or change. The loss can be many things: loss of a body part, loss of health or mobility, loss of a job (including retirement), loss through moving house, loss of a pet, loss of a marriage through divorce, loss through death of a friend or loved one, and loss through failure of any kind. Also every loss tends to be a multiple loss as other parts of our lives are affected (so-called secondary losses). For example, when my father lost a leg at 82 years old in an accident, he experienced the "phantom limb" phenomenon, a pain in his foot that he did not have, which kept reminding him of how active he used to be right up to retirement at 80. When my first wife had a full mastectomy she grieved over the loss of her breast, as she felt mutilated and that part of her femininity had been lost.

Summing up, we are very much on a continuum of losses as we tend to grieve over the loss of anything that is important to us. As Parker says: "Between birth and death there are a thousand griefs and a million hurts."[1] In fact, "We face minor grief almost daily in some situation or another."[2] When counseling, we need to remember that what is a significant loss for one person may not be significant for

[1] Parker (1981: 16).
[2] Westerberg (1962).

another. Also, the impact of a particular loss can depend on a person's role in a family of origin's life-cycle and what developmental stage they are at with respect to their own family life-cycle.

Losses can be described as external, for example, (1) loss of relationships (e.g., death of a loved one), (2) loss of external or treasured objects (e.g., theft or destruction of something), and (3) loss through environmental changes (e.g., a natural disaster). The losses can also be "internal," for example, (4) affecting our identity (e.g., failure, arrest, and rape) and (5) natural or accidental loss (e.g., injury and miscarriage). Each of these five subcategories can also be divided into apparent losses (examples just given), loss as a part of a change (e.g., divorce, moving house or job, and change in pace), and unnoticed "loss" (e.g., marriage, birth of a child, and promotion, where something positive can lead to a loss such as loss of freedom).[3] Another way of categorizing losses is real losses, threatened losses, and imagined losses; they can also be concrete or abstract. For further details about these latter losses see Section 9.3.2. An interesting catalogue of 43 losses and changes ranked numerically from 100 down to 11 in terms of their effect was given by Holmes and Rahe (1967).[4]

Some losses are difficult to deal with because their resulting grief is not recognized socially, for example, a miscarriage, an abortion, giving up a baby for adoption, loss of a clandestine lover, loss of a gay partner, immigration, and death of someone facing public disapproval (e.g, a drunken driver). This type of grief is usually referred to as disenfranchised grief. For specific losses, grief counseling is often provided through support groups (e.g., abortion, suicide). One cannot deal with a loss without recognizing what is lost.[5] Also there is a need to negotiate and renegotiate the meaning of the loss over time.

Unless a person is stuck in grief (which is discussed later in Section 11.6), it is important for us to remember that grief is not something that needs fixing or curing! It is not an illness nor a psychological problem. Grief is what a person experiences as they go through the process of grieving (some use the term "mourning"). I will now consider some of the more significant losses that people face.

11.2   DEATH OF A LOVED ONE

11.2.1   Overview

There is a very extensive literature on this subject giving a number of different approaches to this kind of grief.[6] Clearly a single chapter on this subject will be just a beginning so the best I can do is to try and achieve some sort of integration of various basic ideas that may be useful for the therapist. Because of different approaches, there will be some repetition and overlap of ideas. One of the best things a therapist can do is listen; listen to stories of what life was like before the bereavement and how life has changed since.

[3]See Frears and Schneider (1981: Table 1, page 342).
[4]http://en.wikipedia.org/wiki/Holmes_and_Rahe_stress_scale (accessed November 2010).
[5]Klass, Silberman, and Nickman (1996: 18–19).
[6]For a very comprehensive handbook for caregivers covering a wide range of grief topics see Jeffreys (2005).

Death of someone close is always a painful experience,[7] and the resulting grief depends on the person that has been lost. For example, death of a mate will affect us differently than the loss of a child. Death by suicide is hard for those left behind. Suicide leaves so many unanswered questions, and there is sometimes a legacy of guilt with the words "If only I'd ...." Finally, death after a long illness, especially when the caregiver is left exhausted and too numb to grieve, may leave the caregiver feeling guilty that he or she is relieved it is finally over. However, such caregivers may find that there is a huge void in their life, once filled by caring for the loved one, and this can affect decision making.[8]

Jeffreys suggests that there are three conditions of grief relating to the degree of attachment bonding, namely:[9]

1. Broken or altered bond. This can occur when there is death or permanent separation from an attachment figure.

2. Threat to a bond. For example, a relationship at risk, a loved one with a terminal illness, a workplace reorganization, and a recently detected breast lump, can all bring on a grief response as intense as if the loss had already occurred.

3. Unestablished bond. This represents something that never has or never will happen such as "the relationship you never established with an alcoholic father or mother, the child you were never able to conceive, the promotion you never obtained, or the partner you were never able to court." These losses can become linked up with current losses.

People may come for counseling at different stages of their grief, for example after six months or even years later, and often when immediate support is fading. Strong feelings of grief can reoccur over a lifetime; they are not continuous after an initial period of the first few days or weeks. Sometimes a client will come for some other issue and it is found that unresolved grief is an underlying problem. A woman I counseled for some other matter still looked for her husband in a crowd sixteen years after his death. Empty chair work can be used in such a situation, where the client addresses the person who has died.

11.2.2 Grief Models

Models Based on Stages

A number of models have been proposed for stages of the grief process. For example Kübler-Ross (1978) suggested the following stages that a dying person may go through after the initial shock, namely denial, anger, bargaining (with God?), depression, and acceptance (acronym DABDA).[10] It has also been applied to other types of grief as well. However, there seems to be a lack of empirical evidence for this model and its application to bereavement in spite of the popularity of the model.[11]

---

[7]My first wife died many years ago at the age of 46 after a six - year battle with cancer.
[8]Johnson (1987: 31).
[9]Jeffreys (2005: 40–41).
[10]Corr (1993) discussed some weaknesses of this model.
[11]See, for example, the Letters in the *Journal of the American Medical Association*, (2007), **297** (24).

Westerberg (1962) has a 10-stage model that describes the stages of grief that a bereaved person may go through, namely: shock, emotion, depression and loneliness, physical symptoms of stress, panic (because we can't get the loss out of our mind), guilt (e.g., because of wrongs and/or unfinished business), anger (e.g., at God or caregivers for allowing the death), resistance (e.g., we don't want to get back into life again as we don't want to minimize the loss, or because life is too painful), hope (which slowly filters through), and affirmation of reality (and our spirituality). There are a number of other models associated with names like Lindemann, Bowlby, Engel, and Parkes, for example,[12] and they all have similar basic ingredients.

How useful are such models? One weakness is that they do not allow for the individuality of grief. We are all different and the grieving person needs to be told that there is no right or wrong way to grieve, or an appropriate length of time for grieving. For example, a husband and wife may grieve very differently with a different time frame over the death of a child, and this can lead to marital stress and problems. Sometimes our closest friends can be the hardest people to be around as they may want us to snap out of it and feel better, which can be maddening. They may even give well meaning but irritating advice like, "You have to get over it and move on with your life."

People should give themselves permission to grieve in their own way and according to their own schedule. However, models may be helpful as they can at least give the therapist something of a framework, though it must be born in mind that not everyone goes through all stages, nor in any particular order; in fact they may switch back and forth and even miss out stages. The danger of using a model is that when a person reaches the last stage the assumption might be that the person has completed their grieving! These models are more descriptions of observed behaviors rather than required stages for healing grief.

One thing all the models seem agree on is that the first stage is shock (tranquil or hysterical) and a temporary escape from reality. We often hear phrases like "I feel numb" and "I seem to be on autopilot." Being in this stage will take a person through the funeral and receptions and everyone may think that as the person seems to be scoping so well that they will be okay in the future. Westerberg (1962) suggests that during this stage the bereaved person should be encouraged to carry on as much of their usual activities as possible. This will help them come out of their "trance" and get on with their grieving. Doing nothing is not going to help. Westerberg has the analogy of recovery from surgery; these days they get you moving almost straight away, as it speeds up recovery. Attig[13] describes this initial stage as experiencing

> shock, disbelief, longing, preoccupation with the deceased and an acute awareness of sights sounds, or smells that call the person to mind, yearning and searching for the deceased, numbness, withdrawal in defense, and denial.

Attig describes a second common stage as experiencing somatic distress when we are burdened with "acute and intense emotions such as sadness, depression, anxiety, despair, helplessness, anger, frustration, and guilt." As preoccupation with the dead person recedes, loss of motivation, isolation, hopelessness, and purposelessness can creep in. Humphrey and Zimpfer[14] believe that a feeling of total aloneness is a

---

[12]See for example Attig (1996: 42) and Jeffreys (2005: 54–60).
[13]Attig (1996: 42).
[14]Humphrey and Zimpfer (1996: 39).

universal experience in this early period of acute grief. Attig says that emotions then settle down and we move into the third and final stage of acceptance. These comments apply not only to bereaved adults with deceased adults, but also to those with deceased children.

As we have seen above, symptoms of grief are complicated and numerous, and Johnson[15] suggests that it is helpful for a therapist to categorize them, namely feelings, physical responses, and behavioral reactions, when assessing symptoms; she also gives three detailed lists of common symptoms. For example, feelings can include loneliness, yearning, and sadness, as well as those mentioned by Attig above; physical responses can include migraine headaches, odd aches and pains, sleep disturbances, fatigue, and panic attacks; and behavioral responses can include appetite disturbances, social withdrawal, concentration difficulties, and preoccupation with the dead person.[16] If grief is not allowed direct expression it will find another indirect way of expression, leading to a whole range of possible somatic symptoms.

Models for Moving Forward

The above stages models focus on what happens to the grieving person. I now want to look at the grieving process from the point of view of what might need to happen. Based on the work of Lindemann and Bowlby, Worden[17] describes grieving as a process that requires four steps or "tasks," namely

1. Accept the reality of the loss.

2. Fully experience and work through the pain of grief.

3. Adjust to an environment in which the deceased is missing.

4. Emotionally relocate the deceased and move on with life.

Rando[18] extends these ideas and describes three phases and a six 'R' model as follows:[19]

1. *Avoidance phase.* This involves helping the client to **RECOGNIZE** the loss.

2. *Confrontation phase.* The bereaved person must **REACT** to the loss and fully experience the pain of both the loss and and any resulting secondary losses or symbolic losses. Past losses need to be considered as well. Also, the client needs to **RECOLLECT** and re-experience the relationship with the deceased through reviewing and remembering, and **RELINQUISH** the old attachments to the deceased and assumptions about the world at that time.

3. *Accommodation phase.* This involves **READJUSTING** to the new world without forgetting the old and **REINVESTING** in a meaningful life.

Rando believes that a problem in one of these six processes can lead to complications with the grieving process. As already mentioned, everyone's experience of grief is

---

[15] Johnson (1987: chapter 3).
[16] For further comments on this topic see Worden (2002: 11–22).
[17] Worden (2002: 27–38).
[18] Rando (1993).
[19] See Humphrey and Zimpfer (1996: 7–8) for a summary.

different and the above is provided, along with the stages models, to give the therapist some way of measuring progress with the grieving process and to help uncover any problems. It will be helpful to examine now what may be regarded as an extension of the accommodation phase.

Grieving as Relearning

Attig[20] claims that grieving for a loved one is a process of relearning the world. Rather than debate the pros and cons, he presents some very detailed case histories that clearly support his thesis. These personal histories not only demonstrate the individuality of grief but also show the uniqueness of each person's learning about being in the world prior to bereavement, as well as their coping with the disruption to their life, and their learning of new ways of being in the world after the bereavement.

Attig sets out some broad principles about what bereaved people are looking for, namely:

1. *They seek general understanding.* People want others to understand them and appreciate something of what they have been through. They long for someone who will listen patiently to the details of their stories of life with the bereaved, the events surrounding the death, and their lives since the death. No story of loss replicates any other. They also want self-understanding as what has happened is life-shattering. There are so many unanswered questions, and they come against not just problems but mysteries that are more difficult to deal with. They now face a radically new life-landscape that can threaten to overwhelm them.

2. *They seek respect for individuality.* This has already been alluded to above. What is not wanted is people saying that they know how the person feels, but rather they want respect for the uniqueness of their experience and want people to hear all the details of the challenges they are facing in every avenue of their life.

3. *They seek ways to deal with helplessness in grieving.* Bereavement is a choice-less event that a person has little or no control over, and they have no control over the havoc it brings into their lives. Although grief is an emotion we may experience as overwhelming, grieving is a coping process that is not choice-less but involves active participation in addressing tasks, for example, dealing with items that belonged to the deceased, returning to an activity that the deceased introduced into their life, returning to work, and so forth. People may adopt various coping mechanisms such as the idealization of the deceased. A women who maintains she was married to an ideal man means that she was okay and the belief helps to remove unpleasant past memories.[21] Also Attig says:

> As we relearn how to be in a world that is drastically changed by what has happened, we always have options in how we meet the emotional, behavioral, physical, social, and intellectual and spiritual challenges we face.[22]

[20] Attig (1996).
[21] Klass et al. (1996: 151).
[22] Attig (1996: 19).

The bereaved relearn their physical surroundings, their places in space and time, their relationships with fellow survivors, their understanding of themselves, and their spiritual position. They can choose how to reshape their lives and find purpose, meaning, and hope again.

4. *They seek guidance for caregivers.*

Attig's comments above also help spell out some of our role as therapists.[23] With regard to (1) and story telling, Johnson[24] encourages her grieving clients to tell and re-tell their stories and she notes details of what, when, and where, and also what is included and excluded, when the tears come, nonverbal messages, and themes. Each time the story is told it becomes more complete, which increases resolution and peace; any reduction of breakdown in the telling can indicate healing. She also recommends recording their story in some way (e.g., journaling), as memories fade in time.[25] Another idea of hers is to ask clients to bring to counseling recent and past photos of their family and important people in their lives. Such photos can provide information about family dynamics and physical changes in time. Writing a letter or letters to the deceased can help a client express their feelings and take care of unfinished business.[26]

With regard to (3) in the above list, we can help the bereaved person to recognize the variety of challenges mentioned in the above quote from Attig that they might face, and help them to engage actively in identifying tasks and options and in redefining new daily life patterns. Clients should be encouraged to look after themselves with regard to their physical well-being (see Chapter 2). It is important for bereaved people not to rush into making any major changes in their life until emotions have settled down and they are able to think more clearly. Some tasks are very painful, such as cleaning out clothing and personal effects of the dead person. Generally it is best to do it over a period of time rather than all at once, but only when ready to do it. Getting through special days such as anniversaries, birthdays, and holidays is not easy, so it is helpful for the bereaved person to try and plan these days with perhaps help from the therapist and support from friends.

11.2.3 Some Metaphors

The best thing a client can do with grief is grieve! Paradoxically, when we hurt the most we are perhaps doing the best job with our grief. We don't control grief. We can only experience it and let it roll over us, wave after wave. Sometimes there will be reminders and triggers that bring another wave, for example holidays, anniversaries, music, and night time. A lot of the time there is no explanation for the wave, and when a wave comes we may feel that we have made no progress. However, it does provide an opportunity for further growth. The client needs to acknowledge how they feel, and act according to their feelings and not according to what they or others think they should feel. As mentioned above, grief generally gets worse for a time as it goes deeper and the full impact of the loss is felt, but in time the waves do become less frequent and less overwhelming.

[23] Attig (1996: 23).
[24] Johnson (1987: 154).
[25] This topic is discussed further below under the title of "Continuing Bonds."
[26] Worden (2002: 68).

A metaphor I find helpful with clients is that grief is a like a black cloud over the whole sky. In time the cloud shrinks and blue sky, white clouds, and birds begin to appear around the edges until eventually the black cloud is small and swamped in light and color. This cloud won't completely disappear but simply becomes part of the landscape of life; for most people the pain of grief never completely goes. When counseling, a metaphor will be used by the client at some point and it will be helpful to explore that metaphor perhaps with drawing.

Another good metaphor, suggested by Manning (2002),[27] is that experiencing grief is like peeling an onion — no two onions are the same and no two people peel them the same way. As with the above models, he describes the first layer as shock, where everything is both real and unreal, and there is often denial. Mental confusion reigns and one's minds whirls with questions. A typical question is: "How long will I hurt like this?" Although every one is different, there seems to be a consensus that it takes about two years to go through the whole grieving process, but it may take longer. As already mentioned, a person needs to proceed at their own pace and not be dictated by others as to how to grieve. One guideline for recovery from grief is when one is able to think of the deceased person without pain. There will always be sadness in losing a loved one, but it won't have the physical manifestations that go with intense grief.

According to Manning, the second layer of the onion is facing reality. My own experience with the death of my first wife was that I was able to get through the funeral and the following weeks, and then it began to hit me as I faced the reality of being alone and bringing up two boys. Often people can return to work soon after a death, but may need time off later when the crash comes. We can act better than we are really are and hide our pain from others. However, we all need someone we can talk to honestly. Talking helps us to release our feelings and often gives us insight, rather like talking about a problem may help us see the solution. Although no one fully understands how we feel, as our pain is unique, talking at least helps us to recognize that we are no longer alone in our pain. It helps to legitimize our feelings and enables us to move on. We all need safe people who will listen rather than try to explain things away or offer advice.

The final stage in peeling the onion is reconstruction. There comes a time when we decide to move on with our life and begin again. There will be moments when we begin to feel normal again! However, there will also be times when we experience triggers and the tears flow so we need to give ourselves permission to let them flow freely. There is freedom in giving ourselves permission to grieve. We also need the freedom to let ourselves laugh again, love again, and live again. We don't need to live our lives according to what we think our departed loved one would want; we need to give ourselves freedom to change traditions, if necessary. Rituals are important such as grave visiting, especially during the initial months and on special occasions such as birthdays.

11.2.4 Significance of Loss

When something bad happens to us, we want people to really notice what has happened and understand the significance of the event to us. We like to share bad

[27]This is an excellent series of small booklets used by funeral homes, and ideas from these booklets are used in this section.

news as well as good news! We may need to tell the story over and over again until we believe that the story has actually been heard. It may sound like a cracked record played over and over to the outsider, but when heard by an understanding friend it brings healing.

The need for significance is paramount—if we can establish it we can move on. We may also need to establish not only the significance of our loss but also the significance of the person who has gone, both to ourselves and to others. When there is grief and loss we sometimes build a wall and we don't want to venture out and become socially active or, alternatively, we may try to kill the pain by an incessant round of social activity.[28] There is a danger that we can become self-centered instead of being outward looking and reaching out to other people who are in need.

11.2.5 Anger

At some point grief can often create anger. As noted in Chapter 3, there is nothing wrong with anger as it is a normal emotion in response to some form of pain, and is therefore neutral. It can provide a driving force to "fight back" and get us going again. Unfortunately anger needs a focus, and where it focuses matters. We may be angry with our loved one for dying and leaving us like that. If our loved one committed suicide we may be angry that he or she took the easy way out and left us to clear up afterwards. We may be angry with God for allowing the death to happen, or angry with the church for not being there when it mattered most, or angry with the way the funeral was conducted. If, after an inquest, it turned out that the death was caused by negligence (e.g., by a doctor or hospital) then we may be angry with the people who were negligent. We may be angry with our partner over the death of a child. Friends may say the wrong things and we get angry with them and their "good intentions" and "advice." We may be angry with ourselves, and what sometimes comes to mind is the phrase "If only." We can get obsessed with the idea that we might have contributed in some way to the death, or have regrets over unfinished business. There is always unfinished business and we have to accept this. If the death was not sudden, should we have talked about death at the time or was it better to just leave things be and not say our final goodbyes? We make our decision at the time and accept the fact that it was the best we could do under the circumstances.

Worden[29] makes some useful comments about raising the issue of anger with a bereaved person. Often the person does not associate their anger with the deceased and direct it elsewhere. If it is not directed at the deceased or deflected elsewhere, it may be turned inward and experienced as depression, guilt, or lowered self-esteem. The therapist can help the client to get in touch with his or her anger and process it in a safe place. However, it is usually not productive to tackle the anger issue directly and Worden suggests an indirect method such as asking, "What do you miss about him?" followed by questions like "What don't you miss about him?" and "How did he disappoint you?" The aim is to obtain a better balance between the positive and negative feelings, but not just leave the bereaved person with negative feelings.

[28] This is particularly the case with divorce.
[29] Worden (2002: 58–59).

11.3   COUNSELING FRAMEWORK

Much of what has been discussed above, along with the various models, will provide the therapist with some ideas for counseling. I now want to suggest just a few general principles for these counseling sessions. The principles can apply to other losses, with appropriate rewording. Education remains an important part of this counseling as some clients may not understand the grief process and need to learn about it from the therapist.

11.3.1   Initial Sessions

In the initial session(s), the therapist can consider the nature of the loss as well as any previous losses and their impact on the client. It is helpful to know the role of the deceased, the nature of the attachment, the mode of death, and the social support available including the client's perception of the support.[30] In assessing past losses, Humphrey and Zimpfer[31] suggest listing each loss and at what age, along with feelings and behaviors at the time (e.g., what was happening internally and what was happening externally in the environment), any unanswered questions (e.g., using how, what, when, and so on), and what changes occurred as the result of the loss. They also suggest looking at the client's perspective on how the loss or losses have affected the client from philosophical, spiritual, psychological, sociological, and physical perspectives, where appropriate.[32] We now consider these perspectives in more detail.

Client Perspectives

The philosophical perspective relates to the client's outlook on life and what questions the current loss has triggered, and whether the feelings are similar to those felt with previous losses. Spiritual perspectives can be considered through questions that relate to a client's relationship, if any, with a Higher Power, and how this has been impacted by the loss. If the client attends some religious organization, he or she can be asked what help they are receiving from that organization and what rituals have been helpful.

Psychological perspectives will continue to emerge throughout the counseling sessions with different aspects arising at different times. Humphrey and Zimpfer[33] suggest constructing a table assessing psychological needs under the following categories:

Love: Which family and friends love me that I can trust and love in return?

Belonging: What do I belong to that I feel comfortable with and feel part of?

Self-worth: What do I do or like about myself that makes me feel good about myself?

Recognition: Who appreciates me and gives me recognition? What do I do that I feel is worthwhile and important to me?

---

[30] Worden (2002: 37–45).
[31] Humphrey and Zimpfer (1996: 36).
[32] Humphrey and Zimpfer (1996: chapter 2); see also Jeffreys (2005: 41–52).
[33] Humphrey and Zimpfer (1996: 29, 58).

Fun: How much fun do I have and how often? How much of it is free?

Freedom: How much freedom do I have to make decisions? What am I in control of in my life?

The top four fall generally under the heading of acceptance, value, and belonging—three things we all need in our lives.

In the assessment stage the therapist can explore how the above needs were met in the past and how they are being met, or not being met, now. The same can be applied to the nature of the relationship that's been lost, finding out what needs it fulfilled in the client's life, and determining how those needs are currently being met, or not being met. This will provide an opportunity for the client to tell his or her story about the relationship right from the beginning. In the course of asking the above questions, the therapist can do some detective work on the type of personality the client has and determine whether there are any underlying problems that can make the grief process more difficult, for example, a dependent or compulsive personality.[34] It is also important to assess clients' grief emotions and how their feelings are expressed as well as their beliefs about such expressions (e.g., seeing grief as a sign of weakness), and their self-talk.

The remaining two perspectives are the sociological and physical aspects of grief counseling. Clients' cultural[35] and sociological background need to be taken into consideration as well as the their family of origin and their status in both the work force and in their society. Many losses in these areas are not always visible or recognized as losses. Family and support systems may be seen as a help or a hindrance, and changes in the environment as a result of the loss can be a painful reminder. Some cultures negate the grieving process and believe it is a sign of personal weakness. Others (e.g., Hispanics) view crying openly as helpful. Finally, physical effects need to be assessed (e.g., sleep and appetite disturbance, lack of energy, aches and pains, nausea), and this can be done by referring to the topics of Section 2.2 in the chapter on wholeness.

All above perspectives can be assessed right throughout the counseling process as they will keep changing with time.

11.3.2 Further Sessions

As already noted, grieving is very individual so it is not possible to put a number on how many sessions may be needed, though Humphrey and Zimpfer[36] talk about early, middle, and late sessions in the counseling process. As the best thing a client can do with grief is grieve, the early sessions will involve the client being encouraged to experience a whole range of emotions, with the therapist supporting the release of these emotions by genuine listening. The grief work will not just be with regard to the individual but will also incorporate all those things associated with the individual. Care is needed in closing a session so that the client is not left hanging. This means probing for feelings early enough to allow time for the client to return to some state of equilibrium; the process can't be rushed!

[34]See Chapter 21.
[35]See, for example, Charles-Edwards (2005: Chapter 11) for some cultural and religious information on bereavement.
[36]Humphrey and Zimpfer (1996: 43–57).

In the middle sessions the focus begins to shift to letting go and making new choices, which is the relearning process described above. Perspectives continue to change, often centering on the psychological and sociological ones. Psychologically the bereaved person begins to feel more in control of their emotions and begin to make new decisions. Sociologically they begin to understand the influence of their cultural background and discard inappropriate messages from that background.

The later sessions focus mainly on "the experience of letting go and making new choices" and it involves investing "mental and emotional energy in the business of living a meaningful life."[37] The list of psychological needs outlined above can be revisited to see how the needs are currently being met, or not being met. The client can then be encouraged to find ways in the future of fulfilling those unmet needs. However, the need for closeness can drive a person prematurely into close or even sexual relationships, and a bereaved person can be very vulnerable to anyone who shows them kindness. Emotions can then become very confused as he or she is sad over the loss, but happy over the new relationship!

11.3.3   Some Aspects of Grieving

Some topics (not in any particular order) that a therapist might need to deal with in grief counseling are listed below.

Anticipatory Grief

A common situation is where death is anticipated (e.g., after a long illness) so that grieving begins while the person is still alive. It is not clear whether this anticipatory grief will make grieving easier after the death or not; it does in some cases. As we see a loved one go steadily downhill, the first stage of the grief process, namely denial, is less likely to be a problem. We also begin to work through some of the grief feelings, though there is often a heightened awareness of one's own mortality, and separation anxiety may grow. It can be helpful for us to begin to rehearse in our minds how we will cope when our loved one has died, especially when children are involved. With the delay there is an opportunity to take care of unfinished business, though sometimes there may be denial on the grounds it is inappropriate to anticipate death in any way. If the illness is lengthy, there can be problems with regard to the emotional distance between the dying person and concerned others. The latter may withdraw because the process is so drawn out and a person may feel guilty for wanting it to end. On the other hand, people may get too close to the dying person to try and compensate for their guilty feelings and ambivalence towards the dying person. The latter will have their own distance problems, which I now discuss.

Withdrawal of the Dying Person

When my first wife drew near to the end of her life after her long illness, she began to withdraw from me, which I found painful. However, I now know that this is normal. As Kübler-Ross notes:

> The most heartbreaking time, perhaps for the family is the final phase, when the patient is slowly detaching himself from his world including his family. They do not understand that a dying man who has found peace and acceptance in his death will have to separate himself, step by step, from his

---

[37]Humphrey and Zimpfer (1996: 56).

environment, including his most loved ones. How could he be ready to die if he continued to hold onto meaningful relationships of which a man has so many?[38]

A grieving client may take some comfort from this knowledge and the normalization of the withdrawal process.

Viewing the Body

This is a very personal matter and will depend on the individual and the state of the body. Generally speaking, it is a good idea to view the body (perhaps with suitable company), say goodbye, and thus have some closure and some "unbinding." For me, the most striking observation about viewing a dead body is that you are aware that the person is gone and that only a physical shell remains. A common problem for people with grief issues is that they were never able to see their loved one or say goodbye to them. They have difficulty believing, on an emotional level, that their loved one has actually gone and, through lack of closure, may have difficulty in forming future relationships. If the person dies at home, the partner may wish to keep the body there for an appropriate time. In some cultures, viewing the body and paying last respects is part of the normal grieving process.

Coping with Change

Death certainly brings changes and secondary losses. For example, if we lose a partner we may find we have to do things that our partner used to do, for example, the widowed wife may have to get the car serviced, while the widowed husband may have to get used to shopping for food. Our life style is altered and we may need to learn a lot of new skills. Our friends may change. Some old friends may avoid us as they don't know what to say or we may feel uncomfortable with the old crowd who don't really appreciate how we feel. We may struggle with our spirituality and reassess our beliefs.

Memories also change. At first they are very painful, but eventually they can become something we can embrace. Rituals can be helpful, like visiting a grave and perhaps leaving some flowers. A year after my present wife's mother died, the family met around her grave and shared stories. Then they all went out to lunch to celebrate her life. There is no right or wrong way of doing this kind of thing, but it may be helpful to have some sort of celebration in a family situation.

Coping with Anxiety

Anxiety is a normal feeling in confronting a death situation and Johnson[39] suggests the following strategies to help control anxiety.

- Avoid changes.
- Don't think about too many things at once.
- Don't force yourself to do something, like read, when you cannot concentrate.
- Don't over-plan your days; allow time out.
- Recognize feelings of anxiety and take steps to alleviate them (e.g., walking, listening to music, and so on).

[38]Kübler-Ross (1978: 177).
[39]Johnson (1987: 85).

- Learn to recognize what you are really feeling; it may actually be anger, guilt, and so on instead of anxiety.

Depression

Depression is usually present at some stage in the grief process. However, it is not easy at times to distinguish between "normal" depression and the development of a Major Depressive episode as the symptoms are very similar. Possible markers for the latter are a morbid preoccupation with worthlessness, prolonged and functional impairment, and a marked psychomotor retardation, though these are not always reliable indicators.[40] A complicating factor with loss is that it may trigger unfinished business from the past so that, as mentioned above, the therapist should always explore a client's previous history for major losses and its effect on the present situation.[41] The depression may actually be due to a past loss so, if possible, it is helpful to deal with any past losses early in the counseling.

Continuing Bonds

Given some of the difficulties of letting go, an important question to ask is what is an appropriate connection between the bereaved and the deceased? In the past there has been a tendency to tell bereaved people to sever their relationship with the deceased and move on, otherwise maintaining a bond with the deceased was regarded as symptomatic of psychological problems. This kind of advice is no longer considered appropriate, so as therapists we should not encourage our clients to completely let go of their loved ones.[42] Attig says, "We need not break our bonds with the deceased but instead redefine the nature of those bonds and their places in our lives." In fact, "We can reassure the bereaved that the desire for a continuing relationship with the deceased is normal and not necessarily, or even usually, morbid."[43] We continue to love the person, but in a different way by letting go and letting be. How bonds are maintained and how they are seen (e.g., normal, pathological, or aberrant) depends on the culture. Care is needed then in grief counseling for people from another culture.

There is a need to continue to love and cherish the stories of the bereaved and to care about the things they cared about. As therapists we can encourage the following:[44]

1. Retell stories about the deceased. This can be done, for example, during the funeral period, or on special occasions such as birthdays or anniversaries.

2. Collect material about the deceased, for example, create scrapbooks, photo albums, and/or a biographical journal.

3. Consider ways of continuing to promote those things inspired by the deceased.

4. Forgive any shortcomings or failings in the deceased.

---

[40] See Section 9.3.3.
[41] Johnson (1987: 87).
[42] Klass, Silverman, and Nickman (1996).
[43] Attig (1996: 174–175).
[44] Attig (1996: 189–191).

5. Relieve any guilt "over new involvements or relationships by urging them to explore whether the deceased's love for them included a desire that they continue to live fully and to flourish."

With the death of a child it is very difficult to let the child go. Anne Finkbeiner,[45] in talking about the loss of her teenage son and in detailing a number of case histories, concluded that letting go of a child was impossible. However, everyone is different and it will depend very much on the circumstances of the death of the child. We never forget the death of a child, but its impact on our life can vary.

11.3.4 Children's Grief

How children respond to grief depends on their age, their relationship with the one who has died, and their type of attachment.[46] Up to the age of five, children do not understand the full meaning of the word "death" and do not appreciate that death is final. They see things concretely so that abstract explanations should be avoided. Explanations need to be simple such as, "Usually when we get sick we get better, but Grandpa died because he was very, very, very sick and his body was unable to go on living so it stopped." Also euphemisms like saying that the dead person is asleep or gone on a long journey may be taken literally, especially as young children are very sensitive to separations. However, there is no reason to doubt that they react strongly to loss even though they may not have the language to explain their feelings.

From five to ten, children begin to understand that death is irreversible and final, and at around seven begin to realize that death is unavoidable and universal. They are still concrete in their thinking and their understanding of the causes of death, so they are helped by concrete expressions of grief such as memorial acts and rituals. From ten through adolescence a child's concept of death becomes more abstract, though concrete memorial acts remain important. At the time of writing this sentence I heard the story of a 12 year-old boy who, after the funeral for his 16 year-old sister, organized the flowers that came to the house along either side of the front entrance and the front hall as a memorial.

It is important to keep reminders of the dead person present, and look at albums and photographs. Children might want to express how they feel in different ways about the deceased person such as producing a scrapbook of memories using drawings, pictures, press cuttings, photos, and their own and perhaps others' writings, and should be helped to do so. It is also helpful to create and notice opportunities to remember and celebrate the deceased person, such as birthdays and anniversaries. Teenagers can find it difficult to reconcile their desire to be with the family with their drive for autonomy, peer acceptance, and social activities.

Clearly bereaved clients with children may need to be more aware of the affect that the death has on their children as we have seen that children grieve differently from adults and we cannot view their grieving through adult eyes. My boys were 11 and 14 years when my first wife died and looking back I recognize that personal grief can stop one from fully appreciating the grief of one's children. As Parker says, "often the grief of a child goes unacknowledged, even unrecognized."[47] Children

---

[45]Finkbeiner (1996: xiii).
[46]Dyregrov (1991: chapter 1).
[47]Parker (1981: 36–37).

need to be allowed to grieve as children. For example, children do not grieve continuously but take breaks, may delay their grief, and may mix grief with play (which can be disconcerting for adults).[48] Children need to be kept informed, in words they can understand, of what is going on so that surprises are minimized. As with adults, every child grieves differently, though some common immediate reactions are:[49]

- Shock and disbelief. They may refuse to accept the death, and parents can be surprised that their children do not react more than they do.

- Dismay and protest. They cry a lot and initially seem inconsolable.

- Apathy and stunned feelings.

- Continuation of usual activities. This can be unsettling for parents, but it is a protection mechanism for the child.

Children need to know that they will be cared for and perhaps reassured that they were not to blame for what happened and that the person did not want to leave them.

As with adults, children can have a wide range of grief reactions,[50] for example: anxiety (e.g., from fear of losing the other parent or dying themselves); vivid memories (e.g., unwelcome repeated thoughts and images); sleep difficulties (e.g., afraid of bad dreams); sadness and longing (e.g., searching for the lost one); anger and acting out (e.g., anger at God, adults, self, and even the dead person for allowing it to happen); guilt, self-reproach, and shame (e.g., blame themselves for their past behavior); school problems (e.g., concentration problems); and physical complaints (e.g., stomach problems).

The death of a parent has the greatest consequences for children when it comes to losing someone close. As a defense mechanism, they may try to keep the event at a distance until they slowly get used to the idea, for example, they may not cry. It is important that a child is not forced into a "surrogate" parent role for the remaining partner. As with adults, sudden death creates other problems with grief for a child as there isn't time to say goodbye; in particular, suicide creates problems for both adults and children.

How adults handle death has a big impact on the children, particularly if the children are not updated as to what is going on. If the children are excluded from the adult world in various ways such as preventing them from seeing the dead person (if they want to)[51] or taking part in the funeral (or any rituals such as visiting the grave), or even seeing the adults' reactions, a difficult situation can be made worse for them. If they see adults in tears, they may feel less disturbed about how they feel. By discussing the death openly and sensitively, the child can learn to do the same. Also the children need structure in their lives so that the usual routines should be maintained. They may have difficulty in sorting out what their friends should be told or dealing with the discomfort that others have with the death.

---

[48] Jeffreys (2005: 96).
[49] Dyregrov (1991: 13).
[50] Dyregrov (1991: 13–24).
[51] However the child needs to be properly prepared by having all the details of the body and room described beforehand.

The aim of the above discussion is not so much to provide guidelines for counseling children, but rather to provide some ideas for the therapist in their supporting role for bereaved adult clients. Counseling help will be particularly helpful for a child bereaved by trauma such as suicide or murder, or for a child having witnessed a death. A child may need professional help if there is excessive crying for long periods, frequent temper tantrums, frequent nightmares and sleep disturbances, extreme changes in behavior, and headaches and other physical complaints. Other things to look for are changes in school performance, general apathy and withdrawal with a loss of interest in friends and previously enjoyed activities, and a negative outlook about the future.

Care of Pets

Any pets involved with the person who died may seem to grieve and need to be talked to and comforted. There are many stories about the responses to death of dogs and cats and these animals seem to go through a grieving process when their master dies. Pets should not be forgotten.

Friends of a Bereaved Person

We may be called upon to counsel the friend of someone who had been bereaved as the friend wants some ideas about how they can help their bereaved friend through the grieving process. It may even be a group of people who want some guidance. For example, there may be a major tragedy in which a man who is leader of a group or organization has lost a child and the group would like to know how they can support him when he returns to work. In the case of a group, the effect of the tragedy is like dropping a stone into a calm pond and watching the ripple spread out far and wide. Many people are affected and everyone's loss will be different in some way so that everyone will grieve differently. People in the group may find some of their own losses and grief get triggered, often from way back in the past, especially if they weren't completely dealt with then. What happens is that the loss and the accompanying emotions go into a person's memory and, when the loss is recalled, the emotions accompany the memory. These emotions will be added to any they have concerning what has happened and there needs to be a safe place where these emotions can be expressed.

The above material on stages and metaphors can be used to convey some basic ideas to a person or a group. A key point mentioned above is that grief is not something that needs fixing so that the friend or colleagues should realize that we don't need to solve anything, or make the person feel better, but simply listen and care. Because of triggers, a small reminder can release overwhelming grief out of the blue. If the bereaved person suddenly bursts into tears, it is important not to be embarrassed but simply be with the person and be silent if necessary. I guess we all tend to be afraid of silence and want to say something at times like these when what is needed most is our presence and for us to not go into fix-it mode!

Some practical information regarding bereavement and the survivor's role in the workplace is given by Charles-Edwards.[52] He notes that some bereaved staff members find it helpful to visit the workplace before returning to work, if only to see the manager or chat with colleagues to break the ice. He suggests that being part-time for a couple of weeks may suit some people but not others, though it

---

[52] Charles-Edwards (2005: Section Four).

will depend on the type of work. As colleagues may not know what to say to the bereaved person, he emphasizes that it is important for those who have any kind of personal relationship with the person to find a way of acknowledging the loss openly, discretely, and as soon as possible so that the relationship will not be impaired. He gives a selection of possible responses that would be acceptable from the heart such as:

- I am so sorry about ..... .

- I have been thinking about you a lot these last few days.

- George, I can't find the words to tell you how sorry I am.

- He was a great person and will be a terrible loss.

- If you ever feel like talking, you know where I am.

We need to keep it simple and genuine as our concern and compassion are more important than our words. Sometimes inappropriate comments are made out of embarrassment, such as "I am sorry he died, but..." (e.g., "I believe it was expected", "it must have been a relief for him/you", "he had a good innings", "it means that you can now get on with your life", "we all have to go sometimes", and "I'm sure you can have another baby.") When they return to work it is important to periodically check up on how they are doing, make time for them, and offer attentive listening or else just be there. It is also helpful to encourage the person to talk about the deceased as well as sharing your own memories about the deceased.

Death in the Workplace

In this situation, debriefing is helpful for affected staff in a workplace so that they can share some of what they have experienced and are experiencing now in order to normalize what they are going through. It also helps to promote "an environment of mutual understanding and support, in which they can talk (without being compelled) with each other about the incident and its aftermath, both for them as individuals and as a group."[53] They can be informed about some of the normal responses and reactions to trauma such as nightmares and irrational fears. It also allows them to discuss any worries about the incident and investigate available support options. The therapist needs to listen empathetically and patiently using both eyes and ears! Anger may also be present. These comments apply to any other type of group such as a football team or a school group.

11.3.5 Suicide and Sudden Death

In the last 45 years suicide rates have increased by 60% worldwide and suicide is now among the three leading causes of death among those aged 15-44 years (both sexes).[54] This means that quite a substantial proportion of a population will have experienced someone close to them dying through suicide.

---

[53] Charles-Edwards (2005: 203).
[54] http://www.who.int/mental_health/prevention/suicide/suicideprevent/en/ by WHO (World Health Organization); accessed November 2010.

People who have lost a loved one through suicide, especially parents losing a child, face a difficult grief journey. The bereaved person may be overwhelmed by a sense of shock and horror at the suicide and this may be compounded by the way it was carried out. They may experience feelings of guilt and shame for not anticipating or even preventing what happened. Some may be angry with the person for taking the easy way out and leaving the bereaved person to cope with the trauma and perhaps problems, unfinished business, and mess left behind. They may also feel that others blame them for the suicide (e.g., suicide of a child or teenager) and feel stigmatized by it. As they may not know anyone who had faced the same situation, they may feel very isolated; support groups can be helpful here. Any guilt and rage need to be acknowledged, listened to empathetically, and normalized, but not supported (and later reality tested). Two big questions a mourner faces is "Why has this happened?" and "How can I make sense of this?" Sometimes a family creates a myth about what really happened, for example describe the death as accidental, and no one is allowed to challenge the belief. Such distorted thinking is not productive in the long run.

As already mentioned above, children should not be forgotten when there is a death, and it can be particularly difficult for a child whose parent has committed suicide. The child needs to realize that they were not to blame and that the person did not want to leave them. They will need to explore the reasons for the suicide and their feelings about it. Charles-Edwards notes that:

> If they think of their parent as mentally ill, it can reinforce the fear that they may one day take the same path. On the other hand, if they regarded them as not especially disturbed, they may feel desolate at the apparent lack of care or love that allowed them to act in a way in which their own needs were so apparently disregarded.[55]

They may also need to consider what other options were available to the parent if the suicide was triggered by despair or acute depression in case the child faces a similar situation on the future.

Worden[56] suggests that therapists can carry out a number of interventions such as doing a reality test on any guilt or blame to disperse wrong thinking. They can also help to correct any denial and distorted thinking so that a survivor can face the reality of of the suicide and be able to work through it. Using uncomfortable words like "killed himself" or "hanged herself" can facilitate this. They may need to help the client process anger and have a reality check on feelings of abandonment. A key issue is to try and help the client find some meaning in the death, though this can be very difficult and may take some time.

Although suicide is a sudden death, there are other examples when a death occurs without warning, for example an accident, a natural disaster, heart attacks, and homicide. In these cases the survivor will usually have a sense of unreality about the loss and, as with a suicide, there can be strong feelings of guilt and anger, and a sense of helplessness. Unfinished business is of special concern and there is often a strong desire to blame someone for the death. There may also be legal and medical ramifications when some form of malpractice such as not having proper safety standards is involved and this can lead to a protracted investigation.

[55] Charles-Edwards (2005: 53).
[56] Worden (2002: 122–124).

The grieving can then be drawn out or even delayed. Worden[57] suggests that some principles of crisis intervention are appropriate here. For example, viewing the body of the deceased may help a survivor actualize the loss, and keeping them focused on the death rather than on the the circumstances of the death can also help. Trauma may be a result of the death and the reader is referred to Section 7.3.4 concerning trauma counseling.

11.4   DEATH OF A CHILD AT ANY AGE

In this section we will cover a range of topics from pre-birth to adult child. Abortion has been added, though there might be some disagreement as to when a fetus is a child. However, if a person comes for counseling it often relates to an attachment problem whether it be to a child or a fetus!

11.4.1   Miscarriage and Prenatal Deaths

A miscarriage or stillbirth has a heightened dimension of loneliness as only the mother knew the child and was bonded at the moment of conception. It is can also be a loss for the father, though he may not appreciate the depth of the loss for the mother if there is no physically bonding for him during pregnancy.[58] A still-born child should be named, if that hasn't already happened, so that the child becomes part of the family. There is a consensus in studies of stillbirths that it is helpful for a parent(s) to see or hold their baby (or at least have the option of doing so) if it is possible; also a photograph may be helpful. It is important to realize that the grieving process has similar features to that experienced in losing a spouse, even though it is more of a loss of an anticipated future.[59] This loss of a potential future can be acutely felt, especially at special times such an anniversary of the loss. Writing a letter to the child can help the healing.

   In the case of a miscarriage, grief is complex as the parents suffer from the effects of a birth and death without usually having a baby to bury or a funeral. Because there is no tangible evidence of the death, people generally don't know how to respond and may be unaware of the grief. In fact the death may be minimized, especially if it occurred early in the pregnancy. It is the strength of the bond and not the length of the pregnancy that determines the depths of a mother's grief. Also the hormonal after-effects of a pregnancy don't disappear immediately after the loss. The death can have an additional impact if it is the first pregnancy, and can also raise questions like "Will I ever be a mother?", "Can I trust my body?", and "Did I do something wrong?"

   The extent of the grief will depend on many factors such as the hopes and expectations of the pregnancy. For example, the pregnancy may have been a replacement for former losses so that such past losses may compound the present loss. The marriage might have been been shaky and the pregnancy might have provided the couple with hope for the future of their marriage. With the loss, a woman may feel pressured by herself or others to try to get pregnant again quickly without allowing adequate time for grief.

---

[57]Worden (2002: 1278–128).
[58]I have experienced both losses and found them very painful.
[59]Archer (1999: 191).

The steps involving a pregnancy are:[60]

- Planning, confirming and accepting the pregnancy.

- Feeling the fetal movement and accepting the fetus as an individual.

- Giving birth.

- Hearing and seeing, touching and holding, and caring for the infant.

Clearly the major part of the attachment process is completed before birth, thus highlighting the pain of the loss. Ideally one would like to help the mother to complete the last step in various ways, but counseling usually occurs some time later when grief has become a problem. Typical grief symptoms can include emptiness, body tension, sadness, anger, guilt, depression, sense of failure, preoccupation with thoughts of the baby, having a desire to be left alone, or not wanting to be alone. There may also be an element of self-blame (e.g., "Was there something I shouldn't have done?") and some blame may be directed toward the husband. The loss can therefore cause distance and communication problems between husband and wife. The husband needs to be especially sensitive to his wife's needs at this time. Friends may not be very helpful so that any inappropriate comments need to be ignored.

Mothers often remember the specific details surrounding the loss for many years, and may be angry with the medical caregivers at the time, even blaming them for lack of care. Helping to find a healthy outlet for anger might be a necessary task for the therapist. One of the problems is that often couples have very few tangible reminders of the baby to help them memorialize the loss. Therapists can encourage memorialization in various ways including putting together a keepsake box of the child with any memorabilia, planting a flower garden or tree in the child's name, giving Christmas gifts to the less fortunate in the name of the deceased infant, and celebrating the birthday of the child. The couple's environment may need to be reassessed, for example, what to do about baby clothes and a bedroom decorated as a nursery. An important question for the couple might be when should they try for another child; grief needs to be fully experienced first.

Other siblings should not be forgotten as they will be aware that something is not right with their parents. They need adequate information even though the loss is invisible, as they may blame the loss on their parents, on themselves, or wonder about their own safety. Also some aftercare in hospital for the mother might be needed. Children need to know that a miscarriage is a common and normal experience and need to be kept informed so that they don't feel left out or confused. If there is a keepsake box, the children might like to contribute something too as a memento, or help plant a tree. They need to know how a parent is feeling and that it is is okay to cry. What the child needs to be told will depend on the age of the child (see Section 11.3.4 above).[61]

11.4.2   Sudden Infant Death Syndrome

Sudden infant death syndrome (SIDS) or "cot death" is not uncommon. It is very distressing as it occurs without warning and for no apparent reason so that guilt

[60]Humphrey and Zimpfer (1996: 143).
[61]For a helpful book see Miller-Clendon (2003).

is usually keenly felt by the parents with sometimes irrational blaming between spouses. As Worden notes,[62] older siblings may have resented the arrival of the baby and may now experience guilt and remorse. Any grandparents may need support. There can also be a communication breakdown between husband and wife, especially as their responses to grief may be very different. Sexual relations may be suspended because of the fear of pregnancy and a repeat of the experience. Some of the comments in the previous section also apply here as well as the last paragraph of Section 11.3.5 on sudden death.

11.4.3   Loss of a Child

The loss of one's child is generally regarded as the most difficult loss to bear,[63] especially if an only child.[64] This is particularly poignant in a culture where one child is the norm. I have already mentioned the death of a baby through a prenatal death or SIDS and its consequent effect. However, for some, the intensity of the grief increases with the age of the child, even into adulthood.

The death of one's child is so unsettling because it is contrary to the accepted idea that children live on after us. It may also have the aspect that the child will not be there to support them in their old age. As Johnson comments, "It brings to the fore ultimate issues of powerlessness, guilt, and the fact that as parents they were unable to protect their own child."[65] The death also carries with it the loss of a potential future that can continue to haunt parents for the rest of their life, especially at special times such as birthdays and anniversaries.

Guilt is a common emotion, as with all deaths of a loved one. However, Miles and Demi suggest five types of guilt that bereaved parents may experience.[66]

1. *Cultural guilt.* Society expects parents to look after their children.

2. *Causal guilt.* This can arise if there was any real or perceived negligence, or if the death was due to some inherited problem.

3. *Moral guilt.* The death may be seen as a punishment for some previous misdemeanor (e.g., an abortion).

4. *Survival guilt.* The question asked is "Why am I alive and not my child?" This is particularly relevant if the family had an accident with the child dying and the parents surviving.

5. *Recovery guilt.* If I move on happily with my life I am dishonoring the memory of my dead child.

It is important that other siblings are not ignored or overprotected. My comments about childhood grief in Section 11.3.4 apply here. Sometimes another sibling becomes a substitute for the lost child, even to the extent of using a similar or identical name.[67] When this happens, the mother might not be able to fully let go of

---

[62]See Worden (2002: 129–131).
[63]Archer (1999: 199).
[64]For helpful histories relating to the death of a child (including adult children) see Finkbeiner (1996).
[65]Johnson (1987: xiii).
[66]Miles and Demi (1991).
[67]Worden (2002: 153).

the dead child and let the "substitute" sibling develop his or her own potential and innate abilities. This can be even more problematical if the sibling is of opposite sex to the dead child so that a girl is encouraged to do boy's activities, or vice versa. It is therefore important that the couple delay having another child until the grief has been worked through.

11.4.4 Abortion and Grief

The internet can be a good source of information on abortion and its after-effects.[68] Abortion rates in some countries are very high and a substantial proportion of women suffer various psychological symptoms after an abortion.[69] They can also experience a post traumatic stress disorder and, when it is related to abortion, it is called Post Abortion Syndrome (PAS).[70] Studies show that women with mental health issues have more psychiatric problems after an abortion than those without such issues.

Often the initial feeling after an abortion is of relief, but this can fade and be followed by uncomfortable emotions and thoughts (e.g., regret, guilt, anger at self or others, anxiety, depression, sense of loss, heartache, and thinking of the baby often, with some of these occurring at different times) with possibly physical problems.[71] The two main defense mechanisms for coping with these emotions are repression and denial so that the woman might try to rationalize away her thoughts and feelings instead of facing them. However, it should be realized that grief is a normal outcome from an abortion because there is a loss.

With pregnancy, the mother's body undergoes changes and her body and mind begin to prepare for the birth. Abortion stops this process and disturbs the mother's mental state. If she lost the baby through an accident or miscarriage, then everyone would expect her to grieve so that it is not surprising that a sense of loss and the resulting grief will still occur after an abortion, even though the loss was caused by the mother. The woman may be told by various people that she shouldn't grieve, which may exacerbate her problem. She may be unable to prevent an emotional crisis surfacing immediately or she may be able to avoid the problem for typically between two and five years, though for some the crisis may occur twenty or thirty years later.[72] Often this delayed reaction is triggered by some event such as her or a close friend having a baby or some life-changing event like finding out that she is sterile.

If a woman comes for counseling for some other issue, the therapist may find that there might have been an unmourned abortion (or more) in the past. If she admits there is some merit in discussing her abortion(s) then she could be asked to relate how she became pregnant and describe her thoughts and feelings as the embryo grew. The therapist can check whether she personified the embryo and used any words of attachment (e.g., as "my baby"), and then find out why she decided to

---

[68]See, for example, http://www.abortionfacts.com and
http://www.unfairchoice.info/pblresearch.htm (both accessed November 2010).
[69]See also www.afterabortion.org/psychol.html (accessed November 2010).
[70]The existence of such a disorder has been denied by some researchers; for some aspects of the debate see, for example, http://www.abortionfacts.com/PAS/PAS.asp (accessed November 2010).
[71]For a list of possible physical problems see also www.afterabortion.org/physica.html (accessed November 2010).
[72]This is similar to the delay experienced with a post-traumatic stress syndrome.

have the abortion. Speckhard and Rue say that "This line of questioning typically begins to uncover the dual thought process of attachment and denial of attachment to the fetal child."[73]

Some questions that a therapist might ask a female client are:

- What was her life like for her before the abortion?
- What were her beliefs and opinions about human life and abortion?
- What sort of relationship did she have with the father of her child? Was she still with him or have contact with him?
- How did she find out she was pregnant? How many weeks into the pregnancy?
- What were her first reactions and later thoughts and feelings?
- Whom did she she tell and what were their reactions and opinions?
- Did she get any counseling? What information was she given?
- How did she make the decision to abort?
- Afterwards, how did she cope in each area of her life?
- How did others respond to her action?
- What was her response (e.g., withdraw, keep it secret, suppress her emotions, have angry spells, bury herself in activities)?

The role of the therapist is to encourage the woman to make a new start to rebuilding her life. A woman will have an abortion for a variety of reasons; these can be explored, as mentioned above. The woman may have been pressured by others (e.g., the boyfriend or parents) or was unable to support a baby for a number of reasons (e.g., being a girl still at school); the nature of her reasons will probably affect how well she recovers from the abortion. She needs to realize that her grief is normal and it should be accepted and worked through, as with any other loss.

The woman may be plagued by remorse for making what she now believes was the wrong decision. At this stage, some cognitive therapy may be needed to help her see that she made the best decision she could make at the time and she should not be too hard on herself. It may be that she was not only pressured or talked into it by others, but inadequate information may have been given to her about any physical and emotional complications that might arise from the abortion or what the abortion would do to the fetus. Forgiving those she may feel misled her whether it be friends, family, or health professionals is important because they thought they were doing the best for her. She may be very angry with them and may need a safe place to express her anger. She will need to accept responsibility for her part in the abortion and forgive herself. If she is religious, she may need to ask God for forgiveness and accept the fact that God is willing to forgive her.

A woman may come to counseling to discuss the pros and cons of having an abortion. The above information can also be used in this context to go through all the pros and cons, as well as considering the risks of after-effects. Recent research

[73]Speckhard and Rue (1993: 23).

suggests that abortion can substantially increase the risk of breast cancer and it is important for the client to be fully informed of all aspects.

Father's Role

The father should not be forgotten in this discussion. He may have been involved in one of several ways:[74]

1. He encouraged or supported the woman to choose abortion.

2. He pressured her to abort.

3. He abandoned her to make the decision alone.

4. He passively left the decision to her.

5. He unsuccessfully opposed the abortion.

6. He learned about it after it happened.

Whatever his role was in the decision, his natural role as a protecting father was denied. In most countries men have no legal rights concerning abortion and, under such laws, their opinion doesn't count. Although his initial reaction to the abortion may have been relief, other unsettling emotions may surface soon afterwards such as anger, resentment, guilt, grief, and a sense of emptiness. He may not realize that his emotions are the direct result of an abortion experience, and he may be in denial about the experience. Some societies (including North Americans) see any sign of emotion as a weakness so that many men hide their true feelings even though they are hurting; their relationships, jobs, families, and responsibilities then suffer. Feelings often come out in destructive behaviors such excessive drinking, drug use, depression, suicidal feelings, risk taking, or maybe running from relationship to relationship unable to make commitments.

A therapist can encourage a male client to forgive the mother if he is angry with her, forgive himself for his part (if he is religious he may need to ask God for forgiveness first), come out of any denial, grieve for the little one no longer living, and grieve for those affected by the loss (e.g., grandparents). He also needs to be there for his partner who will also be hurting and may suffer from the post-abortion syndrome described above.

11.5 JOB LOSS

11.5.1 Introduction

In the past, a job loss generally occurred through being fired, through lack of work being available, or through a company going out of business. Today job loss can also occur through a "down-sizing" of a business in an effort to be more efficient, cut expenses, and increase profits. Job security has become a thing of the past and people can expect several job or career changes in their lives. This uncertainty can add to job stress.

---

[74]http://www.abortionfacts.com/literature/literature_9411FN.asp (accessed November 2010).

As with any other loss, a job loss leads to grief. The level of the grief will depend on a number of factors depending on, for example, the nature and duration of the job, one's age, one's family situation, and how the job loss was notified. People who have dedicated themselves to a particular job for many years are going to be very shocked if they are told tersely and unceremoniously that they are no longer needed. Fortunately there has been a trend by some businesses to try and soften the blow by providing, for example, a transition period beginning with advance notification of job termination and ending with the actual termination. On the positive side it may involve such things as job retraining and outplacement by the company, but the downside is that it only delays the "death sentence" and there can be anticipatory grief. Even if a person finds a new job before unemployment begins, it still means a new environment, new people, and sometimes a relocation. Frequently the change involves a loss of status with a pay cut, a loss of benefits, and a drop to the bottom of the seniority ladder. Any job loss is very much associated with failure. Often people have trouble finding another job, even if there is a transition period.

11.5.2   Grief Process

It has been suggested that the job-loss grief process goes through the various stages of grief like those proposed by Kűbler-Ross (1978) and described in Section 11.2.2 above. For example there is the initial shock and possibly denial, anger towards the company or management (or redirected at friends and family), bargaining with God over another job (not everyone goes through this), depression, and acceptance (getting on with life).[75] There may be concerns about one's financial future, about the possibility of having to move (and possibly uprooting any children), and about what friends will think of one's unemployment status.

Counseling for Job Loss

In counseling a person who is having difficulty coping with the loss, it is helpful if the person is able to be open about what has happened and be able to say, "I lost my job." People are sympathetic, as many have had a similar experience, and it is helpful to be part of a support group. Emotions (e.g., anger, fear, and guilt) need to be processed, for example, any guilt at perhaps letting down one's family or spouse, even if not at fault in any way, needs to be resolved. Renewing and deepening relationships can be a source of strength. After getting over the numbness of what has happened, depression, fear of failure, or embarrassment from being jobless may hinder people from getting on and looking for another job. They may also find it difficult to cope with a loss of routine and loss of lifestyle because of financial restrictions (e.g., having to go on to an unemployment benefit). There may be stress-related problems, family conflicts, and a tendency to blame others. Counseling can follow along similar lines to dealing with a bereaved person (e.g., allowing a person to grieve and to process emotions).

11.5.3   Finding a New Job

To help a client find a new job, a therapist might assume the role of job coach by listening to ideas and helping to identify skills and interests (e.g., using a mind map,

---

[75]See part 3 of http://www.joblossguide.com/ (accessed November 2010).

discussing retraining), by helping with résumés (CVs),[76] practicing interviews,[77] teaching communication skills, and helping with job search strategies (e.g., door knocking; making phone calls; viewing advertisements; and listing companies, organizations, and agencies within driving distance).

It is helpful for the client to have a vision about what the future might be. While looking for a job a client can be helped to set out a (temporary) daily routine that includes exercise to keep the mind focused and promote a feeling of usefulness, and to not give up but persevere with the job search. Helping others can divert one's focus away from one's own problems. Finally, it is important to go into a job with the aim of doing a little more than one has to.

11.6   UNRESOLVED GRIEF FOR A LOVED ONE

Unresolved grief, extreme grief, complicated grief, and other terms, are all used to described grief that can be unhealthy and is not considered normal. This a difficult topic and the client may need to be referred on, though the topic may surface during counseling for other issues. Because grief experiences are all so different, the subject has been long debated as it is not clear what "normal" means. An obvious sign of unresolved grief is a prolonged sense of mourning where a person seems to be stuck and unable to function, plan, and move on with their life. It may manifest itself as eating or sleeping disorders, severe depression, despair, uncharacteristically engaging in reckless behavior such as substance abuse, heavy drinking or promiscuity, or talking about death and loss frequently. Alternatively, there may be a steadfast refusal to talk about death or loss, or to engage in any conversation about the person who has died.

When people are grieving, it is common for them to wish that the deceased was still alive and long for their presence. As everything in their lives is a reminder of the person who has gone, it is therefore not unreasonable for a mourner to go on a temporary retreat from reality because reality is too painful.[78] Also, their staying in grief can help avoid the unknown and it can bring secondary rewards in terms of, for example, attention and sympathy from family and friends. It can also avoid the fear that if they stop longing for the one they have lost, they will stop loving them. However, they do need to move on eventually and learn new ways of living without the loved one. If the mourner becomes stuck so that their longing for the presence of the deceased becomes irrational and their behavior becomes rigid and ritualistic, then the grief is no longer "normal" and the mourner is at risk. Also unresolved grief can be due to unfinished or repressed business from past losses that need to be addressed before the current loss can be dealt with. A suicide, especially of a child, can lead to unresolved grief.

Other clues[79] that suggest unresolved grief are the client still experiencing intense renewed grief when discussing the dead person, or having an intense reaction to a relatively minor crisis such as weeping when they break a dish or learn of someone else's loss. Also, taking many years to clear out the belongings or special objects of the dead person is another sign. Some of the symptoms experienced by the deceased

---

[76]The internet is a good source for advice on writing a résumé (curriculum vitae).
[77]See, for example, "How to succeed at interview" on the internet.
[78]Attig (1996: 34–37).
[79]See for example Worden (1992: 95–98).

before death may be presented by the client, who may also have a compulsion to imitate the dead person. A false sense of euphoria after the death or an unaccountable sadness occurring at a certain time of the year may also be clues. DSM-IV list a number of symptoms defining unresolved grief, some of which are similar to those of a major depression, like a morbid preoccupation with worthlessness, a marked psychomotor retardation, and a prolonged and functional impairment.

Worden[80] lists five factors regarding failure to grieve: relational (e.g., ambivalent or narcissistic relationship with the deceased); circumstantial (e.g., uncertainties regarding the death or having multiple losses); historical (e.g., past complicated losses such as the early loss of a parent); personality (e.g., how one copes, or how well one is integrated); and social (e.g., a socially unspeakable death or lack of support systems). He links these factors to his four steps outlined in Section 11.2.2 under "Models for Moving Forward." Rando[81] maintains that there is complicated mourning when there is some shortcoming in at least one of her six 'R' processes also defined in Section 11.2.2. Based on DSM-IV, she organizes syndromes under three headings:

Problems in Expression. (Absent, delayed, or inhibited mourning.) This can arise because of the presence of both positive and negative aspects leading to ambivalence about the deceased. Worden[82] also gives some possible reasons for delayed grief reactions such as being overwhelmed by the magnitude of the loss at the time, as with a suicide or multiple losses (e.g., all of one's family killed in a car accident or in a natural disaster). Under this topic we can include what Worden calls "masked" grief reaction when it is masked as a physical or psychiatric symptom.

Skewed Aspects. (Distorted, conflicted, or unanticipated mourning.) In the case of distorted or conflicted mourning, the degree of ambivalence is now much stronger with, for example, guilt and anger playing a major role. Unanticipated mourning can occur when a death happens unexpectedly, as in the case of an accident or natural disaster, leaving the bereaved person totally unprepared for the loss.

Problems with Closure. (Chronic mourning.) Here the grief is very intense and continues to last much longer than one might expect.

Under each syndrome Rando determines a problem area in one of the 'R' processes. For example, delayed mourning could be linked to an inability to react to separation, the second R process. Both Worden and Rando believe that in using their respective models it is essential to locate the complication at each stage and work through it before moving on to the next stage.

In counseling for unresolved grief, Worden[83] suggests the following helpful procedures.

- Revive the (positive and negative) memories of the deceased with an emphasis on the positive memories.

[80]Worden (2002: chapter 4).
[81]Rando (1993: 149).
[82]Worden (2002: 91).
[83]Worden (2002: 104–110).

- Check which of the four tasks listed under "Models for Grieving" in Section 11.2.2 was not completed.

- Deal with the affect or lack of it stimulated by the memories.

- Explore and defuse symbolic objects that a survivor uses to externally maintain an obsessive relationship with the deceased (e.g., a keepsake or a special photograph).

- Encourage an acknowledgment of the finality of the loss.

- Deal with the fantasy of ending grieving, for example, "What would you lose in giving up your grief?"

- Help the client say a final goodbye (i.e., exploring what this means and, if necessary, doing it gradually using, say, "Goodbye for now.")

11.7   BIBLICAL VIEWPOINT

11.7.1   Story of Job

The Bible tells an interesting story about a man called Job. He was described by God as an upright and blameless man who feared God and avoided evil, yet he lost everything—his family, servants, possessions, and his health. His loss seemed unfair and unreasonable, and his grief so unbearable that he wanted to die. He spends thirty-seven chapters arguing with his friends and asking some hard questions about why God allowed such terrible things to happen to him. In chapter thirty-eight God appears on the scene and compares Job's credentials with almighty God's credentials. God does not answer Job's questions but simply points out that God is sovereign. In grief counseling there are few answers, if any, as no one can fathom the ways of God.[84] Death is a mystery. All one can do is trust God even when the most appalling things happen.

11.7.2   Death Not the End

On a more positive note, the Bible has a lot to say about death not being the end.[85] Although God restored everything that Job lost, the New Testament teaches that one often has to to wait for the next life for restoration and justice. God is described as being close to those who mourn,[86] though at times it may not seem like it. David experienced the pain of grief[87] that enabled him to write such powerful psalms out of the depth of his experience.[88] Jesus experienced sorrow[89] and is the great burden bearer.[90] Ultimately sorrow and pain will be defeated.[91]

[84]Isaiah 55: 9.
[85]For example, John 3:16, 5:25, 8:51, 11:25–26, 14:3; Romans 8:38–39; I Corinthians 15; Psalms 23:4, 33:18–19, 49:15; and 1 Thessalonians 4:13–14.
[86]Psalms 30:11–12, 34:18, 147:3; Isaiah 53:4, 61:1–3; and Matthew 5:4.
[87]See Psalms 6:6.
[88]For a good insight into the role of emotions in the Psalms see Allender and Longman (1994).
[89]Matthew 11:35, 26:38.
[90]Matthew 11: 28–30.
[91]Revelation 21:4.

11.7.3 Forgiveness

I want to say a few words about forgiveness[92] and grief. Clients may need to forgive God,[93] forgive others, and forgive themselves in order to move on. For example, a client may have great difficulty in forgiving oneself for an abortion, but he or she needs to remember that God is a forgiving God. Some people in the Bible made terrible mistakes involving the death of people, for example Moses and an Egyptian, David and Uriah (the husband of Bathsheba), and Paul and martyred Christians, yet God was still able to forgive and use such people for divine purposes.[94]

---

[92]See Section 2.5.5.
[93]See Section 3.5.
[94]For a pro-life biblical view of abortion see http://www.abortionfacts.com/abortion/bible.asp (accessed October 2010).

CHAPTER 12

ADDICTIONS: GENERAL

12.1 INTRODUCTION

One of the difficulties that a therapist may face in dealing with addictions is deciding the difference between "normal" and "addictive behavior." How people behave may be regarded as a continuum of behavior so that where the line is drawn between "normal" and "abnormal" can be problematical; it can be regarded as a statistical problem and it depends on what is measured and what population of people is under consideration. For example, the normal range of height for a pygmy is very different from other populations. Thus addiction can be viewed very differently in some cultures so that we need to be very careful about attaching addiction labels to people. It may depend on whether the behavior of a client is hurting the client or those associated with the client such as family and friends. What may be regarded as addictive behavior for one person may be regarded as coping behavior for someone else.[1] It should be noted that some people overcome their addictions "naturally," that is without outside help or treatment.

In this chapter we look at some general methods of counseling for addictions. Further ideas are given in the next two chapters on specific addictive substances and behavioral addictions. Although addictions are very different, many of them can be handled by similar techniques including some of the many addictions not

---

[1]This is similar to what Keane (2002) says in her controversial and thought provoking comments about some traditional views of addiction.

included in this book. This chapter should be read first before looking at specific addictions in the next two chapters.

12.2   THE NATURE OF ADDICTION

12.2.1   Definition

There are various definitions of addiction in the literature such as an "overpowering, repetitive, excessive need exists for some substance, object, feeling, act, milieu, or personal interaction."[2] Another definition is, "A pathological relationship to any mood-altering experience that has life-damaging consequences."[3] The difficulty with most definitions is that they do not distinguish between addictive behavior and compulsive behavior. It can be argued that addiction is about gaining pleasure and comfort or pain avoidance so I decided to put some compulsive type disorders into a separate chapter, namely Chapter 8, instead of into my addiction and anxiety disorder chapters.[4]

The term "addiction" is derived from the Latin verb *addicere* meaning "to give assent, to assign or surrender." The word "dependence" is used instead of "addiction" in DSM-IV.[5] Addictive behavior typically begins to take priority over all other life issues, and addicts may sometimes deny their addiction (though, once again, one needs to be cautious about using labels). Addicts tend to develop a tolerance to their addiction so that the addictive activities tend to grow to compensate.

12.2.2   Substance and Behavioral Addictions

Addictions can be divided into substance addictions and behavioral (process) addictions. However, there is a sense in which they are all substance addictions in that in process addictions the brain produces certain substances, namely neurotransmitters such as adrenaline and dopamine, to which a person can become addicted.[6] Even a hug can cause a rise in dopamine, which is produced in the pleasure centre of the brain. For example, some people can become addicted to the "buzz" of having an illicit affair. Also, substance addictions may have a behavioral component, for example in smoking the process of lighting up can be part of the addiction.

There is one important factor that impinges on substance addictions, namely psychological dependence, which explains the persistence of an addiction even when there are no unpleasant effects on withdrawal (e.g., cocaine). The key is the memory as the addict remembers the reinforcing effect of the addictive substance and this can be enough to continue the addiction. In a similar way the memory is a powerful contributing dimension to process addictions. Ritual, an important factor relating to memory, is discussed below.

[2]Hart (1990: 17).
[3]Bradshaw (2005: 35).
[4]I am grateful to Doug Sellman, Professor of Psychiatry and Addiction Medicine at Otago University, New Zealand, for drawing my attention to this problem of classification.
[5]Maddux and Desmond (2000). In this editorial the authors have an interesting historical discussion and argue for "addiction" to be used on the grounds that it more clearly reflects the behavioral aspect.
[6]See Section 1.2.1.

12.2.3   Crossover Effects

It should be noted that there are "crossover" effects of different addictions. For example it is well-known that if you are trying to give up smoking you should not continue to drink strong coffee as nicotine and caffeine both stimulate the same part of the brain: one substance will maintain an addiction to the other even if the other is removed. Hart[7] believes that the same crossover effect can occur with process addictions, for example, excessive TV watching and overeating. It is therefore not uncommon for a person to have multiple addictions or even conquer one addiction but then move on to another.

12.2.4   Goals and Loss of Control

Addictions are about loss of control. The first basic premise of self-regulation theory and its central theme of self-control[8] is that people adapt their behavior to their goals;[9] inappropriate goals can lead to a loss of self-control of emotions and behavior. Some negative aspects associated with goals are:[10]

- failing to set goals needed for well-being

- failing to achieve attainable goals

- setting unattainable goals

- goals too easily attained with consequent boredom or emptiness

- frustration at the delay and effort in achieving goals

An approach to goal setting, with particular reference to gambling, is discussed in Section 14.2.4. The methodology there can be used more generally.

12.3   DIAGNOSIS OF SUBSTANCE ADDICTIONS

The British based ICD-10 criterion (the WHO International Classification of Diseases) for a positive diagnosis of substance dependence is that at least three of the following occur:

1. A strong desire or sense of compulsion to take the substance.

2. Impaired capacity to control its use.

3. Withdrawal symptoms if stopped.

4. Evidence of tolerance.

5. Preoccupation with substance use and decreased interest in other activities.

6. Persistent use despite clear evidence of harmful consequences.

[7] Hart (1990: 15).
[8] Carver and Scheier (1998).
[9] See Section 2.3.2 on goal setting.
[10] Ciarrocchi (2002: 16).

Apart from some subtle differences, this is similar to the American DSM-IV criterion of at least three of the following:

1. Evidence of tolerance (a need for increasing amounts of the substance to achieve the desired effect).

2. Withdrawal symptoms if stopped.

3. Taking the substance in larger amounts or over a longer period than intended.

4. A persistent desire or unsuccessful efforts to control use.

5. A lot of time spent getting, using, and recovering from the effects of the substance.

6. Important social, occupational or recreational activities are given up or reduced because of substance use.

7. Use is continued despite recognition that a physical or psychological problem is caused or exacerbated by the substance.

Some forms of substance abuse and dependence seem to run in families; and this may be the result of a genetic predisposition, environmental influences including conditional learning, or a combination of both.

There is a wide range of questionnaires for assessing the level of various addictions and some of these are mentioned in the next chapter under specific addictions. However, in addition to the internet, a useful reference is Marlatt and Donovan (2005). Some helpful insights on the psychology of addiction are given by Nakken:[11] these are discussed in the next section.

12.4   THE AIM OF AN ADDICTION

The aim of the addiction is to produce a desired mood change, state of intoxication or trance state in order for the addict to cope with life's problems and to obtain emotional fulfillment or pain avoidance. Addicts are attracted to certain types of mood changes or highs such as arousal, satiation, and fantasy.

> Arousal makes the addict believe they can achieve happiness, safety and fulfillment. It also gives the addict the feeling of power while it subtly drains away all power. To get more power, addicts return to the object or event that provides the arousal and eventually become dependent on it.[12]

A satiation high gives the addict a feeling of being so good that it can numb the sensations of pain and distress—a form of medication and self-nurturing. A trance state is particularly useful for describing process addictions such as gambling, spending, and sexual acting out. What happens is that the trance allows the addict to have a temporary detachment from the pain, guilt, and shame they feel. In essence, addiction is a relationship with an object or event with the consequence that relationships with people change, so that they get treated as objects also. However, people around addicts get tired of being treated this way. Addicts

[11]Nakken (1996).
[12]Nakken(1996: 3).

also treat themselves as objects and tend not to take adequate care of themselves. Objects are predictable and so is the associated mood change, being more reliable than any friend; for the addict the object comes first, people second.

The timing, setting, and anticipation of the addictive behavior are an important part of the process. The longer addicts wait, the more they experience the affects of delayed gratification and the more self-nurturing it feels.

One phase of addiction is "acting out" when the addict engages in addictive behavior or addictive mental obsessions to create certain feelings, and be nurtured and have their needs for intimacy met. Addiction follows a logical progression but it is based on "emotional logic," not intellectual logic. Emotional logic can be summed up in the words "I want what I want and I want it now." This creates an internal tension—for example the tension of not gambling versus betting on a "sure thing."

Addictions can form at times of loss, such as retirement or loss of friends. It is also a process of buying into false and empty promises: the false promise of relief, the false promise of emotional security, the false sense of fulfillment, and the false sense of intimacy with the world. Intensity gets confused with intimacy. Acting out is a very intense experience for addicts as it involves going against themselves.

Another way of viewing an addiction is to reframe it as a means of coping with an intolerable kind of stress so that the "problem" is also a "solution." The client is now coping instead of being out of control (although the addiction provides a false sense of control). This does not change the situation, but it provides an opportunity for the therapist and client to rewrite the story so that a glass that is half empty becomes a glass that is half full.

12.5   CATEGORIES OF ADDICTION

It appears that human beings have the propensity to be addicted to almost any behavior, for example shopping, fishing, jogging, reading, gossip, and even religious activities, as well as the more well-known ones such as gambling, pornography, sex, shop-lifting, workaholism, and so forth. Hart[13] describes four classes of addictions:

- addictions that stimulate
- addictions that tranquilize
- addictions that serve some psychological need
- addictions that satisfy unique appetites

Underneath process addictions that stimulate is adrenaline, and too much of this eventually causes undue stress and physical breakdown. The human body can also produce its own tranquilizers; for example the "runner's high" is due to the production of endorphins. The psychological need to succeed or be accepted can lead to workaholism. We are all unique with our own particular likes and dislikes that can lead to very specific addictions. However, in spite of how an addiction arises, people must ultimately take responsibility for their addictions.

[13]Hart (1990).

Addictive substances tend to be either stimulants or sedatives. Stimulants provide positive reinforcement and produce a high, with well-known examples being caffeine, cocaine, "ecstasy," and methamphetamines. Sedatives produce a negative reinforcement and alleviate distress and anxiety, thus returning a person to a normal state. For process addictions, the two main effects can be described as excitement (stimulation) and tension reducing. Unfortunately excitement does not necessarily mean satisfaction! Many addictions reduce tension but then follows shame with more tension, and so the cycle continues. Sexual addiction creates a cycle of creating and reducing tension.

12.6   ADDICTION MODELS

12.6.1   Addictive Personality

The first question a therapist might ask is whether there exists an addictive personality style. Hart[14] asks two related questions: (1.) Are certain individuals prone to develop certain addictions? (2.) Is there a personality style common to all addictions? In the case of substance addiction, personality is one of three possible factors along with the environment and the particular substance. With regard to the first question, people with addictions tend to have certain personality traits such as impulsive behavior, anti-social behavior, negativity, excitement or sensation seeking, feeling alienated from society, being nonconformist, being impatient with delayed gratification, and having a sense of heightened stress. They may exhibit certain behaviors when coming to counseling such as being anxious, depressed, impatient, angry, or arrogant.

With regard to the second question on personality style the answer appears to be no at present as there seems to be no single set of psychological characteristics that embrace all addictions. The answer will be related to brain chemistry.

12.6.2   The Addictive Self

Nakken (1996) proposed a model consisting of three stages of addiction: internal change, lifestyle change, and life breakdown. The first stage begins with mood changes. The initial experiences are often very enjoyable and very intense. A cycle is set up of pain, need to act out, act out and feel better, pain from acting out and so on. When the addict acts out they are saying to themselves one or more of the following:

- I don't really need people.

- I don't have to face anything I don't want to.

- I'm afraid to face life and my problems.

- Objects and events are more important than people.

- I can do anything I want, whenever I want, no matter whom it hurts.

[14]Hart (1990: 50).

The addict's personality begins to change and shame is produced as a by-product, though in the beginning it may be experienced as a general uneasiness. Shame creates a loss of self-respect, self-esteem, self-discipline, and so forth. The addictive personality then starts to take over from the Self, and Self and Addict fight for control as follows:

- The Addict develops its own way of feeling.

- The Self disapproves of the Addict's beliefs, but enjoys the mood change.

- The Addict develops its own way of thinking.

- The Self regularly fights and argues with the Addict, but loses.

- The Addict develops its own way of behaving.

- The Self makes promises to control the Addict, uses willpower to control the Addict, but eventually becomes dependent on the Addict's personality.

The Addict side begins to develop its own way of feeling, thinking, and behaving. When people act out, they get high and feel different, and this changes their thought patterns. Any feeling that creates discomfort becomes a signal to act out. For example, when a food addict feels sadness, the Addict will sense this sadness and interpret it not as real feeling, but as a clue about food. Thus the person's feelings become mental obsessions. By choosing this interpretation of a feeling, the person gets an illusion of control. Addicts chase control to obtain peace and happiness. However, "it's human to be imperfect and powerless, and chasing the illusion of control is really running away from the reality of being human."[15]

When a person starts to internally question what is happening, addictive logic of denial begins to develop, and the addictive relationship is denied, for example, "I only drink like this occasionally," or addictive logic says, "It is too big to overcome." Normal logic tells us it's not right to hurt one's Self; addictive logic says it is all right to hurt one's Self because Self is not important, only the mood change is important. This logic slowly develops into a belief system that becomes more complex and rigid, locking one in but keeping people out who might threaten the addictive relationship.

Returning to the three-stage model discussed at the beginning of this section, we find in Stage 1 that the person behaves mainly within socially acceptable limits. However, in Stage 2 a behavioral dependency starts to develop and the addict becomes dependent on the addictive personality and not on the mood change or the object or the event. The addictive belief system becomes ritualistic and develops into a lifestyle. Lying, blaming others, and withdrawal from others can become a regular occurrence. The addicts' world becomes secretive and goes "underground." They make sense of their behavior through denial, repression, lies, rationalizations, and so forth.

Rituals are important as they link us to our beliefs and values and connect us with like-minded people; they also bring comfort when life is difficult. The ritual strengthens our ties to whatever it represents, for example, family birthdays. The same is true with addicts; the ritual supports the addictive process, enhances the

[15]Nakken (1996: 33).

mood shift, and reinforces the addiction. Also addicts have their own particular rituals. When facing a choice, the addict gets tense: Do I act out or not? This tension can go on for a very long time until released by the addictive ritual and there is peace for the moment. Healthy rituals bind us to others while addictive rituals isolate us from others. As a result, addictive rituals usually take place alone or within a group whose members have no real caring connection with each other except perhaps with their common form of acting out. Addictive relationships are very superficial and very private. The addict likes to be alone or with other addicts who know, accept, and are not scared by his or her rites of addiction. It is important for recovering people to understand that their Addict has preferred ways of acting out and that there are certain things that need to be avoided.

Addicts develop "people" problems as their attachment is to an object or event, which conveniently can't ask questions. They begin to manipulate other people and treat them as objects. People are seen as nosy, and their concern becomes an obstacle. The addicts' mistrust of others grows and they begin to have more confidence in their ability to manipulate others. However, the addict's Self feels more shameful, lost, and isolated. Addicts feel like strangers within themselves. Pain and anger fuel the addictive process and are major byproducts of addiction and those who surround them. As with other addictions, addicts also build up a tolerance so that they need to act out more frequently and more dangerously. More and more energy needs to be redirected towards the addiction and there is a constant battle between Self and Addict. A spiritual deadening takes place, where spiritual involves being connected in a meaningful way to the world and being able to extract meaning from one's experiences.

At Stage III the addictive personality is in total control and the addict's life begins to break down. Acting out no longer produces much pleasure, addictive logic stops making sense any more, coping breaks down, and interacting breaks down. Addicts may totally withdraw, yet deep within they crave connection with others. They seem to be pushing people away, but get upset if the people withdraw. Physical signs of breakdown become evident and there may be thoughts of suicide.

12.7 COUNSELING METHODS

12.7.1 Some General Comments

When addictive clients come for counseling they usually have some idea that something is not right and are initially not prepared admit their addiction. However, an occasion may arise in general counseling that indicates that the client has an addiction and they are in denial of it. The task of the therapist is to then help the client admit their denial and addiction at some stage of their therapy.

In counseling for an addiction, it is important to establish the frequency, intensity, duration, and history of addictive behavior. It will help the therapist to determine how far down the track the addiction has progressed. Some life history will also be helpful as sometimes the beginning of an addiction can be traced to some earlier traumatic event. It can also be helpful for clients to describe a typical day (week) with regard to their involvement with their addiction. In Section 13.3.3 there is a helpful and memorable check list for the therapist that can be used quite generally to determine the extent and effect of an addiction. While its focus is drug addiction, it is still a useful tool.

Nakken suggests that it is helpful to admit the presence of an addictive personality and the dual personalities of Self and Addict. The "practicing addict does not focus on the Self but perpetuates the fight between the Self and the Addict within. The two are always in conflict, struggling for supremacy, with the Addict invariably winning out."[16] The addict needs to understand and listen for addictive logic and then listen and believe in one's Self, not one's Addict. For example, the Addict might say, "If you act out now you will feel much better" whereas Self might say, "Feeling better is only temporary and in the long run you will feel worse."

It is important to help a client understand as much as possible about the nature of his or her addiction. For example, is the addiction maintained through excitement seeking, tension reduction, or both? Hart suggests that excitement seekers should concentrate on learning to be content with ordinary activities and appreciate the "little" pleasures of life. It also means learning how to become accustomed to a life with less arousal. Tension reducers need to learn how to identify painful emotions, face them head-on, and be aware of any denial tendencies. The challenge is how to turn these suggestions into strategies. A key aspect is the role of trigger mechanisms that tend to set off the addictive behavior. There are certain states that may trigger addictive behavior, for example, when hungry, angry, lonely or tired (acronym HALT). Hart adds several more such as anxiety, isolation, boredom, depression, crises, sense of failure, unmet sexual needs, criticism, and selfish needs. Learning how to avoid triggers or finding alternative ways to respond will be discussed with respect to particular addictions in the next two chapters.

The counseling approach used will depend on the type of addiction. There are several psychotherapies that can be effectively used generally. A cognitive behavioral approach will be helpful in looking at situations where addictive behavior might arise. A method called *contingency management* based on operant conditioning theory has been found to be helpful with substance abuse, (e.g., opiate substitution therapy), in the sense of retaining clients in treatment and reducing substance abuse. It is based upon a simple behavioral principle used in everyday life where a behavior reinforced or rewarded is more likely to occur in the future. This approach is more appropriate for people attending a clinic where some sort of voucher or token system might be used as a reward for "good behavior.". The technique may worth trying in the counseling room.[17]

12.7.2   Motivational Interviewing

This important counseling approach has been found useful, especially at the beginning of therapy to encourage further attendance by the client. This is defined as "a client-centered, directive method for enhancing intrinsic motivation to change by exploring and resolving ambivalence."[18] It aims to be non-judgmental and non-confrontational, and its success depends on providing objective feedback based on

---

[16]Nakken (1996: 65).

[17]Some imagination is needed in determining appropriate rewards.
For further discussion about this technique see Higgins and Petry (1999) available at http://pubs.niaaa.nih.gov/publications/arh23-2/122-127.pdf.

[18]Miller and Rollnick (2002: 25).

information given by the client. It attempts to move clients to acknowledging current problems, developing in them a desire to change, and identifying strategies that will enable this change to take place. The method has been found to be effective in brief intervention therapy, sometimes under the label *Motivational Enhancement Therapy* (MET).[19] The key is to provide motivation to change.

Motivation to Change

Miller and Rollnick[20] came up with a number of interesting research findings about change. First, change often happens naturally without therapeutic intervention, and the result of any therapy tends to mirror natural change rather than being a unique form of change. Second, if change occurs in therapy, most of it occurs within the first few sessions and the total number of sessions does not seem make much difference. Third, the key to change is motivation. Clients who believe that they are likely to change have a good chance of change especially if the therapist shares that belief. Fourth, a person-centered, empathetic counseling style is most likely to help expedite change. Finally, the "self-talk" the client employs about change is important. Positive motivational statements are good predictors of success, whereas arguments against change (or resistance) are not. Miller and Rollnick also suggest that there are three important components for motivating change—being "ready, willing, and able."

1. *Willing.* A key question is, "How important would you say it is for you to ....? On a scale of 0 to 10 where 0 is not at all important and 10 is extremely important, where would you say you are?" A low score would indicate that change is not important and would perhaps indicate a lack of willingness. Follow-up questions might be, "Why have you scored ... and not a lower number (or zero)?", and "What would it take for you to go from ... to a higher number?"

2. *Able.* A key question is, "How confident would you say you are, that if you decided to ... you could do it? On a scale of 0 to 10 where 0 is not at all confident and 10 is extremely confident, where would you say you are?" A low score would suggest that they have little confidence in their ability to succeed. The same follow-up questions as those in (1) can be used.

3. *Ready.* A client may be willing and able to change but they say that it is not the most important thing right now: "I'll quit next year."

Ideally, one would like high scores on all three categories as this would indicate that the client has good prospects of giving up the addiction. Often a low score occurs with (2) above, say three, so that the client's motivation needs to be strengthened. In the definition of motivational interviewing, the word "ambivalence" is mentioned. Clients are generally ambivalent about whether they want to change or not, and ambivalence itself in life is a normal human behavior. Addiction leads to an *approach-avoidance* conflict where a person can't live with their addiction and can't live without it! The aim of the therapist is, to change the metaphor,

[19] For a useful manual for therapists authored by Miller that is focused on drug addiction (including alcohol) see http://www.motivationalinterview.org/clinical/METDrugAbuse.PDF (accessed October 2010).
[20] Miller and Rollnick (2002: 9).

to tip the balance towards change. One technique is to help the client fill in the following balance sheet, where "stop" and "continue" refer to the addiction.

Table 12.1   Balance Sheet.

	Stop	Continue
Good things (Benefits)	1. ...	2. ...
Not so good things (Costs)	3. ...	4. ...

The client fills in the four gaps; adding scores as well might be helpful. This should be done early on in the counseling as it will help motivation. Looking forward and asking the so-called "miracle question" can also help this process, namely, " If you woke up tomorrow and found you were free of the addiction what would it be like for you?" Similar questions might be: "What would be the best results you could imagine, if you make a change?" or "How would you like things to turn out for you and what would this be like?" It is important to encourage the client to express what concerns them about their addiction. This helps to highlight the conflict produced by their ambivalence and increase the *discrepancy*, which generates discomfort, between where they are and where they want to be.

The therapist should deeply explore any of the concerns raised as this reinforces the discrepancy and can lead to *change talk* statements. These statements indicate an interest in changing, for example: problem recognition ("Maybe I have been doing this too often"); expressions of concern ("I am really worried about what is happening"); expressing advantages of a change ("I would save a lot of money if I stopped doing this"); showing optimism for change ("I have stopped doing this for a time once before so I guess I can do it again"); and intention to change ("I think it's time I thought about quitting"). The client should be encouraged to elaborate further on their change talk (e.g., "What else?"). Affirming change talk ("That sounds like a good idea") and summarizing change-talk statements can be helpful.

Exploring extremes can be useful such as "What concerns you the most?" or "What are your worst fears about what might happen if you don't make a change?" Looking back at times before the problem emerged may bring out an observation about increased tolerance, or what initiated the problem. If there have been previous occasions when the problem was overcome (e.g., temporarily gave up smoking) then the therapist can ask what strategy was used at that time. In looking forward, one can use questions like, "If you decide to change, what are your hopes for the future?" or "How would you like things to turn out for you?"

A helpful summary of components that will facilitate change described by Miller and Sanchez (1994) and summarized by the acronym FRAMES is as follows:

- Feedback of personal risk or impairment to the client.

- Emphasis on personal Responsibiliity of the client for change.

- Clear Advice to change.

- A Menu of alternative change options for the client.

- Therapist **E**mpathy.

- Facilitation of client **S**elf-efficacy or optimism.

Basic Principles

In motivational interviewing the therapist should not adopt the role of being too confrontational or directive (this can lead to resistance and denial, though resistance is normal in any case), or argue with the client about change (logic often does not help as you may be dealing with the addictive side of the client's personality), or even warn the client. Some wrong kinds of questions are: "Why don't you want to change?", "Why don't you just ...?", and "Why can't you ...?" The aim is to encourage the client to voice their own arguments and reasons for change. Summing up, the main counseling principles in motivational interviewing are:[21]

1. *Express empathy.* This is part of the person-centered approach in motivational interviewing. The emphasis is on listening rather than telling; purposeful questioning is important as the therapist can ask the client his or her own feelings, ideas and concerns, and then respond with empathetic reflection, affirmation, or reframing. The therapist needs to avoid appearing to be the expert and should avoid labeling or blaming.

2. *Develop discrepancy.* Here we depart somewhat from the person-centered approach and become more directive towards the resolution of ambivalence.

3. *Roll with resistance.* This involves avoiding arguing for change; reflection is more important than arguing. Taking the opposite side will act out the ambivalence and reinforce the client's opposition to change. In fact the client may talk themselves out of making a change. Resistance is a therapist problem. It may take the role of arguing, interrupting, negating, and ignoring. It is a signal for the therapist to respond differently and not directly oppose the resistance. New perspectives are invited but not imposed; reframing can be helpful here, where new meaning is given to what has been said and current problems are placed in a more positive or optimistic frame. Another approach is to suggest small incremental changes rather than a full abrupt change.

4. *Support self-efficacy.* This refers to supporting a client's belief in his or her ability to change. A small series of steps with plenty of affirmation and encouragement will be effective. It's the client's responsibility for choosing and carrying out any changes. The aim of the therapist is work toward eliciting client self-motivational statements.

Summarizing periodically is helpful, particularly towards the end of a session, including and thus reinforcing the client's self-motivational statements. Elements of reluctance or resistance can also be included to lessen a negating reaction from the client. The first session is particularly critical for any later success.

When a client decides to make a change, a plan needs to be set in motion, but it needs to be the client's plan. It is a good idea to brainstorm and consider a range of change options. Some things need to be elicited from the client such as

[21] Miller and Rollnick (2002: 36–48) and the eight strategies of Miller and Rollnick (1991).

"What is the first step?" and "How will you go about it?" Specific actions need to have a time frame, and it is helpful to list friends who can help with change and the ways they can assist. Obstacles to change can be listed as well as strategies for dealing with them. Brainstorming on how to deal with high-risk situations will help to develop coping skills. There are two main types of coping: anticipatory (e.g., avoiding a high-risk situation such as attending a certain bar) and immediate (e.g., turning down an offered cigarette or a drink);[22] here cognitive-behavioral therapy can play a useful role.

Coping skills can be introduced two ways depending to some degree on the addiction being considered. One approach is for the therapist to determine what skills are needed and then help the client to learn these. An alternative strategy is a guided "self-management" approach where the emphasis is on identifying and capitalizing on the client's own strengths. For example, a client faced with social pressure to drink could be assertive, or less assertive and say that they are following doctor's orders, or leave the situation. The second approach might be a good way to start and then both methods can be used. In the case of substance abuse, a particularly useful skills set for coping is given in the second half of Section 13.3.3. In planning for a change it is important not to rush the client into action as ambivalence is still likely to be present. The shift from contemplation to action may be gradual and tentative rather than a discrete decision.

Homework is important in addiction counseling. Each session can begin with a review of how the client fared in putting into action lessons and strategies learnt in a previous session. With most addictions it is helpful to keep a journal or daily record of how clients are coping with their addictions, so this can be reviewed as well.

Advice Giving

Care is always needed when a client asks the therapist for his or her opinion, for example, "What do you think I should do?" There is no problem if it is simply a request for factual information in which case therapists can simply respond to the best of their ability. It can then be helpful to ask the client what he or she thinks of the answer. The danger of giving your opinion is that it is not client-driven therapy. Miller[23] suggests an approach like the following in dealing with drug and alcohol addiction:

> I'm not sure I should tell you. Certainly I have an opinion, but you have to decide for yourself how you want to handle your life. I guess I'm concerned that if I give you my advice, then it looks like I'm the one deciding instead of you. Are you sure you want to know?

When it comes to "how to's," Miller suggests it is often best not to prescribe specific strategies but ask the client what they might do. I find this helps to tap into the client's resources.

Wheel of Change

Prochaska and DiClemente (1982), and in subsequent papers, give a useful six-stage model (TTM, or Transtheoretical Model) for change, also called the wheel of change. They begin with the first stage of pre-contemplation when the person

---

[22]Shiffman et al. (2005: 100).

[23]See http://www.motivationalinterview.org/clinical/METDrugAbuse.PDF (accessed October 2010).

is not aware of a problem and the therapist's task is to raise doubt, or the person is maybe aware of the problem behavior but is unwilling or discouraged when it comes to discussing or changing it. This stage is then followed by the stages of contemplation, determination, action, maintenance, and either exit or relapse. If a relapse occurs (which we discuss below), then the therapist can either continue where they left off or, more usually, go round this cycle again beginning with contemplation—it depends on the nature of the addiction. In the contemplation stage, the client is usually ambivalent about wanting to change and not wanting to change. The therapy then endeavors to tip the balance. In the determination stage, where the client decides he or she needs to do something about the problem, there is an opportunity for the therapist to work with the client to choose the best course of action to effect change. The client is then encouraged to take steps towards change in the action stage. In the maintenance stage, the client is helped to identify and use strategies to prevent relapse. If a relapse occurs, the therapist guides the client to renew the processes of contemplation, determination, and action, without the client becoming stuck or demoralized because of the client's relapse. The TTM approach seems to fit in well with motivational interviewing and can be used in conjunction with the latter, then usually called motivational enhancement.

Relapse Strategies

A distinction needs to be made between a single lapse and a full-blown relapse. As relapse is very common with addictions, it can be helpful for therapists to inform their clients that each lapse (slip) or relapse can bring them closer to recovery. This is not encouraging relapse (which might reduce resolve) but normalizing and re-motivating. Smokers, for example, can go round the cycle three to seven times (or even more times for some) before quitting. People who choose to lapse may find themselves vulnerable to the so-called *Abstinence violation effect* (AVE) which is self-blame, guilt, and loss of perceived control.[24] However, a relapse can be viewed as a mistake that the client can learn from rather than a behavior for which they are judged. It can also be regarded as a unique response to a difficult situation rather than personal weakness or failure. It is important to find out what happened before and after a relapse and look for AVE affects. If a relapse occurs, it is important for the client to try and cut the episode short to minimize the consequences.

Marlatt and Witkiewitz[25] suggest a number of intrapersonal factors that relate to the probability of relapse. There is self-efficacy (the degree to which an individual feels confident and capable of performing a certain behavior in a specific situational context), outcome expectancies (the anticipated effects that an individual expects will occur as the result of a substance consumption), motivation (action towards a desired goal), coping skills (especially in handling high-risk situations), emotional (affective) states, and craving. The main interpersonal factor is the level of social support or lack of it. A change for the worse of any of the above factors will raise the probability of a relapse. Three of these in particular, namely negative emotional states, interpersonal conflict, and social pressure, are likely to precipitate a relapse, especially with alcohol abusers.[26]

[24]Marlatt and Witkiewitz (2005: 3).
[25]Marlatt and Witkiewitz (2005: 8–20).
[26]Cummings, Gordon, and Marlatt (1980).

Craving is one of the above factors that is not well understood. It is sometimes differentiated from an "urge," which is regarded as being less severe than a craving (though the distinction is not clear in the literature). Dealing with an urge to drink or take other drugs is a coping skill, and a helpful metaphor proposed by Alan Marlatt comes from surfing on a wave, namely "surf the urge."[27] A helpful summary of this technique is now discussed.[28]

Fighting an urge simply feeds it.[29] Instead we examine the urge and focus on physiological effects while maintaining steady breathing. The key is that urges rarely last for very long, especially if there is no opportunity to use. The urge is like a wave that will swamp us if we try to struggle against it. Instead we go with it (or surf it) and watch it peter out. The technique, referred to as *mindfulness meditation*,[30] is to carefully observe where in our body we feel the physical sensations associated with the urge, noting the intensity, boundaries, and quality of the sensations, and observing how they change with time and with the in-breath and out-breath. Notice is taken of our thoughts and, without judging them or fighting them, gently bring our attention back to the sensations and our breathing. The process is then repeated, noting any changes. What happens is that we replace the anxiety and stress engendered by the urge or craving with curiosity and an interest in the urge. We face it rather than fighting it knowing that it will pass! It is a kind of interested detachment in which our focus is on the present. Bourne describes mindfulness as

> paying attention without judgment to whatever comes up in the present moment of your experience. It is witnessing your immediate experience just as it is, without trying to change, react to, or interfere with it.[31]

One way of practicing the technique is to relax in a chair until one has an urge to do something like move, scratch an itch, and so forth, and then go through the procedure.

Marlatt and Gordon[32] outline an intervention procedure for preventing relapse. They recommend that the client be encouraged to learn the following:

1. Situations that are a high risk for them. (This means becoming more self-aware and learning to recognize the danger signs.)

2. Skills to cope in high-risk situations. High-risk rehearsal can be carried out using role play.

3. Relaxation and stress management skills.

4. Examination of positive outcome expectancies from addictive behavior and focus on the realistic outcomes (e.g., follow the drink through to its inevitable outcome). In this way beliefs about positive outcome expectations can be challenged, as in CBT.

[27] Marlatt and Kristeller (1999).
[28] See www.mindfulness.org.au by Chris Walsh for a helpful summary and some useful exercises (accessed April 2011). References are also given there to support the idea that suppressing a thought, feeling or sensation (including pain) ultimately increases it.
[29] The same thing tends to happens with panic attacks!
[30] See Marlatt and Witkiewitz (2005: 15) for some references; note also web references. A helpful book is Kabat-Zinn (2004).
[31] Bourne (2005: 388).
[32] Marlatt and Gordon (1985).

5. Immediate and delayed effects of the addictive activity (see Table 12.2 below).

6. Action to take if a relapse occurs.

7. Control over behavior through programmed relapse. For example, the client may be required to have an alcoholic drink or smoke a cigarette under clinical conditions so the lapse can be observed and reflected upon therapeutically. The aim is to "challenge the positive expectancies of the lapse by comparing them with the reality of the experience immediately after it has occurred."[33] It can bring home the realization that the lapse is not as rewarding as anticipated. It is meant to be an intervention of last choice to use when other interventions are not working. Care is needed in using this technique, which is regarded by some as controversial.

In the case of stress control, Hart[34] suggests using self talk, planning ahead for periods of high demand, building in recovery time, avoiding the adrenaline emotions (anger, resentment, frustration, and irritation), and developing alternative ways of dealing with pressure (e.g., laughter, music, talking).

Also recommended by Marlatt and Gordon is an examination of the client's life-style and development of positive addictions or substitutions for the addictive behavior. They also recommend the creation of an "observatory role" (the mindfulness meditation mentioned above) where clients learn from their addictive urges to simply observe them rather than act on them, as well as the development of the client's "relapse warning system" so that early warning signals of relapse can be heard. A useful tool is the decision matrix of Table 12.1 under "Motivation to Change" above or the extended matrix table below for some addictions (e.g., alcohol) that needs to be completed early on.

Table 12.2   Extended Balance Sheet.

	Immediate Consequences		Delayed Consequences	
	Positive	Negative	Positive	Negative
Stop/remain abstinent				
Continue/resume				

Further prevention activities from Nakken (1996) are:

• Time the length of the urge to usage.

• Log recovery experiences.

• Role play (acting out relapse-triggering activities).

• Guided imagery (focussing on positive thoughts and images while simultaneously imagining the difficult situation).

[33] O'Donohue and Levensky (2006 : 159).
[34] Hart (1990: chapter 12).

- Use the empty chair (carrying on a dialogue with opposing parts of self—the Addict and Self— by being the opposite self in each chair).

When there are frequent relapses, a model proposed by Muraven and Baumeister[35] that may be helpful is the *self-control strength model*. It uses the analogy of self-control being like a muscle that can become overworked; it's overuse leads to a depletion of glucose in the brain. When a person exerts self-control in one situation, it can therefore undermine his or her ability to exert self-control in a later situation. It is therefore better to develop habits rather than have to exercise willpower on every occasion. Detailed evidence for this model is given by Baumeister and Tierney (2011).

A number of groups are available for helping people with all kinds of substance and process addictions, for example the AA (Alcoholics Anonymous), NA (Narcotics Anonymous), OA (Overeaters Anonymous) and GA (Gamblers Anonymous). Information is available about these groups on the internet.[36] They all use a 12-step program, originally introduced by AA and adapted to each addiction. The advantages of a supportive group include: feeling less alone, knowing others have similar struggles builds confidence, helping to break any denial, helping others leads to more self-help, being in a group shifts the focus from blaming others or circumstances for one's problems to oneself, and other group members can be significant social reinforcers for positive change.

Couple Counseling

With some addictions it can sometimes be helpful to involve a caring significant other person (CSO) such as a spouse or a support person in the counseling process. For drug and alcohol addictions, Miller[37] gives some useful ideas about the role of the CSO who should be encouraged to participate and be actively engaged in the treatment whenever possible. Emphasis is placed on the need for the client and CSO to work collaboratively on resolving the addiction problem.

12.8 BIBLICAL VIEWPOINT

From a biblical perspective, an addiction has been described as causing a person to be lured and enticed by one's own desire that ultimately can lead to destruction.[38] Christians are not immune to having addictive issues. The Christian message would argue that we do all tend to have addictive tendencies because of what the Bible refers to as our fallen natures. Paul says that one's body should not be used as an instrument of unrighteousness, but rather as an instrument of righteousness for God so that sin will not have mastery.[39] The Christian message says that the believer can be set free from the yoke of slavery and from the law of sin and death.[40] Christians are admonished to walk by the indwelling Spirit of God and focus on

---

[35] Muraven and Baumeister (2000).
[36] http://www.addictionrecoveryguide.org/resources/recovery/ (accessed October 2010).
[37] See the latter part of http://www.motivationalinterview.org/clinical/METDrugAbuse.PDF by William Miller (accessed October 2010.
[38] James 1:13–15.
[39] Romans 6:11–14.
[40] Galatians 5:1 and Romans 8:2.

the things of the Spirit and things above that are pure and honorable, rather than things of the flesh.[41]

As humans we want to have absolute freedom, but that is not possible as only God is completely free. Because we are made in the image of God we have some limited freedoms, restricted by the restraints of time, space, and natural and moral law. There is also the specter of death that we must all face eventually. Lenters[42] suggests that these two ideas of freedom and death are behind addiction proneness.

Here is a suggested 12-step recovery program for Christians wrestling with addictions:

1. Admit that we are powerless over certain areas of our lives and that our lives have become unmanageable.

2. Believe that through the Holy Spirit power has come in the person of Jesus Christ who is greater than ourselves and is able to transform our weaknesses into strengths.

3. Decide to turn our will and our lives over to the care of Jesus Christ, as we understand Him, learning to comprehend His will more fully.

4. Make an honest searching and fearless moral inventory of ourselves, our strengths, and our weaknesses.

5. Admit to God, to ourselves, and to another trusted individual the exact nature of our addiction or tendency to unhealthy compulsions.

6. Become entirely ready to let Christ heal those defects of our character that are preventing us from having a more enriching spiritual lifestyle.

7. Humbly ask God to transform our shortcomings.

8. Make a list of all persons we may have harmed and be willing to make amends to them all.

9. Make personal amends to such persons except when to do so would injure them or others.

10. Continue to take a personal lifestyle inventory and when we falter, promptly admit it, and when we are right, be thankful to God for His guidance and to those assisting us.

11. Seek through prayer and meditation to improve our conscious contact with God, as we understand Him, praying for a better knowledge of His will for us and for the power to carry it out.

12. Having experienced a new sense of spirituality as a result of these steps and realizing that this is a gift of Gods grace, we should be willing to share the message of Christs love and forgiveness with others and to practice these principles of spiritual living in all our affairs.

Biblical verses can be associated with each of the twelve steps.[43]

[41]Galatians 5:16–17, 24–25; Romans 8:5–9; Colossians 3:1–3; and Philippians 4:8–9.
[42]Lenters (1985: 27).
[43]See, for example, http://www.alcoholicsvictorious.org/12-steps.html (accessed October 2010).

CHAPTER 13

SUBSTANCE ADDICTIONS

13.1 INTRODUCTION

People can become addicted to almost any substance that can alter mood or help them to forget life's difficulties. This discussion however will be confined to just nicotine, alcohol, and some of the more common drugs. Unfortunately humans have the propensity to invent new party drugs! According to Enright and Fitzgibbons, "Many therapists identify substance abusers as their angriest, most abusive and most violent patients."[1] As therapists we need to help such clients find ways of coping with these problems and their resentments.

13.2 SMOKING

13.2.1 Nicotine Addiction

Smoking is highly addictive and harmful and can be equally addictive as heroin and cocaine. According to the American Heart Association, "Nicotine addiction has historically been one of the hardest addictions to break."[2] A person may continue smoking even though they are dying of lung cancer! Most smokers want to stop and in fact usually try, but about one in three (or even one in two for long-term

---

[1] Enright and Fitzgibbons (2000: 156).
[2] http://en.wikipedia.org/wiki/Nicotine.

smokers) who continue will eventually die because of this habit.[3] "On average, they will die 10 to 15 years earlier than they would have died from other causes."[4] One cigarette can shorten a person's life by at least 5 minutes; 20 cigarettes a day by five years. There are further health issues discussed below.

A major problem with smoking is that the addiction can develop very quickly. Smoking usually begins in early adolescence, and those who begin smoking at an early age are more likely to develop severe nicotine addiction than those who start later. Also, the relapse rate after giving up is quite high. Much of the methodology of Chapter 12 applies to smoking. In the case of nicotine, some clients might prefer to use a substitute such as nicotine chewing gum, patch, lozenge or nasal spray. Helpful non-nicotine substances that interact with the brain are now available. Patches, for example, slowly deliver a fixed amount of nicotine through the skin, and the amount is then steadily reduced. Gum, and particularly spray, deliver nicotine more quickly and can be useful for handling acute cravings. Unfortunately some people end using up patches or gum as well as cigarettes! There are also alternative tobacco products on the market.[5]

As with all addictions, there is the question of harm reduction (i.e, cut back on smoking) versus total abstinence. Shiffman et al.[6] discuss the pros and cons and conclude that tobacco harm reduction (THR) is "controversial and risky."

13.2.2   Products of Cigarette Smoke

Smoke Substances

Tobacco smoke is a mixture of gases and small particles made up of water, tar, and nicotine. The tar is a mixture of hundreds of toxic chemicals, with at least 43 being carcinogenic (e.g., nitrosamines and benzpyrene). Many of the gases are harmful, such as carbon monoxide, nitrogen oxides, hydrogen cyanide, and ammonia. There are also phenols that destroy the bronchial cilia, and other irritant chemicals that cause coughing, shortness of breath, and wheezing. The burning end of a cigarette acts like a chemical factory churning out other nasties! Over 4,000 chemical substances have been identified in tobacco smoke.

Nicotine

Nicotine, a natural insecticide that stops insects from eating the tobacco plant, is a highly toxic[7] and addictive substance.[8] Its chemical structure is so similar to

---

[3]For some statistics see http://smoking.ygoy.com/smoking-statistics-general-facts/ (accessed November 2010).
[4]See www.ehealthmd.com/library/smoking/SMO_whatis.html (accessed October 2010). The same article mentions that only 2.5% of smokers successfully quit each year.
[5]See for example
http://www.ndp.govt.nz/moh.nsf/indexcm/ndp-publications-noveltobaccoproductshealthrisk
(accessed October 2010). See also "alternative tobacco products" on the internet as new ones are appearing all the time.
[6]Shiffman, Kassel, Gwaltney, and McChargue (2005).
[7]Drop for drop it is more lethal than strychnine or diamond rattlesnake venom and three times deadlier than arsenic, cf. http://whyquit.com/whyquit/LinksAAddiction.html by John Polito (accessed October 2010).
[8]Kandel et al. (2005). This article shows that about 87% of students who smoke nicotine at least once daily are chemically dependent under DSM-IV mental health standards.

the important neurotransmitter acetylcholine, which orchestrates a whole range of neurotransmitters, that once inside the brain it can fit a large number of chemical "locks" (receptors) permitting direct or indirect control over the flow of over 200 neurochemicals. The brain's defense against this "apparent" excess of acetylcholine is to carry out some protective adjustments such as growing more acetylcholine receptors so that there is a new neurochemical sense of what is normal, based on nicotine. Any attempt to stop the influx of nicotine will herald a brain reaction bringing anxiety and powerful mood shifts. The effect of the nicotine is reinforced by the fact that it activates the "pleasure centers" of the brain (the nucleus accumbens, a structure in the so-called limbic system) with the release of the neurotransmitter dopamine. Also, it appears that a chemical in cigarette smoke blocks the action of a mopping-up enzyme called MAO B, which removes excess dopamine.

With a low dose (e.g., quick puffs) nicotine can act like a stimulant, while with a higher dose (e.g., slow deep puffs) it can have a calming effect. However, it should be noted that smoking may not really relax or calm a person down—smoking could merely relieve the situation that smoking created in the first place, namely the need for nicotine!

Research suggests that in dopamine-rich areas of the brain, nicotine behaves remarkably like cocaine, which could account for nicotine's addictive power. As the addictive substance wears off, the newly created receptors on the neurons begin to "scream for stimulation." Clearly the potential for addiction may depend on a person's natural levels of dopamine, along with genetic makeup and social environment.

As nicotine enters the body, it is distributed quickly through the bloodstream and takes about seven seconds to reach the brain when inhaled—quicker than an intravenous injection! The body's nicotine reserves decline by about a half every two hours (the so-called *half-life*) and it can take up to 73 hours for the blood-serum to become nicotine-free and 90% of nicotine's metabolites to be eliminated via urine. It is then that reactions like anxiety peak in intensity and begin to gradually decline. Just one decent dose of nicotine and the smoker has to face another 72 hours of detox anxieties.

Nicotine addiction is enhanced by psychological and emotional factors. It is essentially a learning process where smoking is linked to other activities, places, and people that trigger the urge to smoke (e.g., after meals, with coffee or alcohol, taking a work break, or meeting people). These triggers can be numerous and varied. For example, a trigger can be an emotional one; anxiety can trigger a desire to smoke because of the calming effect. The smoking addiction is therefore an addiction with three parts: nicotine addiction, habits, and feelings.

What about cigarettes with a low level of nicotine? What happens is that smokers regulate their nicotine intake by the way they smoke, for example, change the puff rate and the amount of inhalation until the intake is at their preferred level; this level may end up the same as with higher level nicotine cigarettes. Low-tar cigarettes however are likely to be less harmful.

13.2.3   Health Aspects

The effect on health is generally the greatest motivation for giving up smoking. It is helpful for the therapist to have a detailed knowledge of the health risks, which are varied and extensive. The onset of minor ailments such as coughs, sore throats, breathlessness, and indigestion, as well as feeling unfit and generally off-color, are early signs that the body has had enough. Here are some basic facts about the health risks of smoking (from U.S. data):

- Heart disease. Smoking is responsible for 30% of all heart attacks and cardiovascular deaths.

- Cancer. Smoking is responsible for at least 30% of all cancer deaths and 87% of lung cancer deaths.

- Lung problems. Smoking is responsible for 82% of deaths due to emphysema and chronic bronchitis. However, if a person stops smoking before or during middle age (age 35 to 50), they will avoid about 90% of the lung cancer risk.[9]

- Sterility. Smoking impairs erections in middle-aged and older men and may affect the quality of their sperm. It seems to sedate sperm and impair their mobility. This is reversed after stopping smoking. Smoking reduces women's fertility and delays conception after they stop using oral contraceptives.

- Menopause. Smoking advances menopause by an average of 5 years.

- Osteoporosis. Smoking accelerates the rate of osteoporosis, a disease that causes bones to weaken and fracture more easily.

- Circulation. Smoking causes an impairment of blood flow and reduces the oxygen-carrying capacity of the blood at a time when the heart needs more oxygen because of the nicotine's stimulation effect. Nicotine also disturbs the heart's rhythm.

- Face. Smoking reduces skin elasticity and can age the face by 5 years on average.

- Pregnancy. Smoking during pregnancy can seriously damage the baby.

- Side-stream smoke. There is the well-known danger of passive smoking from side-stream smoke. It can be particularly unpleasant for nonsmokers and even cause them headaches.

- Brain. Smoking affects mental capacity and memory.

- Senses. Smoking affects the ability to smell and taste.

13.2.4 Motivation to Stop

Some motivating reasons to stop smoking are as follows:

1. *Personal health.* This has already been discussed and for many this is the greatest motivator.

2. *Health of others.* The health of babies, young children, and spouse are particularly vulnerable to passive smoking.

[9]See www.ehealthmd.com/library/smoking/SMO_whatis.html (accessed October 2010).

3. *Expense.* It is a sobering exercise for a client to work out how much smoking costs them each year, if they have not already done so.

4. *Setting an example.* Parents and people in responsible positions involving children (e.g., teachers) need to set a good example.

5. *Social pressure.* In some work places it is difficult to give up smoking because everybody is doing it. However, in public places, smoking is regarded as anti-social or even weakness because of passive smoking, and restrictions are increasing. Non-smokers generally dislike the stale smell of cigarette smoke that seems to permeate everything.

6. *Control.* A smoker may get little pleasure from smoking and realize that they have lost control, which they want to regain.

7. *Aesthetic.* People may get tired of the smell and messiness of smoking.

13.2.5   Counseling Process

The first thing that a therapist will usually face with regard to addiction is the ambivalence a client will show towards whether they want to give up their addiction or not. Motivation is the key to change and overcoming addiction.

As a general framework, the six-stage wheel-of-change model of Section 12.7.2 can be helpful, though where one starts will depend on the client. Most clients know they should give up so they may be in the *contemplation* stage where they are ambivalent about wanting to change and not wanting to change. At this point the therapist can ask the client the pros and cons of continuing or stopping so that Table 12.1 or Table 12.2 of Section 12.7.2 can be filled in. Clients also need to list what concerns they have about giving up smoking and what difficulties they might experience.

Deciding to Quit

There are a number of useful booklets on the internet to help the quitting process (e.g., look up "The quit book" on google).[10] Much of what follows is given in these sources. Before the client actually quits, some pre-planning can be helpful. For example, keeping a record sheet of smoking activities can help the client sort out as many triggers for smoking as possible. Such a sheet will enable the client to determine when they are most vulnerable and devise alternative strategies and habits to avoid smoking in these high-risk situations. One such sheet is given in Table 13.1 below.

Once clients have decided to quit, they should choose an "easy" time and date when they won't be under too much pressure and feel good. The day before they should clean up and remove anything to do with smoking (especially smell) from their house, car, workplace, and so forth. A concern of some smokers is that they might put on weight when they stop smoking as smoking seems to increase the metabolic rate and nicotine is an appetite suppressant. In practice about 80% to 85% gain weight, with the remainder staying the same. Average weight gains of 5 to 10 pounds are extremely common especially in the first few months of cessation

---

[10] A book which seems to have been very successful is Carr (2006).

Table 13.1   Smoking Record.

Time	Habit	Feelings	Craving	What I could do instead
7am	Wake up		5	Get into shower immediately
10am		Upset	3	Deep breaths
11am	Coffee	Stressed	4	Go for a walk

1 = I could do without it; 2 = I feel like it; 3 = I need it;
4 = I really need it ; 5 = I'd kill for it

and 15% to 20% may gain more than 30 pounds.[11] Therefore having a good exercise plan and sensible diet will help weight control. Supportive friends and family or a quitting partner can be very helpful. Before actually quitting, some people find it helpful to begin cutting down their smoking or delaying the first cigarette by an hour each day.

Withdrawal Symptoms

Once a person quits, they will be faced with withdrawal symptoms (preferably called "recovery symptoms" with the client) for a few days while the body rids itself of nicotine. These symptoms will vary from person to person and will generally include cravings, a wide range of unpleasant feelings and moods (e.g., irritability, anger, sadness, and anxiety), digestion and stomach upsets, headaches, coughing (the little hairs or cilia that clean the lungs are doing their job again), sleeping problems, and hunger. However, it will all pass! Drinking plenty of water can help cleanse the body of toxins and reduce the hunger. As mentioned in Section 12.2.3, there is a crossover effect of other drugs so that the client should cut back on caffeine and alcohol. In fact it might help to switch to decaffeinated coffee or herbal tea until cigarette free for two months.

Five Ds for Quitting

The following 5Ds are helpful:

- Declare repeatedly, "I choose to be a nonsmoker".

- Delay. Wait for 10 minutes. Most cravings will only last 3–5 minutes.

- Deep breathing. The key is to relax. Two or three deep breaths will help.

- Drink water. Slowly sip a glass or two. Water helps ease several discomforts associated with nicotine such as constipation, coughing, the hunger/urge to eat, and the craving to smoke. It also helps flush out residual nicotine out of the body.

- Distract. Do something else to take one's mind off smoking, for example, doodle when on the phone.

Some people might wish to add one more.

[11] The popular "one-third" statistic is unfounded: see Kleges (1995: 61–62).

- Depend on God (higher power).

Most recovery symptoms will only last a few days, but some take a few weeks to settle down. Cravings can continue at times in the future, and for some smokers the craving for nicotine can last a year or more after giving up.[12] Apart from delay, one key to handling cravings is to change one's habits. For example, at a cigarette break eat a piece of fruit or some healthy snack food. A cigarette habit could be switched to a nut habit—four nuts in their shells for every cigarette. This gives the hands and mouth something to do. It has been suggested that sunflower seeds can be a good substitute as they contain ingredients that mimic some of the effects of nicotine.[13] One problem with smoking is its social aspect, a major factor with youth, where the smoking habit often begins as a result of "peer pressure"; almost 75% of all first cigarettes are smoked with another teenager.[14]

Relapse Prevention

We need to distinguish between a single lapse (slip) and relapse back into smoking. However, relapse is common with nicotine; it only takes one puff to begin the cycle all over again. Just one cigarette can set things off, though several glasses of water will help flush out the effects of the nicotine and ameliorate the slip. In any case, the client should be encouraged to just simply start again. The slip or relapse can be normalized as most smokers relapse several times before they finally quit permanently. The more days they have smoke-free the closer they will get to achieving their goal. A possible problem is that of mixed messages; the client is told to stop smoking on the one hand, but it is okay if it happens on the other. A good analogy is that: "Having a cigarette after quitting is like playing with fire—one must know what to do once a fire starts."[15]

If the client has a lapse, then suitable messages might be: "Think of the slip as mistake rather than as evidence you are a failure"; "As with other mistakes, use the slip as a learning experience"; "Even if you are upset, don't beat yourself up"; and "Quit again immediately while your nicotine level is lower." Such self-talk will help minimize AVE, the abstinence violation effect (cf. Section 12.7.2).

Shiffman et al.[16] note that the success of relapse prevention depends on identifying those high-risk situations and developing some coping skills. They describe coping skills as either cognitive or behavioral. For example, the first D above is cognitive, and one might add thoughts about the health effects of smoking on self and others (e.g., children). The next four Ds are behavioral and one might add chewing something, getting up and walking around, and stimulus control (e.g., change routines, sit in non-smoking sections, and avoid coffee or alcohol in risky environments).

From recent research, Shiffman et al. state that cognitive methods are more effective than behavioral ones. They also give reasons to support the idea that it is better to learn a few coping skills well so that they can be easily triggered and executed, rather than learning many coping responses. It could be helpful for the client to practice some responses like when a friend offers them a cigarette (e.g.,

[12]Ashton and Stepney (1982: 63).
[13]Kenton (2004: 30).
[14]World Health Organization (1992: 60).
[15]Shiffman et al. (2005: 114).
[16]Shiffman et al. (2005).

some "empty-chair" work). Exercise can be used as a "positive addiction" that can substitute for smoking and it can have other health benefits such as relieving stress and controlling weight gain (especially with women who are generally less successful at quitting).[17] However, the authors suggest that there is little evidence that exercise per se prevents relapse. Finally, as noted above, such things as nicotine gum and spray can be used to prevent a lapse in a high-risk situation.

13.3   ALCOHOL

13.3.1   Physical and Social Effects

Physical Effects

When a person drinks alcohol, the alcohol is absorbed by the stomach, enters the bloodstream, and goes to all the tissues. The effects of alcohol are dependent on a number of factors such as a person's size, weight, age, and sex, as well as the amount of food and alcohol consumed. The disinhibiting effect of alcohol is one of the main reasons it is used in so many social situations. Other effects of moderate drinking include dizziness and talkativeness; the immediate effects of a larger amount of alcohol include slurred speech, disturbed sleep, nausea, and vomiting. Alcohol, even at low doses, significantly impairs the judgment and coordination required to drive a car safely. Hangovers are another possible effect of heavy drinking; a hangover consists of a headache, nausea, thirst, dizziness, and fatigue. Prolonged and heavy use of alcohol can lead to addiction (alcoholism).

Alcohol greatly upsets the central nervous system, hindering the ability to retrieve, consolidate, and process information. Too much alcohol can destroy brain cells, which can lead to brain damage. While even moderate amounts of alcohol can affect cognitive abilities, large amounts interfere with the oxygen supply of the brain causing a blackout when totally drunk. Alcohol addiction may also inflame the mouth, esophagus, and stomach, and could cause cancer in these areas, especially in drinkers who also smoke. Binge (splurge) drinking may produce irregular heartbeats, and abusers experience a higher risk of high-blood pressure, heart attacks, and other heart damage. Alcohol also can harm vision, impair sexual function, slow circulation, and be the grounds for malnutrition and water retention. It can also lead to skin and pancreatic disorders and weaken the bones and muscles, leading to decreased immunity.

Young people reach full maturity in their early to mid 20's and excess alcohol before then can damage the hippocampus and effect brain function and development. Alcohol is also linked to cancer in women.

Long-Term Effects

Suddenly stopping long-term, extensive drinking is likely to produce withdrawal symptoms, including severe anxiety, tremors, hallucinations, and convulsions; care is needed in doing this as it can be dangerous. Long-term effects of consuming large quantities of alcohol, especially when combined with poor nutrition, can lead to permanent damage to vital organs such as the brain and liver. A large portion of the alcohol ingested is broken down in the liver, which processes the alcohol at a

[17]Perkins, Donny, and Caggiula (1999).

fixed rate. This means that if the liver is overused, disorders and malfunctions can result, so that the liver becomes a primary target.

Liver damage can occur in three stages. The first stage is liver enlargement whereby liver cells are penetrated with abnormal fatty tissue. The second stage is alcoholic hepatitis whereby liver cells swell, inflame, and eventually die. The third stage is cirrhosis in which fibrous scar tissues are formed, hindering the flow of blood through the liver. Alcoholics who do not stop drinking reduce their life expectancy by 10 to 15 years.

Metabolism and Absorption

Although units of measurement vary, alcohol levels are usually measured in terms of percentages, for example 1 mg of ethanol in 100 ml of blood is referred to as 0.01%.[18] Although metabolic rate varies with body weight, sex, and percentage body fat, alcohol is metabolized at roughly 0.02–0.025% per hour. One standard drink[19] can raise the blood alcohol level of a male weighing 200 lbs (approximately 89 kg) by about 0.02% in 20 minutes, and higher for a lighter person. It is important for clients to understand tolerance, which is different from blood alcohol level. Those with a high tolerance to alcohol won't feel as intoxicated as someone with lower tolerance, and they may gauge their alcohol level by how they feel, not realizing that their judgment is still impaired and that they are over the legal limit for driving! It should be noted that women tolerate alcohol less well than men because of physical and biochemical factors.

Some Effects on Children

A serious issue is that mothers who drink alcohol during pregnancy may give birth to infants with fetal alcohol syndrome.[20] These infants may suffer from mental retardation and other irreversible physical abnormalities; often the symptoms are not readily observable but are reflected in abnormal social behavior. In addition, research indicates that children of alcoholic parents are at greater risk than other children of becoming alcoholics.

Social Effects

The social effects of excess alcohol are well-known. Low to moderate doses of alcohol can increase the incidence of a variety of aggressive acts, including domestic violence and child abuse. Alcoholism can lead people into serious trouble, and can be physically and mentally destructive, not to mention failure to hold down employment or professions. Currently alcohol use is involved in about half of all crimes, murders, accidental deaths, and suicides.

Scientists say that those with an alcoholic addiction in their family are more likely to develop alcoholism if they choose to drink. Alcoholism can also develop or worsen depending on a person's environment and traumatic experiences in life. These factors may include culture, family, friends, peer pressures, and lifestyle.

[18]This is based on the fact that 1 gm of alcohol is approximately 1 ml and 100 ml is 0.1 liters; this gives a value of 0.0001 liters of alcohol per liter of blood or 0.01%. For more information and maximum levels for driving in various countries see alcohol blood levels and wikipedia on the internet. Most countries have 0.05% or less except for some countries like the U.S, U.K., and New Zealand for example which, at the time of writing have 0.08%.
[19]See Section 13.3.4 on harm reduction below for a definition.
[20]See the internet for information.

13.3.2   Alcohol Assessment

People with alcohol problems are often divided into two groups, *chronic* alcoholics who have alcohol dependence, tolerance, and withdrawal symptoms on stopping, and *problem drinkers* whose heavy drinking causes problems but their life does not revolve about drinking and they do not suffer withdrawal symptoms. The difference between these two groups is discussed in some detail by Sobell and Sobell (1993), who present clear evidence that different methods of treatment are needed for the two groups. Less intensive brief therapy and self-management seems more appropriate for the problem drinking group. This approach is based on the idea that many people with alcohol problems can solve them on their own if sufficiently motivated and supported. Also the problems are not necessarily progressive but come and go with the drinking, and outpatient treatment is no less effective than inpatient treatment.

As a first step in assessment, the CAGE questionnaire, named for its four questions, is one example that may be used to screen patients quickly in, say, a doctor's office. Two "yes" responses indicate that the respondent should be investigated further. The questionnaire asks the following questions:

Have you ever felt you needed to **C**ut down on your drinking?

Have people **A**nnoyed you by criticizing your drinking?

Have you ever felt **G**uilty about drinking?

Have you ever felt you needed a drink first thing in the morning (**E**ye-opener) to steady your nerves or to get rid of a hangover?

The four key things indicating alcohol dependence that apply to other addictions as well are: craving, impaired control (unable to limit one's drinking), physical dependence (withdrawal when alcohol is stopped after a period of heavy drinking) and tolerance. There is also a preoccupation with alcohol use to the detriment of other activities and there may be a persistence with alcohol in spite of clear signs of harmful consequences. A useful assessment tool is the 25 item Alcohol Dependence Scale (ADS) questionnaire[21] due to Harvey Skinner.[22] Dichotomous items are scored 0, 1; three-choice items are scored 0, 1, 2; and four-choice items are scored 0, 1, 2, 3. In each case, the higher the value the greater the dependence, and total scores can range from 0 to 47. If the score is 0 there is no evidence of dependence, though this does not mean that the person is free of dependence symptoms. A score of 9 or more is highly indicative of alcohol abuse or dependence; a score of 1–13 indicates a low level of dependence and that moderation strategies may be appropriate along with brief counseling; a score of 14–21 suggests an outpatient program is appropriate; and anything above 21 suggests that an intensive in-patient program is appropriate.

A less complex questionnaire is the revised Michigan Alcohol Screening Test (MAST).[23] Here 3–5 represents an early or middle problem drinker and 6+ a problem drinker. Shorter questionnaires are Alcohol Use Disorders Identification Test

[21]See http://www.emcdda.europa.eu/attachements.cfm/att_4075_EN_tads.pdf (accessed October 2010).
[22]Skinner and Horn (1984)
[23]See   www.alcoholism-and-drug-addiction-help.com/alcoholism-test.html   (accessed   October 2010).

(AUDIT)[24] and the Short Alcohol Dependence Data (SADD) questionnaire, which is particularly suited to the therapist counseling mildly to moderate alcohol dependence.[25]

Two other assessment tools are the quantity and frequency (QF) method and the time-line follow-back technique. In the QF method the client determines such numbers as the average number of drinking days per week and the average amount consumed each day and each week. Unfortunately this method does not take into account any extreme drinking episodes and it forces a person to impose a pattern on his or her report of drinking. In the second method the client endeavors to record his or her past drinking on a daily basis using a blank calendar over a particular representative interval of time such as the the past 90 or more days. Here reliance is placed on the client's memory, though there is some evidence that indicates that this works quite well in giving the general picture.[26] Here the aim is to identify the pattern of drinking and determine how often large amounts (e.g., 12 or 15 SD's, see below) and small amounts (2 or 3 SD's) are drunk.

13.3.3   Counseling Strategies

It is preferable that clients are alcohol free or significantly sober when they attend counseling sessions. An important step is to determine the effect alcohol is having on the life of the client. A helpful check list is as follows:[27]

Amount and Tolerance. Is usage increasing and is more needed to produce the desired affect?

Behavior. Has alcohol caused behavioral problems with friends, the general public, and the law.

Coping. Is drinking used to cope with problems and how well is it working?

Dependence. How difficult is it to do without drinking and have alcohol-free days, for example?

Emotional Health. Does alcohol affect emotional states (e.g., anxiety, guilt, and depression).

Family. What effect does drinking have on the family?

Good About Self (Self-Esteem). How does drinking affect a client's view of self? Does he or she feel ashamed, guilty, or out of control?

Health. Has alcohol contributed to ill-health, injuries, fatigue, or poor eating habits?

Important Relationships. How has alcohol affected relationships with loved ones and friends?

---

[24]See http://www.drugnet.bizland.com/assessment/audit.htm (accessed October 2010). This may be more useful for older people, white women, and African- and Mexican-Americans.

[25]See http://www.emcdda.europa.eu/attachements.cfm/att_4128_EN_tsadd.pdf (accessed October 2010). This questionnaire is due to Raistrick et al. (1983).

[26]Sobel and Sobel (1993: 59).

[27]See http://www.motivationalinterview.org/clinical/METDrugAbuse.PDF by William Miller (accessed October 2010).

Job (Work and School). What affect has alcohol had on a school (college) or employment?

Key People. What do key people in the client's life think about his or her alcohol use?

Loving Relationships and Sexuality. How does alcohol use impact the client's physical attractiveness, sexual drive, sexual relationships, safe sex practices, and so forth?

Mental Abilities. What affect has alcohol had on a person's memory, ability to concentrate and learning?

The reader can perhaps add some more of their own using the remaining letters of alphabet (e.g., recreation and sport).

A key issue for the client is to determine his or her treatment goal, namely abstinence versus moderation (harm reduction). Goals that are self-chosen, provided they are sensible, are more likely to be achieved. Clearly abstinence should be pursued if there are medical problems or the client loses control when they start drinking, while moderation may be more appropriate for a drinker who is not addicted or consider themselves to be not alcoholic. Even though abstinence may recommended by the therapist, some clients may insist upon moderation. This can be tested by allowing the client to drink a substantially reduced amount of alcohol and see if they can handle it. Frequently an abstinence goal becomes a moderation goal! Guidelines for safe drinking are given below in Section 13.3.4 on harm reduction.

A helpful question to ask a client is whether it would be easier for them to not drink at all or limit their drinking to only one or two drinks a day. If they say not at all, it may be that because of tolerance and not getting the desired effect from drinking they may be tempted to drink more. If they decide for moderation and set reduced drinking goals, they can be asked whether they ever drank at that reduced level before. If the answer is no, they can be asked whether they believe that they could achieve it now and how they would go about it. At the time of goal setting it is appropriate to provide some alcohol education about such things as health issues; absorption, metabolism, and disposition of alcohol by the body; blood alcohol level; standard drink conversions; and tolerance.

Ambivalence, a problem with addictions, is particularly troublesome with alcoholism. From a cognitive-behavioral vantage point, alcohol dependence can be viewed as a set of learned behaviors acquired through experience. What were neutral stimuli become triggers for cravings as a result of repeated association of those stimuli with alcohol use, in common with other addictions. High-risk situations need to be identified and coping skills developed. To do this the therapist needs to help the client identify the *antecedents* or factors leading to alcohol use and the consequences that follow. The antecedents can be of a social, situational, emotional, cognitive, or physiological nature,[28] and a number of questionnaires are available such as the Inventory of Drinking Situations with either 100 or 42 questions (ISD-100 and IDS-42). As these don't seem to be freely available on the internet at the time of writing, a useful source of questions and ideas is the Situational Confidence

---

[28]Kadden and Cooney (2005: 72).

Questionnaire (SCQ), which is a selection of 39 questions from ISD-100 given by Helen Annis that assesses self-efficacy.[29] For consequences, there is the Drinker Inventory of Consequences listing 50 questions (DrInc-2R).[30]

As with other addictions, Motivational Interviewing, as described in Section 12.7.2, is a useful counseling method. A summary of a training guide for teaching coping skills is given under the following headings.[31]

1. *Managing urges to drink.* The technique of "surfing the urge" described in Section 12.7.2 under "Relapse Strategies" can be helpful. There is also the recalling of unpleasant consequences that resulted from drinking, anticipating the benefits of not drinking, distracting oneself, delaying the decision about whether or not to drink, leaving the situation, and seeking support. Seeking support might simply being able to talk to someone on the phone until the urge passes.

2. *Anger management.* Anger is a very common antecedent to drinking and clients need to be able to spot external and internal signs of impending anger so that they can use avoidance strategies. Aspects of anger management are discussed in Chapter 3.

3. *Negative thinking.* Negative thoughts can be high-risk for drinkers and depression is often comorbid with alcoholism. Clients need to learn to identify negative thoughts and negative self-talk and replace them by positive ones.

4. *Pleasant activities.* Stopping drinking frees up time that can then be used profitably in pleasant activities. These can be identified and explored with the client.

5. *Decision making.* A relapse can arise through a series of seemingly innocuous decisions that lead to risky situations. Clients can be helped to see the risks and learn to make better decisions.

6. *Structured Problem solving.* This is a difficult skill to teach (see Section 9.4.2). However, once high-risk situations are identified, solutions for handling them can be found and practiced. The method teaches a client to have several alternative choices rather than just yes or no.

7. *Planning for emergencies.* This is like the previous one but applies to more overwhelming situations.

8. *Drink refusal.* Knowing how to say "no" convincingly and in a variety of situations is an important skill that can be practiced through role play and empty-chair work.

9. *Handling criticism.* Keeping anger out of giving or receiving criticism about drinking (and in fact anything else) is important. Looking for common ground with the criticizer can lead to helpful compromise rather than negative antagonism.

[29]http://www.emcdda.europa.eu/attachements.cfm/att_4472_EN_tscq.pdf (accessed October 2010).
[30]See http://casaa.unm.edu/inst/DrInC-2R.pdf (accessed October 2010).
[31]Adapted from Kadden and Cooney (2005).

10. *Relationship problems.* Past drinking may have led to relationship break-downs, particularly with partners, so that communication and listening skills will probably need to be developed.

11. *Enhancing social support network.* Since alcoholism creates so many life problems including loss of supporters, a client's support network may need re-establishing and possibly building up.

12. *General social skills.* A client may need further social skills to help them cope better with social situations that could put them at risk for drinking, for example dealing with any feelings of social inadequacy that could make them vulnerable.

13. *Coping skills training with significant others.* It can be helpful to bring a significant other, such as a spouse, into the training to discuss joint strategies for reinforcing the alcoholics's efforts to change.

13.3.4   Harm Reduction

The standard measurement of alcohol is the so-called *standard drink* (SD), which is 10 gm of alcohol, and alcoholic drinks have the number of equivalent SDs on their labels. One SD is equal to:

- 12 oz (355 ml or one can) of beer (5% alcohol).

- 1.5 oz of hard liquor/spirits (e.g., whiskey)

- 5 oz (148 ml or one small glass) of table wine (11-12%)

- 3 oz of fortified wine such as port and sherry (20%)

The following are some reduced-drinking guidelines that might be helpful in encouraging clients to formulate some goals for their drinking. (They should determine their own goals and how they might go about achieving them.)

- Decide a realistic cut-off point for a maximum daily limit, for example no more than 4 SDs per occasion for women and 6 SDs for men.

- The cut-off should be a meaningful reduction, not just 1 or 2 SDs but a sizable reduction.

- Keep a weekly limit of no more than 21 SDs for men, and 14 SDs for women.

- Abstinent days, for example, 2 or 3, are important for two reasons: habitual components of drinking are minimized, and tolerance is reduced. The effects of abstinence can also be monitored.

- Don't drink on high-risk occasions.

- Drink at a rate of less than one SD per hour (for 70kg male) if driving. (Information can be given to the client regarding metabolic rates and the country's legal alcohol limit when driving.)

- Pace yourself. To do this determine the following: How much are you going to drink and how long will you spend drinking, then work out how long each drink should last. It may help to alternate with non-alcoholic drinks ("spacers") or low alcohol drinks, and sip slowly rather than gulping. Drinks can also be watered down using a mixer, especially in the case of spirits.

- Learn to refuse a drink politely.

- Change your drink to break old habits.

- Occupy yourself; don't just drink.

- Never drink on an empty stomach (but beware of salty chips and peanuts as they make you thirsty).

- Make a contract with a significant other before drinking to space drinks. It is good to be accountable to someone.

- Know how much you have drunk.

- Impose a thinking period of 20 minutes between deciding to drink and acting on that decision, particularly if it leads to breaking one's goal.

- Reward yourself materially and mentally with some positive reinforcement for successes.

- Chart your progress.

Charting Progress

With regard to the last recommendation above, keeping track of daily alcohol consumption can be very illuminating for clients as they typically underestimate the amount they drink. A more detailed form is provided by Sobell and Sobell[32] that may be "reproduced by book purchasers for professional use with their clients." This form has seven rows for days of the week with columns headed date, number of standard drinks (subdivided into types of beverage such as beer and wine), situation (subdivided into "alone," "with others," "private place," and "public place"), and thoughts and feelings (experienced just prior or after drinking). They also include a column entitled "Able to resist problem drinking" (1= yes, 2=no, 3= no urge); this could be replaced by, for example, "Ability to maintain goal (yes or no)." Another row for the weekly total could be helpful for monitoring weekly progress. For some people the table might need to allow for more than one episode of drinking on a a particular day and allow for adding in time, place, and with whom. By noting whether the consequences are good or bad, one can then determine the circumstances common to troublesome drinking and the circumstances common to trouble-free drinking.

Finally, in their chapters 8–10 and in particular their Readings 1 and 2, Sobell and Sobell give useful summaries of some counseling approaches. We now consider the question of alcohol withdrawal.

---

[32]Sobell and Sobell (1993: 83).

Alcohol Withdrawal

When a person with alcoholism stops drinking, withdrawal symptoms begin within six to 48 hours and peak about 24 to 35 hours after the last drink.[33] During this time the inhibition of brain activity caused by alcohol is abruptly reversed. The central nervous system becomes over-excited and the person becomes stressed exhibiting stress symptoms, aggressive behavior, and various mental disturbances. People going through severe withdrawal symptoms need to be managed in a clinic or hospital setting with the immediate goal of calming the patient, using anti-anxiety medication (e.g., benzodiazepines) if necessary. People with symptoms of delirium tremens need immediate treatment as it can be fatal. Those with moderate symptoms can usually be treated as outpatients with possibly temporary medication. There are some medications that help with abstinence.

Relapse Prevention

A very high percentage of people (say 80% to 90%) treated for alcoholism relapse, with social pressure and uncomfortable emotional states being common causes. Kadden and Cooney[34] describe the primary counseling tasks for relapse prevention as (1) identify as many as possible of the needs being met by alcohol use, and (2) develop coping skills that provide alternative ways of meeting those needs, thus reducing the likelihood of relapse. As previously mentioned, it is important to identify high-risk situations. As consequences tend to be delayed with alcohol, Table 12.2 of Section 12.7.2 is appropriate here. In the case of moderation, it is more appropriate to think of a relapse as a violation of a rule imposed by the client and the resulting effect as a "rule violation effect" rather than an abstinence violation effect (AVE).

In addition to relapse prevention, there is the question of relapse management. It has two components.[35] The first concerns how clients react to the onset of a relapse. They need to realize that the quicker a relapse is interrupted the better the outcome; harm is minimized by cutting the episode short. The second deals with the effects of a relapse on future motivation for change; the client needs to try to view the relapse as a learning experience and move on.

13.4   OTHER DRUGS

A large number of substances are abused in one way or another, and we shall confine this discussion to the more well-known drugs. This subject area is perhaps more appropriate for the clinician, as regular blood tests and urine samples are often part of the program to monitor progress. However, a therapist might find the information given in the next section helpful as a drug issue often arises in the course of normal counseling. For further information, one can search the wikipedia on the internet for the drug concerned. There is a world-wide self-help organization called *Narcotics Anonymous*. The techniques used for alcohol addiction can be used here.

[33]http://www.jwoodphd.com/Addictions/alcoholism.htm (accessed October 2010).
[34]Kadden and Cooney (2005).
[35]Sobell and Sobell (1993: 46).

13.4.1 Stimulants

A wide range of drugs come under the stimulant umbrella, but the most widely abused drugs in this category are cocaine and methamphetamine ("P"). The "rush" that accompanies the use of these drugs is due to the rates of high levels of dopamine released into the brain. The half-life of cocaine is about 1 hour, giving a short-lived high of 20–30 minutes, while the half-life of P is 12 hours, giving a duration of effect ranging from 8 to 24 hours. In reviewing these two drugs, Carroll and Rawson[36] describe the immediate effects as including euphoria; increased blood pressure, body temperature, heart rate, sex drive, and breathing rate; and decreased fatigue and appetite. The long term effects include tremor, high body temperature, stroke, and cardiac arrhythmia, along with anxiety, insomnia, paranoia, and hallucinations. Chronic use can produce severe weight loss, fatigue, headaches, powerful craving, and intense preoccupation with getting and using the drug. Also some parts of the brain become sensitized, which can produce severe paranoia. It is these psychotic effects that are particularly dangerous as they can lead to violence. A bewildering array of questionnaires are available for assessing level of drug use.[37]

A detailed list of important areas of assessment is given by Carroll and Rawson including determinants of drug use, for example, severity of abuse or dependence, patterns of use, triggers and cues, sources of access to drugs, access to money, and the role of the stimulants in the client's life as well as what is happening in the social, environmental, emotional, and cognitive domains. In the social domain, key questions are: Who are the people the client spends time with (both with or without the use of drugs)? What are the environmental "cues" and triggers for the client's drug use? Cognitively, what thoughts typically precede drug use? Finally, there is the question of what skills and resources does the client have including such things as coping skills (e.g., handling craving), strengths in achieving past abstinence successes, and the network of support. As with all addictions there are also the "ready, willing, and able" aspects of change and the counseling methods of Chapter 12.

Carroll and Rawson[38] note the usefulness of group therapy and self-help groups, and in individual counseling refer to the "20/20/20" rule. Here the first third of the session is devoted to assessing substance use and general functioning in the past week as well as hearing any concerns; the second third is more didactic and devoted to skills training and practice; and the final third is devoted to planning and new skill implementation for the week ahead. Much of what is discussed on alcoholism above, including the training guide, is relevant here. For example, the question of total abstinence versus harm reduction is always a key issue with drugs. Harm reduction is not just a matter of moderation, but also includes health and safety issues such as needle use and purity of the drug.

13.4.2 Opioids

The main drugs under this category are heroin and narcotic analgesics for pain relief. Morphine, a derivative of the opium poppy, acts directly on the central

---

[36] Carroll and Rawson (2005).

[37] For example www.drugnet.bizland.com/assessment/assessme.htm (accessed October 2010) is a very helpful website. See also Marlatt and Donovan (2005).

[38] Carroll and Rawson (2005: 136–137, 166).

nervous system and is one of the most effective drugs in the management of severe pain. It is highly addictive, and tolerance and dependence develop very quickly. Heroin, which is synthesized from morphine, crosses the blood-brain barrier soon after its introduction into the blood stream, whether injected, snorted or smoked. It is then converted into monoacetylmorphine and morphine. These substances mimic the action of endorphins and create a sense of extreme well-being. As heroin is also a pain-killer, it is a legal prescription drug in some parts of the world. Occasional usage does not lead to withdrawal symptoms but sustained use over a few days followed by an abrupt stop can lead to withdrawal symptoms. Also tolerance can build up quickly. It should be noted that a high proportion of people treated for opioid dependence will have coexisting psychiatric and medical disorders.

In aiming for harm reduction, opioid *agonists* can be used. These are medications that can be used to replace illegal opioids like heroin, for example methadone and levo-alpha-acetylmethadole (LAAM). Methadone can be useful in preventing relapse: it is taken orally under a controlled regime, thus avoiding some risks; it is longer acting than heroin so that some of the ups and downs of intoxication and withdrawal are smoothed out; and it has the same effect as heroin on opiate receptors. However, methadone has a similar addiction potential to heroin and its withdrawal symptoms generally last much longer.

There are also narcotic *antagonists*, which are medications that counteract the effects of narcotics. For example, naltrexone occupies the brain's opioid receptor sites thus counteracting the medical effects of heroin. If heroin is then used, it can't displace the naltrexone and the heroin is therefore rendered ineffective. A more recent treatment for heroin dependence is buprenorphine, which has both agonist and antagonistic properties so that its effects and side effects are less than those of full agonists. Such medications can strengthen a person's ability to remain abstinent, as well as providing an alternative to illegal drugs, and thus support an addict through the counseling process.

13.4.3 Cannabis

Cannabis is a genus of flowering plants that produce cannabinoids, substances that produce mental and physical effects when consumed. Different species are used for fibre (hemp), medicinal purposes, and a psychoactive drug usually referred to as hashish (oil) or marijuana. According to a 2006 U.N. World Drug Report it is estimated that about 4% of the world's adult population use cannabis annually and 0.6% daily. It is estimated that 11–16% of marijuana users in the U.S. qualify for the diagnosis of dependence.[39] The criteria for determining dependence are given in Section 12.3. Marijuana comes as a green, brown, or gray mixture of dried, shredded leaves, stems, seeds, and flowers. Cannabis plants all contain THC (delta-9-tetrahydrocannabinol), the main active chemical in marijuana,[40] as well as more than 400 other chemicals. When smoked, marijuana contains more toxic substances than tobacco (e.g., 20 times more ammonia, a carcinogen; 5 times as much hydrogen cyanide or prussic acid, which can cause heart disease; and nitrogen

---

[39] Roffman and Stephens (2005: 179). For a discussion of the debate about cannabis dependence see Earlywine (2002).
[40] Through new breeding and cultivation techniques the THC content of marijuana has been steadily increasing since the 1970s.

oxides, which can cause lung damage). THC is rapidly absorbed by fatty tissues in various organs, and traces (metabolites) of it can be detected by standard urine testing methods several days after a smoking session. However, in chronic heavy users, traces can sometimes be detected for weeks after they have stopped using marijuana.

The way marijuana affects each person depends on many factors. Some people feel nothing at all when they smoke marijuana. Others may feel relaxed or high. Sometimes marijuana makes users feel thirsty and very hungry— an effect called "the munchies." Short-term effects include memory and learning problems, distorted perception, and difficulty thinking and solving problems. Some users may suffer sudden feelings of anxiety and have paranoid thoughts. This is more likely to happen when a more potent variety of marijuana is used.

13.4.4 Hallucinogens

LSD (lysergic acid diethylamide) is generally regarded as the most representative among the class of hallucinogenic (mind altering) drugs, with a range of psychological, physiological, and behavioral effects. For example, the senses are affected so that sounds, smells, and colors are highly intensified. The effects on an individual are very unpredictable and a user can experience some severe and frightening psychological reactions ("bad trips").

13.4.5 Party Drugs

There are now so many of these that our discussion will be limited to ecstasy,[41] ketamine, and GHB.[42] For further details see Kilmer, Cronce, and Palmer (2005). Further details about these drugs are available on the internet.

Ecstasy

Ecstasy is a synthetic derivative of amphetamine that has both stimulant and hallucinogenic qualities. It is one of the most dangerous drugs affecting young people today. The positive psychological effects of ecstasy include euphoria, increased sociability, and connection with others. Elevated energy levels take effect in under an hour and can last up to six hours. Negative rebound psychological effects include depression, irritability, paranoia, and anxiety. Common physiological effects include elevated blood pressure and pulse, and the upsetting of the regulation of body temperature. Water is often drunk in large quantities to help control body temperature following rigorous exercise (e.g., dancing), which can cause health problems such as disrupting the body's electrolytic balance. There are a host of other possible health problems including memory impairment. One potentially serious one that is still under investigation is the possibility that ecstasy is neurotoxic, that is, it can damage neurons in the brain. Ecstasy is also a dangerous drug as its effects vary from person to person and the effects can be quite serious after only one or two uses. Furthermore, it is often used in conjunction with other drugs including alcohol.

[41] 3,4-methylenedioxymethamphetamine (MDMA, E, X, or XTC).
[42] gamma-hydroxybutyrate.

Ketamine

This drug has a legitimate use as an anesthetic in some special situations (e.g., on the battlefield and in veterinary medicine) and induces a state referred to as "dissociative anesthesia." Because it is tasteless and colorless in liquid form, it has become associated with sexual assault as it can be slipped into someone's drink. Some of the effects are similar to those experienced with ecstasy, except for a sense of detachment, distorted perceptions, and vivid hallucinations, and it acts more quickly.

GHB

This drug occurs naturally in the human body. In its manufactured form it acts as a depressant of the central nervous system, and induces euphoria. Effects include intoxication, increased energy, happiness, talking, desire to socialize, feeling affectionate and playful, mild disinhibition, and so forth. However, many people report having bad reactions such as nausea, headaches, drowsiness, dizziness, amnesia, vomiting, loss of muscle control, respiratory problems, loss of consciousness, being conscious but unable to move, and even death. As it is tasteless and colorless like ketamine, but with a slightly salty taste, it has been used in sexual assault and gang rape.

13.5 BIBLICAL VIEWPOINT

A biblical view concerning general addictions is discussed at the end of the previous chapter. The Bible reminds followers of Christ that their bodies are in-dwelt by the Holy Spirit and that they should offer their bodies as living sacrifices.[43] Our bodies are therefore regarded as important and need to be looked after and not drugged or abused in any way. Paul talks about having a desire to do the right thing but being unable to carry it out.[44]

Drinking too much is criticized in the Bible, and its negative effects are clearly spelt out both physically and economically.[45] Causing someone else to get drunk is also condemned.[46] Paul exhorts Christians not to get drunk on wine but instead be filled with the Holy Spirit.

Having an addiction is a form of slavery.[47] Regular prayer can help with a craving and God can provide strength to help overcome an addiction. It is a matter of one day at a time, each addiction-free day being a victory. Phoning a Christian friend can help the craving to pass, as cravings are generally temporary.

---

[43]2 Corinthians 12:1.
[44]Romans 7:15, 18–19, 22–23.
[45]Proverbs 20:1, 21:17, 23:20–21, 29–35; and Isaiah 5:11, 22, 24:11
[46]Habakkuk 2:15–16.
[47]2 Peter 2:19 and John 8:34–35.

CHAPTER 14

ADDICTIONS: BEHAVIORAL

14.1 GENERAL COMMENTS

Behavioral (or process) addictions that involve the repeating of certain behaviors are very similar in terms of brain chemistry, progression of the addiction, and the build up of tolerance to the substance addictions discussed in the previous chapter so that the general principles of Chapter 12 apply here. There is also a link with compulsive behaviors so that Chapter 8 may also be relevant to this topic. Drawing a parallel between substance and behavioral addictions may be helpful with some clients. As there are many substances a person can become addicted to, so there are many different behaviors that can become addictive. This chapter will concentrate on the most common, namely gambling, sexual addiction (including pornography), internet addiction, addiction to another person, workaholism, and compulsive eating.

14.2 GAMBLING

14.2.1 When is It Addictive?

Gambling opportunities have increased throughout the world (e.g., internet gambling) and so have the proportion of problem gamblers (currently about 12% lifetime prevalence rates in some Western countries). Unfortunately a high proportion of problem gamblers fail to to seek treatment. Females have generally caught up with males in the incidence of problem gambling, though their profiles on types of gambling are different and females are far less likely to go for treatment.[1]

When does gambling become problematical or pathological? Pathological gambling is characterized by a loss of control over gambling, deception about the extent of involvement with gambling, and life disruption. Detailed assessment procedures are described below. As so often with addictions, gambling is frequently comorbid with other problems such as alcohol dependence, depression, and particularly suicidal ideation.[2] These additional problems can make the therapy more difficult so that the approach will probably need to be tailor-made for the individual. There could be an integrated treatment by one therapist, or parallel treatment with different therapists at the same time, or sequential treatment in which the issues are treated one at a time by the same therapist.

A question arises as to whether a client should choose total abstinence or moderation (harm reduction). Some clients may be put off if they think they will be told to stop gambling completely. However, at the time of writing this, it is not known which factors must be present to support a moderation approach. Until more is known, abstinence is the preferred goal. Although this may not be the initial goal of the client, hopefully abstinence will be achieved by the end of the counseling sessions. It would be helpful if clients could at least abstain for the duration of the counseling. Generally, however, abstinence tends to be achieved gradually.

At present there is a lack of reliable information on effectively treating pathological gambling. As with other addictions, motivational interviewing along with cognitive-behavioral therapy (CBT) receives support in the literature as an appropriate method.[3] This approach assumes that thoughts and beliefs lead to problem gambling, and CBT aims to help the client recognize erroneous thoughts, dispute them, and replace them by more appropriate ones. As gambling often tends to lead to isolation, the therapist may need to help the client reactivate relationships and perhaps develop some social skills. One can also use the wheel-of-change (stages-of-change) model of Section 12.7.2 to describe the various stages of the counseling process.[4]

Why do people gamble? There are many theories put forward to explain problem gambling, but it is unclear about which is best as there is a lack of in-depth research.[5] Three common reasons given for gambling are the lure of monetary gain, the need to escape life's difficulties, and the adrenaline driven excitement that goes with risk taking. The excitement can be like a drug so that gamblers may have withdrawal symptoms when they give up gambling. Impulsivity also plays a key role.[6] Another angle is given by Ladouceur et al. who comment that, "Gamblers become full of the feeling of being powerful and admired, which reinforces their behavior and insidiously drives them to become addicted to gambling."[7] Gambling establishments tend to treat their customers like royalty!

[1] Ciarrocchi (2002: 16).
[2] Ciarrocchi (2002: 23) notes that about 15–20% of pathological gamblers report a significant suicide attempt.
[3] For example, Ladouceur and Lachance (2007a). They also have an associated workbook (2007b).
[4] Combining motivational interviewing with the stages model is also referred to as motivational enhancement.
[5] Ladouceur, Sylvain, Boutin, and Doucet (2002: chapter 2).
[6] Ciarrocchi (2002: 34).
[7] Ladouceur et al. (2002: 30).

14.2.2   Assessment

The majority of pathological gamblers who come for counseling do so when their problem has reached a critical stage and they are struggling with the consequences of their gambling so that it is fairly easy to recognize their problem. However, recognizing the problem is only the first step, and other issues such as the intensity and frequency of gambling and lifestyle consequences also need to be assessed. A helpful place to start is the DSM-IV diagnostic criteria (with just yes/no answers required) for pathological gambling, namely:[8]

1. *Preoccupation.* The gambler is preoccupied with thoughts about gambling, whether past, future, or fantasy and it may involve thinking of ways to get money with which to gamble.

2. *Tolerance.* The gambler needs to gamble with increasing amounts of money in order to achieve the desired excitement.

3. *Loss of control.* The gambler has repeatedly been unsuccessful in attempting to control, cut back, or stop gambling.

4. *Withdrawal.* The gambler is restless or irritable when attempting to cease or reduce gambling.

5. *Escape.* The gambler gambles as a way of escaping from problems or relieving a particular mood (e.g., feelings of helplessness, guilt, anxiety, and depression).

6. *Chasing.* The gambler tries to win back gambling losses with more gambling.

7. *Lying.* The gambler lies to family members, his therapist, or others to conceal the extent of his or her gambling.

8. *Illegal acts.* The gambler has committed illegal acts such as forgery, fraud, theft, or embezzlement to finance gambling.

9. *Risked a significant relationship.* The gambler has jeopardized or lost a significant job, or educational/career opportunity because of gambling.

10. *Bailout.* The gambler relies on family, friends, or another third party for financial assistance money as a result of gambling.

At least five of the above criteria must be met for a diagnosis of pathological gambling. Some people use additional categories: at-risk gambling (one or two criteria) and problem gambling (three or four criteria).[9] Working through the above items, and then asking the client to enlarge where appropriate can give the therapist a good idea of the gambler's lifestyle and his or her current living situation.

These ten criteria are discussed in detail by Ladouceur et al.[10] and Ciarrocchi[11] who note that the criteria lack specificity with regard to intensity, frequency, and

---

[8]See http://en.wikipedia.org/wiki/Problem_gambling (accessed November 2010).
[9]A related questionnaire using the above criteria, called NODS, can be downloaded from the internet using http://govinfo.library.unt.edu/ngisc/reports/attachb.pdf (accessed October 2010).
[10]Ladouceur et al. (2002: 41–51).
[11]Ciarrocchi (2002: 72–84).

duration of certain behaviors. Also gambling subtypes are not recognized. A further weakness is that only one criterion refers to financial problems, which are invariably present. There is another companion instrument available called the South Oaks Gambling Screen (SOGS).[12] This screen should not be used on its own as it tends to overestimate the number of pathological gamblers, while NODS may underestimate.

Ladouceur and Lachance,[13] in their pretreatment assessment, have several other questionnaires also available in their workbook; these are downloadable.[14] For example, their "Gambling Related Questions" include the level of perceived control (0–100%), the urge to gamble in the past week (0–100%), and the gambling frequency over the past week as well as time spent and money wagered. As with all addictions, high-risk situations need to be investigated, including those games that lead to a partial or complete loss of control.[15] It can be helpful if the client keeps a diary similar in spirit to the form for alcohol in Section 13.3.4 under "Charting Progress" for noting some facts and feelings about consumption. This diary can be used to determine the triggers (e.g., thoughts, emotions, and events) that lead to excessive gambling.

As inferred in the introduction above, suicidal ideation is prevalent among pathological gamblers so that any past history of this needs to be considered early on. Questions like, "Have you ever *seriously* thought about committing suicide?", then if yes, " Had you ever thought about a way to do it?", and "Was this thought mainly linked to your gambling problem?", and so forth (see also Chapter 10 for further details).

14.2.3   Understanding Chance

Ladouceur and Lachance[16] stated that a crucial research finding was that the majority of gamblers have wrong conceptions about chance and probability, and confuse games of chance with games of skill; "luck" and "chance" are also confused. Many believe they can control the outcome by adopting different strategies, the conviction being strong with pathological gamblers. This misconception will be addressed below, especially with regard to games of skill versus gambling, lotteries, and horse racing.

Statistical Independence

Speaking as a past teacher of statistics I have found that a concept that is often misunderstood is that of statistical independence. For example, given a "fair" coin, that is one in which heads or tails are equally likely, then every time we carry out the experiment of tossing the coin the two outcomes remain equally likely irrespective of what has happened previously. For example, if I tossed the coin seven times and got five heads, then some would say that on the eighth toss that tails would be

---

[12]See http://www.stopgamblingnow.com/sogs_print.htm (accessed October 2010).
[13]Ladouceur and Lachance (2007a: chapter 2).
[14]See www.oup.com/us/ttw (accessed October 2010). Click on "Downloadable Tools," then scroll down to "Overcoming Your Pathological Gambling" and click on the desired item (username etc. is not required).
[15]Another questionnaire, "Perceived Self-Efficacy Questionnaire" is available asking the client to give a percentage score on their ability to control their gambling in each situation.
[16]Ladouceur and Lachance (2007a: 5–6).

more likely as the numbers of heads and tails should even out "in the long run." Of course eight tosses is a short rather than a long run and on the eighth toss heads and tails will still remain equally likely, as the outcome of the eighth toss is independent of the outcomes of the previous seven tosses; this will remain true no matter how many tosses are carried out. This is because the conditions of the experiment are essentially the same even if we chose which side of the coin is up before the toss. If we didn't believe in the independence of events we would not toss a coin at the beginning of matches to determine some aspect of play. It's like a gambler saying, "I have had a run of losses ('heads') so I should have an increased chance of a win ('tails')." However, most games of chance are not equal 50–50 odds like tossing a coin, but are weighted against the gambler. Games of chance are often designed to let the gambler believe that it is possible to predict a win and it is just a matter of mastery! For example, the outcome of a gambling machine is determined *before* a stop button is pressed; stopping provides entertainment value only. Also, complex devices are used to encourage gamblers to observe a sequence, thus creating a false impression that they can do better than chance.

A game of chance is then a bit like tossing a coin where heads represents the "house" or establishment winning, while tails represents the gambler winning. Unfortunately the coin is weighted towards the house so that although there is the occasional win for the gambler, they cannot predict when it will occur and most times the house wins; technically, there is an expected loss by the gambler. There is no "beating the system," though false stories do circulate about "beating" games of chance. The same ideas apply to randomly selecting a marble from a set of white and black marbles with the marble returned to the mix each time. The chance of selecting a white marble, say, is always the same and previous selections do not affect the current outcome. Time works against gamblers as they eventually lose; the more they gamble the more they accumulate losses.

The misconception that a win must follow a series of losses is usually the driving force to keep a person gambling. An accumulation of losses tends to reinforce the conviction that the gambler is close to winning. It also creates the urge to recoup losses—called "chasing the losses"—which helps maintain the gambling. Early winning can create a belief in personal control and it can foster the idea that gambling is easy. Wins can also be seen as confirming personal skill and losses seen as due to uncontrollable factors.

Games of Skill Versus Gambling

With a game of skill you can get better with practice, but with games of chance this does not happen. Casinos and slot machines only offer games of chance and use some mechanical or electronic means of random generation (e.g., spinning a roulette wheel). However, they may be disguised as games of skill especially if they give the gambler some choices, thus giving a false sense of control. It should be noted that there may appear to be a pattern to outcomes, but this is imaginary as the human mind is very good at making up patterns. What happens is that as we continue to observe more outcomes the "pattern" changes randomly. Even random sequences can give an appearance of regularity. If patterns are a problem with a client, then the therapist could design a suitable random experiment such as repeatedly tossing a coin and, after a prescribed number of tosses, asking the client to look for a pattern to predict a future outcome.

Lotteries

Since lotteries are a common form of gambling, some comments on these are appropriate. One misunderstanding is the idea of a "near win," for example, having just one digit different from a win. This is not fate saying, you should continue! There are only two possibilities — win or lose. If I phone a friend and get one digit wrong, we don't connect. Another misconception is that a person choosing their own set of numbers has a better chance of a win than with a set of numbers chosen at random; there is no difference in odds between the two.

Horse Racing

Some might argue that there is skill in betting on horse races. However, some research has shown that experienced horse gamblers achieve the same level of payout as rookies; analyzing past information about races and current information about the distance, track condition, and so on, apparently do not increase the chances of winning![17] This of course assumes that the jockeys are not in an illegally "fixed" race! The recent issue of spot betting in cricket exemplifies how corrupt gambling practices can be. Sporstmen are bribed to conform to the bookmakers specific requests during a game.

Summary

Following Ladouceur and Lachance (2007b), we summarize some principles relating to chance that a client could do well to remember:

1. Chance gives a false impression about the likelihood of winning.

2. Results cannot be predicted.

3. Each play is independent.

4. No strategy works as there is no way to control the outcome.

5. Negative expected winnings means that there is more to lose than to win.

14.2.4 Counseling Strategies for Gambling

First Steps

We will examine some aspects of a 12-session program by Ladouceur and Lachance (2007a). The first step is a careful pre-assessment using questionnaires like those described above in Section 14.2.2 as well as looking for the presence of other addictions and disorders both now and in the past. Is there a history of gambling habits? A comprehensive questionnaire, called the Diagnostic Interview on Pathological Gambling, gives the history and evaluation of the gambling problem and is available for personal use.[18] Asking the client for reasons they have come to counseling can be helpful in determining ambivalence issues.[19]

---

[17]Ladouceur and Lachance (2007a: 70). They also list some common illusions of control for various other types of gambling.

[18]Ladouceur and Lachance (2007a: Appendix) and Ladouceur et al. (2002: Appendix 2).

[19]Asking them to define gambling can be helpful, but have a dictionary definition handy!

The next step is to help clients by using motivational interviewing to explore and resolve ambivalence using the tools of Section 12.7.2, for example filling out Table 14.1 below (based on Table 12.2 in Section 12.7.2) with regard to the advantages and disadvantages of gambling. The "ready, willing, and able" questions of that

Table **14.1** Gambling Balance Sheet.

	Immediate Consequences		Delayed Consequences	
	Positive	Negative	Positive	Negative
Stopping gambling				
Continue gambling				

section can also be used here.

Useful homework topics for the client at this stage will include reasons for liking or hating gambling, reasons for stopping gambling, and goals aimed for by the end of the counseling.

High-Risk Situations

It is important to equip the client with strategies for handling high-risk situations, for example, some gambling establishments allow self-banning contracts while in others it may be possible to have a self-imposed limit on a machine. A helpful approach to a high risk is to ask the client to describe the situation and identify the spontaneous thoughts that trigger the urge to gamble. A good place to start is with a very recent risky situation that led to gambling. By in-depth questioning, the therapist can get below the automatic thoughts to the underlying erroneous beliefs, which can then be challenged.

Managing Emotions

Common emotions associated with pathological gambling are depression, guilt, and anxiety. Depression is discussed in Chapter 9 with emphasis on a cognitive model in which one has negative perceptions of self, the world, and the future (Beck's triad). Given the sorry state that pathological gamblers (PGs) can get into, dealing with their self-image may not be easy. A cognitive approach can help the client to get a balanced view of self and find hope. A PG often has a pessimistic world view. Ciarrocchi[20] suggests two negative beliefs about others: "People think I am a failure and a loser and I will never be respected," and "Others fail to support me and give me what I am entitled to," (e.g., others holding me accountable or withholding affirmation).

With a PG, guilt often goes with depression making it difficult to separate the two. Inappropriate guilt can be challenged cognitively, but appropriate guilt poses a significant therapeutic task. Appropriate guilt has a real positive place and encourages the client to engage in restitution. Gamblers Anonymous encourages this aspect.

[20]Ciarrocchi (2002: 174–175).

Financial Strategies

Financial strategies are needed to reduce the amount of money available and restrict access to it, for example, canceling credit cards, not carrying an ATM card, using cosigners for cash withdrawals, and having someone with them when depositing money in a bank account. High-risk situations can arise without the proximity of a gambling establishment. For example, lack of financial resources such as lacking money for a bill, food, and clothing, and a birthday present for a loved one. Clients should also be aware of crossover effects of addictions, for example drinking while gambling or contemplating gambling.

Review a Gambling Session

A very helpful technique is to ask the client to recall a gambling session (say, his or her last one) together with what happened leading up to the session and what followed after the session. Detailed questions can be asked like what game/table did they choose and why, and how much did they gamble and why. The therapist can ask who, what, when, where, how, why, how often, and how much.[21] The aim is to reconstruct the client's interior dialogue in great detail in order to determine erroneous thinking without commenting on it or digressing (tempting though it may be!).[22] These thoughts can then be examined later with the aim of providing alternative thinking. Some typical erroneous thoughts include[23] superstitions (certain moods, practices, and charms all supposed to increase the gambler's odds), selective memory (a few wins are better remembered than past losses; gamblers are not always aware of the money lost), illusions about chance (chance is controllable and contagious if lucky elsewhere in life), and anthropomorphisms (e.g., a "friendly" slot machine or table).

Goal Setting

Ciarrocchi,[24] in his self-regulation approach, emphasizes the importance of keeping focused on long term goals (especially for younger clients), as pathological gambling "leads to tunnel vision regarding the future." He suggests using 10, 5, and 1 year goals for the following categories: abstinence/recovery, developmental, family, recreational/entertainment, health, financial, and spiritual/religious/personal character goals. The most important goal for immediate action is chosen from each group and given a score of importance level, and then steps for carrying them out including steps to overcome any obstacles are listed. He[25] mentions four strategies for resolving the conflict between two goals A and B, say: list advantages and disadvantages of achieving A versus B, and advantages of not achieving A versus B; set priorities; use a two-chair technique (continue arguing the case for A in the first chair and for B in the second until resolution); and visualization (visualize all the consequences of each of A and B to see which one is of more benefit).

Couple Counseling

Counseling with a significant other present such as a partner or spouse can be beneficial in helping to manage the gambler's environment. Such a person can, for

[21]Ciarrocchi (2002: 147).
[22]Ladouceur and Lachance (2007a: 50–53).
[23]Ladouceur et al. (2002: 68).
[24]Ciarrocchi (2002: 127).
[25]Ciarrocchi (2002: 141).

example, help build a fence around obtaining money for gambling. In the case of an intimate relationship, gamblers often use secrecy, and this needs to be removed by the gamblers telling their partner everything on the assumption that their partner knows nothing. This means revealing the state of mind and patterns of behavior when gambling and the gambler's methods of deception with family members as well as sources of gambling money.[26] For further references on couple or family approaches see Ciarrochi.[27]

Relapse Prevention

There are a number strategies a client can use to avoid relapse or cope with relapses.[28] For some, participation in a self-help group like Gamblers Anonymous (GA),[29] which functions on the same principles as Alcoholics Anonymous with its 12-step program, can provide support and encouragement. It appears to be helpful with the more severe gambling problems. A client may need to attend several different groups before deciding that GA it is not for them. Strategies such as keeping a photo of a loved one to remind the client not to gamble out of respect for that person, avoiding free time, taking up new activities or reactivating old ones (to fill the space originally taken by gambling), carrying round cards with written motivating sentences, and surfing the urge (mindfulness meditation). When facing overwhelming urges or slips, a useful memory aid from Ladouceur and Lachance (2007b) is as follows:

- I stay calm; I distance myself and reflect on what just happened (mindfulness meditation).

- I identify any thoughts that tell me to exceed my limits.

- I recall the five principles of chance given in the previous section.

- I recall all the effort I have made so far.

- I remember all the advantages of controlling my gambling listed in my gambling balance sheet.

- I get help if all of the above fail.

The technique of recalling a gambling session described above is very useful for relapse prevention, or for recovery from a relapse using the session when they slipped.

14.3 SEXUAL ADDICTIONS

14.3.1 What is Sexual Addiction?

Sexual addiction is defined as any sexually-related, compulsive behavior which interferes with normal living and causes severe stress on family, friends, loved ones,

---

[26] Ciarrocchi (2002: 151) calls this process "disarmament" whereby pathological gamblers comes clean with all their "tricks of the trade."
[27] Ciarrochi (2002: chapter 14).
[28] Ladouceur and Lachance (2007a: 42–43).
[29] It is essentially based on a medical model, that is, pathological gambling is an irreversible disease requiring total abstinence.

and one's work environment. It is a pattern of out-of-control behavior that can't be stopped despite adverse consequences; for example, it may lead to the ending of an important relationship because of the addict's inability to curtail sexual activities in or outside of the relationship. Sex becomes the organizing principle of addicts' lives so that they are willing to sacrifice what they cherish most in order to preserve and continue their behavior. The addiction may lead to unsafe sex or going to unsafe places to have sex, and having inappropriate boundaries leading to involvement sexually with people they don't know. Love and sex get confused and intimacy and commitment are feared. Addicts may devote enormous amounts of time to the pursuit of partners, or to fantasizing and self-stimulation. For example, a person may become addicted to masturbation and this may be driven by pornography, as discussed below. Sex becomes a form of escapism to relieve anxiety or cope with problems.

Sexual addiction in the literature can take on a variety of forms including, for example, compulsive heterosexual and homosexual relationships, repeated affairs, one night stands, pornography, cybersex, compulsive masturbation, sexual fantasizing, child abuse, rape, sexual harassment, prostitution, exhibitionism, voyeurism, and indecent phone calls. As with other forms of addiction, one has to be careful with the use of labels, as sexual practices vary considerably in society and across cultures.

Some screening tests for sexual addiction are available,[30] for example, SAST (general),[31] G-SAST (men),[32] and W-SAST(women).[33] In commenting on possibly earlier versions of these tests, Keane says that "many of the questions seem to almost guarantee affirmative replies from any member of a culture which constitutes sexuality as a central yet problematical aspect of the individual."[34]

Puff[35] notes that an addict's behavior can range from monogamous relationships in which the sexual aspect is over-emphasized, to extremely perverse behavior. Encounters are not characterized by genuine emotional intimacy, as this requires both partners to be in touch with their feelings. Sex addicts suppress their real feelings and they are not emotionally available to the partner if there is one; they may even be overtly abusive.

Addiction to Romance

Puff also refers to the related problem of a "sort of addiction" to romance. In one form, addicts keep finding new love interests to take up their time and thoughts. Typically they have short, serial relationships with a pattern of breaking up or moving on as soon as the relationship gets "boring" after the initial exciting infatuation stage has passed. In another form, addicts have long term, rocky relationships where there is an alternating cycle of passionate fighting and loving; the relationship is never allowed to settle down and the two feel inexplicably drawn to one

---

[30] Carnes (2001).

[31] www.sexhelp.com/sast.cfm by Patrick Carnes (accessed October 2010).

[32] www.sharonohara.com/article08.html by Patrick Carnes and Robert Weiss (accessed October 2010).

[33] www.sharonohara.com/article07.html by Patrick Carnes and Sharon O'Hara (accessed October 2010).

[34] Keane (2002: 143).

[35] http://searchwarp.com/swa498938-Other-Forms-Of-Addiction-People-Use-To-Avoid-Feelings.htm (accessed October 2010).

another. For both types of romance addicts, an ordinary long term relationship with a stable partner will not do. Such a relationship is not consuming enough to serve its purpose, and it is deemed boring because it does not provide adequate distraction from whatever the addict is running from.

14.3.2   Role of Pornography

The Nature of Pornography

What is pornography (which we abbreviate to porn)? It has been defined as the commercial exploitation of sex, designed to stimulate sexual appetite and having a particular interest in perversion and sometimes violence. It presents distorted information about human sexuality. People will draw the line where porn begins in different places along the continuum of sexually explicit material. We hear terms like "soft" porn (e.g., nudity) and "hardcore" porn (e.g., explicit sexual penetration) and, with the continual pushing of sexual boundaries on television, there is the danger of viewers becoming insensitive to some of the dangers of porn.

With the advent of the internet, we have seen a rapid increase in the viewing of porn. Because people are loathe to admit to a porn problem, it is not easy to get accurate figures about viewing. However, it appears that in the U.S. at least about 75% of men and 20% of women have some difficulties with porn, for example, x-rated movies, x-rated software, videos, CDs, explicit magazines, and porn sites on the computer. Internet viewing seems to provide much stronger and more addictive porn because of its easy availability, its affordability (at least initially when it is free), its explicit nature, and the privacy that online viewing offers.[36]

Therapists have different views about the seriousness of porn and some would even dispute applying the term addiction to porn overuse. Some therapists recommend the watching of sexually explicit material to stimulate sexual intimacy in a marriage, though I personally don't support this as there is some evidence that it does more harm than good. However, irrespective of one's viewpoint, porn can cause serious problems and seems to be a major cause of marriage breakdown (e.g., having an affair with porn). Dependence upon porn is characterized by obsessive viewing, reading, and thinking about porn and sexual themes to the detriment of other areas of one's own life. Porn can become the primary relationship in a person's life. As with alcohol, some people can take it or leave it, while others get addicted almost straight away; some people may always have a potential problem so that they need to avoid porn completely. The addiction is no respecter of persons and can occur across all boundaries, cultures, and areas of society.

Why do men view porn? For some it might mean a confirmation of their maleness, especially if abused as children by men. Others might do it for an easy emotional release or as an antidote for boredom. Those unhappy with their wives' sexual responses may engage with porn as kind of payback or as an easy alternative to trying to fix sexual problems in their marriages. If they are afraid of failure or feel controlled by women (e.g., family members) in their life, porn can provide a means of vicariously controlling women.

---

[36]For some disturbing U.S. statistics see http://www.blazinggrace.org/cms/bg/pornstats (accessed October 2010).

Women also view porn, and ready internet access has seen an increase in the number of women addicted to porn (see details on the internet). In fact women are slowly beginning to catch up on men with the number addicted. Women are also involved with child pornography and are more likely to be involved with a chat room than men.

The progress to addiction can be described in terms of the following stages:

1. *Early exposure.* I have found that men who get addicted have often been exposed to porn at an early age, perhaps through reading material in the home or exposure on the internet.

2. *Addiction.* Porn begins to become a part of a person's life as he or she keeps coming back to it.

3. *Escalation.* As with addictions, tolerance begins to build up so that the images viewed become more and more graphic; porn previously found to be disgusting is now seen as exciting.

4. *Desensitization.* This is the consequence of the previous stage. The viewer begins to become insensitive to the images and is no longer excited by the most graphic porn.

5. *Acting out sexually.* At this stage, men start acting out the images they have viewed, and take the behavior into the real world, often in destructive ways.

In addition to checking up on the above sequence, the following are some criteria for assessing a client for possible addiction:

- Regularly seeking out pornography.

- Spending parts of the day looking forward to viewing pornography.

- Feeling out of control and unable to stop.

- Often comparing one's wife or girlfriend to the women in pornography.

- Refusing to tell others about the struggle with porn.

- Telling lies to hide the struggle.

- Looking at porn has caused serious life problems.

Effects of Pornography

Porn can have a damaging effect on both interpersonal and intrapersonal aspects of a person's life. Some of these are as follows:

1. *Sexual Addiction.* Porn is often a gateway into a sexual addiction. It can begin slowly and then steadily grow until it takes over a person's life. It can, for example, lead to promiscuity and sexual deviancy.

2. *Escalation and desensitization.* As with other addictions, the craving for more and more intense porn grows until soft porn is no longer stimulating enough and there is a shift to hardcore porn. Clients sometimes realize how

far they have spiraled downwards when they compare early internet pictures with what they are watching now.

3. *Addiction to masturbation.* Those addicted to porn are almost always addicted to masturbation, often in front of the computer screen. The sexual urges become so strong that masturbation is the easiest way of finding release from the tension. For further comments about masturbation see Section 2.2.6.

4. *Unwelcome feelings.* Feelings of fear, guilt, and shame are common, as well as depression. There may be a fear of being found out, and this fear can cause a person to associate fear with sexual pleasure. Guilt frequently accompanies exposure to pornography, while shame is a dominant emotion. Self-esteem is seriously affected.

5. *Dissatisfaction with one's sex life.* Spouses of addicts can be affected as sex no longer satisfies the addict as much as it used to. Men who look at porn become part of a fantasy world in which women are idealized sex objects doing idealized things so that men can end up being dissatisfied with their wife's appearance and/or performance; they need to remember that pictures these days are enhanced. Porn destroys intimacy in marriage and many wives have a difficult time surviving the fallout from porn, some describing it as visual adultery.

6. *Undesirable memories.* These can become imprinted in the brain. As noted in Section 1.2.4, repeated exposure can lead to the establishing of certain ego states that are readily activated. Clients often claim that they can't get certain undesirable images out of their heads even years after they have given up watching porn.

7. *Secrecy.* Porn addicts generally keep their addiction secret so that they can become very lonely and end up with dysfunctional relationships. As the addiction grows, they become even more clandestine and deceitful about what they are doing.

8. *Disrespect for women.* This occurs in in various ways.

   • Women are regularly exploited in porn. Many women have disclosed how they and others were abused and coerced into degrading activities to sexually please the male characters in the making of porn films.

   • Women in porn are viewed as less than human, as mere property and just sex objects, and something to compete for. There is a pattern of sexual conquest of people who exist to be used.

   • Women are portrayed as being always available and willing at a moment's notice to fulfill every man's sexual whim.

   • Women (and men) are portrayed as being no more than animals interested in sex.

9. *Acting it out.* There is a tendency for those who view porn to act out those sexual behaviors on others, no matter what the cost. This can include rape, group sex, having sex with children, and so on. Men can become desensitized

to violence, and this can lead them to trivialize rape. Many convicted rapists confess to the regular use of porn.

10. *Financial aspects.* In some situations, escalating porn can lead to escalating costs as tolerance increases.

Signs of Partner's Pornography

A client may suspect that his or her partner is involved with porn and there are several indicators that might suggest this conclusion.[37] One sign is the partner spending excessive amounts of time on the internet and being less social with unexplained absences and expressing little interest in making time for others. There may also be a lack of interest in sex or sexual unresponsiveness, and the partner may be emotionally distant during sex with a decrease in physical affection and non-sexual touch. The partner may need more and more sexual stimulation to be sexually aroused and may want to engage in some fringe sexual practices that feel physically or emotionally uncomfortable for the client. For example, the partner may initiate practices that are uncharacteristically demanding or rough during sex. Since pornography is often about fantasy people, another sign might be criticism about the client's appearance, weight, and shape and whether the client is sexually attractive "enough." Insensitive sexual comments may be made. Often there is evidence of hiding, lying, and secretive behavior, and straight answers are not given, especially when asked about porn. There may be a change in the partner's demeanor such as self-dislike, changes in moods and interests, and emotional outbursts. It is important not to put too much weight on any one of these signs but several of these together may suggest that something is not right.

Counseling for Client's Pornography

The first step is the acknowledgment by the client that pornography is a problem and that he or she is powerless to control it. Clients are sometimes in denial about their problem and blame others for it; progress can only be made when they come out of denial. Sometimes a person has been caught by a partner so that he or she comes for counseling to try and save the relationship and to try and regain trust. Pornography is very damaging to a marriage as it can be regarded as having an affair, say with a computer.

As with other addictions, counseling begins with obtaining a history of the addiction and how it is currently affecting the client's life. With men, it often begins in their teens; inappropriate parenting may have led to childhood isolation and insecure attachment, thus paving the way for their attachment to porn. They may have been exposed to porn at an early age through material in the home or through male sexual abuse. Being aroused by porn may remove doubts they might have about their own sexuality because of the abuse. Their history of sexualization is therefore relevant to what is happening now and they need to understand their own history.

Porn may have happened almost accidentally in adulthood when images popped up unheralded on the computer and aroused curiosity. Some people may find life boring or lonely and turn to porn for excitement and a buzz. Others may use it as

---

[37]See http://www.foxnews.com/story/0,2933,364749,00.html#ixzz164fShaTG (accessed November 2010).

a form of self-medication or self-soothing to provide some release from the stresses and difficulties of life. If porn is being used as some kind of substitute, then there is no point in getting rid of it unless the ensuing gap in their life is filled with something positive. The question to be explored is then what to put in its place.

As well as using the general methods spelt out in Chapter 12, we now consider a number of strategies that a therapist can pass on to help a client deal with pornography addiction.

1. Encourage clients to get rid of all pornography from the home and especially from the computer.

2. Discuss with clients how to safeguard their computers. Some suggestions are:

    • Install an appropriate internet block to keep porn out. Any password to remove the block should only be known to someone else. If the client has a good knowledge of computing it might be best for an experienced person to install the block so that the client cannot "hack" in when feeling the craving.

    • Where feasible, keep the home computer in a public place if a family or others live there. It might help to keep home and work computers separate, if circumstances allow.

    • In the initial stages, have someone sitting next to the client when he or she is using the computer, if possible.

    • Attach something to the computer screen such as a religious symbol (e.g., a cross) or a photograph of one's wife or partner to provide a reminder for the client. One can also use a suitable picture for a screen backdrop.

    • If possible, avoid using the internet when alone.

3. Help clients to list times, places, and circumstances, namely high-risk situations, that trigger the craving for pornography. Discuss with clients ways of distracting themselves in these situations. The acronym HALT (hungry, angry, lonely, or tired) from Section 12.7.1 can provide some ideas. Find things that clients like to do when they are alone, for example take up new hobbies or some form of exercise, so that they can learn to enjoy their own company. It also helps to realize that we can all feel lonely occasionally, as it is part of life.

4. Pornography can lead to isolation and a shutting down of individual and social activities. Clients can be helped to expand these activities again to get some balance back in their lives using for example ideas from Chapter 2.

5. Help clients to develop thought control (see Section 1.4.4) so as to steer away from inappropriate thoughts. Encourage them to replace negative thoughts by positive ones.

6. Teach men to guard their eyes. Men are wired to be sexually aroused by sight.

7. Encourage clients to work out how much the pornography costs, if anything, and to put aside each porn-free day a fixed amount of money that they can afford. After so many days clients can reward themselves by buying or doing

something good for themselves. A client should keep a tally on the total number of porn-free days. If they fail, then they have to give the money away to some charity. After a certain number of successful abstinence days (e.g., 100) they can reward themselves with a special treat.

Counseling for Masturbation Addiction

Frequently masturbation is the outcome of pornography, but it may be a separate issue with some people.[38] Some of the above strategies for dealing with porn apply here by replacing the word "pornography" by the word "masturbation." If people use masturbation to anesthetize emotional pain, they can become emotionally stunted. A therapist can help a client find out what masturbation is substituting for in the client's life.

Masturbation can also cause guilt feelings or at least a sense of "this is not normal."[39] It all begins in the mind, not the sex organs, and controlling fantasies becomes a major issue. Masturbation can make a person susceptible to unfaithfulness in marriage. With the concentration on self and one's own orgasm, masturbation can lead to selfishness in marital sex. Being done quickly, it can lead to premature ejaculation for men. Resisting the desire to masturbate can make a person stronger. Further comments follow in the next section.

14.3.3   Counseling for Sexual Addiction

There comes a time when the sex addict realizes that life is out of control because of his or her sexual behavior. The moment of truth may occur with public or family exposure or with a spouse ending the marriage. Fear of discovery, fear of abandonment, and shame are uppermost for the addict. When addicts are found out, their spouses may believe that they have the power to stop the addiction, but efforts at control generally make things worse as the addiction has taken over.

Clients may come to counseling at first for reasons other than sexual difficulties because of the stigma attached to sexual addiction. Their addiction will be fed by false beliefs and rationalizations such as: I'm over-sexed; once more won't hurt; everybody does it; I really care for him or her; I deserve it; it gives me pleasure; it relieves my stress; and it won't affect my marriage. Other more painful beliefs might be: I am not a worthwhile person; other people wouldn't like me or meet my needs if they knew all about me and my addiction; and sex is my most important need as it gives me what it promises, for the moment. Addicts lead a double life, the addict's world and the real world, where the former becomes more real and the addict is in denial. As the addiction is based on the addict's belief system, cognitive restructuring can be used.

Pornography is often a main player in sexual addiction so that some of the above counseling suggestions for dealing with pornography apply more generally. If masturbation is a problem, then it needs to be tackled like any other addiction. For example, situations that lead to masturbation and sexual addiction generally need to be recognized, and ways to avoid these situations put into practice. This may involve being on guard when on one's own such as being careful in choosing what

---

[38] See also Section 2.2.6.
[39] Hart (1994).

is read or what is seen on TV and places visited, spending less time in the shower, exercising, or taking up some fun activities. Men, in particular, need to guard their eyes as they are aroused by what they see. Explicit images cannot be avoided as they tend to be everywhere in our society, but they don't require a second look! One method of reducing the frequency of masturbation is to delay gratification and then slowly extend the delay.

Pornography and sexual addiction are forms of escapism and generally prevent people from getting in touch with their true feelings. There may be past negative experiences that a person wants to bury. Therapists can help clients to discover what is driving the addiction.

A number of groups exist to help sexual addicts such as Sexaholics Anonymous and Sex Addicts Anonymous, for example, that use a 12-step program like Alcoholics Anonymous.[40]

14.3.4 Sexual Anorexia

Sexual anorexia (SA) or hyposexual desire disorder is an obsessive state in which the physical, mental, and emotional task of avoiding sex dominates one's life. There is a fear of intimacy or any sexual pleasure. Like self-starvation with food or compulsive dieting or hoarding with money, deprivation with sex can make one feel powerful and being able to defend oneself against all hurts.

As with any other altered state of consciousness, such as those brought on by substance or behavioral addictions, the preoccupation with the avoidance of sex can seem to obliterate one's life problems. The obsession can then become a way to cope with all stress and all life's difficulties. Yet, as with other addictions and compulsions, the costs are great. In this case, sex becomes a furtive enemy to be continually kept at bay, even at the price of annihilating a part of oneself. This obsessive state can be caused by underlying social phobia or extreme shyness, or it may have been brought on by a devastating rejection or trauma (e.g., rape). It can also be the effect of a rigid, morally strict upbringing. SA is experienced primarily by women but can also occur in some men. Symptoms of people with SA can include withholding love, sex or praise, being unwilling or unable to share feelings, and blaming or criticizing others for their problems in a relationship.

Counseling can investigate what led to SA as there can be many possible causes. Irrational beliefs and cognitive distortions may need to be challenged and some communication skills taught. There may also be other sexual dysfunction such as an erectile problem, premature ejaculation, or inorgasmic functioning.[41]

14.4 INTERNET AND ELECTRONIC DEVICE ADDICTION

14.4.1 Diagnosis and Assessment

Internet addiction (IA) or, more generally, pathological computer use is a new and growing problem with about 6% of people in the U.S. seriously affected by

[40]See http://www.safefamilies.org/12steps.php (accessed October 2010).
[41]See also http://www.sexaddict.com/eBooks/SAeBk.pdf (accessed November 2010).

it.[42] Even more people have some difficulty in keeping away from the internet, especially with social networks like Facebook and Twitter. IA is frequently related to internet pornography, though the addiction does not need to be of a sexual nature as children and adults can become addicted to computer games, gaming, shopping, investing, surfing on the internet (cybersurfing), and taking part in internet chat rooms. It does provide a distraction from life's problems and can be stimulating, thus providing the addictive "buzz." Unfortunately it can lead to self-neglect, self-destructive behavior, and social isolation. With new electronic devices such as i-phones, smart phones, and i-pads, people and particularly youth are becoming addicted to these devices as well. I will include these under the general umbrella of IA.

There is some debate as to whether the urge to go on the internet is actually an addiction or a compulsion, or a symptom of other existing disorders. A number of questionnaires are available for assessing whether or not it may be a problem, for example Greenfield's 15 item test[43] or Young's 20 item Internet Addiction Test (IAT).[44] For general references see Greenfield (1999) and Young (1998).

IA is not listed under the DSM-IV criteria, but there are those who believe it should be listed under the future DSM-V. However it is labeled, it generally includes the following features:[45]

1. *Excessive use.* For example, having a loss of the sense of time. The internet is accessed more often or for longer periods of time than intended, often despite excessive fees. Other examples are spending less and less time on meals at home or work, eating in front of the monitor, and checking one's internet mailbox too many times a day. There is a lack of control and an inability to stop.

2. *Withdrawal.* For example, having feelings of stress, depression, or anxiety, engaging in obsessive thinking about the internet, and voluntary or involuntary typing movements of the fingers when the computer is inaccessible. The internet may be used to relieve or avoid withdrawal symptoms.

3. *Tolerance.* For example, needing better equipment, more software, and more hours of computing.

4. *Negative repercussions.* For example arguing, lying, being fatigued, and being socially isolated. Also jeopardizing a significant relationship, job, or educational or career opportunity.

In assessing a client for IA, these four aspects can be looked for as well as distress due to computer over-use and/or detrimental effects on his or her physical, psychological, interpersonal, marital, economic, or social functioning (e.g., important activities like work and social life are reduced or given up because of internet use). Other characteristics can be identified such as irritability or restlessness when trying to cut back internet usage, using the internet to escape from problems and

[42]See http://en.wikipedia.org/wiki/Internet_addiction_disorder (accessed November 2010).
[43]http://www.virtual-addiction.com/pages/a_iat.htm (accessed October 2010).
[44]For example, http://www.healthyplace.com/psychological-tests/internet-addiction-test/ (accessed October 2010); scores from one (rarely) to five (always) with total 40–69 moderate and 70–100 severe addiction.
[45]Block (2008: 306).

negative emotions, and lying to family members or friends about the extent of computer usage. Most of these aspects are common to any other behavioral addiction like, for example, gambling or workaholism. Some people are addicted to texting on their cell phone, which has become their friend. With one client I suggested they repeat the rhyme, "When I am alone, I don't need my phone."

This leads me to digress to cell-phone addiction. It appears that as much as about 30% of people say they can't live without their cell-phone, so that they are becoming addicted to it. Breaking away is made harder as friends and family often expect you to reply to messages and texts promptly! I therefore wish to comment briefly on cell-phone addiction. Signs of this are:

1. Checking your phone when you wake up and right before you go to bed.

2. Sleeping with your cell-phone so as not to miss any messages during the night.

3. Checking your phone when it doesn't ring.

4. Having your cell phone with you all the time, even in the bathroom.

5. Feeling anxious when unable to access your cell phone.

6. Allowing checking of your cell-phone to interfere with social activities, e.g., at the dinner table, going out, talking, and being intimate.

7. Allowing the checking of your cell-phone to get in the way of safety, e.g., texting while driving (this is illegal in New Zealand).

8. Being afraid of being without your cell-phone (called nomophobia). A high proportion of the population have this problem. How long do you think you could go without a mobile device?

9. If you are a woman, would you prefer to leave home without your makeup or without your cell-phone?

10. Has your cell-phone use increased significantly?

11. Have you had problems with family or friends because of your cell-phone use?

12. Is your cell-phone bill out of control?

Having such an addiction tends to reduce interpersonal activity so that there is less face-to-face contact, less outdoor activity, less conversation, less intimacy, and less reliance on one's own fund of knowledge and ability to structure time and tasks. It is related to the fear of missing out.

14.4.2   Counseling for Internet Addiction

Internet overuse may be self-correcting as new users are more likely to be temporarily addicted. If the problem remains, the methods used in previous chapters on addiction can be used here. There is one main difference from most addictions in that it generally does not make sense in this electronic world to give up the internet entirely (as with the telephone), but rather focus the counseling on reducing the total use of the internet. Counseling methods include motivational interviewing to assess how motivated clients are to change their behavior and cognitive-behavioral therapy to change any distorted thinking. As with other addictions, "triggers" for the compulsive behavior need to be identified and alternative responses introduced. Focusing clients on how their behavior adversely affects significant others can provide a motivation for change. Similar comments apply to phone addictions.

To help clients see the problem areas and identify triggers (e.g., time of the day) it can be useful for them to keep a log of non-work related use of the internet. Setting goals for the amount of usage is important, for example, turning off the computer the same time every night, scheduling usage for certain times of the day, or setting a timer for usage. The aim is to make small changes and try to use the computer for necessary tasks only. Internet usage needs to be replaced by more healthy activities, hobbies, and interests not related to the computer or the internet to avoid the urge when, for example, bored or lonely. Having more relationships in real life and joining common interest groups will minimize the need for social interaction from the internet. Sharing problems with friends and family can provide support and stop social isolation. Reducing the amount of TV watching may also be helpful as TV can trigger other addictions.

Care is needed in handling online relationships and certain boundaries need to be in place to avoid cyber-affairs, especially when the client already has a partner. Some of these are: avoiding intimate conversation, controlling the information one gives out, not believing everything one reads or hears, giving priority to offline relationships and established commitments, and being prepared to go offline if the communication from the other person becomes inappropriate.[46]

Clients may need to be helped with other emotional problems or addictions and encouraged to increase coping skills (e.g., overcoming shyness, assertiveness training, and relaxation techniques for stress). Exercise is particularly helpful, as with other addictions, to help deal with stress, depression, and those neurotransmitters in the brain such as serotonin, adrenaline, and dopamine stimulated by addictions.

With regard to cell-phone addiction some further suggestions are: recognize the problem, turn off the ringer from time to time, turn off any notification device such as a light, screen calls, set aside times for checking and responding to messages, and reduce the time spent on the phone.

There is a support group called Internetaholics Anonymous that has a 12-step program.

14.5   RELATIONSHIP ADDICTION

14.5.1   Recognizing Relationship Addiction

Relationship addiction, also called love addiction, is added to this chapter because some relationships have all the characteristics of addiction. This topic should be read in conjunction with codependency (Section 17.4). The main references for this section are Halpern (1982), Mellody, Miller, and Miller (1992), who focus on love

[46]http://www.aplaceofhope.com/internet.html and click on "cyber-affairs." (accessed October 2010).

addiction and its links with codependency, and Forward (1986), who describes an addicted woman as a woman that loves too much. She draws parallels between an addiction to a relationship and an addiction to alcohol.[47] Mellody et al.[48] make the same connection with the following stages of love addiction: (1) increasing tolerance of inappropriate behavior from another person, (2) greater dependence on the person, (3) decrease in self-care, (4) numbness to feelings, (5) feeling trapped and helpless to fix the relationship, or escape the pain of ending it, and (6) in the final stages addicts feel abused by their partners, can be abusive toward their partners, make unreasonable demands, and see everything in a negative light. A very helpful self-help book, which I shall also refer to below, is Forward and Torres (1986).

How does one recognize a relationship addiction? The answer is when a person is stuck in a bad relationship and wishes he or she wasn't. It is more than just the normal ups and downs of a relationship, but rather the relationship seems to be a dead end! Some specific signs are:[49]

1. The person realizes the relationship is bad, that it won't improve, but he or she takes no effective steps to change it or break it off.

2. The person gives inappropriate reasons for staying in the relationship.

3. The idea of ending the relationship is terrifying and causes even greater attachment.

4. Taking steps to end the relationship can lead to acute withdrawal symptoms.

5. Fantasizing that the relationship is ended can lead to feeling lost and empty.

The above will be associated with self-deceiving beliefs such as rationalization (e.g., "Although he doesn't show it, I know he loves me beneath his coldness" and "Love is forever") and irrational beliefs (e.g., "If I leave her I will be alone forever" and "I can't live without her"). Another example of irrational beliefs that can arise is when a husband has an affair. The wife may believe that if someone else wants him, he must be better than she thinks. If he wants someone else, the other person must be better than her and she is being dismissed because she is undesirable.[50] The key feature is that of attachment, which can be like an addiction in being compulsive, inducing panic at the idea of breaking up the relationship, and creating withdrawal symptoms when the breakup occurs. Somatic symptoms can occur along with sleep problems and a craving to go back to the relationship.

Some questions that a therapist might ask a female client about her partner are:[51]

- Does he assume the right to control how you live and behave?

- Have you given up important activities, dreams for yourself, or people in your life to keep him happy?

---

[47] Forward (1986: 185–186); her book is a good source of case studies.
[48] Mellody et al. (1992: 32–34).
[49] Adapted from Halpern (1982: 10).
[50] Halpern (1982: 73).
[51] Forward and Torres (1986: 10, 165).

- Does he devalue your opinions, your feelings, and your accomplishments?

- Does he yell, threaten, or withdraw into angry silence when you displease him?

- Do you walk on eggs, rehearsing what you will say so as not to set him off?

- Is your life based on trying to please him so as to avoid his wrath or disapproval?

- Does he bewilder you by switching from charm to rage without warning?

- Do you often feel confused, off-balance, or inadequate with him?

- Is he extremely jealous and possessive?

- Does he blame you for everything that goes wrong in the relationship?

- Do you constantly excuse his behavior to yourself or to others?

Forward and Torres say that an answer of yes to most questions suggests that the man is really a woman-hater (misogynist). There is a need for the woman to develop some self-awareness of what is actually happening and she needs to be asked about what makes a good relationship. They also give the following list of ways for a woman to develop self-awareness:[52]

1. Become an observer and note how you respond to your partner's negative comments (e.g., "Every time he is mad at me I feel ...").

2. Choose to continue to behave as before but without any outbursts (i.e., don't challenge him). You need to recognize that his behavior is his choice.

3. Write down all the labels he uses against you and compare what he says you are (e.g., bitchy) with what you really are (e.g., gentle). Focus on the positive labels.

4. Picture your partner behaving at his worst with someone else and therefore recognize that his behavior is not okay and has very little to do with you. Also ask the question, would you want somebody you value to be treated this way.

5. Change the way you see your partner. Is any of what he does reasonable?

6. Slow down and check how you are treating yourself. Use thought stopping and replace bad thoughts by good ones.[53]

Although the above focus is on an abused woman, certain aspects also apply to an abused man.

Often the relationship starts off with a very romantic whirlwind courtship, with love being blind and overlooking potential problems. Things can suddenly change after marriage and he may switch from being loving to being angry and critical; she may be expected to read his mind. She may find that he must be in control,

---

[52] Adapted from Forward and Torres (1986: 174–183).
[53] See Section 1.4.4.

for example, in the bedroom, financially, over their social life and extended family connections, and can use anger, implied threats, verbal attacks, and unrelenting criticism to get his way. Tactics include denial, rewriting history, shifting the blame, being possessive, not allowing her to be upset, and telling her how to feel. He keeps her hooked into the relationship through addictive love and dependency reinforced by his swings between love and abuse, and the hope that he will change. In response she may rationalize his behavior or even blame herself for his behavior.

Attachment Problems

Considering love addiction more generally, Halpern uses the useful term "attachment hunger" to describe the addictive process whereby a person feels incomplete without the other person. Mellody et al. describe the love addict as assigning a disproportionate amount of time, attention, and "value above themselves" to the other person in an obsessive way, expecting too much from the other person in unconditional positive regard, and not adequately caring or valuing themselves.[54] Love addicts find themselves in a bind with two conflicting fears—a conscious fear of abandonment and an unconscious fear of intimacy. They believe that they can't take care of themselves and are looking for someone to do it for them. Furthermore, they become repeatedly disappointed in their partner, who can never live up to their expectations of love and care and satisfy their insatiable desires.

The roots of attachment begin with the infant and mother (see Section 2.5.2). A broken attachment, difficulties with differentiation and independence, or a failure to achieve gratification can drive a person to try to get back the loss of parental attachment by attaching to another person who becomes the "absent parent." People with attachment hunger can therefore have unfinished business with parents such as making parents more responsive and trying to solve childhood wishes. This can reflect in their choice of partners and I refer to Section 19.2.3 where one often chooses a partner with the negative traits of a parent with the aim of fixing those traits. This attachment can be confused with the idea of "falling in love," but after the honeymoon phase the unhealthy addiction continues.[55]

Threatened Losses

The addiction process can be fed by threatened losses that can trigger memories largely forgotten; the events are forgotten but the feelings are remembered. Bodily memories frequently originate before words, so that the body remembers. A client needs to claim the feelings about what happened in childhood and modify any childish thinking still present. Comments like, "Someday, someone will provide me with everything my parents didn't give me," and "Life should be fair" can indicate childish thinking.[56] Connecting with one's childhood is discussed in detail in Section 17.4.3 on codependency.

Partner Relationships

Forward[57] gives another angle on choosing a partner like a parent. With this partner the person is able to feel the same feelings and face the same challenges

---

[54]Mellody et al. (1992: 9–12).
[55]Halpern (1982: 22).
[56]Mellody et al. (1992: 103).
[57]Forward (1986: 77).

encountered with growing up. Here the atmosphere of childhood is replicated so that the person feels at home with familiar feelings, even though the feelings are uncomfortable. In the stories she recounts, a common theme is that the women needed to be of service and to help men they became involved with, helping being the main aspect of their attraction. They were attracted to inadequate men who could be dominated through efforts to help them. The men, for their part, indicated that they had been searching for someone who would help them, control their behavior, and "save" them. The man is redeemed by the woman's all-accepting love.[58]

Sexual Attitude

Being addicted affects how a woman relates sexually to men. Forward[59] says that the woman is not so concerned about how much she cares for the man but rather is concerned with how much he loves or needs her. She is motivated to get him to love (or need) her more using sex as the tool for manipulation. Her concern is to gratify her partner and his excitement becomes her excitement. She gets a buzz in trying to give herself sexually to a needy man who is not there for her; nice, caring men she can find "boring." She can also go all out to catch a man who is not readily available, enjoying the excitement of an illicit affair, but once he is available she loses interest. Such women have often grown up with alcoholism in the family and exhibit aspects of codependency (see Section 15.4.2), for example: low self-esteem, a need to be needed, a strong urge to control others (as anyone in an uncomfortable situation seeks to control the situation), and a willingness to ignore their own needs.

Identity Problems

Identity can be a problem with addicted clients. They may use another person to define who they are and may define themselves in terms of what the partner says. For example, a wife may define herself as bad when her husband says she is bad and as good when he says she is good. Consequently the addicted person can be very much up and down emotionally, for example swinging between love and hate, trust and jealousy, and joy and depression. Halpern calls this process mirroring and it may reflect inadequate parenting and the parent's lack of mirroring individuality.

Parental Models

Forward and Torres (1986) have some helpful comments about how inappropriate parental behavior can lead to a man who tries to inappropriately control his partner. For example, as a boy he may have been made to be too dependent on his mother through her demands or he may have been overwhelmed by her neediness and pushed into an inappropriate adult caring role. The resulting rage he feels for his mother is transferred to his wife. He may be caught in the conflict between his need for the woman's love and his deep-seated fears of her power to hurt, engulf, or abandon him. He sets out to make her less powerful and dependent on him.

The man's father may have been very controlling and abusive, thus modeling how to treat a woman; his message may have been, "You can't trust women." On the other hand, she may have been brought up to believe that women are helpless

---

[58]Forward (1986: 125).
[59]Forward (1986: 39).

and that they must have a relationship with a man at any price. There may have also been the fear of losing a father's love irrespective of his behavior toward her.

Codependence

Mellody et al. have a slightly different slant on the nature of love addiction and define a love addict as "someone who is dependent on, enmeshed with, and compulsively focused on taking care of another person."[60] Although this is often described as codependence, the authors maintain that codependence is a broader and more fundamental problem area; codependency can lead to love addiction but not all codependents are love addicts. From a counseling perspective, a person will probably have elements of both.

Four Steps

Love addiction can be approached in the same way as other addictions are dealt with in Chapter 12. Mellody et al. suggest four steps: (1) Confront the addiction by acknowledging that the symptoms are operating in one's life; (2) examine the harmful consequences created by the addiction issues; (3) intervene on the addictive cycle; and (4) experience withdrawal.[61] Twelve step programs can be helpful for various addictions and there exists one called Sex and Love Addicts Anonymous (SLAA); details can be found on the internet.

14.5.2   Counseling for Relationship Addiction

What Keeps the Addiction Going

What keeps the attachment going? The therapist can look out for some of the following, some of which have already been mentioned above:[62]

1. *Rationalization.* "It's not that she doesn't love me; she is just afraid of commitment."

2. *Idealization.* Here a person has an unreal idealistic picture of his or her partner (e.g., "If he disagrees with me, I must be wrong").

3. *Unfounded Hope.* Here the hope is not based on legitimate ideas (e.g., there are times he admits that he gives her a hard time, and that always gives her hope that he'll stop).

4. *Maintaining an Illusion.* "If I remain connected to this person, my life will be good; if I can't my life will be terrible."

5. *Control through Weakness.* "I am weak and I will fall apart if you leave me."

6. *Control Through Servitude.* "If I make myself indispensable, he will never be able to do without me."

7. *Control through Guilt.* "If you were nicer to me, maybe I wouldn't have to drink."

[60]Mellody et al. (1992: 2).
[61]Mellody et al. (1992: 75–79).
[62]Adapted from Halpern (1982: chapters 10 and 11).

Some Recovery Steps

In the the case of an abused woman, one aspect is the need for her to deal with past memories, past anger, inappropriate childhood beliefs, and parental opinions of her. There may also be a need to reparent the inner child, for example, write a loving letter to her. The empty-chair method can be used to address a parent. Forward and Torres[63] emphasize the need for a woman to realize that past ways of reacting to mistreatment don't work such as apologizing, pleading, crying, arguing, defending oneself, trying to get him to see it your way, and yelling. Statements need to be more positive, such as: "This is what I think", "This is what I believe," "This is what I will do (or not do)," "This is what I want," and so forth, rather than phrases like "I'm sorry," "Is this okay?" and "Do you like it?" She needs to have a list of things she wants for herself as well as a list of things that she won't permit anymore. A personal bill of rights can also be helpful for a client.[64]

Summing up, Forward gives the following general steps to help a woman to recover from the addiction:[65]

1. *Go for help.* Clearly this has already happened if the person is a client.

2. *Make your own recovery your first priority in your life.* This means transferring all the fruitless energy you would use to try and change your partner into changing yourself. You will need time to get well otherwise you will be too busy doing all the things that keep you addicted

3. *Find an understanding support group of peers.* Stick with the group for at least six meetings before deciding how useful it is as it takes time to fit in. Helpful models are Al-Anon and CoDA (Co-Dependents Anonymous). Many of the programs follow the 12 -step program of Alcoholics Anonymous.[66] Forward gives some suggestions in an Appendix on how to start your own group.

4. *Develop your spirituality through daily practice.* Here "spirituality" is interpreted in its broadest sense (see Section 2.6.2); for example, contemplating some aspect of nature. Doing this helps to change one's perspective and has a calming effect.

5. *Stop managing and controlling him.* This means not helping him nor giving advice; it is learning to say and do nothing. This will not be easy for you when his life becomes a struggle for him. It means detaching and paying more attention to yourself than to him. He is more likely to change if you don't pressure him and simply leave him to himself. After all, previous efforts at changing him have not been successful.

6. *Learn not to get hooked into games.* An example of this is shifting roles in the rescuer-persecutor-victim Karpman Triangle (see this triangular model in Section 19.2.2). It's avoiding those battles!

7. *Courageously face your own problems and shortcomings.* It helps to list personal likes and dislikes, successes and failures, as well as what makes you feel

[63] Forward and Torres (1986: 207).
[64] See Section 2.5.4.
[65] Forward (1986: chapter 10).
[66] For a list of over 30 such programs see http://en.wikipedia.org/wiki/List_of_twelve_step_groups.

good or unhappy. Focus on particular problem areas in your life and write it all down. Time lines are helpful (e.g., one each for relationships, family of origin, work, and spiritual journey). Are there any patterns?

8. *Cultivate whatever needs to be developed in yourself.* Don't wait for him to change but get on with your own development and what you want to do with your life. It may mean actively pursuing interests given up because of him, undergoing new training, taking on a new career, or pursuing that project you always wanted to engage in. Also stretch yourself by doing a couple of things each day you don't want to do. Indulge yourself and enjoy some of the more "mundane" things of life (e.g., watch a sunset; see also Section 9.6 for some ideas).

9.. *Become healthily selfish.* This means putting your own well-being and activities first instead of last. If you are a parent of small children, then incorporate some "selfish" activities during the day. This may mean having to tolerate disapproval. Avoid arguing, apologizing, or self-justification, and endeavor to remain as cheerful and even-tempered as possible.

10. *Share with others what you have experienced and learned.* This will help others to recover and help maintain your own recovery.

The final stage is to help clients to set limits with their partners. For example, non-defensive responses such as "You're right, dinner isn't ready," "I don't blame you for being upset," and "Perhaps I'll do better next time." New assertive statements can be rehearsed such as "It is not okay for you to talk to me this way." He probably has a problem with insecurity, and loss of control will exacerbate this, so there will be some resistance.

Choice of Partner

Love addicts frequently are drawn to what Mellody et al.[67] call avoidance addicts. The authors explain the former love addicts as focusing on the partner and the relationship, while the latter endeavor to avoid intimacy in the relationship and tend to focus on substance or behavioral addictions. This type of connection can exist within almost any two-party relationship (e.g., parent-child, child-child, and so forth). When the avoidance addicts' lives become unmanageable, love addicts often end up taking care of them, which makes the latter angry. Love addicts stay in the relationship because they are afraid of being alone, but their anger can make them very controlling and abusive. They can't leave, because they fear abandonment; but they are not comfortable staying, because they are not rescued and cared for. Avoidance addicts tend to be male and love addicts female, but sometimes it's the other way round.

Mellody et al.[68] describe avoidance addicts as having the following characteristics that contribute to avoiding intimacy: (1) They replace intensity within a relationship by creating intensities in external activities (usually addictions), (2) they back off from the relationship to avoid engulfment and control by the neediness of the other person, and (3) they avoid intimacy using various distancing techniques (e.g., building walls instead of healthy boundaries, using distractions

[67]Mellody et al. (1992: 7–13).
[68]Mellody et al. (1992: 7–13).

like playing sport or having a radio on in the partner's presence, or controlling the relationship through financial control or abuse). According to Mellody et al. they have the same two fears as love addicts, except that the fear of abandonment is now unconscious and the fear of intimacy is now conscious.

A person may be alternate between being a love addict or an avoidance addict; partners may swop roles from time to time. Both addicts go through certain cycles of emotion described by Mellody et al. that tend to complement each other, forming what might be called a co-addicted relationship. Each partner is both attracted and repelled by the other so that they end up in the paradox of not being able to live with the other person and at the same time not being able to live without that person. One is running while the other is chasing most of the time. The avoidant addict likes being pursued by the love addict, but when the latter stops out of frustration the roles are reversed with the former often using seduction.

When to Leave

The big question for the client is whether or not to finish the relationship, and this should not be taken lightly. Halpern[69] suggests listing all the pros and cons of leaving or staying (and one can add scores), and one suggestion is to refer to the five general categories of Chapter 2, namely physical, emotional, mental, social, and spiritual. Questions like, "What do I like or dislike about my partner?" and "Does the relationship help or hinder me?" are helpful. Halpern also suggests examining the role of self-centeredness in any decision. The hunger to attach to the perfect mother may bring about inappropriate inner child behavior. As noted earelier, the idea of actually leaving a partner can generate intense feelings of panic. There may be certain beliefs, usually unconscious, about the permanence of marriage that can add to the anxiety. The therapist needs to be aware of the danger of the client switching the addiction to the therapist or the therapy.

In the case of a woman who tries to put strategies into place, things might get worse as he feels he is losing control and becomes even more punitive. She may then reach a breaking point and decide that it is time for her to leave the marriage. However, knowing when to actually leave may not be easy for her. The more she has given up her self-confidence and belief in her abilities, the harder it will be for her to go out on her own, and she may be afraid to take this step; ambivalence is often a problem. She may feel she owes the man something for taking care of her and may feel guilty or disloyal if she leaves and abandons him; she may even decide to try harder at the relationship. A therapist can help her to work through her fears and any faulty thinking, and turn any desperate fears into solvable problems. Any children will complicate her decision and friends and family may try to convince her to stay in the relationship. They are often unaware of what is really happening as a man can be quite different when out in public. His response to the threat of leaving may be pathetic, self-destructive, threatening, or to not take it seriously.[70]

Once a client decides to leave his or her relationship, Halpern suggests a number of strategies, including the following:

- Keep a relationship log that focuses on feelings.

[69]Halpern (1982: 136).
[70]Forward and Torres (1986: 257–259).

- List the physical attributes and personality characteristics of each person involved with in the past and look for patterns (e.g., always involved with a "loser").

- Write reassuring memos to the inner child (e.g., "You will feel afraid of the loneliness, but that is an infant's view").

- See the connection between the past child and the feelings experienced now.

- Have a supportive network of friends especially during withdrawal and the re-entry as a separate and unattached individual.

- Use sentence completion to define self without the partner (e.g., "The main thing about me is ....", "When I feel happy I like to ...," and "Most of all I really want ...."

- Use thought stopping when it comes to thinking about the partner (see Section 1.4.4).

If the client is considering staying in the relationship, Mellody et al.[71] discuss strategies for putting the relationship on hold and withdrawing from aspects of the relationship. As with other addictions, there needs to be a period of "detoxification." Withdrawing does not necessarily mean separation or divorce, but it may mean some sort of physical distance. It doesn't mean there is no contact, and rather refers to avoiding any contact that leads to fighting, intensity, or painful feelings. Intimacy can include physical, sexual, emotional, and intellectual intimacy, and couples can be helped to negotiate those aspects that may be causing the problems. It means treating each other in a very pleasant way, then going about one's own business and avoiding areas of intimacy that are off-limits or irritations. The aim is to remain well-mannered and pleasant with one's partner no matter what happens. Teaching relaxation methods can be helpful for keeping emotional control and preventing reactions like anger or even seductive behavior. Such reactions can happen from both parties when abandonment issues surface. Self- and other-awareness are important; noting what is happening to oneself as well as to one's partner.

Mellody et al. suggest using the three "gets" of AL-ANON and these are:

1. *Get off your partner's back.* It means noticing but not responding to what your partner is doing or not doing. If this is too hard, then avoid even noticing and observing your partner as much as possible.

2. *Get out of your partner's way.* This means not interfering with your partner's life including not giving advice or helping your partner to avoid a catastrophe or any consequences of his or her actions. Make the partner's behavior none of your business.

3. *Get on with your life.* You need to learn to take care of your own needs and stop trying to get somebody else to do it for you. It also means learning to value yourself, to set boundaries, and to own your own reality.

[71]Mellody et al. (1992: chapter 8).

14.6   WORKAHOLISM

14.6.1   The Nature of Workaholism

Workaholism is not easy to detect for various reasons. First, work itself is regarded as morally good, and hard work can be very rewarding and even wholesome. Second, unlike other addictions, this lifestyle addiction to work is usually socially rewarded both in the workplace (and in the church). Also a hard worker may appear to be a workaholic when he or she may not be. Third, it is a "hidden" addiction for three reasons:[72] addicts are unaware of their addiction (at least in the beginning); society generally does not recognize it as an addiction, as already mentioned; and like some other behavioral addictions, the addicting mechanism is not fully understood. Finally, like other addicts, work addicts often refuse to face the fact that they are addicted. When Wayne Oates realized he was an addict he laughed, no doubt at the irony of it![73] He defined a workaholic as

> a person whose need for work has becomes so excessive that it creates notice-able disturbance or interference with his bodily health, personal happiness, and interpersonal relations, and with his smooth social functioning.[74]

Hart describes workaholics as having the following characteristics:[75] They are so immersed in and dependent on their work that they are not free to do other things such as recreational activities, and they have a neurotic desire to work other than a genuine desire to be gainfully employed. Apparently there is a crucial stage in the life of a workaholic when he or she faces a choice brought on by a physical or interpersonal collapse.[76] They either move towards chronic workaholism and their work totally takes over, or they move towards rehabilitation. It seems that dependence on overwork (work compulsion) is psychologically very similar to drug dependency so that the methods of Chapter 12 can be used. It should be noted that a person does not even have to be employed to be a workaholic as it is possible to be a workaholic housewife or mother. Also it is not just a matter of abstaining from work as there will be a craving for work, as with other addictions.

14.6.2   Counseling Strategies for Workaholism

There are various reasons why a person may be driven to perpetually work. For example, a workaholic may be driven by a deep need to prove that he or she is good enough or valuable enough to be accepted by others such as parents or even by God. In this case one approach would be to investigate the addict's self-esteem. The process of recovery from workaholism tends to follow a similar path to other addictions. Hart proposes the following steps:[77] own up that it is a problem; don't minimize or excuse the addiction; identify the harmful aspects; and change habits. Ryan and Ryan[78] use food addiction as an interesting analogy for workaholism. Addicts should practice "fasting from work on a daily and weekly basis." This might mean not working past a certain time, not taking work home on certain days,

---

[72]Hart (1990: 15).
[73]Oates (1978: 4).
[74]Oates (1978: 7).
[75]Hart (1990: 113-114).
[76]Oates (1978: 13).
[77]Hart (1990).
[78]Ryan and Ryan (1993: 10).

and not taking mobile devices to non-work events like vacations, kid's activities, family occasions, and so forth. Addicts should also "practice moments of resting, playing, reflecting and relating" and "learn to say no to overcommitment." They may need to get off the perfectionist treadmill. Some suggestions similar to those of the Ryans are:

1. *Rest.* We function better and even work more efficiently if we allow ourselves to rest on a regular basis. If this seems to be impossible for the client, then a starting place might be time management discussed below. Clients need to learn to enjoy relaxing; feeling good about relaxing can be difficult, as there may be guilt feelings. Relaxation techniques may be helpful. The old adage applies here, "time taken to sharpen the axe is not wasted."

2. *Ask for help.* Workaholics tend to be very independent and believe that they should be able to do it all on their own and should always operate at the very highest level. In many cases childhood criticisms and lack of approval messages are driving factors. Words like "should," "must," and "ought" reflect critical parent messages.

3. *Smell the roses.* Work addiction robs a person of the simple pleasures of life and takes away the joy of living. The challenge for the addict is what will provide true satisfaction. New activities may be needed such as a hobby.

4. *Humility.* We all want acceptance, value, and belonging, and for some, work provides these. Unfortunately, it is often related to statements like, "If I don't do it, it won't get done, or it won't be done right." The value for the work addict comes with believing they are being indispensable; this belief can be challenged and reassessed.

5. *Revive relationships.* Work addicts tend to be lonely, depressed, and often exhausted. Their work becomes their primary relationship and other relationships are squeezed out including, for example, family and friends.

6. *Have some fun.* A question for the work addict is, "When did you last have some fun?"

Ineffective time management can lead to stress, burnout, and ultimately illness. It can also contribute to workaholism. For further information about dealing with time management problems see Section 5.3.

14.7 COMPULSIVE EATING

14.7.1 Relationship with Food

Compulsive eating means eating without regard to physical cues signaling hunger or satisfaction, which are suppressed. A compulsive eater feels out of control about what he or she eats. The eating may be fairly continuous ("grazing") or be more like binges.[79] People suffering with compulsive eating have been described as having an "addiction" to food. They use food and eating as a way to hide from their

---

[79]See Section 8.6.6 on binge eating disorder.

emotions, to cope with boredom, loneliness or feeling deprived, to fill a void they feel inside, and to cope with daily stresses and problems in their lives. Although an eating addiction is about a substance, namely food, it is the process involved in how food is used that can become the problem. It is about trying to make the whole of life better through food and eating; their self-esteem hinges on what they weigh and how they look. Some of the addictive features are experiencing a "high" after a large consumption of food, abstinence from certain foods leading to withdrawal symptoms, and feeling the need to eat greater and greater amounts of food.

Multiple factors are involved with the addiction including behavioral factors (e.g., lack of exercise because of a more sedentary lifestyle), psychological factors (e.g., using food as a coping strategy), and social factors (e.g, the wide availability of convenience foods and society's obsession with body image). Compulsive eating is also motivated by emotional factors and, along with compulsive dieting, is part of an addictive cycle. Orbach[80] says that dieting can turn normal eaters into people who are afraid of food. For some people, their weight goes up and down (so called "weight cycling") because of dieting attempts, and this weight variability is associated with negative health outcomes such as increased morbidity and mortality.[81] It is very common to find that people who lose weight put it all back on again! People who take appetite suppressant drugs (anorectic drugs) will find that they regain lost weight when they stop taking the drug, though such drugs can play a useful role. What is needed in the long run is a change of lifestyle such as less stress and better sleep combined with better nutrition, drinking plenty of water, and increased exercise. Some drugs such as atypical antipsychotics and certain antidepressants can cause a significant weight gain.

Women tend to have a complicated relationship with food. Being nurturers, they have a traditional (and unequal) role that includes choosing, buying, and cooking food for others, but they can also try and conform to a particular slim image by denial and constantly policing what they eat. The Western image of the "ideal" woman, which is aimed at creating body insecurity, seems to get slimmer each year. This contrasts, however, with the fact that we are getting fatter.

Some individuals are more susceptible to weight gain than others, and this is due to a combination of genetics and environment; obesity tends to run in families. The fact that obesity is on the increase probably indicates that the main factors for it may be psychological and social. We can all use food from time to time as a form of self-medication to fill a void or cope with stress and negative affective states, but when the eating becomes compulsive, then there needs to be an assessment of underlying psychological causes. Compulsive overeaters tend to be overweight and at risk for various health problems. For example, weight has a strong positive correlation with both Type 2 diabetes and high blood pressure. Obesity also predisposes a person to cardiovascular, gall bladder, and respiratory diseases increasing the probability of cancer, arthritis, and gout.

Overeaters are usually well aware that their eating habits are abnormal, but they struggle with society's tendency to stereotype the "overweight" individual. Words like, "just go on a diet" are as about as helpful as telling a person with depression to "lighten up," or an anorexic too "eat up." Compulsive eaters may hide behind

[80] Orbach (1982: 30).
[81] Brownell (1995: 58).

their physical appearance, using it as a wall against society (common in survivors of sexual abuse). They feel guilty for not being "good enough" and feel shame for being overweight. With a low self-esteem and often a constant need for love and validation they will turn to obsessive episodes of bingeing and eating to dull the pain and alleviate the longing for affection.

14.7.2 Assessment

The symptoms for compulsive eating overlap with those for a binge eating disorder (see Section 8.6.6). Several lists are given on the internet and the following is a selection including some signs of emotional eating.

- repeated failure at dieting with the consequence of being overweight
- bingeing or grazing (snacking constantly), usually while engaging in other activities
- having an urge to eat after experiencing a painful emotion, worry, or stress
- eating when not hungry or when full, wanting more of the taste of the food
- feeling angry (which is suppressed) when eating alone is interrupted
- thinking a lot about food and eating
- keeping private stashes of food, hoping that others will not find them
- making a lot of demeaning remarks about one's food consumption and body weight
- seeing food as a friend
- emotional hunger comes on suddenly and feels urgent (normal physical hunger comes on slowly)
- craving specific foods (usually unhealthy ones)
- unconscious eating occurs
- feeling guilty after eating
- eating something and not stopping until it's all gone

The usual tables for determining the Body Mass Index (BMI) are not always helpful as body weight is not necessarily a measure of the amount of fat a person is carrying. For example, a thin person may have too much fat while some athletes like weight lifters have muscle that is heavier than fat.

14.7.3 Counseling for Compulsive Eating

In addition to dealing with the psychological aspects of overeating, a goal for counseling is to help the client eat comfortably and with one's hunger, and to know when to stop. Keeping a journal on eating behavior can be very helpful as the key is to learn about oneself. I need to know at what times I am hungry, why I am hungry, and what I am hungry for. As with all addictions it is important to identify triggers. Clients can use a food chart showing time of day, circumstances and feelings before eating, what and how one ate, whether the food was satisfying or not, feelings after eating, and whether the eating was with someone else or in front of people.[82]

Overcoming prejudice and discrimination is a major obstacle for overweight people. They need to realize that their self-worth does not depend on their weight, in spite of public perceptions to the contrary. Clients need to able to discuss their feelings freely (e.g., about the effect of obesity on their lives, or about their successes and failures in weight management). They also need to be actively involved in any decisions about the goals and methods of treatment; their competence and value are then acknowledged. Poor adherence to a weight loss program by a client can be frustrating not only for the client but also for the therapist who then needs to remain objective and supportive, avoiding criticism and exploring the reasons behind the behavior. One aspect of weight loss mentioned in Section 8.6.2 is the so-called *set-point theory* that says that genes tend to stabilize the weight[83] and the body resists dieting when that weight is reached. It is important to remember that obese people use more energy than people of normal weight so that their energy intake needs to be higher,[84] a fact not always not appreciated.

Low self-esteem may precede dieting efforts as a means of self-improvement or it may stem from failed dieting attempts. Those who struggle with a diet-binge cycle need to review past eating behavior in a journal to prove that dieting seldom works. Dieting can upset the appetite system causing the body to give confused messages with regard to hunger and satiety. In this case Orbach[85] suggests that a first step for compulsive eaters might be to stop dieting and not have any food restrictions. She recommends focusing on what they would most like to eat, to eat it slowly enough to taste it, and then see how much they want of it on this particular occasion. She then asks, "Can you stop when you have had enough?" An important step is for overeaters to realize that they are entitled to food as much as anyone else and that they can enjoy food irrespective of their weight, shape, or opinions of others. There is no need to be ashamed. It is healthy learning to eat without guilt and being generally comfortable with food.

The role of exercise in reducing overweight needs to be carefully introduced. Only moderate fitness is needed to make a substantial improvement to one's improved health and survival chances. This can be achieved by having about 30 minutes or more of incremental, moderate-intensity exercise for at least 5 days a week that includes activities like walking, gardening, cleaning the house, sweeping, and raking leaves as well as the usual sports activities. A 30 minute session can even be replaced by three 10-minute sessions.[86] An important benefit of exercise is feeling better psychologically, rather than losing weight.

[82]Adapted from Orbach (1982: 168).
[83]See the internet, for example, http://medweb.mit.edu/pdf/set_point_theory.pdf (accessed October 2010).
[84]Smith and Gibbs (1995:15).
[85]Orbach (1982: 36–37).
[86]See www.acsm.org/ and click on "Physical Activity and Public Health Guidelines" (accessed October 2010).

Dieting tends to lead to bingeing but not necessarily to bulimia if there is no predisposition to pathology. Some practical steps for breaking the binge cycle are as follows:[87]

1. Clients should slow down, sit, and take a moment to reflect on the fact that they are bingeing. They should accept the bingeing and not fight it, but ask themselves some questions like (a) do they choose a specific food when bingeing, (b) do they taste the food, (c) do they enjoy the food, (d) is it the right food, and (e) what do they really want to eat? Going one step further, what is it that they really want from life?

2. Clients should identify the feeling that led them to eat and ask what would be so terrible about having those feelings. Further questions can be asked about what is to be achieved by the eating, what is their eating trying to express, and what would be so difficult about facing their emotions if they were thin?

3. Clients should ask themselves what will happen if they sit with their feelings and then see if they can experience their feelings directly, even if only for a minute or two.

Orbach[88] mentions that when food and eating get overloaded with emotional meaning and the satiation mechanism is continuously abused, people may not be able to respond to physical cues that they are full. They may need to learn to recognize fullness. One way of interrupting mindless overeating is to pause half-way through every snack or meal just briefly, say for a minute, reflect on whether you are beginning to feel satisfied and full, and decide if you want to continue eating or not. You have the right to continue to eat if you want to. Food takes a long time to be digested so it may be a matter of sitting with a feeling of wanting just a little more and then checking 20 minutes later to see if more food is required. Interrupting the eating may require a huge amount of effort and create considerable tension, but the reward for having exercised control is substantial. Stopping is more difficult if you were not hungry for food when you started eating so it is best to avoid this stress and learn to say no without embarrassment. Related to this is the ability of being able to leave food over. Difficulties in doing this may stem from childhood training to "clean the plate," or from a fear of offending someone, or even feeling deprived if food is left.

Overeating is typically used to avoid or deny certain issues, decisions, emotions, or feelings, and these should be explored with the therapist. Orbach notes that eating cannot make feelings go away or fill any emotional emptiness; it only provides temporary relief and postpones difficult emotions. She emphasizes that feelings are to be recognized and experienced, not necessarily solved. Once experienced, feelings become less frightening. With regard to body image, most women are uncomfortable with their bodies so they need to ask what their "fat" is expressing, whether it is self-dislike, a desire to be different, or rebellion. Being content with your body is an important goal for a healthy mental state. It can begin with noting all your good features and encouraging yourself to love your unique body.

[87] Orbach (1982: 43–44).
[88] Orbach (1982: 434–45).

Some people find being in a group helpful. One such organization is Overeaters Anonymous (OA); this has a twelve -step program like Alcoholics Anonymous.[89]

14.7.4   Relapse Prevention

Maintaining weight loss can be difficult for clients because of physiological factors (e.g., adaptive thermogenesis), environmental factors (e.g., extensive advertising of fattening foods), and psychological factors (e.g., a negative reaction to an initial weight gain triggering a sense of hopelessness).[90] Strategies suggested are similar to those used for dealing with any addiction: identify high-risk situations and learn to cope with them, review past patterns of relapse, use cognitive restructuring to cope with slips and relapses, improve problem solving to avoid lapses, have good social support, and continue physical activity to maintain one's metabolic rate. High-risk situations that might lead to an overeating "slip" are negative emotional states (e.g., anger, anxiety, and especially depression), occasions of low arousal (e.g., lonely, bored, tired), social influence situations (e.g., social meal times with family or friends, interpersonal conflict), and positive emotional states (e.g., birthday or family celebrations).[91]

Effective coping skills need to be put in place, including the provision of positive alternatives to eating (or lack of it). Where aspects of overeating are involved, exercise, relaxation techniques (e.g., to handle stress, urges, and cravings), and various forms of recreation can be effective in providing a positive alternative to eating.

14.8   BIBLICAL VIEWPOINT

14.8.1   Gambling

The Bible does not specifically condemn gambling, betting, or lotteries, but it does warn against the love of money.[92] Scripture also encourages people to stay away from foolish attempts to "get rich quick."[93] Gambling is focused on the love of money and certainly tempts people with the promise of quick easy riches. The tenth commandment about not coveting is relevant here.[94] Gambling done occasionally and in moderation could be better described as a stimulating risk and a waste of money rather than as evil.[95] However, there remains the ethical principle of obtaining something for nothing at the expense of others. The practice of gambling takes away from the Bible's principals of economics – working, saving, and giving. It is true that the Bible in several places refers to the luck of drawing lots with regard to making an impartial choice, but that is a slightly different

---

[89]See, for example, http://www.oa.org.wvproxy.com/ and click on "Twelve Steps" in the text (accessed October 2010).
[90]Perri (1995: 547).
[91]Marlatt (1995: 543).
[92]1 Timothy 6:10 and Hebrews 13:5).
[93]Proverbs 13:11; 23:5; Ecclesiastes 5:10; and 1 Timothy 6:9.
[94]Exodus 20:17.
[95]For further comments see http://www.gotquestions.org/gambling-sin.html (accessed October 2010). There are many websites dealing with this problem.

matter.[96] Such methods were also used in Old Testament times as a vehicle for priestly inward illumination and decision making before the promised guidance of the Holy Spirit to make wise choices.[97]

14.8.2 Sexual Addiction

Paul talks openly about sexual immorality that was prevalent in the Corinthian church and says that sexual sins are sins against one's body. He reminds the Corinthians that a Christian's body is a holy place, in fact a temple of the Holy Spirit. Because they have been bought with a price he admonishes them to glorify God in their bodies.[98]

There is clear evidence today that Christians unfortunately indulge in pornography. For them, sexually explicit images can become idols to help them through difficulties instead of relying on God. They often find it difficult let go of their "best friend" on the computer and let God in so there is a crisis of faith. This is predominantly a male problem. A man may tend to blame his wife, his job, his family, his circumstances, and even God for his struggles. He needs to take the log out of his own eye when others have just a speck in theirs.[99] It is helpful for those addicted to actively recall those times when they experienced God's goodness and redemption free from pornography or other forms of immorality. Sharing with a few trustworthy Christian men[100] whom he can trust and who will help to hold him accountable can strengthen commitment to change this habit. The story of the prodigal son[101] (and the forgiving father) can encourage repentance. Pornography entraps through fantasy and deception and usually has an element of secrecy and dishonesty. Freedom comes through knowing and living open truth. The Bible describes that truth as residing in the words of Jesus.[102] Although focus here is on men, women also can become addicted to immoral fantasy and chat room computer access as well as other forms of pornography.

Paul talks about living in the Spirit to avoid sinful acts[103] and lists the fruit of the Spirit as the outcome of a spirit-led life.[104] He exhorts Christians to be holy, to avoid sexual immorality, and to control one's own body in an honorable way.[105] The members of our body should be presented as instruments of righteousness to God,[106] and our mental focus should be on worthy things.[107] Christ brings freedom to the obedient Christian and provides strength for them to choose to be able to overcome.[108]

[96]Leviticus 16:8: Joshua 18:6; 1 Samuel 14:40-45; Luke 1: 8; and Acts 1:24.
[97]See the use of Urim and Thummim; these weren't used after the reign of David.
[98]1 Corinthians 6:18–20.
[99]Luke 6:41–42.
[100]Preferably before being "caught".
[101]Luke 15:11–32.
[102]John 8:31–31.
[103]Galatians 5:16–21.
[104]Galatians 5:22–23.
[105]1 Thessalonians:4:3–4.
[106]Romans 6:11–14.
[107]Philippians 4:8–9.
[108]Galatians 5:1; Romans 8:2; and Philippians 4:13.

14.8.3   Workaholism

Christian workers are not immune to becoming workaholics without realizing it as they may perceive their work as a Christian duty that should come before everything else; being a servant is for them a demanding key principle.[109] Therefore they see setting boundaries and saying no as somehow against their Christian principle of servanthood. Unreasonable expectations from others may also drive this belief. Christian pastors often don't have a realistic job description so that there may be no guidelines as to what is expected from them and what can be delegated. The Bible talks about being still and knowing God, and Jesus himself recognized the vital need to draw aside from people to a quiet place and rest.[110]

Too many Christian workers suffer burnout, some symptoms being overcommitment, a loss of joy in serving Christ and in life generally, overwhelming fatigue, having a feeling of always giving out and not receiving, feeling a failure, and resenting the people being served. Life is meant to be abundant and enjoyed.[111] God expects us to use only the abilities that we have been given. Then he will give us more, but not before.[112] We need to love ourselves as well as God and others.[113] The Sabbath rest was instituted by God for a purpose.[114] The Christian's first priority (and first commandment) is to God.[115]

14.8.4   Religious Addiction

In conclusion we need to briefly mention Christian religious addiction, which can be driven by spiritual abuse (Section 16.7). The focus of the addiction is usually the local church rather than God, and the addiction is driven by erroneous beliefs that fuel a toxic faith. A sample of such beliefs is as follows:[116]

- Problems in my life must result from some particular sin or failure on my part.

- A strong faith will protect me from all problems, pain, and sickness.

- All ministers are truly men and women of God and can be trusted never to fail.

- I must always totally submit to those in spiritual authority.

- I can work my way to heaven, earning grace by my efforts.

- Security and significance with God completely depend on my behavior.

- The more money I give to God, the more money God will give back to me.

---

[109] John 13:12–16.
[110] Psalms 46:10 and Matthew 6:31.
[111] John 10:10.
[112] See the parable of the talents in Matthew 25:14–15.
[113] Matthew 22:37-40.
[114] See Section 2.7.2.
[115] Matthew 22:37.
[116] See http://www.philosophy-religion.org/criticism/toxicfaith.htm by Bill Jackson (accessed October 2010).

- If God does not heal me or someone else I pray for, then my faith or their faith or both is not sufficient.

- Material blessings are a sign of spiritual rightness and strength.

- Having true faith means waiting for God to help and bless me and doing nothing until God does.

- God alone will find me a perfect mate.

Religion becomes unhealthy when a person's attendance in church and his or her service is driven by a need to be loved and find worth. Rather it should be out of the acceptance of Christ's grace and favor and a simple faith and worship of God. It has all to do with motive. Religious addicts may be very good workers in the church so that their dysfunction is not only overlooked but unfortunately can also be rewarded. Addictive thinking is also driven by the following: all or nothing mentality; global thinking (using words like "never" or "always"); hearing only the positive or the negative, thus distorting reality; self-condemning at not being able to measure up; thinking with the heart rather than the head; and codependency on doing things for others as well as being in control. Such addicts need to focus on God alone to take away any pain of the soul and meet their deepest longings; they should find their worth in God's sight rather than in the evaluation by their church.

CHAPTER 15

ADULTS ABUSED AS CHILDREN

15.1 INTRODUCTION

This is the first of two chapters on abuse and focuses on adults abused as children, while the next chapter considers the abuse of adults. Clearly there is some overlap between these two chapters. Often abuse as a child can lead to abuse as an adult and abusive adults. This chapter is also linked to the topic of codependency considered in Section 17.4 and to Chapter 7 where trauma and Post Traumatic Distress Disorder are discussed in Section 7.3.

Child abuse of various kinds is unfortunately prevalent in our modern society. Briere says, "The majority of adults raised in North America, regardless of gender, age, race, ethnicity, or social class, probably experienced some level of maltreatment as children."[1] Abuse of any kind strikes at the heart one's very being and usually leaves a person wounded for many years, exhibiting a lack of trust, avoidance of feelings, low self-esteem, a sense of helplessness, and difficulty in relationships—all issues for counseling.[2] Abuse can occur as sexual, physical, emotional or psychological (including verbal) abuse, and also as emotional neglect.

With child abuse, traumatization affects children during the most informative period of their lives when they are learning about themselves and their world and

---

[1]Briere (1992: xvii).
[2]Farmer (1989: 18).

developing coping skills. Neglect or abuse can lead to attachment difficulties[3] for the child leading to various problems in later life. As most child abuse occurs "in the context of relationships or intimacy ... it is not uncommon for abused children to fear, distrust, or experience ambivalence about interpersonal closeness."[4] They may either "(a) avoid interpersonal closeness altogether or (b) accept some level of aggression in intimate relationships as normal or appropriate."[5] For women, this can lead to a form of codependency (fulfilling the female stereotype role of giving to others), while for men this might lead to victimizing others in turn. As the formation of trust receives a major blow by the abuse, the victim may even see the therapist as a threat or as one who needs to be manipulated into providing interpersonal safety. It's important for the therapist to challenge the notion that close relationships are dangerous. A key point is that therapy is not a cure for a sickness called "child abuse"—it is about better coping mechanisms and better survival (e.g., replacing any self-harm by an alternative tension-reducing behavior).

There is another related topic worth consideration in this chapter, namely divorce. Although abuse is not necessarily implied, divorce can have a huge affect on a child that can continue into adulthood and even old age. Some marriages are merely marriage in name only and have been described as emotionally divorced; the effect on children can be the same as legal divorce. As Kalter says: "It is possible for an emotionally divorced home to produce the same negative psychological development in the children as if the parents were legally divorced."[6] It is the dysfunction, not the actual divorce, that is the problem. A dysfunctional family usually produces a dysfunctional person lacking in various developmental stages[7] unless the child is rescued by the intervention of some person or event. I will later discuss adult children of legal or emotional divorce in Section 15.4.1 and the related topic of adult children of alcoholics in Section 15.4.2.

An useful topic relating to counseling is the notion of ego states, and a number of ego-state therapies have been developed for healing the wounded "inner child."[8] They are based on the idea that we all have different parts of self, rather like a family, and these parts sometimes have different agendas leading to internal conflict. The aim is to use the adult parts of self to comfort the disturbed child part and bring about inner healing.

15.2   SEXUAL ABUSE

15.2.1   What is it?

A major focus of this chapter is sexual abuse, but much of this material will apply to other forms of abuse as well. In this section we consider the counseling of adult victims (or, using a better term, "survivors") of childhood sexual abuse rather than the counseling of children. The term "victim" is more appropriate for children,

---

[3]See Section 2.5.2.
[4]Briere (1992: 50.
[5]Briere (1992: 52).
[6]Kalter (1987).
[7]For example, parts of Erikson's eight-stage model—especially trust and intimacy.
[8]See Section 1.2.4.

emphasizing the fact that the abuse is not their fault because they were not able to give mature consent to the sexual activity.

Clients who come for counseling often won't present their problem as sexual abuse because of the shame attached to it, or they may have chosen to forget or repress it. They may believe that since it happened such a long time ago it is no longer a relevant issue and they have got over it and moved on. Very often this is not the case in spite of their protestations otherwise. It is sometimes easier for survivors to deny the past, the memories, and the pain, and the current struggles that may be related to the abuse. Entering the past in this issue is usually very disturbing and traumatic so that there may be a reluctance to acknowledge the abuse. Clients may come to counseling because of self-harm (e.g., to deal with overwhelming emotions or self-hate stemming from the abuse), anger and aggression, addictions and compulsions (representing long standing coping mechanisms to deal with intolerable emotions), and relationship issues (e.g., due to relational patterns of abuse and victimization). These presenting issues need to be addressed first.

Because of denial and some confusion about what constitutes sexual abuse, it is important to have a definition. Although there is no universal definition of sexual abuse, the following is helpful.[9]

> Child sexual abuse is a form of child abuse in which a child is abused for the sexual gratification of an adult or older adolescent. In addition to direct sexual contact, child sexual abuse occurs when an adult deliberately exposes his or her genitals to a child, asks or pressures a child to engage in sexual activities, displays pornography to a child, or uses a child to produce child pornography.

This word "contact" can be broadened to include "interaction," whether visual, verbal, or psychological, and these may overlap.[10] Sexual contact ranges over a spectrum of severity covering (1) forced or unforced touching (or sexual kissing), or (2) forced or unforced manual stimulation (or penetration), or (3) forced or unforced intercourse, oral sex, or anal sex. On the other hand, sexual interaction is a lot harder to acknowledge because physical touch is not involved and the abuse doesn't initially seem as severe. In fact it can be so subtle that the survivor wonders what has really happened and whether it was just his or her imagination. In addition to what is mentioned in the above definition, visual abuse might be voyeuristically gazing at the child in the shower or in a state of undress; seductive verbal interactions may involve inappropriate sexual language, sexual cues, and innuendos.

Psychological abuse can occur when there is an unwarranted non-parental and intrusive interest in a child's sexual development or activity, or when a parent turns a child into a confidante about the adult's sexual problems, thus crossing the parent-child boundary. Although, as an adult, one tends to grade such abuses in terms of severity, the most important thing for the therapist to remember is that all abuse is damaging and that sexually abusive words can produce the same damage as sexually abusive contact.[11] Abuse is damaging because it is always a violation of personal boundaries and relationships, irrespective of the severity of the abuse.[12]

---

[9] Adapted from http://en.wikipedia.org/wiki/Child_sexual_abuse (accessed November 2010).
[10] Allender (1991: 30, 34).
[11] Allender (1991: 33).
[12] Allender (1991: 74).

Prevalence

It is difficult to get accurate prevalence statistics for various countries because we don't know the level of under-reporting, which is generally substantial especially for abused male children; boys are less likely to disclose than girls. Also the statistics depend on the definition of abuse. A few statistics will at least give some idea as to the magnitude of the problem.

It seems that about one fifth to one third of all women in Western countries report some sort of childhood sexual experience with a male adult. This doesn't include abuse of girls by women. The rates for boys are lower and take up a proportion of approximately one fifth to one third of all abuse victims, though much higher rates have been reported in the U.S., and we need to include abuse by women.[13] These figures are very rough as the various studies have a wide divergence of prevalence rates. However, the key fact from a counseling perspective is that because the figures are high, the therapist always needs to be on the lookout for sexual abuse as it may not be originally presented, but turn out to be the underlying problem by a client. When the pain is too great, the pain and the knowledge of what caused it are often repressed and locked away to enable the victim to survive. The question of memory suppression/repression is discussed further below.

Because of the high prevalence of child abuse, there is a real possibility that the therapist may also have been abused as a child. This raises possible problems for the therapist about objectivity such as counter-transference, over-identification with the client, projection (where the therapist confuses his or her own issues with those of the client), and boundary issues.[14]

Offenders: Who are They?

A high proportion of offenders are male, though the abuse by women is probably under-reported.[15] Both men and women abuse boys and girls, and sometimes there are multiple abusers. Over 80% of offenders are by people the abused child actually knew. Nearly half of the offenders are relatives and nearly a quarter are fathers or stepfathers, with stepfathers being much more likely to abuse children in their care than biological fathers.[16] The term *extrafamilial* is used to describe abuse by someone outside the family, usually someone known to the family, and *intrafamilial* or incest by someone inside the family. Abuse by someone a child trusts such as a parent is far more damaging, and the damage will generally be in direct proportion to the degree it disrupts the parental bond. What happens is that the source of safety becomes a source of danger and there is a loss of healthy attachment[17] and proper social and emotional development through interruption. Such a betrayal can lead to a loss of trust in future intimate relationships; the protector fails to protect. The effect of the abuse will depend on two factors—the abuse and the revelation of the abuse. Abuse by a neighbor, for example, will have a far greater impact if the child fears that he or she might not be believed or may even be blamed in some way for the abuse, should it be revealed.

[13] The statistics for New Zealand are about 1 in 4 for females and 1 in 8 for males, many before the age of 16; see http://www.rapecrisis.org.nz/ (accessed October 2010).
[14] Briere (1992: 160–162).
[15] MacDonald, Lambie, and Simmonds (1995: 4).
[16] Macdonald et al. (1995: 4).
[17] As per John Bowlby.

Pedophiles, namely adults who see children as desirable possible sexual partners, are often well informed about what children like or need. Usually they will select a lonely child or one who is in some way vulnerable. For a helpful discussion and references relating to sex offenders and their treatment see MacDonald et al.[18] and for survivors who also become offenders see Draucker.[19]

15.2.2 Stages of Abuse

A fertile environment for abuse exists when a child is in a home where there is relationship distance, emotional isolation, and a lack of appropriate intimacy. The child may be empty of love and yet be dependent on adults for that love, leaving the child vulnerable to a "take over." Also, children may be given adult roles that are not appropriate for children. In most cases abuse doesn't happen suddenly, but is carefully planned, sometimes over a considerable period of time. It usually goes through four stages described by Allender.[20]

In the first stage, sometimes referred as the "grooming" stage, there is a development of intimacy and secrecy. The perpetrator reaches out to fill a gap in the child's life by offering an intimate relationship, special privilege, and rewards. Allender notes that this stage tends to produce a desire for more of the same, and "relationship pleasure is enhanced through the bonding of secrecy and privilege." This stage is the beginning of entrapment and may involve some physical touch like hand-holding and hugs. He also mentions that the child or adolescent "feels loved and longs for the fatherly or motherly touch of the adult who is bonding with her."

The second stage usually involves physical contact that appears to be appropriate. The touch may move to the beginning of physical and sensual bonding, which, for the child, is generally not sexual at this stage but is pleasurable and increases relational intimacy. Physical touch then becomes sexualized for the child. Although the child may feel uncomfortable and uncertain boundary-wise as to what is happening and experience guilt or shame about the touching, the situation is clouded by the experience of being cared for. Children do not recognize the progression as abuse and, having enjoyed the non-sexual touching and being treated as an adult, feel somewhat responsible for their complicity. Allender comments that they are thus effectively silenced and their fate sealed.

Stage three is when sexual abuse proper begins and Allender describes this stage as a betrayal of the child's trusting relationship. When the abuse is overt and physical (e.g., genital contact), the child or adolescent may experience sexual arousal so there is ambivalence about hating what is happening and yet enjoying the feeling. As Allender comments, "The tragedy of abuse is that the enjoyment of one's body becomes the basis of a hatred of one's soul"[21] and "the part of ourselves we hate the most is our longing to be wanted and enjoyed."[22] Being unable to accommodate opposing feelings like hate and shame versus pleasure and desire can lead to blocked feelings. It is better to feel nothing at all than cope with the ambivalence of rage

[18]MacDonald et al. (1995: chapter 12).
[19]Draucker (2000: 93–98).
[20]Allender (1991: chapter 3).
[21]Allender (1991: 86).
[22]Allender (1991: 49).

over the betrayal and terror of losing the relationship with the abuser and others in one's family.[23] As noted above, huge damage can be done to a child's sense of self, even when the abuse is non-physical such as inappropriate remarks of a sexual nature.

Stage four involves the maintenance of the abuse and the secrecy through a variety of physical or psychological means. Although stage four is similar to stage one, pleasure from the initial attention is now gone and the abuser forces the child into silence and compliance using fear and/or privilege. Offenders may use violence or physical threats including the threat to hurt the victim, or someone dear to them, or even a pet. They may use psychological means such as telling the child they won't be believed. The silence is very seldom broken, and the child tries to find some way to endure. One way is to block out memories and emotions; we consider memories in the next section.

15.2.3   Effects of Sexual Abuse

Memories

Some child abuse victims block out the memory of their abuse from their conscious mind and can experience various degrees of dissociative amnesia. As children they were unable to fully understand their feelings and express them openly so the feelings got suppressed and stored in implicit memory.[24] Memory suppression can take place quickly. For example, Sandford[25] recounts a story of a young man, abused by several schoolmates, who was terribly afraid when he caught sight of some of them only a few days after the trauma, but he did not know why! What happens is that the suppressed feelings can be triggered later in life by various events, but the victim does not know their source. These memories can be physical or "body" memories where a physical symptom seems to appear out of nowhere, or a "feeling" memory where there is an unexplained overwhelming emotional experience that suddenly occurs.[26] For example, there is the woman who always experienced a choking feeling when she heard a man eating as she had been forced as a child to have oral sex. Another example is where a person develops a fear of water because of abuse in a swimming pool.

Hydes[27] comments that survivors can come under tremendous pressure from memories and reactions around the age of forty as they no longer have the energy to hold these memories away from their conscious mind. There may be times when memories are too deeply buried in the subconscious or the child was too young to recall them. Sometimes the stress of a trauma is so great that the hippocampus is affected to the extent that the explicit memory of the event is fragmented or permanently missing. It is important to remember that the amnesia is not so much a pathological process but is more of an adaptive strategy for coping. For this reason, some memories are too traumatic to be recalled and using special techniques like hypnosis or guided imagery can run the risk of re-traumatizing the client or planting false memories.

[23] Allender (1991: 88–89).
[24] See Section 1.2.3.
[25] Sandford (1988: 39).
[26] Mellody et al. (1989: 134).
[27] Hydes (1995: 31).

An important question, then is "Why recall past memories?" Regaining memories helps to remove denial, reclaims back self and the past, and moves toward real change in the future. The past and present are tied together so that facing past memories brings control and avoids the sabotaging of the present by the past buried in the subconscious. Memories often return slowly but may gradually hone in on the worst experience so that care is needed in order that the survivor won't be destroyed by the devastating memory. Trying to force memories into existence won't work, but a client being open, honest, and curious will help. Draucker says that:

> Free narrative recall in which clients are encouraged to discuss thoughts, feelings, and experiences in response to open-ended, non-suggestive questioning often yields significant information about past events without increasing the risk of memory error.[28]

Often, no special techniques for enhancing the memory are required. If they are needed, one can perhaps use context reinstatement combined with free recall, which involves having the client focus on a period of time in which the abuse probably occurred; this is slightly more open to false memories. According to Brown et al.

> Recovery of memories is not about gathering information about the past. It is about mastery over what has been unclear or avoided in memory, making meaning out of one's personal history, and achieving integration.[29]

It can be problematical to trigger memories in later life as they may not recall accurately what really happened. There is an extensive literature on recovered memories and their validity,[30] and lawsuits have resulted from false memories about sexual abuse.[31] Repressed memories are discussed further in Section 7.3.3 with regard to post-traumatic stress disorder.

There are two views on suppressed memories, that is memories that are voluntary and one attempts to forget, summarized briefly by Drauker.[32] One is that recovered memories are "confabulations" induced by questionable therapeutic practices or self-help literature, and the other is that they are typically accurate and should not be met with skepticism by therapists. She recommends that therapists keep an open mind with regard to memories presented by clients in therapy and avoid leading or closed-ended questions, premature conclusions, and uncritical acceptance of memories as historical truths. It can be helpful to inform clients that memories can contain a mixture of accurate and inaccurate information so as to avoid impulsive actions based on the information. However, Richmond[33] makes the point that even a false memory can be helpful to the therapist as there will be circumstances surrounding that memory. It is not a question of the therapist believing whether the event in question happened exactly as the client recalls it, but rather that the therapist believes in the client's pain. It is a matter of listening to the wounded inner child.

There is controversy as to whether or not most or all memories of abuse should be accessed and worked through for client recovery, especially as many clients will

[28] Draucker (2000: 22).

[29] Brown, Scheflin, and Hammond (1998: 481).

[30] Pope and Brown (1996).

[31] See, for example, the writings of Elizabeth Loftus and internet references such as http://en.wikipedia.org/wiki/False_memory_syndrome (accessed November 2010).

[32] Drauker (2000: chapter 2).

[33] http://www.guidetopsychology.com/repressn.htm (accessed October 2010).

never recall some memories.[34] Gradual recall through building up the therapeutic relationship seems to be the way to go, since working through available (or eventually available) memories reduces the power of unavailable memories.

Identification with the Aggressor

There is a psychodynamic process called "identification with the aggressor" in which the abused child, in trying to make sense of something essentially senseless, comes to believe that the abuse must somehow be justified. The child then unconsciously seeks to befriend and even imitate the abuser[35] with the result that blame and anger toward the abuser becomes turned toward the self, thus beginning the repetition of an unconscious, self-inflicted abuse. Because the child is powerless to stop the abuse or to convince anyone to help, the child begins to blame the world for being unfair. They also blame themselves for not being "good enough" to put up a successful fight against the world. Since the world can't be punished, blaming and punishing self can provide immediate and controlled satisfaction. The child therefore grows into an adult harboring bitterness against the world for its unpunished abuses. At every disappointment he or she may find some convenient, secret means of self-sabotage, and will then feel justified in saying, "Look what they did to me! Its not fair!"

Adult Sexual Effects of Abuse

Adults abused as children may find that their ability to enjoy sexual experiences has been compromised. They may view their relationship and sexual arousal in terms of their past victimization. Consequently they may have a lack of interest in sex or feel disgusted by it, even though they can function sexually. For example, a woman's lack of interest may bring her relief by avoiding unpleasant emotional realities and foster revenge through withholding intimacy and pleasure. Also, the stress associated with the past abuse reinforces the memories of the abuse, especially the accompanying emotions, which makes the brain hyper-vigilant or overly watchful for anything that resembles possible abuse. Sometimes all it takes is something small like some kind of movement or reaction from a partner during love-making to trigger a physical response that stems from the past abuse, even if the abuse is not consciously remembered. Consequently the person may feel uncomfortable and pull away from the partner. One client I had could not sleep with her back to her partner. Another struck out at her partner if he grabbed her unexpectedly for a hug; she need to be warned so her thinking neocortex could override her amygdala's emotional esponse.

There can be a variety of circumstances where a person may feel uncomfortable with his or her partner present (e.g., being in a state of undress or being in the shower) due to the circumstances surrounding the abuse. In fact any situation that the survivor experiences as sexual can trigger a fear response. It is important to identify triggers and avoid them during sex. A woman might go from one partner to another leaving them when they get too close emotionally or when they do something she does not like. Such a person can unconsciously become a man-hater as she is trying to punish her past abuser. A survivor may also act out sexually to feel psychologically in control and may endeavor to master feelings about sex by

[34] Briere (1992: 135).
[35] See Stockholm syndrome on the internet.

being with many partners. Other behaviors for men like watching pornography or having paid sex can also be the result of abuse. For further details about sexual problems see Section 19.4.3.

General Effects of Sexual Abuse

Sexual abuse can lead to such issues as fear, anger, shame, major depression, poor self-esteem, sexual dysfunction (mentioned above), a variety of physical complaints, and compulsive disorders and addictions (e.g., alcoholism, self-harm, eating disorders). Concerning bulimia, we have the implication that, "A strange combination of relief and revenge is found in the process of purging."[36] A high proportion of people with addictions like alcohol, substance abuse, eating disorders, and self-harm have a history of some form of abuse, including a significant number of children and adolescents attempting suicide. Other effects can include the intrusive symptoms of post traumatic stress disorder (PTSD) such as flashbacks, which are often triggered by events or stimuli that are abused-related, and intrusive thoughts centered around themes of danger, humiliation, sex, and guilt.[37] Four possible damaging effects of sexual abuse are traumatic sexualization, stigmatization, betrayal, and powerlessness. As the last three are cognitive they can "alter the child's cognitive and emotional orientation to the world and create trauma by distorting a child's self-concept, worldview, and affective capacities."[38] The tendency to blame the victim carries with it a stigma and a general discomfort about recognizing the presence of sexual abuse. Many women who were abused as children and disclosed their experience to others have had their experience denied completely or invalidated. Care is therefore needed in who the abused shares his or her history with. Some people will have relatives or friends who will minimize or deny what happened. This may mean the abused person accepting some ambiguity about what happened and some uncertainty about specific details.

Those abused may not be confident in their perceptions and judgments about themselves and others, and second guess their own emotional reactions. They don't trust themselves or others. In particular, abused clients will usually have a distorted image of self. For example, when a daughter is abused by her father, there will be a confusion of identity in which the sense of being what she was created to be as female, daughter, wife, and mother is damaged at the core; she feels like a nothing, a nobody. She can therefore argue as follows:[39]

1. I am being hurt by a parent.

2. Based on a child's thinking, this abuse is because I am bad or my parent is bad.

3. I am taught that parents are always right and do things for my own good; when they hurt me it is for my own good (it is called punishment).

4. I am being hurt so it must be my fault and I deserve the punishment.

5. I am hurt often and/or quite deeply so I must be very bad. (This logic is applied to any kind of child abuse, including physical abuse. As alluded to

[36]Allender (1991: 150).
[37]Briere (1992: 21).
[38]Finkelhor and Browne (1985: 180).
[39]Briere (1992: 28).

above, sexual abuse can lead the survivor into promiscuity, or it can lead to frigidity in a marriage.)

Being powerless as an abused child can have far-reaching consequences in adulthood such as experiencing self-doubt, despair, and deadness, with the deadness often being achieved by a process of splitting, denial, and loss of memory. Here splitting is an unconscious process of dividing memories and feelings into separable categories of good or bad. A wall of denial is then built between the "good" and "bad" selves.[40] Another aspect of splitting is that thoughts and feelings are dissociated from the physical experience, or the feelings are blocked off from the thoughts. Without a proper expression of feelings a person cannot learn what hurts them so that they doubt their own feelings and thus lose their perspective and their sense of judgment. There is a danger that they may enter into inappropriate relationships and be victimized again. They may even believe that they are not worthy of a better relationship and see themselves as inadequate.

A woman may want to be close but be afraid of being too close and not in control. She may form a relationship with someone who is insensitive with a "macho" image as she knows he won't get too close or be capable of forming a close relationship. This ambivalence can lead to confusion about a person's desirability, and can give rise to a chronic sense of irrational responsibility for the past abuse. Emotions can be confused, for example, pleasure becomes highly suspect and dangerous and needs to be controlled.

As most abusers are known to an abused child, betrayed trust also has after-effects. If the abuser was a father, betrayal can lead to a loss of trust in authority figures. Survivors can be angry and ashamed that they allowed themselves to be taken advantage of, and may assume that they could have prevented the betrayal if they were less needy or naive. Guilt, therefore, can weigh very heavily as survivors may feel they are responsible in some way. They may feel they should have resisted or told someone. The abuser might have said, "You made me do it." Guilt can then become the crippling bondage of shame. Furthermore, they may feel betrayed by the family for not being there for them prior to abuse, betrayed by the perpetrator, and betrayed by the non-offending parents for not protecting them. For example, they may ask "Why did my mother let this happen?" or "Where was she when it happened?" This leads to an ambivalence about love/hate feelings towards parents. The role of non-offending parents may have been: (a) they had no knowledge of the abuse, (b) they suspected but did not acknowledge the abuse, (c) they knew of the abuse but did not intervene, or (d) they knew of the abuse but condoned it.

A further consequence of betrayal is that survivors may believe that relationships can neither be trusted, nor expected to last. They need a new working model for relating to others, for example with regard to authority figures or to current romantic relationships. How people behave towards others can be an indicator as to how much they have got over the abuse, irrespective of what they may declare about their recovery. Allender[41] suggests that there are certain styles of relating to people that can be typical of an abused woman, namely:

1. *Good girl.* She is the woman who does everything for everybody else no matter what the cost, as she wants others to be pleased with her. However,

[40] Allender (1991: 104).
[41] Allender (1991: chapter 9).

she is detached and dead inside, is passionless and largely disengaged from her emotions and wounds of her soul, except perhaps for guilt. She is more willing to give her hands than her heart.

2. *Tough Girl.* She is the tough minded, controlling, taking charge, no-nonsense woman who has built a wall that she lives behind to keep people from getting too close. Emotions are to be conquered and controlled so that she won't be hurt again, and she refuses to be dependent on anyone. She is suspicious, hostile, critical, and views compliments as "buttering up." Consequently people keep their distance so she ends up a lonely woman.

3. *Party Girl.* She is the complicated, easygoing, good time lady who is capricious, inconsistent, and hard to pin down in close relationships. She will go from one relationship to another looking for satisfaction; once the fun eases off or commitment is needed or a storm brews, she ends the relationship. Her manner can be warm and inviting, then she can quickly become irascible and demanding. She has both a hunger for and a hatred of relationship.

A person may exhibit all three characteristics with different people at different times. Allender notes strategies for helping all three: the Good Girl can "reclaim her voice with her spouse or friends for the sake of their spouse and friends;" the Tough girl can "pursue feedback rather than intimidate those around her into never expressing their anger and hurt;" and the Party Girl can "acknowledge her tendency to bail out" when things get difficult and "deepen her commitment to talk over her dread of relationship and how it shows itself in manipulation."[42]

For men, the three corresponding roles might be: the uninvolved, withdrawn "nice guy;" the macho mentally or physically tough and emotionally distant man; and the sexually addicted non-committed male.[43]

Cloiter et al. (2006) found from their studies, including client complaints, that interpersonal problems, emotion management problems, and symptoms of PTSD contributed a total of 42% to functional impairment in abuse. This led to their following symptom profile of childhood abuse survivors;[44]

1. Symptoms of PTSD.

   (a) Reexperiencing symptoms including nightmares, flashbacks, and intrusive thoughts related to trauma.

   (b) Avoidance and emotional numbing, including avoidance of thoughts, people, places, or activities that produce reminders of the trauma, and a loss of interest in things that used to give pleasure.

   (c) Hyperarousal leading to irritability, exaggerated startle response, and problems with sleeping and concentration.

2. Emotion regulation problems such as emotional reactivity to minor stimuli (e.g., fear, rage, avoidance), losing one's sense of equilibrium, tendency to disassociate under stress, engaging in self-harm, and excessive use of drugs or alcohol to cope.

---

[42] Allender (1991: 215–216).
[43] Allender (1991:249–250).
[44] Cloitre et al. (2006: 36, Box 4.1).

3. Interpersonal problems including difficulty with intimacy and trust, sensitivity to criticism, inability to hear other viewpoints, difficulty in standing up for oneself, tendency to quit relationships and jobs without negotiation, and a history of repeated victimization (e.g., domestic violence, date rape).

They proposed a *resource loss model* for trauma generally, as well as for sexual abuse, and believed that enduring symptoms occur when the resources are insufficient relative to their need. Like a physical injury, recovery will depend on one's resources. Childhood abuse is a trauma that overwhelms a child's resources. The key then is to build up a client's resources using phase 1 of their two-phase program call STAIR, which stands for Skills Training in Affective and Interpersonal Regulation, and the symptom targets are emotion regulation difficulties and interpersonal problems. The focus is on increasing emotional awareness by identifying and labeling feelings along with relaxation breathing techniques, using positive self-statements and imagery, using positive feelings as a guide to decision making and action, identifying goals, working with fear and anger, and accepting negative emotions. Emotion regulation is important as some people experience intense negative emotions and they need to have options as to how they might respond to them rather than being carried away by them. With interpersonal problems there is a need to change relationship patterns including revising interpersonal expectations, role playing different interpersonal relationships, and teaching the client about the role of trauma-based schemas and their self-fulfilling nature, as well as helping to generate new schemas. Here schemas, which are organized patterns of thought or behavior, play a fundamental role in this therapeutic model, as there is a need to replace maladaptive schemas by more positive adaptive schema, and changing interpersonal schemas to relate better with people. This is essentially a CBT approach. They consider the activating event, feelings, and beliefs about self, expectations about others, and the resulting action can be documented along with alternative feelings, expectations, and actions. [45]

15.2.4   Counseling Strategies

First some general comments. In counseling adult child-abuse victims, irrespective of how much they are aware of the abuse or not, it is essential that we provide a safe, caring, and loving environment where the client can express feelings such as anger and rage openly, knowing that we will hold those feelings out there for them. It is important for a therapist to acknowledge expressed feelings and help the client to connect facts with feelings through open-ended questions. Some families may discourage the expression of feelings and this can be addressed by the therapist, for example by asking where a certain message came from.

Because of the high prevalence of sexual abuse, we need to be on the lookout for characteristics that suggest possible abuse. If we think this is the case, it is not up to us to impose this on the client as we may re-traumatize them. If they are aware of the abuse they may reveal it in their own good time if we stay with them, for what might turn out to be a long journey. Otherwise probing might close them down or destroy their coping strategy and leave them vulnerable. If they are not aware of the abuse, they may in time eventually experience flashbacks and feelings,

[45]Cloitre et al (2006: 208).

with the ultimate return of memories or partial memories of what happened and how they felt at the time. This can be terrifying for the client, and clearly the therapist needs to handle this very carefully and gently, without rushing. Clients should be warned at the beginning of such a session about this possibility, which can be reframed (e.g, getting "worse" before getting "better"). Section 7.3 on post traumatic stress disorder may be relevant here to help a client to manage trauma symptoms. However, if healing is to begin, this catharsis, or outpouring of the heart, needs to take place through the client going back over the abuse experience, with considerable attention to any details recalled. This point is also emphasized by Ann Hart in her horrific story.[46] Mourning over missed opportunities and losses due to the abuse may also surface.

Revisiting the Abuse

The revisiting of the abuse needs to done in a way that empowers the client and does not reinforce the original feelings of powerlessness. The repeated telling allows clients to evaluate and organize their memories and determine their place in life history. They learn to see that they are just memories and have no real power over the client. The client can also identify self and interpersonal beliefs, realizing they belong to a traumatic childhood. Cloitre et al.[47] mention other benefits such as: reducing feelings of alienation, reducing the strength of the bond to the perpetrator, enhancing self compassion, learning to know self better, improving interpersonal relationships, and providing liberation and growth. Draucker suggests beginning with factual, verbal memories, as these tend to be processed first and are less overwhelming, and then moving to sensory memories (including sight, hearing, smell, and touch) about physical sensations and affects. Initially the focus is on the big picture. Care is needed in asking for details to avoid any impression that the therapist is voyeuristic! Draucker[48] notes that on disclosure by the client it is important for the therapist to avoid a shock response, disbelief, blaming, and any minimization. She suggests a number of helpful responses such as showing calm concern (e.g., "Sexual abuse can be very painful for children and it can impact adulthood"), acknowledging the difficulty of disclosure (e.g., "I respect your courage"), reinforcing the client's control of the disclosure process (e.g., "I will proceed at your pace"), and acknowledging feelings and assessing safety (e.g.,"Do you feel unsafe in any way?").

The process of revisiting the abuse is the second phase of Cloitre et al's treatment program, which they call Narrative Story Telling (NST), and it involves the emotional processing of the traumatic events in the context of a safe and supportive environment. They particularly focus on fear, shame and loss followed up with strategies to ground the client in the present. They mention four different shame themes: self as inferior, self as bad, self as annihilated, and self as identified with the perpetrator. They take a different approach to revisiting the abuse. They suggest first selecting the trauma memory that elicits the most distress as other memories will be easier to handle. However, this is preceded by practicing with a narrative of a neutral memory to help the client to get used to the idea. In retelling the story they suggest taking a SUDS score both before and after telling the story.[49]

[46]Pike and Mohline (1995: 46).
[47]Cloitre et al. (2006: 289–290).
[48]Draucker (2000: 31).
[49]See 6.3.3 under exposure methods.

Briere[50] mentions the importance of focusing the therapy on the abuse to allow the survivor "to discover and address the basis of his or her discontent" and to rework the injured child's cognitive reactions and impressions, replacing them with an adult understanding of the victimization. It is a matter of helping them to get in touch with the child within. Cognitive restructuring can therefore play a helpful and important role in therapy. When clients revisit the difficult past from a position of present strength, they are able to feel compassion for the young persons they once were and appreciate more their current achievements both in and out of therapy. They need to let go of the past in favor of the present, where they can feel at home.

Traumatic events that led to dissociation need also to be re-experienced so that the simultaneous contradictory feelings experienced at the time of the abuse that led to a shut-down of feelings can be re-experienced without significant damaging dissociation. This enables the history of the abuse to be rewritten from an adult point of view. The abuse history also helps the therapist to be aware of potential problems, for example, abuse by a father may impact on a client's view of authority.

The therapist needs to be aware that this process of giving up survival strategies and facing painful memories can be very difficult and requires courage and trust in the therapeutic relationship from the client. Because of the client's potential pain, the therapist will usually meet initial resistance. Clearly there needs to be a balance between exploration and consolidation;[51] the therapist deciding whether to proceed with further uncovering (which might be too painful at that stage) or to concentrate on stabilizing and supporting gains made thus far.

Issues needing to be reframed from an adult perspective include survivors' self-blame for the abuse, guilt about physical pleasure from sexual arousal during the abuse experience, the enjoyment of the attention from the abuser, wondering why they were singled out for the abuse (not because of personality defects or seductive behavior), and why they kept the abuse a secret.[52] Reframing the abuse experience can be reinforced in various ways and narrative therapy is extremely effective for creating a space for a new story with new meaning in the experience. Clients viewing photographs of themselves at the time of the abuse can help them reenter the world of the child and realize that as children they were incapable of initiating or consenting to such sexual behavior.

Other useful techniques are to use the empty-chair method whereby clients address the "abuser" imagined sitting in that chair using their new insights, or to write an unsent letter to the abuser or others with whom clients wish to share their new beliefs. The purpose of these procedures is to create the possibility of some form of tangible or remembered measure of closure.

Contempt with self or others can be a serious consequence of past abuse. Because of her contempt, a woman may hate her longing for an intimate relationship with a man as she believes it may descend into "lust or revenge."[53] The contempt can range from very severe, in which a person wants to physically harm oneself or another, to a milder form in which a compliment from another person causes

[50]Briere (1992: 87).
[51]Briere (1992: 102).
[52]Draucker (2000: 53–56).
[53]Allender (1991: 65).

discomfort due to either a sense of unworthiness (self-contempt) or doubt about the sincerity of the kind word (other-centered contempt). It is therefore "a good rule of thumb to listen to how people talk about their natural abilities, intelligence, and accomplishments to get an initial assessment of the nature and intensity of their contempt."[54] Contempt and other self-negating beliefs are best dealt with using careful cognitive restructuring and providing feedback in a supportive and non-blaming manner, for example, "I notice that when you …... Tell me more about that," not "Why do you always put yourself down?" It is important to challenge such beliefs, otherwise the client will interpret the silence as agreement. As previously mentioned, the focus is not on "sickness" or "dysfunction" but on surviving in a healthier way in the future. Counseling areas for further work include self-esteem, boundary setting, and developing trust.

Initial Enquiry

Because of the prevalence of sexual abuse in society generally, some therapists believe that enquiring about it should be part of an initial assessment. In doing so, Draucker[55] suggests asking specific questions rather than ask a general question like "Have you ever experienced sexual abuse?" as clients will differ on what they consider sexual or abusive. She suggests questions like, "As a child were you ever touched in a way that felt uncomfortable to you?" or "As a child, did anyone hurt or use you in a sexual way?" These questions can be added to historical questions like, "Tell me about your first sexual experience", and "How did you feel about this and subsequent sexual experiences?" The aim here is to determine whether the experiences were harmful, irrespective of whether the client labels them as abusive or not.

Memory Recall

The role of remembering the past in counseling has already been referred to above, especially with regard to repressed memories. The process of memory recall begins with the available memories, and these need to be frequently revisited so that painful affects can be reduced or eliminated through repeated exposure. What happens is that the repeated emotional processing of the memories during therapy helps the client to build up tolerance without being overwhelmed or resorting to inappropriate tension-reducing behaviors. This revisiting requires attention to both "verbal" and "imagery" systems of memory so that the combination of the two can facilitate a a less dissociated re-experiencing of the abusive events. McCann and Pearlman[56] suggest accessing these two memory systems by, respectively, asking questions about memories concerning the beginning, middle and end of the abuse, and questions about mind pictures, colors, clothing, smells, sounds, and bodily sensations. In recalling images and sensory information, a nonverbal medium like drawing therapy can be really helpful.

Recalling available memories will usually encourage repressed material to emerge as the client's conscious memory is expanded, and allow emotions to be released (catharsis) in a safe place, but now from an adult perspective. However, a client may suppress or withhold conscious memories in counseling because of various reasons such as disgust, anxiety, fear of losing control, fear of therapist reaction, and so

[54] Allender (1991: 110).
[55] Draucker (2000:26–27).
[56] McCann and Pearlman (1990: 290).

forth. Here the therapist needs to be active in clarifying a neutral role in accepting the painful information without judgement.

One technique for handling painful memories is for the client to work through them progressively and, at some appropriate point when things become difficult, stop the thinking by carrying out some action like clicking a ball-point pen. By extending this period of recall, a person can thereby steadily be helped to gain personal control over the painful memories.

Coping With Heightened Awareness

Briere[57] notes that clients who begin well can sometimes appear to deteriorate, even though there may be clinical improvement. What is happening is that the client's heightened awareness and increased sensitivity to repressed feelings is bringing such things as anxiety, flashbacks, intrusive memories, and nightmares into sharper focus. This can be unnerving for the therapist and scary for the client who may begin to feel that he or she should leave memories well alone and stop the therapy.

The therapist will need to decide if (a) there are some aspects of the therapy that need correcting, or (b) the therapy is working but needs a change of pace or a greater focus on consolidation, or (c) what is happening is a natural part of the therapy. In the case of (a), the therapist should consult his or her supervisor and may even need to refer the the client on to another therapist. Otherwise aspects of (b) as well as normalization and reframing the negative aspects in a positive light will be helpful.

In counseling, therapists will discover that it is at times helpful to treat male and female clients a bit differently because of gender stereotyping.[58] We now consider some differences.

Gender Differences

A male survivor may be deterred from coming to counseling because of his cultural view of what it means to be a man.[59] For example, he may believe that only women are victims and not men (at least not to the same extent), and he may feel ashamed that he did not protect himself or achieve appropriate revenge against the offender. If abused by an older woman, the abuse may be misinterpreted as a plus (even if there are misunderstood long-term effects), while if carried out by another male it may reflect on the survivor's own sexual orientation. In the latter case there may be confusion about the survivor's male sexual identity because he was passive or experienced sexual arousal during the same-sex abuse (a normal reaction to sexual stimulation) and wonder if he has latent homosexual feelings. This confusion can result in him avoiding any behaviors regarded as feminine, including emotional intimacy with other males. It can lead to exaggerated efforts to assert his masculinity and become involved with the dynamics of power and control, macho behavior, homophobia, and sexual aggression. He may also engage in compulsive sexual behaviors.

Males, then, may need to be reassured that they are no less manly (irrespective of sexual orientation) because they have been abused by a male, and therefore do

---

[57]Briere (1992: 143–144).
[58]Briere (1992: 157–158).
[59]Struve (1990: 38).

not need to "prove" themselves by aggression. On the other hand, female clients can be helped to be assertive and not feel responsible in some way for their abuse (the "seductive female" stereotype). The two sexes often express their feelings differently, with males tending to externalize and females tending to internalize. They also see their abuse quite differently.

Some Client Goals

Allender suggests that one of the keys to moving forward is honesty, and the following truths should eventually be acknowledged by a survivor—clearly helpful guidelines for a therapist.[60]

1. I have been abused.

2. I am a victim of a crime against my body and soul.

3. I am not in any way responsible for the abuse, no matter what I might have experienced or gained as a result of the abuse.

5. Abuse has damaged my soul.

6. My damage is different from anybody else's and is worthy of being addressed and worked through.

7. It will take time to heal and the process must not be hurried.

8. I must not keep a veil of secrecy and shame over my past, but I don't need to share my past with anyone I feel is untrustworthy.

Briere frequently mentions the term "self work" and says that:

> The goal of self work is to help the survivor build a positive source of identity, so that he or she is able to monitor internal states, call upon inner resources at times of stress, maintain internal coherence in interactions with others, and foster affect regulation.[61]

It means a client knowing who they are so that they can better understand their needs and motives, and be better able to care for themselves without going down a self-defeating path.

Confrontation

Some clients want to confront their abuser, perhaps with a support person present. They may, for example, want to know why the abuser acted that way and why they were chosen by the abuser. All the ramifications of confrontation should usually be discussed with the therapist prior to any action; for example, to decide how it should be done (e.g., face to face, by phone, or by letter). The desire to do this must be initiated by the client because of the real risks involved. This is a difficult topic and confrontation may not be in the best interest of the client. The question that needs to be explored carefully with the client is, "What do you hope to gain from confrontation?"

---

[60] Allender (1991: 184).
[61] Briere (1992: 113).

Role of Forgiveness

This is another difficult topic. Should abused people extend some sort of forgiveness to the offender?[62] If they do, then this may help the client to find release from the control of the offender, even if the offender is now dead. However, this is a big ask as childhood sexual abuse is generally regarded as being among the most "unforgivable" of transgressions; incest is particularly damaging to core beliefs. Forgiveness must be initiated by the client and be free of pressure from the counselor.[63] Interestingly, there is a difference of opinion over the importance of such a step. For example, Macdonald et al. comment that: "it is not necessary for the survivor to forgive the abuser or to have some form of confrontation or disclosure," and "they need to let go of any desire for revenge and to feel free to put their energy into other pursuits."[64] Bass and Davis[65] also comment: "Never say or imply that the client should forgive the abuser. Forgiveness is not essential for healing."

On the other hand, Heitritler and Vought state: "Without forgiveness, incest trauma will never be resolved," and "The purpose of forgiveness, however, is not forgetting the events, but to stop the tape from continuing to replay the lingering pain."[66] According to Allender, "The role for forgiveness in the healing process may seem profoundly difficult, but clear and necessary" and "Forgiveness is not something to be pushed on the abuse victim."[67] Noll, after examining the limited empirical literature on the topic concluded that "a forgiveness intervention may be effective for some sexual abuse victims and that many aspects of forgiving (letting go of anger, cessation of revenge, moving on with life) would likely benefit the recovery process."[68] Clearly clients' attitudes toward forgiveness will depend to some extent on how they perceive forgiveness and its role, the nature of the abuse, and their spiritual background, if any. Premature forgiveness needs to be avoided in situations of abuse.

If the abused client has a religious dimension in his or her life, then forgiving God for allowing the abuse to happen may be the first step.[69] Then guilt feelings like those described above (e.g., "enjoying" aspects of the abuse[70]) may need to be dealt with, and clients may feel they need to receive forgiveness from God for these. Once the client feels accepted and forgiven by God, he or she may be in a position to extend forgiveness to the abuser. Clearly it is a personal matter that is important to some but not to others, and may take a long time to achieve.

If clients are willing to consider the possibility of forgiveness, one approach is to using the empty-chair method. For example, if I was the victim I could imagine the abuser sitting in the chair and then I would tell him or her how much he or she hurt me. I then sit in that chair and try to express what he or she might say back to me. I then return to my chair and offer genuine forgiveness.

---

[62] For a general discussion on forgiveness see Section 2.5.5.
[63] Benner and Hill (1999: 1152).
[64] Macdonald et al. (1995: 43).
[65] Bass and Davis (1988: 348).
[66] Heitritler and Vought (1989: 82–83).
[67] Allender (1991: 223–224).
[68] Noll (2005: 368).
[69] See Section 3.5.
[70] It is not the child's fault for feeling this way, but forgiveness can deal with the guilt.

MacDonald et al.[71] mention that when forgiveness is important to clients, the therapist needs to check whether they see forgiveness as assisting in their healing or as something they owe the offender or to compliantly please the therapist. Generally it is not helpful for clients to feel some obligation to the offender and, as part of their healing, they need to recognize that they are not responsible for the offender's behavior.

Closing a Session

Towards the end of any session, the therapist should bring the client back to lower levels of arousal so that he or she can face the outside world with composure. Care is also needed in the termination of the whole counseling process as there may be issues of separation, abandonment, and re-stimulated loss. Some attachment with the therapist is likely to occur during the process, which is not necessarily unhealthy, but care is needed to ensure that the development of autonomy is done at the client's own pace. While unconditional caring support is necessary from the therapist, there must be a very clear delineation of the therapist-client boundary and therapists need to address this issue in their regular supervision.

Therapist's Role

The transition to focused attention on the trauma memories is often associated with increased anxiety and discomfort, and sometimes for the therapist as well. Self-care is therefore important for the therapist exposed to the trauma of clients as it can be upsetting, and good supervision is important for the therapist. Cloitre et al. (2006: 96–100) give five helpful guidelines for therapy, namely:

Actively support the client rather than take a neutral position and don't avoid raising the issue (the traumatic experience needs to be talked about).

Use **B**ehavioral descriptions rather than value judgments. For example, not "When you were a child were ever sexually abused which means defining abuse, but rather "When you were a child were you ever touched in places that made you feel uncomfortable?"

Contain the client's narrative. This means not too much detail initially as it may make the client feel too vulnerable.

Don't avoid. This has to be balanced with **C** as the story needs to be told.

Expect more as further sessions will reveal more details.

In the above treatment of sexual abuse I have not expressed in detail a step-by-step program of counseling as each client will be different. If a detailed and very specific program is required the reader can refer to Cloitre et al. (2006) for example.

15.3 PHYSICAL ABUSE

In any society where physical pain is often used by adults to control children, it is difficult to determine when physical correction becomes regarded as physical abuse, as physical abuse can be "disguised" as discipline. In New Zealand, for example,

[71]MacDonald et al. (1995: 43).

there has been a lot of controversy over certain anti-smacking laws. Unfortunately too many parents cross the boundary with the consequence that too many children are maltreated. When a child is physically abused, the child may come to believe that his or her body is not worth being respected and the child has no right to control what happens to his or her body. When a parent uses an implement to administer punishment rather than using a hand, such an action is shaming and the parent may have no idea how painful it might be. Watching someone else being physically abused is deeply abusive. Physical abuse can also take the form of physical neglect, where a child's basic needs such as food, clothing, warmth, and medical/dental care are not provided. This however does not even begin to address the horror of child abuse in terms of brutal war or terrorism, but the therapy process remains fundamentally the same. The methods used for trauma counseling and sexual abuse can also be adapted to physical abuse.

15.4   PSYCHOLOGICAL ABUSE

This type of abuse is not so easy to define, but it remains one of the most common forms of child maltreatment. Briere lists the following behaviors indicating abuse: rejecting, degrading/devaluing, terrorizing, isolating, corrupting, and exploiting; denying essential stimulation, emotional responsiveness, or availability; and unreliable and inconsistent parenting.[72] Although emotional neglect is different from psychological abuse and is also difficult to define, its effect is similar. Children who are brought up by unloving, unresponsive, or otherwise emotionally neglectful parents have a damaged self-image with consequent psychological problems later on. For example, lack of approval in childhood can lead to perfectionism, which engenders insecurity, the need to completely control one's life, and a fear of risk (because of fear of failure). It can also lead to dissatisfaction with self and personal accomplishments (and therefore a low self-image, anger, guilt, and paralysis), and a fear of intimacy and therefore of vulnerability.[73] In addition, boundaries may be inadequate, having not been properly developed in childhood, and such adults may not honor other people's boundaries.[74] Low self-esteem is common and it makes such a person prone to manipulation through a little bit of praise.

Mellody et al.[75] mention that psychological abuse can be verbal and take the form of screaming, name calling, ridiculing, and listening to verbal abuse being done to someone else. It can also be social, where the parents directly or indirectly interfere with a child's access to his or her peers. For example, such children may not want to bring their friends home to a dysfunctional parent, or they may not be allowed to. Mental abuse occurs when there is no room for a child's ideas, or for a child to think differently from a parent; a child is not allowed to query an adult's thinking. Some aspects of trauma and sexual abuse counseling can also be adapted here.

Emotional neglect often arises as the result of divorce, which I now discuss.

---

[72]Briere (1992: 9–10).
[73]Conway (1990: 52–58).
[74]See Section17.2.
[75]Mellody et al. (1989: chapter 12).

15.4.1   Effects of Divorce, Legal or Emotional

We are only too aware of the damage caused by family-of-origin problems such as divorce[76] and inadequate upbringing on adult clients, though the extent of the damage is not always fully appreciated by clients and sometimes not even by the therapist. Much of this section is based on Conway,[77] who includes in the word "divorce" both legal divorce and "emotional divorce." The latter is where the parents were married but dysfunctional and married in name only. Children suffer not only from the fallout of a divorce but also from a dysfunctional marital relationship through neglect and sometimes abuse. They end up lacking a suitable role model of marriage and generally don't know how to positively process and negotiate conflict.[78] Children of alcoholic parents are especially at risk, as discussed below. Children from a divorce usually feel unhappy, powerless, helpless, lonely, afraid, angry, rejected, worthless, and suffer emotional neglect. They can become perfectionists, judging self and others, and trying to control others. Such children can experience a number of losses such as:[79]

- loss of parental models

- loss of a secure and stable foundation for adult life

- loss of parental guidance

- loss of ability to love, appreciate, and be at peace with themselves

- loss of the ability to be intimate and close, or to trust others

A therapist who has not been through similar childhood experiences can easily underestimate the long-term effect of divorce on a child.

A divorced child can become an "adult child," that is an adult on the outside but a needy child on the inside.[80] Bradshaw makes the following comment:

> Being abandoned through the neglect of our development dependency needs is the major factor in becoming an adult child. We grow up; we look like adults. We walk and talk like adults, but underneath the surface is a little child who feels empty and needy, a child whose needs are insatiable because he has a child's needs in an adult body. This insatiable child is the core of all compulsive/addictive behavior.[81]

Children usually tend to see everything as black or white and regard parents as being always right. If children find their feelings or thinking in conflict with a parent, they will think that they are wrong. This leads to a mistrust of parents, mistrust of self, and mistrust of anyone else (even God).[82] This pattern of mistrust and self-blame can carry over into adulthood, with the result that many doubt their ability to form and maintain intimate relationships, and can be afraid of relationships. They want to be close, but not too close, for if they love too much

---

[76] For further comments concerning children see Section 18.2.3.
[77] Conway (1990). This is a useful self-help book.
[78] Wallerstein, Lewis, and Blakeslee (2000: 56).
[79] Adapted from Conway (1990: 32).
[80] For a list of some characteristics of an adult child see http://gods_mark.tripod.com/Roles.html (accessed October 2010).
[81] Bradshaw (1988: 58).
[82] Conway (1990: 18).

they are afraid they will get hurt. As a result they are afraid of rejection and being vulnerable, and can become people-pleasers, constantly seeking approval. Because of fear that a friendship won't last, they will often prefer to terminate it first to avoid the pain; conflict is to be avoided as it triggers childhood conflict. In a legal divorce, the child may assume some blame for the divorce and be afraid that the caregiver may leave too.

For children from a divorce, their childhood is often not just unhappy but a matter of survival, where part of self is suppressed. They end up experiencing pain in adulthood, but not knowing where it came from. They also tend to feel cheated out of part of their life, for example, with legal divorce both parents may be too busy trying to sort out their own lives, either as single parents or with a new spouse (the new focus of love) and possibly other step-children. Sometimes one of the parents may have manipulated the child into the role of being a supportive parent (parentification). Children sent to a boarding school in their early years (e.g., from six to fifteen years of age) because of parental break up by well meaning parents can feel cheated out of parental experiences. In many modern western family situations the father is missing either physically or emotionally.

Such adult children often fail to integrate their past into the present by, for example, blocking out memories and feelings, which leaves them with a sense of unfinished business. They frequently try to compensate for what they missed or they forget their early years through such "substitutes" as drugs (including alcohol), food, or a new relationship, and consequently become addicted. Healing comes through the adult facing the past and its pain, but dealing with the past now through the eyes of an adult. For example, a client can visualize a difficult event that happened to them as a child and then the therapist can ask the client to visualize going into that scene as an adult and saying what he or she would do or say now. For instance, what would you say to the frightened child and what would you say to the abuser.

It also helps to tell one's story as it "breaks the cycle of silence that keeps the hurt alive" and makes it possible for a client to get in touch with feelings, hear the story aloud for perhaps the first time, become more strongly in charge of life, and loosen the grip of old pains.[83] It is not always easy to remember one's past and it may be helpful for the client to write down some family history or construct a time line.

Boundaries are an important issue with adult children as inadequate parents tend to have children without boundaries, damaged boundaries, or resistant walls instead of boundaries.[84]

Summing up, counseling may take some time as the problems and behaviors can become deeply ingrained. Mood swings involving anger, guilt, and depression can occur and there will be a tendency to mistrust, to control, and want to make everything perfect. The therapist can provide a safe place for emotions for the client to feel the pain, express anger at past violations, and grieve over what was lost. Constant encouragement will be important for the client. In dealing with a damaged past, Conway suggested the following healing steps: deciding to be healed and committing time to the healing process, developing a spiritual link, joining

---

[83]Conway (1990: 158–159).
[84]Mellody et al. (1989: 11–13).

a recovery group, remembering the past, grieving losses, shaking off the victim mentality, forgiving the past, working on problems, and maintaining and enjoying a new life.[85]

An important question we now consider is what should adults do about parents who were not there for them when they were children.

Forgiving the Parents/Care-givers

Depending on the degree of abuse or neglect, a client may be able to offer their parent(s) a degree of forgiveness. Bloomfield[86] suggests that the client should list all the specific things and events (not vague generalities such as "I hate my mother") that caused pain in childhood. This will help to externalize anger. The therapist can then use the empty-chair method. Clients choose one or two events and then express their feelings and pain to their parent imagined as sitting in the chair opposite them. They can then sit in that chair themselves and endeavor to respond in a way that they think the parent might respond. By recalling specific instances, a client could then say something like: "I understand that you did want to care for me and I now freely offer you my forgiveness, which I now symbolize by tearing up my list into little pieces." Forgiveness can, of course, be offered face to face, if appropriate. For further comments about forgiveness see Section 2.5.5.

How can the parents themselves facilitate their child's forgiveness process? Possible steps are: (a) admit their mistakes and acknowledge and witness their child's pain (even though it may have happened differently to how it is told), (b) offer a genuine and non-defensive apology, (c) recognize and be prepared to reveal their contribution to the injury, (c) endeavor to earn back trust, and (e) forgive themselves.[87]

15.4.2 Adult Children of Alcoholics

Children who are particularly prone to difficulties in adult life are those with a parent or parents with an addiction like alcoholism. The earlier literature focused on this problem. The abuse encountered can be somewhere on a wide spectrum ranging from total neglect to physical violence, and codependence can be a feature of the family's dysfunction. There is a continual undercurrent of tension and anxiety as the children never know what to expect. Such children tend to have a low self-esteem as parental warmth, clearly defined limits, and respectful treatment, all contributing to self-esteem, generally are missing. Children end up taking on extra jobs or specific roles to keep the family together and to help themselves to survive.

Various roles have been described in the literature including the hero (the model, responsible child who assumes responsibility for other family members and gives the family self-worth), the lost child (the withdrawn child hiding in a shell, attempting to be invisible), the scapegoat (the child who draws attention away from the family's problems by always getting into trouble; the family's way of not looking at what was really happening), the mascot or clown (the child draws attention away from family problems by providing humor and mischief), and the enabler (the child who

---

[85]Conway (1990: part III).
[86]Bloomfield (1983: 30–34).
[87]Spring (2004).

supports and "covers" for the alcoholic).[88] These unhealthy roles may relate to birth order and get carried over into adulthood.[89] Consequently adult children may not be sure what their role is as a partner and often project parental roles from their family of origin onto their partners. They can also be unsure about their parent role with their own children.

If the father was the alcoholic, he could be loving, warm, and caring on one occasion, and unreliable, aggressive, and uncaring on another when drunk. In this situation the mother may have had to work and was tired, irritable, and grouchy through having to manage the family and cover up for her husband. If the mother was the alcoholic, the father had already left or worked late or ended up taking over his wife's jobs (e.g., preparing lunches, sewing on buttons). The child soon learned to cook, clean, and shop, help any younger siblings, and try and help the mother. Being a family secret, the children had to keep their feelings to themselves. Making friends was problematic as the children did not want others to know what was going on and were afraid they would lose any friends if others found out. The child was afraid of inviting friends over to his or her house, not knowing what to expect from the alcoholic parent. It also may have been impossible to stay after school and play, not knowing what was happening at home.

Woititz[90] suggests that adult children of alcoholics may end up with some of the following perceptions and behavior that can be investigated in counseling; brief recommendations are also given.

1. *They guess at what normal behavior is.* Life was chaotic and confusing as a child. Double standards were a problem and there was no idea about how a normal household should function.

   Reading a book on child development and the various stages can be helpful, particularly with understanding one's own children.

2. *They have difficulty in following a project through to the end.* They grew up in an environment where there were lots of promises but nothing got done.

   Proper planning and suitable goals are the key here.

3. *They tend to lie when it would be just as easy to tell the truth.* Lying was a basic family trait, generally disguised as denial, coverups, broken promises, and inconsistencies. It can become a habit, even when it accomplishes nothing.

   Acknowledging and replacing the habit is the key.

4. *They judge themselves without mercy.* Constant criticism, especially when it was unfounded and made no sense, can lead to negative self-judgment. Life is full of "shoulds."

   The aim here is to process feelings and focus on the positive.

5. *They have difficulty having fun.* Not knowing what it meant to be a carefree spontaneous child can lead to growing up too quickly and missing out on a normal childhood. There was not much fun in the family.

---

[88] Wegscheider-Cruse (1981: 85–88).
[89] See, for example, http://www.joy2meu.com/DysfunctionalFamilies.htm for details (accessed October 2010.
[90] Woititz (1990).

The answer is to spend time with children and adults who know how to have fun and timetable some fun activities.

6. *They take themselves very seriously.* The pressure to maintain an adult role as a child keeps the child suppressed; being childlike is foolish as life is a serious business.

   Creating space for oneself away from work to do other things (e.g., music, theatre, sport) is a beginning.

7. *They have difficulty with intimate relationships.* The problem is that they have no model of what a healthy, consistent, and intimate relationship might be. There is the inconsistency of being loved one day and rejected the next, with conflicting messages like "I want you—go away."

   A first step is to ask oneself which of the following need some work: vulnerability, understanding, empathy, compassion, respect, trust, acceptance, honesty, communication, compatibility, personal integrity, and consideration.[91]

8. *They tend to overreact to changes outside of their control.* This stems from living in a chaotic household where you can't rely on others so it became important to take charge of your own environment and look after yourself.

   Becoming more self-aware and having a more flexible routine can begin the change.

9. *They constantly seek approval and affirmation* This arises because parental love was conditional and the child received mixed messages. Missing affirmations became internalized as negative.

   Acknowledging good things that one does, no matter how small, along with accepting the support and encouragement of others can begin the change.

10. *They usually feel different from other people.* Feeling different began in childhood because a normal childhood did not happen and the feeling can continue in adulthood, even if not warranted.

    Joining a group that shares feelings can help to reduce such feelings.

11. *They tend to be either super responsible or super irresponsible.* As a child there is a tendency to take it all on or give it all up, with no middle ground.

    Coping with perfectionist tendencies, setting boundaries, and learning to say no are useful steps.

12. *They are extremely loyal, even when the evidence is that the loyalty is undeserved.* Loyalty and excusing behavior were part of the family life. It is better to stay with what you know as there is safety in an established relationship. Fear of being abandoned may lead to fear of abandoning others.

    Examining unfair relationships and learning to take appropriate action is the beginning. Once again setting boundaries is important.

[91] Woititz (1990: 78–79).

13. *They tend to be impulsive.* Drinking tends to be an impulsive act without consequences being considered. Living in a continual crisis situation encourages a sense of urgency. Also outcomes were unpredictable so that there was no learning curve about consequences.

Learning to pause and ask oneself who is going to be affected and in what way can introduce some control on impulses.

15.5   BIBLICAL VIEWPOINT

There is no record of a single instance in the Bible where a child is being deliberately sexually abused by a parent. Unfortunately child sexual abuse tends to be a taboo topic in church circles. Children had a special place with Jesus who welcomed them and blessed them.[92]

15.5.1   Child abuse

The Bible has some harsh words to say about child abuse.[93] Also fathers are not to provoke their children.[94] There are some controversial Old Testament passages about discipline that need to be examined as they can appear to condone abuse. In Proverbs it talks about the use of the rod for discipline,[95] which was the case in those times. However the word "rod" is also used symbolically in various verses in the Old Testament (e.g., Assyria was the rod of God's anger[96]), and it has a connotation of direction. The rod was the shepherd's crook, not used to hit the lambs with but rather to pull them out of difficult places and get them on the trail with the rest of the flock. David in the twenty-third psalm (verse 4) refers to the rod comforting him not thrashing him!

Abuse is the result of sin and God allows it to take place as a consequence of God's gift of free will to humankind. God is not to blame and He can be trusted, though trust is generally a difficult issue with a survivor.[97] The Bible is very clear on the fact that God cares for the survivor and understands his or her pain.[98] Sexual abuse damages a person's being (his or her "soul") and the way forward spiritually is for the person to face the problem honestly and patiently, believing that with God's help hope can be found again.

An important aspect of recovery is to be open to past memories, leaving God to slowly do the prompting in a way that allows the survivor to face and cope with emotions that are unleashed.[99] God promises to listen to the person who seeks God wholeheartedly.[100] Another aspect is to ask God for forgiveness for the damage done by turning one's self against life with little thought of others. This can

[92]Mark 10:14–16.
[93]Leviticus 18: 6, 10–12 and Luke 17: 2.
[94]Ephesians 6: 4 and Colossians 3:21.
[95]Proverbs 13:24, 22:15, 23:13–14, and 29:15.
[96]Isaiah 10:5.
[97]Care is needed here as the client may have a distorted view of God, especially the concept of Father.
[98]1 Peter 5:7 and Matthew 11:28–30.
[99]Psalms 139:23–24.
[100]Jeremiah 29:11–13.

help survivors to open up their emotions, move away from self-protective patterns, and shift their focus to the well-being of others. It is a refusal to be dead and passionless. They certainly do not need forgiveness for their coping actions as a child in their experience of powerlessness, betrayal, and ambivalence. The question of extending forgiveness to the abuser has been discussed above and further aspects relating to Christian attitudes towards the abuser are discussed by Allender (1991). For further comments about forgiveness see Section 2.5.5.

One area where guilt can surface is the result of being abused, whether it was physical, psychological, or sexual. Victims unfortunately sometimes take the blame for what happened thinking that somehow they were responsible for the abuse. The residual effects of abuse might be anger, bitterness, hatred and distrust, and may lead to repeating the abusiveness toward others. Such feelings can be dealt with by learning to forgive the abuser irrespective of whether the abuser has repented or not, or shown remorse. It does not mean having to have anything to do with the abuser as it is a matter between the abused person and God. The so-called Serenity Prayer of Alcoholics Anonymous mentions asking for the courage to change the things we can, and that begins with changing ourselves.

Similar comments apply to adults whose parents divorced when they were children. What can shift a person's focus away from God are negative thoughts about parents. One way to handle this is to pass the parents and the hurt on to God; this release and surrendering control to God can promote healing.

CHAPTER 16

ABUSED ADULTS

16.1 INTRODUCTION

We live in a world of violence, war, and terrorism, with abuse the eventual outcome. We see it in business, politics, and regrettably sometimes in churches. It is reflected in our media and films (especially in some reality shows) and is glorified in a variety of sports (e.g., boxing and martial arts). It is therefore not surprising that bullying manifests itself early in preschool and eventually surfaces in most educational institutions. As long as we applaud power and control we endorse some form of abuse and victimization!

Abuse of adults can take the form of sexual, physical, psychological (including verbal and emotional), financial, and spiritual abuse. At the more extreme end of the spectrum there is rape, gang rape, and life-threatening violence. All forms of abuse tend to relate to the desire for control by one person over another, so this is the first topic considered below. This chapter is linked with Chapter 17 where issues of control are considered under the topics of boundaries and codependency.

16.1.1 Control

Helping a client cope with a controlling spouse, family member, or boss is not easy. We may face the reverse situation when our client is controlling as in codependency, discussed in Section 17.4. A spouse may be controlling because of modeling after a controlling parent. Many of those abandoned or neglected as children may be controlling in their adult life as compensation for the lack of security that they experienced. If both partners in a relationship or marriage have experienced this, they may struggle for control so that arguments soon escalate. Some people are controlling because of their narcissistic personalities, which result in their insistence on always having their own way. They can achieve control through overreacting in anger.

This section will address some general ideas about being on the receiving end of control such as recognizing it, living with it, and coping with it. This will partly overlap with the other sections on abuse. There will be a brief discussion on counseling someone who is a controller.

Recognizing Control

There are various forms of control such as verbal, emotional, physical, sexual, and financial. The first question to ask is how much do we alter own personality, plans, and beliefs to fit in with others; we are often expected to change our plans for them so that we end up doing something we didn't really want to do. Do we always give in? Are they isolating us from friends and family by causing trouble, and do they tell us how we should feel, contrary to how we really feel? They may try to control our emotions. How much do they try to control what we buy, what we wear, how we look and speak, or even criticize our opinion? They will want to control every aspect of our lives. How much do they need to know all the answers up front, and do they apply constant questioning and badgering? Are they extremely jealous, always asking us about the people we meet and how much time we spend with them? They will want to know why we spend more than the required time with the group, and want to dictate things about the kind of people we are supposed to meet.

People who are controlling tend to be moody, impatient, short-tempered, won't take "no" for an answer, and get angry when we disagree with them or do not do as they ask. Everything must be done their way as they don't trust other people's competence. They may play mind games and often assume erroneously that they know how we think so that they get frustrated when we ask normal questions. Such people are never wrong, are very critical of others, and try and divert attention from themselves by saying that we are the ones with the problem when we point out their mistakes, or else change the subject. They can also achieve control through putting us in a place of obligation by being generous and giving us things. The strategies they use to assert their superiority may be criticizing others (especially those held in high regard by others) and refraining from complimenting others (or doing it in a backhanded, derogatory way). They may also psychologically induce physical problems on themselves such as back pain to gain our attention, concern, and sympathy.

Some people have normal forceful and persuasive personalities. However, if they allow us to be free to be ourselves and don't try to unduly influence our behavior, they are not really controlling.

Counseling Controlled Clients

When counseling a client on the receiving end of control it is helpful to point out that controllers can be male or female and are generally insecure people with few close friends. When they try and shift the blame away from their own mistakes, clients need to stand firm and then end the discussion before the blame gets shifted. The stronger clients are, the harder controllers will work to exercise control. Controllers won't like those who stand up for themselves about issues important to them so that even if the controller loses his or her cool and tries to manipulate, which is likely, the client should be encouraged to stay calm, speaking slowly, clearly and softly in difficult conversations. The client can agree with the controller's intentions and arguments, but not yield to the controller's demands or agree with his or her conclusions. If the controller becomes abusive, a person should leave or say goodbye and hang up the phone. Training in assertiveness (Section 2.5.4) and boundary setting (Section 17.2) may be needed to teach offenders how we want them to treat us. Clients may also need to distance themselves from those who are trying to control them, though spouses face a more difficult situation. In the latter case a client needs to learn how to have that difficult conversation (Section 17.2.4). It is helpful to avoid lengthy explanations and simply go ahead and make any changes, as control is not the client's problem but the controller's.

Kirkwood says that, for abused women, greater control by abusers is achieved by "weakened self-esteem, loss of identify, decreased control over their physical state and debilitating depression related to a loss of hope."[1] An important step is to help clients to become aware of the negative changes (e.g., self-doubt, inability to function, lack of confidence, and indecision) that have taken place in themselves (and possibly the children) and why this has happened, and link this to their partner's behavior.

Clients should be encouraged to live their own lives by pursuing their own activities, especially those that build up self-esteem, and by doing the things they enjoy (even if support is withdrawn from the partner). They need to decide that they are not going to be controlled and perhaps tell the controller that they don't need another parent telling them what to do. If they make plans, they should not let the controller cause them to change or break them. It is unnecessary to acknowledge or respond to the controlling behavior, and it does not help to look for approval or other reactions from the controlling person. It is important to maintain relationships with others as the controller will try to sever those relationships.

In the case of verbal abuse and demeaning language, clients should refuse to listen to it and firmly excuse themselves from the conversation. They need to say that they will be happy to listen when talked to with respect, but not when verbally abused. Dealing with emotional control can be more difficult to cope with, especially the withdrawal of affection and "love" when demands, sexual or otherwise, are not met. This is generally the pattern whenever the controller is upset with the client. Emotional abandonment is a very painful form of control and manipulation, and a client may find this hard to resist and end up giving in. Such clients need help to build up their self-esteem and fight back by reminding themselves that they are worthy of unconditional love and don't need to perform for it; they need to dismiss the controlling behavior and emotional barbs without giving in.

Financial control occurs when a client has to ask permission to buy something basic for themselves (or even the children), has to account for every sum of money spent, or has to meet certain expectations to "earn their keep." Many men struggle

---

[1]Kirkwood (1997: 67).

to accept that in a relationship everything earned regardless by whom becomes relationship property and is equally owned by law in some countries. The message is that love must be paid back and the client doesn't deserve access to the money. Obtaining some kind of financial independence, for example through employment, may give the controlled person a greater degree of freedom. It depends on whether the equal ownership of relational income and assets is fully appreciated by both parties. In the end, unless there is evidence of a willingness for the controller to change the abusive behavior the client may need to get out of the relationship permanently. Eventually anger can be a positive motivating force to take that step.

One way a client can "defuse" a controlling person, say in a work situation, is to use reflective listening (Section 10.6.2). This powerful approach allows the controlling person to be aware of what he or she is saying by hearing paraphrases and summaries. The client is not agreeing or disagreeing with the comments made but is simply raising the awareness of the controller so that he or she is forced to think about what has been said, especially if it is inappropriate or simply incorrect. Some skills in assertive behavior (see Section 2.5.4) can be helpful here.

16.1.2 Counseling the Controller

Controlling people usually refuse to come to counseling as they probably don't believe they need counseling, or if they turn up will attempt to "control" the whole process! If they do come, generally under coercion, they simply won't recognize the authority of the therapist or admit that they are controlling. The first step for a therapist is to create some self-awareness for such a controlling client; a spouse may be present as well, if possible. A checklist based on the above comments about recognizing signs that a person is being controlled can be used. Controlling people need to be asked how much stress do they think they cause people. Who in their lives can they be really open to about their true feelings as any true friendship cannot be built on control?

16.2 PHYSICAL ABUSE

16.2.1 Prevalence

There is considerable variation in the statistics of abuse, depending on the method of sampling (e.g., representative versus clinical or criminal surveys) and the prevailing culture so that the rough figures below are given to simply highlight the widespread occurrence of abuse. Other factors can complicate the statistics such as geographic location (e.g., rural women), race, immigrant status, and sexual orientation.

In the U.S. it appears that about 20% to 30% of all women will be physically assaulted by a partner or ex-partner at least once in their lifetimes, and numbers are generally underreported.[2] A helpful resource book for domestic violence in the U.S. is Berry (2000).[3] A substantial proportion of women are even attacked during pregnancy, sometimes causing miscarriage, still births, or even death of the woman. Cook concludes that for the U.S.:

[2]Marin and Russo (1999: 18–19).
[3]See Berry (2000: chapter 2) for a brief history of domestic abuse.

As of this writing, there are over 200 published peer-reviewed studies coming to the same essential conclusion: that women and men in intimate relationships assault each other at equal rates and initiate assaults at equal rates.[4]

He also notes that about 50% of those surveyed report both spouses to be violent.[5] This means that the percentages for the categories men:women:both of those who are violent are very approximately 25:25:50.[6] However there are those that maintain that the percentage of men who are violent is much higher so that there isn't complete agreement. The percentage of men abusers is particularly high in countries where patriarchal ideas are very strong.

As women tend to have a greater number of injuries (including death), an emphasis on the abuse of women is not unreasonable. For the purposes of counseling, I don't want to enter into a debate about male versus female violence as statistics vary, but I do want to provide a more balanced picture and note that patriarchy is not the only factor behind the male abuse of females.

In the U.S., Canada, and New Zealand, violence is more severe and more prevalent for cohabiting couples (common-law unions) than for married couples.[7] There is also substantial risk of violence against the woman after a couple has separated,[8] though more research is needed on the topic of post-separation violence. Most marriages are ended by women, which puts them at a substantial risk during separation.

Feminist lesbians also engage in in domestic violence and Renzetti[9] found that lesbians batter each other at about the same rate as couples in heterosexual relationships. Gay men can face similar problems. There is evidence that battering may occur in up to one in three same-sex relationships.[10] Unfortunately homosexual couples are at a disadvantage in obtaining appropriate support because of social attitudes. Such attitudes may make it difficult for homosexuals to find compassion and cope with isolation, and they will need to reveal their sexual orientation if they want help from a social service, for example, a women's refuge.

16.2.2   Men's Violence Against Women

There is no typical abuser, and no typical abused woman. The question of why men are violent against women is a controversial one and often avoided because of men's reactions and defensiveness. Typically these are denial, minimizing, or entitlement, and there may be attempts at excusing men or justifying violence. Sometimes domestic violence is brushed aside as a "family matter" or "no big deal" by the men who batter, the criminal justice system, and the public.[11] Men always make excuses for their abuse such as blaming women for "provoking" the abuse, using their tongues to attack a man emotionally and not shutting up, having the house in mess, not controlling the kids, not providing for his sexual needs, and

---

[4]Cook (2009: 9).
[5]Cook (2009: 17).
[6]For domestic violence statistics in the U.K. and some other countries, see
www.womensaid.org.uk/core/core_picker/download.asp?id=1602 (accessed October 2010).
[7]Brownridge (2009: 28).
[8]Brownridge (2009: chapter 5).
[9]Renzetti (1992).
[10]Berry (2000: 65).
[11]Berry (2000: 14).

so forth. There are a myriad rationalizations like "I hardly touched her!", "She bruises easily", and "I was trying to grab her when she fell." Women may not be believed when approaching others for help. Non-religious men may even misquote the Bible to justify their behavior!

We find then that too much violence exists in marriage, casual and de facto relationships, and in same sex relationships. Threats of violence can be as effective as actual violence in obtaining control. Such abuse is a world-wide problem and ranges from inequitable social structures through to harassment, rape, and physical violence. In a relationship it tends to escalate with time. Children are often abused as well or witness partner violence, which can have serious repercussions later on.

Children who witness violence often end up as adults who abuse partners and children, as patriarchal values are passed down from generation to generation. Patriarchal values might include: men have the right to have power over women; the male head of a household should be in charge; femininity is defined by weakness, powerlessness, and submissiveness; masculinity is defined in terms of power and domination; and female sexuality is a particular threat to male power and should therefore be under the control of men, specifically fathers and/or husbands.[12] Violence, then, can be passed down through the generations with one generation providing a model for the next. Men therefore need to shape a post-patriarchal image of masculinity for their children.

Professionals together with feminists rightly view rape and other types of male violence as merely forms of abusive power and control. Unfortunately too many cultures teach women that they are of less value than men. They are not taught self-respect, personal confidence, and assertiveness—all of which can help diminish the evil of domestic violence. Instead the overemphasis is on being nurturing and care-taking others, submissiveness, learned helplessness, over-evaluation of relationships, and an over-emphasis on marriage and motherhood. Even in New Zealand where we led the world in women suffrage and many of the highest offices in politics and business are held by women the unfortunate stereotyping of women remains.

There are three categories of abuse of power: gender-role devaluation, gender-role restriction, and gender-role violation.[13] For example, Nutt[14] notes that "young women get little encouragement for developing independence, problem solving, abstract thinking, risk taking, and career maturity," which is a gender-role devaluation. We see gender-role restriction in women's culturally driven focus on the pursuit of beauty and being thin. According to most media, the current ideal female figure is becoming more like an adolescent male.

Why then are men so violent toward women? Some partial answers or factors can be suggested, and the effects of these can be conscious or unconscious. One factor relates to the negative portrayal of women in society and the patriarchal, sexist structures that promote unequal power between men and women, along with learned sexist attitudes (e.g., men are superior to women). A second factor could be biology—a combination of genetics and environment. A third factor could be gender-role socialization, where boys and girls are brought up to fit in with cultural norms and beliefs determined by a male dominated culture. This can lead to a

[12]Marin and Russo (1999: 20).
[13]Nutt (1999: 118–119).
[14]Nutt (1999: 127).

man fearing femininity and emasculation, and to developing defense strategies to cope with perceived threats to his masculine identity. Gender-role conflict can lead to questions like, "How am I perceived as as man?", "Do I appear masculine?", and "Am I inadequate?"[15] Many modern men in Western civilization appear to be quite threatened by even the just claims of the feminist movement for a measure of equality.

A fourth factor involves distorted thinking, for example: power and control are essential to proving one's masculinity; feelings should not be expressed (restrictive emotionality); and masculinity is equated with heterosexuality and femininity with homosexuality (leading to homophobia). Expressing feelings is seen as being weak and feminine, leading to exposure and the loss of power and control, and expressing vulnerability can result in being taken advantage of by others.[16] The male ill-informed stereotype is primarily about competition, status, achievement and success, toughness, and emotional stoicism. There is therefore a drive to obtain authority, dominance, and influence over others. However, fear of failure in this aspect can lead to addictive behaviors such as alcoholism, compulsive exercise, and overeating, as well as to defense mechanisms (e.g., repression, denial, projection, displacement, and so forth).

A fifth factor is that the man may be terrified of abandonment and will do anything to trap and enclose his partner. He may place the full responsibility for all his happiness or unhappiness on the woman in his life. Studies regularly show that men who exhibit dominating behavior are usually extremely insecure, vulnerable, and dependent.[17] There are a number of other variables that might be involved that relate to psychological, psychosocial, and relational factors.[18]

When separation of a couple occurs, usually initiated by the woman, a man is likely to see this as a severe challenge to his patriarchal authority. This engenders the belief that he is entitled to a relationship and expects obedience, loyalty, and dependence. During separation, men may even attempt to or actually use violence to reclaim their rights and dominance over their former partner. Anxious male attachment and the perception of separation as abandonment can also lead to male violence.[19] There is some evidence that real violence may occur in some cases after separation and is precipitated by the separation itself.[20] Stalking and forms of obsessive control are often a factor after separation.

16.2.3 Women's Violence Against Men

This topic is even more controversial than the previous one as the feminist literature generally either ignores or downplays this, except in the case of lesbian abuse.[21] Some would argue that although women can also act violently towards men, it is often in self-defense; rarely is it used to subjugate or control men.[22] Cook says

---

[15]O'Neil and Nadeau (1999: 100).
[16]Adapted from O'Neil and Nadeau (1999: 97, 100–104).
[17]Berry (2000: 40).
[18]See, for example, O'Neil and Harway (1999: chapter 12) who use a multivariate statistical model.
[19]Brownridge (2009: 60, 67).
[20]Brownridge (2009: 91–92).
[21]For example, Whelan (1996).
[22]Anderson and Schlossberg (1999: 138).

this is not true in the majority of cases (though it will inflate the numbers).[23] As noted in the prevalence statistics above, mutual violence predominates. Men tend to minimize or downplay acts of violence against them because it presents them as less than the "boss" they wish to be seen as.

Women who use physical means of attack lend themselves open to severe retaliatory male violence. As women tend to have a greater number of injuries, an emphasis on the abuse of women is not unreasonable. For the purposes of counseling, I don't want to enter into a debate about male versus female violence as statistics can vary, but I do want to provide a more balanced picture and note that patriarchy is not the only factor behind abuse. Where alcoholism or other drug addictions are concerned both sexes can act out of control and be physically abusive.

Some of the reasons for men's violence against women apply also to women abusing men. Women may believe they have the right to control their partners by telling them what to do and expecting obedience, using force to maintain power and control, controlling the finances, and not accepting responsibility for the abuse. Women tend to use different forms of physical abuse from men and make up for a lack of physical statue by throwing objects, using weapons, scalding, poisoning, biting, kicking, using sleep deprivation, and attacking a sleeping partner.

Women may sometimes threaten to use extended male family members to attack their partner (as with some cultures), threaten to tell the police that their partner is responsible for committing the domestic abuse, threaten to remove the children, and destroy personal items. They may also tell family members, friends, employers, sports clubs, and other organizations that he is the abuser. Women, like men, can wear a mask that goes on in public but comes off behind closed doors.

Men are generally bewildered by female abuse as there are no rules as to how to respond.[24] Some will respond with violence while others, because they were brought up not to hit women, will refrain from hitting back and try to withdraw or restrain the woman in some way. It is regretted that sometimes restraining a striking arm can leave bruising that is then used as evidence of male assault. Men (and women) will try to hide any signs of physical damage or blame it on an accident. Men may have a sense of shame that they are not able to handle the problem and fear being called a "wimp" or unmanly if they mention the abuse to friends or family. There is still a lack of public recognition of the problem of female abuse as well as disbelief; sex discrimination is common. Provocation itself is no defense for abuse, and anger management teaches the wisdom of walking away or fitting some safety catch to the trigger of provoked anger.

16.2.4   Counseling for Physical Abuse

Violence has no place in any relationship; either the violence ends or the relationship will. Getting out of the relationship may be the only option.The first step for a therapist will be to ensure the safety of the client and any children in some form of safe-house. In this case there is generally no point in joint couple counseling as there are safety issues both at the time of counseling and afterwards. Clients

---

[23]Cook (2009:17).
[24]Cook (2009: 52–65).

need to be able to express themselves freely without fear of later recrimination. Also, batterers may already have a court no-trespass order forbidding them to have contact with their spouse. Some psychologists conclude that battering relationships rarely change for the better and that form of unequal balance of power is resistant to change.[25] Individual counseling is then the first step and may involve some form of controlling and redirecting anger as discussed below for the batterer, and individual and/or group counseling for the abused person. If joint counseling is eventually possible, the initial focus should be on stopping the violence before exploring what has lead to it, and teaching conflict management (see Section 19.6.4). Couple counseling may be possible after the abuser has undergone a therapeutic program but care and discretion by the therapist is required.[26]

Women (and men too) in an abusive relationship need to have three safety plans: a plan for staying in the relationship, a plan for leaving, and a plan for after leaving.[27] If they decide to stay, Berry[28] has a useful list of 38 ideas on what a woman can do if she decides to stay for the time being, for example: get information, call a crisis line, pack an emergency bag, inform trustworthy people, get important documents together, and so forth.[29] If she leaves, she may fear retaliation so she will endeavor to ensure her safety and protection in various ways. Berry has comprehensive security plans for a woman's residence, work, car, and person.[30] Unfortunately abuse from ex-partners and stalking does take place. There may also be grief over the loss of a dependent relationship.[31]

In counseling, a key step might be to help clients understand the nature and extent of their abuse, and help them to recognize that the abuse is more than just physical. A useful tool for initiating this is the so-called Wheel of Power and Control developed in Duluth in the 1980's for abused women by the Domestic Abuse Intervention Project. This is available for downloading from the internet.[32] The wheel has been translated into other languages and is also reproduced in various modified forms for specific populations. It pictures the use of intimidation, emotional abuse, isolation, children, privilege, economic abuse, coercion and threats, as well as minimizing, denying, and blaming as eight spokes of a wheel. Below each spoke is an expansion of the spoke; for example, using intimidation involves making her afraid by using looks, actions, and gestures, smashing things, destroying her property, abusing pets, and displaying weapons. The wheel is particularly useful in helping women to identify the tactics used against them and to more fully understand how their batterer could exert such control over them.[33] It is also used in women's groups where they can see that they are not alone in their

---

[25] Berry (2000: 17).
[26] A good time to listen to one's supervisor!
[27] An example of all three is given at http://www.womensrefuge.org.nz/ under "Factsheets and Resources" (accessed October 2010).
[28] Berry (2000: 248–255).
[29] See http://www.ncadv.org/protectyourself/SafetyPlan_130.html for a list (accessed October 2010).
[30] Berry (2000: 256–262).
[31] See "Stockholm syndrome" on the internet, e.g., Wikipedia.
[32] See http://www.ncdsv.org/publications_wheel.html (adapted October 2010).
[33] For a more extensive list of abusive behaviors for consideration by a client see http://www.ywcaofmissoula.org/?q=node/53 (accessed October 2010).

experience. Group therapy, involving sharing with other abused women, is highly recommended.[34]

There is a second wheel called the Wheel of Equality,[35] where the spokes are, in some sense, opposites of the previous ones, namely non-threatening behavior, respect, trust and support, honesty and accountability, responsible parenting, shared responsibility, economic partnership, and negotiation and fairness.

A third wheel is available called the Power Wheel for Same Sex Relationships. It is a modified form of the first wheel mentioned above.[36]

Finally there is a fourth wheel called the Advocacy Empowerment Wheel[37] for particular use by the therapist. It refers to: respecting confidentiality (without other family members present), believing and validating her experiences (acknowledging her feelings and letting her know others have her experiences), acknowledging the injustice (it is not her fault), respecting her autonomy (to make her own decisions), helping her plan for her future safety, and promoting access to community services.

Counseling the Abuser

The wheels described above can also be used in counseling and education groups for men and women who batter to help them to identify the tactics they use to establish and maintain control, to explore the beliefs leading to the battering, and to consider alternative ways of being in a relationship with a person that is free of violence and controlling behavior. Stoneberg[38] notes that in a group, men in particular can allow themselves to be vulnerable and accountable to one another without being judged for being less of a man. Boys need models showing them that vulnerability is not unmanly.

A type of anger management course involving emotion regulation for both men and women batterers has been developed by Stosny[39] called HEALS[TM], where the acronym HEALS refers to the following steps: "Heal" through compassion as blame is powerless and compassion has the true power to heal; "Explain" to self the *core* hurt and pain masked by anger; "Apply" self-compassion for one's pain instead of reacting with anger; "Love" is shown to self and partner to heal the core hurt through love rather than anger and compassion instead of abuse; and "Solve" the problem. The idea is that self-love is more powerful than self-control; kindness and compassion replace violence and hostility. The program is practiced at least 12 times a day for 12 weeks. In counseling violent men there may be issues of transference and countertransference and Chapter 3 on anger can be used here. Violent men know how to to frighten others (including therapists) and play on their fears.

Men may suffer from a lack emotional literacy and empathy toward others because of socialization and upbringing. Stoneberg points out that when one is aware

[34]Berry (2000: 101).
[35]See http://www.ncdsv.org/publications_wheel.html (accessed October 2010).
[36]See http://www.womensrefuge.org.nz/ under "Factsheets and Resources" and then click on "Lesbian power and control wheel." (accessed October 2010).
[37]See http://www.endingviolence.org/files/uploads/AdvocacyEmpowermentwheel.pdf (accessed October 2010).
[38]Stoneberg (2002: 62–65).
[39]Stosny (2006); for some background see http://compassionpower.com/reviews.php (accessed November 2010).

of his or her feelings there is the option of verbal expression, which improves impulse control. However, when emotional awareness is missing, such people may resort to expression through movement or action. The one emotion that men will tend to accept who are in the typical masculine mold is anger; this will provide them with protection against vulnerability, and unfortunately provides a replacement for emotions like shame, guilt, sadness, grief, and even love. Men sometimes displace their anger towards fathers who were physically or emotionally absent onto women. By exploring their relationship with their fathers, some men's own pain and hurt can be identified and they can become more open to see how hurtful the control of their wives can be.

Poling,[40] from his experience in working with male batterers, comments that therapists are usually faced with lying, denial, and minimizing so that it may be nearly impossible to discern the real truth. He says that such men may be out of touch with the emptiness and isolation of their own lives, and externalize their own problems by blaming others. They feel entitled to the emotional control of the women and children in their families and resent any outside interference. Concerning sexual violence, denial is the typical defense against accountability and is the most serious problem preventing batterers seeking the treatment they need.

Marks of a Healthy Relationship

A healthy relationship should be based on mutual **RESPECT** for each other and will give importance to:[41]

Rights (paying attention to and respecting each other's rights)

Equality (giving equal importance to each other's needs)

Sharing (exchanging thoughts, experiences, and feelings)

Patience (realizing that relationships take time and effort)

Exploring differences (accepting people are different)

Communication (talking things through openly and honestly)

Trust (an essential foundation for any relationship)

16.3   ADULT SEXUAL ABUSE

I referred above to the patriarchal values of society that can lead to the control of women. Unfortunately through this sexual socialization, women can develop various misconceptions about sexuality and sex roles such as the following: sexual relations should primarily meet the male's needs and desires; the role of the female in sexual activity is to be submissive and dependent; women are the property of men; women must satisfy the male's sexual desires, which are powerful and uncontrollable; and sexual activity is a prerequisite for receiving emotional support.[42] Such serious and ignorant misconceptions can leave the door open to sexual abuse that can lead to

[40]Poling (2003: 90–91).
[41]Donnellan (2002: 2).
[42]Draucker (2000: 90).

rape, even in marriage. A helpful starting point in dealing with such misconceptions is the "Sexual Bill of Rights," which includes basic ideas such as: I have a right to own my own body, I have a right to state my own sexual limits, I have a right to say no, and I have a right to experience sexual pleasure.[43] Women can also sexually abuse men through sexual harassment, withholding sexual intercourse, forcing sex after physical assaults, and using sexually degrading language. In marriage, sexual abuse may be one part of physical abuse, where one partner is afraid not to give in to the other partner.

16.3.1 Rape

In U.S. criminal law rape is any forced, unwanted sexual intercourse. Koss[44] conservatively estimated the prevalence of rape on females as at least 14%, with some studies reporting over 20%. Most rapes are committed by men between the ages of 20 and 50, and more than 50% of all rapes reported in the U.S. occur against females under 18 years of age. Strangers commit about one-half of all rapes, while the other half are committed by men who are well-known to their victims. About 9% of all rape victims are male. In the U.K., the appalling statistic is that 1 in 7 of all married women are raped by their husbands.[45]

Nearly a third to a half of people in the U.S. who experience rape suffer from rape-related post traumatic stress disorder (RR-PSTD).[46] Victims may suffer from depression, thoughts of suicide, and drug and alcohol problems. They usually go through various stages. The few days after the rape involve anger, physical problems due to the rape, confused emotions (e.g., shock, guilt, shame/self-blame), fear of how friends will react (Will she be believed?), and will be looking for emotional support and someone to believe her. She may then face the fear of pregnancy, AIDS, or a sexually transmitted disease and require unpleasant anti-pregnancy and anti-venereal medicines. There is also the question of a possible abortion if she does become pregnant or the implications of unchosen solo parenthood if against abortion. Legal aspects of the rape, PSTD symptoms, and various emotions and beliefs need to be dealt with, including any sexual difficulties, issues of safety, loss of self-esteem, issues in re-establishing intimate relationships, and regaining trust in men. In addition to all of this there is the real fear of a court case and a horrific examination accusing her of consensual sex or even initiating the act, and having to confront the rapist.

Because of all the above problems, rape victims may find it very difficult to ask for help. Having supportive friends is important, in particular having support people accompanying the victim to all appointments, meetings and discussions, no matter how minor, that relate to the rape (even when talking to family members or having brief meeting with such people as a landlord, boss or teacher). The reasons for this is that there is still a strong tendency to blame, disbelieve, or ostracize rape victims so that reactions by others can be witnessed by a support person. Support people can also act as prompts in remembering information and recalling

---

[43] There are several versions of the Bill on the internet and a basic one is at
http://studenthealth.oregonstate.edu/sexual-health-bill-rights (accessed October 2010).
[44] Koss (1993: 217).
[45] Donnellan (2002: 10).
[46] See Section 7.3.

what questions need to be asked; they should also take notes. They need to be kept informed about what is happening and their role made clear; it may include making phone calls for the victim or helping to get accurate information. Support persons will be essential if a court trial ensues.

Rape victims should endeavor get all their questions answered as soon and as accurately as possible, especially from the authorities. They should keep pushing for the truth if any answers seem unsatisfactory. It is also a good idea for them to keep a journal of everything that happens and prepare a professional two or three minute summary of their case to avoid being sabotaged by emotions when talking about it. Before a meeting they should prepare and rehearse what they will communicate and what questions they will ask. Final, on-the-spot, decisions on important matters should not be made quickly or over the phone or in meetings. Rather say that they will get back with a complete and accurate answer after they have had some time to think clearly. Unprofessional people without rape experience such as work, union, or church officials should not be relied on to investigate the rape; they may even have a conflict of interest in the case.

A major problem is that people will sometimes side with the rapist! We live in a male-dominated society and sexist views might arise. Also the rapist is often known to the victim so that when it all becomes public, surrounding people may be forced to take sides. All the old clichés tend to surface such as she provoked him, she was acting too sexy or dressed inappropriately, she drank too much, she wanted it, and so forth. In addition, the authorities might not take the victim seriously. Having a good victim advocate from a rape crisis center is a good idea; it needs to be someone with authority such as a therapist or other suitably trained and qualified professional.

Rape also occurs in same sex relationships. Waterman et al.[47] found that 12% of gay males studied reported being victims of of forced sex by current or most recent partners, and 31% of lesbians studied reported forced sex.

In the above discussion I have not specifically mentioned counseling processes. However I have endeavored to raise some of the issues that a therapist might meet and have to deal with. Each situation will be different so that the therapist needs to provide appropriate support and a safe place for the victim to process emotions and set down strategies.[48] The fundamental principles of therapy and supervision apply equally here as to other presenting issues.

16.4 PSYCHOLOGICAL ABUSE

Verbal, mental, and emotional abuse are included this section as they are part of psychological abuse; abusive control is also an important feature. Financial abuse can have a profound psychological effect, for example, he may totally control the family income so that permission to spend is required, and every sum has to be accounted for. She may run up huge bills in his name or default on payments. Both are forms of psychological control or a reaction to it.

---

[47]Waterman, Dawson, and Bolgna (1989).
[48]For further details, including information in dealing with the justice system in the U.S. see http://www.justicewomen.com/tips_index.html (accessed October 2010).

Psychological abuse may also be combined with physical abuse so that all the topics, including control, might be subsumed under "domestic abuse." For example, continual derogatory comments, being shouted at, made a fool of, and verbal abuse that attacks a person's self-esteem (e.g., "You are stupid, ugly, and useless.") can be as harmful as physical violence; both leave scars of different kinds. The psychological abuse can have a significant emotional impact which the victim takes on board, perceiving that he or she is of low human value and "useless." An example is that of a romantic relationship where the batterer repeatedly tells his victim, "If you leave me, no one will want you." Over time, she comes to believe that and, when considering whether to leave, she has to confront the very real possibility that she will never have another relationship – and accept that perhaps she will never have sex again. Never again will a man touch her with love and caring!

Kirkwood has identified six components of the emotional abuse of women that are interwoven and mutually reinforcing:[49]

- degradation (e.g., put-downs and devaluing)

- fear (e.g., for physical and emotional safety)

- objectification (e.g., viewed as objects, told what to do or how to act),

- deprivation (e.g., economic and social deprivation; coping with possessiveness; and intense isolation)

- overburden of responsibility (e.g., to maintain the emotional and practical issues of their relationship and the family)

- distortion of subjective reality (e.g., what women perceive and what their partners maintain eventually lead to women questioning the validity of their own subjective reality)

Most of the above also apply to the emotional abuse of men by women. Unfortunately there is an unbalanced image in the media with the emphasis on just the physical abuse and not the emotional abuse. The latter is not understood by friends and family because of stereotypes based on physical abuse. The topic tends to be avoided by everybody a few months after the abused person leaves their partner.

16.5 WHY PEOPLE STAY WITH ABUSIVE PARTNERS

16.5.1 Abusive Men

The majority of battered woman do not stay in the relationship (up to 75% in the U.S.).[50] However, for those that stay, there may be a number of beliefs a female client has to explain to the therapist as to why she stays that need to be explored. It is helpful to recognize the significant difference between why a woman chooses to stay and why she feels she cannot leave. In the latter case, a common reason given is that women accept violence for economic reasons, having to choose between staying in an abusive relationship and being homeless and/or poor. This difficulty

---

[49]Kirkwood (1997: 46–58).
[50]Berry (2000: 48).

is compounded when children are involved (the care of pets may also be at factor).

She may also stay because she believes that all children need a father; he may be good with the children even though he hits her. Children primarily need love and security, which they can get from their mother and other healthy adults, more than they need a dysfunctional man as a "father figure" who is abusive to their mother.

A woman may feel she must have a man to be a whole person. Others may feel that they don't deserve more in a relationship and do not deserve to leave it. Because of low self-esteem, they may blame themselves for the violence, especially if he is only violent with her, which is usually the case with at least 80% of violent men.[51] The man may even say that his partner caused him to be violent and blame her (a societal myth). Some women believe that if they stop making mistakes and improve themselves, then the violence will stop. They stay because of guilt. Some women buy into the myth that women are masochists who actually like being beaten, otherwise they would leave.

Women may engage in mind-reading and interpret their partner's violent behavior as a sign of distress or mental illness, especially if he was mistreated as a boy. Being motivated by pity and/or a mothering instinct she may believe that she is the only one who can help him overcome his problem. However, the only thing that will help him is for him to be accountable and stop the abuse.

Between violent episodes the batterer may express contrition and mild affection or even be romantic and loving, which gives the woman hope and encourages her to stay in the relationship. She goes through what has been described as the cycle of violence: a tension building phase when the woman tries to please, an explosion phase when the batterer takes control, and the contrition stage when the batterer becomes loving and apologetic. She continually seeks the third phase, which generally gets shorter and shorter.[52]

Abused women may have been brought up in a home where abuse happened regularly so that abuse is accepted as natural; the more she was hit by her parents, the more likely she is to stay in an abusive relationship. Her childhood message was that it is okay to hit someone you love when they have done something wrong.

A woman may stay because she is afraid of her partner who may take revenge if she breaks up with him or he is reported; she may even fear for her life. She may also incur the wrath of the extended family. If reported, he might even lose his job, the only source of income for the family.

Another reason for staying could be her isolation, as her partner may be her only support system psychologically. He may have systematically destroyed her other friendships either directly or indirectly by making others uncomfortable. Continual violence can lead to a form of brainwashing and a learned helplessness that engenders the idea that she cannot escape. Childhood factors linked to learned helplessness are: witnessing or experiencing battering in the home; sexual abuse; periods of loss of control through parental alcoholism, frequent moves, or poverty;

[51]Berry (2000: 46).
[52]Whalen (1996: 63).

rigidly traditional sex-role training; and health problems.[53] Some women have a strong religious conviction not to divorce, but no reputable religious movement in the Christian tradition condones marital abuse. She may not choose divorce but must consider separation. Some eastern and third world non-Christian religions tolerate maltreatment of women and the therapist is well advised to be informed of these practices when working with an adherent of such religious systems.

16.5.2   Abusive Women

When men are abused by women, they may have a more difficult time admitting they are victims and therefore seeking help, and find it more difficult to leave an abusive relationship. A man may stay in an abusive relationship for economic reasons as moving out will still leave him responsible for supporting his family and obtaining a separate residence for himself that is liable to be small and not as comfortable as his home. He may lose some of his possessions. She may use emotional blackmail and threaten to kill herself if he leaves. As women tend to end up with most of the custodial care of the children, and the father only having visiting rights or restricted access, the man may be afraid of losing contact with the children if he leaves, especially if she abuses the children when he is not there to prevent it. Also leaving the relationship will bring home to the man his loss of power and force him to accept failure. He may find authorities like the police unsympathetic toward him and tending to believe her rather than him; restraining and/or trespass orders may be biased. She may file false charges.

I also mentioned in a previous section that lesbian abuse is relatively common. Lesbians may stay in a secret abusive relationship because of a threat of exposing one's sexual orientation to family, employers, and so forth.

16.6   ABUSE OF THE ELDERLY

It seems that abuse and neglect of the elderly is on the increase in many parts of the world including developed countries, The problem is exacerbated by some populations getting older, especially with the most developed nations. People are also living longer and are therefore becoming more prone to degenerative diseases. Although helping the elderly is somewhat outside my brief as more than counseling is generally needed, I would like to raise some issues so that therapists are aware of possible risk factors.[54]

There are several types of abuse, namely physical, sexual, psychological, emotional, and financial, while neglect can be passive (e.g, carers' inadequate knowledge, illness, or lack of trust in prescribed services) or active (conscious and intentional deprivation of an older person under care). Forms of abuse have been set out in the form of an Abuse in Later Life Wheel, similar to the Power and Control wheel described above.[55] This is a useful wheel for determining factors indicative of abuse and it makes a distinction between emotional and psychological abuse.

[53]Berry (2000: 54).
[54]See, for example, the Appendices of http://www.moh.govt.nz/moh.nsf/pagesmh/6565/ and entered under "Publication availability" (accessed October 2010).
[55]See http://www.ncall.us/docs/Later_Life_PCWheel.pdf (accessed October 2010).

Illnesses such as dementia that can cause at times disruptive and aggressive behavior can lead to abusive reaction by the caregiver. Aging can bring many problems because of increasing physical (and sometimes mental) challenges, isolation, and poverty. The term *ageism* is used to describe some of the disadvantages of being old. For example, the elderly have a poor social image such as being "retired" and unproductive, asexual, intellectually inflexible and forgetful, and they tend to get stereotyped in a negative fashion in the media. Ageism can lead to inadequate services for older people and the violation of their legal and financial rights.

Some risk factors associated with elder abuse are mentioned below.

1. Living with others can be high risk, while living alone has the lowest risk. An exception is financial abuse where the reverse is true, i.e., living alone poses a greater risk.

2. Social isolation from family and friends (apart from the person they may be living with) heightens the potential for abuse, particularly when family stress is present. Such isolation renders the older person extremely vulnerable and can serve to conceal the abuse.

3. Financial abuse and exploitation can a problem.

4. Most abuse and neglect comes from family members, usually because of internal family problems or both spouses having to work. A supportive extended family network is the best protection against elder abuse and neglect.

5. Unfortunately some residential care can be inadequate or even abusive. The quality of care varies a great deal depending on staffing issues with the care; low paid, undertrained staff adding to abuse risk. Neglect can include medication errors, high use of psychotropic drugs, and poor management of challenging behaviors.

6. There may be a lack of social support and connectedness that is compounded by inadequate public transport and community facilities.

Abusers may have problems with their own mental illness, substance abuse, or depression, and have inadequate caregiving skills. They are often overstressed with insufficient support and little or no triangular supervision.

16.7   SPIRITUAL ABUSE

I am indebted to Johnson and VanVonderen (1991) for many of the ideas in this section.[56]

16.7.1   Defining Spiritual Abuse

"I am the pastor so that I am right. If you disagree with me, then you are wrong and there is something wrong with you spiritually." Although these words are a parody of what might be said they are sometimes implied. This scenario is an

---

[56]For further comments see http://www.spiritualabuse.com/?page_id=58 and http://www.watchman.org/cults/precond1.htm (both accessed October 2010).

example of spiritual abuse when a person comes to someone perceived as having spiritual authority and is left feeling ashamed of his or her lack of spiritually. What then is spiritual abuse? Johnson and VanVonderen define spiritual abuse as follows:

> Spiritual abuse is the mistreatment of a person who is in need of help, support or greater spiritual empowerment, with the result of weakening, undermining or decreasing that person's spiritual empowerment.[57]

Examples of this are:

1. A leader uses his or her spiritual position to control or dominate another person as in the above opening scenario. Spiritual abuse comes from a place of power or perceived power. For such leaders image may be everything to them and their place of honor is important.

2. People are judged because they don't live up to a particular "spiritual standard." Spiritual performance is used to measure a person's spirituality without regard to a person's wellbeing (e.g., "You should pray for one hour every day").

3. A person's family can also be an abusive system where, for example, the husband sets down spiritual rules. He takes seriously a verse of scripture like "wives respect their husbands" and ignores the context and other admonitions (see Section 16.8.1). Older members of the extended family can also play similar roles.

Spiritual abuse is not new and there are biblical examples of it described in Section 16.8.3 below.

16.7.2   Recognizing an Abusive System

The first sign is when the leaders are focused on their own authority and remind others of it; what can be referred to as power posturing. Followers come to believe that the leaders are the only ones who can discern God's word so that the leaders' interpretation is the right one, which becomes the mindset of the followers. Authority then becomes legislative so that there is a preoccupation with the performances of the members in the system leading them to obedience and submission. Spirituality becomes equated with doing the "right thing" as determined by the leader rather than with who you are (e.g., knowing your income so that you give the right amount of money to the church). Such leaders may quote verses referring to being subject to the leaders (e.g., 1 Peter 5:5, Hebrews 13:7),[58] and use "proof" texts, where a sequence of texts, even taken out of context, are used to "prove" a point. This approach is what the followers learn to use without a proper exegesis of the texts. For example, some areas where texts can be used in a legalistic way are as follows:[59]

- self denial (e.g., 1 Corinthians 15:31, Matthew 16:24)

- giving (e.g., Malachi 3:8, Luke 6:38, 2 Corinthians 9:6)

---

[57] Johnson and VanVonderen (1991: 20).

[58] But note Acts 5:29 when Peter disagreed with the religious leaders on the grounds that we must obey God rather than men.

[59] Adapted from Johnson and VanVonderen (1991: chapters 7 and 8).

- peace in the church (e.g., Matthew 5:9, Philippians 2:2, Ephesians 4:3).

- church discipline (Matthew18:15–17, 1 Corinthians 5:5)

- never resist (Matthew 5:39)

- wives submit at all costs (Ephesians 5:24)

- keep on forgiving, even if abused (Matthew 18:21–22)

- no appealing to a secular authority (1 Corinthians 6:1–2)

- forget the past (Philippians 3:13–14)

It is not my intention to discuss the appropriate context of these verses but to simply point out that when taken out of context they can be used ignorantly as weapons.[60]

Spiritually abusive systems have unspoken rules that generally involve someone's personal interpretation of a biblical principle. One example is that you must never disagree with the pastor or church authority, especially openly or publicly. If you do you may be ignored or shunned, possibly openly censured or asked to leave. As mentioned above, if you raise a problem out loud you become the problem. The message is "Don't rock the boat" as everything is fine. There is a pretend peace[61] and the system is protected through secrecy. An over-spiritualizing of emotions may occur, with certain emotions demanded and others condemned by a twisting of scripture. The result is a "don't feel your real feelings" rule.

An abusive system is out of balance where either valid subjective expression is excluded or it is pushed to the exclusion of scriptural objectivity. Such objectivity is when everything is so black-and-white that there is no room for a people's individual experiences and people have to fit into the system. Extreme subjectivity is when people's gifts and experiences are given the ultimate authority even if one's personal experience or scripture says otherwise. Therapists need to note and advise Christians to be careful when someone, even a pastor, says to them, "I have a word from the Lord for you." Such clients should be advised that God can guide them personally and that's the role of the Holy Sprit, according to traditional Christian theology.

Johnson and VanVonderen describe an abusive system as shame-based as it is based on messages of shame, for example,

> You are so weak and defective that you are nothing without this relationship. Shame becomes the glue that holds things together. It is the force that motivates people to refrain from certain behaviors and to do others.[62]

They go on to say that if families, churches, or groups are shame-based, they are more than likely sending messages to their members that they are:

> not loved and accepted; not even lovable or acceptable; only loved and accepted if, when, or because they perform well; not capable, valuable, or worthwhile; very alone, not really belonging anywhere, to anything, or with anyone.

---

[60]See http://www.philosophy-religion.org/criticism/toxicfaith.htm by Bill Jackson (accessed April 2011) for a good discussion on "toxic" faith.
[61]Compare Jeremiah 6:14b.
[62]Johnson and VanVonderen (1991: 55).

Characteristics of shame-based relationships are:

1. Out-loud shaming. The overt message is that something is wrong with you.

2. Focus on performance. What you do is more important than who you are.

3. Manipulation. This is done through unspoken rules or inuendoes.

4. Idolatry. The system, which is impossible to please, is a false god. The group is not God either.

5. Preoccupation with fault and blame. Watch out if you don't perform properly.

6. Reality is obscured. Contrary views are ignored or denied. There is guessing at what is "normal."

7. Unbalanced interrelatedness. Members are either neglected or over-involved (enmeshed) with others. There are no clear boundaries between people so it is hard to say no, and everyone is responsible for everyone else.

A key aspect of an abusive system is that it is usually very difficult to leave. There is a belief by the members of the system that they are more enlightened, that others won't understand unless they join too, and that others will respond negatively. In the case of a church, it may view itself as being persecuted by the world, the media, and other Christian churches, which are denounced. The system isolates the abusers from accountability and people don't want to leave as they will then become outsiders. It also means that these people don't get the help they need. Disloyalty to the system is seen as disobeying God and those who decide to leave may be submitted to scare tactics and humiliation (e.g., "God will destroy your business.") and may be are shunned by other members.

16.7.3 Hallmarks of a Spiritually Abused Person

The abused person suffers from learned powerlessness. Johnson and VanVonderen[63] give the following list of possible indicators of an abused Christian:

1. A distorted image of God (e.g., God is fickle and never satisfied with us).

2. A distorted image of self as a Christian (e.g., not realizing what it means to be a new creation in Christ; having a shame-based identity).

3. Not understanding grace and being able to accept it.

4. Lacking boundaries (e.g., personal rights versus "death to self").

5. Having difficulty with personal responsibility, for example, being under-responsible in one's relationship with God or others through finding it all too difficult to live up to and virtually giving up, or being over-responsible and trying to fix everybody else's problems.

6. Having difficulty admitting the abuse because of "brain washing."

7. Having difficulty with trust.

[63] Johnson and VanVonderen (1991: chapter 3).

8. Lacking living skills because of the emphasis on avoiding contact with the evil world.

9. Only feeling loved and accepted when he or she performs appropriately.

16.7.4   Why Stay?

Why do people stay in spiritually abusive relationships? Sometimes there is too much at stake to leave because of time invested and friends made. They may be afraid of threats if they leave or are so dependent that they are unsure of surviving emotionally or financially if they leave. They may blame themselves for being abused and believe untruths about God, themselves, and their relationships. For example, they may believe that leaving the system is equal to leaving God and God's protection. They may also be afraid to leave because they are worried about the evils outside the system; it is not safe outside. Sometimes when they are about to leave things improve for a while so that they keep changing their mind.

The abusive spiritual system may be likened to a trap with many kinds of bait[64] such as: promising right standing with God through self-effort;[65] having the approval of others; having religious status or position; getting a pay check; being promised things will improve; or having "an opportunity to be shamed and mistreated in a way that is consistent with their sense of deserving to be punished for being so 'bad'." However, they don't realize that the goal posts keep moving so that they become more deeply involved with the system.

16.7.5   Counseling for Spiritual Abuse

People may come to counseling because of side effects of spiritual abuse such as depression, stress, or shame, for example. Unfortunately there is no diagnostic test for spiritual abuse, only spiritual clues such as lack of joy in the Christian life,[66] being tired of trying to measure up, being disillusioned about God and spiritual things, uneasiness, lack of trust, or fear of those who care about spiritual things, even legitimately.[67] The first step for the therapist is to recognize that they are spiritually abused using, for example, material from the above sections, and then encourage them to ask for help for the abuse. Trust may be an issue for clients so that it is important to build up a good relationship with clients. The second step involves a cognitive restructuring, described in biblical terms as the renewing of one's mind,[68] because of brainwashing by the system. For example, ideas that grace and approval are gifts from God can be explored.

Care is needed in using God-language as the language may mean something different to clients. They need to realize that leaders are not more favored by God over others and all struggle spiritually, including leaders. Everyone is in a different stage of spiritual growth and everyone makes mistakes, including leaders. Everyone can learn to hear God's voice for themselves and have their own separate relation-

---

[64]Johnson and VanVonderen (1991: 184–185).
[65]But see 2 Corinthians 11:13–15.
[66]Cf. Galatians 4:15, 5:7.
[67]Adapted from Johnson and VanVonderen (1991: 194).
[68]Romans 12:2.

ship with God; they don't need to remain spiritual children who must submit to parental leaders. We all have something to give and we are valuable to God.

The therapist then helps to establish a safe relationship where healing can take place and clients can recover their sense of identity as they often don't know who they are anymore, having been lost in the system. The client needs to decide on a plan of action—either stay in the system and try and change it, or leave it altogether. Both options need to be explored. Key questions might be:

- " Are you supporting what you hate?"

- "Can you stay and stay healthy, both at the same time?"

- "Can you set boundaries and stick with them?"

- "Can you set a limit on how much effort you will put in before seeing a change, and sticking with the limit?"

- "Is it possible that the system might need to die?"

- "Are you trying to sow your seed in the wrong place?"[69]

- "If you came today knowing what you know now about the system, would you stay?"

Answering these questions might lead to the client leaving. If the client is going to stay and fight, then Johnson and VanVonderen[70] offer the following advice:

- Decide whom you serve.

- Be ready for resistance.

- Keep telling the truth.

- Know who your enemy is.

- Hang on to God.[71]

16.8   BIBLICAL VIEWPOINT

16.8.1   Control Issues

Since the Bible arose out of patriarchal societies, some scriptures have a male focus and have consequently been misused. For example, Genesis 3:16 talks about the husband ruling over the wife. This is not the norm, which is set out in Genesis chapters 1 and 2, but rather the result of the Fall; sin can lead to this. With regard to control, some husbands use biblical verses that exhort wives to be subject to their husbands[72] to justify their endeavor to take control, but conveniently forget the injunctions to love their wives as Christ loved the church, love their wives as

---

[69]See Mark 4:3–9 and Matthew 10:14.
[70]Johnson and VanVonderen (1991: chapter 21).
[71]See Isaiah 40:29–31.
[72]I Corinthians 11:3; Ephesians 5:22–24, 32; and 1 Peter 3:1–6.

their own bodies, and be considerate to and bestow honor on their wives.[73] Phrases like "the husband is head of the wife" are taken out of context, filtered through popular culture, and are used to justify controlling behavior. In contrast, verse 21 of Ephesians chapter 5 talks about mutual submission, and the Greek word *hupotasso* for "submit" can also include "behaving responsibly." The Greek word for "head" (*kephale*) can also mean "source" or "origin," which reflects the interdependence of men and women; each comes from the other.[74] When it comes to sexual relations we again see the equality of husband and wife with regard to sex and control.[75] The idea of headship is best replaced by authentic partnership.[76]

With regard to the control of children, scripture can again be misused to justify authoritarian and abusive attitudes toward children, thus ignoring the injunction not to provoke children or put a stumbling block in their way.[77] Poling notes that: "Parents often expect children to obey them without question, to run errands and do chores for the parent's benefit, and to accept the suffering that comes with punishment and abuse."[78]

Marriage is about sacrifice and partnership, and not about control. Wives can also endeavor to take control in various ways, and one of the most effective ways is the withholding of sex. However such an action is not surprising if the husband is already abusive. A wife who complains to some church authorities about abuse may find she is not believed; after all her husband is a man of God and she should obey him! There are also injunctions as to how Christians should behave to one another; husbands and wives are not exempt.[79]

From a Christian perspective, controlling people may lack a trust in God and need to reassess their belief.[80] Relinquishing control to God can relieve anxiety and bring peace.[81]

16.8.2   Partner Abuse

As mentioned above, some churches do not take a victim's abuse seriously or even believe the person. For example, in the case of a battered wife someone might say, "You made a vow before God to stay with him in sickness and in health until death do you part. Clearly he's sick, so it's your duty to stay with him and help him." Christians are taught, "God never gives you a burden greater than you can bear." However, nowhere in the Bible is spousal abuse sanctioned, and in the previous section we see that marriage is based on love and respect.[82] Genuine love is spelt out clearly in 1 Corinthians chapter 13. The victim's safety is paramount.

Given the high level of abuse in society, which will also unfortunately be reflected in the church, there needs to be a greater level of awareness of the problem shown

---

[73] Ephesians 5:25–30 and 1 Peter 32:7.
[74] See, for example, 1 Corinthians 11:11–12.
[75] 1 Corinthians 7:2–5.
[76] Gender equality is seen in the passage Galatians 3:26–29.
[77] Exodus 20:12; Ephesians 6:1–4; and Matthew 18:1–7.
[78] Poling (2003: 185).
[79] Galatians 5:13 and Philippians 2:3.
[80] Proverbs 3:56.
[81] Matthew 6:25–34; 1 Peter 5:7; and Philippians 4:67.
[82] See also Colossians 3:18–19.

by religious leaders. In stressing this point, Poling[83] points out that salvation can also involve safety and freedom from death and suffering (e.g., Hagar and Ishmael from starvation, Joseph from a pit, the Israelites from slavery, Jeremiah from the cistern, Daniel from the lions, and Paul and Silas from prison). Violent behavior is also a prison that an abuser can be released from. Paul was struck by a blinding light and Jesus asked him, "Why are you persecuting me?"[84] An abuser needs to go through the steps of confession, repentance, sanctification (living a new life), and restitution.

For a church family in some ill-informed churches, the leaders may automatically require unconditional forgiveness from the abused person before some healing has taken place, or any appropriate safety measures are put in place, and before there is genuine repentance and restitution from the abuser. The abuser, when confronted (if he is), may then ask for and be given prayers of forgiveness from the pastor and sent back to the family to reoffend.[85] Forgiving an offender, therefore, is not straightforward as the repentance may not be genuine. We recall that there are differences of opinion about forgiving sexual abuse (Section 15.2.4 under "Role of Forgiveness"). Forgiveness ultimately involves the restoration of one's relationship with God. Some survivors see forgiveness as the last step in a process involving safety from violence, grief over losses from the violence, reorganizing one's life, and reconnecting with God.

We have an interesting case of familial rape in the Bible in the story of King David and three of his children, sons Amnon and Absalom, and daughter Tamar, Amnon's half-sister.[86] Amnon becomes infatuated with Tamar and arranges a situation where he rapes her. She protests but is overpowered; Absalom shelters her and then murders Amnon. Poling suggests that there are several ways of looking at this story from an ethical viewpoint. We see a violation of the ten commandments, destructive consequences causing an ongoing system of family violence, a violation of community standards ("Such a thing is not done in Israel"), and Tamar disempowered and marginalized. It is interesting to read the story from Tamar's point of view and think about what emotions she must have experienced.

16.8.3   Spiritual Abuse and the Bible

Spiritual abuse is described in the Bible. For instance, in the Old Testament we have an example of false prophets and greedy priests who spiritually neglected God's people.[87] In the New Testament Jesus accused the religious leaders of burdening the people with legalism that weighed them down, which can be contrasted with his role of providing rest.[88] He called these leaders a brood of vipers and accused them of being evil.[89] The Jews of that time suffered under a performance-based religion, something echoed today with some modern religious communities. Jesus also warned about false prophets who are disguised as sheep but inwardly are

[83]Poling (2003: 27).
[84]Acts 9:4.
[85]Poling (2003: 30).
[86]2 Samuel 13.
[87]Jeremiah 5:30–31 and 6:13–14.
[88]Matthew 23:4 and 11:28–30.
[89]Matthew 12:34 and 23:33.

ravenous wolves.[90] What were these religious leaders like? They gave money, attended the synagogue, and had more scripture memorized than anyone else. How did they respond to the out-loud criticism by Jesus? He was treated as the problem as he said there was a problem.

Blue notes several symptoms of abusive leaders based on Matthew 23; they do the following:[91]

- base their spiritual authority on their position or office

- often say one thing but do another

- manipulate people by making them feel guilty for not measuring up spiritually

- impose heavy spiritual loads that keep getting heavier

- are preoccupied with looking good and stifle personal criticism

- seek special titles and privileges that elevate them above the group

- do not communicate in a a straightforward manner, especially when defending themselves

- major on minor issues to the neglect of important ones

- are conscientious about religious details but neglect God's larger agendas

Paul struck similar problems with some religious leaders. In Ephesus he warned the Christian community about wolves arising from among them when he left.[92] Then some demanded that new Christians become circumcised because Moses had been circumcised. However Moses' belief in God was what counted, not circumcision.[93] Paul raised an important point that is relevant today and it is reflected in the words "they desire to have you circumcised, that they may boast in your flesh."[94] This is an example of meeting one's spiritual needs through someone else's performance. Paul describes the damage done in Galatia throughout the letter to the Galatians, namely, people followed a different gospel and were disturbed (1:7), they were brought into bondage (2:4), bewitched (3:1), suffered persecution from this teaching (4:29), were hindered from obeying the truth (5:7), and felt the loss of the sense of blessing (4:15).

[90] Matthew 7:15.
[91] Blue (1993: 134–135).
[92] Acts 20:29.
[93] Genesis 15:6 and Galatians 5:6.
[94] Galatians 6:12–13.

CHAPTER 17

DYSFUNCTIONAL RELATIONSHIPS

17.1 INTRODUCTION

This chapter is somewhat diverse as it deals with some very different but connected themes such as boundaries, codependency, and coping with difficult people
in various environments. The common denominator is that of dysfunctional relationships, and the emphasis of this chapter is to help a client cope with such
a relationship, generally without the therapist having access to the other party.
Clearly some aspects of couple relationships will be relevant here, but most of that
topic is considered in Chapter 19, where the emphasis is on helping both members
of the couple.

17.2 GENERAL BOUNDARIES

17.2.1 Nature of Boundaries

The role of a boundary is to protect us from others, protect others from us, and
help give us our identify and allow us to have as many gates through the boundary
as is mutually desirable. Our internal boundary separates our thoughts, feelings,
and actions from others so that we are not controlled by others or control others,
while our external boundary maintains an appropriate physical and sexual distance.
Boundaries can be too rigid or too weak (diffuse) instead of being flexible so that
there is a balance between maintaining personal identity and allowing others in.

Counseling Issues: A Handbook for Counselors and Psychotherapists. By George A. F. Seber **441**
Copyright © 2013 G. A. F. Seber

A boundary is not a matter of building a wall, but rather defining what you will do or won't do. It does not mean that you are demanding anyone to respect your boundaries, though when they are crossed some appropriate confrontation will be needed.

Boundaries need to be taught, as very young children have no boundaries to protect themselves from abuse or from abusing others. Both parents therefore need to first demonstrate their own safe boundaries and then protect and respectively confront their children so that the children grow up to have a healthy and firm understanding of what boundaries mean and when to permit them to be flexible. Children brought up in dysfunctional families may have real problems with boundaries such as[1] (a) no boundaries (and therefore do not recognize the boundaries of others), (b) damaged boundaries (i.e., boundaries with holes so that there is only partial protection), (c) walls instead of boundaries (e.g., walls of anger, fear, silence, and words, with no intimacy), and (d) fluctuating boundaries (e.g., back and forth from walls to no boundaries).

17.2.2   Some Boundary Principles

Cloud and Townsend[2] proposed ten principles or "laws" relating to boundary setting that provide a helpful summary. These are as follows:

1. *Sowing and Reaping.* This allows consequences to happen rather than rescuing or being codependent.

2. *Responsibility.* We need to understand what it means to be responsible to ourselves and to others. With respect to others we have a responsibility to treat them as we would want to be treated, yet we also need to set limits on someone else's irresponsible behavior

3. *Power.* We can reclaim our power to change, and we have the power to ask others (and a Higher Power) for help.

4. *Respect.* We need not fear that others won't respect our boundaries and our "nos." Our focus should not be determined by others. However, we do need to respect other people's boundaries.

5. *Motivation.* We should be motivated by love and not by fear of losing love, fear of loneliness, and others' anger.

6. *Evaluation.* We need to evaluate the effects of our boundary setting and be aware of the difference between hurt and harm as others may be upset with our boundary setting.

7. *Proactivity.* Our boundaries need to be proactive and not reactive. Our initial response may be reactive, but we don't need to stay there.

8. *Envy.* This can arise because we feel that we may be lacking something. We need to ask for help (from others or our Higher Power) to understand why we don't have what we envy and whether we really need it.

[1]Mellody, Miller, and Miller (1989: 13–16).
[2]Cloud and Townsend (1992: chapter 5).

9. *Activity.* We may have boundary problems because we lack initiative.

10. *Exposure.* Boundaries need to be made visible to others.

There are some misconceptions that people have about boundaries, some of which I now list as follows:[3]

1. *Setting boundaries is not selfish.* It doesn't mean that "good" people must always say "yes," but rather it indicates self-awareness, self-care, and self-esteem. It is often a way of being kinder and showing more care toward others.

2. *Setting boundaries doesn't mean hurting those we love.* In fact the opposite is true as allowing others to walk all over us robs them of personal growth. Always rescuing them is not in their best interests as they never learn to stand on their own feet nor realize that their actions have consequences.[4] Love does not mean always saying yes.

3. *Setting appropriate boundaries is not manipulation.* The difference between setting a boundary in a healthy way and manipulation is that when we set a boundary we let go of the outcome.

4. *Setting boundaries is not the same as being angry.* However, anger may lead to the setting of a boundary and consequently the receiver may get angry over the boundary put in place and try to exert control through anger.

5. *Setting boundaries does not mean that they are permanent.* If there are changes, renegotiate.

A key aspect of setting boundaries is learning to say and hear both yes and no at the right times. This is discussed in the next section.

17.2.3 Recognizing Unhealthy Boundaries

Some signs of unhealthy boundaries are as follows:[5]

- Not noticing when someone else displays inappropriate boundaries.
- Not noticing when someone invades your boundaries.
- Allowing others to take as much as they can from you.
- Giving as much as you can for the sake of giving.
- Letting others direct your life.
- Going against personal values or rights to please others.
- Accepting food, gifts, touch, or sex that you don't want.

---

[3] (1)–(3) are adapted from "Drawing the line," *Grapevine*, (2001), Issue 4, 15–23, Auckland, New Zealand.

[4] This is related to the concept of "tough love," where you have to be tough to be kind in the long term.

[5] A selection from http://www.recovery-man.com/coda/boundaries.htm (accessed October 2010).

- Telling all.

- Talking at an intimate level at the first meeting.

- Touching a person without asking.

- Falling in love with anyone who reaches out.

As mentioned in the previous section, people with unhealthy boundaries have problems with yes and no. The following table[6] sets out four categories of people with problems in this area.

Table 17.1   Choosing Yes or No.

	Can't say	Can't hear
No	The Compliant	The Controller
Yes	The Non-responsive	The Avoidant

Compliant (push-over) people who can't say "no" and end up saying "yes" to the bad is the most common of the four. Such people don't have boundaries, tend to be overworked and take on too much, and are always available to the detriment of their own needs. They feel guilty and/or controlled by others, and they find it hard to be independent and to admit that they have a problem. It is very difficult to have a relationship with someone who has no boundaries. They also minimize their differences with others so as not to upset anyone and tend to be self-condemning.

Controller (take-over) people, who can't hear no, manipulate and violate the boundaries of others. They will try and dump tasks on others that they should do themselves or are too tough or unreasonable. Controllers are unable to see or set their own boundaries so they cannot respect people's boundaries and may even hold others responsible for their problems. Their typical tactics are to fast-talk and bulldoze their "victims" (e.g., "If you would just lend me some money I won't get in a mess again") or put them on guilt trip (e.g., "I thought you would make time for an old friend"). They have problems with delayed gratification and can't function on their own in the world, needing people to spend time with them which they achieve through threats and manipulation. Otherwise they fear abandonment.

Non-responsive (cold-shoulder) people, who can't say yes, set boundaries against responsibility to love. They don't show empathy, and don't understand why some-one in difficulty can't simply "pull themselves together" and "get over it."

Avoidant (strong-silent) people, who can't hear yes and say no to the good, prefer to go it alone as they see dependence on others as a sign of weakness. They confuse healthy interdependence and "helplessness" and have boundaries when they shouldn't.

People may be combinations of the four types, for example, compliant/avoidant where they get lumbered with a controller's load but won't share the load, or

[6]From Cloud and Townsend (1992: 59).

controller/non-responsive where they dump on others without showing any empathy. With couples, the compliant and the controller may end up together—a typical situation in counseling couples.

Saying No

A therapist may find the following alternative ways of saying no helpful to pass on to a client.[7]

1. *Valid no.* "I have been out too many nights and need to spend time with my family."

2. *No after a previous yes.* "Sorry, I have to say no. I made a mistake and have overcommitted myself. I am very sorry but I will have to back out."

3. *The no-comeback no.* "No doubt it is a great cause, but I will have to pass it up."

4. *A not-now no.* "I have done it before and I'll do it in the future but I can't do it just now."

5. *The polite no.* "I'm sorry but I can't take on any more obligations this week/month/ year."

6. *Diplomatic no.* "It was so kind of you to think of me. I'm flattered you asked. I'm sorry I won't be able to do it."

7. *Absolute no, when all else fails.* "I simply cannot do this. I don't have the desire, the time, the interest or the energy."

The idea is to start with something "soft" followed by something "hard," then finishing with something soft. For example: "I would like to help but I have already been out three times this week. Perhaps I could do it next month."

17.2.4 Counseling for Boundary Issues

The first step with clients is to determine the nature of their boundaries. The most common situation faced in counseling will be with a client who has weak or no boundaries, and some of the ideas expressed above can be used to formulate open-ended questions. In endeavoring to establish boundaries, the first step for clients is to be honest with how they feel about the current situation and to own their feelings (e.g., "I feel angry when I am treated this way").[8] They need to know that it is okay to feel the way they do for that is who they are. It is important that they don't play the blame game like "You make me. . ." (e.g., angry, sad) and "How could you do that after all I have done for you," which may have carried over from childhood.

The next step might be to encourage clients to see that they have every right to take care of themselves.[9] Some help with self-worth (Section 2.5.3) and assertiveness

---

[7]Adapted from Arp and Arp (1993).
[8]Emotional processing can be used here (see Section 1.4.2).
[9]See for example the Personal Bill of Rights at
http://www.adoptioncrossroads.org/PersonalBillofRights.html. (accessed October 2010).

training (Section 2.5.4) may be appropriate. How to set up boundaries will depend on the situations that the client has to face, and different situations will be discussed separately below. However, there are a number of general guiding principles that may be useful to get a client thinking:

1. *Determine whose problem is it?* When clients are put under pressure to "go the extra mile," they need to ask the question, "Whose problem is it?" and not to take the problem on board and react to the way it was introduced. For example, they need to recognize when someone is trying to talk them into doing what he or she wants or whether the person is trying to put them on a guilt trip. Such tactics may need to be exposed and some suggestions for doing this are given below under the tile of "Difficult Conversations." They may of course end up fulfilling the request, but that needs to be done for the right reasons, for example, on the basis of love and freedom and not guilt.

2. *If possible respond, but don't react.* The only person I can put a boundary on is myself. Clients need to realize that they cannot control how others will react—that is not the client's problem. Nor can they demand that others do something or even respect one's boundaries. However, boundaries need to be communicated verbally followed by actions, and they need to be clear and unapologetic. Passive resistance needs to be avoided.

3. *Allow people to suffer the consequences.* Fear of this leads to blurred boundaries. People need to reap what they sow to bring about change.

4. *Sometimes boundaries need to be negotiated.* In fact it could be argued that most boundaries are more of a negotiation rather than simply "drawing a line in the sand."

In formulating boundaries, clients need to understand that they have the right to protect and defend themselves and take responsibility for how they allow others to treat them. This means being able to tell other people when they are acting in ways that are unacceptable to the clients. Others need to respect and honor the client and recognize that he or she has the right to be heard and the right to have feelings. One is often faced with the decision of setting limits and risk losing a relationship or not setting limits and remaining a prisoner to the wishes of another. Fearing loneliness or trying to overcome guilt to feel good about one's self can sabotage boundaries. Some people will put up with a bad relationship as they are afraid of being alone.

Cloud and Townsend[10] comment that we need other people to help us set and keep boundaries. For example, if someone has been subject to another's addictions, control, or abuse for some years through giving too much to the relationship, he or she can learn to to say no to abuse and control through receiving strength from a support group. Those who continue in a bad relationship may do so because they are afraid of being left on their own, whereas a support group can help take away that fear. The group, or a therapist, can encourage those who have been taught by their church or family that boundaries are unbiblical, mean, or selfish to stand against the guilt engendered by those old "tapes" that tell them lies and keep them in bondage.

[10] Cloud and Townsend (1992: 37).

Setting Boundaries

How one sets boundaries will depend on the other person, for example one's boss, one's spouse, or one's children, so a number of different strategies will be given.

One strategy[11] begins with expressing how you feel to the other person by saying, "When you ... I feel ... and I want ...." This wording avoids blaming statements like " You behaved badly." The word "when" describes the behavior and it needs to be very specific. For example, instead of saying "When you get angry ...", which is an interpretation, it is better to be more specific such as "When you shout and clench your fists ...." People often have no idea what their behavior looks like and may even try to minimize it; I have heard anger described by one client as just being "firm" or "forthright." In describing the behavior, it might also give the person making the statement some insight as to why he or she finds it upsetting and perhaps bring some recognition of triggers from the past. It can also help recipients to become more aware of their own behavior (e.g., the fact that they are shouting). It is important to stop interpreting and start communicating.

The "I feel ..." part of the communication refers to expressing emotions in an honest and healthy way. For example "When I try to talk to you and you get up and walk out of the room I feel angry, unimportant, and unloved, and I feel that I am being punished." It may be possible to add what was triggered from the past, for example, "When you talk to me as though I am a child I feel angry as my mother used to use the same tone and treated me as the child she never wanted." The "I want..." part refers to asking specifically for what you want. For example, "I want you to listen to me and look at me when I talk to you."

In setting a boundary we need to describe specifically the behavior we find unacceptable and, if necessary, spell out what action will be taken if our boundaries are violated. One could use the words, "If you ..., I will ..." so that the consequences are clearly spelt out and are enforceable. Following through on consequences is particularly important in dealing with younger members of one's family, but some flexibility allowing gradual change may be appropriate in adult relationships. It depends, of course, on the nature of the behavior; abusive behaviors are out of the question. We need to have in mind what we will do if the behavior continues and we may need to spell it out with the words, " If you continue this behavior...;" for example, "If you continue this behavior I will go to the police."

In dealing with significant others who hate limits, one can try saying no to them in some area and see what happens. The outcome will either be an increased intimacy or a realization that there was little intimacy to begin with. Boundary setting needs to be done gently as it can generate anger, usually because of ignored past boundaries. As the limits are set, the anger will subside.

Difficult Conversations

As discussed above, there are times in our lives when people treat us badly and we need to have that difficult heart to heart talk. Cloud and Townsend (2003) discuss this problem and I will draw on their book for some general principles to add to the above.

---

[11] Clearly described by Robert Burney at http://www.joy2meu.com/Personal_Boundaries.htm (accessed October 2010).

We may feel there is nothing we can do to change another person and the only person we can change is ourselves. Certainly we need to see what we contribute to the problem, but change is possible if gone about the right way. Confronting, without anger, needs to be done in a loving way so that the person confronted is affirmed and valued. Listening with understanding and tuning into a person's feelings are important (see Section 19.6.2). Before having the conversation, we need to be very clear about what the specifics of the problem and its effects are, and what we want to change. As noted above, we need to use "I" rather than "you" statements, concentrate on feelings, and be careful not to lose focus as the other person will try to divert attention and use "red herrings." We can also use a type of "we" statement such as "I get upset when we are always running late."

Resistance can be expected and we need to hear the person out to a point, but be persistent in getting back on track. If the person has a habit of diversion this can be pointed out, for example:

> I have noticed that whenever I talk about our problem you ... (diversion). I really do want to own my part, and I will be glad to deal with it as we deal with your part. However it is hard for me as you keep diverting things. Can you tell me what goes on when I bring up problems, or how I can give you feedback in a better way.

Other responses might be: rationalization (give inappropriate reasons), minimizing ("It's no big deal!" or "Lighten up!"), blaming someone else ("Our family always did that"), or denial (the problem does not exist). It is important not to react to reactions. If the answer is no, seek to know the real reason. Either accept the no, acknowledge your sadness, and move on, or deal with any defensiveness and emphasize real consequences.

Summing up, we have the following rules from Cloud and Townsend that a therapist might find useful:[12]

- Choose the right time and the right place.

- Be prepared (be convinced that confronting is the right thing to do; be clear about the change you want; practice and role-play in advance).

- Acknowledge and apologize for any part you play in the problem.

- Stay in control of yourself! Be careful what you say when upset or angry.

- It is not a debate; persist and give it time.

- Avoid "should" (judgmental and parental) and "must" (command). Instead of "You should have ...." you can say, "It would have been really helpful if you ...."

- Avoid the line "we need to talk." Use alternative words, such as "There are some things I would like to discuss with you over a cup of coffee."

- Be specific and don't generalize. Not "I want you to be more helpful", but "I would like you to help me with ....

- Have consequences ready if needed, but avoid trying to control.

[12] Cloud and Townsend (2003: Part II).

- Don't confuse forgiveness (the past), reconciliation (present), and trust (future). Keep the future clearly differentiated from the past.

- Be clear and direct, but loving.

- Presume innocence. Until we know better, we assume a person is innocent of bad motives and approach the person accordingly. We may need to help the person become more self aware, aware of the effect on us, the effect on him or her, and the effect on others.

- Make a plan for after the conversation. For example ask questions like: "What do you think we should do if you do it again?" or "How about if I let you know if I notice it again. Will you be open to hearing that?"

It is helpful to allow the person confronted to have some power to make suggestions for both parties. For example, "When we go out I find that there are times when I feel criticized in front of others. I find this very upsetting. What can *we* do to avoid this from happening again?"

17.3   PARTICULAR BOUNDARIES

In this section we discuss boundaries with respect to self, marriage/cohabitation, family, friends, and work, beginning with a boundary check list. The general principles of boundary setting such as, for example, the ten laws described in Section 17.2.2 can be adapted to each situation. Hopefully the following comments will provide some suggestions for counseling. I am greatly assisted by the work of Cloud and Townsend (1992).

17.3.1   Boundary Checklist

When there are boundary problems between two people a check list like the following from Cloud and Townsend[13] can be useful:

1. What are the symptoms?

2. What are the roots of the problem?

3. What is the boundary conflict?

4. Who needs to take ownership?

5. What do they need?

6. How do they begin?

7. How do they set boundaries with each other?

8. What happens next?

Examples of using this list are given below under "Boundaries and Friends."

[13]Cloud and Townsend (1992: 138–139).

17.3.2   Boundaries with Self

Many clients have lives that are out of control because of serious boundary problems. They may not have had adequate boundaries as children and now find they have all sorts of problems as they are not able to say no to self or have boundaries on self. For example, there may be addictive behavior in areas like food, alcohol, drug abuse, and sex. Many people have problems with money such as impulsive spending, careless budgeting, living beyond one's means, credit problems, and chronically borrowing from friends. Others have lost control of their time and are always late in attending meetings. They may have unrealistic expectations about what they can achieve, they don't plan ahead, or minimize the stress and inconvenience they cause others through their lateness. A related problem is their not being able to finish tasks on time often because they are readily distracted or can't say no to other people and projects. An uncontrolled tongue that repeatedly interrupts or monopolizes the floor can indicate boundary problems. The above boundary checklist can be adapted here with "they" replaced by "you" for the client concerned.

17.3.3   Boundaries and Partners

Boundaries in a relationship help a couple to determine who is responsible for what. This may be a first step in counseling a couple, namely helping them to see what part each is responsible for, and what behavioral changes are needed by each person when there are problems. Almost all marriage problems are contributed to by both partners. Cloud and Townsend[14] emphasize that people need to realize that they are not at the mercy of their spouse's behavior or problems, but they are actually free agents with freedom to respond, with boundaries defining the extent of the freedom. Also, freedom brings responsibility and provides the environment for love. As mentioned above, boundaries are not something we try and enforce on the other person, but rather they are about one's self. For example, you can't stop a person speaking a certain way, but you can say, "If you speak to me that way again, I will walk out of the room."

Cloud and Townsend note that important ingredients for boundary setting are truthfulness, namely letting the partner know one's true feelings rather than hiding them, and establishing consequences that are followed through when boundaries are not observed. Some people stay in denial until they suffer some consequences (e.g., emotional distance), which may provide a wake-up call. Some partners, particularly passive ones who want a life of their own, decide on separation. This may provide some breathing space but it generally does not solve the problem or allow the establishing of boundaries; this requires being in and working on the relationship. Some partners distance themselves because they have poor boundaries and withdrawal is the only boundary they have.

It is important to deal with boundaries and limits with self[15] without being in denial, being irresponsible, self-centered, or judgmental, or withdrawing from the relationship. It is a matter of taking ownership of one's own life before focusing on a partner and applying the same rules you want to apply to your partner to yourself.

[14]Cloud and Townsend (1999: 22–25).
[15]Cloud and Townsend (1999: 70–75).

I want to now briefly consider the ten rules of Section 17.2.2.[16] The first boundary law of sowing and reaping is that partners need to know that their actions have consequences. (e.g., overspending leads to cutting back on necessities). When people do loving responsible things their partners draw close, but if they are unloving or irresponsible, partners draw away. The law of responsibility implies being responsible *to* each other (e.g., to love each other) but not *for* each other, nor does it mean trying to control (e.g., override a "no") rather than influence each other. Related to this is the law of power. Boundaries are not a means of asserting power over a partner but rather power over self.

The law of respect implies respecting the other person's boundaries (e.g., respecting no) if you want your own respected. It means enquiring as to whether you cross your partner's boundaries and attack when receiving a no. The law of motivation is about being free to say no before being able to freely and wholeheartedly say yes without fear (e.g., fear of losing love if non-compliant). The law of evaluation requires evaluating the pain our boundaries cause others, bearing in mind that because a person is in pain it does not mean that something bad is happening. The law of proactivity emphasizes that we need proactive boundaries, where the emphasis is on finding solutions, rather than reactive boundaries, where we blow up. The law of envy states that partners will not get what they want if they focus on what others or their partner has. In solving problems, partners should actively take the initiative and not be passive—the law of activity. The tenth law, the law of exposure, means communicating one's boundaries.

Boundaries are particularly relevant when partner *A* tries to control partner *B*, as indicated by, for example: not respecting a "no" from *B*; punishing *B* for making a "wrong" choice that *A* does not like (e.g., an accusation of not caring); *A* endeavoring to enforce a "right" decision and not valuing *B*'s freedom; and *B* responding negatively to the control.[17] Tactics include *A* putting *B* on a guilt trip, *A* getting angry, *A* continually attacking *B*'s boundaries, and *A* withholding love. What can happen is that *A* behaves like a master with a slave or like a controlling parent; *B* may then go and have an affair, or leave. It seems to me that having an affair is never an excuse for a partner's failings; an act of unfaithfulness is something one person does, not two. Affairs tend to be destructive of all parties involved and don't generally last. However, it is important to have outside supportive and appropriate people as "Marriage simply does not have all the resources a couple needs."[18] Partners also need to be empathetic, allow each other to have the freedom to be different, and not assume ownership over the other person.

17.3.4   Boundaries and Family

Boundary issues can occur in childhood thus interrupting the boundary process. For example, there may be injuries from detachment (e.g., emotional inaccessibility), abandonment (e.g., connecting then leaving), inconsistency (e.g., parent is unstable as a love object), criticism (e.g., unloving attacks on one's needy aspects), and abuse that destroys trust.[19] Parents may provide conditional love that is withdrawn when

[16]Cloud and Townsend (1999: chapter 2).
[17]Cloud and Townsend (1999: 76–77).
[18]Cloud and Townsend (1999: 152).
[19]Cloud and Townsend (1995: 71).

the child misbehaves or is angry (e.g., "It hurts us when you are angry"). The child then becomes compliant or even a peace maker and learns to distrust and hide the more aggressive, truth-telling part of self. Also, the child becomes responsible for parents' feelings and realizes this, and so takes on an inappropriate parental role. Some parents are hostile to their child's boundaries (e.g., "Don't question your mother," or "If you disagree with me I'll ....") or punish a child for his or her growing independence (e.g., "You'll do it my way or else.") They don't allow the child to disagree. Children may be over-controlled or lack limits, or have inconsistent limits, as is often the case in an alcoholic family. In the case of control, it may be aggressive (e.g., hurting the child), passive (e.g., leaving the child), or repressive (e.g., guilt messages) if the child says no; otherwise there is no control with nobody ever saying no to the child.[20]

If the children have learned early in life that they are responsible for their parents, when they become adults they may find it difficult to set boundaries with parents. The adult children may end up having to care for their parents, and if the children try to have separate lives, they feel selfish. Parents can also create guilty feelings by reminding their adult children of all that they did for them. Although children have some responsibility toward their parents, some parents can sometimes be tyrants, putting guilt trips on their adult children, criticizing how they bring up their children, and making unreasonable demands on their time.

A sure sign of a boundary problem is when a member of one's family of origin has the power to affect one's own family and relationships with others. Interfering relatives can cause a lot of disharmony if boundaries are not put in place. This is sometimes the case with some cultures and cross-cultural marriages where one spouse may pay more attention to a parent than the other spouse, who gets leftovers. One area where there can be problem is when there is financial dependence on parents. Siblings can also cause problems as they can create guilty feelings (e.g., "I have to bail him out as he is my brother.")

In counseling, the client needs to be encouraged to identify the problem, the conflict, and the need that drives the conflict. In the beginning, boundary skills are best practiced in situations where the client will be honored and respected, for example, by learning to say no to people in one's supportive group. With family members, the wish to reconcile may be very strong so that care is needed not to get into a controlling situation again. Responding but not reacting is the key to staying in control.

17.3.5 Boundaries and Friends

Interaction with friends can depend on each person's ability to say yes or no appropriately. Table 17.1 in Section 17.2.3 can suggest some of the problem combinations in friendships, for example compliant/compliant, compliant/aggressive controller, compliant/manipulative controller, and compliant/nonresponsive. Cloud and Townsend[21] discuss each of these and use the above boundary checklist to analyze each one. In the case of the compliant/compliant combination, one symptom might be dissatisfaction; its roots lie in a background where one has to say no to keep other person happy. The conflict arises from both of them denying their own

[20]Cloud and Townsend (1995: 73).
[21]Cloud and Townsend (1992: chapter 8).

boundaries to keep the peace so they need to take ownership for attempting to appease the other person. They need to have supportive friends or therapists and can perhaps see less of each other and enlarge their circle of friends.

With a compliant/aggressive controller combination, the symptoms might be that the compliant feels controlled and the controller feels nagged. The roots for the compliant might lie in being taught as a child to avoid conflict while the controller might have never learned about delayed gratification. The conflict is due the compliant being unable to set clear limits while the controller has no respect for the compliant's limits. The compliant needs to own the fact that giving up power is actually a means of control through appeasement, while the controller needs to hear no and accept the limits of others. The compliant is the unhappier one who needs a network of supportive friends where boundary setting can be practiced while the controller needs someone to talk honestly about running over people. The compliant sets a boundary and the controller has to face any consequences of inappropriate actions. Finally, they may renegotiate their friendship with the compliant promising not to nag and the controller promising not to be critical. In practice a therapist will most likely see only one member of the friendship. However, much of the above can still be used.

Boundaries certainly need to be set in romantic relationships right from the beginning before emotions take charge. The order should be the will first, then the mind, and finally the emotions— not the other way round. Individuals with mature boundaries sometimes suspend them in the early stages of dating in order to please the other person. Honesty with self and with the other person is what is needed!

Needy friends are perhaps the most difficult to set boundaries with. We do need to be there for others but we also need to protect ourselves from unreasonable demands.

Safe and Unsafe People

A client having problems with friendships can be asked what makes a good friend. Possible skills needed to develop and maintain friendships might be:[22]

- sharing

- caring

- empathy

- concern

- self-disclosure

- give and take

- positive reinforcement

- complementarity

The therapist can discuss various skills like the ones above with a client to determine where problems might lie and what has led to the problems. Methods of expressing these skills can be explored.

[22]Lazarus (1981: 234).

Clients may need help to recognize the difference between safe and unsafe people, including friends and relatives. They may also need to determine which category they are in themselves! Cloud and Townsend (1995) have written a very helpful book on this topic, and I have used a few of their ideas in the following brief discussion.

If there is a problem with a friend, or there is a problem with choosing appropriate friends, then a question might be: "What are the characteristics of a safe or unsafe person?" An unsafe person might have characteristics such as the following: starting but not finishing a friendship; being critical of others; being irresponsible and not taking care of oneself or others; exhibiting no mutual give and take; or lacking in confidentiality. Traits of unsafe people might include ignoring closeness instead of connecting, ignoring their personal weaknesses, avoiding dealing with their problems (e.g., not thinking they have any, blaming others for their problems), being unforgiving, apologizing without a behavioral change, lying, gossiping, being defensive, being self-righteous, and being religious instead of spiritual.[23]

Friendships are damaged by self-centeredness, for example, a person contacting you only when he or she has a problem instead of simply spending time with you, or treating your needs superficially. Further examples of not getting the safety we need are: not being able to open up about our real feelings and problems (people withdraw if we do) ; not receiving emotional and spiritual support (e.g., people not being prepared to lovingly confront us or tell the truth about ourselves); our personal connections revolving more around activities than relationships; and choosing people who invariably let us down.[24] Some reasons for choosing unsafe friends are: inability to judge character, lack of connection and fear of abandonment, merger wishes (trying to make up for internal shortcomings by fusing with someone else), fear of confrontation, romanticizing (idealizing), wanting to rescue, having guilt, being a perfectionist, and having a victim role.[25]

In the case of romantic friendships there is a need to watch for those who try to play on our emotional side to gain our trust early in the friendship. They may play mind games with us. People who are just out of a relationship or divorce are particularly vulnerable to such a "take-over." Controlling people will try to tell us how to run our lives and spend our money.

Boundaries and Work

For some, setting up a boundary to separate work and one's personal life can be difficult. As work tends to expand to fill the available time, misplaced priorities can lead to not saying no to the unimportant and not budgeting time. Bosses can be very demanding, expecting a staff member to continually stay late to the detriment of the staff member's family, or dumping an extra load of work with the expectation of it being all done in the original time frame. When the latter happens, a response might be, "I work for twenty hours and you have given me thirty, so which twenty do you want me to do?" or "I don't have enough time to do all this extra work so what do you want me to leave?" Difficulties with authority may be due to past childhood dealings with authority figures so that reactionary feelings, perhaps due to transference, need to be explored.

[23]Adapted from Cloud and Townsend (1995: chapters 2 and 3).
[24]Adapted from Cloud and Townsend (1995: 87).
[25]Adapted from Cloud and Townsend (1995: chapter 6).

There is also the need to say no when someone other than the boss tries to off-load his or her responsibility onto you. Knowing how to deal with difficult co-workers and critical attitudes relates to internal boundary setting. The only person I can change is myself and not the other person. So if I just see the other person as the problem to be fixed I am allowing that person to have some power over me instead of changing my reaction to the person. We need to take responsibility for our own feelings and allow the other person to face their own consequences for not getting things done on time.

With regard to an overcritical coworker there is no point in trying to gain his or her approval or getting into arguments or discussions as you can't win and only end up feeling controlled. Either confront the coworker and tell that person how you feel about his or her attitude or else use the company's grievance policy. If confrontation does not work, then explain that you will keep your distance.

People have to be careful not to take their work-stress home. Conflicts at work need to be sorted out there so that they don't affect the rest of one's life. A boundary needs to be put onto the "spillage" into one's personal and family life. Not having adequate boundaries can also lead to a person disliking his or her job.

17.3.6   Resistance to Boundaries

When you set a boundary, external resistance to it can come in the form of an angry reaction; this is the other person's problem and feeling, not yours. The key is not to react to the anger by being angry yourself or doing something inappropriate, but simply let the other person feel the anger without rescuing the person. Sometimes it may be appropriate to say that you will not stay in the room while being yelled at and will go into another room until the other party is prepared to discuss the problem without personal attack. People will not change as long as they can control you with their anger because what they are doing is working effectively for them. They need to learn self-control, perhaps for the first time.

Another form of resistance is trying to put you on a guilt or blaming trip, for example, "How could you do this to me after all I have done for you?" or "You could think about someone else other than yourself for once." Religion can sometimes be use as a guilt weapon, for example, "I thought Christians were supposed to think of others?" When faced with a guilt message we need to recognize it as such, that it is probably anger in disguise perhaps hiding sadness and hurt, and if it works on us realize it is our problem not theirs. What we don't do is try to explain or justify our position. We can, however, empathize with the other's distress making it clear that it is their distress, for example, "I understand you are very unhappy about what I have decided to do and I am sorry you feel that way." There may also be countermoves and consequences by the other party, and this kind of problem is discussed further in Section 17.4.1. We need to be prepared to accept the consequences of our boundary setting. It can be very difficult personally if the other person has real needs, but we do need to protect ourselves at all times from burnout.[26] Empathize yes, but perhaps delegate rather than allow personal overload.

[26] Especially with therapy work.

Internal resistance may be another problem as we struggle to set boundaries. We may have unmet developmental needs, unresolved grief and loss, feelings of guilt, fear of abandonment, and unresolved forgiveness all hindering boundary setting.

17.4 CODEPENDENCY

17.4.1 Definition and Nature of Codependency

Codependency can be defined as an excessive tendency to put the needs of others before your own so that your own feelings, desires, and basic needs are ignored and your life becomes defined by the needs and problems of others. This topic is particularly pertinent to people married to alcoholics or other addicts and is linked with Section 14.5 on relationship (love) addiction.

Beattie, a pioneer in this field, defined a codependent person as one "who has let another person's behavior affect him or her, and who is obsessed with controlling that person's behavior."[27] Originally, the *other* person referred to an alcoholic as the concept of codependency arose out of years of studying interpersonal relationships in families of alcoholics and it was popularized by twelve-step movements such as Adult Children of Alcoholics. However, the definition was widened by Beattie to include anybody such as a child, family member, friend, or co-worker, and the behavior may refer to anyone with an addiction, or to a mentally or chronically ill person.

Characteristics of Codependency

Codependent people often desperately need to be needed; they tend to rely on others and how well they care for others for their self-esteem. They may make excuses for another person's behavior, and thus inadvertently help to perpetuate the other person's needy addiction or condition. They end up either wanting to control or "fix" others, or else are controlled by others and may even take the blame for abuse. Saying no and having appropriate boundaries can be a problem (see Section 17.2.3). Although feeling responsible for others, they often believe deep down that other people are responsible for them; they blame others for their unhappiness. Furthermore, while feeling controlled by people and events, they are overly controlling and don't allow events to happen naturally. They know best and try to control others in a variety of ways such as using threats, coercion, helplessness, or manipulation. I have added the word "excessive" in my definition as caring for a partner or someone desperately in need, for example, does involve at times a huge amount of self-sacrifice, and there is a continuum of behavior that ranges from normal to abnormal.[28] Appropriate interdependency implies reciprocal giving without one person giving until it hurts, while in a codependent relationship one partner does almost all the giving and the other does almost all the taking, most of the time.

---

[27]Beattie (1987: 31).
[28]For further comments on this see http://www.marriagebuilders.com/graphic/mbi8110_cod.html (accessed October 2010).

There is no clear agreement about the nature and treatment of codependency; for example, it is not listed in the DSM-IV-TR diagnostic manual.[29] Sadock and Sadock state that

> The term has been used in various ways, and there are no established criteria for codependence, a concept that some writers have expanded far beyond its origins to encompass any personality trait that involves difficulty in expressing emotions.[30]

However, those who identify with the label consider it to be an emotional disorder. In some cases it may be that the caregiver only requires some assertiveness training skills[31] and the addict some accountability for managing his or her addiction. Codependency can then be viewed more as a caring personality trait, but taken to excess. Some say that codependency is a normal reaction to abnormal people. Whatever the view, recovery for codependents does not lie with changing the other person, but in changing themselves with regard to how they let other people's behavior affect them and how they try to affect other people.

Dysfunctional Families

Mellody et al. believe that "dysfunctional, less-than-nurturing, abusive family systems create children who become codependent adults."[32] They describes children as being valuable, vulnerable, imperfect, dependent, and immature.[33] If children are brought up to believe they are not good enough or are devalued, their self-esteem can be damaged. If the parents have inadequate boundaries, the children may also have inadequate boundaries and be too vulnerable so that they are not able to protect themselves properly. Parents may expect too much from their children and apply harsh discipline instead of allowing for the fact that a child, like anyone else, is imperfect. A child's dependency in a dysfunctional family may be dealt with by (a) enmeshment, with the child not being allowed to do anything for himself or herself, (b) attacking or criticizing the child for having needs and wants, or (c) ignoring the child. Dysfunctional parents may treat their children as being more or less mature than they really are.

Such behavioral patterns experienced as children can carry over into adulthood, for example, a codependent adult may have poor self-esteem, have inadequate boundaries, be a perfectionist and controlling, have no awareness of personal needs and wants, and be immature or over-controlling in relationships. Mellody et al. believe that it is the emotional damage suffered that most profoundly sabotages the life of a codependent, particularly with regard to anger and shame.[34] This topic is closely linked to Chapter 15 on childhood abuse.

Codependency can arise from being brought up in a dysfunctional family where there is some problem or secret such as, for example, (a) a family member with a substance or behavioral addiction, or (b) a family member with a chronic mental or physical illness, or (c) physical, emotional, or sexual abuse. All the family's energy goes into supporting the family member who has the problem by always making

---

[29] However, the related idea of dependent personality disorder is listed (see Section 21.4.3).
[30] Sadock and Sadock (2005: 1163).
[31] See Section 2.5.4.
[32] Mellody et al. (1989: 4).
[33] Mellody et al. (1989: chapters 4 and 5).
[34] Mellody et al. (1989: 90).

allowances for that member and covering up or making excuses for him or her. They place that member's health, welfare, and safety before their own, and can lose contact with their own needs, desires, and sense of self. The family generally does not acknowledge that the problem exists so that it is not discussed or confronted. The message given is that it is not alright to talk about problems; feelings should not be expressed openly but rather should be kept to one's self. You mustn't be selfish or rock the boat! As a result, family members learn to repress their emotions and disregard their own needs. They detach themselves in order to survive. Children can pick up this learned behavior by watching and imitating other family members; it can lead to a damaged self-esteem. Such children can become codependent adults who have a greater tendency to get involved in relationships with people who are perhaps unreliable, emotionally unavailable, or needy, and they look for anything outside of themselves to make them feel better such as a sense of being needed. They try to provide and control everything within the relationship without addressing their own needs or desires, thus setting themselves up for continued unfulfillment. Codependency can be passed down from one generation to another.

17.4.2   Assessment

Detecting codependency is not easy. For example, a couple may come to counseling because one partner has an addiction. This partner can end up being the focus of attention whereas the therapist may not realize that other partner is codependent. Part of the problem is that there is a continuum from being a caring person to being strongly codependent, where the caring becomes compulsive and defeating; it becomes a question of degree and where to draw the line, if there is one. Some women were even taught that these caring excessive behaviors were desirable feminine attributes.

A helpful list of patterns and characteristics of codependence is given by Co-Dependents Anonymous.[35] They don't give a diagnostic questionnaire, which is perhaps appropriate given the breadth of the subject and the variations in the different lists put forward, but they do have a 12-step program.[36] However, a useful set of questions that the therapist can use is given on the internet.[37]

The difficulty in diagnosing codependence is reflected in the fact that many lists of symptoms are given in the literature.[38] Mellody et al. (1989) suggests that there are five core symptoms of codependent people, namely:

1. *Low self-esteem.* They tend to get their self-esteem from exterior things such as status, money, job, education, achievements, and what others think.

2. *Inappropriate boundaries.* They have difficulty in setting appropriate boundaries, whether external or internal.

3. *Reality problems.* They have difficulty in owning their own reality in four areas of their lives. (This can arise when children are denied the right to appropriately express themselves.)

---

[35] See http://www.coda.org/tools4recovery/patterns-new.htm (accessed October 2010).
[36] See http://socalcoda.org/12steps.php (accessed October 2010)
[37] http://www.allaboutlifechallenges.org/codependency-test-faq.htm (accessed October 2010).
[38] For extensive lists of characteristics see Beattie (1987: 37–45).

(a) *The body.* This involves not "seeing" their appearance accurately or being aware of how their bodies are operating.

(b) *Thinking.* This involves such things as faulty thinking, being unaware of what their thoughts are, or not being able to share their thoughts if known.

(c) *Feelings.* They are either unaware of their feelings or, if aware, are overwhelmed by their feelings.

(d) *Behavior.* They are either unaware of their behavior or have difficulty owning their behavior and its impact on others.

4. *Confuse needs and wants.* They have difficulty acknowledging and meeting theirs needs and wants, and perhaps confusing the two. These may have been denied to them as children.

5. *Immoderate expression.* Difficulty experiencing and expressing their reality moderately. They are unable to act moderately and this may be reflected in one or more of the four areas of (3) above.

There are many other symptoms of codependent people given in the literature and on the internet that may be described as either "core" or "secondary" symptoms, and I have selected the following from various sources:

- controlling behavior

- avoidance of feelings as in item 3(c) above and ignoring personal needs

- resentment (at others harming our self esteem)

- in denial over what is happening (i.e., avoiding reality)

- difficulty in sustaining intimacy

- distorted or nonexistent spirituality

- self-blaming

- feeling uncomfortable in receiving from others

- care-taking behavior with an exaggerated sense of responsibility for the actions of others

- seeing one's self as a victim when the care-taking becomes compulsive

- tendency to do more than one's share, and becoming hurt when one's efforts are not recognized or complimented

- unhealthy dependence on relationships

- sense of guilt when asserting or doing something for one's self

- extreme need for approval and recognition

- distrust in self and/or others

- perfectionism and being afraid of making mistakes (not allowed to enjoy or feel good about the things they do)

- fear of being abandoned or alone

- inability to develop behaviors that get needs met (related to boundary problems)

- initiating relationships with people who are not good for them

Mellody et al.[39] refer to "negative control" whereby the controlling behavior by codependents can be either trying to control others by telling them who they should be (so the codependents can be comfortable), or allowing others to control the codependents by dictating who the codependents should be (to keep others comfortable). Either form of control sets up negative responses in the person being controlled that cause codependents to blame others for being unable to be internally comfortable with themselves.

There is a questionnaire of 20 questions to identify signs of codependency on the internet,[40] though it is stated there that not everyone experiencing these symptoms suffers from codependency.

17.4.3 Counseling for Codependency

There are number of strategies that can be used by the therapist and the choice will depend on the individual needs of the client. After hearing the client's story and making an initial assessment, a sensible first step for the therapist might be to help the client understand the nature of codependency, which may involve an exploration of early childhood issues to see the connection with what is happening now. If the current situation involves the care-taking of someone with an addiction, then the therapist can help the client to learn all about the addiction and how it impacts on the client's relationship. The client may need to be aware that conquering an addiction is not simply a matter of will power or the client behaving in a particular way. The sort of questions a client might be asked are:[41]

- "How do you find a balance between your own needs and the needs of others?"

- "How do you feel about asking others for what you want?"

- "What are you like at saying no to needs of others when you need to?"

- "How responsible are you for other people's problems?"

- "How much can you make another person change?"

- "How do you feel when you can't fulfill another person's expectations?"

- "How perfect do you have to be to be accepted and loved?"

A second step might be to help the client get in touch with and experience his or her feelings that may have been buried in childhood or suppressed in adulthood.

---

[39]Mellody et al. (1992: 3).
[40]See, for example, http://www.nmha.org/go/codependency (accessed October 2010).
[41]Adapted from Bourne (2005: 218).

This self-awareness should then extend to identifying self-defeating behavior patterns such as covering up for an addict's behavior thus "enabling" the addict to continue with the addictive behavior. For example, a wife might call in sick for her husband when he is hung over. A client may need to say "no" and insist on some boundaries—sometimes called "tough love."

I now want to list a number of issues that the therapist might wish to consider.[42]

1. *Detachment.* This is "based on the premises that each person is responsible for himself, that we can't solve problems that aren't ours to solve, and that worrying doesn't help."[43] It does not mean that we don't care. We simply need to let others deal with their own responsibilities and tend to our own instead. We also need to determine what we can change, and accept what we cannot change. The therapist can ask such questions as, "What might happen if you detach?" and "What would life be like if that particular person was not in your life?"

2. *Self-awareness.* This involves helping a client to develop a self-awareness of their reacting so as to avoid overreacting so much or so quickly. Working through various scenarios and discussing coping mechanisms with the client can be helpful. A relaxation technique or some diversionary tactics may help the client to face what appear to be crisis situations more calmly and to deal with them more effectively.

3. *Build self-esteem.* This includes not taking other people's behaviors or their rejection as a reflection of the client's self-worth, and not taking everything personally. This topic is discussed more fully in Section 2.5.3.

4. *Relinquish control.* This involves helping the client set himself or herself free from the need to rescue and control others. A helpful exercise is to get clients to list all the things that they think are their responsibility in every area of their lives. They then list what responsibilities belong to others. If responsibilities are shared then they decide what percentage is their responsibility. Beattie discusses rescuing in terms of the Karpman Drama Triangle: the client rescues the addict but the addict is not grateful so that the client becomes the persecutor whereby the addict becomes angry and persecutes the client so that the client becomes a victim! Control tactics can range from bulldozing to helplessness, and the tactics used and their success or (more likely) failure can be discussed. Cognitive therapy can be used to examine faulty beliefs about the need to control. Often the addict will accuse the client of trying to control him or her when it is actually the other way round! The client has to realize that you cannot control an addict's behavior, only the addict can do that.

5. *Relinquish dependence.* This is linked with attachment discussed in (1) above and the term used by Beattie[44] is "undependence" where a person is not happy living with the partner, but can't live without him or her. Such people becomes dependent on others for their presence, approval, and love but may

[42]Adapted from Beattie (1987).
[43]Beattie (1987: 56).
[44]Beattie (1987: 92).

feel they are unlovable. They need someone to be there for them, but the person they have chosen cannot or will not do that. A therapist can help their client to connect to those ego states laid down in childhood that clamor for attention when least expected, and also encourage the client to be self-dependent.

6. *Feel feelings.* Anger can be a problem and clients may have false beliefs about it, for example: (a) it is wrong to feel angry, (b) if others are angry with us it must be our fault, (c) others shouldn't get angry with us, and (d) if we feel angry then it is someone else's fault and they should fix our feelings. The client can be asked what they believe about anger and also "What would you think would happen if you started feeling your angry feelings?"

7. *Set boundaries.* This includes setting limits on what a client does for others and what the client will allow others to do for him or her, which won't be easy. There may be some resistance as others may try to make the client feel guilty so that the boundary is removed, and there is a return to the old system of being used again. Typical boundaries might be: not supporting lies, not rescuing an addict from the consequences of their behavior, not financially supporting an addiction, and not allowing someone to spoil the client's fun, day, or life.

8. *Self-love.* The client is encouraged to look after himself or herself in each area of life as described in Chapter 2. It is being able to accept one's self and say "I'm okay." Clients can be asked to list the things they like or don't like about themselves. Are the things they dislike about themselves actually true?

9. *Set goals.* This needs to be done regularly and as needed (see Section 2.2.3). Check off goals when they are reached.

Mellody et al.[45] emphasize that it is important for a client to review his or her past history for three reasons: (a) to understand how the parenting affected the client, (b) to replace the childhood perception of what happened by an adult perception, and (c) to avoid relating to similar dysfunctional people. In reviewing, they suggest using the word "dysfunctional" instead of "wrong" or "bad" to describe inappropriate or abusive behavior suffered by the client, and using the word "functional" instead of "right" or "good" to describe supportive behavior. They emphasize that it is important not to focus on whether the abuser meant to harm the client or not as this may lead to minimizing what happened. Abusers should be held accountable, but a client should not get hooked into the "blame game" because it ties the victim to the offender. Also a client should focus on his or her caregivers rather than the client's role as a caregiver.

Codependency can relate to an excessive need for approval and Bourne[46] suggests three guidelines to cope with this need. The therapist can help their client to (a) have a realistic view of other people's approval (e.g., "Not everyone will like me"), (b) learn from criticism, if valid, and (c) recognize and let go of over-dependency.

[45]Mellody et al. (1989: chapter 8).
[46]Bourne (2005: 229–230).

It may help a client to link up with an organization such as Codependents Anonymous (CoDA)[47] and Adult Children of Alcoholics[48] (ACoA or ACA), each with its own twelve-step program.

Finally, a therapist should be aware that when a client depends on the addict to the extent that he or she needs to enable the addict, the client may feel uncomfortable and threatened when the addict begins to recover and may even sabotage the addict's efforts.

17.5 BIBLICAL VIEWPOINT

17.5.1 Boundaries

Some Biblical Principles

Being clear about one's yes and one's no is a theme in the Bible.[49] We should confront people who sin against us in a spirit of gentleness remembering that we too can make mistakes.[50] The Bible also warns against giving to others reluctantly or under compulsion.[51] Jesus did say some hard things about giving to others that need to be put in perspective.[52] A key biblical principle is that we reap what we sow[53] so that we are responsible for our own actions, not other people's actions. People need to face the consequences of their actions.[54] Physically removing oneself from a situation can sometimes help to maintain boundaries, whether it is to get respite after continually giving out, separating from those who continually hurt us, or getting away from danger and evil.[55]

Setting Boundaries

Some Christians have difficulties setting boundaries because of the way they interpret the injunction to "bear one another's burdens"[56] and thus fulfill the "law of Christ," which is the law of love. The word "burdens" here means excess burdens or burdens that are so heavy that they weigh us down. It is true that Christians have a responsibility to help such people who struggle under burdens that are too heavy. However, this must be balanced by another statement which says that we all must carry our own load.[57] Here the word "load" refers to the "burden of daily toil," namely the everyday things we all need to do. Boundary problems arise when "burden" and "load" are confused; the injunction does not say we should be responsible for another person's "load." It also implies, however, that we must not be so overloaded already that we can't step in and help when needed.

---

[47]http://www.coda.org/ (accessed October 2010).
[48]www.adultchildren.org (accessed October 2010).
[49]Matthew 5:37 and James 5:12.
[50]Matthew 18:15–20 and Galatians 6:1–5.
[51]2 Corinthians 9:7.
[52]Matthew 5:38–42
[53]Galatians 6:7.
[54]2 Thessalonians 3:10.
[55]Proverbs 22:3.
[56]Galatians 6:2.
[57]Galatians 6:5.

We need to be careful about giving to others what is important to us in case they misuse it; we need to keep the pearls in and the pigs out.[58] At the same time as setting boundaries to keep the good in, we need to get the bad out. The Bible teaches that inner cleansing comes through the confession of sin which leads to forgiveness and a new beginning.[59] When it comes to friends, a safe relationship is one that draws us closer to God and to others, and helps us to become the person God wants us to be.

God and Boundaries

It can be argued that God respects our boundaries. First, God respects free will and leaves things for people to do. Second, God allows us to experience the consequences of our behavior so that we will change, but is not willing for any to perish and takes no pleasure in our destruction.[60] Finally, there are a number of instances where the Bible teaches that we can influence God.[61]

Resolving Conflict

We need to exercise self-control (a fruit of the Spirit), not other control.[62] Sometimes we need to take the plank out of our own eye before trying to take the speck out of someone else's eye.[63] Adam and Eve each blamed someone else for their own failings.[64]

17.5.2   Codependency

When it comes to codependency, the Bible teaches that the only one a person should be dependent on is God. A positive goal is not to be dependent on others in an unhealthy way.[65] There is a need for care in interpreting biblical injunctions such as, "Love your enemies," "Go the extra mile", and "Be cheerful givers." They are not a mandate to caretake another person. Christians need to feel good about their giving out and who they give to, and give from a position of strong self-esteem. They don't continue giving long after it hurts.

---

[58]Matthew 7: 6.
[59]1 John 1:9.
[60]2 Peter 3:9 and Ezekiel 18:23.
[61]For example, Genesis 18:16–33 and Luke 11:5–13, 18:1–8.
[62]Galatians 5:22–23.
[63]Matthew 7:5.
[64]Genesis 3:11–13).
[65]2 Thessalonians 4:11–12.

CHAPTER 18

DIVORCE

18.1 GENERAL COMMENTS

Relationship breakup statistics are difficult to calculate because of a number of factors including people marrying at an older age and the rise in the number of de facto relationships. For those under 25 years, the number of de facto relationships apparently exceeds the number of marriages, and that is only the relationships on record as many these days drift in and out of multiple relationships. However, roughly speaking, the chance of a breakup is approaching 50%, while for second marriages it is more like 60-70%.[1] These are very crude average rates as they are affected by many factors such as age, culture, and multiple divorces. There are so many people affected by a divorce, including extended family and friends, that divorce has a very significant affect on society. Children unfortunately are particularly affected, and in most western countries such as New Zealand we find as much as one third of all children will experience parental divorce before they are 18 years old.

---

[1]Detailed statistics can be found on the internet under the tile of "divorce."

18.1.1   Grief from Divorce

Grief is an important aspect of divorce as the loss of one's partner is a significant loss, ranked in magnitude only below the death of a partner by some writers.[2] For some, divorce is worse than death. The reason for this is that there is one important difference: death can lead to some sort of closure, while divorce can leave unfinished business as the corpse is still walking around! In divorce, people can go through a cyclical stage: they climb from a negative to a positive state and then something happens which sends them spiraling back down again to a negative state. Triggers for this vary and some examples are: seeing an ex-husband with the "other" woman, custody battles with respect to children, legal confrontations over marital property, and an unexpected phone call from the ex-spouse. This cyclical pattern appears to be a normal part of the divorce process. The therapist can normalize this pattern and encourage the client to see this to be expected as a painful but routine process. Fortunately the cycles get less frequent and less devastating. Although time does help in the healing process, time itself is not a healing force. I dislocated my artificial hip some years ago and as I lay on the ground in agony I could either wait for time to bring some healing or go by ambulance to the hospital to have my hip put back in place. Healing from a divorce requires a person to be proactive about recovery rather than just reactive. As Smoke[3] mentions in the introduction to his book, the aim is to *grow* through divorce rather than just *go* though divorce.

Various models of grief can be carried over to divorce. For example, Wiseman[4] refers to denial, loss, anger, reorientation, and acceptance as common emotional responses to divorce.[5] Other writers include shock, depression, and mourning. The divorced person will usually struggle with a variety of emotions and the therapist should help the client to identify these emotions and work through them. Typical emotions include:

- Confusion ("Where did I go wrong?")

- Guilt ("If only I had been more ....") Guilt can be marital (marriage failed), family (let parents down), social (loss of friends, particularly joint ones) and possibly divine (let God down).

- Shame ("I feel ashamed that I am divorced.")

- Anger ("I am angry with my ex-spouse because he has hurt me.")

- Doubt ("Can I ever trust a woman again?").

- Fear ("I am afraid of ever letting anyone get close again.")

- Loneliness ("I don't like being on my own, especially on weekends and public holidays.")

- Depression ("I will never be happy again.")

Clients can be encouraged to make their own list; the therapist could suggest a list like the following: joy, jealousy, boredom, caution, sorrow, hope, uneasiness,

[2]Holmes and Rahe (1967).
[3]Smoke (1995).
[4]Wiseman (1975).
[5]For other models see Chapter 11.

relief, love, sadness, elation, hate, uselessness, embarrassment, uncertainty, pride, pain, loneliness, weariness, happiness, grief, calm, anxiety, fear, rejection, confidence, silliness, anger, gladness, discomfort, contentment, hopefulness, confusion, depression, frustration, guilt, bitterness, shock, numbness, betrayal, emptiness, and hostility.[6] Therapists can help their client to realize that emotional chaos after separation and divorce is normal and to say to themselves, "Emotions are normal. My emotions are natural."

Smoke describes the pain of divorce as follows:

> But whether a person is left by his or her spouse or decides to take that step personally due to painful circumstances, feelings of rejection will probably be overpowering. These feelings can shake self-worth and self-esteem to their roots. .... But however loss happens, the process of grief cannot be hurried."[7]

The therapist should also be aware that, from a psychodynamic perspective, some of the emotions experienced may also be a reflection of past childhood experiences that have now been triggered.[8] For example, anger towards the spouse (or even the therapist) may arise from separations that took place earlier in life, and the therapist will need to help the client to distinguish these from the current situation. An adopted person who is angry at being abandoned by a spouse may subconsciously be reflecting and transfering the anger at being abandoned by a birth mother.[9]

Bradshaw[10] notes that both partners often learn from experience early in the marriage that certain areas are very touchy, and unconsciously agree to stay away from these trouble spots. The role of such unconscious agreements, which are like a shared secret, can help to maintain a desired status quo. With divorce, the lid usually comes off and the result is often explosive and acrimonious. Many of these unconscious mutual contracts of inattention are extended to the children who also buy into the secret to please the parents. This can lead to a loss of awareness by the children as a defense against the possible loss of security, and this can lead to later problems.

18.1.2   Attachment Issues

One of the features of divorce, which may be surprising to the therapist, is the ambivalence that the client may have about separation from the spouse even when the client has been emotionally or even physically damaged by the spouse. Once people have been bonded together their attachment persists and resists dissolution even when love begins to go and there is hurt and anger. There is a difference between attachment and love.[11] Detachment from the previous marital role may therefore need to be part of the recovery process. Allowing clients to work fully through the grief process may help them to avoid an unrealistic attachment to an ex-spouse. Also, they need to appreciate that although their marriage has failed, they are not a failure and that divorce needs to be reframed as a positive step toward change rather than be seen as their failure.

[6]See also the table in Section 2.4.2.
[7]Smoke (1999: 12–13).
[8]For example, Spira (1981).
[9]Adoption is discussed in Section 20.5.
[10]Bradshaw (1995: 74).
[11]Attachment is discussed further in Section 2.5.2

Two important tasks of human development that need attention continually throughout various stages of our life-cycle are *intimacy* (closeness) in relating to another individual and *identity*, which emphasizes separation (individuation). In human development we all want to be close, yet periodically autonomous. Divorce may require clients to redefine these two processes and readdress the balance between these two aspects of their life; how these two tasks are handled can affect their self-esteem.[12]

Divorce, with its consequent rejection, will damage one's self image (so-called "narcissistic injury" discussed below) so that those divorced may wonder if they will ever be able to obtain intimacy again and be loved and lovable. Their identity will change dramatically because of the loss of their role and status among family, friends, and the community. Switching from the role of wife to the role of being single can be particularly difficult for the woman who was brought up to view marriage and motherhood as their ultimate "careers." The therapist can help their clients to realize that their sense of being lovable and their self-worth don't depend on being intimate with or married to their ex-spouse. They can come to affirm that (a) they love themselves without needing the love of another person, and (b) be themselves without being the spouse of another. It is a matter of independently establishing one's own identity.

18.1.3 Narcissistic Injury

There can be two extreme responses to narcissistic injury (injury to self). One is to avoid future relationships for fear of being hurt again and the other is over-involvement in relationships, especially sexually, to overcome feelings of rejection and restore some self-esteem. Here the role of the therapist is to help clients achieve a balance so that they meet with other people, including those of the opposite sex, but remain wary of entering into a new relationship prematurely. The loss of self-esteem can lead to a number of defensive strategies. For example, the divorced person may overcompensate (through guilt?) by trying to be a super-person, especially a mother who has the major responsibility for bringing up the children and being a wage-earner; he or she endeavors to be both mother and father and keep everything going, which is an impossible task. Alternatively, the divorced person may withdraw from life as he or she believes that nothing good can come from the change in one's life. A third strategy is self-denigration, where the ex-spouse is viewed as a saint and the client takes the blame for the divorce. A fourth strategy is the opposite, where the ex-spouse is viewed as the devil incarnate and is regarded by the client as being totally responsible for the divorce. The role of the therapist is then to encourage the client to see that both parties had some responsibility for the breakup and that there is a need to get the ex-spouse into a correct focus.

Depression was listed above as one of the emotions arising from divorce. In addition to being a natural response to grief and loss, it can sometimes serve as a psychological defense against anxiety and painful feelings by putting a lid on them. It can often represent the internalizing of angry feelings felt towards the spouse before he or she left, or did not meet one's needs or measure up to one's expectations.

---

[12]Self-esteem is discussed further in Section 2.5.3.

Let's now consider consider some of the consequences of divorce.[13]

18.2 THE FALL-OUT FROM DIVORCE

18.2.1 Family and Friends

I have already noted how many people are affected by a divorce, including not only the children, but relatives (extended family), and the friends of both parties. Children grieve differently from adults, depending on their age, but it is just as real for them; they may not have the maturity to express it clearly. Parents have to make sure they don't apply adult criteria in assessing their childrens needs. Children are discussed later in more detail.

Parents and in-laws can become divided over loyalties. For example, the wife sometimes may get on better with her mother-in-law than with her own mother. Because relatives don't know what to do they may do nothing; in fact in-laws can become outlaws!

The response of friends and other relatives can be very mixed. Friends usually know what to say when there is a death, but are unsure about a marriage break-up, whether to commiserate or congratulate! Those who are friends of both parties face a dilemma and so may avoid contact all together—the phone may stop ringing. The therapist should encourage clients to be kind to their friends, helping them if they don't know what to say, and going easy on them with frequent off-loading of their feelings and emotions. Couples who are friends may see a newly single person as a possible threat to their own marriage, especially if their marriage is having problems. Bearing in mind the high divorce rate, this is not a fanciful observation! In particular there is evidence that divorce is contagious in a group of friends (called "divorce clustering"). Having a split up between immediate friends increases one's chances of divorce substantially. The same is true with family members and colleagues. The possible "normalizing" of splits might be a reason.

Men may feel particularly isolated as they often don't freely talk and tend to have fewer friends they could share with. They may shut off their emotions or foolishly jump prematurely into another relationship, which can be catastrophic for them both.

18.2.2 Telling the Children

The therapist will often find that there has been some shortcomings in the way the children were informed about the divorce. The following suggestions can at least act as a checklist and perhaps improve the situation.[14]

1. *Be sure.* It's best if the parents don't say "I think ...." or "We might ...." as their wrestling becomes the child's wrestling. It's important to be positive and say "We are separating." It will be tough and painful for the parents, but indecisiveness is more confusing. Decisiveness is better in the long run.

---

[13]I am grateful to Brian McStay for many of the ideas in this section taken from a past divorce recovery workshop of his.
[14]I am grateful to Brian McStay for providing much of the following material on this topic.

2. *Be together.* The important thing is the child's welfare so both parents should be there when they share with the child. Parents who have been through several divorces still have the high ideals about such things as undying love or everlasting commitment. It is important not to undermine the child's future ideals and being together helps affirm these ideals. It also helps to keep things balanced with the couple and stops a certain amount of unbalanced reporting where comments may favor the father or the mother. The child is also helped by minimizing anything which could be directed more towards one parent than the other.

3. *Be general but honest.* Not "I'm divorcing your mum because she spends too much money," but "Mum and I are separating as we can't live together."

4. *Be cautious.* Parents need to choose their words carefully, for example, avoid saying I don't love him/her anymore. If the father says "I don't love your mummy," the child one day might think that the father will say "I don't love you either." Young children fear abandonment.

Whether the two parents or just one are present, Wallerstein, Lewis, and Blakeslee[15] say it is helpful to explain to the children that when you got married you loved each other and hoped to live together for the rest of your lives. You tried hard but in the end had to call it quits for the sake of everyone, as things between you both would only get worse. Explain that you are both very sad and very sorry. It is important to convey the idea that your failing marriage is not the best example of a marriage. The children also need to be told that you were very happy when the children were born so that the children realize that they were born into a loving family and that they were wanted. It is then a good idea to ask the children what they understand about divorce, what they have learned from their friends' experiences, and listen to any worries or fears they might have. Explain what plans you have in mind and allow them to have some choices. Although they may be frozen into silence, they will be very aware of everything that is said, and won't forget.

18.2.3   Effect on the Children

Wallerstein et al.[16] mention two myths about divorce. The first is that if parents are happier, the children will be happier too; divorce automatically rescues children from an unhappy marriage. Unfortunately this is often not true. The children don't care if parents sleep in different beds as long as the family is together, and they learn at an early age to turn a deaf ear to their parents' arguments. The second myth is that divorce is a temporary crisis that hurts parents and children most at the time of the breakup. Unfortunately the effect on the children is far reaching and usually extends into adulthood, especially when they become involved in serious romantic relationships. Their image of a marriage being a permanent couple is broken!

There is one other factor not appreciated by divorcing parents. Young preadolescent children are not able to make the connection between the parents' behavior and the breakup of the marriage, even if one or both parents cry, yell, or hit.[17] The

---

[15]Wallerstein et al. (2000: 49–50).
[16]Wallerstein et al. (2000: xxiii, 26–27).
[17]Wallerstein et al. (2000: 91–92).

children are generally unaware that their parents are suffering and so splitting the family to solve family problems doesn't make any sense, being not seen by them as a remedy. They don't understand about recurrent patterns of behavior. Wallerstein et al. comment that "in high-conflict marriages, the fighting rarely stops with divorce."[18]

As children also grieve over divorce, it is important for parents to realize that children grieve differently at different ages, and their grief may not be easily recognized.[19] Some typical responses gleaned from a number of sources[20] are given below; all children respond differently so the age divisions are not clear-cut.

Infants (0-18 months): At this age infants can pick up tension in the home and notice changes in parents' energy levels. Older infants notice when one parent is no longer living in the home. Infants may experience changes in eating, sleeping, and their other daily routines. They need to be held and comforted with their favorite objects close by. It is very important for parents to maintain established routines.

Toddlers (18 months to 3 years): Any change in environment is upsetting for toddlers, especially at this age when they are interested in exploring. They will recognize that one parent no longer lives at home. There may be an increase in crying, more attention seeking, some change in sleeping and nappy routines, and they may discover anger without understanding it. Parental focus should be on quality time and maintaining their regular routines.

Preschool (3-5 years): At this age children like to think they are in control of their environment and may unfortunately feel responsible for the divorce. They need someone to talk to about what has happened and be told repeatedly that they are not responsible for the divorce. They probably will have fantasies that the parents are going to get back together again, so they need to be reminded that divorce is actually final. They often have feelings of uncertainty, show sadness, exhibit a regression of the most recent developmental milestone achieved (e.g., toilet training, reverting to thumb sucking), and have nightmares. They often have a fear of separation from the custodial parent and may need reassurance of their safety. There is usually a great deal of yearning for the non-custodial parent so visitation with this parent is important and needs to be encouraged. In most western nations adequate access is legally established and strongly encouraged unless there is evidence of unacceptable behavior by the noncustodial parent.

Early Latency (6-8 years): These children will often grieve for the departed parent. They may believe that their parents will get back together again and may try to manipulate this. As they don't grasp the concept of the permanence of divorce, they need to know that divorce does not mean losing a parent. However, they may blame one parent for the separation and feel abandoned, alone, and rejected by the parent who left the house.

Late Latency (8-11 years): Anger and powerlessness are the predominant response in this age group. They will usually experience grief over the loss of their

---

[18]Wallerstein et al. (2000: 94).
[19]See also Section 11.3.4 on a related topic.
[20]For example, Wallerstein and Corbin (1999).

previous intact family. At this age children begin to interact significantly with their peers and may pick up controversial ideas about divorce. Openness about the divorce and maintaining a regular weekly activity schedule are important. Quality time spent with the children by both parents (preferably usually separately), the reassurance of safety, and encouragement to engage in healthy activities outside of school can be be helpful.

Adolescence (12–18 years): This is a time when adolescents are beginning to become more independent from home and parents, with school and contact with their peers becoming their prime focus. They will be very aware of what is going on in their parents' lives and may tend to be severely critical about the situation, often being overly judgmental on moral issues, and will challenge and criticize their parents' decisions and actions. They may experience anger (even hatred), behave unpredictably, try to take advantage of both parents, or push the blame on to one parent. The danger is to ascribe this behavior to just the divorce itself, whereas teens can behave like this in non-divorce. Adolescents may experience a sense of growing up too soon, perhaps having to take on a parental role with their care-giver, and may start worrying about adult matters such as the family's finances. Keeping lines of communication open with them, establishing and maintaining household rules, honoring family rituals and routines, and keeping them out of parental disputes are some strategies.

There is a great deal of research that indicates that children usually are affected unfavorably by divorce in many areas of their lives. There is a moderate increased risk that they will have social, emotional, or psychological problems affecting academic achievement and relationships in the future.[21] Some of these may include: lower parental supervision, lack of strong parental role modeling, guilt, conflict, less financial support, and change of living circumstances. Courses are available to help the children of a divorce, and divorced parents may find it helpful for their children to attend one. Childhood problems linger on into adulthood and Amato sums up the situation with the comment, "Overall, the evidence is consistent that parental divorce during childhood is linked with a wide range of problems in adulthood."[22] With such children there is a greater risk of divorce when they become adults than occurs with children from non-divorce or separated families. The impact of divorce during childhood on adulthood is further taken up in Section 15.4.1.

18.3   PARENTING AND DIVORCE

When there is shared custody of children we list some of the pitfalls to be avoided.

1. Depending on the level of control and affection there are four parenting styles set out in the following table.[23] What sort of parenting style does each parent have?

    Authoritarian parents. They value control and unquestioning obedience so that the children have to conform or else they are severely and often

---

[21] Amato (2001).
[22] Amato (2005).
[23] Papalia et al. (2001: 300).

Table 18.1   Parenting Styles.

	Low Affection	High Affection
High Control	Authoritarian	Authorative
Low Control	Neglectful	Permissive

arbitrarily punished. These parents usually lack affection and are more emotionally detached than other parents. The result will probably be unsettled and withdrawn children.

Neglectful parents. These parents have low control and low affection, often because they are caught up in their own problems (e.g., stress or depression). Such children can end up with behavioral disorders.

Authoritative parents. They value a child's individuality, but also stress the importance of boundaries generally and not just their own. They guide their children and respect their independence. They are loving and accepting, but also demand good behavior. They will impose discipline if necessary, but in the context of a warm supportive environment. The authority they claim is balanced and reasonable. Such children feel secure knowing they are loved and knowing what is expected of them.

Permissive parents. They value self-expression and self-regulation and consider themselves resources, not models. They make few demands and allow children to monitor their own activities as much as possible. Such children are least self-controlled and least exploratory.

If one parent is on a very different wave-length and has a different parenting style from the other parent, then there can be behavioral problems. Preferably both parents are authoritative with the necessary balance.

2. A child ideally needs two parents. Even if one parent doesn't think much of the other parent, children need a mother and a father! They are the only birth parents that the children have. Unless there are safety issues, it is important for one parent not to deny access to the other parent (often the father) as such denial can have a way of rebounding back. The child needs to be able to move comfortably between the custodial and non-residential parent's homes without guilt or stress.

3. A person cannot be both parents. If parents try to do this they put unrealistic expectations on themselves and can wear themselves out. Just being the best mum or dad the parent can be is the key (even if quality time with the children is limited). Parents need to maintain their own boundaries with the kids. Rules should be consistent with both parents and each parent should endeavor as much as possible to respect the other's parenting values.

4. It is important not to turn children into confidants as it can lead to their "parentification." It places a huge burden on their shoulders as they do not have the experience, objectivity, and maturity to be a therapist to a

parent. They may begin to assume they are some sort of counsellor and that decisions are theirs. Parents in this unhealthy situation can become emotionally dependent on their children and this can lead to bitter custody and visitation fights over who has priority in the child's life. Children can then end up eventually becoming compulsive rescuers when they are adults and suppress their own needs. This is unlikely to be helpful in their future relationships.

5. Ideally parents should not compete with each other. There is the temptation for men to be Disneyland fathers and go overboard in spoiling and spending on their kids. This makes it tough on the mother who usually cannot compete financially.[24] Although children enjoy special treats, everyday experiences with the parent are more important. Children like to simply be with their parent, even just sitting around in an untidy bed-sitter and sharing in ordinary activities such as cleaning the car, shopping, and cooking. Summing up:

- Children need love first.
- Children need their consistent routine and structure.
- During access time parents need to do what they ordinarily do (e.g., do the gardening, clean the car).
- Parents need to respect ritual.
- Children need a "father" and "mother," not a playmate; they need access and quality time.
- Children often want both parents back together again so they may try intimidation or sabotage of either parent's access time and/or future relationships.

6. It is not a good idea for one to take responsibility when the other parent fails to meet his or her obligations to the children (e.g., forgets to turn up or is late). Doing this can backfire later with the present parent being blamed for not being able to fix it. It is important not to make up excuses for the other parent's mistakes (e.g., dad must have forgotten) as that absent parent must be responsible for his or her own failures. If the ex-spouse does not turn up, it may not be appropriate for the parent to ring them up or else the children may think that the present parent is to blame for not fixing the problem. It is best for the child to phone the failing parent, take the disappointment, and then be supported by the present parent. If the children are disappointed, the parent should just put an arm around them and comfort them.

7. By the same token it is important for parents to be careful what they say to children or in their hearing about each other.

- They should avoid loading torpedoes. By this I mean not sending off a child to the other parent loaded with negative comments (torpedo) about them like a torpedo from the submarine. The torpedo may probably sink the target (the other parent) but the torpedo (the child) will also

[24]Research indicates that about 73% of divorced women in the U.S. experience a decline in their standard of living.

be destroyed in the process. Sometimes a torpedo may circle back and destroy the sending submarine parent.

- The children should not be questioned about a partner's lifestyle or lovers. Although it is important to know what is going on for the sake of the welfare of the child, such information is best obtained directly from the parent in question.

- Children should be encouraged to continue their relationship and affection for their mother/father, avoiding put-down comments like you are just like your no good father/mother.

- Parents should be reliable about picking up or delivering children on access days.

- The other parent should be notified, preferably in writing, text, or e-mail, well in advance concerning any proposed changes to an access arrangement, especially illness, birthday parties, holidays, and sports, cultural or religious events.

- Note that children can see through inappropriate behavior. When the opportunity arises, they will willingly go to the parent who is not angry and bitter but is getting on with their life.

8. Parents need to be consistent and keep their word. Children need security.

9. If possible, parents should try to minimize the disruption to a child's life. This means supporting the maintenance of previous friendships, sports, church, and play activities.

10. Parents should avoid all conflict in front of the children as this will disrupt the children's adjustment and is likely to precipitate behavioral problems. Most children are usually very sensitive to conflict especially when it is not demonstrated how to resolve it positively.

11. Children will misbehave irrespective of the divorce or separation. They are just being kids so parents should not ascribe all outbursts to this.

12. Both parents should try to establish a proper home. Many men fail here, initially living in cheap flats with little or no "home" atmosphere. This means having a clean and tidy place with normal things like pictures. Children like to know that they have their own space when visiting. However, in the end, the most important thing for the child is meaningful time with the parent.

13. Both parents need to plan holidays and special events carefully. Children can sometimes end up being a victim of a tug-of-war. They should be at least included in such discussions if they are old enough.

14. Although it may be painful for parents, they should not shy away from recalling and talking about the past with a child. Otherwise the child gets the message that part of his or her life is unacceptable. With smaller children, sitting down and looking at old photos, videos, and so on, and talking openly about such times is a worthwhile exercise from time to time.[25]

---

[25]Hayman (1994: 139).

18.4   LOOKING BACK

18.4.1   Reasons For Breakdown

Up till now the focus on divorce has been on coping in the present. It is, however, very helpful to look back and evaluate if possible why the relationship actually failed so that past mistakes don't just get repeated.

Reasons for Divorce

Here are some reasons for relationship breakdown as follows:[26]

- *The victim divorce.* One spouse leaves the relationship for somebody else. This produces powerful feelings of rejection and worthlessness that can turn easily to anger and the desire for revenge. Rejection is not easy to live with.

- *The problem divorce.* There is a problem with one partner or both partners that may have been there before the marriage. Common problems in addition to emotional or mental health issues are addictions (e.g. alcohol, gambling, pornography), phobias, dysfunctional family background, and career related problems (e.g., workaholism).

- *The little boy, little girl divorce.* They want to partner with their mates but don't want the responsibility of being a lover and spouse or a parent.

- *I was conned divorce.* There has been a lack of honesty before the marriage so that spouses feel cheated and never get what they were led to expect.

- *The mid-life crisis divorce.* This is where there are dramatic changes in the personality or lifestyle of one or both partners. This can occur quite unexpectedly after a long pleasant marriage. The complete change can cause a deep personal hurt and bitterness along with a feeling of being unable to fix the problem, with sad feelings of rejection and abandonment.

- *The no fault divorce.* It just didn't work out and the two just drifted apart. There was no conflict, no affair and no midlife crisis, just boredom and nothingness!

- *The rat race divorce.* The husband and wife both work, the children fight for their own survival, and in the end everybody runs out of steam.

- *The conflict ridden divorce.* Nothing ever gets resolved or settled. There is a continual battle for survival with struggles for control and unpleasant manipulation ending in verbal, psychological, and/or physical violence.

- *The "shotgun" divorce.* This is the result of a "'shotgun" marriage where the bride to be is pregnant and, without love or commitment, the (usually) young couple feels obligation (often from parents) to marry rather than leave the girl a solo mum or face abortion as an option. Coercion is not a good way to start a marriage and gives it at best a shaky foundation.

[26]Smoke (1995: 29–32).

Subconscious Baggage

A high proportion of relationship failure is caused by past subconscious baggage brought into a marriage, for example, parent/child messages and learned behavior from a family of origin ("We always did it this way"), and inappropriate past coping skills ("If I kick up enough fuss I will get my own way!"). The therapist needs to find out out what sort of messages clients received as children as there are both good and bad parent messages that can be brought from their families of origin. The words "should" and "must" are often parent messages. "Men shouldn't cry" is a typical critical parent message instead of "It's okay for men to cry," a nurturing parent message. Again, the message "I mustn't be close" can arise if a parent is inconsistent with feelings, for example, nice one minute and angry the next. The message is then: "I can't trust the way people respond when I get close so that it is therefore safer if I don't get close to people at all."

Such subconscious baggage carried into the marriage is usually below the surface rather like 90% of the iceberg underneath the water. The "below the surface issues" tend to explode when triggered by less serious issues like money, the children, sex, in-laws, and religion.[27]

Partner Choice

The process of how a marriage will go will largely depend on why people choose each other as partners. In Section 19.2.3 we considered the imago model that describes one way how a person might choose a partner, namely someone with traits like a care-giver (especially the negative traits). Another way is choosing someone with complementary traits; as they say, "opposites attract." Clearly, marrying someone with some negative traits can be a recipe for a matrimonial disaster, once the heated initial romance has cooled down. Also opposite traits which can be great to start with can end up being irritating. Exploring a client's family of origin and his or her childhood hurts can perhaps help a client understand what might have gone wrong with the marriage. Unfortunately the cycle of divorce or dysfunctionality ends up all too often being repeated into the future generations unless there is effective therapeutic intervention.

18.5 FORGIVENESS

Some general principals of forgiveness are discussed in Section 2.5.5. In the case of divorce, I would like to suggest a number of steps clients might engage in. Not all of them will be appropriate for a particular client (e.g., depending on one's religious background).

1. *General willingness to forgive and open up again.* When we are deeply hurt, we respond with enormous mental, emotional, and spiritual energy, usually to protect ourselves and to prevent further injury. This energy unfortunately can block the healing process when we determine to "*never* cry again," or respond with "I'll *never* forgive the idiot," or "I'll *never* trust a man/woman again." The vulnerable emotions are often shut down to cope. In time the hate and anger may diminish, but the passing of time does not necessarily

---

[27]Such topics are considered in more detail in Chapter 19.

get rid of it. However, willingly embracing forgiveness does help get hate out of a person's life.

2. *God forgive me.* It is hard to admit our own mistakes. Even if we believe that we are only 5% to blame for the break up we still need God to forgive our 5%. After all, we married our ex-partner in the first place! We need to soberly evaluate our own failures in the marriage and ask God to forgive us for our part. God is forgiving as God forgave Israel again and again. The story of the prodigal son is more about the forgiving father than it is about the failing son asking for forgiveness. Because we are angry with God for letting the divorce happen we may need to forgive God![28]

3. *I forgive myself.* This can be difficult for some clients as sometimes deep feelings of shame and personal blame can be deep-seated. If I believe that God has forgiven me, then surely I can forgive myself. Are my standards higher than God's? Dwelling on "If only I'd ...." is a no-win situation. We can go to a mirror and say: "(Your name), I forgive you!" Forgiving myself can mean:

   - I accept I am part of this fallen world.
   - I accept responsibility for my failures.
   - As God has forgiven me, I can forgive myself for my failures.
   - I can begin again.

4. *I forgive my ex-partner.* This is not condoning my ex's actions, nor minimizing the pain.[29] It doesn't mean that I have to take my ex-mate back, nor do I have to send a note or ring up my ex and say I forgive you. He or she might respond with, "How big of you when it was your fault anyway!" It is an act of will and it involves seeing my ex in a new light and learning to process that forgiveness in a way and at a time that is appropriate. It is helpful to first address (5) below at the same time as (4) here, if this is possible.

5. *I ask my ex-partner for forgiveness.* This is a tough one and its relevance will depend on individual circumstances. It can be argued that even if I am only 1% in the wrong then I need to ask for forgiveness for that part. Does it matter how my ex responds when I ask forgiveness for my part in the relationship breakup? No, that is not my responsibility. Such an act can (a) give me freedom even if I am not forgiven, and (b) make an opening for my ex to reciprocate. Of course we need to be circumspect about when and how we do this and a letter may be the best way to do it. Now may not be the best time to ask for forgiveness and, depending on the circumstances, it might not ever be appropriate.

6. *I ask my children for forgiveness.* Even though our children may have taken sides, they know deep down that we *both* failed. If I failed in a marriage that does not make me a failure or a failure as a parent, but any children are greatly affected. I can ask them to forgive me for the way the failure of the marriage hurt and affected them.

---

[28] See Section 3.5.
[29] See Section 2.5.5.

We may feel that we can forgive but never forget. However time does bring about some change in the vividness of our memories. Through focusing on forgiveness we can begin to shift the emphasis and concentrate on good memories rather than on bad ones. It will depend on the ongoing relationship with the ex, but new beginnings can encourage progress or at least provide a better balance and perhaps a transformation of our memories.

18.6 BIBLICAL PERSPECTIVE

The question of divorce raises real issues for some Christians and the churches they belong to. The interpretation of biblical verses about divorce is controversial and I don't wish to enter the debate. There are four approaches to the subject of divorce: (1) No divorce and no remarriage; (2) Divorce, but no remarriage; (3) Divorce and remarriage for adultery or desertion; and (4) Divorce and remarriage under a variety of circumstances. In House[30] these four approaches are presented from a biblical viewpoint and debated by four theologians, while additional material may be found in Richards[31] and Stott.[32] I have summarized this material into a set of notes which I use for any client concerned about this matter.[33]

---

[30] House (1990).
[31] Richards (1981).
[32] Stott (1990: chapter 14).
[33] A copy can be obtained from me at seber@stat.auckland.ac.nz.

CHAPTER 19

COUPLE RELATIONSHIP COUNSELING

19.1 INTRODUCTION

This is a huge issue as a chapter topic and could easily take up a whole book of its own. Couples come for counseling in a variety of combinations, married or unmarried, heterosexual or same sex, and without or with children (perhaps from one or more previous marriages). Irrespective of whether a couple is married or not, they aspire to a happy and lasting relationship. In this chapter I focus on heterosexual couples, though much of the material applies equally to same sex couples. There is an extensive literature on couple counseling, so my aim is to just provide a variety of strategies from various sources including my own experience. Every couple is different so that no structure will suit everybody. The RELATE program is used extensively in the U.K. and I will make mention of it.[1] For further material on couples' problems see Chapter 16 on abuse and Chapter 17 on dysfunctional relationships.

19.1.1 Who Should Come to Counseling?

In relationship counseling, initially one of the couple may come alone. Frequently it will be the woman. It is important, preferably at the first session, to encourage the client to see if the other partner can also present as soon as possible. The other

[1]Butler and Joyce (1998).

party may want to know what is going on, perhaps being suspicious, or suspecting collusion. There is "her truth, his truth, and the truth!" It is not that they both tell lies, but their perspectives on events and behaviors can be very different, and some have more accurate and detailed memories. Often their separate accounts of events are so different I have been left wondering whether they are talking about the same event! Talking to just one partner can be seriously misleading. Conjoint sessions usually reveal beliefs that each partner might prefer to hide; they may get caught up in the moment and the interaction becomes healthily less personally censored. On the other hand, sometimes either or both cannot talk adequately in the presence of the other partner. They may not be free enough with the other present to be totally honest about whether or not they want to stay in the relationship. If seeing just one partner, the therapist has to be careful not to collude on what the absent partner may be reported to be doing wrong.[2]

Another reason for seeing them together is that members of a couple may function individually quite well out in the world, but the problems occur in their interaction with each other so it is important to see them together interacting. In this way we can discover their pattern of communication and method of resolving conflict. It can be helpful to externalize the discussion of the relationship, for example by writing "The Marriage" or "The Relationship" on a piece of paper and placing it on the floor. Sometimes one member of a couple can be in denial about his or her part of the problem. That member's main concern may therefore be to get the other person "fixed."

Reddrop and Reddrop[3] affirm that "the model or paradigm in marriage counseling has to be joint interviewing," but recognize that sometimes individual interviews might be appropriate. In dealing with an addiction, it is usually essential to see a person individually, depending on the type of addiction. However, with addictions like compulsive gambling and alcoholism, it will be helpful to bring in the other partner either initially or at some stage in order to develop joint strategies. Bubenzer and West[4] also discuss individual versus couple counseling and summarize some research findings to support couple counseling. These include a greater chance of success, shorter treatment time, positive outcomes for affective and anxiety disorders when the focus is on the disorder, and, with early appropriate support, couple stability is encouraged. However, as the authors indicate, conducting objective research on couple counseling is fraught with difficulties.

Sometimes the client is not able to get his or her partner to counseling and if no other approach works then the therapist can contact the other party directly. A letter or e-mail may be the best form of communication,[5] but this is not the preferred option and is best left as an open option. If the other partner decides he or she will come to counseling a long time after the first partner started, it might be more appropriate for another therapist to carry out the joint counseling. The "late arrival" may well assume work done with the therapist without that person may put him or her at a prejudiced disadvantage. On the other hand, if after couple counseling for some time one partner wants to have additional individual counseling, then the therapist will need to determine exactly which of the two is the client. The

[2]Reddrop and Reddrop (1995: 15).
[3]Reddrop and Reddrop (1995: 12).
[4]Bubenzer and West (1993: 20).
[5]For example, ask for help!

problem of collusion can arise so it may be appropriate for a different counselor to see the person individually. However, I have found on some occasions when a partner has some personal (perhaps delicate) issues that individual counseling can be helpful. It should be noted that in couple counseling, the counselor is not neutral but is on the side of the relationship. I often say that I am there for both of them and should be regarded by them both as a team player.

A relationship needs to be established with each individual before positive work can be achieved on the couple's relationship. It is important to remember that it is not the therapist's job to save a relationship; that is solely up to the couple. In fact two people together do not necessarily improve a relationship. Each person, however, making positive progress will improve the relationship.[6] That is why homework tasks are important. They should be closely linked to the counseling session and created in collaboration with the couple in order to give appropriate relevance, and not just be an "add on." The therapist should always follow up on homework given, otherwise it may be seen as unimportant. Men usually like to be given specific tasks to carry out. It does not have to be too complicated and can be as simple as for example, listening and taking his partner walking.

If seeing just one partner only, many of the following ideas can still be used in such counseling. Sometimes positive changes in that person can encourage the other partner to eventually want to come to counseling also.

19.2   MODELS FOR COUNSELING

19.2.1   Life-Cycle Models

Individual Life Stages Model

Erik Erikson proposed a most useful eight-stage psychosocial developmental model we go through from birth to old age.[7] The task of each stage is to re-solve a certain conflict, for example trust versus mistrust. Although the timing of stages can vary with some cultures, the general pattern is very helpful.[8] Each of the couple and also their children are not only negotiating their own stages, but members of their extended families are also dealing with their stages. All of these elements can awaken earlier personal conflicts that are expressing themselves in the couple relationship, for example, mistrust, anger, mutual accusations, and loss of intimacy. Clues for the relevance of this life-stage model (also used by RELATE[9]) can be specific triggers such as arrival of a baby, mid-life changes, death of a parent, and difficult past life events. The therapist needs to recognize the existence of any difficult stage (e.g., adolescence, mid-life), look at the tasks and conflicts associated with that stage, and compare the history of previous transitions.

Family Systems Model

In understanding couple relationships, there are many questions that go beyond just the couple. In addition to the couple's family life cycle discussed above, each

---

[6] Kerr (1985: 130).
[7] Erikson (1995). A ninth stage has been added in Erikson and Erikson (1997).
[8] For further details of the stages see http://en.wikipedia.org/wiki/Psychosocial_development and http://psychology.about.com/library/bl_psychosocial_summary.htm (accessed october 2010).
[9] Butler and Joyce (1998: 75–76).

partner will belong to his or her own family-of-origin life cycle. The members can also each be brother or sister to their siblings, and offspring to their parents. The couple need to be regarded as part of a system moving through time. Trying to maintain all these different roles, especially when they make contrary demands, can lead to much of the couple's role-conflict and problems in the relationship.[10]

If one or both partners come from a dysfunctional or just a different family of origin background or culture, this can eventually create all sorts of problems, which can impinge heavily on a couple's happiness. For example, his small family of origin may have resolved conflicts quietly, while her large family tended to have a noisy free for all, but got over it quickly. Each member is familiar with a different way of handling conflict, and this can lead to confusion in conflict management. It is therefore helpful with couples to construct a genogram (family tree), where several generations and different levels of family background can be included.[11] The therapist can use objects or drawings to identify systems, examine the beliefs of different systems, and assess each partner's roles with an eye on possible conflicts. Boundaries of preferred systems can be strengthened while boundaries of other systems may need to be loosened.

Some therapists prefer to use a family systems approach in their couple counseling and a number of case studies using this approach are given by Gurman (1985). In any case, it can be helpful to see a couple as a system rather than as two individuals and make use of the technique called *circular questioning*. Basically this consists of asking one person about another, for example, asking partners what they believe the other partner thinks about an issue, or why they think their partner behaved a certain way, or how does their partner behave when they are angry/depressed/stressed, and so on. The therapist could also ask what would a parent of a partner think about a certain behavior, or whether either of his or her parents would behave in a similar manner, thus bringing in the intergenerational system (and even checking on the existence of possible triads). Such questioning can, for example, encourage positive communication as the silent partner may feel that he or she is understood, or a partner there under duress will be drawn into involvement even if it is just active listening or needing to correct misinformation. A systems approach is implied in the "too close–too far" system described under the attachment model of Section 19.2.2 below.

Couple's Stages Model

In addition to the stages model for individuals, a similar model has also been developed for the couple defined as a single unit. This family life cycle model discussed by Carter and McGoldrick[12] with six stages focuses on the different stages of a couple's family-life cycle. Difficulties can arise at a transition from one stage to another, for example, when the first child arrives a parental system is added to a marital system. However, it is important to recognize that the stages can be somewhat arbitrary, have many exceptions, and are culturally dependent.[13]

In counseling a couple, it may be helpful to be aware of what stage they might be at, though the situation is sometimes muddied if there are children from previous

[10]The RELATE program call this the systems model approach [Butler and Joyce (1998: 71–72)].
[11]See, for example, http://en.wikipedia.org/wiki/Genogram, McGoldrick and Gerson (1985), and McGoldrick (2007) for details.
[12]Carter and MCGoldrick (1999: 2–3).
[13]Carter and McGoldrick (1999: 4).

relationships. This raises the question of what role children play in a couple's dynamics. With the high divorce rate and even higher rate for second marriages, blended families are playing a greater role in the success or failure of a relationship, and the children, whether "his," "hers," or even "ours," can sometimes hijack relationships. This topic is discussed in Chapter 20.

Clearly some aspects of family therapy are relevant and sometimes the whole family or other members need to be brought in for counseling at some stage, including seeing a child or children on their own. A sand tray with small animal figures or a drawing board with an A3 sheet of paper and thick crayons can help children explore their feelings about members of their family and the relative importance of those members to the child. They can draw themselves, add other family members (including extended family), and be asked about inter-person distances (and relative importance).

The factor of the increasing number of cross-cultural marriages brings further challenges for couples. The stress of immigration and adjusting to a new country has an profound effect on a couple and any children. If a couple has been in "survival" mode in their country of origin, coming out into the new safer society can reveal deficiencies that had been previously ignored because of the threat to life itself in their own land.

19.2.2 Psychoanalytic Models

The RELATE approach assesses aspects of the unconscious using a number of behavior models in the second stage of the counseling process called the "understanding " stage. I shall now discuss three of these models.

Splitting and Projection model

This model relates to ambivalence. This is the state of simultaneously holding positive as well as negative feelings about the same thing— something we all face in our daily lives. Splitting occurs when under stress we "split" our emotions and focus only on the one and suppress the other. However, the denied feelings still exist and may surface under natural stimuli upsetting the balance. To maintain the split, the feelings have to be attributed elsewhere, and this displacement of unwanted feeling is called "projection." In the case of a couple in conflict they may take refuge in a split position and deny the full range of feelings in both themselves and their partners. RELATE uses the following three categories of this type of interaction, giving them colorful names.[14]

1. *Babes in the Wood.* Both parties ignore the negative because such feelings (and any related problems) belong to the outside world, and not to them. They tend not to come to counseling. If they do, they may present sexual problems, as their desires may be regarded as problems and negatives.

2. *Cat and Dog.* Both parties ignore the positive and only see the bad in themselves and their partner. All the positive is projected onto the outside world.

3. *Net and Sword.* Here one partner ignores the positive and the other partner the negative, for example one partner is all love and yearning and the other is all anger and rejection.

[14]Butler and Joyce (1998: 58–59).

In dealing with such couples, the therapist needs to show how to handle ambivalence, divert destructive arguments, encourage open communication, demonstrate how to avoid being drawn into the conflict, and avoid siding with the couple's view that the world is a terrible place, or the couple is awful, or one partner is worse than the other. Signs that the model may be appropriate are:[15] strong "primitive" emotions, a sense that the couple are bound together, simple notions of good and bad are spoken about, words like "ought" and "should" are common in describing preferred actions, and the counselor feels drawn into the struggle. Further comments about projection are made below in Section 19.6.4 under the title of "Criticism."

Attachment Model

Another RELATE contribution is the attachment model based on the work of John Bowlby.[16] The breaking of a secure attachment with a primary caregiver through, say, bereavement or rejection, can lead to detachment problems in adulthood. Detachment problems are real issues in therapy. Another problem refers to the emotional-pursuer—emotional-distancer scenario where one partner is seeking a closer attachment and struggles for it, which he or she has always had to do in the past, while the other partner prefers to be detached, which feels more natural to that person. The couple is caught in a pattern of complementary attachment behaviors and any change in the level of intimacy would feel strange to either partner. However, the tug-of-war is exhausting and destructive to the relationship. Clearly the therapist will need to deal with past issues, and the possibility of detachment factors, perhaps by focusing on specific events.

One example where there is such an imbalance in a couple relationship is when one partner shows compulsive self-sufficiency (avoidant attachment) and the other compulsive care-giving (anxious attachment). In the former case, when the person was a child, a desire for attachment was not met with an appropriate response from the parent (e.g., "Big boys don't cry"). Often the response was harsh and angry when help was needed. Such a partner doesn't need anybody, doesn't like closeness, and doesn't want help, except when the other partner wants more closeness. The compulsive care-giving partner was perhaps not appreciated enough as a child and had to care of a sick mother; the child's message was "please take care of me."

There are many clues for the therapist to identify attachment issues such as: the existence of past separations, affairs, and desertion; recurrent losses in later life such as redundancies and relocations; and isolating work patterns such as long distance driving and armed forces. There are also frequent reference to commitment, rejection, and loss; difficulties over partings and meetings; and attachment to or detachment from the therapist (e.g., frequent contact or, conversely, missed meetings). The therapist needs to examine the couple's expectations around bonding, perhaps address the effects of past losses, uncover and help them mourn past unacknowledged losses, and create a safe place for this in the counseling room.[17]

The dynamics can be different from that described above when both partners can have the same distance problems. Byng-Hall[18] says that a couple can end

---

[15]Butler and Joyce (1998: 80).
[16]See Section 2.5.2 for types of adult attachment.
[17]A helpful book on the role of emotion-focused therapy and attachment issues in counseling couples is Johnson (2008).
[18]Byng-Hall (1985: 2).

up forming a "too close–too far" system in which they are both far enough away to be free of anxiety about intimacy but are so distant that they feel constantly insecure about their autonomy. There is constant tension between trying to get closer with trying to escape. He explains that one partner may develop symptoms that remove the distance conflict by becoming the reason both for staying together and for the lack of intimacy. For example, the husband may become an alcoholic, which interferes with intimacy, but he can't manage on his own and needs her, or the wife develops agoraphobia, which interferes with intimacy because of her intense anxiety, but she needs him to be nearby for her support.

Weeks and Treat[19] describe language as a manager of distance. A spouse who says "You never hug me!" is seemingly communicating a wish for closeness, but the defensive response it provokes actually creates distance. Although the spouse believes he or she is asking for closeness, the spouse may subconsciously be wanting to protect himself or herself against future pain. Who wants to hug someone who verbally accuses, attacks, or complains? A better statement for intimacy is "I need a hug." Distancing language needs to be addressed by the therapist so that couples can understand the impact of their language, especially "you" statements. Language like this can indicate a parent-to-child dynamic with a spouse talking as a parent to the child in the partner as described in transactional analysis, rather than there being an adult-to-adult communication.

Byng-Hall has found that children's ambivalence about their parents' relationship can act as a distance regulator. The child wants them to stay together but not too close so that the child cannot get in between to achieve his or her own ends. He notes that:

> When parents start an escalation, they may find that one of their children acts to disrupt intimacy but also behaves in a way that brings then together if they get too far away. This may provide such relief that the child's ambivalence is given positive feedback.[20]

This amplifies the child's contradictory feelings and reduces the parents' conflict, but the child may develop problems that can then regulate the parents' distance. They "come together as mother and father, which is a non-intimate form of sharing, in order to cope with the child's problem."

In addition to children, others may act as distance regulators. Byng-Hall's aim in counseling is to achieve adequate levels of autonomy and intimacy in the couple by changing their thresholds of anxiety about distance and giving them new experiences of closeness and distance. It is not a question of autonomy versus intimacy but of strengthening both. He notes that one of the situations that the therapist can face is to be triangled into the role of distance regulator, which can be helpful in the earlier stages of counseling, but needs to be dealt with later. In this situation I have found that the counseling room can become almost a safety outlet whereby people feel they can express their concerns and feelings to their partner by addressing me as a mediating party.

Triangular Relationship Models

The first of these models relates to the triangular interaction between parents and a third party, whether it is a child inside the relationship or an affair outside.

[19] Weeks and Treat (1992: 62–63).
[20] Byng-Hall (1985: 3).

In the case of a child, the child may become excluded, or the strong bond between the mother and child may leave the father feeling excluded. The effect of an affair is discussed below. However, even if there is no affair, one partner may feel threatened by the presence of a third party at, for example, a work place or a place of recreation (e.g., a gym). Too many text messages from a third party or if one frequently provides a helping hand to a person of the opposite sex on weekends can be seen as a threat to a relationship. The therapist can examine past triangles, normalize any feared exclusions, encourage nonexclusive triangles, and address any trust issues.

Another type of triangle, called the Karpman drama triangle, frequently arises in couple or family situations and incorporates three roles, namely the persecutor, the victim, and the rescuer, and may involve just a couple or a couple plus one other, such as a child.[21] Under pressure, the triangle comes into full play with individuals shifting their positions, for example they may swop roles. The simplest way to escape the triangle is by one member giving a non-defensive response, for example, "Oh," "I see," and "You may be right," or else reflecting back or agreeing with the previous statement such as responding to "You expect too much of me as I get very tired" with "I am sorry you get so tired."

A third triangular model is Sternberg's[22] *triangular theory of love* in which love is described as a triangle with the three corners representing passion, commitment, and intimacy.[23] A couple can each be asked what they think comprises a loving relationship and give a definition of these three attributes. Weeks and Treat[24] suggest using the triangle to ask five diagnostic questions, namely: (1) Do both partners desire all three components? (2) Do they each require the same level of intensity for each component? (3) Can they identify and express each component openly and freely? (4) Do they each have a realistic perception of what love involves? (5) Do they each have a realistic perception of what they can deliver? This can lead on to talk about intimacy and what it entails.

Various authors give different lists of what constitutes intimacy (= "into me see"). For example L'Abate (1977) lists seeing the good in the other person along with caring, protectiveness, enjoyment, responsibility, sharing hurt, and forgiveness. However, the list will vary from couple to couple and within a couple. There are also various types of intimacy that include not just the sexual (sharing bodies) and physical (openness of touching and feeling, and togetherness in various activities), but also the intellectual (sharing thoughts), emotional (sharing feelings), social (spending time together and discussing time spent apart), and spiritual (soul sharing).

Some people are afraid of intimacy, perhaps because of past abuse or they had experienced the pain of being let down by past partners and didn't want to be hurt emotionally again. In addition to a fear of abandonment/rejection, Weeks and Treat[25] list a fear of the following: dependency (e.g., a man may feel that it is a sign of weakness), feelings (e.g., because they have been suppressed), anger (e.g., unresolved from the past), losing control or being controlled (e.g., fragile self-identity), and exposure (e.g., because of low self-esteem).

[21] See http://en.wikipedia.org/wiki/Karpman_drama_triangle for a definition and an example.
[22] Sternberg (1988).
[23] See http://en.wikipedia.org/wiki/Triangular_theory_of_love for details.
[24] Weeks and Treat (1992: 106–108).
[25] Weeks and Treat (1992: 111–116).

19.2.3 Imago Model

An interesting question that may help us to understand the source of some couple difficulties is, "How do people choose each other?" Hendrix looked at a number of models for romantic attraction[26] and came up with the following theory. We *unconsciously*[27] choose a partner who matches a broad brush imago or image determined by a part of our brain sometimes referred as the "old brain" (the brain stem plus the limbic system[28]), which being timeless in its operation, tries to recreate the environment of childhood. Thus "most people are attracted to mates who have their own care-giver's positive *and* negative traits, and, typically, the negative traits are more influential."[29] That part of our brain is trying to recreate the past so that we can vicariously put things right and heal our childhood wounds. Although this re-creation is uncomfortable, it is in a sense familiar territory again. As no one comes through childhood completely unscathed no matter how good the upbringing, we see that under this model childhood has a profound affect on our partnership.

Role of Past Repression

Repression can play a harmful role in a child's development, whether caused by unhealthy parental discipline or unsatisfactory parental role models. We begin life as potential "whole" persons but end up losing bits that Hendrix calls our "lost self," our "false self," and our "disowned self," described as follows:[30]

1. Our *lost self* is that part of us we had to suppress because of parental or care-giver indoctrination on how we should be in society. This means, "There are certain thoughts and feelings we could not have, certain natural behaviors that we had to extinguish, and certain talents and aptitudes we had to deny."[31] For example, a parent message like, "Women should be homemakers and not have a career," or "Women can't do mathematics," can lead to the repression of self. This is not to accept the limited Freudian concept of the self being the outcome of expressed or repressed drives.

2. Our *false self* is the facade we adopt to fill the void created by the repression and lack of adequate nurturing. For example, a boy brought up by an unloving mother may repress that affectionate part of himself and become a "tough guy" to protect himself.

3. Our *disowned self* consists of the negative parts of our false self that met with disapproval and were therefore denied. For example, the boy referred to in (2) when criticized for being cold and distant denies it and says that he is really strong and independent.

The only parts we are aware of are those parts of our being still intact, plus certain aspects of our false self. The problem bits of one's personality can have a negative affect on a couple's relationship when they can't be fixed. In trying to

---

[26] Hendrix (2001: chapter 1).
[27] Hendrix calls this the "unconscious" marriage.
[28] This terminology has mixed support.
[29] Hendrix (2001: 34); his italics.
[30] Hendrix (2001: 32).
[31] Hendrix (2001: 25).

recover those lost parts, people often choose mates with complementary traits so that they can make up for what is missing in their own lives. Hendrix sums up the imago as follows:

> To guide you in your search for an ideal mate, someone who both resembled your caregivers and compensated for the repressed parts of yourself, you relied on an unconscious image of the opposite sex that you had been forming since birth.[32]

In other words we carry an image we are seeking, hence his imago therapy. But as he teaches, an image is not a real person.

People expect their partners to love them in a way that their parents never did so as to satisfy unmet childhood needs and compliment lost self-parts. In such a situation, people can end up being in love with an image they project onto their partner rather than with the partner. At some stage after the initial flush of romantic love it can seem as though the wounded child within takes over and the relationship changes. Some of the things a person initially liked about his or her partner become a source of irritation as forbidden parts of self are stirred up, and the negative traits resolutely denied in the romantic phase come into sharp focus and begin to annoy! Hendrix notes that: "At some point in their marriages, most people discover that something about their husbands or wives awakens strong memories of childhood pain."[33] For example, a woman with abusive parents comes to recognize a violent streak in her spouse. There comes the realization that one is going to be wounded in a similar way as in one's childhood and these awakened memories can add further injury to old wounds. Sometimes the negative traits of one person are projected onto the other partner so that the partner gets blamed or criticized for all the things the person dislikes and denies in his or her own life.

19.2.4   Cohabitation

Although most of the discussion in this chapter applies to couples that are either married or cohabiting, there are clearly some differences. Given that an increasing proportion of young couples cohabit before they get married, some comments on this topic seem appropriate.[34]

Various reasons are given why people live together first in a trial de facto relationship (common-law union). They may fear commitment on the grounds that they might fall out of love or else be afraid of being hurt again, as with previous bad experiences. They may not want to conform to what other people expect or may even dismiss the need to prove their love with a piece of paper. Perhaps the most common reason is to make sure they are completely compatible, including sexually—"try before you buy." However, the statistics indicate that living together does not divorce-proof a subsequent marriage. The statistics are no better than for those who don't live together. One reason suggested for this is that a de facto relationship is not the same as marriage as the level of commitment is different. In the U.S., about half of cohabiters get married while the other half break

---

[32]Hendrix (2001: 36).
[33]Hendrix (2001: 69).
[34]See also Section 20.3.

up, and half of all cohabitations last less than one year, with 90% ending in five years.[35]

Domestic violence is more severe and more prevalent among cohabiting couples than among married couples.[36] In the U.K., a recent extensive study showed that cohabiting has become a less stable form of relationship compared with 18 years ago, with such couples more likely to separate.[37] In 2006, 75% of couples who had children after they were married stayed together until their child's 16th birthday, while only 7% who were unmarried when their child was born were still cohabiting by the child's 16th birthday. For whatever reason, the statistics show that marriage provides a more stable background for children. The study also showed that never-married couples who live together before marriage were 60% more likely to divorce than those who did not.

19.3 GENERAL PROBLEM AREAS

19.3.1 Couple Issues

Bubenzer and West[38] list the following ten issues for couples:

1. *Economic issues.* Such things as who controls the purse strings, how one or both parties earn and spend money, and who pays the bills, credit cards, mortgage time payments, and debt generally.

2. *Companionship and intimacy.* Companionship is linked to quality time spent with a partner and intimacy relates to the closeness they share, whether sexual or otherwise. A key problem issue is the emotional distance between the partners. Intimacy is discussed further below.

3. *Work and recreation.* Achieving a healthy balance between work and recreation is always difficult, and healthy circumstances can upset this balance, for example, someone sick off work thus temporarily increasing the other's work load. Spending too much time at the office (for example on weekends) or bringing too much work home can lead to serious estrangement.

4. *Parenting.* Parenting is often a minefield for couples, and children will often try to set one parent up against the other. Blended families (which are on the increase) pose even trickier challenges.[39] Both partners need to have similar parenting methods, preferably with a basis of acceptable rules and routines.[40] Sometimes one parent feels that only he or she has the right answer to parenting, so a power struggle arises with one parent becoming over-involved and the other parent becoming marginalized. The couple's problems may get projected onto one or more children causing dysfunction in the child as well as in the relationship.

---

[35] Bumpass and Lu (2000); see also
http://paa2006.princeton.edu/download.aspx?submissionId=61534 by Anna-Marie Cunningham and Zhenchao Qian (accessed October 2010).
[36] Brownbridge (2009: 28).
[37] Hayward and Brandon (2101); based on 30,000 cases.
[38] Bubenzer and West (1993: 7).
[39] See Chapter 20.
[40] See Section 18.3.

5. *Household chores.* The division of household chores is also an issue, particularly if both partners work—a trend which is on the increase. Expectations about household chores and who does what (e.g., gender roles) that have developed from individual family life cycles can have a profound effect especially when the man refuses to take close to an equal share when both work the same hours.

6. *Relationships with extended families.* Relationships with extended family can cause friction particularly if one partner has never really left his or her parents or continually seeks parental advice. Members of the extended family can intentionally or unintentionally interfere inappropriately in a couple's relationship with similar damage.

7. *Religion.* Disagreement over this can be a real issue, particularly when children reach a certain age.

8. *Friends.* Couples can struggle over the issue of friends, especially in the early stages of the relationship when there is a merging of two sets of friends. There can be, for example, going sailing with friends to the exclusion of one's family for the men or endless coffee clubs and girls' nights out for the women, ignoring family responsibilities.

9. *Substance abuse.* Substance abuse (including alcoholism and recreational drug use) is becoming more prevalent in society and its problematic intrusion into a relationship is not always adequately acknowledged or even admitted as a problem.

10. *Communication.* I have found this to be a major problem with most couples who come for counseling and part of this is the way conflict management is handled. Often partners are more interested in being heard than trying to really listen.[41] According to Enright and Fitzgibbons,[42] "Clinical experience indicates that in a marriage each partner has some degree of buried anger that they bring to the relationship ...." This unconscious anger may be from others in the past such as parents or significant others, or from the workplace. Men sometimes have difficulty in facing their issues with their fathers.[43]

Dobson[44] adds the following sources of issues: over-commitment and physical exhaustion, addictions, business failure or even success, and getting married too young. Worthington[45] also mentions unmet expectations (often associated with marital myths like my partner will provide all that I need), difficult situations such as loss of employment or illness, individual problems such as addictions and mental disorders (e.g., depression), selfishness (to which I would add insensitivity), and a lack of balance between closeness and distance (autonomy versus intimacy or independence versus interdependence). Unmet expectations are related to needs, especially the need for acceptance, value, and belonging. Using a family systems model, Kerr[46] maintains that two variables, namely the degree of differentiation of

[41] This topic is discussed further below.
[42] Enright and Fitzgibbons (2000: 194).
[43] Enright and Fitzgibbons (2000: 198).
[44] Dobson (1990: 129–137).
[45] Worthington (1993: chapter 2).
[46] Kerr (1985: 114).

self (e.g., losing self in a relationship) and chronic anxiety significantly affect the thinking, feelings, and behavior of family members.

Epstein and Beaucom[47] also mention different standards of interaction (e.g., how much of one's free time should be spent with your partner) that can lead to conflict. They suggest that the therapist clarify each person's standard; list advantages and disadvantages of each person's standard, with input from both partners; search for commonality in the standards and develop a common standard they can both accept; translate the shared standard into specific behaviors; ask them to try behaving according to the new standards for a trial period; trouble-shoot any problems and modify the standard accordingly. Different expectations over things like housework do create conflict. If he is as perfectionist and she hates doing *any* housework there will be trouble. Or the other way round.

Clearly the number of possible issues seems endless and sometimes there is a failure by one of both partners to even recognize the existence of a problem. However, although the real problem generally lies deeper than what is initially raised "it is usually prudent for the counselor to acknowledge and address the problems presented."[48] Otherwise the counsellor has to convince the couple that what they thought was the problem was not the real problem, and this can lead to some resistance. However, the current problem is a starting point for going deeper and the symptom area can be used to assess how the counseling is going; a drop in symptoms means progress. The therapist often needs to help a couple become aware of some things in their relationships that appear to have become automatic. Emotionally, primary emotions such as anger, hurt, and fear are sometimes covered up by secondary emotions. The therapist needs to provide a safe place for a couple to experience their emotions.

Sooner or later the question of separation or divorce may come up. In this case it can be helpful to put the following questions to the partners.

1. Are you in love? (This raises the issue of the nature of love).

2. Am I sabotaging the relationship?

3. How do I feel about us settling down and growing old together?

4. How do I feel about breaking up and moving on?

5. How will I feel if I bump into my ex in six months later and he or she is with someone else?

19.3.2   Intra-personal Problems

Partners often bring their own underlying problems and "baggage" from the past into a relationship that can end up being dumped on one of the above issues. Sturt and Sturt[49] note that these problems often need attention before there can be much progress with the couple. The partner with the problem needs to take responsibility for it and do something about it. However, although the partner can be seen on his

[47] Epstein and Beaucom (2002: 353–354).
[48] Bubenzer and West (1993: 13).
[49] Sturt and Sturt (1988: 11).

or her own, Sturt and Sturt recommend that the both partners should be involved in the problem, utilizing the strength of the couple relationship. These authors list the following common intra-personal problems with some additional comments added. Hopefully this list will help therapists recognize problems to watch out for.

1. *Immaturity.* Emotional maturity is needed for a satisfactory relationship. Since there is a great deal of emotional growth between the ages of 18 and 25, marriage at a young age may cause problems. If you can't understand yourself how can you understand your partner?

2. *Low Self-Esteem.* If you don't like yourself how can you love your partner? If both parties have this problem, they will find it difficult to give and receive love, and may end up putting each other down to feel better.

3. *Fear of Intimacy.* Fear of intimacy, or at least a difference in the degree of intimacy desired by each person, is very common. This can be a problem if one or both parties were brought up in a home lacking emotional or physical closeness. Walls get built!

4. *Inability to Express Feelings.* In some societies males are encouraged not to show their emotions and can even end up losing touch with their feelings. There can't be real intimacy if feelings are not shared.

5. *Sexual Hang-ups.* These often stem from ignorance or negative childhood experiences such as abuse. If sex is not a problem in a marriage, then it plays a more·minor role in couple interaction, but if it is a problem it can play a very major role. The quality of a couple's sex life can be a good indication of how the relationship is functioning.

6. *Childhood Hurts.* There can be a wide range of these including those previously mentioned. Rejection or parental disharmony are not uncommon. A lot depends on the parenting style.

7. *Emotional and Psychological Disorders.* A partner with anxiety, depression, or a phobia can make life difficult, and such disorders are not uncommon.

8. *Spiritual Difference.* Referring to spirituality in a very general sense (see Section 2.6), if one person takes a deep interest in spirituality and the other does not, the couple will probably face some real challenges as to fundamental values and priority issues.

19.3.3   Inter-personal Problems

Sturt and Sturt[50] list a number of problems that can upset a couple relationship (some of these are revisited later in greater detail).

1. *Differences.* For example:

   (a) Gender. Men and women view things differently. Compared with men, women are generally more relationship oriented, are more emotionally connected in their brains, network better with friends, like to talk a lot

---

[50]Adapted from Sturt and Sturt (1988: 13–15).

more, and, because of hormonal changes, go through a lot more mood changes over a month.

(b) Personality. We saw above that we can be attracted to someone with different personality traits. This can create tension when the initial "honeymoon" phase is over.

(c) Family of origin models. Both partners, coming from different homes, will have seen different models of marriage and may be unaware of that influence. For example, many individuals raised in families where there is little caring or thoughtful acts do not recognize or act on opportunities for such tender behaviors.

(d) Expectations. People come into a relationship with different and/or unrealistic expectations, which may lead to disappointment and friction when these are not forthcoming.

(e) Love languages. Everyone has their own primary "language of love." It is how we express our love, and when used by the other person we know we feel loved. This topic is discussed in detail below. If a couple have trouble finding love in their relationship, Coleman[51] suggests they put aside their concerns about love and focus on caring, or at least on showing consideration for each other.

(f) Learning style. The three main styles, namely visual, auditory, and kinesthetic, are briefly discussed in Section 1.3.3. Different learning styles can lead to miscommunication.

2. *Communication Breakdown.* This is a major cause of a relationship breakdown.

3. *Poor Conflict Resolution.* Conflicts are never resolved by one winning and the other losing; there needs to be a win-win solution.[52]

It can be helpful to find out what are the mental images in a couple conflict that tend to run a ritualistic course. Kantor[53] suggests that upset people be asked to consider what they are feeling right at the time of the conflict. They then go through all their life experiences to come up with a picture or some memory of an experience that is telling them how to behave and feel right. It can be a single event, several events, or a conglomerate experience put together by them. The first memory that comes to mind will do as there is no correct memory; it is the structure of the experience that needs to be brought to the surface to determine its interaction with the present. If they can't think of anything, the therapist can help them make up an image. The image is then explored from thematic, affective, and action perspectives. The action perspective means not just describing the people actually involved with the experience but also those who are not present physically but are somehow part of the memory.

According to Kantor, these images color how we see the world, especially the images with regard to relationships with significant others he calls *critical identity images*. These images guide the actions and the feelings a person has in dealing with

---

[51]Coleman (1998: 85).
[52]Covey (1990: habit 4).
[53]Kantor (1985: 39–40).

others. The image is elicited for each partner, preferably during the same counseling session. For example, because of a disappointing incident that happened with her father, the theme of the female partner's image might be that of being disappointed and controlled by a man, whom she was supposed to trust but couldn't. She couldn't get mad with her father so she gets mad with her partner who psychologically becomes identified with her father. The male partner's theme might be that he is not allowed to express his feelings so that he needs to use power and control, as exercised by his father in the past.

This uncovering of images can lead to change, but Kantor says, "Changes brought about in this way are not expected to be stable,"[54] and are simply part of an evolutionary process. Further memories may also surface leading to an augmentation of the image. For example, her partner might also become identified with her brother because of something controlling that her brother did in the past. An aim of the therapist might be to help transform the the image by, say, reframing, and then cementing in a new image. For example, the female partner might see herself as an on-stage entertainer with men at her feet, and totally in control.

Another area that can contribute to instability in a relationship is when one partner was brought up under the cloud of a family secret. Bradshaw (1995) shows how such secrets can have a profound effect, even though they may be in the subconscious and outside of current conscious awareness. The secret may not have been revealed to the child, but the child can unconsciously know that something is wrong. He says that: "The paradox is that at some mysterious level of consciousness, the secrets are not really secrets."[55] Secrets can be acted out, for example a husband may act out his father's sexual addiction that was kept a secret, or secrets can be acted in, for example a sister of the husband may even go into a convent to "act in" her disdain for sexuality. Bradshaw says that many family therapists believe that everyone in the family knows the secret at some level of awareness and that the greater the denial about the secrets the more they get acted in or out.

19.3.4   Environmental Problems

Epstein and Beaucom[56] propose that the most rewarding relationship is one where the needs of the individuals, the couple as a unit, and their interaction with the environment are all considered. There are a number of external and environmental factors that can place stressful demands on a relationship such as family of origin problems, work related difficulties, moving house, issues with children, and so forth. Sometimes the behavior of one partner is socially embarrassing for the other partner (e.g., drinking too much), or the behavior of both (e.g., with extended family members) can hurt the relationship.

On the positive side, being involved in a community cause such as protecting the environment, community projects, church, and volunteer work can give the couple focus that can help them to reaffirm their values and have a sense of purpose beyond themselves. It is important for a couple not to be so wrapped up in themselves with the daily grind that they are unable to participate in fulfilling activities either individually or together. Ritual celebrations and activities such as holidays,

[54]Kantor (1985: 43).
[55]Bradshaw (1995: 53).
[56]Epstein and Beaucom (2002: 19).

birthdays, anniversaries and extended family events as well as religious, school, and community events help to cement relationships.[57]

19.4   SOME SPECIFIC ISSUES

19.4.1   Forgiveness

Forgiveness is discussed in general terms in Section 2.5.5 and the ideas expressed there can be used in couple counseling. However, the operation and nature of forgiveness in a marriage relationship is much less known.[58] When one partner transgresses, counseling should focus on both partners and not just on the offender using, for example, cognitive-behavioral techniques.[59]

Behavioral interventions can include victim restraint (e.g., not over-reacting and controlling the impulse to lash out when hurt), offender amends (e.g., genuine apologies and heartfelt amends), and couple reconciliation (e.g., working to restore mutual trust). The therapist might also help the couple to re-negotiate the norms that govern a relationship, for example, "How does each partner interpret 'the rules,' what constitutes 'reasonable debt repayment' on the part of the offender, and what are the consequences of future transgressions?"[60]

Cognitive counseling can include dealing with problematic beliefs or expectations. The victim may believe that the offender's transgression shows a complete lack of respect for the victim, or the offender believes that the victim is over-reacting or behaving irrationally. Dragging up past demeanors is a common reaction demonstrating that past transgressions have not been forgiven. Forgiveness can be difficult to give when there are repeated offenses. A helpful strategy towards forgiveness is to encourage the couple to acknowledge their mutual reliance and recall one another's past acts of support and benevolence (e.g., desiring the best for one's partner so that he or she does well).

As noted by Coleman,[61] the therapist should not raise the issue of forgiveness prematurely until feelings have been adequately expressed, trust and and communication with the couple have improved, and a therapeutic alliance has been established. He notes that forgiveness is ultimately a decision of the will and not a matter of waiting to feel forgiving. It can be helpful to explain that the more vengeful the victim is, the less guilty the offender starts to feel; this idea may help reduce a victim's desire for vengeance. Someone once said that getting revenge is like drinking poison and waiting for the other person to die!

Coleman mentions a number of other practical aspects of the forgiveness process. Initially angry flare-ups may occur, but they do not indicate that forgiveness is insincere or lacking; they will subside eventually. The "victim" needs to explore what part he or she may have unwittingly contributed to the problem by enabling and reinforcing objectionable behaviors. There is often the question of whether the victim's response to the hurt was possibly unreasonable. A victim's past hurts and

[57]Epstein and Beaucom (2002: 175).
[58]Fincham, Hall, and Beach (2005: 208).
[59]Rusbult et al. (2005: 200).
[60]Rusbult et al. (2005: 200).
[61]Coleman (1998: 83).

failed relationships can also be unfairly dumped on the offender. Similarly, "guilty" partners needs to examine their motives and accept responsibility for their actions rather than try and shift the blame. An important step is to replace their automatic and defensive reactions to a confrontational partner by nonreactive responses.

One helpful intervention model for couples (and family dyads) is Worthington's five step model based on empathy, humility, and commitment, with the acronym REACH. This is described as follows:[62]

Recall the hurt. This involves acknowledging the offense and realistically assessing its effect.

Empathize with the one who hurt you. Here one endeavors to see the offense and its effect from the offender's point of view.

Altruistic gift of forgiveness. Here the partners explore and consider the impact of occasions when each has received and been granted forgiveness (not necessarily from the partner). This will hopefully recall positive feelings about forgiveness and plant the idea that no one is perfect, encouraging humility.

Commitment to forgive. This happens when the therapist believes that the partners have experienced enough empathy and developed enough humility to take such a step toward a process of forgiveness.

Hold onto forgiveness. The couple will need to do this when past hurts are inevitably remembered.

An affair is a very serious transgression that can destroy any relationship and will involve forgiveness whether there is reconciliation or not. This topic is discussed now as a separate issue, although some of the strategies suggested below can be used generally and not merely for affairs.

19.4.2 An Affair

First some general observations. An affair is destructive, and frequently fatal to the relationship. Trust is lost and it can only be recovered with great difficulty. However, both parties need to be helped as the partnership may well have been shaky before the affair and the offender may have already begun to give up on the partnership for some reason. An affair is very painful and traumatic for the victim, and the offender will usually discover that the affair eventually comes to nothing in the end. When offenders come to their senses it may be too late to save the relationship! There may also be real anxiety about the possibility of contracting sexual diseases such as HIV.

What leads to an affair? It is usually a symptom of other underlying problems. It could be say one of the following: emptiness in the relationship; a demand to be treated as perfect (e.g., by a narcissistic partner); one partner takes on the role of victim with the other being the perpetrator (as in the Karpman triangle) and the former then goes looking for a rescuer; or a boundary problem where an affair is seen as the only way of saying "no" to a partner.[63]

---

[62]Worthington (2001).
[63]Cloud and Townsend (1999: 168–169).

There is one question that I want to raise. Which is more serious, an affair or a "one-night stand?" If a partner has difficulty giving up an affair, it could be argued that the partner is showing a "good" quality, that is they have convinced themselves they have genuine feeling for that person. A one-night stand could indicate impulsivity and a lack of any true feelings other than sexual exploitation and self-centered pleasure seeking with a lack control that could reoccur any time. Both behaviors are very damaging, but which is more forgivable? It depends on the circumstances and the three persons involved.

A useful intervention procedure to help a couple recover from an affair and other trauma is outlined by Gordon, Baucom, and Snyder (2004, 2005). These authors propose a three stage process as follows:

1. ***Stage 1: Impact***. In this stage the couple comes to grip with the impact of what has happened. It involves the following:

   (a) The partners need to be helped to set desired boundaries or guidelines for interaction between themselves and with others. For example, how much time should they spend together or apart, should they sleep together, should they maintain sexual relations, what further contact (if any) should the offender have with the outside affair person, and who should know about the affair (e.g., children, in-laws, or friends).

   (b) The partners need to manage their emotions, which can be very erratic, especially as the victim will usually be traumatized. Typical feelings for the victim are betrayal, fear, hurt, and especially anger, while the offender once past the initial denial may experience guilt, shame, or fear so that the question of self-care for both partners is important (e.g., sleep, diet, exercise, social support, and spiritual support, if appropriate). As feelings run high at times, strategies need to be introduced to help the partners to "back off" or have "timeout" when their level of emotion becomes too high.

   (c) Express and identify each partner's reaction to the impact of the infidelity, bearing in mind that emotions will continue to erupt and the victim may experience "flashbacks" of his or her intense emotional reactions to the affair. Once the couple have reached some stability in individual and couple functioning, the therapist can help the partners to identify the impact of the affair on the assumptions they have about each other and their relationship. For example, typical comments might be, "I don't know what to expect anymore," or "I thought I knew him, so how can I trust my judgments now?" The victim also invariably wants to express to the offender how deeply he or she has been hurt. How the affair was brought to light can be relevant. Letters to each other to end and resolve the affair can be helpful, but the offended partner needs to be fully involved in this, and the exercise needs be monitored by the therapist for some objectivity.

2. **Stage 2: Meaning**. Here the couple explores why the affair happened and what were the contributing factors (e.g., problems with the couple relationship, withdrawal of sex, outside factors such as stress and work, individual characteristics and vulnerabilities, and the developmental history of each partner). Although the responsibility for the affair rests with the offender, it is

important to understand the context of the affair rather than simply blaming the offender. A helpful step with forgiveness is the victim recognizing that no one is perfect and there will have been times when the victim has inflicted pain on the offender. The offender may simply be an insensitive selfish and immoral person but may also prove to have been extremely lonely in the marriage, lacking affection, love, and praise, and may in fact be more angry, frustrated, and confused than the victim.

3. **Stage 3: Moving on.** An important decision is whether to end the relationship and, if not, what needs to be put in place to begin the process of rebuilding the relationship. A key question is, "Can the offender be forgiven?" For many couples this involves examining personal beliefs about forgiveness and exploring what might stop a forgiveness process taking place. If forgiveness is possible it won't be easily given and the offender will generally end up on probation! A key issue will be the restoration of trust, which will always take time. The offender may be eager for reconciliation, but may become impatient with the victim's inability to forgive and with the victim's anger and distance. What will help to defuse the situation is for the offender to disclose that he or she doesn't like the partner's continued anger but understands it and accepts it.[64] Also the offender may need to express genuine remorse on a regular basis.

Forgiveness does not require anger to disappear completely and, although thoughts and feelings associated with the event will reoccur, in time they won't be as severe or disruptive as they once were.[65]

Can love be restored again? If this is a problem, Coleman[66] suggests that the couple put aside their concerns about love and focus on caring, or at least on showing consideration for one and other. Trust and friendship need to be restored before love can be evidenced.

19.4.3 Sexual Problems

The issues surrounding sexual problems are complex and the following merely aims to provide some general information. It is important to remember that if a relationship is not going well, then usually sex is not going well either. Sex, for a woman, is only meaningful in the context of a caring relationship where the man really listens to her and is affectionate.

A key question in couple counseling is: What is normal sexual desire and behavior? It is no easier to define this than to define a normal eating desire and behavior, so it is not a straight-forward area for counseling. For this reason, sexual problems should generally be handled by a therapist with some specific knowledge in this area, who has a good understanding and knowledge of sexual response, and is aware of how it differs for men and women. For example, women like to be emotionally and physically close after sex. After-play is as important as foreplay, otherwise she may feel "used" if the man just rolls over and goes to sleep. A woman is more aroused by words and touch, while male arousal is more stimulated by what he sees and

[64]Coleman (1998: 85).
[65]Gordon et al. (2005: 409).
[66]Coleman (1998: 85).

by visual imagery. For example, he will like to see her in nice lingerie and may not be too excited by her heavy woolen pyjamas! Generally speaking, women like to be emotionally connected while men like to feel physically connected. However, men can also have strong emotional needs and women strong sexual needs. Dealing with a specific sexual dysfunction will generally require specialist counseling as inappropriate counseling can simply make problems worse.

Butler and Joyce[67] have a short but clear and factual summary explaining what happens with the stages of sexual arousal in which there is desire, excitement, plateau, orgasm, and resolution, though everyone is probably quite different in their sexual response and stages. Patience and timing is essential as men and women's arousal patterns differ substantially, and women's style of lovemaking is different from men's. Women tend to prefer a gradual approach, though not necessarily on every occasion. As we have seen above, women attach great importance to words and talking. She may be happy with no orgasm, one orgasm, or several orgasms. Generally women have an orgasm (or several) through clitoral stimulation rather than through vaginal stimulation. Conventional wisdom has it that most women consistently seem to associate love with sex, while men tend to seek pleasure and emotional release through sex. Both claim to value love and affection in sexual relationships, but men often avoid physically expressed affection, because it may seem to be associated with being weak or even homosexual.

When might there be a need for sex therapy? Hawton[68] suggests the following indications:

1. The sexual problem has a long duration (at least several months).

2. The couple have been unable to solve their problem.

3. The problem is likely to have been caused or maintained by psychological factors (e.g., bad past sexual experiences, performance anxiety, poor self-esteem).

4. The problem is threatening to destroy the relationship.

Some Myths

Before beginning any interventions, some myths may need to be exploded as the media and some romance novels operate in fantasy land; the following myths taken from various sources may be helpful for both men and women in exploring difficulties.

- For men, all touching is sexual and should lead to sex.
  Actually touching fulfills other purposes as well; we all need to be hugged or held from time to time.

- Sex is not something to be discussed with your partner. In spite of how openly it is presented in the media, sex is often regarded as a private affair and not to be discussed.
  Actually, intimate communication for a man should be more than just having

---

[67]Butler and Joyce (1998: 117–121).
[68]Hawton (1989: 381).

sex; sex needs to be talked about, as with any other important subject. For example, each should find out how the other likes to be touched and stimulated, and be able to suggest changes that they would like to happen. The principle of taking responsibility for one's own sexual pleasure is important.

- Sex should be spontaneous, with no planning and no talking, so that asking for it can spoil it.
  In fact, sexual concerns need to be expressed openly and men generally need to be more expressive before, during, and after sex. Sexual activity generally needs to be planned, especially if both partners lead busy lives.

- Men should know all about sex. They may not feel manly if they admit ignorance!

- Men must initiate sex.

- Performance is what counts for a real man.

- All gay men are promiscuous.

- Women's sexual feelings are not as strong as men's.
  In fact, a woman's clitoris contains as many nerves as the head of a man's penis, but in a much smaller area, so her feelings can be just as strong.

- Men are always interested in sex and are always ready for it.
  In fact sometimes all they really want is to be hugged (without sex) and either don't realize it or are afraid to ask as it may somehow reflect adversely on their manhood.

- A large penis stimulates more than a small one.
  In fact penis size matters little as the clitoris and outer third of the vagina are the most sensitive areas, and the vagina is like a closed elastic sleeve. Too large an erect penis can cause discomfort for some women.

- You must orgasm together.
  In fact, women's orgasms are more problematic than men's, though women can sometimes have more than one orgasm through manual stimulation.

- Sex equals intercourse.
  However, Zilbergeld[69] argues that intercourse should not always be a mandatory part of sex that follows foreplay; there are alternative ways of providing satisfaction. Anxiety about erections can lead to erection problems. He also argues that an emphasis on an erection and intercourse fails to take into account the affect of age, illness, disabilities, medication, last stages of pregnancy, and having recently given birth.[70] He suggests that "making love has to do with feelings rather than specific acts."[71] Our skin is our largest sex organ, especially for a woman, and our mind the most powerful one. Zilbergeld describes how masturbation, whether self or other initiated, can play varied roles in a couple's sexual options.

[69] Zilbergeld (1999: 29–30).
[70] Zilbergeld (1999: 42).
[71] Zilbergeld (1999: 43).

The therapist needs to have permission to explore some of the myths, fantasies, and taboos surrounding sex and the the sex life of a couple so as to make sense of why their sexual relationship is failing. Also, some of a person's earliest sexual memories may be having an impact now on a couple's relationship. Because of cultural expectations, sexual stereotyping, double standards (e.g., female promiscuity seems to be frowned on more than male promiscuity, and a woman should not be known as sexually experienced to avoid negative labels), and the lack of realism in the media and fiction, people often have unrealistic expectations about sex and sexual performance. For example, in contrast to being a woman, it is not enough just to be a male physically, but he has to somehow earn his manhood. A man has to perform sexually, stay erect for a long enough time (with a part of his body he cannot control), and give his partner a wonderful sexual experience; this can lead to stress and anxiety with consequent dysfunction and sexual difficulties. Zilbergeld[72] says that "Good sex is not about using any particular organ, following any particular script, or doing any particular act. Rather, it has to do with the emotions generated by whatever you and your partner do." Pornography can have a very destructive effect on a relationship as it can create unrealistic expectations.[73]

Sexual Dysfunction

There are some sexual dysfunctions that can affect a couple's relationships.[74] For a male there can be erectile failure,[75] where he is unable to obtain or sustain an erection. This inability may have a physiological or psychological basis, or a combination of both. If a man can have an erection at other times, for example, awaking in the night to an erection,[76] then the problem will generally not be due to any kind of abnormal functioning. A high proportion of men will have erection problems at some time in their life (about 50% of men between the ages of 40 and 70) and this fact will help a therapist to "normalize" the problem. It is important to get help with the difficulty as soon a possible, especially to make sure there is no physical problem. Also the partner may feel that he or she is inadequate in some way. However, as mentioned above, a normal process such as aging, or other health effects such as medication (e.g., drugs for blood pressure, some antidepressants, and tranquilizers), long-term smoking, and alcoholism can affect an erection. In fact anything that interferes with blood getting to the penis and staying there, or the nervous system's lack of control over blood flow, can cause erection problems.

Often a reason for failure is psychological, where fear of failure, say on some past occasion, causes anxiety and stress, stress being a major "dampener" on sexual activity. Men generally have concerns about sex and their performance, and there is often a need for them to lower expectations and realize that they can no longer be as sexually responsive as in their youth or younger days. It should be noted that a man can have an orgasm without a full erection. If erections tend to be spasmodic, the man should take note of the time, place, circumstances, and emotions when a problem arises and when things goes smoothly to determine the best conditions

---

[72]Zilbergeld (1999: 38–39).
[73]For further details see Section 14.3.2.
[74]Butler and Joyce (1998: 111–112).
[75]This can be *primary*, when it has always been a problem, or *secondary*, when it is a more recent problem.
[76]From baby to old age, males usually have several erections in the night during dream (REM) sleep.

for sex. He can also obtain permission from his female partner to satisfy her with nonintercourse sex (i.e, without an erection) until he is able to have satisfactory erections. Knowing he can satisfy her in other ways will reduce his anxiety about erections. However she may not be happy with his idea and professional help may be needed from a doctor or sex therapist. A number of procedures and medications are available including drugs like viagara, cialis, and levitra that enhance blood flow and, with arousal, can lead to erections.[77]

Premature ejaculation is a very common male problem (affects about 30% of men) and tends to affect younger men. Its cause is not fully understood and, although it is regarded as mainly a psychological problem, there can be biological factors as well, especially if the problem has been lifelong. A man with an erectile problem may suffer premature ejaculation because he is trying to rush a sexual encounter. Stress can also be a factor. However, the problem is very fixable through appropriate exercises[78] that require cooperation of the partner (e.g., the squeeze and the stop-start methods, and sensate focusing discussed below). A few men have some form of retarded ejaculation when it takes excessively long to occur. This is a more difficult problem to deal with.

For a female there is vaginismus, where penetration (and not just sexual) is impossible because of an involuntary spasm of the muscles surrounding the entry of the vagina. Given there is no underlying physical cause of the problem, it is almost 100% treatable without drugs.[79] Dyspareunia is a similar problem, where penetration is possible but painful, and often is due to a physical rather than a psychological problem.[80]

Finally, a common problem for a female is orgasmic dysfunction (anorgasmia) in which there is never an orgasm. This so-called primary dysfunction affects perhaps 10–15% of women.[81] If orgasms are not happening now but happened in the past, this is called secondary dysfunction. About 33% to 50% of women experience orgasm infrequently and are dissatisfied with how often they reach orgasm.[82] One problem is that orgasms are not always felt; one recommendation is to breath out when it seems to be coming.[83] Oral contraceptives can have an affect on a woman's libido.

Anxiety about performance is believed to be the most common psychological cause of orgasm problems. Negative attitudes towards sex from childhood experiences and past abuse, as well as trying too hard, can exacerbate the problem. As mentioned above, most women require clitoral stimulation to reach an orgasm and incorporating this into sexual activity may be all that is needed. As with men, some drugs (e.g., some antidepressants, high blood pressure medications, and alcohol), depression, and stress can impair orgasmic responsiveness. Learning about one's self and arousal patterns can be done through masturbation and various couple exercises. A very helpful technique for a couple with sexual problems developed by Masters and Johnson is called "sensate focus" that involves various stages of touch-

---

[77]There is plenty of information on the internet under the heading "erectile dysfunction," for example www.mayoclinic.com/health/erectile-dysfunction/DS00162 (accessed October 2010).
[78]See, for example Zilbergeld (1999: chapter 20).
[79]See, for example, www.vaginismus.com (accessed October 2010).
[80]Heim (2001), available at http://www.aafp.org/afp/20010415/1535.html.
[81]The statistics vary widely.
[82]http://www.nlm.nih.gov/medlineplus/ency/article/001953.htm (accessed October 2010).
[83]See http://www.kadir-buxton.com/page10.htm (accessed October 2010).

ing, both individual and mutual.[84] For the toucher, the focus in on sensations of touch, and initially breast and genitals are avoided. In conclusion, the most effective treatment for sexual problems is in establishing a close emotional relationship with one's partner.

19.5 COUNSELING STRUCTURE

19.5.1 Some General Principles

Set out below are some basic principles of couple counseling.[85]

1. *Establish a good therapist/client relationship.* Both partners need to feel comfortable with the therapist.

2. *Establish a good information base.* This includes a history of the relationship and relevant previous relationships, relevant health data, any previous counseling, family of origin background and upbringing, expectations, how they communicate, sexual relationship (it may be better or easier to talk to them individually about this at first), and, where appropriate, spiritual interest.

3. *Establish a diagnosis.* However, this will usually only evolve over time as the therapist gets below the surface of what is going on. Sometimes it is more helpful to get a consensus about where they want to be in the future rather than a consensus about the nature of the problem.

4. *Establish a contract to work.* The therapist's task is to help the couple define what is wrong with their relationship and what they wish to do about it. Some provisos may need to be put in place such as both parties having an equal right to be heard, and put-downs and destructive criticism being totally unacceptable. Homework needs to be done.

The RELATE program has a similar structure with corresponding stages of exploration, understanding, and action. Having established some broad principles I now want to look at the counseling process in more detail.

19.5.2 Setting the Scene

When the first session is with the couple rather than individuals, Bubenzer and West[86] give an outline of how the counseling program might proceed based on ideas from Haley's strategic family therapy, Minuchin's structural therapy and de Shazer's brief therapy. They use Haley's five stages for conducting the first session, namely the social stage, the problem stage, the interaction stage, the stage for defining the desired changes, and the stage involved with ending the interview; a similar pattern can be used for subsequent sessions.

In the initial telephone contact, the therapist can mention that it is preferable to see them together, that the first couple of sessions will be spent getting to know

[84]See Hawton (1989) and internet references such as http://healthguide.howstuffworks.com/sensate-focus-dictionary.htm (accessed October 2010).
[85]From Sturt and Sturt (1988: 17–19).
[86]Bubenzer and West (1993: chapter 3).

them and their concerns, and at some stage they could be asked to contract for a certain number of sessions. However, determining even a minimal number may be difficult if one or both of the partners is a reluctant participant so that initially the contract may be only from one to week to the next. Hendrix suggests at least twelve sessions as the majority tend to quit somewhere between the third and fifth sessions.[87] He says that this is about the time it takes for unconscious issues to begin to emerge and for people to begin to experience some anxiety that they want to avoid. The RELATE program usually has between six and sixteen sessions, and even a single session can greatly relieve stress.[88] Clearly there is no hard and fast rule for the optimum number of sessions as each couple's problems are unique. However, it is important that the couple at least stays together for a certain number sessions. It is deflating for the therapist to be told in the second session that the couple has separated; very little can be practiced or worked on when they are apart unless both are willing to work on issues separately with a view to joint sessions, if this can be achieved.

Since a presenting problem is often not the real problem, contracting in blocks of sessions may be more appropriate.[89] In any case it is important not to rush the counseling process or overwhelm the couple with too many things to do or practice. At the same time the importance of homework should be stressed. Ideally, the homework should contain at least one of two ingredients, a thinking part and/or a doing part.[90]

19.5.3   First Session

The counselor can begin the session by briefly describing what he or she knows from the initial phone call. The social stage, with its initial introductions, is more "lighthearted" and is aimed at putting the couple at ease. It is a time for finding about each partner such as what they do for work or recreation, any children they have, the existence of medical conditions and medications, any previous counseling, and so forth. At this point, a little self-disclosure might be helpful if related to what the couple does. Also, a genogram (family tree) could be started as the therapist picks up odd background items of information, though one would not normally discuss the genogram at this stage. Body language, tone of voice, any negative self messages, and black and white thinking related to words like "must," "always," and "never," and so forth, will often give some early clues about couple dynamics.

At the problem stage, each partner is asked to clearly describe what they see as the presenting problem perhaps without too much elaboration at this point. It could be helpful to find out why they have come for counseling now and not some other time (e.g., because of family life-cycle events). Generally, neither partner should talk for too long as the other partner may feel left out and suspect collusion. It is up to the therapist to try and maintain some sort of balance, though sometimes one partner is happy to let the other partner do most of the talking. When I am counseling a heterosexual couple I am aware that there are two men and one woman in the room, so I have to ensure that the woman feels comfortable

[87]Hendrix (2001: 201).
[88]Butler and Joyce (1998: 8,15).
[89]Butler and Joyce (1998: 48.
[90]Bubenzer and West (1993: 116).

and not "overwhelmed." It is important for the therapist to keep an eye on the listening partner to note any reaction to what is being recounted, for example, raised eyebrows or rolled eyes, and perhaps ask about this later.

Some questions that might be asked of the couple are: "What do you think is wrong?", "When did you notice your problem started?", "What have you done to try and fix it and how successful has that been?", and "What are the good bits about your marriage?" It is always helpful to focus on the positive in couple counseling rather than focus on alleviating the negatives. As Epstein and Beaucom[91] note, "Unfortunately much less emphasis has been placed on increasing positive behavior, positive cognitions, and positive emotions ....A decrease in ... negative behavior does not necessarily lead to an increase in positive behavior."

After the honeymoon is over there is often a decrease in positive behaviors rather than an increase in negative ones. A helpful question might be, "What positive things does the relationship bring out in you?" Reminiscing together about positive events from their past can be helpful for a couple. I also believe that trying to encourage hope should be a key ingredient in couple counseling. With regard to the health of the marriage, some therapists use various self-report questionnaires to assess this.[92]

With the interaction stage, the counselor directs the couple to interact with the aim of demonstrating how the couple deal with or handle their problems. For example, if there is conflict in their relationship the counsellor may ask them to discuss and try and resolve some specific and contentious issue. The counsellor can then look for behavioral patterns as well as "listening for a possible third person, activity, or illness that has been triangled into the relationship,"[93] and also listen for "I" and "you" statements. Reddrop and Reddrop[94] describe a useful model (schema) of dyadic response called *circular interaction* in which A affects B and then B affects A, and the cycle is repeated or escalates. Examples given are criticizing/protesting, accusing/avoiding, and correcting/placating. Here the emphasis is not on what an argument is about but rather what default position is taken up when arguing. For example, we can have a situation when A wants B to respond in some way but B backs away, which makes A try harder and B shut down even more. Sometimes A and B both struggle for control, especially if both parties have had little control of their lives previously or bring into the couple relationship unhealthy convictions about control itself. In assessing the pattern, the therapist initially keeps to a behavior description rather than looking for underlying motives. Body language and how they sit relative to each other can also play a role in this assessment. Individual partners and couples have a tendency to repeat the same, or nearly identical behavior across time. For example, he sits down and reads the paper when he comes home after work, and when they argue they don't listen but repeatedly interrupt each other.

An important part of assessment is to determine any distancing patterns of the couple. Epstein and Beaucom[95] describe four inappropriate patterns of interaction,

[91]Epstein and Beaucom (2002: 19).
[92]For example, the Marital Adjustment Test of Locke and Wallace (1959), which still has relevance (e.g., Freeston and Plechaty (1997). See also Epstein and Beaucom (2002: chapter 7).
[93]Bubenzer and West (1993: 35).
[94]Reddrop and Reddrop (1995: chapter 4).
[95]Epstein and Beaucom (2002: 404).

namely mutual attack, demand-withdrawal (one pursues and the other withdraws—the most common), mutual withdrawal (reciprocal distancing to avoid clashes), and unilateral or mutual disengagement (no impact on each other).

In defining the "desired changes" stage, the therapist endeavors to find agreement on the goals of counseling for the couple, for example, reducing some problem behavior and possibly increasing some desired behavior. It is always a good idea to close a session with some kind of homework even if it is just asking them to observe what things about their relationship they would like to continue, thus giving a positive focus. In the case of circular interaction they can be encouraged to notice when they engage these behaviors; he points out to her when *he* is doing it, and vice versa, thus helping to create self-awareness. It is helpful to ask questions like what happens and how, when, and where it happens. If there are several problems, and this is often the case, they need to be prioritized by mutual agreement.

19.5.4   Other Sessions

A number of things can be done in the second session. For example, the couple can be asked for further information about themselves and their extended family. In the latter case the information can initially be collected using a genogram as a focal point. Information about current social relationships outside the extended family can be added along with any individual information about past histories such as any previous or ongoing counseling, past medical conditions, and the existence of any legal proceedings. After discussing the homework, the therapist can explore the feelings and the beliefs behind the behaviors. Either then or in later sessions the context as well as the circular behavior can be considered so that a diagnosis can be made. The first two sessions might be regarded as the *exploratory stage* of the RELATE program.

Using a similar pattern to that used in the first session, an "easing in" social stage in the following sessions allows the couple to talk about their social experiences during the previous week and provides an opportunity for the therapist to join in, perhaps with some brief self-disclosure from the therapist to help create empathy. In reviewing the presenting problem, the therapist can ask the couple to individually report to the therapist (rather than to each other) on how the week went. Here the focus can be on the positive aspects of their interaction with the highlighting of any exceptions to the usual dysfunctional interaction. Also any homework can be checked up on. If the homework is not done, then Bubinger and West, following suggestions from Haley, propose several approaches: the therapist may wish to express regret over a lost opportunity and even suggest that he or she misunderstood their desire to resolve the problem, or else ask whether they should slow down the process of working towards change. When the couple have had a good week it is helpful to find out from each partner what was happening that made a difference rather than focusing on any negative aspects, as mentioned above.

If things didn't go well, then the couple can be invited to interact again on a chosen topic with the therapist highlighting any inappropriate communication. If the therapist suspects that things might become heated in a particular counseling session, he or she should initially have asked permission of both parties to interrupt at any stage. Sometimes just by saying, "Remember you have given me permission" may be enough to get things back on course. However, allowing a discussion to become a little heated can give the therapist some real insight as to couple dynamics. Weeks and Treat maintain that managing the intensity of the couple interaction through appropriate intervention is an important part of the therapy and say that, "Too much emotional energy can create destructive dynamics and enmeshment. Too little energy can prevent change, behavioral application of new ideas, and couple intimacy."[96]

Early on in the counseling process it can helpful to ask the couple how they met and what attracted them to each other. I find that this can encourage feelings of warmth and a rejoining in a shared memory, which can be used later. Byng-Hall says that it is a powerful method of joining with the couple "through the emotional experience of telling and being told what is likely to be their most moving story."[97]

Visiting the genogram together is usually a fruitful exercise as many things about the couple's current interaction can often be linked to family of origin behavior. It can be helpful to find out which stories have been told repeatedly as they enshrine family rules about how things should be done now. It is also helpful to ask for stories about how people got on with each other rather than about individual characteristics. This "generates information about interaction that is in the same mode as the therapy in the room."[98]

The above models can provide the therapist with some ideas for the *assessment stage* leading into the final *action stage*. The RELATE program focuses on the therapist encouraging the couple to challenge each other's behaviors, questioning unacknowledged strong family beliefs, and facing up to discrepancies in their verbal and non-verbal language.[99] For example, "Although my face is red and steam is coming out of my ears I am not angry, just very positive!" The therapist can also challenge any self-defeating thinking.

Reframing is another useful tool. Couples often label their partner's behavior in a derogatory manner so that a relabeling by the therapist can encourage hope, for example, labels like withdrawn (thoughtful, cautious), passive (accepting), angry (involved), stubborn (steadfast, stable, committed), oversensitive (aware), insensitive (protecting oneself), critical (forthright), and immature (fun-loving), with the relabels in brackets.[100] When viewing the couple as a system, a problem can sometimes be reframed as belonging to the couple rather the individual. The idea of reframing is not a question of restating the truth but rather giving a different viewpoint that is more conducive for change to occur. For example, a couple who are always fighting can be told that they must care a lot about each other to invest so much time and energy into fighting, and a new narrative can be constructed about how this energy might be used more fruitfully. One can argue that the opposite of love is not hate but apathy. Another example is that a wife's insomnia protects their relationship as she does not have enough energy to get angry and he cannot tolerate anger. For a literature review and further couple examples about reframing see Weeks and L'Abate (1982).

[96]Weeks and Treat (1992: 86).
[97]Byng-Hall (1985: 5).
[98]Byng-Hall (1985: 10).
[99]Butler and Joyce (1998: 82).
[100]Bubenzer and West (1993: 63).

When endeavoring to bring about behavior modification or change, a lot of patience is needed because behavior patterns may have been imprinted for many years. Generally the therapist will try and maintain a balance by indicating how each member of the couple has contributed to the problem. However, the therapist may need to unbalance the couple system by shifting the position of one of the partners to break the pattern (e.g., stop behaving in a certain way). As mentioned above, there needs to be an agreement of the changes the couple wanted, and these changes need to be specific, achievable, and observable, sometimes requiring compromise to be achieved. For example, never to go the pub again may be unrealistic, but the time spent there needs to be discussed and revised. The broad abstract ideas of change need to be broken down into smaller realistic ideas,[101] and each partner should be asked to do an equal amount of work.

19.5.5   Some Dos and Don'ts of Evaluation

Using Weeks and Treat[102] as a focus, I have pulled together a check list from the above discussion for the therapist's evaluation stage.

We should avoid taking sides. We are there for both of them and need to keep them both on our side by not focusing too much on one partner or making one of them feeling more uncomfortable. When one partner makes a negative statement about the other partner, my favorite response is "So your perception is that ...," thus avoiding collusion. The couple system needs to be kept balanced as we want them both to come back again! This balance should also be reflected in the seating arrangement and in the amount of eye contact. However, sometimes the response is not equal from both of them, for example, she may share her feelings more freely or he might not be forthcoming in taking some responsibility for the negative communication, and some mild confrontation might be appropriate.

We should take our time. This means having as much data as possible and having an understanding of the couple system (e.g., the nature of the circular interaction described above) before trying to change it. We should avoid premature interpretations.

All problems are important, even small ones. By not minimizing problems and listening carefully, we can encourage the couple to open up to deeper issues later, especially if those issues are sensitive or embarrassing to the couple (e.g., abuse, sexual problems).

Abstract problems should be made concrete. Problems presented abstractly or nonspecifically such as "He doesn't listen" or "She is always nagging" need to be turned into concrete examples by asking who, when, what, and how questions.

Be aware that their perceptions of the problem will differ. This is why they have come to counseling. We need to give them permission to express their differences and to help them understand why partners see things as they do.

---

[101] Butler and Joyce (1998: 87).
[102] Weeks and Treat (1992: 4–8). This book has very useful material for a beginning therapist that also applies to individual counseling.

We need to prevent an escalation of differences and emotions. More emotional and controversial issues can be dealt with at a later session.

Avoid letting the couple tell long stories. Couples should be encouraged to get to the point rather than wasting a lot of time in giving every single detail.

Stay in charge of the process. This is tricky at the beginning of the counseling as some couples can be very controlling and the therapist does not want to appear too rigid or controlling.

Avoid being hung up on the past. There is a danger that the couple may play the same old cracked record over and over again. They will if they can't process the issue to some resolution.

Avoid getting hooked into a partner's theories or explanations. A helpful question is, "What is your theory about the problem?" thus not giving the theory the status of absolute truth.

Avoid answering questions from the couple until ready. This refers to those "loaded" questions from a partner which indirectly relate to the other partner and which, for example, encourage the therapist to take sides. The question can be reflected back for an opinion, or responded to by a "don't know at this stage" answer.

Problems and goals need to be clarified before moving on. Part of this is to decide what to work on first.

19.6 COUPLE COMMUNICATION SKILLS

There are three key areas where there is often a communication breakdown. The first is not listening. The second is what I call "mind reading" or "second guessing" where one party makes an assumption about his or her partner's communication based on incomplete information (e.g., body language, though there may be a contradiction in verbal and non-verbal messages). The third is a failure to share feelings. We can also add inflexibility in problem solving and a lack of mutual empathy.

Patterns of communication often get passed down from a family of origin and this aspect can be explored. A serious communication breakdown needs a commitment of time, close contact, some eye contact, freedom from distraction (e.g., from TV or the children), and should be planned (e.g., make a date). Communication skills involve both speaking and listening, and for convenience I have separated these two interconnected skills in the following discussion.

Bolton[103] lists 12 barriers to communication grouped in three categories, namely:

1. *Judging.* For example criticizing, name-calling, labeling, diagnosing (e.g., "You did this because . . .," a form of labeling), and praising evaluatively (e.g. not all praise is helpful, for example, when it is used in a manipulative way).

[103]Bolton (1987: 17).

2. *Sending solutions.* For example, ordering, threatening, moralizing (e.g, "It's the right thing to do"), and excessive/inappropriate questioning.

3 *Avoiding the other's concerns.* For example, diverting (e.g., changing the subject), logical argument (e.g., appealing to facts without considering emotional implications; "If you hadn't done this then ….."), and reassuring (e.g., not allowing the person to feel the negative emotion being experienced).

Some of the above can be appropriate.

19.6.1   Conversing

When a couple won't listen to each other, the following simple exercise called "mirroring" can be used to promote listening. The couple decide on a "neutral" topic to discuss that is not too controversial or too demanding emotionally, for example, a movie that they saw recently, or what their day was like. When one of them, A say, holds a certain object (e.g., a pen) he or she holds the floor. In a few sentences A describes what he or she feels about the topic, then says to B "What can you hear me saying?"; B then has to reflect back or paraphrase what was said. At the end, A corrects or adds anything missing, then hands the object to B, who goes through the same process, and so on. The key is to keep the communication reasonably short at first so that memories are not strained! It is not a memory test but a listening practice. After some practice, a more emotional topic could be discussed, for example, talk about some marital problem or future goals.

Another variation of the above[104] is to have a dialogue with a sharing of feelings rather than ideas. A topic is chosen, for example disciplining the children. Person A focuses on himself or herself concerning what A wants or how A feels rather than on what other person B does or does not do, and talks for say three minutes.[105] The task of B as listener is two-fold: firstly, find out as much as possible about A's views and feelings on the topic by asking questions, and secondly summarize at the end what A said and what B thought A felt. After A's input about anything left out, the roles are reversed. The therapist can observe the dialogue and, as a coach, provide feedback to the couple about how clearly thoughts and feelings were expressed and how well the recipient listened. They can be encouraged to keep focused on the topic without sidetracking, and to make clear statements.

The above kind of dialogue can be carried out by the couple at home on a regular basis; delicate topics can be raised there in privacy. For example, if sex is an issue, then the dialogue can focus on family of origin background and the couple's experiences together. Each person can share what their sex education (or lack of it) was like, what attitudes were passed on by their parents about sex (e.g., any taboos), how nakedness was viewed, and how much physical touch and expressions of love were observed between parents and received from the parents. Concerning the couple, each partner can say what their needs are in love making, what they think their partner's needs are, things that turn them on and turn them off, how they respond to a "no" from their partner, and what barriers interfere with

---

[104]Bubenzer and West (1993: 51–52).
[105]Some visual timer such as an egg-timer or miniature hour-glass can provide some fun.

love making.[106] The couple may or may not want to share the outcome of such a dialogue with the therapist.

One of the games a couple often plays is the "blame game" where each accuses the other for causing the problems in their relationship. A useful exercise is for each person to carefully answer the question, "What would it be like to be married to me?"[107] This enables each person to identify and accept their own responsibility for the problems in a way that couldn't have been done when accusations were flying around! Such disclosure and being vulnerable encourages trust in the relationship, which is often missing. It also engenders hope and motivation for change.

A variation of "holding the floor" can be used in a family setting. A family has a "family night" where each member including the children takes a turn at holding the object (e.g., a salt shaker; [108] this entitles them to hold the floor and say their piece without interruption before passing the object on. This approach can be used with just the couple, without any mirroring.

In communicating with each other it is important that the couple use "I" statements instead of "you" statements. For example, in the stereotypical case of a nagging wife, she would say, "You always ..." or "You never ...," and the husband sees this as nagging or attacking and switches off his attention. It would be more productive if she were to say, "I get angry when you continually ...."

19.6.2   Art of Listening

Men are not usually very good at listening to their wives, especially as women generally like to talk more than men.[109] Men and women also differ in the way they communicate, especially with regard to problems. Although women are usually more self-disclosing than men, both in their own way will share their problems and worries with their partners. Unfortunately they tend to interpret the other partner's needs in different ways.[110] Many women, to create empathy, will offer help to their partners by expressing sympathy and sharing examples of their similar experiences. In contrast men are more likely to help by offering practical solutions to the problem. Women want to nurture while the men want to fix. Both approaches, although caring, usually don't go down too well! A woman can interpret his response as a lack of connectedness while he can interpret her response as a devaluation of the relationship.

An interview with Dr John Gray[111] provides the following very useful strategies for male-female interaction, specially with regard to problem solving. Gray says that "Brain chemistry is at the heart of our relationships," and when people are mildly upset a woman experiences in her emotional system "a reaction eight times as great a a man's." He notes that women have a hormone oxytocin that is stimulated with compliments, flowers, being listened to, and so on, while men have the hormone testosterone[112] that is stimulated by, for example, action, goals, and

---

[106]Sturt and Sturt (1988: 59).
[107]Bubenzer and West (1993: 53).
[108]On a maori marae (New Zealand tribal meeting place) a carved tokotoko stick held by the speaker gives him the right of public announcement.
[109]It has been suggested five times as much.
[110]Tannen (1990).
[111]Grant (2004: 66–68).
[112]Ten to twenty times as much as women have.

problem solving. Both feel better when their respective levels are increased. For many women it helps them to relax and lower stress levels. Men on the other hand feel energized. When communicating, "Women are always trying to feminize men: to get them to talk, share their feelings, cuddle and co-operate. Most men actually like to do these things but, according to Gray, it does lower their testosterone levels."

When a women has a problem she wants to talk about it as this actually brings her emotional release, while a man quickly wants to solve it. When she talks about a problem (frequently with other women), serotonin is released allowing her emotional system to calm down after being disturbed by the problem. She can then relax and feel more feel comfortable in assessing the problem and working towards a solution. Sometimes she may not be clear as to what is bothering her and by talking about it she begins to understand the nature of the problem. When men have a problem, any communication about it is for gathering information so they can mull over it and then take appropriate action. So when a woman talks to a man about a problem she does not want him to jump in and try solve it; she wants him to listen and share, perhaps ask questions, and empathize with her by acknowledging and reflecting on her emotions. She is getting her serotonin! If she later wants some help with a solution or suggestion, she will simply ask for help. Normally the man would either get frustrated because of lack of a solution or not listen to avoid discomfort, with a consequent drop in his testosterone levels. However, if he realizes that he is doing something productive by listening, his testosterone levels won't drop and we can have a win-win situation. Gray points out that women in the workplace often have to take on testosterone boosting roles (e.g., be competitive and take risks) that cause them stress. They may need listening to even more so when they get home from work.

It is particularly important for a man to listen and stay with a woman when she is angry with him or complaining. In this situation it is vital for her to be heard and essential that the man does not shut down or walk away. It will actually encourage her to be more accepting of him if she knows he is really listening. He needs to address the issues if he can, agree with her when he can, be prepared to ask what she means if necessary, and then decide with her what together they can do about it. Nagging tends to occur when a woman feels she is not being heard and the man does not open up. If appropriate, he needs to quickly apologize once he accepts what has happened. This involves[113] expressing sincere regret, accepting responsibility, making restitution through her love language, genuinely repenting and setting goals for change, and actually asking for forgiveness. The danger with Gray's thesis is that it runs close to gender stereotyping, but in general has added helpfully to the literature.

I find it helpful to explain to men (and women) the following basics of listening, especially identifying feeling words:

- reduce environmental distractions to the minimum (e.g., turn off the TV or stereo at home)

- give full attention, with appropriate eye contact and not doing other things while listening

---

[113]Chapman and Thomas (2006).

- adopt an appropriate posture (e.g., facing squarely and inclining toward the speaker; being at an appropriate distance from the speaker, say three feet or a meter; and maintaining an open position with arms and legs uncrossed)

- listen for feeling words

- refuse to interrupt

- respond with minimal encouragers (e.g., yes, okay, uh huh)

- using reflective phrases, for example, "I had a hard day so I felt terrible when I got home after fighting the traffic" is reflected as "So you felt terrible when you got home"

- use paraphrases (saying the same thing but in different words)

- being aware of when using open or closed questions (with not too many questions)

- periodically give a summary (a brief summary of what has been said tells the speaker that he or she is being heard)

- observe body language (e.g, clenched fists, trembling hands, tears, furrowed brows, and eye movement) and check that it is giving the same message as the words; ask for clarification if uncertain (a very high proportion of communication is through body language, and tone and volume of voice, with about 7% just through the words themselves)

- use a perception check (related to the previous one) using phrases like "You sound discouraged" or "You look a bit anxious"

- focus on the speaker's chosen metaphor without adding one's own interpretation[114]

- use attentive silence

- express understanding

- ask if there is anything you might do

Closed questions are usually unhelpful unless they are fact finding as the answer will usually just be yes or no. Open questions begin with "what," "how," "when," and "where;" for example, "What was it like for you when you...." Such questions encourage further exploring of feelings. Instead of asking "Why did you ...," which can seem confrontational for some people, a gentler approach is to ask, "I wonder why ...." One can also use the art of supposing, such as "I suppose you find it difficult ..." and "I expect you get pretty tired when you ...." For most people direct eye contact is crucially important as it indicates full attention, but others especially from other cultures (e.g. some Maori or Pacific Island communities) may find it invasive. Some people lean forward and even touch during a conversation, while others may find that action both invasive and intrusive.

---

[114]See, for example, the "clean language" concept at http://www.cleanlanguage.co.uk/ (accessed October 2010).

Weeks and Treat give two other aspects of effective listening.[115] The first is the need to distinguish between intent and effect. For example, he may feel upset by what she says because of his baggage from the past or a misunderstanding even though it was not her intent to upset him—exemplifying mind reading. I find this frequently happens. Cognitive therapy can be used here to determine his belief and then challenge it with a more helpful counter belief. The second aspect is encouraging the couple to adopt the following three assumptions:

1. The assumption of commitment (i.e. the couple are committed to each other and to therapy).

2. The assumption of good will and intent (i.e., recognizing the difference between intent and effect).

3. The assumption of understanding (i.e., hang in there even if the communication is muddled).

19.6.3   Feelings Contract

To improve communication, the therapist can introduce a four-part "feelings" contract.[116]

(a) *I will own my feelings.* This means openly identifying, acknowledging, and accepting responsibility for them.

(b) *I will share my feelings with you.* This will be done in an honest and caring way.

(c) *I will not hurt you with my feelings.* This may need some discussion with the couple as to what "hurtful" might mean.

(d) *I will ask you to help me with my feelings.* This means serious listening to my feelings without trying to change them, and accepting that they are real and significant to me.

19.6.4   Conflict and Disagreement

Some Gender Differences

Poor communication is usually present when any of us are angry or in disagreement. It is important to remember that men and woman generally deal with conflict differently.[117] Most men tend to become more stressed so that the pulse rate goes up, and during a tense exchange may find her criticism provocative and even overwhelming. However, she may merely see such exchanges as potentially increasing love between them so her pulse stays the same. Unfortunately, he may see the exchange as an argument in which he is apt to lose control of the situation and also lose some self-respect. In an attempt to calm himself down he may "stonewall" by going quiet or moving away. She may see this as unloving abandonment while he

[115]Weeks and Treat (1992: 128–130.
[116]Sturt and Sturt (1998: 152).
[117]Eggerichs (2004: 60).

loes not, as it is his way of trying not to react or escalate the conflict. Apparently about 85%[118] of men stonewall their partners during conflicts, which leads to them stepping up the complaining so that he shuts down even more. She needs to be less confrontational and he needs to listen longer, hang in there, and not shut down or disconnect.

Common Strategies

Some common strategies that people use for handling conflict are as follows:[119]

- avoidance

- giving in

- passive-aggressiveness

- bullying

- problem solving

- honor (giving the other person what they want because it pleases you to please them)

Using a positive problem solving approach, a number of steps are available for a couple to achieve resolution of their disagreements. The initial step is for them to first define the issue so that they know what they are arguing about and then agree to discuss that specific problem. When there is more than one issue, focussing on one issue at a time will prevent disruptive hopping from one subject to another. If the situation is feeling quite unmanageable, it would be best to postpone the discussion and agree to address it at a set time later. One way of dealing with disagreement is to use the method of mirroring or reflecting described above, which is best done in two steps. In this first step it is important to get all the feelings out and understand how your partner is feeling. The second step is then to work on solutions listing *all* ideas and not just the ones that you think will work best. Eliminate those that you both decide won't work and choose the ideas that might work and that you can both live with. If none of them work, agree to do some more research and agree to revisit the topic again within, say, 48 hours. It is important to realize that conflict can be positive if dealt with appropriately, as it enables the couple to redress any wrongs and to process unresolved tensions or anxieties.

Dos and Don'ts with Disagreements

Some general dos and don'ts for handling disagreements are given below.

- Discuss issues as soon as possible (after you have both cooled down!), otherwise your partner will suspect that you have been saving them up to use as weapons.

- Choose a good time and an appropriate place, where undisturbed. It is best not to argue in the bedroom, as the bedroom should be associated with rest and intimacy, not arguments.

[18]Gottman (1994).
[19]Ursiny (2003).

- Remain seated and maintain eye contact without glaring at each other.

- Let small and borderline things go. Important issues and feelings are what you are concerned with. Stick to the subject in hand.

- Attack the issue, never the person. Don't play the blame game and avoid cheap sarcasm or put downs.

- Don't expect to get it all your own way. Agreement usually requires some compromise, so go for a win-win situation.

- Agree that either can call time-out if things are getting out of hand.

- Admit mistakes and allow for simple misunderstandings.

- Utilize each other's decision-making strengths.

- Equal say is always the desired process in a mature relationship.

- Don't assume that you know what your partner is thinking or prejudge how he or she will react until you have checked out the whole issue in plain language.

- Don't put labels on your partner or make sweeping judgements about the authenticity of partner's feelings or opinions.

- Always give your partner the benefit of the doubt—trust until it hurts.

- A genuine apology or honest explanation should be wholeheartedly accepted. The incident ideally should then be forgiven for all times.

- Be sure you are influenced by all the facts and not simply by your feelings or needs of the moment.

- Be prepared to fail at all times because that's human! The important thing is to carry on accepting this imperfect humanity after you have slipped. Start again from scratch the next day and try not to fail again.

- Understand that many issues cannot be completely resolved. Differences are deeply rooted in personality and personal histories, and some issues that cause discomfort may need to be accepted.

Anger

If anger triggers the conflict then the couple needs to understand the nature of anger and its role. Both couple and family-of-origin history will help reveal attitudes and beliefs about anger. For example, being brought up in a family where parents did not control their anger or simply denied it will have a profound affect.

Criticism

In many situations the original source of the conflict can be deep-seated, for example where one partner has a narcissistic personality and splits off an unacceptable part of self that gets projected onto the other person. The projector then attempts to get rid of this "projected" behavior perceived to be in his or her partner's problem all along! This leads to conflict. This type of problem requires in-depth therapy. However, the concept of projection does have a huge bearing on the handling of criticism. A couple needs to know how to handle criticism. It can be constructive or destructive, and they need to be able to recognize the difference. Hendrix introduces the following psychological principles:[120]

1. Most of your partner's criticisms of you have some basis in reality. By accepting an element of truth in the criticisms instead of getting defensive, there is the possibility for future growth and change.

2. Many of your repetitious, emotional criticisms of your partner are disguised statements of your own unmet needs. To learn from this there is a need to examine thoughts, feelings, and childhood memories when faced with the criticism in order to uncover childhood wounds.

3. Some of your repetitious, emotional criticisms of your partner may be an accurate description of a disowned part of yourself. There may be a need to separate your own negative traits from those of your partner and withdraw your projections.

4. Some of your criticisms of your partner may help you identify your lost self. There may be something you see in your partner that you would like in your own life.

These ideas also relate to the splitting and projection model described above in Section 19.2.2.

19.6.5 Love Languages

Adults

We all want to be loved and have a full love tank. However, we all have different love languages, the language by which we give and receive love. One person may see a hug as an expression of love while another may see the making of a cup of tea as such an expression. If two people have different love languages, this can lead to a lot of misunderstanding. For example, he brings home a bunch of flowers, but what she really wants is time to talk. Chapman (2000) identifies five love languages:

1. *Physical touch.* This includes hugs, kisses, touches, hair stroking, shoulder and back rubs, holding hands (e.g., in the theatre or church), and sitting close. Foreplay and sex are of course part of it, but physical touch as a love language should not be confused with just sex. Sex may well be a physical driving force for men but touch language is more deeply psychological and incorporates non-sexual touching. Hugs are always important especially in a crisis situation.

2. *Words of Affirmation.* This includes compliments, encouragement, and words of appreciation. Compiling and then sharing a list of the good things one likes about the other person is helpful. Aim for a compliment a day. Compliments

---

[120]Hendrix (2001: 137–140); see Section 19.2.3 above concerning repression for the terms "disowned" and "lost".

are even more powerful when expressed in front of a third party, including children.

3. *Quality time.* This includes quality attention with eye contact and not just proximity (i.e., not just watching TV together), quality conversation (which focuses on listening and feelings, as described above), and quality activities together. Mutually compiling a list of things to do together is helpful. Quality time with any children is so important for them to develop their full potential.

4. *Gift Giving.* The act of giving is what really matters regardless of the cost or size of the gift. In fact any visible token of love will give happiness. A very expensive gift may only register as just one gift, and a gift costing nothing may be appreciated just as much. Also, one should not wait for just a special occasion to make a gift. Make a list of things your spouse enjoyed receiving in the past and note anything that caused special interest, for example, "I really like that." The greatest gift is the totally giving of self.

5. *Acts of Service.* This includes simple chores around the house, performed not out of obligation (a doormat mentality) but out of spontaneous kindness. It is important to know which chores are important for the love tank as a couple with this same love language can clash because of different priorities. It may need one to step out of the typical (cultural) gender role from time to time, for example, he washes the diapers (nappies) while she cleans the car. Doing humble chores can count for a lot for those whose love language is acts of this sort.

A brief description of these love languages is given on the internet.[121] We usually have a mixture of love languages and a more detailed questionnaire is available that will give an automated response.[122] A clue about a person's love language can be indicated by any criticisms of his or her partner's behavior, for example, "She always has the house in a mess" or "He is always watching TV and never talks to me." As Chapman comments, "People tend to criticize the spouse most loudly in the area where they themselves have the deepest emotional need. Their criticism is an ineffective way of pleading for love."[123]

Some people feel that they have fallen out of love when in fact their love tank is simply empty. So often what draws a couple together initially (e.g., when courting) is because they both make an effort at the time and each feels that his or her love tank is being kept full. However, after a while they begin to take each other for granted and their love tanks begin to empty. Ultimately, feeling in love is an act of will.

I have personally found the love languages questionnaire to be a very useful tool helping couples to understand and communicate with each other much better. Once they know their partner's particular love languages, they can focus on communicating through those languages. Initially a partner may not feel like doing this as such behavior may feel "foreign." However, resistance can generally be avoided by

---

[121] See http://www.fivelovelanguages.com (accessed October 2010), which also has a brief questionnaire that just picks out the most predominant language.
[122] See http://www.clickalifecoach.com/questionnaire/lovelanguage.aspx (accessed October 2010); a hard copy is given by Chapman (2000: 194–203).
[123] Chapman (2000: 107).

.

asking them to pretend, even if they don't feel like it, thus acknowledging their feelings yet encouraging a new behavior style in the relationship. It is important for a couple to accept their fundamental differences and recognize that some things cannot be changed because they are deeply rooted in their personalities. Some sacrifice is needed from both parties.

When a couple's relationship is dysfunctional, this usually has a serious "fallout" on any children. It can therefore be helpful for parents in therapy to discover and focus on the love languages of any children, which I now discuss.

Children

It is harder to determine a child's love language—it is usually done by trial and error and careful observation.[124] Every child has an emotional tank that needs to be filled and refilled with unconditional love, and then it is possible to train and discipline the child. Children raised with conditional love learn unfortunately to love only conditionally themselves. If the child's response to a parent's question "Do you feel that I love you?" is sometimes "no", then this needs to be explored.

Although children may have their own special love language, they need some of the others as well. For example, all children need to be touched and held. Boys may prefer vigorous contact, while preadolescence girls especially need various expressions of love from their fathers. Children need to be affirmed when they are seen doing something good, and each child needs individual focused attention irrespective of whether he or she is pleasing the parents or not. Positive eye contact, quality conversations, and helping them to understand their feelings are important. Gifts need to be genuine and not just for services rendered! However, there needs to be a balance in gifts and acts of service as too many of them can lead to self-centeredness and selfishness.

There are several ways one can determine the love languages of children. For example, observe how they express love to others, take note of their most frequent requests and complaints, and take notice of the things with which they are most appreciative. Determine what lights up their candle. We can also give a child two options and see which one they choose (this will be age-dependent), or else focus on each love language for two weeks, with a break in between, to see what happens. Teenagers at times make it difficult for us to fill their emotional tank as they will often just push our boundaries to see if we really love them or because they are bored!

19.6.6   Role of Birth Order

Birth order is defined as a person's rank by age among his or her siblings, and some believe that it has a profound and lasting effect on psychological development. However, as noted in Section 2.5.6, this is a a contentious topic and there is inconsistent evidence of a consistent personality pattern correlating with birth order. A major difficulty is that personality is not yet a well defined concept.[125]

For those who support the idea of a pattern, it is said that firstborn siblings may tend to bear the pressure of the parents' rules and expectations and the parents'

---

[124]My notes on this topic are based on Chapman and Campbell (1997) and Chapman (2000: chapter 13).
[125]See Section 1.3.

projected hopes for continuity and survival. Being an only child and the center of attention for a while, they may resent the arrival of a second child. Bradshaw[126] says that firstborns tend to bear a special relationship with the father and may assume responsibility if he is not fulfilling his role. They may become overly responsible toward their mother to compensate for their father's lack of responsibility, or they may protect their father from their mother's attacks on him.

According to Bradshaw, second-position siblings may try and maintain the family's emotional needs and feel especially responsible for the mother. They may focus on feelings and symbolic meanings, absorb other people's feelings as if they were their own, and have difficulty with ambiguity. He says that third-position children feel responsible for maintaining the quality of the marital relationship. They need to be connected to both parents and their self-esteem is connected to the stability of the marriage. They may also take on the responsibility of all dyadic relationships in the family and feel threatened by interpersonal conflict, which tends to shut them down. Bradshaw also explains how the siblings tend to respond differently to a family secret such as a parent's addiction or some form of abuse.

As far as counseling couples is concerned, all that can be said about birth order is that it may be helpful to keep the idea in the back of one's mind when exploring family of origin backgrounds with each of the couple.

19.7   SOME MISCELLANEOUS INTERVENTIONS

A couple usually comes to counseling with each having very different feelings about the continuation of the relationship. Therefore, as already mentioned above, expressions of hope by the therapist at an appropriate stage and positive motivation towards strengthening the relationship are important ingredients in therapy. This can happen when empathy has been established between the therapist and the couple so that the therapist is not seen as underestimating the couple's problems. Personally I find humor very helpful as long as it is not seen as trivializing the couple's problems. Humor can help to relax the couple and "normalize" what is happening to them both.

Once the pattern of dysfunctional interaction has been established, the aim of the therapist is to destabilize it and suggests ways of altering the pattern.[127] In the case of a complementary relationship, for example one partner becomes more demanding and the other more submissive, tendency to monologues can be interrupted by using mirror listening described above or using a stop watch to equalize talk time. Alternatively, one can encourage the more submissive partner to explore assertiveness without aggression or accepting constantly being controlled. Also the question, "What would it be like married to me?" as described above, can be used. When the relationship is more "symmetrical" and there is a real struggle for unhealthy control, destabilizing can be done through the following.[128]

1. The therapist triangles herself or himself into their arguments so that they talk to the therapist rather than each other and a distance is created between them. As previously mentioned in Section 19.5.4, if that authority can be

[126]Bradshaw (1995: 66).
[127]Bubenzer and West (1993: chapter 6) discuss methods of doing this.
[128]Bubenzer and West (1993: 96, 126, 131).

claimed and actioned the therapist can ask permission at the beginning of a session to intervene at any time.

2. The therapist uses a paradoxical intervention, a useful counseling technique whereby the therapist focuses on the opposite to what the couple want, namely asks them if they really want to give up their familiar pattern of interacting. If they fight, then the therapist can say how important fighting must be to them and asks them to fight at least as much or more so on certain days they decide on, but have the other days free of fighting.

3. The therapist asks the "miracle" question, namely how would they like their relationship to be and how could they achieve this.

4. If one partner is perceived as having wronged the other in the past, some kind of penance can be proposed to achieve "absolution." Forgiveness may also need to be part of this process.

Weeks and Treat[129] refer to dealing with reciprocal patterns of communication that are universal with couples and give an example where one says "I don't like you," and the other replies "I don't like you either," or "I don't care." Here the reply is *reactive*, whereas a *responsive* reply might be "What is it you don't like about me?" The authors suggest that in dealing with the reactive reply the therapist might apply shock treatment and say, "You know I don't like either of you," then immediately ask them to respond. If their reply is "I don't like you either" then tell them it is a reaction and confront them again until there is a responsive reply.

19.8 COUPLE EXERCISES

There are a number of useful exercises gleaned from various sources that a couple can fruitfully engage in either on their own or with a therapist.[130]

1. The aim of this exercise is to find some things that each member of the couple can work on to improve their relationship. John gives the therapist two things that *he* will carry out to improve the relationship; Janet contributes two more for John to do. The roles are then reversed. After discussion, John and Janet then select two from his four and Janet two from her four that they will endeavor to carry out during the next week.

2. The main aim of this exercise is to find out what each member of the couple regards as important in a relationship. Janet and John each draw up a list of what is important to them in a relationship and the therapist then reads out their individual lists, checking with Janet for any omissions from her list, and the same with John. (John and Janet are hearing each other's lists as well as the lists being heard by the therapist.) John then adds an item from Janet's list that he has omitted, and vice versa, thus encouraging some learning about each other. They both score the items on their lists from 1 to 10 according to priority (10 being very important and 1 being not important). They then look at the high scores and John is asked which of Janet's scores are most

---

[129]Weeks and Treat (1992: 66–70).
[130]For example Hendrix (2001) lists 16 helpful exercises that have been tested.

difficult for him. Janet then does the same with John's scores. These two sets
of high scores can then be discussed at perhaps another session. Homework
consists of each person dealing with one thing on his or her partner's list.
An additional activity is for each partner to give scores on the other's list
indicating how difficult it would be them to carry out that item, ten being
the most difficult. I remember with one couple she gave the same scores on
gardening and sex, which caused some hilarity. (Some therapists may prefer
to use a scale of 1 to 5 instead of 1 to 10, similar to the so-called 5-point
Likert scale.)

3. The aim of this exercise is to increase understanding within a couple. The
therapist has two columns on a large sheet of paper (say size A3). Under
John's column, the therapist writes down one item that John believes is important to a relationship and John gives a score of 1 to 10, 10 being most
important. In Janet's column John gives a score on how he believes she scores
on that item. It is now Janet's turn to suggest an item to be written in her
column along with a score and a score for John in his column. The item can
be the same as before or a different one. When the lists are finished they can
be compared.

4. This is a lengthy exercise aimed at each partner finding out the other's deepest
needs and finding ways to fulfill those needs.[131] Janet begins with a list:

I don't like it when you ...

- drive too fast
- criticize me in front of the children
- read the newspaper during dinner, and so forth

On a second sheet of paper Janet writes after each of the above her *desire*, for
example, after the first she might write "I would like to feel safe and relaxed
when driving" followed by a specific *request* "When you are driving, I would
like you to obey the speed limit and drive even more slowly if the conditions
are bad." The request has to be specific (not vague like "Be a safer driver")
and positive ("When you are mad at me I would like you to use a normal
tone of voice" rather than "I would like you to stop yelling at me when you
are upset"). John does the same, lists are shared and desires and requests
are clarified, if necessary. Janet then gives each of her requests a score from
1 to 10, 10 being most important. Lists are exchanged again and John gives
a score for each request on Janet's list describing how difficult he would find
it to carry out the request, with 10 being the most difficult. John keeps
Janet's list and endeavors to fulfill three or four of Janet's easiest requests
each week, irrespective of how he feels and regardless of how many changes
Janet is making. The couple is encouraged to add more items to the lists as
time goes on.

5. The aim of the exercise[132] is to identify and close "exits." Hendrix[133] defines
an exit as "acting out one's feelings rather than putting them into language."

[131]From Hendrix (2001: exercise 12, 272–274).
[132]From Hendrix (2001: exercise 8, 264–267).
[133]Hendrix (2001: 110–113).

The exercise is carried out early in the counseling process and it is based on the idea that a couple can avoid being intimate with each other and avoid putting energy into their relationship by engaging in other activities. Some activities are legitimate, but if one reason for carrying out that activity is to avoid spending time with one's partner, then Hendrix describes that activity as an "exit". A very simple question that can be asked to generate a list of exits is, "What does your partner do to avoid you?" One aim of this exercise is to ensure that a couple stays together during counseling and that they gradually increase their level of intimacy.

The procedure is for Janet to make a list of her exits and then make a second list giving what she perceives to be John's exits. They then share and discuss each other's lists, seeking clarification where necessary; additions can also be made to each list. The mirroring technique described in Section 19.6.1 is helpful here. As an exit is trying to fulfill a need, it is helpful for each partner to explain why a particular exit is needed and the reason for the acting out behavior. Janet then ticks the exits she is willing to eliminate or reduce and puts an "X" beside the ones she finds difficult to change. She then writes out an agreement as to what changes she will make that week to reduce exits. Catastrophic exits like divorce, separation, suicide, violence, or insanity are agreed to be closed at the beginning for a prescribed period.

19.9 BIBLICAL VIEWPOINT

19.9.1 Marriage Model

The Bible has a great deal to say about marriage themes so I will focus on just a few. The role of marriage in the Bible is two-fold, companionship and procreation.[134] A model that has found to be helpful in a secular or religious context for heterosexual relationships is described in the following verse: "For this reason a man will leave his father and mother and be united to his wife and they will become one flesh."[135] There are three key Hebrew words here: "leave" or forsake, which implies a change of loyalty from one person or group to another, unite or "cleave," which generally has no special sexual significance, but rather refers to a closeness, a unity of purpose, or covenant relationship, and one flesh or "weave," which refers mainly to a sexual relationship. The words can also be crudely described as the legal act of leaving home (wedlock), love, and sex.

These three ideas of leave, cleave, and weave form a triangle, which is a stable structure, but if one corner of the triangle is incomplete there are problems with stability. For example, some spouses never really leave the parents (i.e., lack of differentiation) and change their allegiance so that in-laws can play too big a role in a marriage; extended family can dominate one partner's time and priorities. This can happen in cross-cultural or inter-racial marriages where the role of extended families is different for each partner. Another aspect of leaving is that there may be no legal contract with accompanying vows.

[134]Genesis 1:28 and 2:18.
[135]Genesis 2:24.

Other relationships may begin at the sex corner so that there may be inadequate opportunities to really get to know each other before marriage, and real love and unity are missing. The idea is to marry one's best friend rather than just marrying one's lover. Finally, there may be sexual dysfunction or lack of sexual intimacy—a deficiency in the third corner of the triangle. Spouses rarely have equal sexual desire, and not all spouses are sensitive to the sexual desires of the other partner. Wives often have difficulty in keeping up with the sexual needs of their husbands because of their different levels of testosterone. That is why Paul talks about fulfilling one's marital duty and not depriving each other.[136]

19.9.2   What is Love?

These days there is some confusion over the word "love," and a common excuse for separation and divorce is "I have fallen out of love." The meaning of the word love in the New Testament depends on the Greek word used, namely *storge* (friendship), *philia* (family), *eros* (sexual), and *agape* (desiring the best for the other person), which is the meaning of Christian love. For the Christian, this kind of love is an essential ingredient in a marriage. The attributes of love, which also apply to a couple, are spelt out in I Corinthians chapter 13. Another view of love is to build a pyramid from bottom up with the words[137] faith (in the marriage), goodness (a scarce commodity), knowledge (about the marriage), self-control, perseverance, godliness, kindness, and finally love at the top of the pyramid. If we stand the pyramid on its tip with love as the foundation, the pyramid will fall over! Love is actually a choice and a commitment.

19.9.3   Who Is in Charge?

There is one other passage of scripture relating to love in a marriage that has some controversial elements, namely Ephesians 5: 21–33. Verses sometimes used by husbands to justify their behavior are verses 22 and 23 which say that wives should be subject to their husbands, as to the Lord, and the husband is head of the wife. One has to consider the context, namely verse 21. This verse talks about being subject to one another out of reverence for Christ, which, according to the Greek, means mutual submission. Society was such that women at the time were already seen as being in a supposedly submissive role so that verse 22 describes the manner of submission, namely "as to the Lord." Verse 23 then gives a model of the husband-wife relationship, namely the Christ-church relationship, which implies sacrificial love (verse 25) and servanthood.[138] It tells men how to love their wives and it explains what it means for a husband to be first among equals; he must be prepared to die for his wife. Authority brings responsibility. We then have the injunction for a husband to love his wife as his own body (verses 28–29).

The equality in marriage is endorsed by Paul when he says that each partner has authority over the other partner's body;[139] and they are mutually dependent.[140] We also have Paul's general statement that there is no distinction between male

---

[136] 1 Corinthians 7:3–6.
[137] 2 Peter 1: 5–7; my thanks to Brian McStay for this observation.
[138] For example, John 13:12–16, Luke 22:24–27).
[139] 1 Corinthians 7:4.
[140] 1 Corinthians 11:11–12

and female.[141] Other texts (e.g., 1 Peter 3:1–7; fellow-heirs) can be brought into the discussion, but space does not warrant a full-blown theological debate![142]

19.9.4 Love and Respect

We now look more closely at verse 33 of our Ephesians passage that says that husbands must love their wives as themselves and wives must respect their husbands. The two ideas of "love" and " respect" are used by Eggerichs[143] to form the basis of a powerful approach to couple transformation. Women seem to be wired for love and generally understand the idea of unconditional love. However, when they don't get it from their husbands they lose respect for their husbands who, in turn, love their wives less and less, and things spiral downhill. The wife may add that he now has to earn her respect before she will give him any love and, faced with having to provide both love and respect, he shuts down![144] What is interesting is that some surveys suggest that a majority of men would choose being respected over being loved,[145] something that I have found when I have asked my own male clients. Women fear being unloved and show love through respect while men fear being disrespected and held in contempt and show respect through love. In the middle of a conflict, men feel that they are not respected rather than not loved.[146]

If a wife says that she loves her husband but does not respect him, the therapist can ask her how she would feel if her husband said that he respected her but didn't love her. Women may find it very difficult to respect their husbands when the men are behaving badly and may feel that giving respect puts the women in the role of a doormat.[147] They may feel that they cannot give respect if they don't feel respectful and it would be hypocritical to do so. It is helpful if she makes a list of what she respects about him, which may not be easy, and he needs to make a list of the things he loves about her. In the end it comes down to the will so that the husband decides to unconditionally love his wife and his wife decides to give unconditional respect to her husband irrespective of what the other partner decides to do. Forgiveness and being able to say sorry (which is usually harder for men) are important ingredients, and men respond positively to praise (for effort not perfection). If he says something unloving or she says something disrespectful then one response might be to simply say "ouch." Two conversation stoppers are the words "drop it" and "whatever."

The big question is, "Who makes the first move?" Eggerichs'[148] answer is, "the one who sees himself of herself as the most mature." Men need to decode what their wives are telling them, for example, when she is ventilating her pain she may be crying out to be loved. He needs to avoid shutting down and not avoid conflict

---

[141] Galatians 3:28.
[142] The scriptures mentioned clearly provide a basis for a marriage that is free from physical, sexual, and emotional abuse.
[143] Eggerichs (2004).
[144] Eggerichs (2004: 44).
[145] Eggerichs (2004: 49).
[146] Eggerichs (2004: 58).
[147] Giving respect involves neither a "mothering" role nor being a doormat.
[148] Eggerichs (2004: 74).

but to hang in there, listen, and respond with unconditional love. In the the end it is a matter of stepping out in faith.

19.9.5 Adultery

Finally, what about affairs? God hates adultery, as reflected in the seventh commandment,[149] and Jesus extends the concept to adultery in one's heart. We need to be faithful, as God is faithful even if we are unfaithful.[150] There is a warning about the destructiveness of adultery.[151] Jesus forgave a woman caught in the act of adultery.[152]

---

[149] Exodus 20:14.
[150] 2 Timothy 2:13.
[151] Proverbs 2:16–19; 5:3–20; and 6:23–25.
[152] John 8:2–11.

CHAPTER 20

BLENDED FAMILIES

20.1 INTRODUCTION

There is a famous line that says, "The more we are together the happier we shall
be." Unfortunately this does not always happen with blended families. I have
titled this chapter "Blended Families" instead of the usual term of "stepfamilies"
for three reasons. First, there is some disagreement among family scholars over
what constitutes a stepfamily. Second, the term stepfamily has tended to be used
in the past in the more narrow setting, defined by the U.S. census, of remarried
couples who have children (of either spouse or both) from previous marriages that
are under 18 and living in the household. The definition I shall use comes from
Stewart,[1] namely, "A stepfamily results when there is no biological relationship
between one's children and one's serious romantic partner." One reason for this
shift is the increase in the number of women having children outside of marriage.
Today the term "illegitimacy" has lost a lot of its stigma and in the U.S. about one
third of all births are to unmarried women. The rate is similar in other European
countries, but within a country rates vary significantly with race. Other reasons for
the shift include the increase in unmarried couples having children, the variety of
living and custodial arrangements of children after divorce or splitting up, changes
in women's work roles, older age when getting married, married women having

[1]Stewart (2007: 2).

fewer children, reduction in the age of onset of puberty, various demographic and racial changes, and greater toleration of gay and lesbian relationships.

My third reason for using the term blended families is that I want to include not just those that fit the the broader definition of stepfamily, but also children adopted through an adoption agency.[2] Partners sometimes legally adopt the biological (or adopted) children of their spouse and there is disagreement among scholars as to whether this situation constitutes a stepfamily. Since what happens in childhood affects us as adults, I finish the chapter with a section on the triad of adoption, namely adults adopted as children, adoptive mothers, and birth mothers.

It is hard to get prevalence figures for all the various types of blended families, but the proportion of such families is high and its effect on society is considerable. There is also rather limited research available on stepfamilies. Stewart comments that "the majority of Americans are connected to or will be connected with a stepfamily in some way."[3] Unfortunately, in the the U.S., about 70% of stepfamilies dissolve within ten years, and arguments about children are the main factor in the breakup of second marriages.[4]

There is one other topic about mixed parenting that may possibly come up in counseling and that is related to the role of sperm donors. There are a huge number of people conceived from sperm and egg donations in the U.S., and there is at least a million American adults who are biological children of sperm donors. Such people may be grateful to the fertility industry, yet at the same time be uneasy about the way they were conceived— a bought-and-paid for child.

Although there are various ways a stepfamily is formed, I shall consider just two cases, stepfamilies from divorce and remarriage, and stepfamilies from cohabitation,[5] as they can be regarded as being at two ends of the spectrum of types of stepfamily.

20.2 STEPFAMILIES FROM REMARRIAGE AND DIVORCE

This section also includes remarriage where either partner may have had a mate who has died as well as divorce and remarriage.

It appears that most remarried couples who have children from previous marriages have no real idea what they have let themselves in for! It seems that about half the time children are not discussed before marriage and step-mothering is generally found to be more difficult than anticipated. Couples usually have to focus on the children's needs to the detriment of their own relationship. If some people knew what was in store for them, they may not have got married in the first place! It is therefore perhaps not surprising that second marriages have a higher divorce rate than first marriages.

[2]This is a subject close to me as I have two adopted sons.
[3]Stewart (2007: 23).
[4]Douglas and Douglas (2000: 1).
[5]This is defined as a heterosexual couple living together without being legally married.

20.2.1 Some Problem Areas

There are a number of problems that can arise with stepfamilies. Some of the difficulties encountered may have arisen prior to the marriage. There is always "fallout" before, during, and after divorce and the breakup of relationships, which is discussed in Section 18.2. Children are particularly affected as they may have had to cope with the caregiver's multiple dating and various partners prior to marriage, or with one parent's absence (often the father) or declining involvement. Some feelings experienced by children are discussed in Section 18.2.3. The level of parenting tends to decline with solo parents as they have to cope with work, school schedules, and often a reduction in income so that stepchildren come into a stepfamily with a deficit. Smoke[6] sums it up well when when he says that there are three things that never seem to be totally resolved in most marriages: the ongoing relationship with the former spouse, the fair and even treatment of the children on both sides, and the constant strain of stretching the family budget over two households. He also comments that a first family is grown together, while a second family is thrown together! The marriage needs to be strong to survive these pressures. We shall now consider these and a number of other common problems.

Stress

Changes in living arrangements always create tension with one or both partners having to move into a new home; adequate privacy may be a problem. Coping with the visit of someone else's children from time to time can be very unsettling, especially for a stepmother. Also extra children can cause "territorial" problems with the children originally there. Two first-borns may clash or they may work together for the family. Then there is the possibility of having to meet or interact with new family members and friends. Disagreements between parents and ex-spouses and between stepfamily members can occur, and there can be problems with custodial arrangements for the children. Sometimes there is a big age gap between partners that can cause some problems.

Stepchildren tend to have more turbulent lives than other children. For example, they usually have to cope with many changes including living in more than one place when there are joint custodial arrangements, and coping with different parenting styles. Other factors affect stability such as the genders of stepchildren (e.g., boys may be more accepting of stepparents than girls) and the gender composition of the siblings (e.g., sexual interactions may cause problems).

Holidays, birthdays, anniversaries, weddings, and special times like Christmas and Easter can be very stressful for stepfamilies as the wider families of both parents can also get into the act! Meeting up with ex-partners can be very upsetting and family traditions can be a major source of conflict.

Stepchildren show stress in different ways. Hayman[7] mentions that they may revert back to more juvenile behavior such as babyish behavior, temper tantrums, attention demanding, and with younger children even bedwetting. She says that they may behave differently inside as opposed to outside the home. For example, they may behave badly at home but behave perfectly normal at school or with other relatives and friends, or vice versa. The bad behavior can involve harm to others

---

[6]Smoke (1995: 111).
[7]Hayman (1994: 107–108).

(e.g., bullying at school) or harm to self (e.g., truancy, risk taking, performing badly at school).

A stepmother has a particularly difficult role because when she tries to do her best for the stepchildren, they may see her as trying to usurp their mother's role. On the other hand, the man will usually be off to work to leave his wife to cope with the children and provide some sort of mother figure.

Interpersonal Priorities

In a high proportion of divorced families, the mother gets the primary custodial role of the children so that the vast majority of stepparents in a traditional stepfamily are stepfathers. This means that the stepfather's priorities with regard to children may tend to lie outside the marriage. As a general rule, stepparents take a less active role in the lives of their children than do biological parents, and stepchildren get less financial support than biological children.[8]

So often in counseling I have heard one partner complaining of having a lower priority than the children of the other partner. This not surprising as a parent knows his or her children longer than the stepparent. Priorities become even more difficult when there are his children, her children, and their children. It is important for the couple to have time alone to help build their relationship; perhaps have a regular "date night." It is also important for children to have quality time with their natural parent as well as the stepparent.

Parenting

Before marriage a number of issues need to be resolved. For example, what kind of parenting style will be used?[9] If the husband is authoritarian and the wife permissive, or vice versa, there will be problems. All adults concerned need to mutually agree on rules of behavior (e.g., privacy), if at all possible.

It is important for stepparents to realize that that they are not the birth parents and the child-parent bond is there permanently, even if an absent parent is a bad parent; the stepparent role is different. In fact stepparents are often resented by the stepchildren whose goal may be not to forget a deceased parent or to achieve a reconciliation of their separated parents. They may therefore seek to sabotage the new marriage by playing one partner off against the other. Often children feel powerless over what has happened to them and so it is important to try and give them some measure of control over their own lives; allowing them to choose clothes, food, the occasional family menu, and so on, can all help.

Biological parents should not shy away from recalling and talking about experiences in the first relationship with their biological children, even though it may be painful for them, or they might want to protect the partner's feelings or the feelings of the partner's children. They need not be afraid of looking at and discussing old photographs. All children want to know where they come from and ignoring the past can give the message to the child that one part of self is unacceptable.[10] It is essential to help children have good feelings about both biological parents, where

[8]Stewart (2007: 72).
[9]See Section 18.3.
[10]Hayman (1994: 139).

possible.[11] All the adults involved need to decide what to do in the event of a tragedy, such as one parent in the stepfamily dying.

Children may wonder what they did to lose the absent parent's love so that when a new partner comes along he or she may bear the brunt of all the children's fears, worries, and anger. They will naturally wonder about the role of the new parent coming into the home and wonder if this person will be kind, harsh, loving, or mean? A major question for them is how will their lives be affected by this new relationship. They will also want to test out the new person so see if he or she will also give up on them. If they like the new person, they may even feel guilty about letting down their parent in some way. On the other hand, stepparents may feel guilty if they don't love or even like their partner's children. However, being friends of the stepchildren may be the best one can hope for, and a good strategy is to let the children be the guide as to how fast or how slow to go in achieving this friendship. It is helpful to remember that there are times when we would like to give our own children away so we can't expect to always like the stepchildren![12] It is important to remember that all children will misbehave at some stage.

The age and gender of children are important factors in adjustment. For example, those under ten may adjust more easily being accepting of a new adult and have more daily needs to be met. On the other hand, adolescents (aged 12-14) have the most difficult time adjusting to a stepfamily as they need more time to bond to the stepparent and may be as sensitive, or more sensitive, than young children when it comes to needing love, support, discipline, and attention. Teenagers fifteen and older are less involved with stepfamily life as they are in that process of separating from family toward their peers and forming their own identities. However, they still want to be treated as significant persons so that they feel they are important, loved, and secure. Boys seem to accept a stepfather more quickly than girls who tend to be uncomfortable with displays of physical affection by their stepfather.

Smoke[13] sums it up nicely with the following recommendations for stepparents:

1. Give new relationships with stepchildren time to grow.

2. Work at it; respect has to be earned.

3. Make stepchildren feel as important as your children.

4. Remember that you are not a replacement parent.

5. Be friendly to your partner's ex-partner.

I would also add that it is important for stepparents to respect the new children as people and help create security and trust. Young children may not understand adult emotions, but they can be very perceptive. Children may cope better with losing a parent through death than through divorce. Even though one parent would prefer complete child separation from the other parent, it is not helpful or usually healthy to deny contact with, or the recognition of the role of, the other parent. The child can be told that the stepparent is not a replacement for the absent mother

[11] It may not be possible if violence or abuse were present.
[12] Hayman (1994: 91).
[13] Smoke (1995: 112).

or father but simply another person to love and support them (e.g., a friendly aunt or uncle).

If the parent has leaned heavily on the child for emotional or practical support, the child may find it hard to give up this position to a new partner.[14] On the other hand, if stepchildren harbor serious resentment toward their birth parents, they may redirect their anger to caregivers or stepparents. Forgiveness can be a way forward here. A contentious issue is how should the children address the stepparent; insistence on using the title "mum" or "dad" or any other title the stepchildren are unhappy with will cause conflict.

Disciplining the Children

Parents generally need coping strategies and ideas for dealing with difficult children and the couple need to sit down and discuss this. It is important that parents do not disagree on this matter in front of the children as children can be stirrers! Any conflict should be discussed behind closed doors until a united resolution is achieved. This may even need to happen in the middle of a disciplining session. The danger is that a parent may stand up for his or her own children's behavior and point a finger at the stepchild. Alternatively, a parent may accuse the spouse of unfair discipline toward one's own child.

A number of issues need to be decided by the parents. An important one is agreeing on who is the primary disciplinary in the home, bearing in mind that both have the right to keep all members accepting the agreed family rules. This person needs to be backed by the other parent. When a stepfather tries discipline, the child may respond negatively with, "You're not my father." The answer is to agree with child but point out we all have to abide by the agreed family rules and have the mother standing right behind in support. The mother does not step in and take away the father's control unless they have agreed to such a move in advance. Children may also use arguments like, "But mum used to let me do this!" If members of the couple each have their own children living with them, then it is best for each parent to normally discipline his or her own children. This can lead to problems if each of the two sets of children have very different ages, which will generally be the case if members of the couple have very different ages. All children struggle with issues like jealousy, resentment, and sibling rivalry, and not just those in blended families. It is a good idea for the biological (custodial) parent to be mainly responsible for the discipline of his or her own child(ren) until the stepparent has developed solid bonds with the children.

Another important question is: What are the the rules? It is important to establish a list of family rules (e.g., how family members communicate with each other and rules of privacy for the children) and discuss them with the children before posting them in a prominent place (e.g., refrigerator door). How then will a misdemeanor be relayed to the children, for example, will there be a first warning or three strikes and you are out! Finally, what are the consequences of breaking the rules? One idea that can be helpful is to get the children or adolescents themselves to come up with what the consequences should be for various misdemeanors, and perhaps keep them on the refrigerator door. Children can then be sent their rooms to think about which one of three consequences to accept. If they refuse all three,

---

[14]Hayman (1994: 53).

they can be given all three! Children can be given a yellow or eventually a red card for repeat misbehaving, followed by their having to choose one of say three consequences. The key here is to teach the child the connection between *their* choice of behavior and *their* choice of consequences. The parent is not being the one deciding the consequence and is therefore not "punishing" the offender. The offender is therefore learning that one's choices in life will have cause and effect. The parent can then be the parent to help the child understand this instead of being seen as the executioner !

Finances

Often one of the stepparents, usually the stepfather, has to make child support payments especially if the ex-wife is unable to work because of the ages of her children. These payments can make a substantial drain on the stepfamily's finances and the children may find a substantial reduction in money spent on them. Because of lack of finance, a stepfamily may not be able to afford to move into a bigger house to accommodate extra children, with resulting territorial problems. Other pressures occur when the absent parent spends more on the children when they visit the parent than what the stepparents can afford to spend.

20.2.2 Counseling and Blended Families

Counseling may consist of seeing just one partner, both partners together, or the whole family.[15] The ideas in Chapter 19 on couple counseling are relevant here. Sometimes I have found it helpful to see a parent with one of the children, or even the children on their own (depending on their ages). In the latter case drawing or using a sand tray can be helpful.

In counseling couples, the therapist can raise issues commonly met by stepfamilies to increase partners awareness of these demands, normalize the issues, and discuss ways to address the difficulties. The therapist can also ask each member of the couple to describe his or her expectations of what life in the stepfamily would be like and how the expectations lived up to reality. This discussion can unearth any potentially unrealistic expectations and standards (e.g., stepchildren should automatically like and respect their stepparent), and the therapist can help the couple to set out their own standards with regard to them and the children. Ways of involving the stepparent with the stepchildren can be discussed so that bonding with the latter can take place and the stepparent can earn the right to be accepted as an authority figure. Children can be brought in on the plan with the parents presenting a united front and establishing the couple as a significant family unit. Topics like mediating conflicts between siblings or with hostile former spouses concerning the children can also be considered.

Children need to be able to have a reasonable say as long as the tail does not try to wag the dog!. A good strategy is for the couple to choose one night of the week around the dinner table to have open discussion. An object such as a salt or pepper shaker can be passed around; whoever has the shaker has the floor without interruption for an agreed space of time, say three minutes using an egg timer on the table. This enables each person to air any problems or grievances and to encourage group listening. Even if this is not possible or does not work, it is

---

[15]Ideas for family or child counseling are not included in this book.

still also important for each member to have a one-to-one conversation with other family members. Each parent should endeavor to have one-on-one time with each child, including parents with each other.

As with all marriages, the strength of a stepfamily will depend on the strength of the bond between the parents. It is much more difficult for parents of a stepfamily to maintain an appropriate boundary between parents and children and avoid "triangling," where there is a bond between one parent and a child that excludes the other parent. This raises the question of which comes first, the couple or parent-child relationships, as they are both important. Some therapists suggest that unless you love each other as the primary love, different and of greater priority than with children, you should not proceed into the new bonded relationship.

20.3   STEPFAMILIES FROM COHABITATION

In the U.S. and especially in Europe the majority of stepfamilies are formed through cohabitation.[16] However, many of these couples will eventually marry, but such take longer than childless couples to make the transition to marriage. Some couples, especially older ones who tend to have more stable relationships, prefer not to get formally married. However, in spite of the prevalence of cohabitation, "it is not equivalent to marriage in terms of relationship duration, union stability, and childbearing, even in Europe."[17] Stewart comments that cohabiting stepfamilies are increasingly being maintained by biological fathers and their female partners. Also, about 40% of all U.S. children can expect to spend some time in a cohabiting family, that is with a mother and her cohabiting partner. A smaller percentage of children (11%) are actually born to cohabiting couples, suggesting that few couples see child rearing within cohabitation as desirable.[18]

What counseling issues might arise with cohabiting couples? Cohabiting couples and their children are vulnerable in many ways. For example, in the U.S. they don't receive the same legal rights and protections as married couples.[19] A cohabiting stepparent's role may seem less defined than a married stepparent so it's the children who often provide the motivation to marry. Also cohabiting relationships are generally brief compared to marriage; a high proportion ending in separation.

Stewart notes that cohabitors have lower levels of psychological well-being than married people, especially when children are involved. For example, she referred to studies that showed that cohabiting couples with children have higher rates of depression than married couples with children, and divorced and female cohabitors with children have especially high rates of depression. There are often gender inequalities in cohabitation with women tending to get the heavy end of the load. Stewart says: "In general, research indicates that cohabitation is not an ideal living arrangement for children."[20] She says that children raised in cohabiting stepfamilies have worse outcomes than children in married stepfamilies, and about the same or worse than for children raised by a single parent. Finances pay an important role

[16]Stewart (2007: 94, 111).
[17]Stewart (2007: 111).
[18]Bumpass and Lu (2001).
[19]Though this is different in other countries, e.g., Sweden where no distinction is made.
[20]Stewart (2007: 107).

as cohabiting stepfamilies are generally less well off and have less resources than married stepfamilies. However, much more research is needed on this comparison.

20.4 BLENDED FAMILIES WITH SAME SEX PARENTS

Some gay and lesbian people bring children from previous relationships or are choosing to become parents, for example through artificial insemination. Gay and lesbian unions dissolve at about the same rate as heterosexual cohabiting couples, a rate that is however higher than the rate of dissolution for married couples.[21] Others are finding adoption, where this is legally permitted, to be their preferred method of bringing a child into their family. Most of the research on the topic comes from the research on gay and lesbian parenting rather than on adoption. Also most of the research is based on lesbian rather than gay parents.

There is significant debate, which I don't propose to enter into, about gay marriage and allowing lesbian or gay adoption. There are however some misunderstandings that need to be cleared up.[22] First, children are no more likely to be molested by gay men than heterosexual men and, in fact, most pedophiles are heterosexual. Second, a child is no more likely to become gay if brought up by gay parent(s); most gay and lesbian adults grew up in heterosexual families, and sexual orientation does not seem to be determined by family of origin. Third, children will not necessarily be stigmatized or emotionally traumatized. However, they may face some problems from their peers at school and have to be discreet about revealing their family situation. Fourth, children won't necessarily be exposed to HIV/AIDs (if living with two men). Finally, children won't necessarily have disapproval from the religious community although their caregivers might. Earlier studies suggest that the children of lesbian and gay parents probably grow up as happy, healthy, and well-adjusted as the children of heterosexual parents. However many of these studies were not statistically sound because of small samples or biased sampling methods. A recent study based on nearly 3000 adults by Regnerus (2012) concluded that children of parents who have had same-sex relationships didn't do as well as those with married parents on a number of factors. It can be argued, however, that good parenting is determined by a parent's ability to create a loving and nurturing home, rather than on whether a parent is gay or not gay.

20.5 ADOPTED CHILDREN

In the drama of adoption there is a triad of main players, the adopted child (referred to as the adoptee), the birth mother, and the adoptive mother. All of these experience some life-changing loss. Although fathers do not play a central role, they are still important and will be referred to briefly later. I write this section as an adopting parent myself with two adopted sons. I am particularly grateful for the book by Verrier (1993) and her insightful comments. From a counseling perspective, my focus will be on each member of the triad who may end up in the counseling room. But first some general comments.

[21] Patterson (2000).
[22] Adapted from Stewart (2007: 170).

20.5.1   How Well Do Adopted Children Do?

Triseliotis et al.[23] quote a number of studies that suggest that, on the whole, children adopted when very young seemed to do as well on a number of factors as non-adopted children. Verrier,[24] however, paints a somewhat different picture of adopted children being over-represented in psychotherapy. There is some debate over this question and Brodzinsky concludes:

> Taken as a whole, the research literature generally supports the view that adoptees are at increased risk for various behavioral, psychological, and academic problems compared with non-adopted individuals. However, the majority of adoptees are well within the normal range of adjustment.[25]

Apparently, problems tend to arise mostly during the primary school years and adolescence, and these are generally problems such as low self-esteem, academic problems, and "acting out" behavior (e.g., aggression, stealing, lying, hyperactivity, argumentativeness, and running away).[26] Adoptees tend to settle down more as they get older.

There are several factors that contribute to stability in adoption.[27] First, it seems that the younger they are when adopted, the better the outcome in the long term, but many older placed children can do well and some very well. Second, it is important that the child is not too disturbed at the time of placement, especially for children over the age of nine. Finally, for the older child, being well prepared beforehand for the adoption and maintaining some form of contact with a parent and/or sibling or grandparent after placement is helpful.

The Nature of Bonding

Bonding, which is different from attachment and much deeper, occurs between a mother and child before birth so that a baby can recognize mother and mother's voice when he or she is born. We now realize how much a baby is aware of what is happening when in the womb and the baby experiences the separation as abandonment. Verrier asserts babies do not initially have a sense of themselves as a separate being from their mother so that post-natal separation causes what she calls "the primal wound." The baby experiences loss, followed by rage and protest, then hopelessness and despair, detachment, and a kind of resignation before beginning to attach to the new mother.

She also claims that although the memory of the separation event is probably forgotten, the feelings that went with it are still there, which can be disconcerting. Therefore separation anxiety is common in early years and it can be mistaken for a strong attachment. It is also seen in the anxiety that may occur upon entering day care or school or going away to a camp. There may also be psychosomatic, chronic childhood illnesses caused by grief and loss such as stomach aches, migraines, asthma, allergies, and chronic fatigue that can persist into adulthood. These may be triggered by later experiences. Other possible behaviors mentioned

[23]Triseliotis, Shireman, and Hundleby (1997).
[24]Verrier (1994: xv).
[25]Brodzinsky (1993: 157).
[26]Triseliotis et al. (1997: 22).
[27]Triseliotis et al. (1997: 33).

by Verrier include stealing and hoarding, and a desire to control to avoid any future losses.

Adoptees can suffer from the anxiety of wondering whether they would be abandoned again and the anxiety can show up in testing-out behavior. They may try to provoke the very rejection that they fear in order to test the parents' commitment and, at the same time, reject the adoptive parents before the adoptee is rejected. The idea of allowing oneself to love and be loved is too risky. An adoptive mother may find that no matter how hard she tries to show how much she loves her child, she may feel there is an impenetrable barrier. Although the distancing is caused by the child, the child may through the defense mechanism of projective identification[28] against vulnerability see the distancing as coming from the mother instead.

Intimacy can be a a problem for the adoptee who may find that he or she cannot discuss intimate feelings with the mother except perhaps on the telephone or by texting or e-mail, which are not so threatening. Such acting-out behavior, which can be antisocial, provocative, and destructive, is hard for the adoptive parents to handle, but at least the child's pain is brought into awareness. Sometimes adoptees will act out before or during special occasions like their birthday parties.[29] However, the adoptee should not be threatened by the adopter with abandonment. Unfortunately the acting-out can be so severe that when the child is older he or she may either be kicked out of the home or simply leave home, possibly as a defense against being kicked out.

The very opposite kind of behavior can also occur whereby the adoptee is too compliant, acquiescent, and withdrawn. This may give adoptive parents a false sense of security when, in reality, such adoptees can never really bond with anyone as they are not being their true selves. Given these two conflicting attitudes of the adoptee, what happens when there are two adoptees in the family? According to Verrier's experience and research,[30] one tends to adopt the acting-out role and the other is probably compliant, regardless of the birth order, sex, or personalities.

Tasks for an Adoptee

An adoptee faces a number of tasks.[31] Three of these are: the process of re-attachment to new parent(s); obtaining an awareness of being adopted; and forming an appropriate identity.

The first task is not so daunting when the child is adopted as a baby. Studies suggest that children under the age of nine re-attach themselves reasonably well to new families. Older children tend to be separating from parental figures so that re-attachment is perhaps not the best description.

The second task relates to the awareness of being adopted. This involves several aspects.

1. *Coping with the knowledge of being adopted.* When is the right time to tell children they are adopted? As they get older there will be two balancing factors to consider: If children are told too soon it may make the them feel

[28]See Section 21.5.
[29]Verrier (1994: 15).
[30]Verrier (1993: 63).
[31]Adapted from Triseliotis et al. (1997: 35–42) and Verrier (1994).

insecure and rejected, whereas if left too late they may wonder why they have some unsettled and uneasy feelings that they can't explain. It seems to be a matter of *when* rather than *if*. Disclosure needs to be part of a "drip feed" process usually beginning about the time children begin to ask questions about babies and sex. It is suggested that it should start early enough so that a child can feel that he or she "always knew." However, understanding cognitively rather than just knowing won't occur until around age six or seven; and so the debate continues. As Keefer and Schooler note,

> Omission or simplification of some facts may be necessary while the child is very young, but harmful when the omission continues beyond the child's ability to understand.... parents should remember that they usually underestimate their child's sophistication.[32]

The general consensus seems to be that it is better to know than not to know, and knowing strengthens rather than undermines the relationship with the adoptive parents. Keeping the adoption secret can be a disaster once the secret is out. Bradshaw[33] comments that:

> Children believe that if they're not allowed to know something about themselves and their past, then it must be bad. This is a powerful argument against preserving adoption secrets—even when the truth to be uncovered is distressing or disruptive.

It would seem that adoptees have an unconscious knowledge of the supposed secret and sometimes they complain of never feeling part of the family and not being understood. The fact that many adoptees demonstrate little if any reaction when they are told about their adoption may be testimony to their "prior knowledge."[34]

Keefer and Schooler list ten important principles of telling the adoptee.

- Initiate conversation about adoption (like conversations about sex!).
- Use appropriate adoption language (e.g., birth and not real parents, made an adoption plan rather than gave up for adoption, my child rather than adopted child, etc.).
- Never lie to a child about the past or a birth family member.
- Allow a child to express anger towards a birth family member without joining in. It is a matter of not negating the child's feelings or giving excuses for the birth parents behavior (e.g., they couldn't cope so they couldn't help drinking and using drugs).
- Omissions are okay until age twelve, but after that all information should be shared.
- If information is negative, use a third party (e.g., a therapist) to relate the most troublesome details (e.g. about drug or criminal behavior, or promiscuity, for example).[35]

---

[32] Keefer and Schooler (2000: 20).
[33] Bradshaw (1995: 42).
[34] Sorosky, Baran, and Pannor (1978).
[35] There is an old saying about "killing the messenger," so don't be the messenger.

- Don't try to "fix" the pain of adoption.
- Don't impose value judgements on the information.
- A child should have control of telling his or her story outside the immediate family. Parents can help adoptees with what to say by helping them to develop and rehearse a "cover story." This can involve discussing questions people might ask, the situations the child might encounter, and what sort of information should be shared.
- Remember that the child probably knows more than you think he or she does.

2. *Having gradual access to family history, when available.* What is available depends on whether the adoption is open, partly open, or closed.[36] Baby photos can be a great help here. Children like to know, as part of their identity, where they come from, how they came to be adopted, and circumstances of their adoption. It might help them to understand why they have particular personality traits and genetic characteristics, which may be very different from those of the adoptive parents. In fact most adoptees want to know about their genetic past and research indicates that it is normal and healthy to want to do so. Finding out genetic information can help with self-esteem and the establishment of one's identity.[37]

3. *Understanding and accepting the idea of having more than one family or two sets of parents.* Adoptees sometimes fantasize about their birth mothers or birth families. Although they may understand why their birth mother gave them up, they may still have uncomfortable feelings and fear a second rejection. They may feel they can't trust anyone and have to be self-sufficient right from the beginning. They may also use the defense mechanism of splitting[38] whereby they assign all "good" tributes to one set of parents and all "bad" attributes to the other.

There are other pressures that come with the knowledge of adoption. For example, adoptees may be told that they are special and were "chosen." This may not go down too well as they may feel they had no choice and that the parents simply chose to have someone, not necessarily them, being the luck of the draw. They may even feel they were stolen from their birth mother. "Special" may be interpreted as perfect, an unattainable goal, which may reinforce feelings of not being good enough for one's birth mother. It also may engender the belief that you have to be good enough otherwise you will be abandoned. You mustn't complain as you will appear to be ungrateful.

4. *Coping with loss and rejection.* The questions that the adopted child faces are, "Why was I given up for adoption?" and "Was I wanted and loved before being given up?" As we saw in Chapter 11 on grief, other losses may trigger the adoption loss. The loss can damage self-esteem and self-worth and can trigger anger. The adoptee may have to cope with the belief that they must have been bad in some way to be given away, and this can lead to shame.

---

[36]See Section 20.5.2 below.
[37]See http://www.childwelfare.gov/pubs/f_issues.cfm (accessed October 2010) by the Child Welfare Information Gateway, 2004.
[38]See Section 21.5.

5. *Divided Loyalties.*[39] In spite of the issues of rejection and trust, the adoptee may have a profound sense of loyalty stemming from the deep connection with the birth mother that can sabotage bonding with the adoptive mother. However, because of gratitude to the adoptive parents, the adoptee may struggle with divided loyalties and have difficulty deciding whether or not to search for the birth mother for fear of upsetting the adoptive parents. If the adoptive parents seem very willing to assist with the search the adoptee may misunderstand their intent and wonder if they are wanting to get rid of their adopted child.

What needs to be realized by all parties concerned is that in the same way that parents can love more than one child, children can love two sets of parents. It is important for the adoptee to check with the adoptive parents to see how they feel about the search. If adoptees have a strong urge to seek out the people to whom they are biologically related, most therapists say they should follow it, but have a supporting network such as an adoptee's spouse and children, adoptive family, good friends, therapist, support group, or a combination of several of these.

The third task relates to forming an identity that includes the above. Separation at birth can lead to a loss of self, which is identified with mother at birth, so that a search for self seems to be closely connected to the search for birth mother. What can happen is that the real self is hidden behind a mask and a false self is created, which is constantly seeking approval, is polite, and generally good. If the false self is rejected, the real self remains intact.

We note that the first stage of Erikson's stages of development,[40] which goes from birth to eighteen months, deals with the crisis of basic trust versus basic mistrust. Adoption means that mistrust continues. The fifth stage, which encompasses adolescence (ages 11 or 12 to 18), is the confrontation of the crisis of identity versus role confusion. This stage sees a shift from past development that depended on what was done to the child to the development that depends on what the child does for himself or herself. Adolescents are neither children nor adults and they begin to find their identity separate from the family and as a members of society. They ask questions like, "Who am I and how do I fit in?" and "Where am I going in life?" They also begin to develop ideas about their strengths, abilities, needs, interests, and desires so that they can be expressed in a social context.

Teens try on different identities, going through an identity crisis, and they use their friends as mirrors; their peer group becomes very important to them. Some degree of role confusion is normal and can explain the apparent chaotic nature of much adolescent behavior and teenagers' painful self-confidence. Three major issues need to be resolved: "the choice of occupation, the adoption of values to believe in and live by, and the development of a satisfying sexual identity."[41] Adolescents who survive the crisis develop the "virtue" of fidelity, which is a sustained loyalty to others and a set of values of their own choosing. Adoptive parents may wonder what they have struck when an adopted child goes through this stage. What they

[39] Verrier (1993: 91–92).
[40] Erikson (1995).
[41] Papalia et al. (2001: 448).

need to realize is that the behavior is not necessarily the result of the adoption, as non-adopted children go through the same stage!

Finally, some comments about a possible reunion with the birth mother are given below in Section 20.6.4.

20.5.2   Open Adoption

In open adoption, the contact is open so that the birth parent(s) and the adoptive parents are able to share information and possibly meet. This type of adoption can raise issues for the adoptive parents as they may have to cope with visits by the birth parent(s) (usually the mother). They may feel threatened by the visits and fear possible interference, but the advocates of open adoption maintain that the child should come first and not the feelings of the birth or adoptive parents. However, some situations can be difficult. For example, a birth mother may choose confidential (closed) adoption because of rape or incest, or the birth mother may have never told her husband, family, or closest friends. She may want to contact the child eventually, but only when she is ready. For older children, there may have been questions of abuse or neglect that negate open contact. However, open adoption may alleviate some of the negative feelings, for example guilt, of the birth mother associated with relinquishment and give her an opportunity to explain the circumstances leading to the adoption. Also it may help alleviate some of the grief involved, which will be similar to that from other grief events.[42] Contact with the birth mother will inevitably lead to comparisons that may be disconcerting for both the birth mother and the adoptive mother. For example, the adoptee may be very glad he or she was brought up by the adoptive parents, though this won't negate the bond with the birth mother.

Without any tangible contact, birth parents may struggle through life wondering what is happening to their children, wondering if they are even alive, and wondering what they look like at each age. So many questions! With closed adoption, young adults may set out to find birth parents and become almost obsessed about finding them, making use of various organizations that are available to assist them in their search. Birth parents may do the same.[43]

Transracial and inter-country adoption raise a number of issues. It seems that such adopted children do as about as well as same race adoption, though they may face problems with racism as they are growing up. In the end it comes back to the quality of the parenting. Many parents adopt children with special needs, which raises other issues relating to adopting older children who have been in care.

20.5.3   Single Parent Adoption

Whatever we might feel as therapists about single-parent adoption or gay and lesbian adoption, both are here to stay and our role as therapists is to help those who seek our help, whatever the background of the client. It is estimated that the percentage of single-parent non-related adoptions, mainly by women, in the U.S. has grown from about 3% in 1975 to roughly 30% today.[44] Given the high percentage

---

[42]See Chapter 11.

[43]For various pros and cons of open adoption see Triseliotis et al. (1997: chapter 4).

[44]Reliable statistics are not available for the present time.

of single parents today, single parent adoption seems more acceptable now though they face some of the same problems as single parents, for example, less income, social isolation, difficulty in obtaining a break from parenting especially when there is difficult behavior to contend with, and role strain that comes from trying to be both mother and father.

Children in a single-parent family may not have the opportunity to interact with a single, important adult of the opposite sex over an extended period of time. Also friends of singles are not always as enthusiastic about the adoption as are friends of couples. Supportive networks are important for the parent. Some of the strengths of single-parent adoption are:[45] commitment to the child and the adoption; strength and capacity to handle a crisis; a relatively simple family structure; and self-confidence, independence, and ability to develop and use supportive networks. Single parent clients can be encouraged to join a support group and to make use of community resources such as holiday programs, sports clubs, and school and summer camps.

20.6   THE ADULT TRIAD

All three members of the triad (adoptees, adoptive mothers, and birth mothers) are generally unprepared for the impact of the adoption; reason and feelings are often at odds. They may have problems with denial and avoidance being used as defenses against painful feelings, and these can be unconscious on the part of the person using them. The loss that each feels is often denied or suppressed, which can cause problems. They can also struggle with feelings of guilt: the birth mother feels guilty for having given up her child, the adoptive mother feels guilty for somehow failing to adequately take her place, and the adoptee feels guilty for having been born.[46] All three members yearn for understanding, but they are often not very understanding of one another, especially when it comes to reunions. In all cases, feelings need to be owned otherwise they can be projected on to other members of the triad. Before discussing some ideas that might be useful in counseling all three people, I want to mention fathers briefly.

20.6.1   Fathers

The birthfather of the adoptee may struggle with various emotions such as guilt for the pregnancy and for not being able to provide for the child. If he sees and even holds the baby, he may also experience some loss, especially if he wanted the birth mother to keep the baby. He often has very little to say about what happens to their child. He may be told not to concern himself but to maintain secrecy and just get on with life. He won't have to assume parental recognition or have any responsibility. However such goals for secrecy fail miserably.[47] Wherever he goes there will always be the thought that the young lady (or man) walking past him may be his birth child.

In the case of adoptive fathers, some adoptees find it easier to connect with them than their adoptive mothers. For those fathers who are not distant, "the

[45] Triseliotis et al. (1997: 218).
[46] Verrier (1993: 93).
[47] Schooler and Norris (2002: 6).

:elationship seems more straightforward and easier to define than that with the mother. Fathers are often confused by the conflict between the child and the mother, because he is not directly affected by it."[48] The father does not realize that the child is trying to connect to the mother but is afraid of doing so. It is important for the father to be aware of these problems as the situation becomes even more complicated if there is a divorce or the death of the adoptive mother.

20.6.2 Adults Adopted as Children

The usual presenting problem by an adult adoptee is difficulties in relationships. The reason is that many of the symptoms described above for children carry over into adulthood including relationship difficulties, which may lead to the avoidance of intimate relationships for fear of possible rejection again. Underneath there may be symptoms of depression and anxiety that are related to a sense of loss and basic mistrust that can interfere with healthy relationships.[49] Verrier suggests that "the closest diagnosis might be best described as post-traumatic stress disorder."[50] The idea of reacting to a trauma that cannot be remembered is completely foreign to the adoptee, yet traumatic memories intrude in the form of emotional or bodily sensations, as feelings have memories. Adoptees can therefore be encouraged to explore their feelings, for example, when there is fear, guilt/shame, and anger/rage. They usually face issues of identity and feelings of loss, especially with special events such as graduation, marriage, the birth of a child, or the death of an adoptive parent.

Those adopted need to challenge any beliefs about being undeserving or unworthy. As mentioned above, an adoptee can take on a false self or a mask to avoid abandonment again. If someone rejects your external mask then that is not so bad, but if you let someone know who you really are inside and they reject you, then that is real rejection.[51] Using a metaphor like drawing a wall and asking the client to describe what is behind the wall can be helpful.

Adoptees may feel they don't deserve a good relationship and end up sabotaging it; this can include work relationships as well. Because they feel undeserving, they may also unconsciously sabotage other activities. The therapist may need to deal with feelings of unworthiness that are linked to rejection and the feeling of being a bad person because only a bad baby would be given away. Asking the client, after carefully looking at a picture of a baby or even holding a baby, how bad is the baby can be helpful. They may also be angry at having been manipulated as a baby.

In dealing with their feelings, adoptees may project their feelings onto another more convenient person, such as a partner, or they may want someone to become a mother figure. They, including female adoptees, may even be mistrustful of females and have separation difficulties, for example have stomach pains when separated from their spouse. Being manipulated at the beginning of their lives may make them manipulative and controlling in their relationships. They may feel victimized and therefore need to move out of victim role. They may also have poor frustration tolerance or impulse control, with the slightest thing stirring up anger.

[48]Verrier (1993: 63).
[49]Verrier (1994: 50).
[50]Verreir (1993: 71).
[51]Verrier (1993: 35).

With adult adoptees, there is a strong possibility that adoption was closed and secrecy surrounded the adoption, reflecting the approach of adoption of a previous era. This secrecy led adoptees to be unable to mourn their loses and obtain information about their origins. When they learn of it they feel totally betrayed and may experience absolute shock and relief—shock that they were not told and, when the dust has settled, relief because there had always been a suspicion that something was not right. They now had confirmation that those almost unconscious feelings were there for a reason. Can the parents be forgiven? Adoptees may not be prepared to offer forgiveness for various reasons such as:[52] (a) wanting to punish the parents, (b) wanting power over them to make up for the original loss of power, (c) not condoning what they did, and (d) not wanting to do the difficult forgiveness work when the outcome is uncertain. However, forgiveness can bring healing and reconciliation.

20.6.3   Adoptive Mothers

Adoptive parents, no matter how loving, start with some disadvantages.[53] First, the mother has not had the advantage of a 40 week gestation period to bond with the child. Second, neither parent may have been alerted to the trauma experienced by the baby through being separated from the birth mother. Although the adoptive mother usually attaches to the baby very quickly and loves the baby as her own, she may not be aware that she can never quite replace the birth mother and that the baby is mourning for his or her birth mother. The baby wants to connect, but that could be dangerous as a mother cannot be trusted and may be an abandoner. The baby may vacillate between seeing the adoptive mother as the rescuing mother and as the abandoning mother. If an adoptive mother has a child who acts out his or her pain, this unrest may become noticeable by the age of eighteen months to three years. This can undermine the mother's confidence in what she is doing. If she has a compliant child, she may not notice anything at all until adolescence when the child faces the identity issues mentioned above. The problem is that for a mother who has not birthed children it is hard to know what is normal behavior.

A third disadvantage is that many adoptive parents have not dealt with their own losses, including the loss of fertility, loss of a dream, loss of a pregnancy experience, loss of biological heredity, and loss of continuity of inheritance. Without the resolution of these issues can lead to a variety of emotions and may lead to difficulty in fully accepting an adopted child. Also, in some societies, childlessness still carries some shame and stigma, even when health issues cause birth problems rather than infertility. Both parents and grandparents may also be very disappointed to see the end of the family line, especially if the adoption is not going well. It's easy to blame the birth parents and say, "We wouldn't have these problems if the child was really our own flesh and blood."

Resolution with regard to the loss of fertility can mean several things: deciding that to keep trying to have a birth child is not a priority anymore, determining to have a family by means other than birth, and working through the loss and consequent grief. The feelings of loss may help the adoptive mother to have some

---

[52]Schooler and Norris (2002: 61–62).
[53]Verrier (1993: 53–54, 160-161) plus other material.

understanding of the losses felt by the adoptee and the birth mother. Events can trigger the grief like the pregnancy of a friend and the subsequent birth. In considering the loss of biological heredity, I have found the following ideas helpful: (a) in natural birth each parent only passes on half of his or her genes so that the gene pool is soon "watered down" after several generations until the original genetic link is lost; (b) nurture is just as important as nature in the development of a child, (c) adoption is generally much better than foster care and it is an opportunity to provide a long-term family for the child, and (d) children are always a gift, whether adopted or not.

A fourth disadvantage is the problem of having to deal with social perceptions about adoption. Adoptive families sometimes tend not to be regarded as real families in some cultures. People make insensitive statements like, "Oh, I thought he was your own," "So you are not her real mother," and "What's the real mother like?" thus confusing birth mother and adoptive mother.[54] The media may also play a very negative role by focussing on those situations where a birth mother claims back her child.[55] There is a social perception that adoptive parents are somehow "lucky" and that adoption is an easy way out of having a child instead of through childbirth. People may also comment that, " I can't believe anyone would give up their child." Others may see adoptees as "damaged goods," for example, teachers may attribute behavioral difficulties to the fact that the child was adopted.[56] Because of misconceptions, adoptive parents may be ambivalent about disclosing their adoption in various social interactions. For example, the mother may feel "put on the spot" when questions about bottle-feeding versus breast-feeding come up so that she may feel forced to disclose the adoption, or when people notice how thin she is with a such a young child.

A fifth disadvantage arises with those parents who already have biological children and have not adequately explored their reasons for wanting to adopt nor realized the impact the adoption will have on their family life.

A sixth possible disadvantage is not knowing what will happen if her child eventually wants to look for the birth mother and then finds her, as the adoptive mother instinctively knows that her relationship with the child will then change in some unknown way. The reunion will raise all kinds of feelings. After all, she did all the hard work of parenting, while the birth mother just appears on the scene; yet the birth mother has every right to be there. During the initial "honeymoon" phase of the reunion, the birth mother may feel rejected and left out and will need to be very patient. Helping an adoptee to search is one thing, but being expected to like it is something else. The adoptive mother needs to realize that she did the best she could and recognize that she is not able to replace the birth mother. She should also understand that the child's desire to search does not mean that she has done anything wrong.

If a reunion occurs, it will be an emotion charged time for the adoptee and birth mother and the adoptive parents will need to back off while the reunited pair sort out what is happening. If the adoptive parents do this and give the adoptee permission to pursue this new relationship in whatever ever way seems best, their own relationship with the adoptee will be much stronger. The adoptee should realize

[54]Weir (2003: 47–49).
[55]This is particularly the case in the U.S.
[56]For a summary of the social perceptions see Weir (2003: 97–99).

that a reunion does not necessarily solve all of one's issues, but it will generally help.

The above discussion admittedly may appear to been rather negative, when in fact there are many very positive outcomes. However, as the success stories are less likely to come for counseling a full discussion was considered valid. Issues for counseling are likely to be related to infertility, ambivalence about social disclosure, adjustment to rapid parenthood, and adoptees searching for and meeting birth mothers.

20.6.4   Birth Mother

Stifler[57] estimates that about 2% of women living in the Western World choose to give up their children for adoption, and there are long-enduring effects of this loss.[58] First of all a birth mother will have to face any stigma and shame associated with her pregnancy, face possible censure by her parents and relatives, and wear the stigma of giving up her child. She may feel very pressured, may not have access to adequate counseling, and be forced to keep a family secret. Because of the stigma, she may be encouraged to bury the experience and quickly "get on with her life."

An ill-informed social worker might even have told her that she had given up all right to know anything about her child, that she was to forget her child, and that it would be wrong for her to ever intrude in her child's life and upset the child's adoptive family. Unfortunately this does not really help as there are unhealed losses that can later lead to low self-worth, failed or multiple marriages, struggles with parenting, and feelings of inadequacy as a mother. She may also experience emotional numbness, have an unconscious fear of sex, and be prone to addictions and/or anxiety disorders.

Often the birth mother was just a teenager at the time and was going through Erikson's fifth stage described above with respect to the adoptee, where there is crisis of identity versus role confusion and all sorts of identity issues. She may struggle with the guilt and shame of giving her child away and may have deep longings to actually see her child again if the adoption was not an open one. She will feel the pain even more if she is not able to conceive again as there is a high rate of secondary infertility for reasons not fully understood.[59] She may also have a sense of loyalty to the missing child, which perhaps can lead to her not wanting to have another child. She may often later regret giving up that child. If the adoption was closed, she will long to know how her child is doing and what he or she has become but may have not done anything to find the child because of fear of rejection and recrimination. If she eventually meets up with her child, she will usually be acutely aware of the lost years.

There are also other aspects of her loss beside the loss of her child. She may feel that she has lost her virginity and her wholeness, her sense of control of her life, and her sense of trust and self-worth. She may also have lost a home, lost or suffered damaged relationships with members of her family, lost acceptance by society, and lost an important part of her schooling. If it was her parents' first grandchild, they

[57]Stifler (1991).
[58]See Davidson (1994).
[59]Verrier (1993: 92) suggests it may be as high as 40% in the U.S.

may also grieve, compounding her loss. She may also have lost her relationship with the birth father because of issues like unresolved guilt and mutual blame.

With every loss there is grief. Since with adoption the grief is not usually acknowledged by society it is known as disenfranchised grief.[60] Although the literature on grief is extensive, there is very little dealing with the grief of giving up a child for adoption. One problem is that it is particularly difficult to grieve the loss of a child when that child is still alive and not dead. The hope for some future possible reunion may also arrest the grieving process. Even with open adoption, there may not be much real connection with the child, which can become even less with time, or else the connection is shallow as neither party feels confident about opening up emotionally for fear of making the other person feel bad. The birth mother may not feel happy about how her child is being brought up, but is powerless to do anything about it.

The grief process is discussed in detail in Chapter 11 where various models of the process are given. I iterate once again that everyone seems to grieve differently. A stages' model might take the form of the following steps:

1. *Shock and denial.* It is a real shock for her to give away the life she has created and lived with for many months. As the shock wears off and the painful reality sets in, she may then go through a period of denial by minimizing what has transpired, for example in an open adoption by telling herself that the loss was not so great. By being positive about the adoption she may even deny there has been any loss at all. Denial and repressed grief however cannot be maintained for too long without a psychological impact.

2. *Depression.* Once the extent of her loss sinks in, there can be real sadness with depression not far behind.

3. *Anger.* This can take her by surprise and the anger can be directed at a number of targets including the birth father and even God for allowing what happened.

4. *Regret and Guilt.* Guilt has already been referred to above and can take various forms. For example, she may feel guilty for her weakness in sexual temptation or whatever led to the pregnancy, about not being in a position to be able to keep her baby, and having to surrender her role as mother.

5. *Acceptance.* This does not mean that her loss has gone, but that it has been integrated into her life experience. It also means being able to to talk comfortably about the adoption with others.

The therapist can help the birth mother in the following ways[61]

- Take good care of herself.

- Discretely free herself from any secrecy. She may have been encouraged to maintain certain goals of secrecy such as being able to resolve her feelings about placement more easily, not accepting from others or herself the label

[60]See Section 11.1.
[61]Adapted from Davidson (1994) and others.

of "fallen woman," and be able to forget the child and get on with her life. These goals tend to fail miserably.[62]

- Tell and retell her story and be heard without judgement.

- Validate her feelings and express any denied emotions.

- Forgive that younger part of herself. After all, she did the best she could at that time and age.

- Forgive others who were involved, for example, critical parents, others who pressured her to give up her baby, and others who judged her. Help her let go of blame.

- Validate her sense of her own goodness and inner wisdom.

- Create rituals for grieving.

- Raise her level of self-esteem.

- Develop new relationships with supportive people.

- Take part in a workshop and support groups with other birth mothers.

- Understand the needs and losses of birth mothers, adoptees, and adoptive parents. Reading and education are important tools for growth and empowerment.

- If needed, begin a search for her child if the adoption was not open (which may be the case with older clients). She should only search if she is prepared to "hang in there" no matter what the adoptee does and there is no possibility of her abandoning her child again.

- Find out the best way to actually make contact with an adoptee and/or adoptive parent(s). She should be aware that at any reunion she may bring with her a younger traumatized self.

- Deal with any feelings and behaviors that take place after the reunion.

As with other counseling, a genogram is particularly useful. Inner child and ego state methods of therapy can also be used.[63]

Reunion with the Adoptee

Finally, I want to make a few comments about the reunion with the adoptee, if it occurs. First, it needs to be carefully planned; questions like how to contact (e.g., letter or phone, preferably the latter to check whether the right person is being contacted), where will the reunion take place, who will be present, and when is an appropriate time for it to take place.

Second, on meeting, it is very likely that the adoptee will regress as there is a desire to go back to that mother-child relationship that was severed on relinquishment.[64] The mother will want it too. The adoptee may then want to be in

---

[62]Schooler and Norris (2002: 6).
[63]See Section 1.2.4.
[64]Verrier (1993: 170).

continuous communication, which is alright for a while until the trust is regained and the bond re-established. However, the birth mother will have to stop "mothering" the adoptee at some stage as part of the "growing up process." Some adoptees might begin by being receptive, then suddenly cut off communication for a while. The birth mother needs to be patient as the adoptee may be struggling with emotions or may be testing her just as he or she may have tested the adoptive parents. If mutually accepted, the birth mother may stay in touch with texts, e-mail, letters, cards, or phone calls.

A third reaction on meeting is that there may be a kind of genetic sexual attraction between mother and adoptee. This arises because sensual and sexual feelings are natural to the early experience of babies and their mothers. An adoptee who is a man may want to get back inside his mother and therefore be tempted to have sexual intercourse with her, and she may feel the same urge. Acting out on this would be an unacceptable betrayal of trust and violates the taboo placed on incest by virtually every known culture.

20.7 BIBLICAL VIEWPOINT

20.7.1 Blended Families

The Bible does not have anything to say about stepfamilies as we know them today, but has something to say about Christian families in general. It places a very high value on the family and taking care of one another; the principles apply to all types of families.[65] One of the biggest problems that parents face is providing a united front in the disciplining of the children, which is needed for the children's sake.[66] Getting the balance right between under- and over-disciplining of the children is not easy in a stepfamily. Children are admonished to obey their parents, but fathers are not to provoke their children to anger.[67] This can be difficult for a stepfather who may feel disempowered if not adequately supported by his wife. It is important for a Christian couple to sit down and discuss rules as they relate to Christian principles and for the wife to express her feelings. There will be problems if one partner thinks the other partner is too lax with discipline. Humility, patience, and making allowances are needed[68] along with encouraging words, kindness, and having a forgiving nature.[69]

20.7.2 Adoption

What does the Bible say about adoption? There are two examples where God has used an adoptee to fulfill God's purposes. A Hebrew woman called Jochebed, who bore a son during a time when Pharaoh had ordered all Hebrew male infants to be put to death,[70] put her son in a waterproof basket and placed it in river. He was found and adopted by one of Pharaoh's daughters and named Moses. He went

---

[65] For a number of books on stepparenting see
http://www.christian-parenting-devotion.com/parenting-tip.html (accessed October 2010).
[66] Proverbs 12:1, 23:13–14, and 19:18.
[67] Ephesians 6:s1–4.
[68] Ephesians 4:2.
[69] Ephesians 4:29, 31–32.
[70] Exodus 1:15-22.

on to be greatly used by God. Also, in the book of Esther, a beautiful girl named Esther, who was adopted by her cousin after her parents' death, became a queen, and God used her to bring deliverance to the Jewish people.

The New Testament speaks about Jesus Christ being conceived through the Holy Spirit instead of through the seed of a man. He was "adopted" and raised by his mother's husband, Joseph, who took Jesus as his own child.[71] The idea of adoption plays an important role in the New Testament. We are told that once a person becomes a Christian he or she becomes part of God's family, not through the natural process of human conception, but through adoption.[72]

Clearly adoption, both in the physical and spiritual sense, is shown in a favorable light in the Bible as a means of blessing. However, the process of adoption can have a negative effect on spirituality. For example, an adoptee may be angry with God for allowing such a terrible thing as a separation of a mother from her baby to happen. An adoptee may also feel betrayed by both the parents and the church for not supporting him or her in their dilemma. Some religious organizations can be very judgmental toward unwed mothers. It is then a matter of separating the spiritual from the religious and understanding that it is man and not God making the judgments. On the other hand, many adoptees have found great comfort in a religious faith realizing that they are children of God, and therefore of real value.

[71]Matthew 1: 18–24.
[72]Romans 8:15–16; Ephesians 1:5; John 1:12, 2; Corinthians 6:18; and 1 John 3:2. See also http://www.bible-topics.com/Adoption.html (accessed October 2010).

CHAPTER 21

PERSONALITY DISORDERS: GENERAL CONCEPTS

21.1 INTRODUCTION

The subject of personality disorders is big one so I have decided to split my material on it into two chapters. This chapter is for the reader who just wants some general information about the disorders as well as some background to defense mechanisms, which are of wider application than just this topic. In the next chapter the disorders are discussed in more detail along with some general and specific counseling strategies.

A personality disorder (PD) is defined to be "an enduring pattern of inner experience and behavior that deviates markedly from the expectations of the individual's culture, is pervasive and inflexible, has an onset in adolescence or early adulthood, is stable over time, and leads to distress or impairment."[1] It is a long-standing and maladaptive pattern of perceiving and responding to other people and to stressful circumstances. Its prevalence seems to be of the order of about 10%, according to the criteria. This is a difficult subject area as we don't fully understand the nature of personality or have an agreed model for it that will provide a clear scientific basis for categorizing personality disorders. Benjamin[2] notes that it is much easier to ask questions about symptoms for Axis I disorders[3] such as depression

---

[1] American Psychiatric Association (2000a).
[2] Benjamin (1996: 5).
[3] I am referring to the so-called *multiaxial* model which describes PDs as Axis II disorders.

and anxiety disorders than questions about a personality disorder. For example, you can ask a client about how he or she is sleeping, but can you ask a client, "Do you manipulate and exploit people?" Clearly counseling a client with a PD is for experienced therapists. It is important to note that while a person may exhibit any or all of the characteristics of a personality disorder, the main concern is whether the person has trouble leading a normal life due to these issues. With personality traits being somewhat fixed, it is a matter of shifting a client into a more normal range of functioning rather than changing the personality. As the primary audience for this book is therapists in their earlier stages of counseling, I have included this chapter for three reasons.

My first reason is that I believe that all therapists need to have some general knowledge of the topic as "No sharp boundaries exist between normality and pathology. Instead, personality styles slowly shade into personality disorders. As the level of pathology increases, so does the likelihood that difficulties will be created in every avenue of human life ...."[4] For example, we have a spectrum of dependency ranging through codependency, dependent personality, and dependent personality disorder. Clearly there is a certain arbitrariness as to where you draw the line and therapists won't necessarily agree on the final diagnosis as there is a strong subjective element involved in the assessment. For example, it can depend on whether you rely on a score on a questionnaire to make your decision or more subjectively on the perceived degree of harmful dysfunction.[5] Also some of the disorders can include personality traits that actually interfere with the flow of information used for assessing.

Knowing the statistical difficulties in categorizing people, I am therefore somewhat loathe to possibly stigmatize a client with the label "personality disorder" and I agree with Magnavita[6] that the term "dysfunction" might be a better term to use than "disorder." Also, personality disorders are one of the most controversial areas of psychopathology. Being aware of the various personality traits however may help the therapist to recognize when a particular trait surfaces and hopefully will find this chapter helpful in providing some strategies. Generally speaking, if one to three of the criteria for a particular PD are present, then the corresponding personality trait is regarded as being present, while if at least four or five are present (depending on the criteria) then a disorder is specified.

My second reason for this chapter is that we need to know enough about these disorders to sense when a client suffers with this disorder and, if necessary, be able to refer him or her on to a more qualified therapist. This involves having some diagnostic criteria to hand on. I won't be giving exact details of these criteria because of their copyright, but I will provide internet references where the extra details can be accessed. My final reason is that there may come a time when we feel we have experienced enough to tackle some of the more amenable personality disorders ourselves, especially when their symptoms are mild or marginal.

One of the difficulties in assessing clients for a possible PD is that their presenting symptoms may be those of an Axis I clinical disorder such as depression, anxiety disorder, addiction, or phobia. For example, borderline PD may be expressed as

---

[4]Millon and Davis, with Millon, Escovar, and Meagher (2000: 141). These authors also discuss the spectrum from normal to abnormal for each disorder.
[5]Magnavita (2004: 6).
[6]Magnavita (2004: 9).

self-harm, or narcissistic PD expressed as depression. In fact a personality type can incline a person to certain clinical disorders rather than others. Another difficulty is that there are, at present, about ten or more different disorders that have been classified, the main classification systems being the Diagnostic and Statistical Manual of Mental Disorders (DSM-IV-TR) and the International Statistical Classification of Diseases and Related Health Problems (ICD 10). Some writers have suggested that within each disorder there are a number of subcategories, as described for example by Millon et al. (2000). At present the DSM system is under revision and there is some debate over how personality disorders are to be included.[7] Given the problems of classification, we need to be flexible in our thinking about the disorders and not be too driven by criteria.

We note that any classification scheme is not static and undergoes changes over time. This is not surprising as the DMS classification is simply a method of using empirical information to attach labels to selected sets of symptoms and can be culturally dependent and change with new knowledge and experience. There is therefore some controversy over the validity of the DSM classification.[8] As was the case with categorizing depression (see Section 9.3.1), it is not easy to put people into separate "personality" boxes as there will always be a certain degree of overlap, with some people having a few symptoms from several categories. However, as clinical experience has built up over the years, such a classification can be valuable and help us find some sort of path through the maze of human behavior! It provides a rather crude broad brush picture where each disorder roughly describes a family of people with similar characteristics, but there is still a lot of variability within each category and doesn't allow for fine tuning. Another problem is the degree of overlap in diagnosis, which is reflected in the fact that the DSM allows multiple PD diagnoses to be assigned; combinations of two, three, or even four personality disorders are not uncommon.[9] The degree of overlap can be as much as 30–50%.[10] This problem of overlap is a serious one and Benjamin[11] discusses the issues involved.

Another approach to the classification problem is to use a "dimensional" approach, where people are categorized by their score or position on each of several dimensions. For example, Siever and Davis (1991) use the Axis I dimensions of cognitive/perceptual organization, impulsivity/aggression, affective instability, and anxiety/inhibition. This kind of approach has been reflected in the development of a number of trait models with different numbers of traits or factors, with special emphasis on the five-factor model.[12]

The pros and cons of using DMS categories versus dimensions are discussed by Widiger and Frances (1994), who favor the dimensional approach. Benjamin (1996) uses the analogy of "orthogonal" or "independent" dimensions that one meets in mathematics and statistics to develop an interpersonal model using two two-dimensional graphs called the Structural Analysis of Social Behavior (SASB) model that she uses to complement the DSM categories and help with the problem of overlap. The first graph has an interactional focus on another person and endeavors

[7]For some idea of the problems see Bartlett (2011).
[8]For example, see Kutchins and Kirk (1997).
[9]Millon et al. (2000: 72).
[10]Morey (1988).
[11]Benjamin (1996: chapter 15).
[12]Costa and Widiger (2002).

to show (1) how a client relates to his or her partner or other person (the scale ranges from hostility/hate to friendliness/love) and (2) how the partner or other person responds, that is what is achieved by the client (the scale ranges from enmeshment/taking control to differentiation/giving autonomy). The second graph has an interactional focus on the self and endeavors to show (1) the effect of the spouse or other on the client (the scale ranges from reactive hostility to friendliness) and (2) how the client responds (the scale ranges from submission to autonomy). I shall not describe the method as it is moderately complicated, but I do refer to some of the results in the next section.

What factors lead to a person having a PD?[13] Since a major part of our personality and temperament is genetically determined (nature), it is likely that there will be a genetic predisposition to personality dysfunction. Also, the quality of attachments (nurture) will be significant and traumatic events can also play a major role, especially where there is neglect or emotional or sexual abuse. Dysfunctional families play a role in producing dysfunctional people, though there is the possible confounding of environmental with genetic factors. One final factor might be the role of society and culture, especially in a fast changing society. There is considerable debate as to the stability of personality and how much of it can be transformed, if at all. Generally speaking, personality disorders tend to be managed in therapy rather than "cured."

Finally, one might ask how useful is medication for PDs? In the past, the consensus would have been none at all except for concurrent Axis I conditions or target symptoms such as insomnia. However, Sperry[14] notes that there has been a major shift in attitude on this issue and the thinking is now towards a combination of various therapies along with medication, where the medication is targeted towards the basic dimensions that underly the personality, for example, serotonin blockers to deal with impulsiveness and aggression in borderline and antisocial personalities.

21.2   GENERAL PSYCHOLOGICAL ASSESSMENT

As therapists we may be asked to provide a general psychological assessment and below I give several suggested methods of assessment relating to a person's background and his or her present mental status. I then consider a more specific assessment that relates to determining whether a person may or may not have a personality disorder.

21.2.1   Gathering Information

Background Questions

In addition to general demographic data such as name, gender, date of birth, ethnicity, occupation, and so forth, we can find out the following:

1. What does the client see as his or her problems? These need to be distinguished from those you know and observe.

---

[13]See Magnavita (2004: 16–18).
[14]Sperry (2003: 5, 23–24).

2. What is the previous history of physical and mental health (including past history and present use of illicit and legal substance use)? Make a note of any medication used and how well it is working for the client.

3. What is the client's social history including family, education, work, life events, and pre-morbid personality? It may be helpful if some of this information can be obtained from others such as family members.

4. What is the client's daily pattern of living and are there any associated disturbances? What is normal for him or her? Some appropriate topics for consideration might be sleep, nutrition, exercise, sexual activity, work, leisure, and self-care (see Chapter 2).

5. What support does the client have? Who can he or she rely on? This involves investigation of the client's relationships, availability and amount of contact, and perceived attitudes of others.

6. How would you describe the client's mental state right now?

Benjamin[15] describes the interpersonal assessment of a client as exploring for each individual and social relationship the "input" to the client, the "response" from the client, and "internalization" by the client using what she calls a dynamic assessment interview. Here all the usual background information is collected including the chief complaint, current symptoms, present and past interpersonal circumstances, DSM checklist for a likely diagnosis, connection between present symptoms and interpersonal patterns and early experience, and treatment plan (interventions for problem input, responses, internalizations, and goals). Care is needed in case the obtaining of so much information is stressful for the client.

Defining Characteristics

Sperry[16] suggests obtaining the following information to construct a psychological profile of a client and does this for each disorder.

Triggering Event(s.) What are the triggers that initiate a characteristic maladaptive response in family or intimate relations, in social situations, or in work settings? The triggers can be interpersonal or internal, such as failing an exam.

Behavioral Style. What is the usual way the client reacts personally to the triggering event (e.g., impatience)?

Interpersonal Style. What is the usual way the client relates to others (e.g., exploitative, pleasing, or blaming)?

Cognitive Style. How does the client usually perceive and think about a problem, and then thinks up and implements a solution (e.g., analytic, cautious, or careless)?

Emotional/Feeling Style. How does the client usually respond to emotions and moods (e.g., anger, elation, or mood fluctuation)?

[15]Benjamin (1996: 69–70).
[16]Sperry (2003: 34–35).

Temperament. What is a client's inborn, characteristic response pattern with regard to experiencing and expressing emotions (e.g., inhibited, impulsive, or reflective)?

Attachment Style. What is the client's pattern of relating that reflects the past emotional bond between parent and infant? The style will be either secure or insecure (see Section 2.5.2).

Parental Injunction. What parental expectations were imposed on the client as a child as to what the child should be or how he or she should act (e.g., "You can't do it by yourself")?

Self-View. What is the client's personal conception of self, including a self-evaluation of abilities, personal worth, potential, and goals (e.g., "I need the attention of others to feel important and worthwhile")?

Worldview. How does the client view life, others, and the world in general (e.g., "Life is unfair" or "Others should take care of me")?

Maladaptive Schemas. What are the client's enduring and self-defeating patterns concerning his or her world view that were developed during childhood and elaborated throughout one's lifetime (e.g., defectiveness, social isolation, self-sacrifice, and approval-seeking)?

Optimal DSM-IV-TR Criterion. This refers to the single criterion for a given disorder that is most useful in diagnosing the disorder. These are given below.[17]

21.2.2   BAATOMI Assessment

There may be times when a therapist is asked to provide an "official" assessment of the client. One set of assessment guidelines based on the acronym BAATOMI follows.

Behavior. Look for such things as degree of motor activity, restlessness and fidgeting, sluggishness, hypervigilance, movements (e.g., tremors, tics, or hair-pulling), degree of cooperation and concentration, and attention span.

Appearance. How would you give a police description of your client? This would include clothing, physical characteristics and condition, posture, hair, and distinguishing marks (e.g., tattoos, body piercing, or scars that might be associated with self-harm).

Affect. How is the client's mood right now (e.g., anxious, depressed, elevated, or inappropriate)?

Thought. This will be reflected in the client's way of speaking such as rate and volume, degree of ambivalence (e.g., strong positives and negatives), repetition (e.g., perseveration), drifting off the subject, and in the content of their speech (e.g., helplessness, hopelessness, guilt, shame, suspiciousness, phobias, preoccupations, worries, obsessions, compulsions, antisocial attitudes, blaming others, suicidal ideation, and so forth).

---

[17]Allnutt and Links (1996).

Orientation. How connected is your client to the real world at present, in terms of time, place, and person?

Memory. How good is your client's memory, short term and long-term? Any amnesia or blackouts?

Intellectual. How good is your client's use of language and his or her ability for abstract and concrete thinking? What about judgement and awareness of problems and causes?

21.3   INDICATIONS OF A PERSONALITY DISORDER

People with a PD tend to get stuck in the same reoccurring coping strategies making matters worse, rather than adapting. They are rigid and inflexible and their failure to change means that pathological themes dominating their lives are repeated like a cracked record. How do we know that our client may have a PD without us having to go through the criteria for all the disorders? The following, adapted from DSM-IV-TR, give features common to all personality disorders that can be used as a starting point.

1. An enduring pattern of symptoms relating to experience and behavior that differs considerably from the expectations of one's culture. The symptoms show up in two or more of the following areas:

    (a) *Cognitive* (ways of looking at the world, thinking about self or others, and interacting). For example, this could involve suspicion and mistrust of others.

    (b) *Affect* (the appropriateness, intensity, and range of emotional functioning). This would be indicated by, for example, frequent mood swings, angry outbursts, and difficulty in controlling feelings or behavior.

    (c) *Interpersonal functioning* (relationships and interpersonal skills). For example, parts of one's personality may make it difficult to live with self and others. Such people experience the following: difficulty in making and keeping relationships with friends, family, and work colleagues; upsetting or harming other people because of distress; difficulty keeping out of trouble; stormy relationships; and social isolation.

    (d) *Impulse control.* There may be poor impulse control and a need for instant gratification.

2. The enduring pattern is inflexible and pervasive across a broad range of personal and social situations and is not a result of alcohol or drugs or another psychiatric disorder. However, there may be alcohol and substance abuse as well.

3. The symptoms have caused and continue to cause clinically significant distress or negative consequences in different aspects of the person's life, especially in occupational and social performance.

4. The pattern is stable and the symptoms have been present for an extended period of time. They can be traced back to adolescence or at least early adulthood.

In order to diagnose an individual under the age of 18 with a personality disorder, symptoms must be present for at least one year. Antisocial personality disorder, by definition, cannot be diagnosed at all in persons under 18. However, people under 18 years old who fit the criteria of a personality disorder are usually not diagnosed with such a disorder, although they may be diagnosed with a related problem.

There are a number of psychological tests for detecting the existence of a PD. Some of these are readily found on the internet, but I am uncertain about their validation.[18] The most popular inventory for use with people suspected of having a PD is the Millon Clinical Multiaxial Inventory version 3 (MCMI-III) of 175 items that also covers Axis I disorders (anxiety and mood disorders, and so on).[19] A topic that will assume greater importance in the future is the role of defense mechanisms, as it appears that certain defense mechanisms tend to be used by people with specific disorders, as we see in the next chapter. This topic is discussed further below.

21.4   CATEGORIES OF PERSONALITY DISORDERS

Before looking at individual disorders in greater detail in the next chapter, I want to first mention the DMS method of dividing the PDs into categories or clusters, of which there are four. These are summarized briefly below. Benjamin[20] provides what she calls "necessary and exclusionary" criteria or descriptors for each disorder to help with the problems of overlap referred to above, and these are also given below along with the main wish associated with each disorder.[21] The "optimal criterion" for each disorder is also mentioned.[22]

21.4.1   Cluster A

The disorders in this category demonstrate odd or eccentric behavior and are as follows:

Paranoid. This is characterized by irrational suspicions and mistrust of others, and others' motives are interpreted as malevolent. The necessary descriptor is the expectation of harm when it is not there and exclusionary conditions include worry about abandonment and deference to authority. The optimal criterion is: "suspects, without sufficient basis, that others are exploiting, harming, or deceiving him or her." The main "wish" is: "You were extremely abusive to me, and now I am the same to my loved ones. This proves that I love you so please love me." This PD should not be confused with paranoid schizophrenia, another totally different type of mental disorder where the patient has constant feelings of being watched, followed, or persecuted.

Schizoid. There is a lack of interest in and detachment from social relationships and seeing no point in sharing time with others. There is not much awareness of one's own feelings or the feelings of others. The necessary descriptor is a general social withdrawal. Almost any other conditions are exclusionary

---

[18] For example http://similarminds.com/cgibin/newpd.pl (accessed October 2020).
[19] Millon, Davis, Millon, and Grossman (2009).
[20] Benjamin (1996: 389).
[21] Benjamin (1996: 106–107).
[22] Allnutt and Links (1996).

such as strong affect, manipulative skills, concern for abandonment, and so forth. The optimal criterion is: "neither desires nor enjoys close relationships, including being part of a family." This is an uncommon disorder.

Schizotypal. This is characterized by bizarre behavior or thinking. There is an avoidance of social relationships out of fear of people and acute discomfort in close relationships. The necessary descriptors are social withdrawal and thought disorders that imply "autistic control," and the exclusionary conditions are fear of autonomy, proud disregard for social norms, and demanding dependency.

21.4.2   Cluster B

The disorders in this category are characterized by erratic, emotional, and dramatic presentations and are as follows:

Antisocial. This is characterized by a general disregard for the law and the rights of others. Such people are unruly, irresponsible, deviant, and self-serving, and see themselves as free and independent. Necessary descriptors are the need for the control of others as well as autonomy for self, detachment, and lacking remorse, while exclusionary descriptors are fear of abandonment, entitlement, and dependency. The optimal criterion is: "criminal, aggressive, impulsive, irresponsible behavior." The main wish is: "I could never count on you for anything but hassle, so I'll make sure I am always in charge or unavailable."

Borderline. There is extreme "black and white" thinking, and instability in relationships, self-image, identity and behavior. Such people are unpredictable, manipulative, and experience widely fluctuating moods. They see themselves and others alternately as all-good or all-bad. Necessary descriptors are a fear of abandonment that is handled by getting others to provide protection and nurturance, and self-sabotage for doing well or being happy, while an exclusionary descriptor is long term comfort with autonomy. The optimal criterion is: "expectation of meeting personal goals and/or maintaining close relations." The main wish is: "Whenever I was alone you raped me, as you told me it felt good. Now I need you (or your stand-in) to be with me and take care of me so I will never be alone again."

Histrionic. This is predominantly characterized by dramatic and attention-seeking behavior that includes inappropriate sexual seductiveness. Such people have shallow or exaggerated emotions, overact to minor events, and see themselves as charming and attractive. A necessary descriptor is a coercive dependency and an exclusionary descriptor is self-sabotage following happiness or success. The optimal criterion is: "uncomfortable in situations in which he or she is not the center of attention." The main wish is: "You must take care of me and look up to me as you promised you always would."

Narcissistic. This is characterized by grandiosity, a need for admiration, and a general lack of empathy. Such people tend to overact with anger when needs are not met immediately or when facing stress and frustration. Necessary descriptors are a grandiose sense of self-importance and entitlement and an exclusionary descriptor is an uncaring recklessness of self. The optimal criterion is: "has grandiose sense of self-importance." The main wish is: "You must keep confirming your unfounded opinion about how wonderful I am."

This is a difficult group of PDs to counsel and has mixed treatment results.

21.4.3 Cluster C

The disorders in this category are characterized by fear and anxiety and are as follows:

Avoidant. Here we see social inhibition, hesitancy, feelings of inadequacy, extreme sensitivity to negative evaluation, and avoidance of social interaction. Necessary descriptors are defensive withdrawal and wishing for acceptance, and exclusionary descriptors are affective detachment, avoidance of aloneness, instrumental incompetence, and consistent failure to perform. The optimal criterion is: "avoids occupational activities that involve significant interpersonal contact fearing criticism, disapproval, or rejection." The main wish is: "You reject and put me down so much, yet I yearn for and await your love and acceptance."

Dependent. This is characterized by a pervasive psychological dependence on other people and a pattern of submissive and clinging behavior because of an excessive need to be taken care of. There is a tendency to overreact in anger when needs are not met immediately or when facing stress and frustration. A necessary descriptor is submissiveness stemming from a sense of instrumental inadequacy and exclusionary descriptors are complications of dependency (e.g., long term comfort with autonomy, insistence on submission, scorn for authority, and so on). The optimal criterion is: "needs others to assume responsibility for most major areas of his or her life." The main wish is: "You must take care of everything for me as you do it so well and I do it so badly."

Obsessive-compulsive.[23] There is rigid conformity to rules, moral codes, and excessive orderliness. Necessary descriptors are unreasonable control and devotion to perfection, and exclusionary descriptors are irresponsible behaviors, emotional excesses, and contempt for authority. The optimal criterion is: "shows perfectionism that interferes with task completion." The main wish is: "You must love me because I have everything in perfect order."

21.4.4 Other Disorders

Given the problem of trying to classify people, it is not surprising that there are some problems and "loose ends," which I now briefly refer to. Some of these are still under investigation.

DSM Appendices

Four more disorders, referred to by Millon et al.,[24] are listed in DSM appendices, namely the depressive and negativistic (passive-aggressive) personality PDs

[23]Reichborn-Kjennerud et al. (2007) present evidence questioning the placing of this disorder in Cluster C.
[24]Millon et al. (2000).

n DSM-IV-TR and the masochist and sadistic PDs in DSM-III-TR. These disorders, which are still under investigation at the time of writing this book, were
listed provisionally for research purposes only, not having reached the full status of
a personality disorder. However, there is some debate about their importance so
they will be discussed individually in the next chapter.

Not Otherwise Specified (NOS) Group

The problem of classification is shown up very clearly by the existence of a cluster
of PDs referred to as the Not Otherwise Specified (NOS) or Mixed Personality
group. Disorders in this group don't have a sufficient number of symptoms to satisfy
any one of the above ten disorders, but instead have a mixture of symptoms with
some from different disorders. There isn't agreement as to what type of disorders
should be in this group. A person is classified as NOS if he or she experiences
distress and dysfunction in one of more of the the social, occupational, sexual, and
interpersonal areas of life.

ICD-10 Group

A number of the PDs listed in the ICD-10 classification have the same names as
their DSM-IV-TR counterparts. Some of the others are:

Dissocial. This is conceptually similar to the antisocial PD above.

Emotionally Unstable. This consists of an impulsive type and a borderline type
similar to the borderline PD above.

Anakastic. This is the same as obsessive-compulsive PD above.

21.4.5   Treatability

Stone (1993a) has suggested that PDs lend themselves to a three-category classification with regard to treatability. The first has high amenability and includes the
dependent, histrionic, obsessive-compulsive, avoidant, and depressive PDs. The second has an intermediate amenability and includes the narcissistic, borderline, and
schizotypal PDs. The third has low amenability and includes paranoid, passive-
aggressive, schizoid, and antisocial PDs. Unfortunately it is not quite as simple
as this and Stone points that since there is generally overlap with the disorders,
treatability will depend on how much of the disorders in the third category are also
present. Another factor will be the presence of any Axis I disorders.

21.5   DEFENSE MECHANISMS

There are a large number of defense mechanisms or "ego defenses" mentioned in
the literature,[25] but we will concentrate on what seem to be the more common
ones and their relation to PDs. Their definitions vary in the literature and there is
some confusion over the use of some terms. Millon et al. state: "Today, the defense
mechanisms are viewed as so important that they constitute an Axis proposed for
further study, to be considered for inclusion in DSM-V, still some years in the

---

[25]See, for example, http://en.wikipedia.org/wiki/Ego_defenses (accessed November 2010).

future."[26] It should be noted that a defense system is important to a client and it is there for a purpose, irrespective of what we think of it. We don't dismantle it without putting something in its place to fill the gap.

Acting out. Internal conflicts are translated into action with little or no thought. It is the direct expression of an unconscious wish or impulse without conscious awareness of the emotion that drives that expressive behavior. The behavior eases the emotional pain and anxiety associated with the unconscious internal conflict and is often anti-social. For example, a student disrupts a class because he or she is angry over an unfair grade. Another example is acting on the impulse of an addiction such as sexual addiction. This behavior is typical of an antisocial personality.

Denial. A refusal (usually unconscious) to acknowledge some painful external or subjective reality obvious to others. In its extreme form (psychosis), it is a total denial of external reality because reality is too threatening. For example, denial by a mother that her daughter is being sexually abused by her husband.

Devaluation. Attributing unrealistic negative qualities to self or others as a means of punishing self or reducing the impact of the devalued other. For example, a student blames the teaching ability of a good teacher for getting a poor grade from the teacher.

Displacement. Discharging pent up feelings to a less threatening object. It's a form of blame shifting; it is always someone else's fault. For example, a man yells at the cat when he is angry with his wife.

Dissociation. The splitting off the awareness of painful feelings from conscious knowing. For example, a person is unable to remember a traumatic event. This is typical of a histrionic personality.

Fantasy. Tendency to retreat into fantasy in order to resolve inner and outer conflicts. For example, having delusions of grandeur. This is typical of an avoidant personality.

Idealization. Attributing unrealistic positive qualities to self or others. For example, believing that finding a new partner will solve all of one's problems.

Intellectualization. Using only logical explanations without feelings. For example the massacre of a village is described as "the village was neutralized." This is typical of a schizoid personality.

Introjection. Unconsciously incorporating the wishes, beliefs, and values of others as if they were one's own (a deep-seated form of mimicry). For example, a child takes on the problems (and sickness) of the family. This behavior is typical of a dependent personality.

Isolation of affect. Internal conflict is defused by separating ideas from emotions, retaining an awareness of intellectual or factual aspects but losing touch with threatening emotions. For example putting down a litter of animals without any feeling for them. This is typical of a sadistic personality.

[26]Millon et al. (2000: 25).

Projection. Blaming someone else for one's own difficulties or unethical desires. This is typical of a paranoid personality.

Projective identification. Unpleasant feelings and reactions are not only projected on to others, but they are also retained in awareness and viewed as a reaction to the other person's behavior. This is typical of a narcissistic personality.

Rationalization. Attempts to prove one's feelings or behavior are justified; excuses are usually involved. For example saying, "You would have behaved the same way as me if the same thing had happened to you." This is typical of a narcissistic personality.

Reaction formation. Unacceptable thoughts or impulses are contained by adopting a position that expresses the exact opposite; one's real feelings are not acceptable to one's belief system. Such a defense can work effectively for coping in the short term, but it will eventually break down. For example, a wife takes on a parent role for her alcoholic husband, or a person dislikes his or her job but tells everyone how wonderful it is. This behavior is typical of a compulsive personality.

Regression. Returning to an earlier more comfortable development level rather than handling unacceptable impulses or emotions in a more adult way. For example, under stress a person may take on a childlike voice. This is typical of a borderline personality.

Repression. Unconscious and involuntary forgetting of painful memories and withdrawal of forbidden thoughts; the emotion is conscious, but the idea behind it is absent. For example, a woman may forget details of sexual abuse as a child, but feel uncomfortable emotions when alone with a man. This can occur with a histrionic personality.

Splitting. Opposite qualities are held apart and remain unintegrated (e.g., good and bad) resulting in cycles of idealization and devaluation as either extreme is projected onto self and others. For example, fluctuating between treating one's spouse with dignity and respect, and treating him or her as despicable and worthless. This arises in borderline and narcissistic PDs.

Sublimation. Unacceptable emotions and natural drives are channelled into socially acceptable activities. For example, having plants or a pet instead of children.

Suppression. Conscious exclusion from awareness of anxiety producing feelings; these can be accessed later. It involves the conscious decision to delay paying attention to an emotion or need in order to cope with the present reality. For example, not thinking about one's debts while looking for a job.

Undoing. Doing something to counteract wrong doing or feelings of guilt. For example, one takes on some voluntary work. This is typical of a schizotypal personality.

21.6 BIBLICAL VIEWPOINT

In the literature on PDs there is almost no mention of spirituality and the spiritual problems that can lead to personality difficulties. For the Christian, however, there are many verses in the Bible that impinge on some problems associated with the emotions like anger, anxiety, and fear, and the Axis I disorders (e.g., depression, anxiety disorders, phobias, and addictions); these are discussed at the ends of various chapters. There are also a number of positive biblical statements like the injunction to be strong and courageous and not be afraid or discouraged as there is God's continual presence.[27] Learning right thinking is also important. For example, there is the injunction not to be anxious, but to be at peace and focus one's thinking on the "good" things.[28]

The need for a Christian to have good interpersonal relationships is frequently mentioned in the Bible, but has the Bible really anything to say about personality disorders? The answer, of course, is no as they weren't invented then! However, a common underlying factor leading to a personality disorder is parental dysfunction and inadequate attachment. One possible approach for Christian clients might be to focus on God as a parent who won't let them down. For example: Christians are described as being children of God and therefore heirs; God knows everything about them; God is loving and they will never be separated from God's love; God offers more than an earthly father; God provides all the things that they need; God is able to do far more than they can possibly imagine; God gives eternal comfort and hope; and God is close to the broken hearted.[29] There are other verses that have similar themes.

There is the possibility that a client may blame God for allowing abuse to happen and may find the father image abhorrent. There is no reason why a mother image can't be used. In addition to most of the above we can add the following:[30] God is like a hen with chickens; God gives birth to her people; God is like a woman in labor; and God is like a mother who comforts her children.

The problem of characterizing personalities is reflected in an article by four doctors who diagnosed Samson in the Old Testament with an antisocial PD,[31] even though he was described as a man of faith.[32]

---

[27] Deuteronomy 31:6; Joshua 1:9; 1 Chronicles 22; and Psalm 23.
[28] Philippians 4:4–8.
[29] Romans 8:15–17; Psalm 139; 1 John 4:16; Romans 8:38–39; Matthew 7:11; Matthew 6:25–33 and James 1:17; Ephesians 3:20; 2 Thessalonians 2:16; and Psalm 34:18.
[30] Matthew 23:37; Isaiah 46:3, 42:14, and 66:12–13, respectively.
[31] See www.pamweb.org/dsm_103.html (accessed October 2010).
[32] Hebrews 11:32.

CHAPTER 22

PERSONALITY DISORDERS: COUNSELING

22.1 GENERAL COUNSELING STRATEGIES

In the last chapter the emphasis was on providing an overview of personality disorders (PDs). We now look at the disorders individually in more detail and endeavor to give some specific strategies for counseling. A number of counseling modalities can be used including psychodynamic, interpersonal, and cognitive. All three are used by Millon et al. (2000), while Benjamin (1996) has a strong focus on the interpersonal and Beck et al. (2004) on the cognitive. Sperry[1] also suggests mindfulness meditation[2] as a useful tool.

In the previous chapter some general ideas are given about what sort of background information might be obtained from a client. Benjamin[3] suggests five counseling interventions, namely:

1. *Developing a collaborative relationship.* The therapist and client work together to change "it" (the maladaptive pattern). Externalizing the behavior also helps the therapist to accept the client's behavior without affirming it. Codependency of the therapist on the client needs to be avoided and there has to be a balance between bonding and differentiation by the client.

---

[1] Sperry (2003: 24–25).
[2] See Section 12.7.2 under "Relapse Strategies".
[3] Adapted from Benjamin (1996: chapter 4).

Counseling Issues: A Handbook for Counselors and Psychotherapists. By George A. F. Seber **567**
Copyright © 2013 G. A. F. Seber

2. *Facilitating pattern recognition.* It is important to remember that insight by the client into his or her pattern of behavior is only a first step towards the goal of change. Such patterns can be described in very general terms at first and then made more specific as the therapeutic relationship strengthens. Role plays where the client and/or the therapist can take part can be helpful. The therapist can model alternative responses, for example.

3. *Blocking maladaptive patterns.* Here the therapist helps the client to resist the temptation to engage in certain behaviors, at least initially, for brief periods of time.

4. *Addressing underlying fears and wishes.* This may mean cognitive restructuring or desensitization techniques using a hierarchy of fears (see Section 6.3.3). Every psychopathology is there for a reason and is driven by some sort of internalization to help the client achieve his or her beliefs and "love" self. Benjamin uses the insightful phrase, "every psychopathology is a gift of love."[4] Clients won't find it easy to give up old ways and ways of relating to people (or their internalizations) that are associated with those wishes and fears. A decision to do this may lead to loss followed by grief so that the client will need careful support during this process.

5. *Facilitating new learning.* The aim is to not only help clients self-affirm, but also to restructure their lives.

Therapist should try and see things from the client's perspective. In attempting to clarify the client's perception of the present and its connections with the past, Benjamin says that we should assume that the client "makes sense." Care is needed in using empathy as it may unwittingly reinforce the client's pathological patterns. An overzealous focus on getting information can cause client discomfort. Any such counseling errors, including any negative transference, need to be addressed quickly.

To diagnose a person with a specific PD, he or she must satisfy the general criteria in Section 21.3 as well as the criteria specific to that disorder. These criteria are listed on the internet[5] and summaries are given below. Each disorder will be related to possible causes, usually begun in childhood, and I have adapted some helpful comments from Benjamin (1996) that she describes as "pathogenic hypotheses." A number of acronyms for remembering individual DSM criteria for each disorder are available on the internet.[6] The approximate U.S. prevalence rates given below for the various PDs are from Sperry (2003).

22.2 CLUSTER A

22.2.1 Paranoid PD

People with this disorder, referred to briefly as paranoids, are characterized by distrust and suspicion of others as indicated by at least four of the following attributes:

---

[4]Benjamin (1996: 102).
[5]See http://en.wikipedia.org/wiki/Personality_disorder (accessed November 2010) and click on the appropriate disorder. See also Millon et al. (2000).
[6]http://www.personalityresearch.org/pd.html (accessed 2010).

1) unjustifiably suspicious that others are doing them mischief, (2) having unjustified doubts about the trustworthiness and loyalty of friends and associates, (3) being reluctant to confide in others in case the information is used against them, (4) feeling threatened by benign remarks and events, (5) being unforgiving and holding grudges, (6) perceiving personal attacks on character or reputation that are not apparent to others and then angrily overreacting, and (7) having unjustified recurring suspicions of a spouse's or sexual partner's fidelity.[7] Their overt behavior is wariness and their main belief is that people are dangerous.[8] The prevalence of this PD is between about 0.5% and 2.5% .

Paranoids view sincerity with suspicion and can be testy and emotionally closed. They never let their guard down and are hypervigilant in looking for any intrusion into their inner mental sanctuary, believing they are being spied upon. They appear to be guarded, hostile, rigid black and white thinkers, and unfairly accuse others and even life-long friends of various things. They transform innocent remarks into criticism and take some minor incidental fact and grow it into some major conspiracy, thus confirming their preconceived fears. Overtly, they seem arrogant, self-righteous, and easily enraged, but covertly they feel intimidated and inferior, and plagued by doubt and guilt.[9] Projection is used as a defense mechanism (see Section 21.5) to get rid of their guilt about their own aggressive impulses. They do this by attributing their own impulses to others believing themslelves to be the ones who are the persecuted and endangered victims. Paranoids may experience delusional anxiety, mood, and somatization disorders, and may resort to substance abuse. Overlap with other disorders is not uncommon and other personality disorders can also exhibit paranoid traits.

The paranoid's belief of being attacked probably arises from having abusive and/or deceitful parents. The parenting may have been sadistic, controlling, and degrading, and is often passed down from generation to generation. The paranoid may have been chosen as a scapegoat for the family and suffered only criticism and escalating demands. He or she may have been discussed unfavorably by the parents as though the child wasn't present. The child can then become sensitive to and be angry about whisperings, humiliation, and exclusions.

Counseling Paranoids

Counseling the paranoid personality is challenging for the therapist as paranoids generally come to counseling only when coerced by others, for example by a boss or spouse, and want to control the therapy process. They don't come asking for help as such, but instead may seek symptom relief from the effects of their own thought processes and behavior. The therapist therefore needs to look below the surface, but with care, support, and patience as paranoids are secretive, feel exposed and vulnerable, and are not readily open to scrutiny. An appropriate distance needs to be maintained so that the client feels in control. Starting therapy can be stressful for most paranoids and the inappropriate confrontation of delusive ideas simply strengthens their belief that the therapist is just another person attacking them. This reinforces the same vicious circle they experience in real life. It is important

[7]For more details of these criteria see "Personality Disorders" on the internet under Wikipedia and click on "paranoid."
[8]Beck et al. (2004: 21).
[9]Millon et al. (2000: 388).

to remember that any alliance established is fragile and easily destroyed. Because paranoids are often blaming and abrasive, they tend to provoke similar counter-transference reactions so that therapists need to contain their own negative counter-reactions and defensiveness. The therapist will be under close scrutiny so that he or she will need to tread carefully when offering interpretations or comments to the paranoid.

In addition to the five general counseling suggestions of Section 22.1, further strategies are as follows:[10]

1. Provide supportive empathy in contrast to early abuse.

2. Help the client to realize that his or her hostility also puts the client in an abusive role.

3. Help the client to deal with introjects from caregivers that the client feels a need to project.

4. Encourage the client to focus on his or her goals, dealing with the least threatening first.

5. Increase self-efficacy by teaching coping skills and encouraging a more realistic assessment of both objective threats and the client's problem solving ability.

6. Use cognitive restructuring to deal with black and white thinking and over-generalization.

7. Encourage new perspectives on other people, for example, how well they follow through on particular requests, and how well the client does also.

8. Introduce anti-anxiety techniques such as the relaxation response (Section 2.2.5) and the hierarchical desensitization method of Section 6.3.3.

9. Modify social behavior by helping the client to better appreciate social cues through role playing or perhaps watching soap operas with the therapist. This will help the client to become a better observer and be more self-correcting.

10. Encourage a shift in perspective from seeing problems as internally generated to seeing them coming from external causes.

22.2.2 Schizoid PD

People with this disorder, briefly referred to as schizoids, are characterized by a detachment from human relationships and a shutting down of emotions as indicated by at least four of the following: (1) not wanting close relationships (including family), (2) lacking close friends (except immediate family), (3) showing little, if any, interest in sex, (4) invariably choosing solitary activities, (5) taking little, if any, pleasure in activities, (6) showing apparent indifference to the praise or criticism of others, and (7) being emotionally cold and detached.[11]   Their main belief is

---

[10]Based on Millon et al. (2000: 408–409).

[11]For more details of these criteria see "Personality Disorders" on the internet under Wikipedia and click on "paranoid."

hat they need plenty of space and their overt behavior is that of isolation.[12]   A 'primeval strategy" is being autonomous along with the belief that "relationships are messy."[13] The prevalence of this PD is low.

The above criteria focus on what is missing. A schizoid is like a person without a personality, which makes the disorder difficult to describe. Schizoids passively adjust to their circumstances and rarely initiate change. Although the schizoid and avoidant are both interpersonally detached, the schizoid is passively detached, whereas the avoidant is actively detached.[14] The schizoid prefers to be alone, but the avoidant chooses to be alone out of fear. Millon et al. note that "The two personalities may be especially difficult to distinguish during a diagnostic interview, where the avoidant is too fearful or ashamed to be forthcoming, and the schizoid simply has nothing to say."[15]

Schizoids keep to themselves as much as possible and prefer to be on their own so as to be free of interpersonal stress and possible demands from others. They float along untroubled and indifferent, never getting angry or excited, and seem incapable of feeling anything. Schizoids fear engulfment and seek strength and identity in isolation. They can come across as detached, totally unresponsive, and unfriendly, and do not understand the idea of closeness. This desire for privacy and detachment from human affairs can create all sorts of problems for them, especially in areas of employment and family. We all like to be left alone some of the time, but schizoids want it most of the time, yet fail to develop an intimate relationship with self. If they are pressured into social circumstances, they become unresponsive and withdraw even more. Generally they are not motivated to get therapeutic help. Summing up, the key difference of the schizoid PD from other personality disorders is a generalized absence of emotion and lack of desire of interpersonal contact.

What can lead a person to becoming schizoid? Family life may have been colorless, with a focus on just basic social roles. There may have been little warmth, play, or emotional interaction, leading to a very solitary introspective life that modeled a withdrawn parent. The child expected nothing and gave nothing. He or she was socialized, but was not sociable and not attached to self or others.

Counseling Schizoids

Counseling schizoids is difficult and rather bleak as, having no desire for interpersonal relationships and little emotional capacity, they can't see how therapy can help them. They will be indifferent to the praise or criticism of the therapist and find the therapeutic relationship difficult to understand. The biggest trap for the therapist will be to expect too much and get frustrated through lack of progress. In addition to the five general counseling suggestions of Section 22.1, Millon et al.[16] suggest three goals for counseling schizoids.

1. Find something, no matter how small, that the client associates with pleasure.

2. Increase interpersonal contacts, where possible (social anxiety may exist). The therapist can begin by finding out who are actively involved in the daily

[12]Beck et al. (2004: 21).
[13]Pretzer and Beck (1996).
[14]Millon et al. (2000: 312).
[15]Millon et al. (2000: 333).
[16]Millon et al. (2000: 336–337).

life of the client and exploring the client's attitudes, interactions, and feelings (if any) towards these people. It is probably a good idea to bring any significant other that may exist into the therapeutic relationship to hear his or her side of the story. Family members, who may have been passively ignored, can eventually be encouraged to view the client with greater tolerance and understanding through family conferencing. If the client feels anything at all in a family situation, it is likely to be rejection. Significant others can be encouraged to note anything the client seems to find enjoyable or rewarding, as in (1) above.

If the client feels some social anxiety, then that does at least indicate that the client feels something, and techniques for handling social anxiety can then be used (see Section 7.7). Exploring a client's fantasies can be used to uncover any self issues or unfulfilled needs and desires, and the role of isolation in the client's life can be connected to these fantasies.

3. Involve the individual vocationally or educationally, where possible.

Beck et al.[17] suggest helping the client to set up a hierarchy of social interaction goals that he or she may want to accomplish, starting with the easiest. A major goal is to help the schizoid to learn to identify thoughts and emotions arising from such interactions. This can be done two ways. First, the client can be asked to keep a daily diary of automatic thoughts, especially those immediately preceding or following any social encounter, and second, identify and discuss the mental states of others. Social skills can be practiced using role play, real-life exposure, and audio feedback to help identify any problem areas. Questions that focus on positive aspects can help the client to find out what he or she prefers and why, and then the client can be encouraged to repeat those preferences.

22.2.3   Schizotypal PD

People with this disorder, referred to briefly as schizotypals, are characterized by a "pervasive pattern of social and interpersonal deficits marked by acute discomfort with, and reduced capacity for, close relationships as well as by cognitive or perceptual distortion and eccentricities of behavior ...."[18] as indicated by five or more of the following: (1) believing others are referring to him or her (known as ideas of reference), (2) having odd or bizarre beliefs (e.g., magical thinking) affecting behavior, (3) having unusual perceptual experiences (including bodily illusions), (4) showing odd thinking and speech, (5) being paranoid, (6) having inappropriate affect, (7) exhibiting odd behavior or appearance, (8) lacking close friends other than immediate family, and (9) experiencing social anxiety (usually of paranoid nature).[19] The prevalence of this PD is about 3%.

There is considerable overlap of Schizotypal PD with other disorders such as avoidant and paranoid PDs, which makes counseling difficult. There seems to be also a genetic link with schizophrenia, and the boundary between the two is somewhat diffuse. Schizotypals, like schizoids, are relatively asocial, but for a

[17]Beck et al. (2004: chapter 7).
[18]American Psychiatric Association (2000a).
[19]For more details of these criteria see "Personality Disorders" on the internet under Wikipedia and click on "schizotypal."

lifferent reason. They often feel anxious in the company of others, perhaps because of paranoid concerns.

What can lead a person to becoming schizotypal? One possibility goes back to childhood where a parent undermined the child's reality by doing the very things that the child was punished for. The suggestion is that the parent "knew" something important about the child even when the parent was not present, a kind of sixth sense or telepathy. As an adult, the schizotypal claims to have the same ability. Another possibility is that a long history of of severe abuse may lead to a paranoid withdrawal in the adult schitzotypal. The child may have been prohibited from leaving home and found at the same time that being alone in his or her room provided a safe haven to escape from an abusive parent. This isolation interfered with social development and encouraged the development of fantasy.

Counseling Schizotypals

According to Millon et al.[20] schitzotypal PD is perhaps the easiest PD to identify, but one of the most difficult to counsel, taking a very long time. The extreme social anxiety and paranoid problems of the schitzotypal tend to distort the communication between therapist and client making a therapeutic alliance difficult. The need for distance needs to be respected as the client may initially view the therapist with suspicion and retreat as anxiety increases. Therapists need to proceed very patiently and slowly to avoid misconceptions about the therapeutic relationship. Any communication should be simple, straightforward, concrete, and jargon free. The therapist may need to accept some silence. In addition to the five general counseling suggestions of Section 22.1, further strategies are as follows:[21]

1. Establish a more normal pattern of interpersonal relationships by using the therapeutic relationship as a model.

2. Use person-centered (Rogerian) counseling, focusing on the three basics of congruence, unconditional positive regard, and empathy.

3. Once the therapeutic alliance had been established, encourage the client to discuss his or her distortions of reality as they occur.

4. Build self-worth, motivation, and confidence, and focus on positive attributes, all to assist with strengthening social encounters.

5. Use modeling behavior and basic social skills training to help the client to understand what behaviors are appropriate in daily living. (Schizoids have difficulty in sorting out the relevant and irrelevant in interpersonal relationships.)

6. Help the client to have a better understanding of interpersonal realities so as to reduce social anxiety and related paranoia.

Because of its unstructured nature, psychodynamic therapy may not be appropriate, and a combination of medication and cognitive therapy could be helpful. The therapist can identify the client's characteristic automatic thoughts, patterns of reasoning, and assumptions about social interaction, as schizotypals usually believe

---

[20] Millon et al. (2000: 367).
[21] Based on Millon et al. (2000: 368–369).

that others dislike them. Thoughts, including bizarre ones, can be set up as hypotheses and the client taught to test them against the evidence. Clients can also be taught how to collect contrary evidence, particularly evidence that is contrary to their predictions.

22.3 CLUSTER B

22.3.1 Antisocial PD

People with antisocial PD, referred to briefly as antisocials, are characterized by a disregard for the rights of others since age 15 years, and by at least three of the following: (1) lawless acts, (2) repeated lying or deceitfulness and conning others, (3) impulsiveness or no forward planning, (4) aggressiveness as indicated by repeated fights or assaults, (5) reckless disregard for self and others (e.g., substance abuse), (6) consistent irresponsibility with work and finances, and (7) lack of remorse and indifference to mistreating others. In addition there must be evidence of a Conduct Disorder[22] with onset before age 15 years.[23] Their main belief is that others are to be taken advantage of and their overt behavior is attack.[24] A "primeval strategy" is being predatory along with the belief that "others are weak."[25] A typical triggering event can occur when there are social standards and rules. The prevalence rates for this PD are about 3% for males and 1% for females.

A lack of conscience seems to be the most striking characteristic of antisocials, and being intolerant to boredom they need excitement. Since they are predatory, they see others as weak and themselves as needing to be strong and independent. They are generally difficult to get along with and are often manipulative, as they "need to dominate, seize power, gain material reward, or satisfy some concrete need."[26] Their maxim is, "Do unto others before they do unto you." Like paranoids, they are hypersensitive, easily angered, and interpret innocent comments as thinly veiled threats. Unlike sadists, however, they are more focused on their own gratification and people are used to achieve this. The terms psychopath and sociopath are also used for more extreme cases of the disorder. The prevalence of the disorder is about 3% for men and 1% for women. There is some evidence of a genetic link and biological factors.

What can lead a person to becoming antisocial? Children exposed to neglect, hostility, and physical abuse are going to see the world as a harsh and unforgiving place. These environmental factors can interact with biological predisposing factors. Such children learn that having a conscience, being empathetic and sensitive to the emotions of others, or giving in to guilt, are a sign of weakness and therefore to be avoided. Without parental controls and appropriate social role models, aggression is given free reign. If there is violence in the home, children eventually imitate the same pattern as violent parents tend to beget violent children. Sporadic parental control can lead to an adult that fiercely protects his or her autonomy. Inept

---

[22]See http://en.wikipedia.org/wiki/Conduct_disorder (accessed November 2010) for DSM-IV-TR diagnostic criteria.
[23]For more details of these criteria see "Personality Disorders" on the internet under Wikipedia and click on "antisocial."
[24]Beck et al. (2004: 21).
[25]Pretzer and Beck (1996).
[26]Millon et al. (2000: 129).

)arenting can teach the antisocial to model the same behavior and overlook the welfare of others.

Counseling Antisocials

Treatment is usually forced on antisocials and the therapist then has to convince the client to make the best of the time even if he or she doesn't want to be there. Their willingness to hurt others makes their counseling difficult. They can't be trusted, and they may give an appearance of beginning to conform and developing a sense of conscience in order to shrug off any therapeutic constraints. Millon et al. suggest not using psychodynamic approaches as "antisocials are not typically capable of change through insight."[27] As most antisocials have been rejected, a therapist has to be careful of counter-transference reactions to their difficult and often manipulative behavior, otherwise the therapist is seen as one more rejecting person. Forming a nurturing attachment is a major goal for therapy and a frank, relaxed, and nondefensive interpersonal style coupled with a strong sense of humor is beneficial. However, too much empathy may lead to the client taking advantage of the therapist.

In addition to the five general counseling suggestions of Section 22.1, further strategies are as follows:[28]

1. The therapeutic alliance and bonding between client and therapist are of particular importance so that trust can be developed.

2. If therapy has been forced on the client, the therapist can "clear the air" by suggesting that the time might as well be used constructively.

3. Cognitive therapy can be used to raise the level of a client's moral perception of the world by reviewing a client's life, noting specific problems, and identifying cognitive distortions associated with each problem. Rather than accusing or trying to shame a client, a more appropriate focus would be on the long-term negative consequences of his or her behavior.

4. By describing the disorder as having long-term negative consequences such as prison, possible physical harm from others, and broken contact with family and friends, the therapist can help minimize a client's feeling of being accused and encourage the client to continue therapy.

5. It is helpful throughout therapy for both client and therapist to establish clear priorities and consider pros and cons before making important decisions, thus helping the client have an enlightened self-interest.

22.3.2 Borderline PD

Defining what is meant by a borderline personality disorder (BPD) is somewhat controversial and has been repeatedly reformulated in the past. Nearly 90% of those with BPD are also diagnosed with another personality disorder or major mental illness (e.g., depression), thus adding further complications to the profile. It is therefore not surprising that more has been written about this disorder than any

[27]Millon et al. (2000: 134).
[28]Based on Millon et al. (2000: 134–135).

other and there are different sets of symptoms in the literature. In the U.S. about 1% to 3% percent of the adult population have this disorder and the completed suicide rate for this group is about 10–12%.

People with this disorder, referred to briefly as borderlines, are categorized by instability in relationships, mood, and self-image as indicated by five or more of the following: (1) making frantic efforts to avoid real or imagined abandonment, (2) alternating in relationships between extremes like saint and devil or love and hate, (3) having an unstable sense of self so that they come across as very different people in different circumstances, (4) showing impulsiveness in at least two potentially self-damaging areas (e.g., promiscuous sex, eating problems, substance abuse, reckless driving), (5) having rapidly changing emotions, (6) having recurrent suicidal ideation or self harm, (7) having chronic feelings of emptiness, (8) showing intense, inappropriate anger, and (9) exhibiting transient paranoia or severe dissociative symptoms. There are some diagnostic tests and summaries of symptoms on the internet found by searching on "borderline personality test." One particularly useful one is the revised Diagnostic Interview of Borderlines (DIB-R) based on work by Gunderson, Zanarini, and colleagues. The symptoms are summarized under the headings of affect, cognition, impulse action patterns, and interpersonal relationships.[29]

Borderlines are emotionally unstable, frequently angry, and have intense and stormy relationships as their opinion of others undergo sudden shifts between seeing a person as one who is very positive and supporting to one who is very negative and neglecting—from Dr Jekyll to Mr Hyde. They don't like being left alone for very long, they persistently experience separation anxiety, and they can seem dependent and clingy through their fear of abandonment. When they are doing well at something important they suddenly give it up. Because of negative feelings (e.g., anxiety, depression, guilt) they may indulge impulsively in drugs, promiscuity, or self harm. With an unstable self-image, they can suddenly chop and change goals, values, jobs, and opinions, and under stress they can be susceptible to temporary psychotic states and dissociative episodes.[30] Chronic insomnia is a common complaint.

From an interpersonal point of view,[31] they basically have a friendly dependency on a nurturer, but this becomes hostile if the caregiver or lover doesn't deliver enough (and there is never enough). If someone important to them is late, they feel abandoned and go into a panic. A common defense mechanism for borderlines is splitting (see Section 21.5), where good and bad images of objects (including people) are actively separated and held apart, and anger is directed at the bad image. One explanation for the splitting is that a person remains stuck in the separation-individuation stage that he or she went through as a toddler. Like children, they find it difficult to appreciate the "gray areas" of life in between the good and the bad. Attachment is a key issue for borderlines.

There are many possible causes of BPD. Genetics and reduced serotonin levels may contribute as well as childhood trauma and emotional neglect, though some report a fairly normal childhood. One common cause is child sexual abuse, especially

---

[29] See http://www.jwoodphd.com/borderline_personality_disorder.htm (accessed October 2010) for a helpful summary.

[30] Millon et al. (2000: 413).

[31] Benjamin (1996: 124, 126).

when it occurred when the child was alone and unprotected; the message being that autonomy is bad. A second cause might be through being in an extremely chaotic family of origin in which the client may occupy the center stage, as a scapegoat for example. A third cause may be experiences of traumatic abandonment with "aloneness" being linked in some way to "bad person." A fourth possible cause is that the borderline may have learnt that the way to receive parental nurturing is to be needy and miserable. Finally, one possible cause of the disorder is being stuck in the separation-individuation stage so that the future borderline is unable to distinguish between self and other before the image of the mother is internalized as a permanent presence. The fear is that if Mum goes, she goes forever. The borderline keeps having this overwhelming separation anxiety.

Counseling Borderlines

As noted by Millon et al.[32] borderlines are notoriously difficult to counsel as establishing a therapeutic relationship is not easy and there is a high probability of them just quitting therapy. There is always the worry by the borderline that the therapist will not be supportive enough. If there is self-harm involved, this can raise the anxiety level for the therapist. The interpersonal problems experienced by a borderline can carry over into the therapeutic relationship so that the therapist will also experience the swings from being idealized to being devalued. Because of possible threat of suicide and repeated self-harm, and the emotional intensity of the client, the therapist may want to "withdraw" and will therefore need to monitor his or her own countertransference feelings and maintain a healthy level of detachment. Because of the borderline's demands for increased attention and care, the therapist will need to maintain appropriate personal boundaries and avoid blatant manipulations. Borderline PD may be comorbid with other disorders such as negativistic, depressive, histrionic, and avoidant disorders. Borderlines are also prone to somatic symptoms, substance abuse, and eating disorders. They are also inclined to self-sabotage when things are going well (because of a vicious introject), so set-backs can be expected in counseling because of the belief that improvement means an end of therapy and abandonment by the therapist. Ending counseling can therefore be difficult as it may lead to a relapse.

In addition to the five general counseling suggestions of Section 22.1, further strategies are as follows:[33]

1. A strong therapeutic relationship, although difficult, is important as the therapist can be readily classified as malevolent and be devalued, as noted above. Mistrust is a common problem.

2. Care is needed not to overstep the client's boundary as a lack of client trust and consequent fear of intimacy may need to be overcome.

3. Clear goals for therapy (e.g., improved health and ego strength) need to be established right from the beginning and boundaries clarified about the amount of contact outside the counseling room. The therapist can explain that it is not always possible to talk to the client whenever the client calls as it will endorse his or he neediness and weaken rather than strengthen the client. This

[32]Millon et al. (2000: 445).
[33]Based on Millon et al. (2000: 446–448).

would be contrary to a general goal of therapy. As the therapy progresses, phone calls and extra sessions will need to be limited.

4. It is helpful to focus on the strengths of the client and how they can be applied to different situations. The pathology can be externalized and seen as the enemy by the therapist and client.

5. Strategies for dealing with self-harm and destructive behaviors can be used (See Section 8.5.) Fantasies can be explored about who will be pleased by such activities.

6. The therapist can test out the reality of a client's black and white (dichotomous) thinking where it occurs. For example, one can ask the client to define trustworthy and untrustworthy and use the definition to evaluate the people in the client's life. The aim is to show that these people lie in between the two extremes, thus occupying a "gray" position. This cognitive restructuring can encourage the client to identify those automatic thoughts that "caricature the interpersonal world" and help create a better way of experiencing others (e.g., not everyone will abandon or criticize the client).[34] The same approach can be applied to the client's self-image so that he or she realizes that we all have good and bad qualities, and the bad can be worked on. Some appropriate confrontation may be helpful.

7. Role playing and social skills training can be used.

8. Setting goals and maintaining priorities from week to week is a good idea as borderlines find this difficult because of an unstable self-image.

9. Linking the client's early history with present symptoms can bring understanding and relief for the borderline who may have previously been labeled as "crazy."

22.3.3   Histrionic PD

People with this disorder, referred to briefly to as histrionics, are characterized by excessive emotion and attention seeking as indicated by at least five of the following: (1) having to be the centre of attention, otherwise are uncomfortable, (2) being sexually seductive and provocative, (3) having shallow and rapidly shifting emotions, (4) focusing on physical appearance to draw attention, (5) having an impressionistic style of speech lacking detail, (6) being over-dramatic, (7) being suggestible, and (8) seeing relationships as being more intimate than they actually are.[35] Their main belief is that they need to impress, and their overt behavior is drama.[36] A "primeval strategy" is being exhibitionistic along with a belief that "I can go by my feelings."[37] This PD arises much more with women than with men. Prevalence rates are between 2% and 3%.

[34] Millon et al. (2000: 447.
[35] For more details of these criteria see "Personality Disorders" on the internet under Wikipedia and click on "histrionic."
[36] Beck et al. (2004: 21).
[37] Pretzer and Beck (1996).

The most striking characteristic of histrionics is the chronic need for stimulation and attention and always wanting to be "in the lime light." As a result they are lively and enthusiastic, but flirtatious, seductive, dramatic, and capricious in their relationships. Their emotions and thinking tend to be shallow and, although they may know a lot of people, they don't know people deeply including themselves. They don't ponder, concentrate, contemplate, or reflect, and tend to give up on difficult problems.

Histrionics may use repression to keep their world nice and straightforward so that they don't have to think about the deep issues of life or confront their own hyper-sexual manipulation of others. They ignore details of their world and relationships and have only superficial knowledge of their own identity. Instead of taking control of their own lives, they seek to control those who control their future. They may do this by using hypochondriacal concerns and an unfounded somatization disorder to get the support they want. Like dependents, they rely on others to help them, but with the difference that rather than being helpless they try to draw in potential caretakers. Consequently intimate relationships tend to have a superficial quality and their partners get tired of their neediness for attention and stimulation, and withdraw emotionally. Although their basic position is of friendly trust, they will secretly try to force the desired nurturing in various ways such as inappropriate seductive behaviors and manipulative suicidal attempts.[38]

Where does the seductive style come from? One possibility is that when a female client was a child, the doting father reinforced behaviors that were cute and pretty. Although she may have received favorable comments on one occasion however, she might not have received them on another. As the result of inconsistent parenting and a confusion over whether a behavior is rewarded or not, she may have gone into adolescence with an overwhelming desire for love and attention. She may have even been treated as a "showcase" for good looks and entertainment purposes, but wasn't nurtured as a person in her own right. As an adult she may feel reinforced by being attractive and not because of her abilities. Another way that a child may have gained attention was by being sickly and needy.

Counseling Histrionics

Histrionics rarely seek therapy for various reasons.[39] First, with society's focus on good looks and charm, histrionics can get by as there will always be offers. If their primary relationships are satisfactory, then what can be wrong? Second, they may seek therapy just for for immediate relief for some other problem such as anxiety or depression. Third, if they are thinking of having counseling and they are female, they will generally want a male therapist and may be put off by the fact that a majority of therapists are women. A female therapist may get a hard time. Two complicating factors can impinge on the therapeutic relationship, dependency and, for a male therapist, sexual vulnerability. Histrionics will want the therapist to take care of them, which can develop into a pathological neediness, but if they improve and develop new skills, they may fear that they won't be reinforced for being attractive any more and the therapy will be terminated, leaving them feeling

[38]Benjamin (1996: 174).
[39]Millon et al. (2000: 264–265).

abandoned. Benjamin[40] warns that the therapist saying nothing can be construed as agreement, especially when clients talk about their inappropriate behaviors.

In addition to the five general counseling suggestions of Section 22.1, further strategies are as follows:[41]

1. A major aim is to help histrionics to give up their manipulative and demanding dependence that leads them to orchestrate every social interaction. The struggle is to make the unconscious conscious.

2. Cognitively, histrionics need to learn to focus their attention as they are easily distracted and can fritter away the counseling session by talking about tangential themes. Using structure such as a review and a detailed agenda for each counseling session, and formulating short-term and long-term goals can help clients stay on track, though some time can be allocated for more general talk. The goals should be chosen by the client as he or she will want to please the therapist. Also goals that promise more immediate gratification can keep the client focused and in therapy. Bigger goals can be broken down into smaller sub-goals. Encouraging a client to reflect on personal goals, why he or she chose them, and what would change when achieved will help the development of identity and begin to fill the mental void.

3. Help the client to identify automatic thoughts and confront impulsive tendencies.

4. Use assertiveness training (see Section 2.5.4) to help clients put forward their own thoughts and agendas rather than getting others to solve their problems and defining themselves in terms of other people to whom they attach.

5. Teach listening skills.

6. Revisit past experiences to help in the recognition of past repeating patterns and their futility, and focus on better and more adult ways of behaving.

7. Help clients to understand that dramatizing and sexual seduction indicates an intense underlying desperation. Realizing this can increase motivation for change.

8. Explore early family dynamics so that the client can realize the origin of his or her excessive dependency that is now unresolved and unconscious.

9. Praise the client for improved behavior (e.g., self-reliant and nonsexual behavior) as this can begin to counteract the childhood pattern.

22.3.4 Narcissistic PD

People with narcissistic PD, referred to briefly as narcissists, are notoriously difficult to counsel because they see themselves as superior beings and it is sometimes hard to get a word in edgeways! Narcissists are characterized by needing admiration and lacking empathy as indicated by at least five of the following: (1) having a grandiose

---

[40]Benjamin (1996: 183).
[41]Based on Millon et al. (2000: 266–267).

ense of self-importance and exaggerating achievements, (2) being preoccupied with antasies of unlimited success, power, brilliance, beauty, or ideal love, (3) believing hey are uniquely "special" and should only associate with other special or high status people, (4) requiring excessive admiration, (5) having a sense of entitlement and believing they should get special treatment, (6) exploiting others, (7) lacking empathy and ignoring others' needs, (8) being envious of others or believing that others are envious of them, and (9) being arrogant and haughty.[42] Their main belief is that they are special and their overt behavior is self-aggrandizement.[43] A "primeval strategy" is being competitive along with the belief that "I'm above the rules."[44] The prevalence of this PD is less than 1%.

Narcissists see themselves as so special that others should automatically recognize this without needing to do anything to deserve it. However, they are extremely vulnerable to criticism or being ignored. The grandiosity of narcissists feeds into a fantasy life in which they see themselves as brilliant and successful, and they need these fantasies to protect their superior image. They generally regard others as being inferior and expect everyone to recognize their superiority and bow to their wishes. They believe they should be given whatever they need and they get irritated when others fail to assist them in their very important work. Because of their egocentricity, they are indifferent to the feelings, rights, and welfare of others, and sometimes even the law. This indifference is a key feature of narcissism.

Narcissists are always right and when challenged will have every manner of excuse or justification. If necessary, they will reverse the guilt or reinterpret the past (rewrite history) and may resort to belittling, undermining, and sarcasm. When pressed further, they can become even more dismissive and possibly angry. If they have an interpersonal problem it is the other person who is at fault, not them. They may believe that the other person is envious of them and is therefore trying to create difficulties. Note that narcissism may show up differently in other cultures, especially where there is less emphasis on individualism. It may be more exhibitionistic, as in the United States, or closet narcissism, as in Japan.[45] This difference is reflected in the fact that the narcissistic PD is listed in the ICD-10 classification under "Other specific personality disorders." Finally we note that narcissism has a greater prevalence among males.

Narcissists use a variety of defense mechanisms including splitting, grandiosity, rationalization, and fantasy.[46] Splitting involves dramatic shifts in the evaluation of self and others. The person alternates between extremes of idealization and degradation in an attempt to cope with simultaneously dealing with the "good" and "bad" aspects of self and others. What is disconcerting is that such people can hold extreme views of those who are close to them such as friends and family members. On one day they may describe a new acquaintance as the most wonderful person they ever met and on the next day describe him or her as a horrible person. A man can text his separated wife and tell her how much he loves her and misses her and later sends a message telling her that she is a horrible bitch! They also

[42] For more details of these criteria see "Personality Disorders" on the internet under Wikipedia and click on "narcissistic."
[43] Beck et al. (2004: 21).
[44] Pretzer and Beck (1996).
[45] Millon et al (2000: 274).
[46] See Section 21.5.

use rationalization as their self-centeredness often leads them to act unthinkingly without caring about consequences for others or how others view their actions.

There are several different views about the origin of narcissism and, as with other PDs, it is usually linked back to childhood where there may have been a developmental arrest through lack of empathy during infancy. One theory proposes that the self-concept is damaged through lack of unconditional love combined with an overemphasis on some particular ability of the child. The grandiose self becomes attractive to the child because it is the only self the caregivers are prepared to accept. An example of this lack of balance is where an only or first-born male is indulged by a mother for being gifted or special. Another aspect is that the child may be worshipped, but the adoration is not accompanied by genuine self-disclosure so that the narcissist does not get to know about the parent's separate feelings and needs. Narcissism can develop later in life because of the status one achieves (e.g., the rich and famous).

Counseling Narcissists

Millon et al.[47] note some problems that can come up in counseling narcissists. To begin with, narcissists are unlikely to come voluntarily for counseling as they are generally in denial about their own shortcomings. They believe they are getting on quite well on their own in society and their pride may cause them to reject the defective role of "patient." They may come for some other problem like low-grade depression or with a desire to "fix" their partner. They will expect the therapist to agree with them! If they do come because they want relief from nagging feelings of emptiness and powerlessness, their aim will be to get back on the "grandiose wagon" again, which they fell off! When they see that the therapist has different goals, they may put up some resistance and even question the qualifications of the therapist. They may keep their distance and react against any comment that implies deficiency on their part, as the therapist has now joined the ranks of their critics. One of the problems is that if the therapist is too supportive, the narcissist only becomes more grandiose! Interpretation can also raise problems as it could mean (heaven forbid!) that the narcissist has overlooked something, or that the therapist is trying to understand the narcissist whose problems are unique and beyond ordinary mortals. Confrontation to facilitate pattern recognition needs to be gentle, otherwise it may be experienced as extreme criticism that can lead to a rapid termination of therapy.

In addition to the five general counseling suggestions of Section 22.1, further strategies are as follows:[48]

1. Establish a strong therapeutic alliance before confronting any maladaptive patterns, otherwise therapy will terminate. There may be some negative transference toward the therapist and the therapist can help the client connect this with early relationships.

2. Counsel to achieve a balance between helping with the presenting problem and dealing with the underlying disorder. For example, depression can be helped by looking at positive aspects, which allows the client to focus on himself or herself, but not to the point of over-inflating the ego so that the

---

[47] Millon et al. (2000: 304–305).
[48] Based on Millon et al. (2000: 305–307).

real work cannot be done. There is a need to get beyond just symptom relief to the underlying pathology.

3. Provide consistent and accurate empathy that enables the client to deal with unpleasant inner experiences and what caused them. The aim is to help the client decrease entitlement, envy, and arrogant grandiosity.

4. Identify individuals in the client's upbringing who were emotionally centered on the client and then connect how they viewed the client and their expectations of the client with the current situation. This will help the client to see that he or she is unconsciously being controlled by people from the past. The client won't be happy to give anybody so much control over his or her inner world.

5. Helping the client understand the origin of his or her conscious and unconscious anger, directed for example at early attachment figures.

6. Creating a paradox by painting grandiosity as a need, which will conflict with the client's self-image of strength.

7. Address the use of defenses such as splitting, projection, and projective identification.

8. Take responsibility for small errors in order to model how a "status" person can be comfortable with his or her own imperfections without needing to project blame onto others. The client can see that lacking perfection does not imply utter failure.

9. Use cognitive restructuring to deal with automatic thoughts about the client's grandiose view of self, the evaluation by others, and the client's reaction to such evaluations. The aim is to create an awareness about and respect for the feelings of others, and to encourage more empathy and reduce exploitive behavior.

10. Replace unrealistic fantasies by more realistic ones that are more likely to be achieved. This will help desensitize the client to the possibility of failure.

11. Help the client to look for personal similarities with others rather an elevate himself or herself above others, and use the common ground to create more empathy. Role playing can be used to help the client identify the emotions of others and promote beliefs about their significance. Giving compliments can be a start as an alternative way of relating to others. It is also about learning not to take things personally.

22.4   CLUSTER C

22.4.1   Avoidant PD

People with an avoidant PD, referred to briefly as avoidants, are characterized by wanting to avoid being in public view because of being oversensitive to negative evaluations and by at least four of the following: (1) avoiding occupations involving significant interpersonal contact through fear of criticism, disapproval, or rejection, (2) avoiding involvement with people unless sure of being liked, (3) being reluctant to form intimate relationships in fear of being put down in some way (e.g., shame, ridicule, or rejection) due to severe low self-worth, (4) being preoccupied with being criticized or rejected in social settings, (5) being inhibited in new interpersonal situations because of feeling inadequate, (6) seeing self as socially inept, unappealing, or inferior to others, and (7) disliking taking risks or taking part in new activities in case they prove embarrassing.[49] Their main belief is that they may get hurt and their overt behavior is avoidance.[50] A "primeval strategy" is withdrawing along with a belief that "people will reject the real me."[51]

This disorder is often confused with antisocial PD. Clinically, the term antisocial denotes a disregard for society's norms and rules, not social inhibitions. Although avoidants and schizoids both withdraw from interpersonal relationships, they do so for different reasons. Avoidants do it out of hypersensitivity while schizoids are simply detached and socially indifferent. The prevalence of avoidant PD is about 0.5% to 1% of the general population.

Avoidants are painfully sensitive to humiliation and social disapproval. They want to be accepted and loved, but struggle with self-doubt and fear of humiliation so they stay lonely and isolated. They dare not trust themselves to others in case they are exposed for who they are. Because they are hypersensitive to negative evaluation, they don't talk about themselves and seldom reveal their true feelings to others. As a result they have few trusted friends, perhaps only one like a partner or family member. Potential friends must pass strict tests of uncritical support and acceptance before being allowed in. Avoidants try to make themselves invisible socially and avoid anything that might bring them more into public view (e.g., a promotion), because they see themselves as incompetent and don't want to be exposed. This fear of evaluation is very restrictive on their occupational activities so they tend to choose an occupation where it is easy to appear adequate. Wherever they go they feel others always have expectations of them and fear disappointing them. All of this seriously inhibits their lives.

As avoidants are anxious people, it is not surprising that they may suffer from an anxiety disorder such a social phobia, generalized anxiety disorder (GAD), or obsessive-compulsive disorder. Panic attacks can also occur. Those with GAD are always on edge, unable to relax, and have a vague feeling that something dreadful is about to happen, without knowing what it is. The association with social phobia is very close because of the avoidant's fear of social occasions, but there are differences. Millon et al. note that in contrast to those with social phobia, avoidants generally try to "maintain a social façade of poise and self-control that conceals an inner anger, inherited from a developmental history that includes mockery for faults and foibles."[52] They are also prone to depression and panic attacks as well as somatoform (physical) problems. Physical symptoms can be used to solve some coping problems. For example, they provide a wake up to reality when there are

---

[49] For more details of these criteria see "Personality Disorders" on the internet under Wikipedia and click on "avoidant."
[50] Beck et al. (2004: 21).
[51] Pretzer and Beck (1996).
[52] Millon et al. (2000: 162).

eelings of dissociation or they can be used to direct attention away from the person o the symptom, and they can be used to justify social withdrawal.

What leads a person to becoming an avoidant? It can begin with childhood where parents may have been very successful and consequently had very high expectations. If the child was criticized excessively for the smallest mistakes, he or she had to cope with two internal voices, one that demanded achievement and the other overly critical, thus creating a feeling of inadequacy. If the child was overweight or had some physical imperfection, this flaw may have been the subject of continuing cruel family jokes. Such mockery can become internalized, later leaving the adult to be self-critical with a poor self-concept and sensitive to humiliation. Even though the child was rejected, the message was that the family was the main source of support. Loyalty to the family was therefore most important and outsiders were described as likely to be rejecting. Safety was seen as being with the family, whereas the opposite was the case.

Counseling Avoidants

Millon et al.[53] note that one of the difficulties of counseling avoidants is that they will not want to discuss thoughts and emotions and their effect on self openly, one of the requirements for effective therapy. Because of this fear of exposure, avoidants may never come for counseling, and if they do there is always the danger of premature termination. They therefore require a great deal of patience and care to overcome the idea that almost everyone in their lives is a source of negative evaluation. Consequently they need to know that the therapist and the relationship with the therapist will be different. They will need constant reassurance of being accepted and will need to be free to tell the therapist at any time if they feel they are being pushed too hard. Because trust is a key issue, a therapist may be tested at times through the imposition of minor frustrations such as missing appointments or choosing awkward times to see if they still remain accepting, without becoming impatient or critical. Clients may feel disloyal if they talk about humiliations and abuses experienced in their family of origin, and this belief may hinder the counseling process.

In addition to the five general counseling suggestions of Section 22.1, further strategies are as follows:[54]

1. Once trust has been established, the client's feelings of low self-worth can be addressed by disputing his or her automatic thoughts. Care is needed not to seem critical or rejecting as avoidant clients can be easily hurt by therapists. Even minor suggestions can be viewed as put-downs so that anger is often just below the surface. As a check on progress, the client can from time to time be asked to rate the therapist on a trust scale from 0 to 100%.

2. The client can be helped to move away from a continual focus on his or her own faults and instead focus on positive traits that have been pushed aside, thus providing a more balanced view of self.

3. The desensitizing methods discussed in Section 7.7.3 for social phobia can be used to help the client imagine and rehearse social situations that are

[53]Millon et al. (2000: 164–165).
[54]Based on Millon et al. (2000: 165–167).

disturbing. After the client feels more comfortable, a graded hierarchy of anxiety-provoking topics can be introduced and the client asked to predict what will happen in each situation. Client predictions can then be tested, whether by role playing with the therapist as the other person, or by trying out the situations in real life.

4. The client can be encouraged to use anxiety as a signal that automatic thoughts are active. By taking note of these, irrational beliefs can be disputed and realistic coping strategies can be planned.

5. Childhood memories of the client can be analyzed, for example, those of humiliation and embarrassment, and relate these to current behavior and the creation of present emotions. The role of damaging parental and family introjects can explored.

6. Family, couples, and group therapy can be helpful. The therapist may need to deal with any enabling behavior of the partner of the client that perpetrates the avoidance behavior.

22.4.2 Dependent PD

People with a dependent personality PD, referred to briefly as dependents, are characterized by having an excessive need to be taken care of as indicated by at least five of the following: (1) finding it difficult to make everyday decisions without excessive advice and reassurance, (2) needing others to take over responsibility for much of their lives, (3) finding it difficult to disagree with others because they are afraid of losing support or approval, (4) finding it difficult to start or do things on their own through lack of confidence, (5) willing do anything to get care and support from others even to the point of volunteering to do unpleasant things, (6) not liking being alone because they have an exaggerated fear of not being able to look after themselves, (7) when a close relationship ends they need to get into another relationship for care and support, and (8) they are unrealistically occupied with fears of being left to look after themselves.[55] Their main belief is that they are helpless and their overt behavior is attachment.[56] A "primeval strategy" is being help-eliciting along with the belief that "I need others to survive."[57] They see themselves as instrumentally inadequate and wait for strong others to take over.

The dependent PD has some similarities with the histrionic PD. The main difference however is that dependents passively lean on others for everything and encourage others to be active on their behalf through their attitude of helplessness, whereas histrionics are proactive in getting the attention from others that they need. Avoidants and dependents are also similar in lacking confidence, being fearful of criticism, and strongly seeking protection. However, the dependent wants to connect with others, while the avoidant shrinks from others because of fear of rejection and humiliation. Dependents share the fear of abandonment with borderlines.

[55]For more details of these criteria see Personality Disorders on the internet under Wikipedia and click on "dependent."
[56]Beck et al. (2004: 21).
[57]Pretzer and Beck (1996).

Dependents find it almost impossible to take the initiative on their own behalf or even make routine decisions, but instead attach to others for direction, advice, and reassurance. On the surface they are warm and affectionate, but underneath are afraid of doing anything on their own and desperately search for acceptance and approval. Friends will usually see them as generous, thoughtful, and overly apologetic. They are very clingy and quickly submit to their partner's wishes so that the partner won't leave them, an event that would leave them devastated. Their aim is to please others so that they will be regarded as special and will always be looked after. They will therefore avoid conflict at any cost and never disagree with those on whom they depend. Even a request to do something on their own might be seen as rejection. Beck et al.[58] note a number of common cognitive distortions that fuel the disorder. First, dependents see themselves as basically inadequate and helpless, second, their self-perceived shortcomings drive them to find someone to handle their problems in a dangerous world, and third, they are always catastrophizing, especially with regard to relationships. Behind this is black and white (dichotomous) thinking, for example, if they have a difficult problem they see it as impossible or if they are not cared for they see themselves as totally alone. Dependents are particularly prone to anxiety disorders, especially panic disorder and agoraphobia. The latter is linked with the fear of of being left alone or abandoned, which can bring on a panic attack. Dependency is very closely linked with depression because of feelings of helplessness and hopelessness. One "escape route" for dependents is to unconsciously take on some physical disorder so as to solicit the appropriate level of attention.

One common defense mechanism of dependents is[59] whereby the person tries to incorporate the ability, strength, and self-esteem of a stronger figure in exchange for serving the goals of this figure, and the idealization of his or her partner. This idealization of attachment figures is a normal process of growing up, but dependents have difficulty outgrowing this. Although introjection does provide some comfort in being linked to a strong other, it cannot eliminate all sources of anxiety. Consequently dependents make extensive use of another defense mechanism, namely denial, to block feelings of apprehension. This will protect them from acknowledging their anger and hostile impulses, as such feelings may raise the specter of what others might feel or be capable of doing.

What leads a person to become a dependent? One possibility is being brought up in a family where one is always taken care of by others so that there is no development of self-identity or learning to take control of one's life. Every need is taken care of and the child is protected from anything that might be conceived as possibly harmful to the extent of preventing the normal rough and tumble of childhood and discouraging independence. Freedom means unsafe. The family creates the personality trait and the underlying thinking, and does not allow their child to grow up. There can also be an element of overwhelming parental control so that the child's only option is submission. This may be reinforced through being mocked by peers for incompetence. Other factors such as an unusual illnesses or prolonged health issues may prompt a normal parent to become overconcerned or overprotective. A dominant child might force another sibling to adopt a submissive role and run to parents for protection. Alternatively, a hostile child might inspire

---

[58]Beck et al. (2004: chapter 12).
[59]See Section 21.5.

another sibling to be the "good" child who is always obedient and seeks the mother's advice, rewarding the mother's attention and praise with warmth and affection.

Counseling Dependents

Although dependents will not generally seek therapy especially if their support system is intact, the prognosis is good if they do. They may seek help if some aspect of this support gets disrupted. The therapist then assumes a role of caretaker to provide the necessary acceptance, security, and empathy, which will assure continuance of the counseling and provide a willing and motivated client. There is therefore a danger here that the therapist may only reinforce the client's overall pattern of interpersonal dependency. The aim is for the client to become more autonomous and outgrow the therapist. Millon et al.[60] note that it is not just a question of trying to change a client's personality into something which he or she cannot be, but rather a building of strengths, minimizing weaknesses, and breaking old patterns of thinking and behavior. The key is to utilize the dependency in a positive manner without indulging it. The client will want to please the therapist by doing what he or she asks. However, if the dependency pattern is maintained, counseling may go on indefinitely even though the client does everything required by the therapist.

In addition to the five general counseling suggestions of Section 22.1, further strategies are as follows:[61]

1. Because the dependent always wants to please, there is the danger of thinking that therapy is progressing more quickly than it really is. Careful attention needs to be paid to any issues of transference and countertransference.

2. An anxiety hierarchy of behaviors (see Section 6.3.3) can be developed slowly along with role playing and modeling independent living skills. Assertiveness training can be used in targeting submissive behaviors in the counseling room.

3. Exploring family background and upbringing can help the client to understand such things as parental overprotection or sibling interaction that led to the development of dependence. Clients need to realize that without a conscious effort their future will be determined by their past.

4. One can investigate possible defense mechanisms such as introjection, idealization, and denial.

5. Any black and white thinking can be be confronted using cognitive therapy. Automatic thoughts and feelings could be noted by the client in a diary during the week and these processed in counseling. How a client interacts with significant others is especially important. Dependent clients tend to be cognitively immature as they seldom look inside themselves and have only vague ideas about their self-identity and direction.

6. Care is needed in ending counseling, as broaching the subject can lead to a possible relapse with the return of feelings of aloneness and helplessness associated with the possible loss of attachment with the therapist.

[60] Millon et al. (2000: 231–232).
[61] Based on Millon et al. (2000: 229–232).

2.4.3   Obsessive-Compulsive PD

People with an obsessive-compulsive PD, referred to briefly as compulsives, are characterized by being over-preoccupied with rules, orderliness, and perfectionism as indicated by at least four of the following: (1) being preoccupied with details, lists, organization, or schedules to the extent that one loses sight of the purpose of the activity, (2) showing perfectionism that interferes with a project being completed (to the satisfaction of the person), (3) being so devoted to work that recreation and friendship are excluded, (4) being scrupulous and inflexible on morals and values, (5) being hoarders of outdated or useless objects, (6) being unable to delegate tasks or work with others without controlling how things are done, (7) being miserly with money, and (8) being rigid and stubborn. Their main belief is that they must not make a mistake and their overt behavior is perfectionism.[62] The "primeval strategy" is being ritualistic with the belief that "details are crucial."[63] This personality disorder is not the same as obsessive-compulsive disorder (OCD) as compulsives do not generally feel the need to repeatedly perform ritualistic actions—a common symptom of OCD.[64] However, a compulsive might also have OCD. The prevalence of this PD is about 1%.

There are several areas of life where compulsives may feel anxiety. They are always afraid of making a mistake or being accused of being imperfect. Time can therefore become a problem as they may run out of it because they take so long in getting something "right." They are the ones who arrive early and work late to maintain perfection in their work. Consequently they rarely take time out for themselves or their family and lack fun in their lives. Personal and work relationships are often under serious strain because the they insist on being in charge as they are the only ones who know what is the right way of doing things. For some, untidiness may be seen as a lack of perfection, so they may spend considerable time each day putting everything in precisely the right place in precisely the right manner as attention to detail is paramount. Money may be a concern because of fear that things might go wrong in their lives, which can lead to hoarding. In their private lives, compulsives are often rigidly dogmatic with respect to morality, ethics, and values, and everything is done by the book. This rigid thinking often comes across as extreme stubbornness. Compulsives cannot change their minds because that would imply that they are wrong. The attention to detail, order, and perfectionism is a means of coping with an unpredictable world. Compulsives therefore come across as being very formal people, invariably polite, somewhat cheerless, and impersonal, being careful to avoid any revelation of self.

Compulsives make use of a number of defense mechanisms. The most common is reaction formation whereby "compulsives reverse forbidden impulses of hostility and rebellion to over-conform to a rigid ego ideal."[65] They embrace the opposite to what they feel. They may also work out their anger by making others conform to unreasonably strict standards. If others fail, they will either need to acknowledge the superiority of the compulsive or else suffer swift judgement that hides a "sadistic or self-righteous joy behind a mask of maturity."[66] Another defense is

[62]Beck et al. (2004: 21).
[63]Pretzer and Beck (1996).
[64]See Section 8.2.
[65]Millon et al. (2000: 184).
[66]Millon et al. (2000: 184).

isolation of affect, where the compulsive keeps all aspects of experience in separate mental compartments, only allowing intellectual connections and not emotional ones. This prevents any single experience from stirring up any other experience and consequently producing any unanticipated significant emotion or drive.

Where does this disorder originate? One possibility is overcontrol by parents, who may have been fiercely moralistic and who demanded perfection with severe consequences if parental expectations were not realized. This overcontrol is based on the appraisal that children can never be trusted with any amount of autonomy, so that their autonomy could not develop properly. The child is watched very closely and is quickly punished even for minor misdeeds and even when the child does not yet have the cognitive capacity to fully understand the nature of his or her misdemeanor. Such children were taught to feel a deep sense of responsibility and a deep sense of guilt or shame when they failed in their responsibilities. Coupled with this, the parents rarely rewarded or acknowledged the child's legitimate achievements, but simply took them for granted. There was also little warmth shown by the parents. By adolescence, compulsives had taken on the rules and regulations and even the moral sense of superiority of their parents. As adults, their behavior has been described as a form of hostile submission and they displace their hostility onto others. They are the sort of people who are intolerant to exceptions and victimize others with red tape, endless forms, and regulations. No one is allowed to get away with anything! They can rationalize this by asserting that someone has to filter out the unworthy.

Counseling Compulsives

Compulsives tend to view self-exploration as a waste of time and may view counseling as too much of a soft option to spend time on. Because of their stubbornness, they may refuse to admit anything is wrong with them. Underlying the interaction is the inordinate desire to control self and others and, since control is related to hostility, anger is usually just below the surface. They may struggle with the conflict of wanting to defer to the therapist and the fear of loss of control. Another problem for the therapist is that compulsives have difficulty connecting emotionally with anything. Emotions may be equated with being out of control, which is scary for them. Added to this, they are often only fully on display in the home context.

In addition to the five general counseling suggestions of Section 22.1, further strategies are as follows:[67]

1. The way to connect with compulsives is through structure and by appealing to their rationality. They would normally be interested in a therapeutic plan if explained carefully in a logical and scientific manner. Goals can be listed and ranked according to difficulty, with the easy ones solved first. Success with achieving goals will show that change is possible and will provide good motivation for the client. Thought stopping can be used between sessions to minimize inappropriate rumination.

2. Given the approach mentioned in (1) above, the idea that past childhood experience determines the present would be acceptable. The therapist can then help the client to connect with that child and establish empathy with a

[67]Based on Millon et al. (2000: 200–202).

child who was subjected to such cold and demanding parental control. This compassion helps to free compulsives from "a constant, overbearing need to secure approval from internalized, condemning parental images and opens up the way to warmth in current relationships."[68]   The client's identification with the critical parents and their continual faultfinding and its effect on the present situation can then be discussed and investigated.

3. Compulsives are prone to stress so that teaching relaxation techniques can be be helpful.

4. Couple therapy can be helpful[69] as compulsives tend to marry people with complementary personality patterns such as those with dependent or histrionic personality traits. Because compulsives understand rules, they can be enlisted to help establish rules for negotiating trouble spots in the relationship, which will provide a paradoxical method to encourage a relinquishing of control and an equalizing of the relationship.

5. Compulsives can be encouraged to spend more time with their families, especially playing with the children, who can draw out an emotional response.

22.5   OTHER DISORDERS

22.5.1   Depressive PD

People with a depressive PD, referred to briefly as depressives, are characterized by depressive thinking and behavior as indicated by at least five of the following: (1) having their usual mood dominated by dejection, cheerlessness, and unhappiness, (2) having low self-esteem and holding beliefs of worthlessness and inadequacy, (3) being critical, blaming, and derogatory toward self, (4) brooding and tending to worry, (5) being negativistic, critical, and judgmental toward others, (6) being pessimistic, and (7) being prone to guilt and remorse. One further requirement is that this disorder does not occur exclusively during major depressive episodes and is not better accounted for by dysthymic disorder.

The depressive PD, which is still under investigation (and perhaps could be listed under NOS, or Not Otherwise Specified), needs to be distinguished from other forms of depression (dysthymia). As with other personality disorders, the seeds of this disorder are sown in childhood when there may have been inappropriate attachment. For example, there could be an early history of separation or attachment to harsh parental figures. A lack of maternal warmth, affection, or consistent support, and the introject of a critical mother, can all pave the way for a depressive PD. The main style of thinking for depressives is pessimism, which locks them into fearing the worst and believing that life will never get better. They see themselves as inadequate and unable to solve their own problems. This engenders the feelings and beliefs of hopelessness and helplessness that lie at the heart of depressed personalities. These feelings paralyze and prevent them from taking the initiative in their lives to change their future.

[68]Millon et al. (2000: 201).
[69]Benjamin (1996: 257).

Depressives see themselves as failures and prefer not to risk any adventure unless success is guaranteed, thus protecting themselves from further failure. They have low self-worth around others and may feel guilty about not living up to expectations. Others may offer sympathetic support initially, but give up when there is no improvement and no appreciation expressed. They end up avoiding the depressives and feeling hostile towards them. Depressives openly display their moods and troubles to get the sort of support that they want and try and put people on a guilt trip. It is therefore not surprising that they often have few or no friends, only acquaintances. The withdrawal of others confirms the depressive's self-view as being inadequate and valueless, having no praiseworthy characteristics or meaningful achievements. This leads to a withdrawal by the depressive.

The depressives share major traits with several other personality disorders.[70] First, they are like the schizoids and avoidants in being socially withdrawn and not finding pleasure in life. However, unlike the schizoids they do feel emotions, understand the concept of happiness, and remain socially attached as certain relationships are important to them. Avoidants want to join socially, but see themselves as intrinsically defective, whereas depressives just give up and withdraw. Second, they are very similar to masochists except that masochists do participate socially and create unfavorable situations that compound their misery, whereas the depressive remains socially withdrawn and feeling hopeless. Third, they share an abiding pessimism and discontent with negativists, but for different reasons. For negativists, their pessimism is not so generalized and is the result of reaction against the control and authority of others. Unlike the depressives who have given up, they are prepared to fight back passive-aggressively. Finally, they are similar to the borderlines, who get depressed at times, but their emotions are steadily gloomy whereas borderlines are intensely labile.

Counseling Depressives

Depressives may seek therapy through pressure from a significant other or because some life event shakes them up. As with all depression, antidepressants can be helpful, but any improvement in mood may be viewed by the client with skepticism as not lasting, a characteristic of the depressive disorder. Any improvement, however, in mood and increase in energy level can be utilized in counseling. In addition to the five general counseling suggestions of Section 22.1, further strategies are as follows:[71]

1. As with other dependent-type clients, the key is to be careful of the transference relationship with the therapist. The aim is to increase self-efficacy rather than dependency on the therapist.

2. Cognitively, depressives need to shift their focus away from the bad to the good and away from pessimism, their key trait. For them, pessimism is realistic, while optimism about life being worth living is delusionary.

2. Encourage the client to engage the world proactively rather than just resign to fate. One way of doing this is to break large tasks or goals down into smaller more manageable ones and then applaud oneself when each one is completed rather than be self-critical.

---

[70]Millon et al. (2000: 469).
[71]Based on Millon et al. (2000: 470–471).

3. Help the client to stop magnifying problems, dwelling on past failures, and using pessimism to sabotage any effort.

4. Challenge negative automatic thoughts about self, the world, and the future, and help the client to identify such thoughts when they occur and test their validity. Erroneous thinking such as overgeneralization, arbitrary inference, emotional reasoning, and dichotomous thinking can be brought to the surface.

4. Encourage the client to separate psychologically from any dysfunctional relationships and learn to follow one's own agenda rather than put one's self-esteem at the mercy of someone else's appraisal.

5. Help the client to understand that continually expressing helplessness will ultimately push people away, especially if others try to help but get no response.

6. Explore early family relationships and any perfectionist parental expectations that can generate excessive guilt, self-criticism, and low self-esteem. Anger may be present, but not expressed to prevent upsetting any fragile relationships. Once these problems have been identified, separation and individuation can begin.

7. Use social skills training to help develop greater assertiveness in interpersonal relationships.

8. Develop some strategies to avoid relapse. For example, warn the client that some bad times are inevitable and, if possible, warn any spouse or family as well. Group therapy is always helpful as shared experiences can be encouraging.

22.5.2   Negativistic (Passive-Aggressive) PD

People with a negativistic PD, referred to briefly as negativists, have negative attitudes and show passive resistance to demands for an adequate performance as indicated by at least four of the following: (1) passively resisting carrying out routine social and work related tasks, (3) complaining of being misunderstood and unappreciated, (3) being sullen and argumentative, (4) being unreasonably critical and scornful of authority, (5) being envious and resentful of those who seem to be more fortunate, (6) persistently making exaggerated complaints about personal misfortune, and (7) alternating between hostile defiance and contrition. Their main belief is that they can be controlled and their overt behavior is resistance.[72] As with other depressive-type disorders, we have to exclude Axis I disorders by checking that the disorder does not occur exclusively during major depressive episodes and is not better accounted for by dysthymic disorder.[73]

Negativists are people who agree to conform to request for performance, but don't like authority or external control. For example, a boss may require a certain job to be carried out and the negativist responds by, for example, procrastinating, dawdling, being late, being deliberately inefficient, or pretending to be forgetful.

[72]Beck et al. (2004: 21).
[73]For further details and comments see http://www.ptypes.com/passive-aggpd.html (accessed October 2010).

Such a person seems to agree to the requirements of others, but actually passively resists them and becomes increasingly hostile and angry.[74] For instance, a wife may ask her husband to complete a task, which he says he will do, but doesn't get round to doing it. He always has an excuse and gets annoyed when reminded of it.

As noted by Millon et al.,[75] negativists have a problem with ambivalence, for example neediness versus independence, obedience versus defiance, and conforming versus rebelling, and this ambivalence can cause internal turmoil and anxiety. They wish to be loved and nurtured, yet resent control. On the one hand they want to please and be praised for what they do, but on the other hand they see the requirements of others as attacking their free will, thus confusing agreement with submission. They are best off when left to themselves as there is then no ambivalence. Negativists can also be stubborn and irritable, can complain and argue frequently, and can blame their problems on others. They are afraid of competition and dependency, often cannot trust, and tend to avoid intimacy.[76]

Where does this personality disorder have its roots? One possibility is that the parenting started well, but was abruptly withdrawn (e.g., with the arrival of another sibling) and replaced with unfair demands for performance, which can lead to power sensitivity in adult life. This withdrawal of support could have led to anger, any expression of which was dealt with harshly. The child engages in a continual power struggle with his or her caregivers. Such children become disappointed with the caregivers and end up not only disliking or distrusting others, but also not wanting others to be happy and successful. They become pessimistic, seeing the bad and ignoring the good, but instead of giving up as with the depressive they turn adversity to their own advantage.

Counseling Negativists

Although negativists may come to counseling because of vague complaints about "things not going right," they will generally only come when pressured by family, employers, or the legal system. Consequently they may see attendance as punishment and control by others, and be resentful. They may behave true to form by being awkward, such as missing or being late for appointments, wasting time, delaying paying for sessions, sabotaging homework, misinforming, and misreporting their feelings during a session. They might also have a more sadistic agenda, namely a desire to punish those who have a stake in the outcome. This can be done by making themselves suffer so that the therapy fails and the hopes of others are dashed. The therapist can also be seen as another figure of authority, and therefore to be challenged. A classic transference pattern is to sort of comply with therapy but then resist it and covertly sabotage the therapist's endeavors. The client's unconscious goal is to therefore to get worse and then blame the therapist for it.

In addition to the five general counseling suggestions of Section 22.1, further strategies are as follows:[77]

---

[74]This action of being just plain awkward is an example of passive anger (Section 3.6).
[75]Millon et al. (2000: 477–479).
[76]For further passive-aggressive behaviors see Wetzler (1993) and
http://passiveaggressive.homestead.com/PATraits.html (accessed October 2010) for a summary of these.
[77]Based on Millon et al. (2000: 489–490).

1. Because of resistance to external control, negativists should be involved in the treatment planning so as not to feel controlled by it and to maintain some autonomy. They can, for example, choose their own home work assignments from several suggestions and be encouraged to develop their own solutions to problems.

2. There is a need for patience as negativists will test their therapists to see if the latter will become resentful, blaming, and controlling, and therefore repeating what happened to them in their childhood. When progress is not made because the negativist is uncooperative, an appropriate response from the therapist might be, "Nothing seems to be working and I am frustrated with myself that I can't be more helpful" rather than getting upset with the client, which is what the client is expecting to happen.

3. Working with negativists is similar to working with paranoids as both have major concerns about autonomy, are resistant to external control, and believe they will be treated unfairly. Establishing trust is therefore important. Negativists need to feel that they belong and not that they are being used.

4. With trust established, past family patterns can be discussed along with their effect on present interactions with others. An indirect approach is preferred that leads the client to come to his or her own conclusions to avoid rejection of any interpretive comments by an authoritative figure like a therapist.

5. Clients can be helped to become more aware of their automatic thoughts. Rather than debate these thoughts, they can be set up as hypotheses to be tested experimentally.

22.5.3   Masochistic (Self-defeating) PD

The place of this disorder is open to debate and is not listed in DSM-IV, though it was in the appendix of DSM-III-TR. People with a masochistic PD, referred to briefly as masochists, are self-defeating, will undermine good experiences, and won't receive help, as indicated by at least five of the following: (1) choosing people and situations that lead to negative experiences like disappointment even when there are better options, (2) rejecting or rendering ineffective attempts at help from others, (3) suffering depression, guilt, or engaging in painful behavior after a positive personal event, (4) stirring up others to be angry or rejecting, then feeling upset or humiliated, (5) rejecting opportunities for pleasure or being reluctant to acknowledge enjoying themselves, (6) failing to accomplish important personal tasks although they have demonstrated the ability to do so, (7) being uninterested in or rejecting people who consistently treat them well, and (8) engaging in excessive unsolicited self-sacrifice. Such behavior does not occur exclusively in response to or anticipation of being abused in any way or when the person is depressed. The status of this disorder is somewhat uncertain and needs further study.

As noted by Millon et al.,[78] masochists sabotage their lives by deliberately putting obstacles in their own path and seem to end up defeating themselves and courting suffering. They feel uncomfortable when things go well, and any successes

[78]Millon et al. (2000: 493–495).

they attribute to luck, to avoid a sense of pride. Although willing to contribute to the achievement of others, they subtly undermine progress toward their own goals. When it comes to love, they often treat genuinely caring people as tiresome and turn these people into persecutors. In contrast to other personality disorders where people try to succeed but trip up because of their traits, masochists trip themselves up.

How does masochism develop? One suggestion is that a child who receives no attention from a mother except when sadistically abused by the mother is at least attached to the mother. Hate conveys attachment and for the child an abusive attachment is better than no attachment at all (equated with the absence of love). The one way of increasing love is to increase pain. A second suggestion is that to obtain love, self must be made extremely needy. By sabotaging self, a person can check whether a caregiver cares enough to rescue the person. A third suggestion is also about securing love. If parents ignore a child when life is going smoothly, then the child comes to believe that a smoothly running life means that one is unloved and love is only forthcoming when things go wrong. The message then is that displays of competence lead to neglect, but displays of helplessness lead to encouragement and attention.

Sometimes love is needed by an extremely needy parent who is afraid of being alone and unloved. The children of such parents may be required to destroy their own lives so that they always need the parent, thus confirming that the parent knows that he or she is loved. Anger may then be directed at the parent, but it is contained by guilt as only a desperately needy parent would make such a demand. As guilt calls for punishment, the anger is directed against self to avoid expressing it against the parent.

Counseling Masochists

Millon et al. comment that: "The paradoxical dynamics of the masochistic personality make treatment of the disorder long and complex. Because there is no single masochistic personality, there is no single approach to therapy."[79] In addition to the five general counseling suggestions of Section 22.1, further strategies are as follows:[80]

1. The therapist has to achieve an appropriate balance between being sufficiently empathic and being sufficiently distant (e.g., no sympathy or rescuing) so that the therapeutic relationship doesn't become like the client's other relationships. As most masochists present themselves as a suffering child, the therapist may be too nurturing so that the client may want to sabotage the relationship by increasing displays of wretchedness to balance the therapist's authentic support.

2. Developing self respect for the client is important because of feelings such as guilt, self-contempt, and a need for punishment are common.

3. Some clients with appropriate insight may be helped by the identification of their masochistic involvement in various relationships and the tracing back of its beginnings to their family of origin. They can then be encouraged to break the cycle.

---

[79] Millon et al. (2000: 510).
[80] Based on Millon et al. (2000: 511).

.

4. With cognitive therapy, clients can be helped to identify automatic thoughts, especially those in which the client identifies with the aggressor, which tend to evoke punishment.

5. Couple therapy may be useful in some situations, especially to identify and disrupt patterns of abuse from sadistic partners.

6. Clients may be helped by learning some social and assertiveness skills to promote self-respect and limiting abuse from others. It will also help the client to get out of victim role.

22.5.4 Sadistic PD

The validity of this disorder is under question for various reasons and it is not listed in the DSM-IV, but was in the appendix of DSM-III-TR. People with this disorder, referred to briefly as sadists, are characterized by a pattern of cruel and aggressive behavior as indicated by the repeated occurrence of at least four of the following: (1) having used violence or physical cruelty to dominate another person, (2) humiliating or demeaning people in the presence of others, (3) harshly disciplining someone under their control or authority, (4) enjoying the psychological or physical suffering of other people or animals, (5) having lied in order to hurt or inflict pain on others, (6) intimidating others to get what they want, (7) restricting the autonomy of someone they are close to (e.g., spouse or child), and (8) being fascinated by anything to do with violence including weapons. In addition to the above, the behavior has not been directed at just one person such as a spouse, nor is it for the purpose of sexual arousal (as in sexual sadism).

Sadists relate to others through abuse and cruelty, which is often all they know. If they feel their own life is somewhat futile and meaningless, they can use abuse to obtain feelings of superiority and strength, thus providing some compensation. By being sensitive to other people's weaknesses and faults, sadists can point them out, often in public, for a humiliating effect. When it comes to partners, sadists can produce disappointment by anticipating their partner's desires and then doing the opposite. Sadists are callous, act without conscience, and may ascribe malicious motives to everyone they encounter.

Millon et al.[81] note that sadists use a number of defense mechanisms[82] such as isolation, projection, rationalization, and displacement to soften or justify their aggression. Isolation provides detachment from the abuse they inflict, projection allows the transference of their own hostile motives to others, rationalization transforms aggressive bluntness into simply frankness and straightforwardness, and displacement redirects and masks aggressive impulses. Sadists differ from antisocials in that while both are indifferent to the rights of others, antisocials use aggression as a means to an end of getting what they want, whereas for sadists aggression is an end in itself.

How does sadism arise? One possibility is that the early relationships with caregivers were harsh and malicious. The child identifies with the aggressor and, in a sense, takes the abuser into his or her identity. This can preserve a sense of

---

[81]Millon et al. (2000: 520).
[82]See Section 21.5.

attachment and transform the victim into someone who is powerful. The thought is that if the victim is abused it is justified, as weakness deserves to to be punished, and the victim will eventually graduate to being an abuser also. Although attachment is achieved, it is achieved at a cost. The sadist is left with few sentimental or comforting others to provide a basis for a sympathetic understanding of the suffering he or she inflicts. Sadists, if subjected to cruelty themselves in early childhood, see kindness as either hidden self-interest or simply a brief illusion. They want to crush those who show such emotions as their own emotions were once crushed.

Counseling Sadists

In addition to the five general counseling suggestions of Section 22.1, further strategies are as follows:[83]

1. It is important not only to to build the usual rapport with clients but also to try and set clear limits and tolerate less attractive traits. Otherwise the therapist might inadvertently perpetuate earlier childhood abuse. Clients may be afraid that therapy might strip them of their identity, as inflicting abuse is the core of their identity and that they may become weaklings. Submitting to therapy is therefore inconsistent with the sadist's self-image.

2. Clients can be taught different methods of conflict resolution other than domination. They can also be assisted in learning that interpersonal relationships can be mutually rewarding, even without any destructive elements. Developing restraint, compassion, and an awareness of their effects on the lives of others are important goals. Learning to put away expectations of abuse and learning to trust others are important ingredients for developing rewarding relationships.

3. It can be helpful to teach anger management skills. For example, the therapist can help the client to construct a hierarchy of anger-arousing situations to work through using desensitization along with teaching relaxation techniques and alternative forms of coping.

4. Cognitive techniques can be used to help clients evaluate the assumptions and consequences of their behavior. Since sadists expect hostility and aggression from others, the therapist can help them identify good intentions when they occur. By learning to identify automatic thoughts, they may able to prevent a build up of hostility.

5. Problem areas can be identified along with the risks and benefits of various choices. The therapist can perhaps appeal to more self-serving motives by pointing out that a short-term physical victory might not be worth the resulting consequences (e.g., prison or divorce).

22.6   BIBLICAL VIEWPOINT

When it comes to psychopathology of any kind, one is always faced with the question of what is normal. We all have addictive tendencies, though some are more harmful

[83] Adapted from Millon et al. (2000: 528–529).

han others, and we all carry hurts from past experiences. As I have said in several places in this book, we have to be careful about attaching labels to people as people are on a continuum, not in boxes. Labels amongst professionals, however, can be important for psychological research and for helping therapists to provide some tools for counseling.

Having made some comments about personality disorders from a biblical viewpoint at the end of the previous chapter and seeing this is my last section for the book, I want to make a few general comments as a kind of epilogue.

The Bible demonstrates very clearly how imperfect we all are and the portraits of biblical characters show very human flaws. They are not shown to be super-human but are just like us. Yet God was able to use these people, imperfect as they were, because of the faith they had.[84] Paul sums up the difficulties very well when he talks about doing what he hates doing and not doing the good that he wants to do.[85] God can use any Christian who submits to the will and Spirit of God.[86]

God uses people that the world would probably not choose to carry out God's purposes. Tournier[87] gives examples where God reverses how people might measure worth as in the saying, "the last will be first and the first shall be last."[88] God chose a murderer by the name of Moses to be a leader, who was shy, not a ready speaker, and lacking in confidence.[89] Gideon, a man held in contempt and of low status was chosen by God to be a Judge and a military leader.[90] A shepherd boy, David was chosen by God to be a king in the place of Saul, a man of stature and leadership qualities, as God looks on the heart.[91] Amos was another unimportant shepherd sent to prophesy at Bethel.[92] We can also mention Jeremiah, a timid young man, lacking in confidence, and not wanting to be a mouthpiece for God, but called by God to the dangerous task of being a prophet in time of war.

The goal of a Christian therapist might then be to help a client to move closer to God in some way and be open to the Spirit of God. It is a matter of recognizing that it is not possible to help clients to fix every problem in their lives but rather to help them to be able to live a "normal" life, that is live a life that is at least not harmful to self or others; better still, a life that knows the presence of God.

---

[84]Hebrews chapter 11.
[85]Romans 7:14–25.
[86]Romans chapter 8.
[87]Tournier (1972: chapter 13).
[88]Matthew 20: 16 and, for a similar theme, 1 Corinthians 1:27–29.
[89]Exodus 2:13–15 and 4:10.
[90]Judges 6:15.
[91]1 Samuel 16:6–13. This was in spite of the fact that David later committed adultery and was responsible for the death of a man.
[92]Amos 7:14–16.

REFERENCES

Affinito, M. G. (2002). Forgiveness in counseling: Caution, definition, and application. In S. Lamb and J. G. Murphy (Eds.), *Before Forgiving: Cautionary Views of Forgiveness in Psychotherapy*, 88–111. Oxford University Press, New York.

Allender, D. B. (1991). *The Wounded Heart: Hope for Adult Victims of Childhood Sexual Abuse*. CWR, Farnham, UK.

Allender, D. B. and Longman, T. III (1994). *Cry of the Soul*. NavPress, Colorado Springs, CO.

Allnutt, S. and Links, P. S. (1996). Diagnosing specific personality disorders and the optimal criteria. In P. S. Links (Ed.), *Clinical Assessment and Management of Severe Personality Disorders*, 21–48. American Psychiatric Press, Washington, DC.

Amato, P. R. (2001). Children of divorce in the 1990's: An update of the Amato and Keith (1991) meta-analysis. *Journal of Family Psychology*, **15** (3), 355–370.

Amato, P. R. (2005). The impact of family formation change on the cognitive, social, and emotional well-being of the next generation. *Future of Children*, **15** (2), 75–96.

American Psychiatric Association. (2000a). *Diagnostic and Statistical Manual of Mental Disorders DSM-IV-TR*, 4th edit. American Psychiatric Publishing Inc., Arlington, VA.

American Psychiatric Association. (2000b). *Quick Reference to the Diagnostic and Statistical Manual of Mental Disorders DSM-IV-TR*, 1st edit. American Psychiatric Publishing Inc., Arlington, VA.

American Psychiatric Association. (2007). *Practice Guideline for the Treatment of Patients with Obsessive-Compulsive Disorder*. American Psychiatric Association, Arlington, VA. (Available online at http://www.psychiatryonline.com/pracGuide/pracGuideChapToc_10.aspx.)

American Psychological Association. (1998). Final conclusions of the American Psychological Association working group on investigation of memories of child abuse. *Psychology, Public Policy, and Law*, **4** (4), 933–940.

Andersen, A. E. (1995). Eating disorders in males. In K. D. Brownell and C. G. Fairburn, (Eds.), *Eating Disorders and Obesity: A Comprehensive Handbook*, 177–182. Guilford Press, New York.

Anderson, S. A. and Schlossberg, M. C. (1999). Systems perspectives on battering: The importance of context and pattern. In M. Harway and J. M. O'Neil, *What Causes Men's Violence Against Women?*, 137–152. SAGE Publications, Thousand Oaks, CA.

Antony, M. M., Orsillo, S. M., and Roemer L. (2001). *Practitioner's Guide to Empirically Based Measures of Anxiety*. Plenum, New York. (Also available as as an e-book at *e-book ebrary*.)

Archer, J. (1999). *The Nature of Grief: The Evolution and Psychology of Reactions to Loss*. Routledge, New York.

Arp, D. and Arp, C. (1993). *60 One-minute Family Builders: Creative Ideas for Family Fun*. Thomas Nelson, Nashville, TN.

Ashton, H. and Stepney, R. (1982). *Smoking: Psychology and Pharmacology*. Tavistock Publications, New York.

Attig, T. (1996). *How We Grieve: Relearning the World*. Oxford University Press, New York.

Azrin, N. H. and Nunn, R. G. (1973). Habit reversal: A method of eliminating nervous habits and tics. *Behavior Research and Therapy*, **11**, 619–628.

Baer, L. (2001). *The Imp of the Mind: Exploring the Silent Epidemic of Obsessive Bad Thoughts*. Dutton, New York.

Baker, R. (2007). *Emotional Processing: Healing Through Feeling*. Lion Hudson, Oxford, England.

Baldessarini, R. J. and Tondo, L. (1999). Antisuicidal effect of lithium treatment in major mood disorders. In D. G. Jacobs (Ed.), *The Harvard Medical School Guide to Suicide Assessment and Intervention*, 355–371. Jossey-Bass, Wiley, San Francisco, CA.

Bandler, R. (2008). *Get the Life You Want: The Secrets to Quick and Lasting Life Change with Neuro-Linguistic Programming*. Health Communications, Deerfield Beach, FL.

Barrow I. (1985). *Fifteen Steps to Overcome Anxiety and Depression*. Heinemann, Hong Kong.

Barrow, I. and Place, H. (1995). *Relax and Come Alive: A Practical Guide to Overcoming Stress*. Reed Publishing, Auckland, New Zealand. (First published in 1981 with several reprintings.)

Bartholomew, K. and Horowitz, L. M. (1991). Attachment styles among young adults: A test of a four-category model. *Journal of Personality and Social Psychology*, **61**, 226–244.

Bartlett, P. (2011). DSM-5 and ICD-11 on personality disorder: A lawyer's perspective. *Personality and Mental Health*. **5**, 144–151. (See also wileyonlinelibrary.com DOI 10.1002/pmh.165.)

Bass, E. and Davis, L. (1988). *The Courage to Heal: A Guide for Women Survivors of Child Sexual Abuse*. HarperCollins, New York.

Bassett, R. L., Bassett, K. M., Lloyd, M. W., and Johnson, J. L. (2006). Seeking forgiveness: Considering the role of moral emotions. *Journal of Psychology and Theology*, **34** (2), 114–125.

Baumeister, R. F. and Bushman, B. J. (2007). Angry emotions and aggressive behaviors. In G. Steffgen and M. Gollwitzer (Eds.), *Emotions and Aggressive Behavior*, 61–75. Hogrefe and Huber, Cambridge, MA.

602   REFERENCES

Baumeister, R. F. and Tierney, J. (2011). *Willpower: Rediscovering the Greatest Human Strength.* Penguin group, London.

Beattie, M. (1987). *Codependent No More: How To Stop Controlling Others and Start Caring For Yourself.* Harper and Row, New York.

Beck, A. T. (1972). *Depression: Causes and Treatment.* University of Pennsylvania Press, Philadelphia. (Originally published as "Depression: Clinical, Experimental, and Theoretical Aspects," 1967, Harper and Row, New York.)

Beck, A. T. (1980). *Cognitive Therapy for Depression.* John Wiley, New York.

Beck, A. T., Brown, G., Berchick, R. J., and Stewart, B. L. (1990). Relationship between hopelessness and ultimate suicide: A replication with psychiatric outpatients. *American Journal of Psychiatry,* **147**, 190–195.

Beck, A. T., Emery, G., and Greenberg, R. L. (2005). *Anxiety Disorders and Phobias: A Cognitive Perspective.* Revised edition. Basic Books, New York.

Beck, A. T., Epstein, N., Brown, G., and Steer, R. (1979). *Cognitive Therapy of Depression.* Guilford Press, New York.

Beck, A. T., Freeman, A., Davis, D. D., and Associates. (2004). *Cognitive Therapy of Personality Disorders,* 2nd edit. Guilford Press, New York.

Beck, A. T. and Weishaar, M. E. (1995). Cognitive therapy. In R. J. Corsini and D. Wedding (Eds.), *Current Psychotherapies,* 5th edit. F. E. Peacock Publishers, Ithaca, IL.

Beck, J. S. (1995). *Cognitive Therapy : Basics and Beyond.* Guilford Press, New York.

Benjamin, L. S. (1996). *Internal Diagnosis and Treatment of Personality Disorders,* 2nd edit. Guilford Press, New York.

Bender, S. S. , Britt, V., and Diepold, J. H. , Jr. (2004). *Evolving Thought Field Therapy: The Clinician.* W. W. Norton, New York.

Benner, D. and Hill, P. (1999). *Baker Encyclopedia of Psychology and Counseling,* 2nd edit. Baker Books, Grand Rapids, MI.

Benson, H. (1996). *Timeless Healing: The Power and Biology of Belief.* Scribner, New York.

Benson, H. (2000). *The Relaxation Response Updated and Expanded (25th anniversary edition).* Avon, New York.

Berger, H. (2001). Trauma and the therapist. In T. Spiers (Ed.), *Trauma: A Practitioner's Guide to Counseling,* 189–212. Taylor and Francis, New York.

Berman, W. H. and Sperling, M. B. (1994). The structure and function of adult attachment. In M. B. Sperling and W. H. Berman (Eds.), *Attachment in Adults: Clinical and Developmental Perspectives,* 3–28. Guilford Press, New York.

Berne, E. (1961). *Transactional Analysis in Psychotherapy, a Systematic Individual and Social Psychiatry.* Grove Press, New York.

Berne, E. (1966). *Principles of Group Treatment.* Oxford University Press, New York.

Berry, D. B. (2000). *The Domestic Violence Sourcebook,* 3rd edit. Lowell House, Los Angeles.

Beumont, P. J. V. (1995). The clinical presentation of anorexia and bulimia nervosa. In K. D. Brownell and C. G. Fairburn (Eds.), *Eating Disorders and Obesity: A Comprehensive Handbook,* 151–158. Guilford Press, New York.

Beumont, P. J. V. and Touyz, S. W. (1995). The nutritional management of anorexia and bulimia nervosa. In K. D. Brownell and C. G. Fairburn (Eds.), *Eating Disorders and Obesity: A Comprehensive Handbook,* 306–312. Guilford Press, New York.

Bishop, S. (2000). *Develop Your Assertiveness,* 2nd edit. Kogan Page, London.

Block, J. J. (2008). Issues for DSM-V: Internet addiction. *American Journal of Psychiatry,* **165**, March, 306–307.

Bloomfield, H. (1983). *Making Peace with Your Parents.* Ballantyne Books, New York.

Blue, K. (1993). *Healing Spiritual Abuse: How to Break Free from Bad Church Experiences.* Intervarsity Press, Downers Grove, IL.

Bolton, R. (1987). *People Skills: How to Assert Yourself, Listen to Others, and Resolve Conflicts.* Simon Schuster, Brookvale, NSW, Australia. (Reprinted several times.)

Bond, A. J. and and Wingrove, J. (2010). The neurochemistry and psychopharmacology of anger. In M. Potegal, G. Stemmler, and C. Spielberger (Eds), *International Handbook of Anger Constituent and Concomitant Biological, Psychological, and Social Processes*, 79–102. Springer, New York.

Bourne, E. J. (2005). *The Anxiety and Phobia Workbook*, 4th edit. New Harbinger Publications, Oakland, CA. There are many printings of this book.

Bowen, M. (1978). *Family Therapy in Clinical Practice.* Jason Aronson, New York.

Bowlby, J. (1977). The making and breaking of affectional bonds. *British Journal of Psychiatry*, **130**, 201–210.

Bradshaw, J. (1988). *Healing the Shame That Binds You.* Health Communications, Deerfield Beach, FL.

Bradshaw, J. (1990). *Homecoming: Reclaiming and Championing Your Inner Child.* Bantam Books, New York.

Bradshaw, J. (1995). *Family Secrets: The Path to Self-Acceptance and Reunion.* Bantam Books, New York.

Briere, J. N. (1992). *Child Abuse Trauma: Theory and Treatment of the Lasting Effects.* SAGE Publications, Newbury Park, CA.

Briere, J. N. (2004). *Psychological Assessment of Adult Posttraumatic States: Phenomenology, Diagnosis, and Measurement*, 2nd edit. American Psychological Association, Washington, DC. (Also available as as an e-book at *e-Book PsycBOOKS Collection.*)

Brody, S. and Krüger, T. H. (2006). The post-orgasmic prolactin increase following intercourse is greater than following masturbation and suggests greater satiety. *Biological Psychology*, **71** (3), 312–315. (See http://www.ncbi.nlm.nih.gov/pubmed/16095799 for the abstract.)

Brodzinsky, D. M. (1993). Long-term outcomes in adoption. *Future of Children*, **3** (1), 153–166.

Brown, D., Scheflin, A. W., and Hammond, D. C. (1998). *Memory, Trauma Treatment, and the Law: An Essential Reference on Memory for Clinicians, Researchers, Attorneys, and Judges.* W. W. Norton, New York.

Brownell, K. D. (1995). Effects of weight cycling on metabolism, health, and psychological factors. In K. D. Brownell and C. G. Fairburn (Eds.), *Eating Disorders and Obesity: A Comprehensive Handbook*, 56–60. Guilford Press, New York.

Brownridge, D. A. (2009). *Violence Against Women: Vulnerable Populations.* Routledge, Taylor and Francis Group, New York.

Bubenzer, D. L. and West, J. D. (1993). *Counselling Couples.* SAGE Publications, London.

Bumpass, L. and Lu, H.-H. (2001). Trends in cohabitation and implications for children's family contexts in the United States. *Population Studies*, **54** (1), 29–41.

Burns, D. D. (1999). *Feeling Good: The New Mood Therapy Revised and Updated.* HarperCollins, New York.

Butler, C. and Joyce, V. (1998). *Counselling Couples in Relationships: An Introduction to the RELATE Approach.* John Wiley, Chichester.

Buzan, T. (1991). *The Mind Map Book.* Penguin, New York.

Byng-Hall, J. (1985). Resolving distance conflicts. In A. S. Gurman (Ed.), *Casebook of Marital Therapy*, 1–20. Guilford Press, New York.

Carnes, P. (2001). *Contrary to Love: Helping the Sexual Addict*, 3rd edit. CompCare, Minneapolis, MN.

Carr, A. (2006). *Allen Carr's Easy Way To Stop Smoking*, 3rd edit. Penguin Group, London.

Carroll, K. M. and Rawson, R. A. (2005). Relapse prevention for stimulant dependence. In G. A. Marlatt and M. D. Donovan (Eds.), *Relapse Prevention: Maintenance Strategies in the Treatment of Addictive Behaviors*, 2nd edit., 130–150. Guilford Press, New York.

Carter, B. and McGoldrick, M. (1999). Overview: The expanded family life cycle. In B. Carter and M. Goldrick (Eds.), *The Expanded Family Life Cycle: Individual, Family, and Social Perspectives*, 3rd edit., 1–26. Allyn and Bacon, Needham Heights, MA.

Carver, C. S. and Scheier, M. F. (1998). *Attention and Self-regulation: A Control-theory Approach to Human Behavior*, 2nd edit. Springer-Verlag, New York.

Cavanagh, J. T. O., Carson, A. J., Sharpe, M., and Lawrie, S. M. (2003). Psychological autopsy studies of suicide: A systematic review. *Psychological Medicine*, **33**, 395–405.

Chapman, G. (2000). *The Five Love Languages: How to Express Heartfelt Commitment to Your Mate*. Strand, Sydney. (Reprinted many times.)

Chapman, G. and Campbell, R. (1997). *The Love Languages of Children*. Northfield Publishing, Chicago, IL.

Chapman, G. and Thomas, J. (2006). *The Five Languages of Apology: How to Experience Healing in All Your Relationships*. Northfield Publishing, Chicago, IL.

Charles-Edwards, D. (2005). *Handling Death and Bereavement at Work*. Routledge, Taylor and Francis Group, London.

Chiles, J. A. and Strosahl, K. D. (1995). *The Suicidal Patient—Principles of Assessment Treatment, and Case Management*. American Psychiatrist Press, Washington, DC.

Chu, J. A. (1999). Trauma and suicide. In D. G. Jacobs (Ed.), *The Harvard Medical School Guide to Suicide Assessment and Intervention*, 332–354. Jossey-Bass, Wiley, San Francisco, CA.

Ciarrocchi, J. W. (2002). *Counseling Problem Gamblers: A Self-regulation Manual for Individual and Family Therapy*. Academic Press, San Diego, CA.

Clarke, J. C. and Wardman, W. (1985). *Agoraphobia: A Clinical and Personal Account*. Pergamon Press, Rushcutters Bay, Australia.

Claude-Pierre, P. (1997). *The Secret Language of Eating Disorders: The Revolutionary New Approach to Understanding and Curing Anorexia and Bulimia*. Bantam Books, Transworld Publishers, Moorebank, NSW, Australia.

Cloitre, M., Cohen, L. R. , and Koenen, K. C. (2006). *Treating Survivors of Childhood Abuse: Psychotherapy for the Interrupted Life*. Guilford Press, New York. (Also available as an e-book at *e-book ebrary*.)

Cloud, H. and Townsend, J. (1992). *Boundaries: When to Say YES, When to Say No, to Take Control of Your Life*. Zondervan, Grand Rapids, MI.

Cloud, H. and Townsend, J. (1995). *Safe People: How to Find Relationships That Are Good for You and Avoid Those That Aren't*. Zondervan, Grand Rapids, MI.

Cloud, H. and Townsend, J. (1999). *Boundaries in Marriage*. Zondervan, Grand Rapids, MI. (Also printed in Australia and reprinted a number of times.)

Cloud, H. and Townsend, J. (2003). *Boundaries Face to Face: How to Have That Difficult Conversation You've Been Avoiding*. Strand Publishing, Sydney.

Cohen, G. D. (2005). *The Mature Mind: The Positive Power of the Aging Brain*. Basic Books, New York.

Coleman, P. W. (1998). The process of forgiveness in marriage and the family. In R. D. Enright and J. North (Eds.), *Exploring Forgiveness*, 75–94. University of Wisconsin Press, Madison, WI.

Collins, N. L. and Freeney, B. C. (2004). An attachment theory perspective on closeness and intimacy. In D. J. Mashek and A. Aron (Eds.), *Handbook of Closeness and Intimacy*, 163–188. Lawrence Erlbaum Associates, Mahwah, NJ.

Collins, R. L. (2005). Relapse prevention for eating disorders and obesity. In G. A. Marlatt and M. D. Donovan (Eds.), *Relapse Prevention: Maintenance Strategies in the Treatment of Addictive Behaviors*, 2nd edit., 248–275. Guilford Press, New York.

Conway, J. (1991). *Adult Children of Legal or Emotional Divorce*. Monarch, Eastbourne, U.K.

Cook, P. W. (2009). *Abused Men: The Hidden Side of Domestic Violence*, 2nd edit. Praeger, Westport, CT.

Cooper, C. L. and Dewe, P. (2004). *Stress: A Brief History*. Blackwell Publishing, Oxford, U.K.

Cooper, P. J. (1995). Eating disorders and their relationship to mood and anxiety disorders. In K. D. Brownell and C. G. Fairburn (Eds.), *Eating Disorders and Obesity: A Comprehensive Handbook*, 159–164. Guilford Press, New York.

Cooper, Z. (1995). The development and maintenance of eating disorders. In K. D. Brownell and Fairburn, C. G. (Eds.), *Eating Disorders and Obesity: A Comprehensive Handbook*, 199–206. Guilford Press, New York.

Corey, G. (2001). *Theory and Practice of Counseling and Psychotherapy*. 6th edit. Thomson Brooks/Cole, Belmont, CA.

Corr, C. A. (1993). Coping with dying: Lessons that we should and should not learn from the work of Kübler-Ross. *Death Studies*, **17** (1), 69–83.

Costa, P. T., Jr. and Widiger, T. A. (Eds.) (2002). *Personality Disorders and the Five Factor Model of Personality*, 2nd edit. American Psychological Association, Washington, DC.

Covey, S. R. (1990). *The 7 Habits of Highly Effective People*. The Business Library, Melbourne. (This book has been reprinted many times.)

Cummings, C., Gordon, J. R., and Marlatt, G. A. (1980). Relapse: Prevention and prediction. In W. R. Miller (Ed.), *Addictive Behaviors*, 291–321. Pergamon Press, New York.

Damasio, A. (1994). *Descartes' Error: Emotion, Reason, and the Human Brain*. Grosset/Putnam, New York.

Davidson, M. K. (1994). Healing the birthmother's silent sorrow. *Progress: Family Systems Research and Therapy*, **3**, 69–89. Phillips Graduate Institute, Encino, CA.

Davis, M., Robbins-Eshelman, E., and McKay, M. (2000). *The Relaxation and Stress Reduction Workbook*, 5th edit. New Harbinger Publication, Oakland, CA.

Davis, T., Gunderson, J. G., and Myers, M. (1999). Borderline personality disorder. In D. G. Jacobs (Ed.), *The Harvard Medical School Guide to Suicide Assessment and Intervention*, 311–331. Jossey-Bass, Wiley, San Francisco, CA.

De Silva, P. (2003). Obsessions, ruminations, and covert compulsions. In R. G. Menzies and P. de Silva (Eds.), *Obsessive Compulsive Disorder: Theory, Research, and Treatment*, 195–208. Wiley, Chichester, England. (Also available as an e-book at *e-Book netLibrary*.)

DiGiuseppe, R. (1995). Developing the therapeutic alliance with angry clients. In H. Kassinove (Ed.), *Anger Disorders: Definition, Diagnosis, and Treatment*, 131–149. Taylor and Francis, Washington, DC.

Dobson, J. C. (1990). *Love for a Lifetime: Building a Marriage That Will Go the Distance.* WORD, Milton Keynes, U.K. (Reprinted many times by various publishers.)

Doidge, N. (2007). *The Brain That Changes Itself.* Penguin Group, New York.

Donnellan, D. (Ed.) (2002). *Confronting Domestic Violence.* Volume 44. Independence, Cambridge, U.K.

Douglas, E. and Douglas, S. (2000). *The Blended Family: Achieving Peace and Harmony in the Christian Home.* Providence House, Franklin, TN.

Downing-Orr, K. (1998). *Rethinking Depression: Why Current Treatments Fail.* Plenum Press, New York.

Draucker, C. B. (2000). *Counselling Survivors of Childhood Sexual Abuse,* 2nd edit. SAGE Publications, London.

Dryden, W. and Neenan, M. (2005). *Getting Started with REBT.* Routledge, Taylor and Francis Group, New York.

Dunn, A. (2001). Trauma aftercare: A four-stage model. In T. Spiers (Ed.), *Trauma: A Practitioner's Guide to Counseling,* 97–130. Taylor and Francis, New York.

Dyregrov, A. (1991). *Grief in Children: A Handbook for Adults.* Jessica Kingsley, London.

Earlywine, M. (2002). *Understanding Marijuana: A New Look at the Scientific Evidence.* Oxford University Press, New York.

Eckhardt, C. I. and Deffenbacher, J. L. (1995). Diagnosis of anger disorders. In H. Kassinove (Ed.), *Anger Disorders: Definition, Diagnosis, and Treatment,* 27—47. Taylor and Francis, Washington, DC.

Elfert, G. H. and Forsyth, J. P. (2005). *Acceptance and Commitment Therapy for Anxiety Disorders: A Practitioner's Treatment Guide to Using Mindfulness, Acceptance, and Values-based Behavior Change Strategies.* New Harbinger, Oakland, CA.

Eggerichs, E. (2004). *Love and Respect: The Respect He Desperately Needs.* Thomas Nelson, Nashville, TN.

Ekman, P. (1980). Biological and cultural contributions to body and facial movement in the expressions of emotions. In A. O. Rorty, (Ed.), *Explaining Emotions.* University of California Press, Berkeley.

Ekman, P. (1993). An argument for basic emotions. *Cognition and Emotions,* **6**, 169–200.

Ekman, P. (1999). Basic emotions. In T. Dalgleish and M. Power (Eds.), *Handbook of Cognition and Emotion,* chapter 3. John Wiley, Sussex, U.K.

Ellis, A. (1957). Rational psychotherapy and individual psychology. *Journal of Individual Psychology,* **13**, 38–44.

Ellis, A. and Dryden, W. (2007). *The Practice of Rational Emotive Behavior Therapy,* 2nd edit. Springer, New York.

Ellis, A., Gordon, J., Neenan, M., and Palmer, S. (1997). *Stress Counselling: A Rational Emotive Behaviour Approach.* Cassell, London.

Emmelkamp, P. M. G., Bouman, T. K., and Scholong, A. (1992). *Anxiety Disorders: A Practitioner's Guide.* Wiley, Chichester, U.K.

Enright, R. D. (and the Human Development Study Group). (1996). Counseling within the forgiveness triad: On forgiving, receiving forgiveness, and self-forgiveness. *Counseling and Values,* **40**, 107–126.

Enright, R. D. and Fitzgibbons, R. P. (2000). *Helping Clients Forgive: An Empirical Guide for Resolving Anger and Restoring Hope.* American Psychological Association, Washington, DC.

Epstein, N. B. and Baucom, D. H. (2002). *Enhanced Cognitive-Behavioral Therapy for Couples: A Contextual Approach.* American Psychological Association, Washington, DC.

Epstein, N. B. and Falconier, M. K. (2011). Shame in couple therapy: Helping to heal the intimacy bond. In R. L. Dearing and J. P. Tangney, *Shame in the Therapy Hour*, chapter 7. American Psychological Association: Washington, D. C. (Also available as an e-book at *e-Book PsycBooks Collection*.)

Erikson, E. H. (1995). *Childhood and Society*, revised edit. Vintage, London.

Erikson, E. H. and Erikson, J. M. (1997). *The Life Cycle Completed*. W. W. Norton, New York. (An extended version with new chapters on the ninth stage of development by Joan M. Erikson.)

Ernst, C. and Angst, J. (1983). *Birth Order: Its Influence on Personality*. Springer, New York.

ETH Zurich (2008). Why emotional memories of traumatic life events are so persistent. *ScienceDaily* May 11. Available online from http://www.sciencedaily.com/.

Exline, J. J. and Martin, A. (2005). Anger toward God: A new frontier in forgiveness research. In E. L. Worthington, Jr. (Ed.), *Handbook of Forgiveness*, 73–88. Routledge, Taylor and Francis Group, New York.

Fairburn, C. G. (1995). The prevention of eating disorders. In K. D. Brownell and C. G. Fairburn (Eds.), *Eating Disorders and Obesity: A Comprehensive Handbook*, 289–293. Guilford Press, New York.

Fairburn, C. G., Marcus, M. D., and Wilson, G. T. (1993). Cognitive-behavioral therapy for binge eating and bulimia nervosa: A comprehensive manual. In C. G. Fairburn and G. T. Wilson (Eds.), *Binge Eating: Nature, Assessment, and Treatment*, 361–402. Guilford Press, New York.

Faravelli, C., Rosi, S., and Truglia, E. (2003). Benzodiazepines. In D. J. Nutt and J. C. Ballenger (Eds.), *Anxiety Disorder*, 315–338. Blackwell Science, Malden, MA.

Farmer, S. (1989). *Adult Children of Abusive Parents*. Contemporary Books, Chicago.

Ferber, R. (1999). *Solve Your Child's Sleep Problems*. Dorling Kindersley, London.

Fernandes, P. P. (2003). Rapid desensitization for needle phobia. *Psychosomatics*, **44**, 253–254.

Fernandez, E. (2010). Toward an integrative psychotherapy for maladaptive anger. In M. Potegal, G. Stemmler, and C. Spielberger (Eds), *International Handbook of Anger: Constituent and Concomitant Biological, Psychological, and Social Processes*, 349–360. Springer, New York.

Fincham, F. D., Hall, J. H., and Beach, S. R. H. (2005). "'Til lack of forgiveness doth us part": Forgiveness and marriage. In E. L. Worthington, Jr. (Ed.), *Handbook of Forgiveness*, 207–225. Routledge, Taylor and Francis Group, New York.

Finkbeiner, A. K. (1996). *After the Death of a Child : Living with Loss Through the Years*. Free Press, New York.

Finkelhor, D. and Browne, A. (1985). The traumatic impact of child sexual abuse: A conceptualization. *American Journal of Orthopsychiatry*, **55**, 530–541.

Fischer, A. H. and Evers, C. (2010). In M. Potegal, G. Stemmler, and C. Spielberger (Eds), *International Handbook of Anger: Constituent and Concomitant Biological, Psychological, and Social Processes*, 349–360. Springer: New York.

Flanigan, B. (1998). Forgivers and the unforgiveable. In R. D. Enright and J. North (Eds.), *Exploring Forgiveness*, 95–105. University of Wisconsin Press, Madison, WI.

Forward, S. (1986). *Women Who Love Too Much*. Arrow Books, London. (This book has been reprinted many times.)

Forward, S. and Torres, J. (1986). *Men Who Hate Women and the Women Who Love Them*. Bantam Books, New York. (Also available as an e-book at *e-book ebrary*.)

Frears, L. H. and Schneider, J. M. (1981). Exploring loss and grief within a holistic framework. *The Personnel and Guidance Journal*, **59** (6), 341–346.

Freedman, S., Enright, R. D., and Knutson, J. (2005). A progress report on the process model of forgiveness. In E. L. Worthington, Jr. (Ed.), *Handbook of Forgiveness*, 393–406. Routledge, Taylor and Francis Group, New York.

Frooeton, M. H. and Pléchaty, M. (1997). Locke-Wallace Marital Adjustment Test: Is it still relevant for the 1990s? *Psychological Reports*, **81**, 419–434.

Friedman, M. and Rosenman, R. H. (1974). *Type A Behavior and Your Heart*. Fawcett Crest, New York.

Friedman, M. (1996). *Type A Behavior: Its Diagnosis and Treatment*. Plenum Press (Kluwer Academic Press), New York.

Frost, R. O. and Hartl, T. L. (2003). Compulsive hoarding. In R. G. Menzies and P. de Silva (Eds.), *Obsessive Compulsive Disorder: Theory, Research, and Treatment*, 163–180. Wiley, Chichester, England. (Also available as an e-book at *e-Book netLibrary*.)

Frost, R. O. and Steketee, G. (Eds.) (2002). *Cognitive Approaches to Obsessions and Compulsions*. Elsevier, New York. (Also available as an e-book at *e-book ScienceDirect*.)

Furukawa, T. A., Shear, M. K., Barlow, D. H., Gorman, J. M., Woods, S. W., Money, R., Etschel, E., Engel, R. R., and Leucht, S. (2009). Evidence-based guidelines for interpretation of the Panic Disorder Severity Scale. *Depression and Anxiety*, **26** (10), 922–929.

Gardner, F. (2001). *Self-Harm: A Psychotherapeutic Approach*. Taylor and Francis, New York.

Geldard, K. and Geldard, D. (1999). *Counselling Adolescents*. SAGE Publications, London.

George, L. K., Ellison, C. G., and Larson, D. B. (2002). Explaining the relationship between religious involvement and health. *Psychological Inquiry*, **13** (3), 190–200.

Gilbert, P. (1992). *Counselling for Depression*. SAGE Publications, London. Now in a second edition (2000) that is also available as an e-book at *e-book ebrary*.

Girdano, D. A., Everly, G. S., Jr., and Dusek, D. E. (1997). *Controlling Stress and Tension*, 5th edit. Allyn and Bacon, Needham Heights, MA.

Glasser, W. and Wubbolding, R. E. (1995). Reality therapy. In R. J. Corsini and D. Wedding, (Eds.), *Current Psychotherapies*, 5th edit., 293–321. F. E. Peacock Publishers, Itasca, IL.

Goldberg, S., Muir, R., and Kerr, J. (1995). *Attachment Theory: Social, Developmental, and Clinical Perspectives*. The Analytic Press, Hillsdale, NJ.

Goldstein, A. (2001). *Addiction: From Biology to Drug Policy*, 2nd edit. Oxford University Press, New York.

Gordon, K. C., Baucom, D. H., and Snyder, D. K. (2004). An integrative intervention for promoting recovery from extramarital affairs. *Journal of Marital and Family Therapy*, **30** (2), 213–231.

Gordon, K. C., Baucom, D. H., and Snyder, D. K. (2005). Forgiveness in couples: Divorce, infidelity, and couples therapy. In E. L. Worthington, Jr. (Ed.), *Handbook of Forgiveness*, 407–421. Routledge, Taylor and Francis Group, New York.

Gordon, R. A. (2000). *Eating Disorders: Anatomy of a Social Epidemic*, 2nd edit. Blackwell, Oxford, U.K.

Gottman, J. (1994). *Why Marriages Succeed or Fail*. Simon and Schuster, New York.

Grant, I. (2004) John Gray and the chemistry of love. *Parenting with Confidence*, **17**, Winter, 66–68.

Grant, M. (2009). *Change Your Brain, Change Your Pain*. BookPOD, Vermont South, Victoria, Australia.

Greenberg, L. S. (2002). *Emotion-Focused Therapy: Coaching Clients to Work Through Their Feelings.* American Psychological Association, Washington, DC.

Greenberg, L. S. and Shigeru, I. (2011). Emotion-focused therapy and shame. In R. L. Dearing and J. P. Tangney, *Shame in the Therapy Hour*, chapter 3. American Psychological Association: Washington, D. C. (Also available as an e-book at *e-Book PsycBooks Collection.*)

Greenberg, L. S., Warwar, S., and Malcolm, W. (2010). Emotion-focused couples therapy and the facilitation of forgiveness. *Journal of Marital and Family Therapy,***36** (1), 28–42.

Greenfield, D. N. (1999). *Virtual Addiction: Help for Netheads, Cyberfreaks, and Those Who Love Them.* New Harbinger, Oakland, CA.

DiGiuseppe, R. and Tafrate, R. C. (2007). *Understanding Anger Disorders.* Oxford University Press: New York.

Gurman A. S. (Ed.) (1985). *Casebook of Marital Therapy.* Guilford Press, New York.

Hall, J. H. and Fincham, F. D. (2005). Self-forgiveness: The stepchild of forgiveness research. *Journal of Social and Clinical Psychology,* **24** (5), 621–638.

Hallam, R. (1992). *Counselling for Anxiety Problems.* SAGE Publications, London.

Halpern, H. M. (1982). *How to Break Your Addiction to a Person.* MJF Books, New York.

Hamilton, J. G. (1995). Needle phobia: A neglected diagnosis. *The Journal of Family Practice,* **41** (2), 169–175.

Harris, A. H. S. and Thoresen, C. E. (2005). Forgiveness, unforgiveness, health, and disease. In E. L. Worthington, Jr. (Ed.), *Handbook of Forgiveness,* 321–333. Routledge, Taylor and Francis Group, New York.

Harris, J. R. (1998). *The Nurture Assumption: Why Children Turn Out the Way They Do.* Free Press, New York.

Harris, J. R. (2006). *No Two Alike: Human Nature and Human Individuality.* W. W. Norton, New York.

Hart, A. D. (1987). *Counseling the Depressed.* Word Books, Waco, TX.

Hart, A. D. (1990). *Healing Life's Hidden Addictions: Overcoming the Closest Compulsions That Master Your Time and Control Your Life.* Vine books/Servant Publications, Ann Arbor. (Also published by Crossway Books in Eastbourne, 1991).

Hart, A. D. (1991). *Adrenaline and Stress.* Word books, Dallas, TX.

Hart, A. D. (1994). *The Sexual Man.* Word books, Waco, TX.

Hart, A. D. (2001). *Unmasking Male Depression.* Word books, Waco,TX

Havens, L. L. (1999). Excerpts from an academic conference and recognition of suicidal risks through the psychological examination. In D. G. Jacobs (Ed.), *The Harvard Medical School Guide to Suicide Assessment and Intervention,* 210–223. Jossey-Bass, Wiley, San Francisco, CA.

Hawton, K. (1989). Sexual dysfunction. In K. Hawton, P. Salkovskis, J. Kirk, and D. Clark (Eds.), *Cognitive Behaviour Therapy for Psychiatric Problems: A Practical Guide.* Oxford University Press, Oxford.

Hayes, S. C., Strosahl, K. D., and Wilson, K. G. (2012). *Acceptance and Commitment Therapy: The Process and Practice of Mindful Change.* Guilford Press: New York. (Also available as an e-book at *e-book ebrary.*)

Hayman, S. (1994). *Other People's Children.* Penguin Books, New York.

Hayward, J. and Brandon, G. (2010). *Cohabitation in the 21st Century.* Jubilee centre, Cambridge, England. (Available online at http://www.jubilee-centre.org/uploaded/files/resource_344.pdf; accessed October 2010.)

Hazan, C. and Shaver, P. (1987). Romantic love conceptualized as an attachment process. *Journal of Personality and Social Psychology*, **52**, 511–524.

Hazlett-Stevens, H. (2008). *Psychological Approaches to Generalized Anxiety Disorder: A Clinician's guide to Assessment and Treatment*. Springer, New York. (Also available as an e-book at *SpringerLink e-Book SpringerLink*.)

Hebl, J. H. and Enright, R. D. (1993). Forgiveness as a psychotherapeutic goal with elderly females. *Psychotherapy*, **30**, 658–667.

Heim, L. J. (2001). Evaluation and differential diagnosis of dyspareunia. *American Family Physician*, **63** (8), 1535–1545

Heimberg, R. G. and Becker, R. E. (2002). *Cognitive-Behavioral Group Therapy for Social Phobia: Basic Mechanisms and Clinical Strategies*. Guilford Press, New York.

Heitritler, L. and Vought, J. (1989). *Helping Victims of Sexual Abuse*. Bethany House Publisher, Minneapolis.

Hendrix, H. (2001). *Getting the Love You Want*, revised edit. Henry Holt, New York.

Higgins, S. T. and Petry, N. M. (1999). Contingency management: Incentives for sobriety. *Alcohol Research and Health*, **23** (2), 122–127.

Holmes, T. and Rahe, R. (1967). The social readjustment rating scale. *Journal of Psychosomatic Research*, **11**, 213–218.

Holmgren, M. R. (2002). Forgiveness and self-forgiveness in psychotherapy. In S. Lamb and J. G. Murphy (Eds.), *Before Forgiving: Cautionary Views of Forgiveness in Psychotherapy*, 112–135. Oxford University Press, New York.

House, H. W. (Ed.) (1990). *Divorce and Remarriage: Four Christian Views*. InterVarsity Press, Downers Grove, IL.

Hughes, S. (1991). *The Christian Counsellor's Pocket guide*. Kingsway Publications, Eastbourne, E. Sussex, UK. (This paperback has been reprinted several times since 1982.)

Humphrey, G. M. and Zimpfer, D. G. (1996). *Counselling for Grief and Bereavement*. SAGE Publications, London.

Hydes, A. (1995). *Pathway to Freedom from Sexual abuse*. Grace ministries, Auckland, New Zealand.

Jacobs, D. G., Brewer, M., and Klein-Benheim, M. (1999). Suicide assessment: An overview and recommended protocol. In D. G. Jacobs (Ed.), *The Harvard Medical School Guide to Suicide Assessment and Intervention*, 3–39. Jossey-Bass, Wiley, San Francisco, CA.

Jacobs, G. D. (1999). *Say Goodnight to Insomnia: The Six Week, Drug-Free Program Developed at Harvard Medical School*. Owl Books, Henry Holt, New York.

Jacobsen, E. (1938). *Progressive Relaxation*. University of Chicago Press, Chicago.

Jamison, K. R. (1999). Suicide and manic-depressive illness: An overview. In D. G. Jacobs (Ed.), *The Harvard Medical School Guide to Suicide Assessment and Intervention*, 251–269. Jossey-Bass, Wiley, San Francisco, CA.

Jefferson, T., Herbst, J. H., and McCrae, R. R. (1998). Associations between birth order and personality traits: Evidence from self-reports and observer ratings. *Journal of Research in Personality*, **32**, 498–509.

Jeffreys, J. S. (2005). *Helping Grieving people—When Tears Are Not enough: A Handbook for Care Providers*. Brunner-Routledge, New York.

Johnson, D. and VanVonderen, J. (1991). *The Subtle Power of Spiritual Abuse*. Bethany House, Minneapolis, MN.

Johnson, S. E. (1987). *After a Child Dies: Counseling Bereaved Families*. Springer, New York.

ohnson, S. M. (2008). *Hold Me Tight: Seven Conversations for a Lifetime of Love.* Little Brown and Company, New York.

ohnston, F. (1998). *Getting a Good Night's Sleep.* Tandem Press, Auckland, New Zealand.

oiner, T. (2005). *Why People Die By Suicide.* Harvard University Press, Cambridge, MA.

Jones, M. K. and Krochmalik, A. (2003). Obsessive compulsive washing. In R. G. Menzies and P. de Silva (Eds.), *Obsessive Compulsive Disorder: Theory, Research, and Treatment*, 121–138. Wiley, Chichester, England. (Also available as an e-book at *e-Book netLibrary.*)

Kabat-Zinn, J. (2004). *Full Catastrophe Living: How to Cope with Stress, Pain and Illness Using Mindfulness Meditation.* Piatkus, London.

Kadden, R. M. and Cooney, N. L. (2005). Treating alcohol problems. In G. A. Marlatt and M. D. Donovan (Eds.), *Relapse Prevention: Maintenance Strategies in the Treatment of Addictive Behaviors*, 2nd edit., 65–91. Guilford Press, New York.

Kalter, N. (1987). Long-term effects of divorce on children: A development vulnerability model. *Journal of Orthopsychiatry,* **57**, 587–600.

Kandel, D., Schaffran, C., Griesler, P., Samuolis, J., Davies, M., and Rosaria Galanti, R. (2005). On the measurement of nicotine dependence in adolescence: Comparisons of the mFTQ and a DSM-IV-based scale. *Journal of Pediatric Psychology,* **30** (4), 319–332.

Kantor, D. (1985). Couples therapy, crisis, induction, and change. In A. S. Gurman (Ed.), *Casebook of Marital Therapy*, 21–72. Guilford Press, New York.

Kassinove, H. and Sukhodolsky, D. G. (1995). Anger disorders: Basic science and practice issues. In H. Kassinove (Ed.), *Anger Disorders: Definition, Diagnosis, and Treatment*, 1–26. Taylor and Francis, Washington, DC.

Kaufman, G. (1989). *The Psychology of Shame: Theory and Treatment of Shame-Based Syndromes.* Springer, New York.

Keane, H (2002). *What's Wrong With Addictions?* Melbourne University Press, Victoria, Australia.

Keefer, B. and Schooler, J. E. (2000). *Telling the Truth to Our Adopted or Foster Child: Making Sense of the Past.* Bergin and Garvey, Westport, CT.

Kenton, L. (2004). *The Power House Diet.* Vermilion, Random House, London.

Kerr, M. E. (1985). Obstacles to differentiation of self. In A. S. Gurman (Ed.), *Casebook of Marital Therapy*, 111–154. Guilford Press, New York.

Kilmer, J. R., Cronce, J. M., and Palmer, R. S. (2005). Relapse prevention for abuse of club drugs, hallucinogens, inhalants, and steroids. In G. A. Marlatt and M. D. Donovan (Eds.), *Relapse Prevention: Maintenance Strategies in the Treatment of Addictive Behaviors*, 2nd edit., 208–247. Guilford Press, New York.

Kirkwood, C. (1997). *Leaving Abusive Partners.* SAGE Publications, London.

Kiser, B. (2003). The dreamcatcher (Interview with Joe Griffin). *New Scientist,* **2390**, April 12.

Klass, D., Silverman, P. R., and Nickman, S. L. (1996). *Continuing Bonds: New Understandings of Grief.* Taylor and Francis, Washington, DC.

Klerman, G.L., Weissman, M. M., Rounsaville, B. J., and Chevon, E. S. (1984). *Interpersonal Psychotherapy of Depression.* Basic Books, New York.

Klesges, R. C. (1995). Cigarette smoking and body weight. In K. D. Brownell and C. G. Fairburn (Eds.), *Eating Disorders and Obesity: A Comprehensive Handbook*, 61–64. Guilford Press, New York.

Kluger, J. (2007). The power of birth order. *TIME*, October 17. (Available online at http://www.time.com/time/health/article/0,8599,1672715,00.html.)

Koss, M. P. (1993). Detecting the scope of rape: A review of prevalence research methods. *Journal of Interpersonal Violence*, **8** (2), 198–222.

Kramer, M. (2006). Psychology of dreaming. In T. Lee-Chiong (Ed.) *Sleep: A Comprehensive Handbook*, 37–43. Wiley, New York.

Kübler-Ross, E. (1978). *On Death and Dying*. Routledge, London.

Kupfer, D., First, M. B., and Regier, D. A. (Eds). (2002). *A Research Agenda for DSM-V*. American Psychiatric Association, Washington, DC.

Kutchins, H. and Kirk, S. A. (1997). *Making Us Crazy: DSM, the Psychiatric Bible and the Creation of Mental Disorders*. The Free Press, New York.

Kyrios, M. (2003). Exposure and response prevention. In R. G. Menzies and P. de Silva (Eds.), *Obsessive Compulsive Disorder: Theory, Research, and Treatment*, 259–274. Wiley, Chichester, England. (Also available as an e-book at *e-Book netLibrary*.)

Kyrios, M., Steketee, G., Frost, R. O., and Oh, S. (2002). Cognitions in compulsive hoarding. In R. O. Frost and G. Steketee (Eds.), *Cognitive Approaches to Obsessions and Compulsions*, 269–289. Elsevier, New York. (Also available as an e-book at *e-book ScienceDirect*.)

L'Abate, L. (1977). *Enrichment: Structural Interventions with Couples, Families and Groups*. University Press of America, Washington DC.

Ladouceur, R. and Lachance, S. (2007a). *Overcoming Pathological Gambling: Therapist Guide*. Oxford University Press, New York.

Ladouceur, R. and Lachance, S. (2007b). *Overcoming Your Pathological Gambling: Workbook*. Oxford University Press, New York.

Ladouceur, R., Sylvain, C., Boutin, C., and Doucet, C. (2002). *Understanding and Treating the Pathological Gambler*. Wiley, Chichester, U.K.

LaHaye, T. (1988). *Why You Act the Way You Do*. Living Books, Tyndale House, Carol, Wheaton, IL.

Lamb, S. and Murphy, J. G. (Eds.) (2002). *Before Forgiving: Cautionary Views of Forgiveness in Psychotherapy*. Oxford University Press, New York.

Lazarus, A. A. (1973). Multimodal behavior therapy: Treating the BASIC ID. *Journal of Nervous and Mental Disease*, **156**, 404–411.

Lazarus, A. A. (1981). *The Practice of Multimodal Therapy*. McGraw-Hill, New York.

Lazarus, A. A. (2004). Multimodal therapy. In R. J. Corsini and D. Wedding (Eds.), *Current Psychotherapies*, 7th edit. Wadsworth, New York.

Lazarus, R. S. (1999). *Stress and Emotion: A New Synthesis*. Springer, New York.

LeDoux, J. (1998). *The Emotional Brain: The Mysterious Underpinnings of Emotional Life*. Touchstone, Simon and Schuster, New York.

Leibowitz, S. F. (1995). Central physiological determinants of eating behavior and weight. In K. D. Brownell and C. G. Fairburn (Eds.), *Eating Disorders and Obesity: A Comprehensive Handbook*, 3–7. Guilford Press, New York.

Lenters, W. (1985). *The Freedom We Crave*. William B. Eeerdmans Publishing Co., Grand Rapids, MI.

Lerner, H. G. (2004). *The Dance of Anger: A Woman's Guide to Changing the Pattern of Intimate Relationships*. Element, Harper-Collins, London.

Lewinsohn, P. and Gotlib, I. (1995). Behavioral theory and treatment of depression. In E. Becker and W. Leber (Eds.), *Handbook of Depression*, 352–375. Guilford Press, New York.

Lilienfeld, S. O. (2007). Psychological treatments that cause harm. *Perspectives on Psychological Science*, **2** (1), 53–70.

inden, W. (1990). *Autogenic Training: A Clinical Guide.* Guilford Press, New York.

inden, W. (2005). *Stress Management: From Basic Science to Better Practice.* SAGE Publications, Thousand Oaks, CA.

indenfield, G. (1993). *Managing Anger: Positive Strategies for Dealing with Difficult Emotions.* HarperCollins, London.

Linehan, M. M. (1993a). *Cognitive-Behavioral Treatment of Borderline Personality Disorder.* Guilford Press, New York.

Linehan, M. M. (1993b). *Skills Training Manual fot Treating Borderline Personality Disorder.* Guilford Press, New York.

Linehan, M. M. (1999). Standard protocol for assessing and treating suicidal behaviors for patients in treatment. In D. G. Jacobs (Ed.), *The Harvard Medical School Guide to Suicide Assessment and Intervention,* 146–187. Jossey-Bass, Wiley, San Francisco, CA.

Littauer, F. (1992). *Personality Plus: How to Understand Others by Understanding Yourself.* Fleming Revell, Grand Rapids. MI. (This paperback has been reprinted many times.)

Locke, H. J. and Wallace, K. M. (1959). Short-term marital adjustment and prediction tests: Their reliability and validity. *Journal of Marriage and Family Living,* **21**, 251–255.

Lopiano, D. A. and Zotos, C (1992). Modern athletics: The pressure to perform. In K. D. Brownwell, J. Rodin, and J. H. Wilmore (Eds.), *Eating, Body Weight, and Performance in Athletes: Disorders of Modern Society,* 275–292. Lea and Febiger, Philadelphia, PA.

Lynch, J. J. (1985). *The Language of the Heart.* Basic Books, New York.

MacDonald, K., Lambie, I., and Simmonds, L. (1995). *Counselling for Sexual Abuse: A Therapist's Guide to Working with Adults, Children, and Families.* Oxford University Press, New Zealand.

McCann, I. L. and Pearlman, L. A. (1990). *Psychological Trauma and the Adult Survivor: Theory, Therapy, and Transformation.* Brunner/Mazel, New York.

McCullough, M. E. and Root, L. M. (2005). Forgiveness as change. In E. L. Worthington, Jr. (Ed.), *Handbook of Forgiveness,* 91–107. Routledge, Taylor and Francis Group, New York.

McCullough, M. E. and Worthington, E. L., Jr. (1999). Religion and the forgiving personality. *Journal of Personality,* **67** (6), 1141–1164.

McGee, R. S. and Mountcastle, W. D. (1990). *Rapha's 12-Step Program for Overcoming Eating Disorders.* Rapha/Word, Houston, TX.

McGoldrick, M. (2007). *Genograms: Assessment and Intervention.* W. W. Norton, New York.

McGoldrick, M. and Gerson, R. (1985). *Genograms in Family Assessment.* W. W. Norton, New York.

McLeod, J. (1998). *Doing Counselling Research.* SAGE Publications, London.

McMinn, M. R. (1996). *Psychology, Theology, and Spirituality in Christian Counseling.* Tyndale House, Wheaton, IL.

Maddux, J. F. and Desmond, D. P. (2000). Addiction or dependence? *Addiction,* **95** (5), 661–665.

Magnavita, J. J. (2004). Classification, prevalence, and etiology of personality disorders: Related issues and controversy. In J. J. Magnavita (Ed.), *Handbook of Personality Disorders: Theory and Practice.* Wiley, Hoboken, NJ. (Available as an e-book at *e-Book netLibrary.*)

Malcolm, W., Warwar, S., and Greenberg, L. (2005). Facilitating forgiveness in individual therapy as an approach to resolving interpersonal injuries. In E. L. Worthington, Jr.

(Ed.), *Handbook of Forgiveness*, 379–391. Routledge, Taylor and Francis Group, New York.

Manning, D. (2002). *Continuing Care Series. 1. Pain of Grief. 2. Reality of Grief. 3. Dimensions of Grief. 4. Journey of Grief.* 2nd edit. Insight Books Inc, Oklahoma city, OK.

Marcus, M. D. (1995). Binge eating and obesity. In K. D. Brownell and C. G. Fairburn (Eds.), *Eating Disorders and Obesity: A Comprehensive Handbook*, 441–444. Guilford Press, New York.

Marin, A. J. and Russo, N. F. (1999). Feminist perspectives on male violence against women: Critiquing O'Neil and Harway model. In M. Harway and J. M. O'Neil, *What Causes Men's Violence Against Women?*, 18–35. SAGE Publications, Thousand Oaks, CA.

Marks, M. (2003). Cognitive therapy for OCD. In R. G. Menzies and P. de Silva (Eds.), *Obsessive Compulsive Disorder: Theory, Research, and Treatment*, 275–290. Wiley, Chichester, England. (Also available as an e-book at *e-Book netLibrary.*)

Marlatt, G. A. (1995). Relapse: A cognitive-behavioral model. In K. D. Brownell and C. G. Fairburn (Eds.), *Eating Disorders and Obesity: A Comprehensive Handbook*, 541–546. Guilford Press, New York.

Marlatt, G. A. and Donovan, D. M. (2005). *Relapse Prevention: Maintenance Strategies in the Treatment of Addictive Behaviors.* Guilford Press, New York.

Marlatt, G. A. and Gordon, J. R. (Eds.) (1985). *Relapse Prevention: Maintenance Strategies in the Treatment of Addictive Behaviors*, Guilford Press, New York.

Marlatt, G. A. and Kristeller, J. (1999). Mindfulness and meditation. In W. R. Miller (Ed.), *Integrating Spirituality in Treatment: Resources for Practitioners*, 67–84. American Psychological Association Books, Washington, DC.

Marlatt, G. A. and Witkiewitz, K. (2005). Relapse prevention for alcohol and drug problems. In G. A. Marlatt and M. D. Donovan (Eds.), *Relapse Prevention: Maintenance Strategies in the Treatment of Addictive Behaviors*, 2nd edit., 1–44. Guilford Press, New York.

Marsella, A. J. and Kaplan, A. (2002). Cultural considerations for understanding, assessing, and treating depressive experience and disorder. In M. A. Reinecke and M. R. Davison (Eds.), *Comparative Treatments of Depression*, 47–78. Springer, New York

Marshall, C. D. (2001). *Beyond Retribution: A New Testament Vision for Justice, Crime and Punishment.* Wm. B. Eerdmans, Grand Rapids, MI.

Mellody, P., Miller, A. W., and Miller, J. K. (1989). *Facing Codependence: What It Is, Where It Comes From, How It Sabotages Our Lives.* Harper and Row, San Francisco.

Mellody, P., Miller, A. W., and Miller, J. K. (1992). *Facing Love Addiction: Giving Yourself the Power to Change the Way You Love—The Love Connection to Codependence.* HarperCollins, New York.

Menzies, R. G. and de Silva, P. (2003). *Obsessive Compulsive Disorder: Theory, Research, and Treatment.* Wiley, Chichester, England. (Also available as an e-book at *e-Book netLibrary.*)

Miles, M. S. and Demi, A. S. (1991). A comparison of guilt in bereaved parents whose children died by suicide, accident, or chronic disease. *Omega*, **24**, 203–215.

Miller, A. L., Rathus, J. H., and Lionhan, M. M. (2007). *Dialectical Behavior Therapy with Suicidal Adolescents.* Guilford Press, New York.

Miller-Clendon, N. (2003). *Life After Baby Loss: A Guide to Pregnancy and Infant Loss and Subsequent Pregnancy in New Zealand.* Tandem Press, Auckland, New Zealand.

Miller, M. C. (1999). Suicide-prevention contracts: Advantages, disadvantages, and an alternative approach. In D. G. Jacobs (Ed.), *The Harvard Medical School Guide to*

Suicide Assessment and Intervention, 463–481. Jossey-Bass, Wiley, San Francisco, CA.

Miller, W. R. and Rollnick, S. (1991). *Motivational Interviewing: Preparing People to Change Addictive Behavior*. Guilford Press, New York.

Miller, W. R. and Rollnick, S. (2002). *Motivational Interviewing: Preparing People for Change*, 2nd edit. Guilford Press, New York.

Miller, W. R. and Sanchez, V. C. (1994). Motivating young adults for treatment and lifestyle change. In G. Howard (Ed.), *Issues in Alcohol Use and Misuse By Young Adults*, 55–82. University of Notre Dame Press, Notre Dame, IN.

Millon, T. and Davis, R. D., with Millon, C., Escovar, L., and Meagher, S. (2000). *Personality Disorders In Modern Life*. Wiley, New York.

Millon, T., Davis, R. D., Millon, C., and Grossman, S. (2009). *The Millon Clinical Multiaxial Inventory-III Manual*, 3rd edit. Pearson Assessments, San Antonio, TX.

Miltenberger, R. G. (2001). Habit reversal treatment manual for trichotillomania. In D. Woods and R. Miltenberger (Eds.), *Tic Disorders, Trichotillomania, and Other Repetitive Behavior Disorders: Behavioral Approaches to Analysis and Treatment*, 171–195. Klumer Academic Publishers, Norwell, MA. (Also available as an e-book at *SpringerLink*.)

Miltenberger, R. G., Fuqua, R. W., and Woods, D. W. (1998). Applying behavior analysis to clinical problems: Review and analysis of habit reversal. *Journal of Applied Behavior Analysis*, **31** (3), 447–469.

Mines, R. A. and Merrill, C. A. (1987). Bulimia: Cognitive-behavioral treatment and relapse prevention. *Journal of Counseling and Development*, **65** (10), 562–564.

Monnier, J. and Brawman-Mintzer, O. (2003). Generalized anxiety disorder. In D. J. Nutt and J. C. Ballenger (Eds.), *Anxiety Disorder*, 315–338. Blackwell Science, Malden, MA.

Morey, L. C. (1988). Personality disorders in DSM-III and DSM-III-R: Convergence, coverage, and internal consistency. *American Journal of Psychiatry*, **145**, 573–577.

Morrison A. P. (2011). The pschchodynamics of shame. In R. L. Dearing and J. P. Tangney, *Shame in the Therapy Hour*, chapter 1. American Psychological Association: Washington, D. C. (Also available as an e-book at *e-Book PsycBooks Collection*.)

Motto, J. A. (1999). Critical points in the assessment and management of suicide risk. In D. G. Jacobs (Ed.), *The Harvard Medical School Guide to Suicide Assessment and Intervention*, 224–238. Jossey-Bass, Wiley, San Francisco, CA.

Muraven, M. and Baumeister, R. F. (2000). Self-regulation and depletion of limited resources: Does self-control resemble a muscle? *Psychological Bulletin*, **126**, 247–259.

Murphy, J. G. (2003). *Getting Even: Forgiveness and Its Limits*. Oxford University Press, New York.

Murphy, J. G. (2005). Forgiveness, self-respect, and the value of resentment. In E. L. Worthington, Jr. (Ed.), *Handbook of Forgiveness*, 33–40. Routledge, Taylor and Francis Group, New York.

Nakken, C. (1996). *The Addictive Personality*, 2nd edit. Hazelden, Center City, MA.

Napier, N. (1993). *Getting Through the Day: Strategies for Adults Hurt as Children*. W. W. Norton, New York.

Narramore, S. B. and Coe, J. H. (1999). Guilt. In D. G. Benner and P. C.. Hill (Eds.), *Baker Encyclopedia of Psychology and Counseling*, 2nd edit. Baker Books, Grand Rapids, MI.

Noll, J. G. (2005). Forgiveness in people experiencing trauma. In E. L. Worthington, Jr. (Ed.), *Handbook of Forgiveness*, 363–375. Routledge, Taylor and Francis Group, New York.

North, J. (1998). The "ideal" of forgiveness: A philosopher's exploration. In R. D. Enright and J. North (Eds.), *Exploring Forgiveness*, 15–34. University of Wisconsin Press, Madison, WI.

Novaco, R. W. (1075). *Anger Control. The Development and Evaluation of an Experimental Treatment.* Lexington Books, Lexington, MA.

Novaco, R. W. (1977). Stress inoculation: A cognitive therapy for anger and its application to a case of depression. *Journal of Consulting and Clinical Psychology*, **45**, 600–608.

Novaco, R. W. (1985). Anger and its therapeutic regulation. In M. Chesney and R. Rosenman (Eds.), *Anger and Hostility in Cardiovascular and Behavioral Disorders.* Hemisphere, Washington, DC.

Nutt, R. L. (1999). Women's gender-role socialization, gender-role conflict, and abuse: A review of predisposing factors. In M. Harway and J. M. O'Neil, *What Causes Men's Violence Against Women?*, 117–134. SAGE Publications, Thousand Oaks, CA.

Nydegger, R. V. (2012). *Dealing With Anxiety and Related Disorders : Understanding, Coping, and Prevention.* Praeger, Santa Barbara, CA. (Also available as an e-book at e-book ebrary.)

Oates, W. E. (1978). *Confessions of a Workaholic.* Abington, Nashville. (For an on-line version see http://www.oates.org/cos/oateslibrary/books/confessions/weo-coaw-01a.php.)

O'Connell, B. (2001). *Solution-Focused Stress Counselling.* Continuum, London.

O'Donohue, W. T. and Levensky, E. R. (Eds.) (2006). *Promoting Treatment Adherence: A Practical Handbook for Health Care Providers.* SAGE, Thousand Oaks, CA.

Öhman, A. (1993). Fear and anxiety as emotional phenomena: Clinical, phenomenological, evolutionary perspectives, and information processing mechanisms. In M. Lewis and J. M. Haviland (Eds.), *Handbook of Emotions*, 511–536. Guilford Press, New York.

Olmsted, M. P. and Kaplan, A. S. (1995). Psychoeducation in the treatment of eating disorders. In K. D. Brownell and C. G. Fairburn (Eds.), *Eating Disorders and Obesity: A Comprehensive Handbook*, 299–305. Guilford Press, New York.

O'Neill, J. M. and Harway, M. (1999). Revised multivariate model explaining men's risk factors for violence against women: Theoretical propositions, new hypotheses, and proactive recommendations. In M. Harway and J. M. O'Neil, *What Causes Men's Violence Against Women?*, 207–241. SAGE Publications, Thousand Oaks, CA.

O'Neil, J. M. and Nadeau, R. A. (1999). Men's gender-role conflict, defense mechanisms, and self-protective defensive strategies: Explaining men's violence against women from a gender-role perspective. In M. Harway and J. M. O'Neil, *What Causes Men's Violence Against Women?*, 89–116. SAGE Publications, Thousand Oaks, CA.

Orbach, S. (1982). *Fat is a Feminist Issue II: A program to Conquer Compulsive Eating.* Berkley Books, New York.

Orbach, S. (1986). *Hunger Strike: The Anorectic's Struggle as a Metaphor for Our Age.* Faber and Faber, London.

Ortmeyer, C. F. (1974). *Mortality and Morbidity in the United States.* Harvard University Press, Cambridge.

Padesky, C. A. and Mooney, K. A. (2012). Strengths-based cognitiv-behavioural therapy: A four-step model to build resilience. *Clinical Psychology and Psychotherapy*, **19**, 283–290. (doi: 10.1002/cpp.1795)

Palmer, S. (1990). Stress mapping: A visual technique to aid counseling and training. *Counselling Today*, **2**, 9–12.

Palmer, S. (1993). *Multimodal Techniques: Relaxation and Hypnosis.* Centre for Stress Management, London.

Palmer, S. and Dryden, W. (1995). *Counselling for Stress problems*. SAGE Publications, London.

Papalia, D. E., Olds, S. W., and Feldman, R. D. (2001). *Human Development*, 8th edit. McGraw-Hill, New York.

Parker, M. (1981). *A Time to Grieve*. Methuen, New Zealand.

Parnell, L. (1997). *Transforming Trauma—EMDR: The Revolutionary New Therapy for Freeing the Mind, Clearing the Body, and Opening the Heart*. W. W. Norton, New York.

Patterson, C. J. (2000). Family relationships of lesbians and gay men. *Journal of Marriage and Family*, **62**, 1052–1069.

Paul, M. (1992). *Inner Bonding: Becoming a Loving Adult to Your Inner Child*. Harper, San Francisco.

Peale, N. V. (1994). *The Power of Positive Thinking*. Oxford University Press, Oxford.

Pearman, B. (2007). *Forgiveness: The Gift of Love*. Windsor Park Baptist Church, North Shore, Auckland, New Zealand.

Penzel, F. (2003). *The Hair Pulling Problem: A Complete Guide to Trichotillomania*. Oxford University Press, New York.

Perkins, K. A., Donny, E., and Caggiula., A. R. (1999). Sex differences in nicotine effects and self-administration: Review of human and animal evidence. *Nicotine and Tobacco Research*, **1**, 301–315.

Perri, M. G. (1995). Methods for Maintaining Weight Loss. In K. D. Brownell and C. G. Fairburn (Eds.), *Eating Disorders and Obesity: A Comprehensive Handbook*, 547–551. Guilford Press, New York.

Pike, P. L. and Mohline, R. J. (1995). Ritual abuse and recovery: Survivor's personal account. *Journal of Psychology and Theology*, **23** (1), 45–55.

Pingleton, J. P. (1989). The role and function of forgiveness in the psychotherapeutic process. *Journal of Psychology and Christianity*, **17**, 27–35.

Plummer, D. (2004). *Helping Adolescents and Adults to Build Self-Esteem: A Photocopiable Resource Book*. Jessica Kingsley Publishers, Philadelphia, PA. (Also available as an e-book at *e-book ebrary*.)

Pokorny, A. D. (1983). Prediction of suicide in psychiatric patients: Report of a prospective study. *Archives of General Psychiatry*, **40**, 249–257.

Poling, J. N. (2003). *Understanding Male Violence: Pastoral Care Issues*. Chalice press, St. Louis, MO.

Pope, K. S. and Brown, L. S. (1996). *Recovered Memories of Abuse: Assessment, Therapy, Forensics*. American Psychological Association, Washington DC. (Also available as an e-book at *e-Book PsycBOOKS Collection*.)

Portman, M. E. (2009). *Generalized Anxiety Disorder Across the Lifespan: An Integrative Approach*. Springer, New York. (Also available as an e-book at *SpringerLink e-book SpringerLink*.)

Pretzer, J. L. and Beck, A. T. (1996). A cognitive theory of personality disorders. In J. F. Clarkin and M. F. Lenzenweger (Eds.), *Major Theories of Personality Disorders*, 36–105. Guilford Press, New York.

Prinz, J. (2004). Which emotions are basic? In D. Evans and P. Cruse (Eds.), *Emotion, Evolution, and Rationality*, 69–88. Oxford University Press, New York. (Available online at http://subcortex.com/WhichEmotionsAreBasicPrinz.pdf; accessed October 2010.)

Prinz, J. (2005). Are emotions feelings? *Journal of Consciousness Studies*, **12** (8–10), 9–25. (Available online at http://www.imprint.co.uk/books/Thompson_Sample.pdf.)

Prochaska, J. O. and DiClemente, C. C. (1982). Transtheoretical therapy: Toward a more integrative model of change. *Psychotherapy: Theory, Research, and Practice*, **19**, 276–288.

Prochaska, J. O. and DiClemente, C. C. (1988). *The Transthcoretical Approach to Therapy*. Dorsey Press: Chicago.

Puff, R. E. (2002). *Anger Work: How to Express Your Anger and Still Be Kind*, 2nd edit. Well-Spring Press. (Available online at http://www.doctorpuff.com/anger_work.pdf; accessed October 2010.)

Purdon, C. and Clark, D. (2002). The need to control thoughts. In R. O. Frost and G. Steketee (Eds.), *Cognitive Approaches to Obsessions and Compulsions*, 29–43. Elsevier, New York. (Also available as an e-book at *e-Book netLibrary*.)

Qin, P. and Nordentoft, M. (2005). Suicide risk in relation to psychiatric hospitalization: Evidence based on longitudinal registers. *Archives of General Psychiatry*, **62** (4), 427–432.

Rachman, J. (1980). Emotional processing. *Behaviour Research and Therapy*, **18**, 51–60.

Rachman, S. (1997). A cognitive theory of obsessions. *Behaviour Research and Therapy*, **35**, 793–802.

Rachman, S. (2003). Compulsive checking. In R. G. Menzies and P. de Silva (Eds.), *Obsessive Compulsive Disorder: Theory, Research, and Treatment*, 139–162. Wiley, Chichester, England. (Also available as an e-book at *e-Book netLibrary*.)

Rachman, S, and de Silva, P. (1978). Abnormal and normal obsessions. *Behaviour Research and Therapy*, **16**, 233–248

Raistrick, D., Dunbar, G., and Davidson, R. (1983). Development of a questionnaire to measure alcohol dependence. *British Journal of Addiction*, **78**, 89–95.

Rando, T. A. (1993). *Treatment of Complicated Mourning*. Research Press, Champaign, IL.

Rassin, E. (2005). *Thought Suppression*. Elsevier, San Diego. (Also available as an e-book at *e-book ScienceDirect*.)

Reddrop, M. and Reddrop, B. (1995). *For Better, For Worse: A Guide to Contemporary Marriage Counselling*. HarperCollins, London.

Regnerus, M. (2012). How different are the adult children of parents who have same-sex relationships? Findings from the New Family Structures Study. *Social Science Research*, **41** (4), 752–770.

Reichborn-Kjennerud, T. et al. (8 others) (2007). Genetic and environmental influences on dimensional representations of DSM-IV cluster C personality disorders: A population-based multivariate twin study. *Psychological Medicine*, **37** (5), 645–653.

Reinecke, M. A. (2002). Cognitive therapies of depression: A modularized treatment approach. In M. A. Reinecke and M. R. Davison (Eds.), *Comparative Treatments of Depression*, 249–290. Springer, New York.

Reinecke, M. A. and Davison, M. R. (2002). Appendix. In M. A. Reinecke and M. R. Davison (Eds.), *Comparative Treatments of Depression*, 464–490. Springer, New York.

Renzetti, C. M. (1992). *Violent Betrayal: Partner Abuse in Lesbian Relationships*. SAGE Publications, Newbury Park, CA.

Richards, L. (1981). *Remarriage: A Healing Gift From God*. Word Books, Waco, TX.

Richmond, R. L (2008). *A Guide to Psychology and Its Practice*. Available at http://www.guidetopsychology.com/index.html (accessed October 2010).

Riddell, D. (2007). Don't burn out! *DAYSTAR*, December, 20–21. Auckland, New Zealand.

Rodgers, J. L., Cleveland, H. H., van den Oord, E., and Rowe, D. C. (2000). Resolving the debate over birth order, family size, and intelligence. *American Psychologist*, **55** (6), 599–612.

Roffman, R. A. and and Stephens, R. S. (2005). Relapse prevention for cannabis use and dependence. In G. A. Marlatt and M. D. Donovan (Eds.), *Relapse Prevention: Maintenance Strategies in the Treatment of Addictive Behaviors*, 2nd edit., 179–207. Guilford Press, New York.

Rosenberg, M. (1965). *Society and the Adolescent Self-image*. Princeton University Press, Princeton, NJ.

Rothschild, B. (2000). *The Body Remembers: The Psychophysiology of Trauma and Trauma Treatment*. W. W. Norton, New York.

Rothschild, B. (2003). *The Body Remembers Casebook: Unifying Methods and Models in the Treatment of Trauma and PTSD*. W. W. Norton, New York.

Rusbult, C. E., Hannon, P. A., Stocker, S.L., and Finkel, E. J. (2005). Forgiveness and relationship repair. In E. L. Worthington, Jr. (Ed.), *Handbook of Forgiveness*, 185–205. Routledge, Taylor and Francis Group, New York.

Russell, J. A. (1994). Is there universal recognition of emotion from facial expression? A review of cross-cultural studies. *Psychological Bulletin*, **115** (1), 102–141.

Ryan, J. and Ryan, D. (1993). *Recovery from Workaholism*. InterVarsity Press, Downers Grove, IL.

Ryckman, R. (2004). *Theories of Personality*. Thomson/Wadsworth, Belmont, CA.

Sadock, B. J. and Sadock, V. A. (Eds.) (2005). *Kaplan and Sadock's Comprehensive Textbook of Psychiatry*, vols 1 and 2, 8th edit. Lippincott Williams and Wilkins, Philadelphia.

Salkovskis, P. M. (1985). Obsessional-compulsive problems: a cognitive-behavioural analysis. *Behaviour Research and Therapy*, **23**, 571–583.

Salkovskis, P. M. and Forrester, E. (2002). Responsibility. In R. O. Frost and G. Steketee (Eds.), *Cognitive Approaches to Obsessions and Compulsions*, 45–61. Elsevier, New York.

Sandage, S. J. and Williamson, I. (2005). Forgiveness in cultural context. In E .L. Worthington, Jr. (Ed.) *Handbook of Forgiveness*, 41–55. Routledge, Taylor and Francis Group, New York.

Sandford, P. (1988). *Healing Victims of Sexul Abuse*. Victory House Publishers, Tulsa, OK.

Satir, V. (1975). *Self Esteem*. Celestial Arts, Milbrae, CA.

Satir, V. (1976). *Making Contact*. Celestial Arts, Milbrae, CA.

Schacter, D. L. (1996). *Searching for Memory—The Brain, The Mind, and The Past*. Basic Books, New York.

Scheflin, A. W. and Brown, D. (1996). Repressed memory or dissociative amnesia: What the science says. *Journal of Psychiatry and Law*, **24** (2), 143–188.

Scherer, M., Cooke, K. L., and Worthington, E. L., Jr. (2005). Forgiveness bibliography. In E. L. Worthington, Jr. (Ed.), *Handbook of Forgiveness*, 507–556. Routledge, Taylor and Francis Group, New York.

Schmidt, S. J. (2004). *The Developmental Needs Meeting Strategy: An Ego State Therapy for Healing Childhood Wounds*, 2nd edit. DNMS Institute, San Antonio.

Schooler, J. E. and Norris, B. L. (2002). *Journeys After Adoption: Understanding Lifelong Issues*. Bergin and Garvey, Westport, CT.

Schulz, J., Gotto, J. G., and Rapaport, M. H. (2005). The diagnosis and treatment of generalized anxiety disorder. *Primary Psychiatry*, **12** (11), 58–67.

Selye, H. (1978). *The Stress of Life*. McGraw-Hill, New York.

Sexton, T. L, Whiston, S. C., Bleuer, J. C., and Walz, G. R. (1997). *Integrating Outcome Research Into Counseling Practice.* American Counseling Association, Alexandria, VA.

Shapiro, F. (2001). *Eye Movement Desensitization and Reprocessing: Basic Principles, Protocols and Procedures,* 2nd edit. Guilford Press, New York.

Shapiro, F., Kaslow, F. W., and Maxfield, M. (Eds.) (2007). *Handbook of Eye Movement Desensitization and Reprocessing and Family Therapy.* Wiley, Hoboken, NJ.

Shea, S. C. (1999). *Practical Art of Suicide Assessment: A Guide for Mental Health Professionals and Substance Abuse Counselors.* Wiley, New York.

Shear M. K., Rucci P., Williams J., Frank, E., Grochocinski V., Vander Bilt J., Houck, P., and Wang T. (2001). Reliability and validity of the Panic Disorder Severity Scale: replication and extension. *Journal of Psychiatric Research,* **35** (5), 293–296.

Shiffman, S., Kassel, J., Gwaltney, C., and McChargue, D. (2005). Relapse prevention for smoking. In G. A. Marlatt and M. D. Donovan (Eds.), *Relapse Prevention: Maintenance Strategies in the Treatment of Addictive Behaviors,* 2nd edit., 92–129. Guilford Press, New York .

Shneidman, E. S. (1996). *The Suicidal Mind.* Oxford University Press, New York.

Shneidman, E. S. (1999). Perturbation and lethality: a psychological approach. In D. G. Jacobs (Ed.), *The Harvard Medical School Guide to Suicide Assessment and Intervention,* 83–97. Jossey-Bass, Wiley, San Francisco, CA.

Siegel, D. J. (1999). *The Developing Mind: Toward a Neurobiology of Interpersonal Experience.* Guilford Press, New York.

Siever, L. and Davis, K. (1991). A psychological perspective on the personality disorders. *American Journal of Psychiatry,* **148,** 1647–1658.

Silverstone, T. (2005). *Eating Disorders and Obesity: How Drugs Can Help.* IOS Press, Washington, DC. (Also available as an e-book at *e-book ebrary.*)

Steketee, G. and Frost, R. O. (2007a). *Compulsive Hoarding and Acquiring: Therapist Guide.* Oxford University Press, New York.

Steketee, G. and Frost, R. O. (2007b). *Compulsive Hoarding and Acquiring: Workbook.* Oxford University Press, New York.

Skinner, H. A. and Horn, J. L. (1984). *Alcohol Dependence Scale (ADS) User's guide.* Addiction Research Foundation, Toronto.

Smalley, G. and Trent, J. (2006). *The Two Sides of Love.* Tyndale House, Carol Stream, IL.

Smedes, L. B. (1984). *Forgive and Forget: Healing the Hurts We Don't Deserve.* Harper and Row, New York.

Smith, G. P. and Gibbs, J. (1995). Peripheral physiological determinants of eating and bodyweight. In K. D. Brownell and C. G. Fairburn (Eds.), *Eating Disorders and Obesity: A Comprehensive Handbook,* 8–12. Guilford Press, New York.

Smoke, J. (1995). *Growing Through Divorce.* Harvest House, Eugene, OR.

Smoke, J. (1999). *Single Again: The Uncertain Journey.* Vine Books, Servant Publications, Ann Arbor, MI.

Sobell, M. B. and Sobell, L. C. (1993). *Problem Drinkers: Guided Self-Change Treatment.* Guilford Press, New York.

Solms, M. and Turnbull, O. (2002). *The Brain and the Inner World.* Other Press, New York.

Solomon, A. (2001). *The Noonday Demon: An Anatomy of Depression.* Chatto and Windus, London.

Sorosky, A., Baran, A., and Pannor, R. (1978). *The Adoption Triangle.* Anchor Press, New York.

Speckhard, A. and Rue, V. (1993). Complicated mourning: Dynamics of impacted post-abortion grief. *Pre- and Perinatal Psychology Journal*, **8**, 5–32.

Sperry, L. (2003). *Handbook of Diagnosis and Treatment of DSM-IV-TR Personality Disorders*, 2nd edit. Brunner-Routledge, New York. (Available as an e-book at *e-book netLibrary*.)

Spiers, T. (2001a). Trauma assessment. In T. Spiers (Ed.), *Trauma: A Practioner's Guide to Counseling*, 35–68. Taylor and Francis, New York.

Spiers, T. (2001b). An integrated treatment model. In T. Spiers (Ed.), *Trauma: A Practioner's Guide to Counseling*, 6–34. Taylor and Francis, New York.

Spira, L. (1981). The experience of a divorce for the psychotherapy patient: A developmental perspective. *Clinical Social Work Journal*, **9**, 258–270.

Spring, J. A. (2004). *How Can I Forgive You? The Courage to Forgive, the Freedom Not to.* HarperCollins, New York.

Steffens, D. C. and Blazer, D. G. (1999). Suicide in the elderly. In D. G. Jacobs (Ed.), *The Harvard Medical School Guide to Suicide Assessment and Intervention*, 443–462. Jossey-Bass Wiley, San Francisco, CA.

Steffgen, G and Pfetsch, J. (2007). Does anger treatment reduce aggressive behavior? In G. Steffgen and M. Gollwitzer (Eds.), *Emotions and Aggressive Behavior*, 94–114. Hogrefe and Huber, Cambridge, MA.

Stein, D. and Hollander, E. (Eds). (2002). *The American Psychiatric Publishing Textbook of Anxiety Disorders.* Taylor and Francis, Washington DC.

Stein, D. and Hollander, E. (2003). *Anxiety Disorders Comorbid with Depression Social Anxiety Disorder, Post-Traumatiac Stress Disorder, Generalized Anxiety Disorder, and Obsessive-Compulsive Disorder.* Taylor and Francis, Washington DC. (Also available as an e-book at *e-Book Ebsco*.)

Sternberg, R. J. (1988). *The Triangle of Love: Intimacy, Passion, Commitment.* Basic Books, New York.

Stewart, I. (2000). *Transactional Analysis Counseling in Action*, 2nd edit. SAGE Publications, London.

Stewart, I. and Joines, V. (2003). *T A Today: A New Introduction to Transactional Analysis.* Russell Press, Nottingham, U.K. (This book, originally published in 1987 has been reprinted many times with revisions.)

Stewart, S. D. (2007). *Brave New Stepfamilies: Diverse Paths Toward Stepfamily Living.* SAGE Publications, Thousand Oaks, CA.

Stewart, S. H. and Conrod, P. J. (Eds). (2008). *Anxiety and Substance Use Disorders: The Vicious Cycle of Comorbidity.* Springer, New York.

Stiffler, L. H. (1991). Adoption's impact on birthmothers: Can a mother forget her child? *Journal of Psychology and Christianity*, **10** (3), 249–259.

Stone, M. H. (1993a). *Abnormalities of Personality: Within and Beyond the Realm of Treatment.* W. W. Norton, New York.

Stone, M. H. (1993b). Paradoxes in the management of suicidality in borderline patients. *American Journal of Psychotherapy*, **47**, 255–272.

Stoneberg, T. (2002). Moving from vulnerability to empowerment. In J. N. Poling and C. C. Neuger (Eds.), *Mens's Work in Preventing Violence Against Women*, 61–73. Haworth Press, New York. Co-published simultaneously as *Journal of Religion and Abuse*, **4** (3), 2002.

Stosny, S. (2006). *You Don't Have to Take It Anymore: Turn Your Resentful, Angry, or Emotionally Abusive Relationship into a Compassionate, Loving One.* Free Press, Simon and Schuster, New York.

Stott, J. (1990). *Issues Facing Christians Today.* Collins, Marshall Pickering, London.

Striegel-Moore, R. H. (1993). Etiology of binge eating: A developmental perspective. In C. G. Fairburn and G. T. Wilson (Eds.), *Binge Eating: Nature, Assessment, and Treatment*, 144–172. Guilford Press, New York.

Struve, J. (1990). Dancing with the patriarchy: the politics of sexual abuse. In M. Hunter (Ed.), *The Sexually Abused Male: Vol. 1. Prevalence, Impact, and Treatment*, 3–46. Lexington Books, Lexington, MA.

Sturt, J. and Sturt, A. (1986). *A Marriage Enrichment Manual.* Christian Care Centre, Auckland, New Zealand.

Sturt, J. and Sturt, A. (1988). *Christian Marriage Counselling.* Christian Care Centre, Auckland, New Zealand.

Sturt, J. and Sturt, A. (1994). *Created for Love: Understanding and Building Self-Esteem.* Highland Books, Guildford, Surrey, U.K. Also published by Eagle Publishing in 2002 and in New Zealand by Daystar books in 2007.

Sturt, J. and Sturt, A. (1998). *Created to Be Whole.* Eagle Publishing, Washington, DC.

Sulloway, F. J. (1995). Birth order and evolutionary psychology: A meta-analytic overview. *Psychological Inquiry*, **6** (1), 75–80.

Sulloway, F. J. (1996). *Born to Rebel: Birth Order, Family Dynamics and Creative Lives.* Pantheon Books, New York.

Tafrate, R. C. (1995). Evaluation of treatment strategies for adult anger disorders. In H. Kassinove (Ed.), *Anger Disorders: Definition, Diagnosis, and Treatment*, 109–129. Taylor and Francis, Washington, DC.

Tangney, J. P., Boone, A. L., and Dearing, R. L. (2005). Forgiving the self: Conceptual issues and empirical findings. In E. L. Worthington, Jr. (Ed.), *Handbook of Forgiveness*, 143–158. Routledge, Taylor and Francis Group, New York.

Tangney, J. P. and Dearing, R. L. (2002). *Shame and Guilt.* Guilford Press, New York.

Tannen, D. (1990). *You Just Don't Understand: Women in Conversation.* Morrow, New York.

Tavris, C. (1989). *Anger: The Misunderstood Emotion*, Revised Edit. Simon and Schuster, New York.

Taylor, S. (2002). Cognition in obsessive compulsive disorder: An overview. In R. O. Frost and G. Steketee (Eds.), *Cognitive Approaches to Obsessions and Compulsions*, 1–12. Elsevier, New York. (Also available as an e-book at *e-Book netLibrary.*)

Tobin, D. L. (2000). *Coping Strategies Therapy for Bulimia Nervosa.* American Psychological Association, Washington, DC. (Also available as an e-book at *e-Book PsycBooks Collection.*)

Tournier, P. (1972). *Guilt and Grace: A Psychological Study.* Hodder and Stoughton, London.

Toussaint, L. and Webb, J. R. (2005). Theoretical and empirical connections between forgiveness, mental health, and well-being. In E. L. Worthington, Jr. (Ed.), *Handbook of Forgiveness*, 349–362. Routledge, Taylor and Francis Group, New York.

Triseliotis, J., Shireman, J., and Hundleby, M. (1997). *Adoption: Theory, Policy and Practice.* Cassell, London.

Trobisch, W. (1971). *I Married You.* IVP, London.

Trower, P., Casey, A., and Dryden, W. (1988). *Cognitive-Behavioral Counseling in Practice.* SAGE publications, London. (Reprinted many times.)

Tsuang, M. T., Fleming, J. A., and Simpson, J. C. (1999). Suicide and schizophrenia. In D. G. Jacobs (Ed.), *The Harvard Medical School Guide to Suicide Assessment and Intervention*, 287–299. Jossey-Bass, Wiley, San Francisco, CA.

Turner, E.-J. and Diebschlag, F. (2001). Resourcing the trauma client. In T. Spiers (Ed.), *Trauma: A Practictoner's Guide to Counseling*, 69–96. Taylor and Francis, New York.

Worden, J. W. (2002). *Grief Counseling and Grief Therapy: A Handbook for the Mental Health Practitioner*, 3rd edit. Springer, New York.

World Health Organization (1992). *Women and Tobacco.* WHO, Geneva.

Worthington, E. L., Jr. (1993). *Hope for Troubled Marriages: Overcoming Problems and Major Difficulties.* InterVarsity, Downers Grove, IL.

Worthington, E. L., Jr. (2001). *Five Steps to Forgiveness: The Art and Science of Forgiving.* Crown, New York.

Worthington, E. L., Jr. (Ed.) (2005a). *Handbook of Forgiveness.* Routledge, Taylor and Francis Group, New York.

Worthington, E. L., Jr. (2005b). Initial questions about the art and science of forgiving. In E. L. Worthington, Jr. (Ed.), *Handbook of Forgiveness*, 1–13. Routledge, Taylor and Francis Group, New York.

Worthington, E. L., Jr. (2006). *Forgiveness and Reconciliation: Theory and Application.* CRC Press, Taylor and Francis Group, New York.

Worthington, E. L., Jr., Sharp, C. B, Lerner, A. J., and Sharp, J. R. (2006). Interpersonal forgiveness as an example of loving one's enemies. *Journal of Psychology and Theology*, **34** (1), 32–43.

Young, K. S. (1998). *Caught in the Net: How to Recognize the Signs of Internet Addiction— and a Winning Strategy for Recovery.* Wiley, New York.

Zilbergeld, B. (1999). *The New Male Sexuality.* Revised edit. Bantam Books, Random House, New York.

Zvolensky, M. J. and Smits, J. A. J. (Eds.) 2008). *Anxiety in Health Behaviors and Physical Illness.* Springer, New York. (Also available as an e-book at *e-Book SpringerLink*.)

INDEX

Abortion
    father's role in, 303
    grief and, 301
Abstinence violation effect (AVE)
    alcohol and, 342
    relapse and, 322
    smoking and, 333
Abusive partners stayed with, 428
Acetylcholine
    nicotine and, 329
ACTH, 116
Addiction
    advice giving, 321
    behavioral, 310, 347
    categories of, 313
    cell-phone, 365
    coping skills and, 321
    counseling methods for, 316
    crossover effect, 311
    definitions of, 310
    food, 377
    gambling, 348
    high-risk situations, 321
    homework for, 321
    internet, 363
    masturbation and, 362
    pornography and, 357
    process, 310
    relationship, 366
    religious, 384

    sexual, 355
    to romance, 356
    workaholism, 376
Addictive personality style, 314
Addictive self, 314
Adoptee
    tasks for the, 539
    when to tell, 539
Adoption
    adoptee tasks, 539
    adoptive mothers, 546
    adult adoptees and, 545
    Bible and, 551
    birth mother and, 548
    birthfathers and, 544
    gay and lesbian, 537
    grief of birthmother, 543, 549
    guilt of birthmother, 543
    open and closed, 543
    reunion and adoptive parents, 547
    reunion with adoptee, 550
    reunions, 544, 547, 550
    single parent, 543
    telling the adoptee, 540
    triad, 537, 544
Adrenal glands, 116
Adrenaline (epinephrine), 116
Adrenaline
    addiction, 119
    adrenals and, 116

amygdala and, 116
caffeine and, 117
cold hands and, 118
depression and, 238
fear cycle, 146
sexual addiction and, 119
stress and, 116
workaholism and, 119
Adult child, 407
Adult children of alcoholics, 409
Affair
adultery and the Bible, 528
couples and an, 498
recovery from, 499
Ageism, 431
Agoraphobia
and claustrophobia, 177
counseling for, 177
definition, 176
depression and, 177
diagnosis for, 176
some misconceptions, 177
Alcohol
assessment, 336
CAGE questionnaire, 336
counseling strategies for, 337
elderly and, 24
physical effects of, 334
pregnancy and, 335
social effects of, 335
suicide risk and, 271
withdrawal symptoms and, 342
Alexithymia, 12
Alternating bilateral stimulation
definition, 8
pain management and, 10
Ambivalence, 485
Amygdala, 4
pathway to, 14
adrenaline and, 116
danger and, 14
PTSD and, 163
reaction of, 6
Anger, 77
Anger Regulation-Expression Disorder
(ARED), 78
Anger work, 81
Anger
aggression and, 77
boundaries and, 80
catharsis and, 80
codependency and, 91
control options for, 83
counseling strategies for, 82
culturally unacceptable, 78
exercise and, 81
expression of, 80
forgiveness and, 81
from shame and guilt, 78
gender differences, 78
genogram for, 87

grief and, 287
management program, 82
management workshops for, 79
other people's, 91
passive-aggressive, 94
personal, 89
positives and negatives of, 79
PTSD and, 80
reluctant client, 88
thought stopping and, 83
toward God, 92
Angry face universal, 15
Anorexia
assessment of, 219
confirmed negativity condition, 217
depression associated with, 222
description, 216
dieting and, 218
overexercise and, 221
sex and, 218
symptoms of, 220
therapy for, 221
weight tracking, 222
Antecedents
alcohol use and, 338
situational, 142
Anticipatory grief, 290
Anticonvulsant drugs, 272
Antidepressants
main types, 234
suicidal thoughts and, 234, 262
Antisocial personality disorder, 561, 574
suicide risk and, 271
Anxiety disorders
depression comorbid with, 156
medication and, 157
Anxiety hierarchy, 142
Anxiety
anticipatory, 131, 196
counseling for, 139
free floating, 131
refractory (post exposure), 196
situational, 131
ASLEEP acronym, 137
Asperger's syndrome and alexithymia, 12
Assertiveness, 54
anger and, 85
control and, 417
diversionary tactics, 58
LADDER exercises, 57
ladder of exercises, 55
personal bill of rights, 55
techniques for, 56
Attachment
adults and, 50
bonding and, 538
bonding and grief, 281
children and, 49
couples and, 486
divorce and, 467
hoarding and, 200

hunger, 369
insecure, 49
prenatal death and, 299
secure, 49
types of, 49
Atypical depression, 241
Authoritative parents, 473
Autogenics, 40
Automatic thoughts, 160, 181, 183
Avoidance addict, 373
Avoidant personality disorder, 562, 583
  similar to social phobia, 180
Axon, 3
BAATOMI assessment
  psychological profile, 156, 558
Balance sheet
  for addictions, 319
Balanced life, 31
Basic emotions, 15
BASIC ID acronym, 19
BASIC ID
  stress assessment and, 123
Beck's triad of beliefs, 18, 160
Behavioral incident, 267
Behavioral incidents
  sequence of, 269
Benzodiazepines, 138
  anxiety disorders and, 157
Big I/little i diagram, 53
Binge-eating disorder
  assessment of, 228
  prevalence, 228
  therapy for, 229
Bipolar disorder, 242, 254
  suicide and, 271
Birth order, 68, 521
Blame game, 89, 513
Blended family
  stress and, 531
  counseling for a, 535
  disciplining the children, 534
  finances and, 535
  parenting style and, 532
  same sex parents, 537
  stepfamily and, 529
Blood alcohol level, 335
Bodily memories, 369
Body-centered therapy, 168
Body dysmorphic disorder (BDD)
  definition, 207
Body dysmorphic disorder
  compared with OCD, 208
Body mass index, 379
Borderline personality disorder, 561, 575
  self-harm and, 209
  suicide risk and, 272
Boundaries
  anger and, 80
  Christians and, 463
  counseling, 445
  difficult conversations and, 447

family and, 451
friends and, 452
inadequate childhood, 406
misconceptions of, 443
nature of, 441
partners and, 450
principles for setting, 442
resistance to, 455
safe and unsafe people, 453
saying no and, 445, 444
self and, 450
setting of, 447
unhealthy, 443
work and, 454
Brain hemispheres, 4, 24
  balance and, 44
Brain plasticity, 1, 11
Broken-record technique, 58
Bulimia
  assessment of, 225
  characteristics of, 224
  symptoms of, 226
  therapy for, 226
Bulimic anorexia, 227
Burnout, 151
Caffeine
  anxiety symptoms and, 34
  half-life, 117
  palpitations and, 149
  sleep and, 136
Caffeinism, 117
CAGE questionnaire for alcohol, 336
Cannabis, 344
CASE method for suicide risk, 268
Categorizing stimuli, 124
Catharsis, 80
Cell-phone addiction, 365
Cerebral palsy, 78
Change-talk statements, 319
Chasing the losses, 351
Chronic alcoholics, 336
Circadian rhythm, 37, 134, 138
Circular interaction, 89
Circular questioning, 484
Claustrophobia
  compared with agoraphobia, 177
Cocaine, 343
Codependency
  anger and, 91
  assessment of, 458
  characteristics of, 456
  control and, 456
  counseling for, 460
  definition of, 456
  dysfunctional families and, 457
Cognitive-behavioral therapy (CBT), 18
Cognitive distortions, 18
Cognitive unconscious, 13
Cohabitation, 490
  domestic violence and, 491
  stepfamilies and, 536

Competing response training, 205
Compulsions
    persistence of, 192
Compulsive actions, 230
Compulsive eating
    assessment of, 379
    counseling for, 379
    definition, 377
    relapse prevention, 382
Conflict in couples, 516
Contingency management, 206, 317
Control
    assertiveness and, 417
    biblical viewpoint, 436
    codependency and, 456
    financial, 417
    receiving it, 416
    recognition of, 416
Controlling person, 415
Conversing skills, 512
Coping skills
    addictions and, 321
Couple counseling
    gambling and, 354
Couples
    affairs and, 498
    attachment model, 486
    biblical marriage model, 525
    communication skills, 511
    conflict and, 516
    conversing skills, 512
    counseling, 505
    distance problems with, 486
    dos and don'ts of counseling, 510
    environmental problems, 496
    exercises for, 523
    family systems model, 483
    forgiveness and, 497
    imago model, 489
    interventions for, 522
    issues arising for, 491
    life-cycle models for, 483
    listening skills, 513
    love and respect, 527
    psychoanalytic models, 485
    REACH intervention model, 498
    reframing and, 509
    RELATE program for, 481
    sexual myths, 501
    sexual problems for, 500
    splitting and projection model, 485
    stages model, 484
    triangular models, 487
    who should come for counseling, 481
Craving
    urge and, 323
Crisis card, 267
Criticism, 518
Crossover effect, 311, 332
Death of child, 298
Debriefing

    in the workplace, 296
    value of, 163
Defense mechanisms
    list of, 563
    denial, 587
    introjection, 587
    isolation of affect, 589
    narcissist and, 581
    projection, 569
    reaction formation, 589
    sadism and, 597
    shame and sexual abuse, 108
    splitting, 576, 581
    trauma and, 167
Dendrites, 3
Dendritic spines, 3
Denial of the specific, 268
Dependent personality disorder, 562, 586
Depression
    15-step program for, 249
    agoraphobia and, 177
    anorexia and, 222
    assessment of, 236
    atypical, 241
    basic symptoms of, 235
    bipolar disorder and, 242
    causes of, 237
    Christian misconceptions about, 255
    classification of, 240
    counseling strategies for, 245
    dysthymia, 241
    effect on spiritual life, 254
    elderly and, 23
    exercise and, 249
    goals and, 252
    major disorder, 241
    male, 236
    nutrition and, 251
    pleasant activities for, 257
    postnatal (PND), 244
    premenstrual, 244
    prevalence of, 233
    reactive, 240
    ruminating and, 237
    seasonal affective disorder, 244
    sleep and, 236
    spiritual counseling for, 256
    suicide risk and, 233
Depressive personality disorder, 591
Desensitization, 143
    anger and, 83
Developmental needs meeting strategy, 8
Dialectical behavior therapy (DBT), 260, 269
Diaphragm breathing, 40
Dieting
    addictive cycle and, 378
    anorexia and, 218
Differential reinforcement, 206
Difficult conversation, 90
Difficult conversations, 446–447
Disenfranchised grief, 280

Disowned self, 489, 519
Display rules, 15
Dissociative amnesia, 163, 392
Distorted thinking
  self-esteem and, 52
Distracting thoughts
  pain management and, 11
Diversionary tactics
  assertiveness and, 58
Divorce
  attachment and, 467
  baggage and, 477
  children and, 469
  emotional, 407
  family and friends, 469
  forgiveness and, 477
  grief and, 466
  narcissistic injury, 468
  parenting and, 472
  reasons for, 476
DNMS for ego states, 8
Dopamine, 310
  nicotine and, 329
  sexual activity and, 43
  stimulants and, 343
Downward-arrow technique, 141, 160
Dreams, 39
DSM manuals, 2
Dysfunctional beliefs
  body dysmorphic disorder and, 208
  OCD and, 197
Dyspareunia, 504
Dysthymia, 241
Earthquakes, 171
Eating Disorder Not Otherwise Specified, 227
Eating disorders, 215
Ecstasy, 345
EFT acronym, 9
Ego state, 7
Elderly abuse, 430
Elderly brain, 24
Elderly
  safety contracts and, 274
  suicide risk and, 273
EMDR, 8
  trauma and, 169
Emotion-focused therapy, 16
Emotional freedom technique, 9
Emotional processing, 15
Emotional pursuer/distancer, 90, 486
Emotions, 13
  appraisal of, 16
  basic, 47
  beliefs and, 47
  feelings and, 13
  mood matrix of, 47
  primary, 15
  processing difficult ones, 46
  secondary, 15
  somatization of, 47
  the limbic system and, 13

Empty-chair method
  addressing a parent, 372
  anger and, 84
  depression and, 247
  forgiveness and, 405
  forgiving parents, 409
  offender and, 65
  sexual abuse and, 400
  shame and inner critic, 111
  smoking and, 334
  talking to God, 94
Endorphins, 118
Erectile problems, 503
Erikson stages, 23, 483, 542, 548
Eustress, 115
Exercise
  aerobic, 34
  brain power and, 24
  excuses not to, 35
  express anger using, 81
  healthy eating pyramid and, 32
  lifts depression, 249
  physical benefits of, 34
  psychological benefits of, 35
  stress and, 123, 149, 249
  weight control and, 380
Exposure methods, 142
  agoraphobia and, 177
  facts about, 174
  OCD and, 195
  social phobia and, 181–182
  trauma and, 167
  worry and, 160
Exposure response therapy (ERP), 141–142,
    195, 202
Extended balance sheet
  for addictions, 324
Eye movement desensitization and
    reprocessing, 8
False memories, 164
False memory traps, 165
False self, 489
Family systems model, 483
Fear of needles, 185
Fetal alcohol syndrome, 335
Field therapy, 9
Fifteen-step program, 249
Finances
  blended family and, 535
Financial abuse
  control and, 417, 427
  the elderly and, 431
Five freedoms
  denial of, 108
  description, 54
Fogging, 58
Food allergies, 34
Forgetfulness with trauma, 164
FORGIVE acronym for forgiveness, 66
Forgiveness
  anger and, 81

biblical, 73
couples and, 497–498
definition, 59
described, 62
divorce and, 477
FORGIVE acronym and, 66
forgiving God, 404
hasty, 62
misconceptions of, 63
of self, 66
parents/caregivers and, 409
REACH acronym, 66
role in counseling, 60
role of, 59
seeking and receiving, 67
sexual abuse and, 404
steps for, 64
triad, 62
Four life phases (Cohen), 26
FRAMES acronym for change, 319
Friends of a bereaved person, 295
Gambling
  addictive, 348
  assessment of, 349
  chance and, 350
  counseling for, 352
  couple counseling and, 354
  finance and, 354
  games of skill and, 351
  goal setting and, 354
  high risk situations and, 353
  homework and, 353
  horse racing and, 352
  lotteries and, 352
  the Bible and, 382
  understanding chance, 350
Games of skill
  gambling and, 351
Gender-role
  abuse of power and, 420
Generalized anxiety disorder (GAD), 158
Genogram
  for anger, 87
Gentle assumption, 267
GHB, 346
Glia, 25
Goals, 44
  depression and, 252
  gambling and, 354
  SMART, 44
  time management and, 45
Grief
  divorce and, 466
  abortion and, 301
  adoption and, 543, 549
  anger and, 287
  anticipatory, 290
  bereaved friends and, 295
  children and, 293
  continuing bonds and, 292
  coping with change, 291

counseling and, 288
death of a child, 298
depression and, 292
disenfranchised, 280, 549
job loss and, 303
losses and, 240
models for stages of, 281
pets and, 295
prenatal death and, 298
relearning and, 284
rituals for, 286
some metaphors, 285
sudden death and, 297
suicide and, 281, 296
unresolved, 305
viewing the body, 291
withdrawal of dying person, 290
workplace and, 295
Guilt, 100
Guilt and shame
  difference, 100
  together, 105
Guilt
  adoption and, 543
  anticipatory, 101
  bereaved parents and, 300
  biblical viewpoint, 112
  counseling for, 101
  existential, 101
  false guilt, 101
  objective, 100
  real, 101
  sexual abuse and, 396, 400
  shame compared with, 100
  subjective, 100
  survivor, 101
  toxic, 102
Habit reversal training, 205, 230
Habituation, 195
Half-life
  nicotine, 329
  caffeine, 117
  cocaine, 343
Hallucinogens, 345
HALT acronym, 317, 361
Harm reduction
  alcohol and, 338, 340
  drug use and, 343
  gambling and, 348
  opioids and, 344
  smoking and, 328
HEALS program for abuse, 424
Healthy eating pyramid, 32
Hierarchy of situations
  agoraphobia and, 177
  anger and, 83, 86
  anxiety and, 142
  compulsive shopping and, 202
  for fears, 568
  OCD and, 195
  social phobia and, 181

specific phobias and, 184
High-risk situations
gambling and, 350, 353–354
internet addiction and, 366
overeating and, 382
pornography and, 361
smoking and, 331
Hippocampus, 4
damaged, 6
explicit memories and, 6
Histrionic personality disorder, 561, 578
Hoarding, 192
problem solving and, 202
characteristics of, 200
compulsive, 199
Homework
actual incidents, 183
anxiety-causing situations and, 183
desirable features of, 248
exposure and, 168
for addictions, 321
gambling and, 353
practice new behaviors, 161
Horse racing, 352
Hyperventilation syndrome (HVS), 139, 149
Hypochondriasis, 172
Hypoglycemia, 34
I statements
anger and, 47, 85, 90
couple communication and, 513
ICARE for suicide risk, 266
ICD-10 classification, 563
Identifying feelings, 47
Imago Dei, 71
Inner-child therapies, 8, 388
Inner push for elderly, 25
Insulin, 33
Intelligence, 7
crystallized, 7
developmental, 26
fluid, 7
social, 27
Internet addiction
counseling for, 365
description of, 363
Interpersonal psychotherapy, 246
binge-eating disorder and, 229
depression and, 234
Intrusive memories, 15
Intrusive thoughts, 178
OCD and, 194
Irrational beliefs, 18
cognitive distortions, 18
three major ones, 18
Jet lag, 38
Job loss, 303
Karpman drama triangle, 488
Ketamine, 346
L-tryptophan, 136
LADDER acronym, 57
Learning styles, 13

Lesbians
violence and, 419
Life-cycle models, 483
Limbic system, 4
spiritual experiences and, 71
Listening skills, 513
Lithium, 272
Long-term memory
episodic, 5
explicit (declarative), 5
implicit (procedural), 5
semantic, 5
Loss
consequences of, 279
external, 280
internal, 280
significance of, 286
types of, 280
Losses
categories of, 240
Lost self, 489, 519
Lotteries, 352
Love addiction, 366
Love languages
for adults, 519
for children, 521
Lucid dreaming, 39
Major depressive disorder, 241
Masochistic personality disorder, 595
Massed negative practice, 206
Masturbation
addiction to, 362, 356, 359
individual, 43
prolactin and, 43
Melatonin
drug for sleep problems, 138
electro-magnetic radiation and, 136
L-tryptophan and, 136
sleep and, 135
teens and, 138
Memory recall
precautions, 165
sexual abuse and, 401
Memory
repression or suppression, 163
long-term, 5
short-term, 5
suppression, 392–393
working, 5
Menopause, 22
Methamphetamine, 343
Midlife crisis, 22
Midlife reassessment, 22
Mind map
stress and, 124
Mindfulness meditation
generalized anxiety disorder and, 160
personality disorders and, 567
urge and, 323
Miracle question, 125
Mirroring method, 512

Misogynist, 368
Mood graph, 267
Motivational enhancement, 348
Motivational enhancement therapy, 318
Motivational interviewing
  anxiety disorders, 156
  alcohol and, 339
  balance sheet for, 319
  basic principles of, 320
  change and, 318
  definition of, 317
  extended balance sheet, 324
  gambling and, 348, 353
Multi-axial categories
  Axis I dimensions, 555
  Axis II, 553
  list of, 2
  shame and, 99
  Axis I disorders, 155
Multimodal (behavioral) therapy, 19
Muscle relaxation, 40
Narcissistic personality disorder, 561, 580
Narcotic antagonists, 344
Needles, 185
Negative thoughts and biblical texts, 257
Negativistic personality disorder, 593
Neocortex, 4
  pathway to, 14
Nervous breakdown, 144
Nervous fatigue, 144
  sleep and, 151
Neuro-linguistic programming (NLP), 20
Neurogenesis, 25
Neuroleptics, 205
Neurons, 3
Neurotransmitters, 3, 33
  acetylcholine, 4
  addictions and, 3
  adrenaline (epinephrine), 4
  dopamine, 4
  melatonin, 4
  noradrenaline (norepinephrine), 4
  serotonin, 4, 33, 236
Nicotine
  addiction, 327
  alternatives, 328
  half-life, 329
  properties of, 328
  withdrawal from, 332
No talk/listen rules, 108, 217
Nomophobia, 365
Non-equation for over-generalization, 182
Noradrenaline (norepinephrine), 116
NREM, 36
Nutrition, 32
  depression and, 251
  psychological problems and, 34
  supplements and, 33
Obsessions
  nervous fatigue and, 145
Obsessive-compulsive disorder

baseline measurements, 193
compared with BDD, 208
compared with OCPD, 190
description of, 189
diagnosis, 191
dysfunctional beliefs, 197
exposure methods, 195
intrusive thoughts and, 194
Obsessive-compulsive personality disorder,
  562, 589
  OCD compared with, 190
OCD, 189
Offenders of sexual abuse, 390
Open adoption, 543
Opioids, 343
Orgasmic dysfunction, 504
Pain gateway, 10
Pain management, 10
  distracting thoughts for, 11
Panic attack, 146
  ARFT coping method, 149
  coping strategy, 148
  counseling for, 147
  hypoglycemia and, 34
  loss of control, 173
  mindfulness meditation and, 148
  relaxation techniques for, 149
  social phobia and, 180
  symptoms, 146
Panic disorder, 147
  assessment of, 172
  counseling for, 173
  nature of, 172
Paranoid personality disorder, 560, 568
Parentification, 408, 473
Parenting style, 472
  blended families and, 532
Partner choice, 51, 369, 373, 477, 489
Passive-aggressive personality disorder, 593
Passive-aggressive
  anger, 94
  client, 95
Passive anger
  see passive-aggressive anger, 94
Peaceful scene, 41
Pedophiles, 391
PEMSS acronym, 31
Perfectionism
  anxiety and, 133
  shame and, 108–109
Personal bill of rights, 55
Personality disorder
  general counseling for, 567
  Axis II disorder, 553
  cluster A, 560, 568
  cluster B, 561, 574
  cluster C, 562, 583
  definition of, 553
  dimensional approach to, 555
  general indications of, 559
  medication and, 556

optimal criterion and, 558
Personality
  Briggs-Meyers test, 12
  definition of, 11
  five factor model, 12
  models for, 12
  types A and B, 12
Phantom limb phenomenon, 11
Phobias
  categories of, 174
  counseling for, 175
Physical abuse, 418
  counseling for, 422
  counseling the abuser, 424
  of a child, 406
  safety plans and, 423
PLAIDPALS acronym, 263
Pornography
  counseling for, 360
  dangers of, 43
  definition of, 357
  effects of, 358
  signs of, 360
Positive thinking, 29
Post traumatic stress disorder (PTSD), 161
Postnatal depression (PND), 244
Prayer
  relaxation response and, 71
  stress and, 71
Premature ejaculation, 504
Premenstrual dysphoric disorder, 244
Premenstrual syndrome, 136, 245
Prenatal death, 298
Probability of a feared event, 198
Problem drinkers, 336
Psalm 23, 188
Pseudomemories, 165
Psychoanalytic models for couples, 485
Psychological abuse, 427
  of a child, 406
Psychological assessment
  BAATOMI method of, 558
  general, 556
Psychological needs, 288
Psychological profile, 557
Psychosomatic illnesses, 3
Quantity and frequency method, 337
Quit book on smoking, 331
Rape, 426
Rational Emotive Behavior Therapy (REBT),
  17
Rational therapy, 17
REACH acronym for forgiveness, 66
REACH intervention model for couples, 498
Reactive depression, 240
  after a loss, 3
Real-life exposures
  methods, 175
Rebound insomnia, 138
Relapse intervention, 323
Relapse prevention

alcohol and, 342
gambling and, 355
smoking and, 333
Relapse strategies, 322
RELATE program for couples, 481
Relationship addiction, 366
  codependency and, 366
  counseling for, 371
  leaving a, 374
Relaxation response, 41
  agoraphobia and, 178
  rapid, 143
Relaxation techniques, 39
  anger and, 83
  autogenics, 40
  diaphragm breathing for, 40
  muscle relaxation and, 40
  OCD and, 196
  panic attacks and, 149
  peaceful scene and, 41
  relaxation response, 41
  sleep and, 137
  stress and, 126
  tics and, 206
Repressed memories, 164
Resentment bank accounts, 61
Resilience, 45
Resistance to boundaries, 455
Resource loss model, 398
RESPECT method for a healthy relationship,
  425
Restorative justice, 61
Retirement, 27
Reunion with birth mother, 547
Reward system, 3
Rituals
  addiction and, 315
  grief and, 286
Ruminating and depression, 237
Rumination, 17
Sadistic personality disorder, 597
Safety contracts
  elderly and, 274
  informed consent instead of, 276
  need for, 274
  pitfalls of, 275
Safety plans
  physical abuse and, 423
Saturation for obsessive thoughts, 199
Saying no, 498
  alcohol refusal, 339
  assertiveness and, 57
  boundaries and, 444
  children and, 452
  codependency and, 456, 460
  different ways of, 445
  stress and, 121
  to the unimportant, 454
  try, 447
Schizoid personality disorder, 560, 570
Schizophrenia

suicide risk and, 271
Schizotypal personality disorder, 561, 572
Seasonal affective disorder (SAD), 244
Sedatives
  addictive, 314
Self-concept, 51
Self-control strength model, 325
Self-esteem, 51
  counseling for, 52
  depression and, 252
  distorted thinking and, 52
  shame and, 105
Self-harm
  reasons for, 210
  alternative behaviors, 213
  borderline personality disorder and, 209
  counseling for, 212
  description, 209
  diagnosis of, 210
  safety nets for, 213
  suicide and, 209
Self-preservation, 260
Self-talk
  depression and, 250
  negative, 111, 141
  phobias and negative, 175
  positive, 91
Self-worth, 51
Set-point theory for weight, 223, 380
Sex
  aging and, 28
  anorexia and, 218
  shame and, 103, 106
Sexual abuse
  memories of, 392
  confrontation of the abuser, 403
  counseling for, 398
  definition of, 389
  effects of, 395
  forgiveness and, 404
  free narrative recall, 393
  gender differences and, 402
  guilt and, 396, 400
  identification with the aggressor, 394
  memory recall of, 401
  of adults, 425
  offenders, 390
  shame and defense mechanisms, 108
  stages of, 391
Sexual addiction
  adrenaline and, 119
  counseling for, 362
  definition of, 355
Sexual anorexia, 363
Sexual bill of rights, 426
Sexual dysfunction, 503
Sexual myths, 501
Shame-bound relationship, 105
Shame-prone
  anger and, 78
Shame

nature of, 103
  attenuation, 267
  assessment of, 107
  biblical viewpoint, 113
  compared with guilt, 100
  counseling process and, 111
  couple counseling and, 106
  false self and, 104
  forgiveness and, 66
  from a a family system, 107
  interventions for, 109
  intimate relationships and, 105
  natural, 103
  perfectionism and, 109
  sex and, 103, 106
  spiritual abuse and, 434
  toxic, 104, 107
Shaming rules, 107
Single-parent adoption, 543
SIR stimulus response model, 14
Sleep
  benefits of, 36
  body temperature and, 37
  cycles, 36
  depression and, 236
  deprivation and PND, 244
  deprivation from worry, 132
  disorders, 133
  dreams, 36, 39
  how much, 37
  infants and, 38
  insomnia, 134
  naps, 36
  nervous illness, 151
  rapid eye movement and, 36
  strategies for, 134
  stress and, 127
Sleeping pills, 138
SMART goals
  defined, 44
  depression and, 253
  exercise and, 35
  stress and, 126
Smoking
  addiction, 327
  counseling for, 331
  effect on health, 329
  five Ds for quitting, 332
  motivation to stop, 330
  quit book, 331
  record sheet of, 331
  relapse prevention and, 333
  substances from, 328
  wheel of change and, 331
Social networks, 48
Social phobia, 179
  assessment of, 180
  counseling for, 181
  criteria for, 179
Social portfolio, 27, 48
Social skills training

anger and, 85
Solution-focused therapy
  stress and, 125
Soma, 3
SOR model, 15
Specific phobia, 184
  definition, 184
  needles, 185
  subtypes of, 175
Spiritual abuse
  counseling for, 435
  defined, 431
  hallmarks of, 434
  in the Bible, 438
  recognition of, 432
  why stay, 435
Spirituality
  definition of, 70
  health and, 69
  therapists and, 69
Splitting and projection model, 485
Splitting defense mechanism, 396
St. John's wort, 235
Stages of grief, 281
STAIR, 398
Standard drink
  conversions, 338
  definition of, 340
  effect of, 335
Statistical independence, 350
Stimulants and drugs, 343
Stimulants
  addictive, 314
Stress
  adrenaline and, 116
  assessment of, 122
  blended families and, 531
  counseling for, 122
  depression and, 249
  exercise and, 123, 249
  mapping, 124
  monitoring, 118
  nutrition and, 34
  physical effects of, 116
  pressure and, 116
  reduction of, 125
  substances causing, 117
  symptoms of, 118
  Type A personality and, 117
  wheel-of-change model, 127
Structural analysis of social behavior model,
    555
Structured interview, 166
Structured problem solving
  hoarding and, 202
  alcohol addiction and, 339
  couple disagreements and, 517
  generalized anxiety disorder and, 160
  method, 248
  stress and, 126, 128
Stuttering, 230

Substance addiction
  diagnosis of, 311
Sudden infant death syndrome (SIDS), 299
SUDS acronym, 142
Suffering, 93
Suicide risk
  CASE method, 268
Suicide risk, 259
  beliefs about, 264
  alcohol and, 271
  assessment of, 261
  bipolar disorder and, 271
  borderline personality disorder and, 272
  cognitive methods, 266
  counseling for, 266
  elderly and, 273
  gambling and, 348, 350
  hospitalization for, 270
  impossible life and, 265
  PLAIDPALS assessment, 263
  safety contracts and, 274
  schizophrenia and, 271
  trauma and, 273
  uncovering intent, 265
  validation techniques, 267
  writing methods for, 267
Suicide
  biblical viewpoint, 276
  elderly and, 23
  grief and, 281, 296
  viewpoints on, 260
Suppressed memories, 393
Surf the urge, 323, 339, 355
Symptom-matching hierarchy, 267
Symptom amplification, 268
Synapse, 3
Tapping techniques, 9
Temper, 88
Temperament, 11
Testosterone
  effect of gender on the brain, 5
  definition, 42
Thalamus, 14
Thought control
  OCD and, 199
Thought distraction, 41
Thought records, 141
Thought stopping
  anger and, 83
  methods of, 21
  OCD and, 199
  stress and, 127
Thought tracking, 160
Threatened losses
  relationship addiction and, 369
Tic disorder
  classification, 203
  counseling for, 204
Tic disorders
  definition, 203
  motor, 203

phonic (vocal), 203
Time-line and follow-back technique, 337
Time management, 120
  goals and, 45
Time out
  hobbies and, 36
  regular, 36
  vacations, 36
Touch, 44
Tourette's disorder, 204
Toxic faith, 433
Transactional analysis, 8
Transtheoretical change model, 321
Trauma
  assessment of, 166
  client resources and, 169
  counseling for, 167
  defense mechanism and, 167
  earthquakes, 171
  retraumatization and, 167
  suicide risk and, 273
  therapist and, 170
  world view and, 170
Traumatic incident reduction, 169
Triangular relationship models, 487
Triangular theory of love, 488
Trichotillomania, 209, 230
Tunnel vision, 36
Twelve-step program, 69
  addictions and, 325
  Christian version of, 326
  Codependents Anonymous (CoDA), 463
  Gamblers Anonymous, 355
  Internetaholics Anonymous, 366
  narcotics and, 342
  Overeaters Anonymous, 382
  Sex Addicts Anonymous, 363

Sex and Love Addicts Anonymous, 371
Sexaholics Anonymous, 363
Under/over functioning, 89
Universal facial expressions, 15
Unresolved grief, 305
Vaginismus, 504
Validation techniques, 267
Vaso-vagal syncope, 185
Vegetarian pyramid, 32
Verbal abuse, 417
Viewing the body, 291
Violence
  by men, 419
  by women, 421
  lesbians and, 419
Weight cycling, 378
Wheel of change
  gambling and, 348
  addictions and, 321
  bulimia and, 227
  smoking and, 331
  stress and, 127
Wheel
  advocacy empowerment, 424
  of equality, 424
  of power and control, 423
  of power for same sex relationships, 424
Wholeness, 31
Workaholism
  Christian workers and, 384
  adrenaline and, 119
  counseling for, 376
  description, 376
Working memory, 5
World view
  trauma and, 170
Worry, 132